THE COMPLETE BOOK OF

Breast Care

THE COMPLETE BOOK OF

Breast Care

Niels H. Lauersen, M.D., Ph.D. and Eileen Stukane

FAWCETT COLUMBINE · NEW YORK

A Fawcett Columbine Book
Published by Ballantine Books

http://www.randomhouse.com

Library of Congress Cataloging-in-Publication Data
Lauersen, Niels H.
The complete book of breast care / Niels H. Lauersen and Eileen Stukane.—1st ed.
p.   cm.
Includes bibliographical references and index.
ISBN 0-449-90903-4
1. Breast—Care and hygiene.   2. Breast—Cancer—Popular works.
I. Stukane, Eileen.   II. Title.
RG492.L38   1996
618.1'9—dc20   96-25953

Text design by Holly Johnson

Manufactured in the United States of America

First Edition: October 1996

10 9 8 7 6 5 4 3 2 1

To those women and men in research labs, hospitals, health clinics, government offices, and volunteer organizations who dedicate their lives to the betterment of breast health care

Contents

Acknowledgments   xi
Author's Note   xiv
Introduction—Your Breasts: Your Pride and Your Worry   3

PART I—HEALTHY BREASTS ARE ALWAYS CHANGING   **11**

Chapter 1—Understanding the Basics: Your Breasts Over Your
     Lifetime   13

Chapter 2—Transformed During Pregnancy and Breastfeeding:
     Your Breasts Are (Possibly) Better Off Afterward   29

PART II—YOU CAN PROTECT YOUR BREASTS   **45**

Chapter 3—A Breast Self-Examination: When You Have a Good
     Teacher, You *Can* Overcome Your Ambivalence   47

Chapter 4—When to Have a Mammogram: A Recommended
     Timetable   58

Chapter 5—Beyond Mammography: Other High-Tech Breast Tests
     You May Want   74

Chapter 6—Yes, You Can Eat to Keep Your Breasts Healthy: The
     Latest on Foods That Fight Illness   80

Chapter 7—The Surprising Relationship Between Exercise and Your
     Breasts: Another Reason to Work Out   102

Chapter 8—Pollutants, Electromagnetic Fields, and Radiation:
    Exploring the Link Between Your Environment and
    Your Breasts   112

Chapter 9—The Mind/Body Connection: Stress and Your Breasts   125

PART III—WONDERING WHICH COURSE TO TAKE? NEW
    INFORMATION ABOUT MEDICATIONS AND OPERATIONS   133

Chapter 10—How Birth Control Pills and Fertility Drugs Affect
    Your Breasts   135

Chapter 11—How to Decide Whether Hormone Replacement
    Therapy Is for You . . . Even If You Have Survived
    Breast Cancer   141

Chapter 12—When You Want to Reshape Your Breasts: The Latest
    Word on Cosmetic Surgery   151

Chapter 13—When You Are at High Risk for Breast Cancer: Should
    You Consider Preventive Mastectomy?   175

PART IV—WARNING SIGNS THAT YOUR BREASTS
    NEED ATTENTION   181

Chapter 14—Nipples That Have Discharge, Soreness, or Other
    Conditions   183

Chapter 15—A Difference in Your Skin Tone   190

Chapter 16—Your Breasts Hurt: Pain All Over or in One Spot   192

Chapter 17—You Find a Lump: It May Not Be Serious But It Should
    Not Be Ignored   201

PART V—WHEN BREAST CANCER BECOMES A PERSONAL
    BATTLE: DIAGNOSIS, TREATMENT, RECOVERY   213

Chapter 18—Genetic Codes and More: An Overview of the
    Growing List of High-Risk Factors for Breast Cancer   215

Chapter 19—A Suspicious Lump: When a Biopsy Is Needed   232

Chapter 20—After the Biopsy: What the Pathology Report Will
    Tell You   246

Chapter 21—When Your Doctor Says "Surgery," Which Is Best?
    Lumpectomy Versus Mastectomy   258

Chapter 22—Every Breast Cancer Has a Profile, and You Should
    Know Yours 279

Chapter 23—What to Expect During Radiotherapy 284

Chapter 24—When You Need Chemotherapy and Hormone Therapy:
    Seizing the Power of Cancer-Killing Drugs 294

Chapter 25—On the Vanguard of Healing 339

Chapter 26—Breast Reconstruction: Is It for You? 344

Chapter 27—The Wellness Attitude: Healthy Breasts Throughout a
    Lifetime 370

PART VI—RESOURCES **373**

Going On-Line for Information About Your Breasts: How to Use a
    Computer to Find Everything You Want to Know 375
Where to Write, Phone, or Fax for Help 388
Bibliography 400
Index 431

Acknowledgments

Women have sounded the call for improved breast health care, and dedicated physicians and health care professionals around the world have responded. As authors and long-time advocates for women's health, we are grateful for the opportunity to create a book that delivers the latest information from the front lines of medicine, and at the same time, conveys the need for continued research. To produce this book, we received valuable assistance from women and men who are involved in diverse areas of breast health, but who share a commitment to conquer breast cancer. They selflessly offered their knowledge and experience. We extend our deepest gratitude to them, and to each and every person involved in the realization of *The Complete Book of Breast Care*.

Special thanks go to the women among Dr. Lauersen's patients, and among the membership of SHARE in New York City, who took the time to respond to our questionnaires. We asked them intimate questions about their breasts, breastfeeding, breast surgeries, and treatments for different breast conditions and breast cancer, and they gave us honest, thoughtful answers. We are also indebted to the women who allowed us to go beyond the questionnaires and granted personal interviews to broaden the scope of this book. A particular thank you to Eleanor Stukane for allowing her story to be told.

We offer appreciation and praise to the journalists and researchers who helped us meet the demands of individual chapters. Barbara Crook brilliantly unearthed new facts about cosmetic and reconstructive surgery. Paula Dranov's intelligence gave foundation to the chapters on surgery for breast cancer, radiotherapy, and complementary care. Sheila Sperber Haas steered us through the maze of information on the powerful drugs of chemotherapy and hormonal therapy. David Puchkoff explored on-line services, combed the Internet, and helped us create a totally new type of Resources section. From Research Unlimited, David Newman and Claire de Brunner enthusiastically tracked down hard-to-find pieces of information, and fine-tuned the listings of "help" organizations and the bibliography. Lee Martin devoted many personal hours to gathering the studies we needed from medical libraries; she was dauntless. Yanni Antonopoulos and Carrie Puchkoff also took time to assist in research.

We are enormously grateful to Alice Yaker, president of SHARE, and an inspiration to all women to have faith in themselves. She believed in this book when it was embryonic, and allowed SHARE's resources to be available to us. Marlene Bloom was the guiding light who brought us to SHARE and remained our champion.

Media specialists at many of the teaching hospitals, cancer centers, professional associations, and health organizations we contacted extended themselves well beyond our expectations to make this book as timely as possible. This special group of women and men were always ready to help: Stacey Harris at Memorial Sloan-Kettering Cancer Center in New York; Eric Rosenthal and Andrea Bozzelli at Fox Chase Cancer Center in Philadelphia; Catherine Law, Frank Mahaney, and Tom Reynolds at the National Cancer Institute; Joanne Schellenbach and Susan Islam at the American Cancer Society; Michael Bernstein at the American College of Radiology; Chris Kelly at the Armed Forces Institute of Pathology; Mary Ellen Flattes at The United Way; and Beverly Mavus and Steven Clark at Andover Communications.

We owe a special debt of gratitude to the physicians and health care professionals who offered their time and expertise. We spoke to well over one hundred researchers in our effort to gather the latest news from laboratories and medical centers in the United States and other countries. Names of the prominent medical investigators and clinicians we interviewed are cited throughout *The Complete Book of Breast Care*. We sincerely thank each of them, for their availability, and for their interest in informing women about the progress being made in breast health care.

A number of doctors who are highly respected in their fields reviewed individual chapters, and to them we are especially grateful: Dr. Patrick Borgen of Memorial Sloan-Kettering Cancer Center in New York; Dr. Richard A. D'Amico of Englewood Hospital and Medical Center in New Jersey; Dr. Barbara Fowble of Fox Chase Cancer Center in Philadelphia; Dr. Elissa Gretz of Memorial Sloan-Kettering Cancer Center; Dr. David Hidalgo of Memorial Sloan-Kettering Cancer Center; Dr. Michael Lagios of St. Mary's Medical Center in San Francisco; Dr. Doreen Liebeskind of Park Avenue Radiology in New York; Dr. Marjorie Luckey of Memorial Sloan-Kettering Cancer Center; Dr. Silvana Martino of Westlake Comprehensive Breast Center in Westlake Village, California; Dr. Lawrence Reed of Beth

Israel Hospital in New York; Dr. George Raptis of Memorial Sloan-Kettering Cancer Center; Dr. Neil Ratner, New York anesthesiologist; Dr. David Rose of the American Health Foundation; Dr. Mazhar Rishi of The Armed Forces Institute of Pathology; Dr. Melvin Silverstein of The Breast Center in Van Nuys; Dr. John Terzakis of Lenox Hill Hospital in New York; Dr. Maria Theodoulou of Memorial Sloan-Kettering Cancer Center; Dr. James Vredenburgh of Duke University Hospital; and Dr. Grace Yang of New York University Medical Center. Without their attention to detail and accuracy, this book could not have been so complete.

Original artwork for this book was created with care and skill by Enid Hatton. Maya Murphy Puchkoff produced individual illustrations with artistry. Additional drawings were provided by Tony Kramer. Special thanks to Dr. Charles Citrin of HealthSouth Diagnostic Center in Washington, DC, who graciously provided excellent examples of mammography. Our thanks also go to Dr. Richard A. D'Amico of Englewood Hospital and Medical Center, for allowing us to include photographs of his reconstructive surgery, and to Dr. Grace Yang of New York University Hospital, for permitting the reproduction of cell slides. We also thank Ronnie Verebay and Adrian Hirsh, who are always ready to come to our rescue.

Our continued appreciation to our agent, Ellen Levine, who carefully guides our efforts, and to Diana Finch, Deborah Clifford, and everyone on the hard-working staff of the Ellen Levine Literary Agency.

We are fortunate to have worked with a talented editorial staff at Ballantine. We started this project with Joëlle Delbourgo and Sherri Rifkin, who gave us our direction. As we progressed, Ginny Faber and Elizabeth Zack joined the Ballantine staff and once again, we were blessed. Ginny Faber has carefully overseen the project, and Elizabeth Zack has been a dedicated, inspired editor. She has refined and polished our pages. Beth Bortz has also kept the wheels of progress in motion. We are deeply grateful to them, as we are to everyone at Ballantine Books. Their energy and efforts have guided the project and shaped The Complete Book of Breast Care into a reliable resource for today's women.

Authors' Note

For the purpose of simplicity, the authors have chosen to designate the hypo-
thetical doctors in this book with the male gender pronouns—he, his, him,
etc. This gender rendering should not be viewed as a political or chauvinistic
choice, but as a means to a greater clarification, making it easier to distinguish between the patient, who is always a *she*, and the doctor. While in
the past doctors were mostly male, today many more women are entering the
medical profession. Women now have a greater field of choice for selecting a
female or a male doctor.

This book is not intended as a substitute for the medical advice of a physician. The reader should regularly consult a physician in matters relating to
her health, particularly with respect to symptoms that may require diagnosis
or medical attention. The authors have made every attempt to ensure that
the information presented here is accurate up to the time of this book's publication, but due to ongoing research, it is possible that new findings may
invalidate some of the material contained within.

THE COMPLETE BOOK OF

Breast Care

Your Breasts: Your Pride and Your Worry

Your breasts are glands involved in your reproductive system, but their significance goes far beyond their function. Breasts are part of a woman's identity, visible signs of her sex, erogenous zones, and with motherhood, sources of love and nourishment for her babies. Recognizing the vital and varied roles of breasts, we urge you to become involved in their health care *before* a problem occurs. This year alone 184,300 women will be diagnosed with invasive breast cancer and 44,300 women will die of the disease. Our aim for *The Complete Book of Breast Care* is: to offer you the most up-to-date discoveries in *preventive* health care, along with the latest advancements in diagnoses and treatments, to increase your knowledge about what is going on inside your breasts, and to return to you confidence in your body. Daunting as it may seem, it is important for you to be aware of the latest information about preventive care, diagnostic techniques, and improved treatments. The quality of your breast health care improves when you can bring your own understanding of the facts to your doctor's office.

NEVER STOP TAKING A STAND

In 1982, when we wrote *Listen to Your Body* to arm women with information about their gynecological health, women were expected to discover their own breast lumps. At that time, we urged you and your doctor to integrate breast examinations into regular gynecological checkups. We also advised you to ask your doctor to explain fibrocystic breast disease and other benign breast conditions. With activism so strong today, it seems hard to imagine that awareness of breast health care has only existed for about 20 years. But as recently as the early 1970s, when a woman went in for a biopsy, she never knew whether her body would be whole afterward. She signed an agreement that stated if cancer was discovered, while she was still anesthetized the surgeon had her permission to perform a radical mastectomy, removing her breast, the muscles on her chest wall, and the lymph nodes under her arm. This was the famous one-step procedure. Breast cancer was dealt with quickly, in a manner doctors considered "efficient." Now we all know differently.

It was not until the mid-1970s that attitudes began to change. Betty Ford and Happy Rockefeller, admired women in the public eye, openly discussed their breast cancers. Medical writer Rose Kushner was diagnosed with breast cancer and she became an energetic campaigner *against* the one-step procedure and *for* increasing funds for breast cancer research and encouraging breast conservation. Doctors began to consider a possible link between breast cancer and hormones—that the high levels of hormones in birth control pills (levels much higher than in today's pills) might stimulate breast tumors. Once regarded as cosmetic features that could be enlarged or reduced at will, breasts now became a health concern. Discussions of mammography and breast self-examinations appeared in newspapers, magazines, and on television. Everyone was talking about breast health care, but what was clearly growing out of all the talk was an awareness tinged with fear. Women became afraid to touch their breasts. What if you found a lump? *Then* what would you do?

Our belief has always been that *the more you know, the less fearful you will be*. You are not facing decisions about your breast health care alone. Your doctor is there to help you, but to have a valuable partnership, you must bring your own understanding to the table, and that's where we come in. Many women become actively informed about their breast health care only after something goes wrong. Our goal is to increase your understanding of your breasts right now. In *The Complete Book of Breast Care*, we have set out to produce an up-to-the-minute guide for breast health care that is easy to read and enjoyable.

Also, to keep you up to date, we have included a special section on computer research (see Part VI, "Resources") to guide you through the on-line networks that may be available to you. You can learn how to travel the electronic information highway and locate the latest on breast health care. To our knowledge, *The Complete Book of Breast Care* is the first women's health book to pinpoint the best breast health care information in cyberspace.

Today, in the tumult of health care, when major institutions like the National Cancer Institute and the American Cancer Society are at odds over when women should have annual mammograms, when fraud is discovered in a prestigious 15-year lumpectomy study, and researchers are in dispute about whether diet plays a role in breast health, it is more important than ever that you trust your source of information and your instincts.

YOUR GREATEST ASSETS: WHAT YOU KNOW AND WHAT YOU SENSE

The medical experiences of real women continue to support our belief that a mix of information and instinct is essential to good health. Every day, aware that their health depends on *their* choices as well as their doctors', more women are stretching their intellect and searching their souls. To illustrate our point, three informed women who trusted their instincts have allowed us to reveal what happened to them in the course of their breast care:

Stacey's Perseverance

Stacey's aunt had had breast cancer, so Stacey immediately went to her doctor when she felt a small lump. He did not feel anything and was not really concerned. He told her to come back in two months when he would check her again. After reading *Listen to Your Body*, she understood more precisely how to carry out a breast self-examination and realized that sometimes breast lumps can change. She also recognized the importance of a second opinion. A voice within kept telling her to check further. Stacey could not shake the nagging doubt that two months was too long to wait, and even though she was now having a little trouble finding the lump herself, she made an appointment with another doctor for a second opinion.

While this gynecologist also said her breasts felt normal, he sent her for a mammogram. Stacey was only 35, but considering her family history and her strong suspicions, he wanted her to be screened. "Finally," she told us, "I thought I would have my answer." Her mammogram did not reveal anything suspicious but Stacey still was not reassured. "I don't know why—maybe it was my aunt's breast cancer; maybe it was what I had read about missed cancers in the dense breasts of younger women—but I wanted more proof that the lump I knew I felt was gone." The gynecologist told her that she could have a sonogram of her breast, but at the same time he elicited a promise from her that she would accept the results and stop worrying.

The sonogram revealed what looked like a tiny cyst, which the breast specialist conducting the sonogram attempted to aspirate with a fine needle. No fluid came out. "At this point I didn't know what to think," said Stacey. "There was something in my breast." A breast surgeon performed a biopsy and a ductal carcinoma in situ (DCIS)—cancer cells confined to a breast duct—was confirmed. A few days later Stacey underwent a lumpectomy and had "clear" margins. (The outer edges, or *margins*, of removed breast tissue are always examined after surgery to make sure that they are cancer-free or "clear.") Since her in situ tumor was so tiny and her pathology report showed nonaggressive cells, Stacey decided against radiation. Her doctor gave her an excellent prognosis, as long as she visited him every three months for a breast examination and had a mammogram every six months. In time she will be able to return to annual screenings.

"The breast surgeon told me that if I had not pushed for more tests, I might not have been so lucky," Stacey said recently. "I might have needed a mastectomy." She cannot explain exactly why she pursued her gut feeling so strongly, "but I do know that the more I read about examining your breasts, about lumps, about second opinions, the more I wanted to keep going," she says. "Friends told me to stop obsessing, but I didn't think I was obsessing as much as I was being determined."

Hannah's Story

One night after reading an article on breast self-examination, Hannah decided to try it. At the age of 28 and with no history of breast cancer in her family, she was not thinking about finding a lump. She was just curious to see whether she could do a proper breast exam. The inside of her breasts had the texture of cottage cheese, lumpy all over, but a squishy bump, like a soft marble, stood out. She checked the other breast to see if there was a matching bump, but no, only one bump on one breast. Maybe it will go away, she thought, but in the morning it was still there. When it had not disappeared after three days, she went to her gynecologist. By that time she had already stopped drinking caffeinated beverages and started taking antioxidant vitamins C and E.

"It's a cyst," said her doctor after he checked her breasts. "How do you know?" she asked. She was healthy, still in her twenties. Why didn't she believe him? "How do you know your own grandmother?" he answered sarcastically. "I know how cysts feel. It will probably disappear by your next cycle." Not convinced, and wanting positive proof, Hannah asked for a mammogram. Her doctor was against it. It did not make sense to expose her to radiation for a cyst, he told her, but at her insistence he reluctantly sent her to a breast screening center and then to a breast surgeon for a consultation.

"It looks like a cyst," said the breast surgeon, scrutinizing her mammogram, "but I'll examine you." He palpated Hannah's breasts, then paused while he reached for a syringe. Either she was not paying attention when he told her or he didn't tell her that he was going to aspirate the cyst and drain it of its fluid. She was stunned to see him push in the needle an inch or so from her nipple. When no fluid came out, he told Hannah to make an appointment for a biopsy. Without fluid to prove that the lump was a cyst, he needed to cut, he said. She made an appointment for the following week and left his office in a daze. She had pushed for a definitive diagnosis, but she didn't like the course she was on. She hadn't realized a doctor was going to stick a needle into her breast!

Hannah spent practically the whole weekend at her health club, where she worked out and spent time in the steamroom and the Jacuzzi. At home she drank herbal teas and went to bed early. She tried not to touch the lump. She wanted to take her mind off her scheduled biopsy, and she wondered whether she should have simply believed her own doctor, whom she had always trusted. When the possibility that she might have breast cancer arose in her mind, she battled the thought back.

On the day of her biopsy, Hannah examined her breasts before she dressed. She could not feel the lump, but she told herself that she was probably just wishing it away. She arrived at the outpatient area of the hospital and was prepared for the biopsy, which was scheduled to take place shortly. The breast surgeon stepped into the curtained area where she had changed into her patient's dressing gown to ask how she was doing. "Well, I don't feel the lump," she told him as he preoperatively examined her breasts. He did not feel the lump anymore either. "Could it have disappeared?" she asked. "Maybe," he answered. "We should postpone the biopsy, though. I can't cut into something that isn't there. You should have a sonogram before we proceed any further," he said.

Hannah felt as if she had just been granted a stay of execution. Her breast did not have to be cut, at least not on that day. Later, on the table in the ultrasonographer's room, she watched the video screen illuminate the sonogram of her breasts. Everything was normal. No cyst! Maybe she had overreacted initially, she thought. She had put herself through quite an ordeal, but still, she was pleased that she had followed through on her feelings. If she had a chance to relive this episode, she told us, she would still rely on her sense of judgment. "I didn't have a problem this time," she said, "but I'm never going to tell myself I'm being too pushy when it comes to my body."

"My Mother," by Eileen Stukane

My mother called to say that they had found something on her mammogram, her first, at age 72. "Can you believe it?" she asked, and of course I could not. She had no history of breast cancer in her family, had given birth to four children, two in her twenties, the other two in her early thirties, and had breastfed. She exercised regularly, ate mostly vegetarian, low-fat foods, and had never been on hormone therapy. Her only obvious risk factor for breast cancer, other than being female, was that she had lived in an area of the Northeast that had a high rate of cancer.

My father had died six months before my mother's call, only five months after his metastasized cancer had been diagnosed. The shocking discovery and swift progression of his illness had devastated all of us. My mother had been an emotionally strong companion, a loving caregiver, and I had marveled at her inner balance. She had absorbed the traumatic impact of my father's condition remarkably, or so I thought. Now that she appeared to have a cancer of her own, I started thinking about the connection between stress and the immune system, a connection that we explore in Chapter 9,

"The Mind/Body Connection: Stress and Your Breasts." That the stress of my father's illness could have contributed to a growth of a cancer is a theory that I will never be able to prove, but it is one I cannot shake. That my father's illness saved her life may also be true.

Because my father had died from cancer, my siblings and I had urged my mother to get a physical examination. She had not seen a doctor in years, had avoided Pap tests, and had never had a mammogram. The fact that I was researching this book also made me much more aware of the importance of mammography and much more concerned about her breast health care. At last, when winter turned to spring, she went to the doctor.

Her reaction to her first mammogram? "It HURT!" Then her doctor called with the news. There was little question as to what the white star-like spot on the mammographic X ray of her right breast was, although she could not feel a lump. My mother's first response was to say that she would do nothing. "I'm going out with what I came in with," she said. All right, but perhaps she should know what options she was rejecting before she rejected them. She agreed to meet with a breast surgeon, but she offered no promises about considering his advice.

Reluctantly my mother entered the examining room, where the breast surgeon did a fine-needle aspiration biopsy of the lump so that the cells could be analyzed for cancer. The mammographic finding had to be confirmed by pathology. Because the lump appeared only slightly larger than 1 centimeter, he told her that she would have the choice of a lumpectomy with follow-up radiation treatments, or mastectomy, if cancer were confirmed. (If the pathology report was negative, he would perform a surgical biopsy.) He discussed removal of the lymph nodes during a lumpectomy or mastectomy and the fact that chemotherapy would follow the appearance of cancer in the nodes. I could see by the loss of color in my mother's face that she was reeling from the thought of chemotherapy. She had watched my father bravely down the drugs that, in the end, only weakened him. Realizing what was happening, the doctor looked her in the eyes and said, "You don't have to decide anything right now. Your breast cancer is not like your husband's cancer. Even if you need chemotherapy, you will not be as sick as he was. You appear to have an early-stage cancer, which has an excellent—96 percent—rate of survival." Her instincts told her to believe him.

She took a few weeks to make her choice of surgery after the results of the needle biopsy were found to be positive. She consulted another breast surgeon for a second opinion and heard again that she had a choice. Joyce Wadler, author of My Breast, became a smart, comforting adviser who gave her insights into what she could expect from a lumpectomy and how she would feel during radiation treatments. SHARE, the breast cancer support organization based in New York City, put her in touch with other women her age who had chosen either lumpectomy or mastectomy. After a few weeks she decided to have a lumpectomy with a six-week course of radiation to her remaining breast tissue. Her lymph nodes were negative, and no chemotherapy was advised, although over the next five years she will take tamoxifen (Nolvadex), a drug that has been shown to reduce the risk of breast cancer recurring. Eight days after surgery she flew across the country for a family reunion in New Mexico. As I watched her embrace nieces and nephews she had not seen in years, I realized that getting out the best information to her and all women who face breast health crises was the main reason for my writing this book. By understanding her options, my mother was able to become a new woman. I hope you will, too.

HORMONES: THE EVIDENCE MOUNTS

Today the lifetime odds for breast cancer faced by a woman living in North America stand at one in eight, double the risk a woman faced in 1940. We know that since 1940, when Connecticut became the first state to keep good records of breast cancer, new cases have been diagnosed at an increase of 1 percent per year. In the 1980s, that rate soared, reaching a 4 percent peak in 1987. Researchers delved into many areas to find the reason behind the increased incidence of breast cancer. They have investigated heredity and the genes, menstrual history, age at first pregnancy, diet, birth control pills, hormone replacement therapy, environmental factors, and exercise. Although scientists continue to explore these areas, many are now interested in analyzing the timing of, and exposure to, estrogen and progesterone.

Two hundred years ago, women in China and North America reached menarche at the same average age of 17. Today Chinese women still follow that biological schedule. They also have much lower rates of breast cancer than American women. The average age for menarche in the United States is 12.5. Experts think that this may be the result of improved nutrition in childhood. So, with diet leading to earlier menstruation and lifestyles leading to later and fewer births, today's American women experience more years of exposure to cycling estrogen. They also experience higher rates of breast cancer than Chinese women. A Swedish study even found that exposure to estrogen in the womb, before birth, might have an effect on whether a woman develops breast cancer. Researchers at the University of Uppsala reported that daughters of women who suffered preeclampsia, a condition in pregnancy that is associated with a lower than average estrogen level, were significantly less likely to have breast cancer. Evidence for the hormonal connection continues to mount.

Exercise may even affect the hormones that affect breasts. At the University of Southern California School of Medicine, Leslie Bernstein, Ph.D., interviewed 545 women who developed breast cancer by age 40 and an equal number of healthy women. After adjusting for known breast cancer risk factors, Dr. Bernstein found that the risk of women who reported exercising at least four hours a week, for about 35 minutes a day, was approximately *60 percent less* than in sedentary women. Even working out for as little as two to three hours a week was beneficial. Although further study is needed, exercise appears to offer protection against premenopausal breast cancer by lowering the level of estrogen in the body.

Tests are also being developed to measure the level of 16 alpha-hydroxyestrone, a by-product of estrogen, in both blood and urine. High levels have been found in women with breast cancer, and a test that could give a reading of this estrogen by-product may help to predict future trouble in the breasts of healthy women. Without a doubt, you will hear more and more over the next few years about the breast's link to estrogen.

THE BEAUTY OF YOUR BREASTS

At their most idealized, breasts are the world's fertility symbols, timelessly captured by artists. No two women have breasts that look alike, and if you look at your own breasts in a mirror, you can see that even in a pair, no two breasts are identical. Your breasts have been part of your life's most intense experiences. They emerged during your adolescence, reshaped your body, and told the world you were a woman. They were involved in your sexual awakening, and if you have breastfed, they provided a bond like no other for you and your baby. Breasts change with the seasons of your life, but they remain beautiful and important always. We appreciate the opportunity we have been given to help women of all ages understand, in depth, the biology of their breasts and the care they need for good health.

PART I

Healthy Breasts Are Always Changing

CHAPTER ONE

Understanding the Basics: Your Breasts Over Your Lifetime

Like most women, you will probably experience some sort of breast trouble in your lifetime—sore breasts at a particular point during your menstrual cycle or pregnancy; questions about breastfeeding; a certainty that you "feel something" when you are doing a self-examination. Before you are at a crucial point, give yourself an edge by understanding the basics.

YOUR HEALTHY BREAST

What You See

The size, shape, and elevation of your breast, the position of the nipple, and the color of the nipple and *areola* (the circular area surrounding the nipple) are inherited characteristics that vary from woman to woman. In general, the nipple and areola are pink or tan in Caucasians, brown in Asians, and black in African Americans. Your breasts extend from about the second or third rib to the sixth or seventh rib, and from the *sternum*, the breastbone in the center of your chest, into your armpit region, the *axilla*. No pair of breasts ever matches another, however, and no two breasts are alike. It is quite normal for one breast to be slightly larger than the other. You may also be naturally "high breasted" or "low breasted." Your nipple may be inverted or protruding, exactly in the middle of your breast or slightly off center. (Wherever their location, nipples naturally slant toward your armpit, a direction that makes breastfeeding easier.) Hairs may grow from follicles at the edge of your areola, and on the areola itself, you may notice *Montgomery's glands*, a few tiny bumps like pimples.

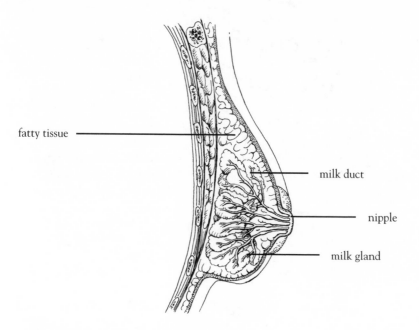

fatty tissue

milk duct

nipple

milk gland

Internal side view of a breast. The breast is made up of fatty tissue, milk glands, and milk ducts which funnel into the nipple.

Inside Your Breast

Your breast is a glandular mass interlaced with *ducts* and supported by a *blood supply*, a *lymph system* (lymph is the clear fluid found in tissue spaces throughout your body), and *fat*. *Fasciae* or *ligaments* are bands of fibrous tissue within your breasts that are attached to the pectoral muscle on your chest wall, supporting your breasts. A highly developed network of nerves and nerve endings connect the breast's glandular activity with the hormonal fluc-tuations of your brain, ovaries, and adrenals. (This important hormonal con-nection is discussed later in this chapter.)

Fat is the main substance in your breasts. The number of fatty cells you have affect your breast size, which gets larger or smaller as you gain or lose weight. An overweight woman will have increased fat and therefore larger breasts. A slim woman usually has less fat and smaller, firmer breasts. Within the fatty tissue in each breast there are 15 to 25 *lobes*. Each lobe contains a system of *milk-producing glands*, or *lobules*, and ducts.

Your breast gets its main supply of blood from the *mammary artery*, which enters from underneath the rib cage, through the chest wall near the *sternum* (your breastbone), and then branches into the breast tissue. The lymph system in the breast closely follows the pathways of the veins and is connected to the lymph glands in the armpit.

HOW A HEALTHY BREAST FUNCTIONS

Each of the 15 to 25 lobes in your breast is formed by groups of lobules. Within each lobule are clusters of up to 100 *acini* or *alveoli*, hollow, glandular sacs that produce and store breast milk. The number of acini varies from woman to woman, but they appear in greatest abundance in the breasts of women 17 to 22 years old. The word *acini* means "grapes" in Latin, and, figuratively speaking, the breast's milk-producing system looks like bunches of grapes (lobules) attached to stems (milk-transporting ducts), which are then attached to larger, stronger vines (main milk ducts). The main milk ducts intertwine in a network, but eventually they all travel through the breast to the nipple. There are between five and nine separate ductile systems in each breast. (See Chapter 2 for more about breast milk and breastfeeding.)

Surrounding each of the acini is the tissue made up of *myoepithelial cells* that give your inner breast the ability to contract. Myoepithelial contraction enables the acini and the duct network to expel milk when a woman breastfeeds. Actually, the ducts deposit the milk in the *ampullae*, the enlarged duct terminals at the base of the nipple. In Latin the word *ampullae* means "jugs," but to avoid an unfortunate translation, they are also called "milk sinuses." To aid the squeezing and emptying of the ampullae, smooth muscle fibers contract and make the nipple erect and firm during breastfeeding.

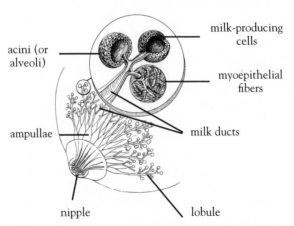

acini (or alveoli)

milk-producing cells

myoepithelial fibers

ampullae

milk ducts

nipple

lobule

Anatomy of the milk ducts and acini. Breast milk is produced in the outer cells of the acini—also called the alveoli—and stored in their hollow sacs. When an infant suckles, the myoepithelial muscle fibers around the acini contract and pump the milk into ducts that transport it to the nipple. This is called "milk letdown."

HOW HORMONES AFFECT BREAST GROWTH AND HEALTH

The Mind/Body Connection and Your Breasts

A holistic approach to breast health care considers your "whole" being. It works with your ability to keep your mind, body, and spirit in harmony—an approach that is as scientific as it is philosophical. What is often called the "mind/body connection" is based on researchers' discoveries of the paths and powers of different hormones, chemical secretions released by the brain, and the endocrine glands located at strategic points in your body.

In a constant internal "conversation," the endocrine glands "listen to" the hormonal messages they receive from the master gland, the *pituitary*. Protectively surrounded by bone, the pituitary is located in the center of the brain behind the nasal cavities, just below an area called the *hypothalamus*. The hypothalamus links the thinking part of the brain, the *cerebral cortex*, to the pituitary. Herein lies the foundation of the mind/body connection.

The endocrine glands respond to the pituitary's hormones by releasing more or less of their own hormones into the bloodstream. The glands also report messages back to the brain. In response to the feedback from the glands, the pituitary sends out a round of hormones again. Technically a hormone acts like a key that can fit into a lock, or receptor, of a cell. Once the hormonal key opens its receptor lock, a physiological process can begin. There are a number of hormones such as estrogen, progesterone, prolactin, and oxytocin that are meant to target receptors in the breast. These hormones are responsible for the way a breast develops, prepares, and releases breast milk. They also contribute to a breast's continuing health.

Breast Development Starts in the Womb

The key hormones in breast development are the female sex hormones, estrogen and progesterone. In the developing fetus, estrogen promotes the growth of ducts in the breasts, and estrogen and progesterone stimulate development of the lobular (milk-producing) glands. Studies have shown that a pregnant woman also produces hormones specifically targeted to the breast growth of her developing baby. Placental hormone, insulin, adrenal steroids, and the pituitary hormones—growth hormone, prolactin, thyroid-stimulating hormone (TSH), and luteinizing hormone (LH)—are all aimed at promoting breast growth in a fetus.

Six weeks after conception, the mammary gland (breast tissue) in the fetus starts to develop. A "milk ridge" forms as paired glands running side by side in parallel rows along the fetus's body appear from above the armpit to the groin area. By the ninth week most of this ridge disappears, except for one pair of glands, which will become two breasts in the chest area. (On very rare occasions a woman may retain vestiges of her

PITUITARY HORMONES AND THEIR POWER OVER YOUR BODY

The following hormones travel from the pituitary gland to different parts of your body:

- Growth hormone—mostly to the bones
- Thyroid-stimulating hormone (TSH)—to the thyroid gland
- Adrenocorticotropic hormone (ACTH)—to the adrenal glands

- Gonadotropins
   Follicle-stimulating hormone (FSH)/Luteinizing hormone (LH)—to the ovaries
   Prolactin—to the breasts to stimulate the acini for the flow of breast milk
- Vasopressin—to the kidneys
- Oxytocin—to the womb during pregnancy to stimulate labor
   —to the breasts of a nursing mother to start the flow of breast milk

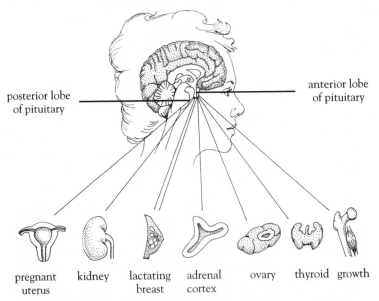

posterior lobe of pituitary   anterior lobe of pituitary

pregnant uterus   kidney   lactating breast   adrenal cortex   ovary   thyroid   growth

The pituitary gland, the master gland, directs sex hormone production, helps maintain pregnancy, governs the kidneys, stimulates the flow of breast milk, affects hormone production in the adrenal glands, ovaries, and thyroid, and controls growth.

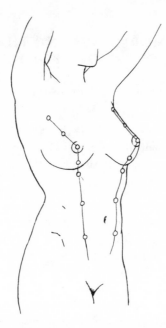

Locations of nipples on the milk ridge that develops in a fetus. Except for one pair of milk-producing glands that become breasts, the ridge usually disappears. On rare occasions, one or two vestigial nipples remain, but they can be removed through plastic surgery.

fetal milk ridge—she may have one or two visible, rudimentary nipples on her body, positioned in places that would be along the length of the ridge. Plastic surgery can remove these extra nipples.) At birth, an infant, whether female or male, may have swollen breasts that leak what's called "witch's milk" until the effects of exposure to the mother's hormones subside.

After 10 or 12 Uneventful Years, the Breast Responds to Puberty

"I never thought my breasts were big enough when I was in high school. I used to try to stretch them by pulling them out by the nipples. They finally grew, but I don't think my stretching technique did it."

—CAROLYN H., AGE 39

"I didn't want to have breasts because I was a tomboy, and I was happy to have small breasts. I've never worn a bra in my life, except when I need support for a strapless dress."

—JULIA L., AGE 63

"I was in a bra when I was 9 years old. I needed a B cup. When we bought it, the saleswoman criticized my mother for waiting too long to put me in a bra and my mother yelled back at her, 'She's only 9 years old!' I remember really resenting my breasts' growth. I couldn't go out to play because my breasts hurt, and the other kids made fun of me and my big breasts."

—MARJORIE T., AGE 41

"The first time I became aware of my breasts, I was coming home from Sunday school with my family and all of a sudden they were really sensitive. I could feel their presence. I told my mother because my nightmare was that I was going to look like her, a 40D. When I was a junior in high school, it happened very quickly—I did start getting like my mother. I became a 38C."

—JANE B., AGE 52

10 TO 12 YEARS OLD

Your breast becomes the first organ of your body to herald your adolescence. Estrogen levels begin to increase at this time, and changes in the hormonal receptors in your breasts make them more responsive to the estrogen surge. The milk glands in the breast start to enlarge. Still, it takes a while for the ovaries to respond to the increasing production of estrogen and to contribute their own formidable share of estrogen and progesterone. Breasts can show signs of change years before a girl's first menstrual period and before hair sprouts in her armpit.

Although the timing of breast growth can vary, most breasts begin to grow when a girl is between 10 and 12 years old. Some girls have fully developed breasts by the age of 10, while others are still waiting to fit into a bra at 14. Researchers do not know why, but African American women start to develop a year or two earlier than Caucasian women. Generally, though, between 10 and 12, a girl can notice her breasts beginning to bud, and at the same time, see pubic hair appearing on her *mons veneris*, which means "mountain of Venus" in Latin and is the medical term for the triangular mound between her legs.

11 TO 15 YEARS OLD

Menstruation begins. Visually, during these years a girl's breasts are becoming more prominent, but her womanly curves have not yet appeared. Starting now, and for the rest of a woman's reproductive years, during each monthly cycle the breasts respond to the hormones released by the brain, adrenal glands, and ovaries as they gear up for pregnancy. Every month the breasts are primed for this change. They swell and become tender. (How hormones fluctuate during the menstrual cycle and their effect on the breasts is described below.) If you *do not* become pregnant during a menstrual cycle, your breasts return to their normal size, until they are stimulated during the next cycle.

15 TO 21 YEARS OLD

You may have inherited the size and shape of your breasts from your mother's or your father's genes, which means that your breasts, whether they are round, egg-shaped, or conical, may have matured according to your maternal or paternal biological timetable. But your genetic foundation could also have been influenced by your hormonal fluctuations, which are influenced by lifestyle choices such as diet and exercise, and weight—the body can convert fat cells into estrogen, for example, so a heavier girl may develop breasts sooner than a thin, athletic girl who has little fat and less estrogen. By age 21, however, every woman's body has reached maturity. Breasts are full; the areolae cap the tips, and nipples, whether inverted or protruding, are clearly centered within the areolae.

From Adolescence Into Your Twenties and Thirties: Your Breasts and Your Menstrual Cycle

The pituitary gland in the base of your brain, the adrenal glands above the kidneys, and the ovaries produce the endocrine hormones that create your monthly cycle and bring on changes in your breasts. As one menstrual cycle ends (at about the time that vaginal bleeding slows to a trickle), another menstrual cycle begins. Like carefully calibrated instruments, the glands release precise amounts of their hormones.

In the first half of your menstrual cycle, approximately two weeks before ovulation, you usually do not see or feel noticeable changes in your breasts. Your breasts ought to be at their normal size and softness. You should not have any tenderness. This is when the hypothalamus of the brain, which controls the menstrual cycle, sends a hormonal message—the *releasing factor*—to the pituitary gland.

When the pituitary receives the message, it releases the *follicle-stimulating hormone*—FSH—into your bloodstream, where it finds its way to the ovaries. You are now well into the first half of your menstrual cycle. Once FSH reaches the ovaries, it stimulates the follicles, the potential egg cells in the ovaries, to grow and produce *estrogen*. Hormone-producing ovarian tissue also adds more estrogen to the buildup. As the estrogen level rises, it affects the skin, which may seem clearer and more radiant; cervical mucus, which changes in consistency; and the breasts, which become larger and firmer as the milk glands swell.

Estrogen output reaches a high level. The increase in estrogen affects the action of the pituitary, which first reduces, then stops its output of FSH to send out the *luteinizing hormone* (LH). While the estrogen level is rising, one follicle in an ovary begins to surpass the other egg cells in its development. That one egg cell, called the *Graafian follicle* or the follicle (egg)-of-the-month, bubbles out on the outside of the ovary. The LH causes the Graafian follicle's bubble to burst and eject a mature egg cell. The ejection of the egg is *ovulation*. The first half of the menstrual cycle, which takes about 14 days, is now complete.

The second half of the menstrual cycle, which lasts 14 additional days (on average), begins as the ovulated egg strikes out on a five-to-seven-day journey inside the fallopian tube to the womb. The scar tissue left behind after the egg pops out of its bubble becomes the *corpus luteum*, the producer of *progesterone*, the pregnancy hormone. Progesterone causes the lining of the uterus to change into a soft, spongy nest rich in blood vessels and glandular tissue that is the perfect bed for the egg coming down the tube. This hormone also (1) changes cervical mucus from clear and stretchy to cloudy and thick to create a natural protective barrier against germs that may enter the uterus, (2) relaxes the uterus to give the egg a better chance to implant itself in the *endometrium*, the transformed uterine lining, and (3) prepares the breasts for lactation, or breastfeeding.

The combined rise in estrogen and progesterone levels affects your breasts more than any single hormonal shift. The high output of this pair of hormones can noticeably enlarge the breasts and contribute to their tenderness. Some women notice a lumpiness at this time. Women who have a tendency to develop cysts (fluid-filled sacs) in their breasts may feel new, cystic lumps that they did not detect in the first half of their cycle. By examining your breasts throughout your cycle, you can become familiar with their "feel" and not be alarmed by these changes. (See Chapter 3 for specifics on breast self-examination.)

The surge of estrogen and progesterone may also bring on symptoms of premenstrual syndrome, menstrual cramps, and/or irregular periods. The menstrual cycle, however, is nearing its end. If the egg has been fertilized by sperm, and conception has occurred, the pituitary continues to send out LH, and estrogen and progesterone levels stay high. The breasts become more tender and painful—they can hurt even without being touched. This breast pain can be a woman's first sign of pregnancy. Throughout pregnancy, the breasts become larger and heavier. They swell until childbirth, when lactation begins. (See Chapter 2 for more information about how pregnancy and breastfeeding affect your breasts.)

If there is no fertilization and conception during a menstrual cycle, the pituitary does not get the stimulus it needs to maintain the corpus luteum. Without the signal from the brain, the corpus luteum disintegrates, estrogen and progesterone levels drop rapidly, and menstruation is triggered. When the sex hormones drop, the level of prostaglandins, hormone-like substances in the lining of the uterus, rises, causing the uterus to contract and shed the endometrium, the enriched spongy lining of the uterus. The endometrium

IS A BRA GOOD OR BAD FOR YOUR BREASTS?

Neither! There is no medical reason to wear a bra, so the decision is yours, based on your own personal comfort and aesthetics. Whether you have always worn a bra or always gone braless, age and breast-feeding will naturally cause your breasts to sag. Here are a few suggestions to consider:

THE COMFORT FACTOR

While some women feel that bras are annoying, many large-breasted women like to wear bras. They say that a bra controls breast movement, which can cause pain and discomfort, and prevents the skin irritation that can occur under the natural fold of a large breast. Among women who have smaller breasts, some who have nursed say that they prefer wearing bras because breastfeeding made their breasts pendulous, and a bra gives them an attractive lift. Many working women admit to feeling more psychologically comfortable wearing bras on the job, but others are relaxed and braless under business suits. The choice is yours.

THE SOFTER, THE BETTER

I recommend soft cotton or Lycra bras, as opposed to underwire bras, which can constrict the breast and cause depressions in the skin. Sometimes the material covering the underwire deteriorates, exposing the metal underwire, leading to skin irritations, perhaps due to an allergic reaction to metal.

NOW AND THEN, GO BRALESS

Allowing yourself to go braless occasionally, whether at home or in a situation you feel is appropriate, is a healthful habit. Ligaments attach your breasts to the pectoral muscle on your chest. When you wear a bra, your supported breast does not allow the pectoral muscle to be exercised as much as it could be. When you *do not* wear a bra, as you move your arms, reach, and lift, your pectoral muscle is strengthened. The muscle can then offer better support to your breasts.

THE PECTORAL SQUEEZE

This daily exercise can strengthen your pectoral muscle, which can give a lift to your breasts. Stretch your arms straight out to the side at shoulder height. Keep your palms up. Bend your arms at a right angle and bring the elbows together in front of your body. Squeeze your elbows together and slowly return your right-angled arms to the side, outstretched position. With shoulders pressed down, repeat the pectoral squeeze eight times twice.

which is useless without a pregnancy, leaves the body as menstrual blood. Without hormonal stimulation, the breasts lose their added fullness, cysts disintegrate, and tenderness disappears. As you start to bleed, one menstrual cycle ends and another begins.

In Your Forties and Fifties: Your Breasts at the End of Your Childbearing Years

The time in your life just before your menstrual periods stop completely is called *perimenopause*. This stage can begin in the late thirties but usually occurs from the mid-to-late forties into the early fifties, when women notice that their menstrual patterns change due to a natural decline in the female hormones estrogen and progesterone. Perimenopause can arrive with well-known change-of-life symptoms, such as hot flashes made obvious by flushed skin and sweats, dry skin, backaches, and menstrual periods that over several months or years can become heavier before they become shorter and lighter. During different menstrual cycles the breasts may become swollen, tender, and cystic as they react to highly unstable estrogen levels. Eventually, as estrogen levels drop more consistently, one or more menstrual periods are skipped, and the breasts go into a resting stage during which engorgement and tenderness disappear. Perimenopause can last anywhere from a few months to several years, although some women never experience this phase at all—one day they just stop menstruating and enter *menopause*.

Menopause, which comes from the Greek word *mens* meaning

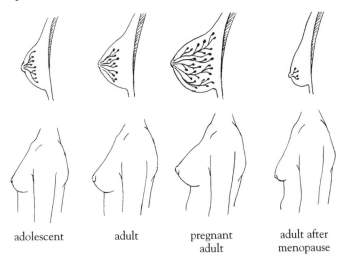

adolescent   adult   pregnant   adult after
                                     adult   menopause

Breast changes throughout life. From left to right, glandular tissue in the breast develops during adolescence, increases with maturity and pregnancy, and diminishes after menopause.

"monthly" and *pausa* meaning "stop," is the time when a woman's monthly menstrual periods come to a halt. When we speak of menopause, we are talking about changes that occur in a woman after she stops menstruating. Unless you go on hormone replacement therapy (HRT), which is covered at length in Chapter 11, your breasts will naturally reshape themselves into softer glands at menopause. Without hormonal stimulation from the ovaries, breasts do not gear up for breastfeeding every month. Because the milk glands are not activated, breast tissue shrinks, and breasts droop more than they did before menopause.

Postmenopause begins after the symptoms of menopause disappear. The array of menopausal symptoms, which vary from woman to woman, and can include hot flashes, heart palpitations, dizziness, nausea, fatigue, and disorientation, to name a few, finally end. At this time, when all the physical and emotional symptoms of this passage have completely passed, a woman feels that her body is maintaining a steady, even balance. As they do throughout a woman's life, the adrenal glands create a certain amount of estrogen by producing a steroid called *androstenedione*, that the body converts into estrogen even after menopause. With the ovaries shut down, the adrenals' hormone-producing activity becomes more important in the senior years.

Your Breasts at Age 60 and Beyond

As you age after menopause, if you do not choose hormone replacement

---

HORMONE REPLACEMENT THERAPY AND YOUR BREASTS

When you are alleviating symptoms of menopause with the estrogen and progesterone/progestins of hormone replacement therapy (HRT), you are also stimulating cell production in your breasts.

- This hormonal stimulation helps your breasts remain firm and full.
- Sometimes women who choose HRT report an increase in breast size.
- With HRT the veins in your breasts may also become more visible.
- While the studies on whether HRT increases the risk of breast cancer are conflicting (see Chapter 11) hormone replacement offers such strong protection against cardiovascular problems and osteoporosis that researchers suggest that each woman discuss her risks with her doctor.

therapy, your estrogen levels fall off, and the drop in hormonal stimulation to your breasts leads to a decrease in breast tissue. Your breasts will droop. Exercise, especially the pectoral squeeze mentioned earlier in this chapter, can strengthen the chest muscles that support your breasts and help give them a lift. Although their appearance undergoes a natural change, your breasts remain as sexually responsive as they have always been during lovemaking.

Throughout your lifetime, but especially as you enter the senior years, it is important to maintain an appropriate weight for your height. Since an enzyme in the body works to convert body fat into estrogen, overweight women have more estrogen, and hence, a greater chance of developing breast cancer. Normally, the risk of developing breast cancer increases with age (see Chapter 18 for more about risk), so during these years every woman should be vigilant about having a mammogram and breast examination by a physician every year.

SEX AND YOUR BREASTS

Only humans—no other animals—integrate breasts into sex play. For the rest of the animal kingdom, breasts are only feeders, but for us, breasts are also sexually responsive. Throughout your life, as long as you are sexually active, your breasts are one of your erogenous zones, although sensations vary from woman to woman. On one end of the sensitivity spectrum are women who say they can achieve orgasm from the oral or manual stimulation of their breasts alone, and on the other are women who do not think their breasts are important to their lovemaking. Still, on the most basic biological level, all breasts become more engorged and reactive during sex.

As you become sexually excited, your heart rate and blood pressure rise, your breasts and areolae swell, and your nipples harden and become erect. A reddish flush emanates from your abdomen and spreads out over your breasts as well. The pituitary gland in your brain releases the hormone oxytocin. You may remember that oxytocin is the hormone best known for starting labor and stimulating the flow of breast milk after childbirth. This same oxytocin level rises during sex, whether you are pregnant or not, breastfeeding or not.

As orgasm approaches, the breasts, areolae, and nipples become even firmer and larger, and the surge of oxytocin creates small muscle contractions in the breasts that are quite pleasurable. These pulsations continue as uterine contractions build during orgasm. If you are pregnant or breastfeeding, you may leak milk from your breasts as you reach your climax.

During pregnancy a woman's breasts can be so large and tender that she considers them more pain than pleasure. On the other hand, the fuller breasts of pregnancy make some women feel more voluptuous and excited about lovemaking. No matter how you feel, a partner's touch should be light and gentle.

During the rhythms of breastfeeding, as the breasts fill with milk and the baby suckles from a mother's erect nipple, there is no mistaking the sexual quality of the experience. Nipple stimulation from a newborn brings on uterine contractions that tighten the muscles of the womb and help return it to prepregnancy size, but as these contractions are akin to sexual arousal some mothers may experience orgasm. This can be pleasurable for some women but disturbing for others. As you and your baby adjust to breast-feeding, both the uterine contractions and the overall intensity of the experience subside. While some women find breastfeeding so fulfilling they are less focused on sex, other new mothers like the heightened sensitivity of their nipples so much, they want their breasts to be caressed and suckled by their partners during lovemaking.

YOUR HEREDITY, YOUR LIFESTYLE, AND YOUR BREASTS

Heredity

Your genetic makeup is the foundation of your body; it provides you with the anatomy and appearance of your breasts and the timetable for their development. The genes that predominate in you may be from either your mother's or your father's side of the family. Thus, you may have a figure like your mother, either of your grandmothers, or one of your maternal or paternal aunts. In the mix of genes you inherited, there may also be a mutated gene for breast cancer, if one exists in your family tree. (See Chapter 18 for the progress being made in genetic research.) The development of your breasts is not solely dependent on genes, however. Since your breasts respond to hormones, lifestyle habits that affect your hormonal fluctuations also affect the look and health of your breasts.

Lifestyle

Whether and when you choose to become pregnant, give birth, and breast-feed your offspring will affect the health of your breasts. The menstrual hormonal cycle is interrupted during pregnancy, and breasts that engorge during the nine months of expectancy empty themselves of breast milk during breastfeeding. The hormonal cycle related to childbearing seems to keep breasts healthy and offer some protection against breast cancer, especially if you give birth for the first time before your thirtieth birthday. (This protective factor is explored more thoroughly in Chapter 2.)

A sedentary or an active lifestyle also influences your breasts. When you gain or lose weight, you also gain or lose in your breasts. Also, the more fat in your body, the higher your estrogen levels are, because an enzyme in body fat converts a steroid from the adrenal glands into estrogen. Current studies are even finding an association between extra body fat that tends to settle in the abdominal area and a higher susceptibility to breast cancer. No matter what your genetic code, when you weigh less, you have less body fat, smaller breasts, and lower estrogen levels. Exercise is one way to keep your weight and the size of your breasts down.

What you eat may also affect the health of your breasts. A lower fat diet will keep body fat and estrogen levels down and maintain the breasts' firmness, but whether a specific *amount* of fat in your diet can be officially regarded as a risk factor for breast cancer is a matter of debate and study. In a 1996 report Harvard researchers pooled data from seven studies that involved 335,000 women in four countries and concluded that there was *no* relationship between the amount of fat a woman eats and her chance of developing breast cancer. Even women who had very low-fat diets—with less than 20 percent of their total calories from fat—had no reduced risk of breast cancer. Yet this is hardly the final word.

Indeed, scientists argue about what a low-fat diet actually *is*. Does a low-fat diet mean that 30 percent of daily calories are from fat? 20 percent? Less? The National Institutes of Health Women's Health Initiative is continuing a nine-year study of 48,000 women eating diets high in fruits, vegetables, and grains, with only 20 percent of dietary calories from fat. Researchers predict a 14-percent reduction in breast cancer in the low-fat group, but that remains to be seen.

It may be that food groups and *type* of fat become more important than amounts. In Greece a survey of 820 women with breast cancer and 1,548 women who were cancer-free revealed that women who ate the most vegetables had 48 percent less cancer risk than those who ate the least, and women who ate the most fruits had a 32 percent lower risk compared with those who ate the least. Breast cancer risk was 25 percent lower among those who consumed olive oil more than once a day, but that effect was observed mostly among postmenopausal women. The olive oil factor brings up questions about whether researchers should focus on levels and/or types of fat in the diet. Greek women typically consume 42 percent of calories from fat, but the source is the monounsaturated fat in olive oil. American women take in about 35 percent of their calories from fat, but little of that fat is the monounsaturated fat of a vegetable oil. Most American women get their fat from meat, and generally that fat is highly saturated. A number of years ago an Italian study found no association between olive oil and risk of breast cancer, but it did report a higher risk of developing breast cancer among women who ate more saturated fat.

When discussing the role dietary fat may play in the incidence of breast cancer, researchers also voice concern that the fat consumed in childhood may make more of a difference to onset of the disease than the fat consumed as an adult. Researchers know that it's time to look at young girls and women of different countries and cultures with different eating habits and fat intake to learn how women around the world can develop a style of living that will promote the good health of their breasts.

MAKING CHOICES FOR BETTER BREAST HEALTH

A woman's breasts will respond to a variety of influences that are under her personal control. While a woman cannot change the genetic makeup of her breasts, she has the power to affect her mind/body connection and her lifestyle. Her decisions about pregnancy, childbirth, and breastfeeding will affect her breasts through a series of hormonal interplays. Day-to-day stress, the amount of time a woman exercises, and the food she eats may also trigger hormones that target breast tissue. By understanding the basics about her breasts, a woman can be alert to her options. Breasts can be cared for when they are healthy, which is why so much of *The Complete Book of Breast Care* is devoted to preventive health care for breasts—in other words, preventing trouble before it starts.

Transformed During Pregnancy and Breastfeeding: Your Breasts Are (Possibly) Better Off Afterward

Pregnancy and breastfeeding are profound events that not only change a woman's breasts while they are happening but leave health effects that linger long after a new baby is grown. The research exploring a link between pregnancy/breastfeeding and breast cancer is dynamic and ever-changing. Pregnancy may offer protection against breast cancer for women when they reach their menopausal years but may offer no protection, and in fact might temporarily increase their risk, while they are young. On the other hand, breastfeeding may lower a woman's risk of breast cancer while she is young but have little effect after menopause. And daughters who were breastfed may have a lower risk of breast cancer throughout their lives.

The power of pregnancy and breastfeeding to have lasting health effects on women's breasts has captured the interest of researchers in different countries. The ramifications of recent findings are discussed later in this chapter. First, though, a woman should understand what she can expect from her breasts during both pregnancy and breastfeeding.

HOW BREASTS RESPOND TO PREGNANCY

When conception occurs, the levels of the female hormones estrogen and progesterone, which normally drop with the onset of menstruation, instead continue to rise in the mother's body. At the time a woman would normally expect her menstrual period, these hormones make her breasts fuller and more tender than ever. In fact, one of the earliest signs of pregnancy is breast enlargement and tenderness. Breasts can also begin to tingle, and nipples can become extremely sensitive.

As pregnancy progresses, the blood supply to the milk-secreting glandular tissue increases to the point that blue veins become visible beneath the skin, and the nipples and areolae darken. Montgomery's glands, small round oil glands that look like pimples, appear on the periphery of the areolae. Toward the end of the nine months, yellowish, watery fluid called *colostrum* may leak from a woman's breasts. It is important to wear a comfortable, well-fitting bra for good support throughout pregnancy but especially as childbirth nears. Nursing pads can be slipped into the bra to prevent staining that may result from leakage.

THE EFFECT OF PREGNANCY ON A WOMAN'S LIFETIME RISK OF BREAST CANCER

If you become pregnant before age 30, you may reduce your risk of breast cancer. Through population studies and the work of epidemiologist Dr. Mitchell H. Gail of the National Cancer Institute, we know that if you give birth before your thirtieth birthday, you lower your risk of breast cancer, and the younger you are, the lower your risk. In comparison, women who either never give birth or who bear children later in life are at slightly higher risk. In a 1992 paper Dr. Gail made this comparison: for every case of breast cancer among women who give birth before age 30, there will be approximately 1.9 cases of breast cancer among women who either postpone childbearing until after 30 or who never give birth at all. (Whether a pregnancy that ends in a spontaneous or an induced abortion affects risk is a controversial issue addressed in Chapter 18.)

Scientists do not yet completely understand how pregnancy reduces risk, so investigations are ongoing. In fact, it may not be as simple as "have a baby before 30 and lower your risk of breast cancer." In 1994 a statistical analysis of thousands of Swedish women born between 1925 and 1960 was published in the *New England Journal of Medicine*. In the analysis, 12,666 women with breast cancer were compared with 62,121 age-matched women in a control group. *Investigators concluded that pregnancy offers a woman protection against developing breast cancer when she is older, but shortly after giving birth her risk may temporarily rise.*

The Swedish researchers speculated that pregnancy might change a group of so-called stem cells in the breast and prevent them from becoming cancerous in later years. This is good news, because during the menopausal and postmenopausal years, when the disease is more likely to strike, you could use added protection.

On the other hand, this study also revealed the cautionary news that for the first 15 years after giving birth, mothers—particularly older mothers who bear only one child when they are over 30—have more risk of developing breast cancer than do women who never give birth. However, until menopause, a woman's "normal" risk for developing breast cancer is quite low, whether she gives birth or not. So new mothers, even though they may be at "higher than normal" risk, are still in the category of women who experience breast cancer infrequently. This recent discovery should be regarded mostly as a reminder that childbirth does *not* offer the powerful protection against breast cancer that many women think it does. Breast self-examinations and medical checkups are important at every age and stage of life.

Another Theory About Fertility and Breast Cancer

In the 1980s a different team of Swedish researchers suggested that the number of menstrual cycles—and fewer are better—between a woman's first period and her first pregnancy were better predictors of protection against breast cancer than her precise age at the time of her first pregnancy. This line of thought—that fewer menstrual cycles are more beneficial—may have some connection to other findings that show that women who were athletes in their teens and twenties have a *decreased* risk of breast cancer.

Athletes and dancers often have fewer menstrual cycles and skip their periods. Their low body fat and weight, a result of their strenuous activities, affect the balance of female hormones, menstruation, and ovulation. Even teenage girls who exercise only moderately have been found to ovulate less, whether or not they continue to menstruate regularly. That's one reason why a doctor will suggest that a woman who has a daily exercise regimen, such as a three-mile run, cut back on her workout when she is trying to conceive. While the estrogen-lowering effect of exercise may be good for breast health, it can sometimes disturb fertility.

WHAT RESEARCHERS DON'T KNOW

Despite all the findings and theories, no one can name the menstrual/reproductive pattern that can give a woman maximum protection against breast cancer. There is no sure course to follow. For instance, what if an athlete who has not had menstrual periods for months becomes pregnant at age 32? Would her risk for breast cancer be the same as a nonathlete who becomes pregnant in her twenties? We do not know. What we are aware of is that among risk factors, menstruating early (younger than age 12) and reaching menopause late (after the early fifties) *increase risk* of breast cancer, probably because the hormones generating the menstrual cycle course through your body so often.

While a woman cannot control the beginning and end of her monthly fertility, she often can decide when to become pregnant. Does research information about a possible lower risk of breast cancer if you give birth before age 30 mean that women ought to start their families before their thirtieth birthday? The fact is that we do not know *how many* women would benefit by becoming young mothers. Despite all the theories, many women who develop breast cancer fall into low-risk categories, i.e., they become mothers before age 30 and have no family history of breast cancer.

Every woman's life is her own to plan and protect. While the facts we have are important, each woman must look at the numbers, weigh her individual needs and risk factors for breast cancer (perhaps consult with a risk-assessment counselor; see Chapter 18), and make her own decisions. Meanwhile, researchers are still probing the connections between pregnancy, hormones, and the risk of breast cancer so that more informed choices can be made.

A Must: Breast Self-Examination During Pregnancy

Breast self-examination (BSE) during pregnancy, as explained in Chapter 3, is a must. Research conducted on 407 women aged 20 to 29 at medical centers in the United States, Russia, the Netherlands, Sweden, France, and the United Kingdom, found breast cancer to be quite aggressive when it appeared in pregnant women under age 30. When young pregnant women in the study were diagnosed with breast cancer, they were over three times more likely to die of the disease than were young women who had never been pregnant. Suspicious lumps stand out even when pregnancy enlarges the breasts, so a monthly BSE is a habit to continue. (For more about pregnancy and breast cancer, see Chapter 18.)

A WOMAN'S BREASTS DURING BREASTFEEDING
A Collection of Reflections

"At first I had trouble breastfeeding. I couldn't get him to take the left breast. Everyone would give me different advice and finally my doctor's nurse said, 'You're blocking the nipple. You have to present it with your hand underneath and your thumb on top.' That seemed to work much better."

—MARYANN L., AGE 39

"I breastfed my daughter for 10 months and I loved it—the naturalness, the closeness to the baby. I'm planning to do it again. And by the way, it's also convenient."

—AMY H., AGE 33

"When I started breastfeeding, my nipples seemed very sensitive. I put olive oil on the tips and let them hang out in the air because I don't want them to crack. Now they've mellowed out."

—CLEO T., AGE 40

"People make breastfeeding seem more difficult than it really is. Until I got the position of the baby right, my breasts were sore for a couple of weeks, but then everything was fine. I'll breastfeed for six months."
—KATHY M., AGE 25

"I breastfed for four months, and that was pretty much all I could do. Socially, culturally, it was hard to breastfeed. I found it tough to go out and do things. I'd be sitting in the car and breastfeeding because I didn't feel comfortable in a public place. As for the breastfeeding itself, once I learned to regulate the flow, I had no problem."
—NATASHA J., AGE 31

"I know people who have breastfed their infants until they were two or three years old. That's definitely not for me, although I like it. It's such a comfortable, relaxing way to bring your infant into his own as much as you can. You have to watch what you eat, but it is so empowering. You can sustain life with your body."
—ELLIE B., AGE 35

The main function of breasts is to feed. The milk-production system in your breasts exists from puberty but remains dormant until you become pregnant. During pregnancy, a woman's breasts are stimulated into producing milk by

A WOMAN'S BREASTS WHEN SHE BOTTLE-FEEDS

A woman who decides to bottle-feed rather than breastfeed can alleviate the discomfort of milk-filled breasts by wearing a tight bra day and night. Ice packs, placed on the breasts intermittently, also lessen the pain. As long as breasts are not stimulated by a suckling newborn, milk letdown will eventually subside, and in two to four weeks, the breasts should return to normal.

Obstetricians used to prescribe bromocriptine mesylate (Parlodel) to stop the flow of breast milk and end swelling and engorgement. This drug blocked the release of prolactin, the milk-producing hormone from the pituitary gland. In August 1994, Sandoz, the manufacturer of the drug, took Parlodel off the market as a lactation suppressant because it had been linked to heart attacks and strokes, a number of them fatal. Parlodel remains on the market mainly as a treatment for Parkinson's disease. Although it is still available by prescription, it is no longer considered safe for new mothers.

the hormone *prolactin*, which is released by the pituitary gland in the brain. As explained in Chapter 1, the pituitary receives the "message" from the nearby hypothalamus to release prolactin. The prolactin level increases slowly during pregnancy until about the seventh month, when, as childbirth nears, it surges. Breasts swell as milk production builds in the *acini*, the glandular sacs that produce and store breast milk. The growing milk supply is held in check by high levels of the female hormones estrogen and progesterone. After the baby is born, however, estrogen and progesterone levels fall, causing a slight decline in prolactin and the beginning of the delivery of breast milk.

The first milk is the yellow-tinged *colostrum*, filled with antibodies that the baby needs to fight off infections, allergies, and asthmatic conditions. This nourishment is moved through a network of milk ducts by the contractions of the myoepithelial cells that surround the milk-filled acini in your breasts. The ducts deposit the milk in the *ampullae*, the enlarged duct terminals at the base of the nipple. When the baby begins to suck, the nerves around the nipple and areola send "messages" to the hypothalamus, which are transmitted to the pituitary. The result is that the pituitary releases the hormone *oxytocin*.

Prolactin and *oxytocin* work together during breastfeeding. The prolactin makes the milk, and the oxytocin delivers it. Oxytocin stimulates the myoepithelial cells and small, smooth muscles within the breast to contract and push the breast milk toward the nipple. When a nursing infant stimu-

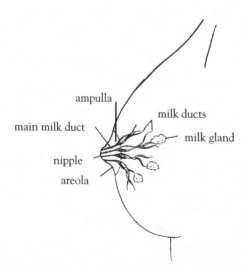

Main milk ducts in the nipple receive milk from a network of ducts behind the areola that are linked to corresponding milk glands. Note the location of the ampullae, where milk collects prior to transport through the nipple.

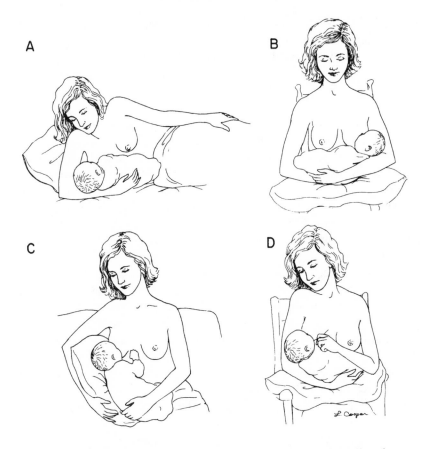

Positions for breastfeeding. A woman should choose a position that offers the greatest emotional relaxation, whether A) lying on her side with her arm around the baby; B) sitting up and cradling the baby on a resting pillow; C) resting the baby on two pillows she cradles to one side of her, which may be helpful after Caesarean birth; D) sitting in a chair with an armrest. Lap pillows can help support the baby.

lates a mother's nipple, the signal to release oxytocin travels from her breast to the hypothalamus, to the pituitary. Oxytocin may also be released spontaneously during lovemaking when the nipples are touched, and some milk may leak from a woman's breasts. This may also happen when a mother hears her baby cry. Oxytocin is released and the *milk reflex* is triggered.

Some type of stimulation to the nipples is always needed to begin and maintain the milk reflex. With suckling or other stimulation, a surge of prolactin kicks in and makes fresh milk, and a surge of oxytocin kicks in and delivers it. It takes about 10 minutes of continuous sucking for a baby to empty one breast. Milk production ends when nursing or other stimulation stops. That's why, for successful breastfeeding, a woman must start and maintain her flow through regular nursing—or by using a breast pump when she is away from her child—until she is ready to wean her baby.

When a New Mother Begins to Breastfeed

As a new mother, if you choose to breastfeed your baby, you should begin either directly after or within a few hours of childbirth. Position yourself comfortably, and rest your baby's cheek against your breast. A baby instinctively knows how to suck, but you may need to guide the baby to your nipple, making sure that his mouth is open wide enough to allow sucking on the areola and not just the nipple. It is important to massage the breast from the outside to the center and gently press the areola to stimulate the release of milk. In the beginning, a woman may experience brief uterine contractions from the surge of oxytocin into her bloodstream. This is normal and is nature's way of helping the womb to get back in shape.

A woman should not expect complete nursing at this point, but the colostrum contained in the few drops her baby will receive in these early stages will be of great benefit. Colostrum helps to coat a baby's stomach, build up immunities, and help prevent bowel and intestinal abnormalities. A mother's milk will actually "let down," or start flowing, within a few days of childbirth, and nature has cleverly arranged for babies not to need much milk in their first few days of life.

NOTE: Massaging the breasts, particularly after placing a hot towel over them, will help stimulate milk let-down. Knead the breast gently in a circular motion, working from the outside toward the center. Some nursing mothers have found it helpful to massage the breast with petroleum jelly or

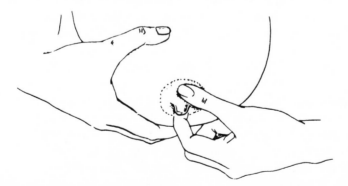

To prevent cracked nipples: Roll each nipple between the thumb and first finger of one hand while massaging the breast with the other hand to stimulate the milk-ejection reflex prior to breastfeeding. A baby will exert less pressure on nipples that have been stimulated.

baby oil. You should also be sure your nipples remain clean, although you should avoid cleansing them with soap. Be sure your nipples are dry after bathing and after nursing so that they do not become dried and cracked.

Do not become discouraged if you and your baby do not become an instant feeding team. Be patient, and above all, try to remain calm and relaxed. For advice and support, these two organizations are extremely helpful:

La Leche League International, 9616 Minneapolis Avenue, Franklin Park, IL 60131, 800-LALECHE(525-3243) or 708-455-7730.

International Childbirth Education Association, Box 20048, Minneapolis, MN 55420, 612-854-8660.

What's in the Breast Milk

During breastfeeding a woman will see changes in the color, texture, and content of her breast milk. The first milk, the *colostrum*, is thick and yellowish. After a few days of colostrum and early breast milk, mature milk appears, which is white and creamy, although it is thinner than the colostrum.

Colostrum, which has antibody protection superior to that of mature milk, continues to flow during the first four weeks of nursing, while the mature milk is coming in. Even if you are only planning to breastfeed a short time, a newborn will receive the benefits of colostrum. As a newborn nurses on colostrum, he or she absorbs a mother's resistance to viruses and infections—a resistance built up over a lifetime. Through breastfeeding a woman gives her baby a protection against illness that lasts several months, until the child is older, stronger, and able to develop his or her own resistance to disease.

Ideally, a baby receives optimum benefits if breastfed for six months to one year. If you know that you can breastfeed only for a shorter time, try to stretch that period over three months before switching to formula. If your schedule is fixed and permits only a few weeks of nursing, breastfeeding your baby during that short time will still give him or her immeasurable benefits. As a mother weans her infant, she will see her breast milk change to a thin, white, almost skim milk.

The calorie/nutrient mix in mother's milk is the exact combination needed for her baby's normal growth. Breast milk contains proteins, minerals, vitamins, fats, sugars, antibodies to fight infection, growth factors for evolving tissue, and hormones that affect a baby's brain development and behavior. Animal studies by Israeli researchers recently have shown that the mammary glands of nursing animals activate a gene that produces the gonadotropin-releasing hormone or GnRH. While scientists do not yet know the precise effects of GnRH, it probably influences the timing of the development of sex organs in a growing child and the child's sexual behavior.

HEALTH TIPS FOR A BREASTFEEDING MOTHER

To prepare herself physically for breastfeeding, a new mother should:

- Eat nutritiously (see Chapter 6), increasing her food intake by 500 to 600 calories a day;
- Drink plenty of liquids, avoiding caffeine, which can keep the baby awake, and alcohol, which can tire the baby and slow his or her eating;
- Continue taking prenatal vitamins or other vitamins recommended by her doctor;
- Test home tap water, and if contaminants exist, install the appropriate water filter;
- Eat only farmed fish to avoid passing on possibly cancer-causing polychlorinated biphenyls or PCBs, which are absorbed by fatty fish swimming in polluted water, and;
- Refrain from gardening, to avoid breathing harmful chemicals from sprayed pesticides.

The latest analyses of breast milk have also found a number of growth hormones, thyroid hormones, the hormone melatonin (which is credited with biorhythms and natural timing), endorphins (the body's natural painkillers or opiates), and a factor called *mammotrope differentiating peptide*, which seems to promote the growth of cells in the pituitary gland. The ingredient list continues to grow all the time.

Complications That May Arise During Breastfeeding

- **Engorgement,** which happens as your mature milk is coming in, can cause breasts to swell, harden, and become quite tender. Sometimes only the areola is engorged, but no matter how extensive the engorgement is, a woman will be in too much discomfort to breastfeed. She can easily overcome this temporary setback with the release of her breast milk:

First, I advise wearing a nursing bra that offers good support night and day. Next, place hot compresses on your breast and massage the area. Heat and massage signal the pituitary to release the hormone oxytocin, which stimulates milk let-down and an end to engorgement. The discomfort will be alleviated with the release, or expression, of milk by hand or by using a breast pump.

To hand-express breast milk, a woman should start with the left breast (since most people are right-handed and work more easily with their right hand). Support the left breast with your left hand. You will be squeezing the milk reservoir behind the areola with your right hand. Place the tips of the right thumb and first or middle finger on opposite sides of the outer edge of the areola. Press your thumb into your breast and then squeeze your finger and thumb together. Repeat this squeezing motion in short, consistent rhythms. You must press firmly and work patiently until the first drops of milk appear. Remember always to stay at the edge of the areola. Never squeeze the nipple alone. Once the milk is flowing, press the other side of the areola to release more milk from other milk ducts.

If you prefer, *use a breast pump* to start your milk let-down. Massage your breasts to increase your flow, position the pump at your nipple, and allow the pumping and sucking action of the device to draw the milk out.

Once milk is expressed, a mother should have no more trouble with engorgement. A hungry baby will drink up the milk supply that her body replenishes.

• **Infections/Mastitis and Breast Abscess.** Breastfeeding offers a situation in which bacteria can thrive. Thickened milk clogs a breast duct and the milk behind the clog cannot get out. If bacteria enter the breast, through a cracked nipple for example, they can travel through the clogged duct, multiply in the backed-up milk supply, and infect the area. Until the blockage is removed, the infection can cause mastitis or a breast abscess.

A breast infection, *mastitis*, can make your breasts swollen, red, hot, and painful. You should see your doctor right away. If mastitis goes untreated, you can experience chills, headache, and a high fever, and the condition can lead to an abscess (see below). The best way to fight the infection is with a broad spectrum antibiotic such as cephalexin (Keflex), ampicillin, or erythromycin, which will not harm the feeding infant. Hot compresses on the breast, massage, and either hand or pump expression of milk help to break down the blockage in the duct and drain away the infection. A woman should continue to breastfeed because the baby's stomach acid kills the bacteria and prevents the infectious organisms from being passed on. Breastfeeding, in fact, is a form of treatment for mastitis because a nursing baby can keep milk flowing and ducts open. If a newborn is reluctant to drink from the breast with mastitis, do not push the infant to feed because the milk may have a sour flavor. In this case, express the milk until the infection is cured.

An *abscess* forms when the infection festers in one spot and the skin turns deep red in that area. Pus builds, and like a boil, the abscess must drain. A doctor usually continues to prescribe the antibiotic given for mastitis in the hope that the drug will cause the abscess to disintegrate naturally. If the antibiotic doesn't work, a small abscess may be aspirated with a needle, but a large abscess may need an incision for draining. The incision is usually made after you have been given a local anesthetic. Sometimes a wick (a small drain) is temporarily inserted in the incision to prevent it from closing up. An incision will not be needed, however, if the mastitis is properly treated at the start.

• **Galactocele.** Sometimes breast milk can thicken in one of the acini, causing a swollen sac, or milk cyst. This is a case of galactocele. A needle aspiration of the cyst remedies the situation.

• **Cracked Nipples.** As a woman begins to breastfeed, she may allow her baby to suck too long and too hard on her breast. Tender nipples can become damaged and cracked. One way to avoid soreness and cracking is to make sure the newborn grasps *most of the* **areola** *along with the nipple* while feeding and does not pull on the nipple when taken from the breast. Any area of soreness should be examined by a doctor, who can supply a woman with a rubber nipple shield. When placed over the areolae, the shield discourages an infant from sucking right on the cracked nipples. It also helps to massage the nipples a few times a day with an antibiotic cream such as Bacitracin to promote healing. The cream should be sponged off with warm water before breastfeeding, and reapplied afterward.

• **Inverted Nipples.** Inverted nipples, nipples that are drawn inward, are being pulled in by an adhesion of breast tissue that occurred during breast development. They do not prevent a woman from being able to breastfeed. A special exercise, Hoffman's exercise, can be started before childbirth to draw the nipples out. Twice a day, place your forefinger and thumb on the edge of the areola, press them into the breast, and then stretch the skin from side to side. Adhesions at the base of the nipple will be stretched out and the nipple released. A new mother can also do this exercise during breastfeeding. To help pull the nipples out, you can also wear plastic breast shields called *Swedish milk cups* for several hours a day at the end of pregnancy and the start of nursing.

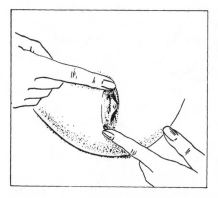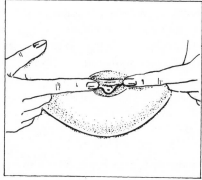

Hoffman's exercise for drawing out inverted nipples can be practiced several times a day during pregnancy and breastfeeding. Press either the index finger of each hand, or thumb and index finger of the same hand, into the edge of the areola and stretch the skin from side to side.

- **Cosmetic Surgery on Breasts,** depending on the type of surgery, may have an impact (see Chapter 12). A breast lift or *mastopexy* should not affect a woman's ability to breastfeed, but after a breast reduction or mammoplasty, only 50 percent of women can breastfeed postoperatively. Many women choose to wait until after their childbearing years to have this latter surgery. Breast augmentation with silicone or saline implants is also somewhat suspect, and you should check with your obstetrician about the latest findings. In a study at Schneider Children's Hospital on Long Island in New York, six of eight babies breastfed by mothers with silicone breast implants developed abnormalities of the esophagus, the tube that transports food to the stomach. Their problems were similar to symptoms related to scleroderma, a rare disease in which a breakdown in the immune system causes skin to thicken and harden. The 17 breastfed infants examined, whose mothers did not have silicone implants, did not have comparable damage to the esophagus.

When Breastfeeding Comes to an End

I advise women who decide that it is time to wean their babies to ease into the change. The longer a mother has breastfed, the less her risk of engorgement when she stops, but no matter how long she has nursed, she still needs to plan a slowly paced transition. I suggest eliminating one feeding a day and offering baby formula in a cup or a bottle. As a mother nurses her baby less frequently, her breasts will not be stimulated to manufacture as much milk, and eventually milk production will stop completely. This transition can take place over several weeks. At this time an infant needs a lot of affection to be reassured that his mother is not abandoning him.

Meanwhile, a mother also may need special attention as her milk supply dwindles. She can reduce swelling and pain by applying ice packs to her breasts while she is weaning. I also advise letting nature take its course and avoiding medication that may speed the drying of milk.

The most popular drug for lactation suppression, bromocriptine mesylate (Parlodel), was removed from the market for this use in August 1994 (see box, page 33) because of a link found between Parlodel, heart attacks, and strokes.

How Breasts Will Look After Breastfeeding

If you breastfed for only a few months, you can massage your breasts and perform the pectoral squeeze exercise described in Chapter 1, and you may be able to return your breasts to their former contours. Sometimes, however, a long period of breastfeeding (more than six months) causes breast tissue to diminish, and breasts settle into a shape smaller than their prepregnancy size.

A LOOK AT THE LINK BETWEEN BREASTFEEDING
AND BREAST CANCER

Whether breastfeeding offers any protection against breast cancer continues to be a matter of research and debate. Until recently the largest population studies had been done among women in China, where long-term breast-feeding seemed to offer a dose of prevention—but here we are talking about almost a *decade* of nursing for any real benefit. While some prevention was observed among women of all ages who had breastfed, it was the post-menopausal Chinese women who had breastfed up to nine years who had the greatest benefit: about half the risk of women who had never breastfed. Meanwhile, the postmenopausal Chinese women who had breastfed up to a year shared the same risk as those who had never breastfed.

A population study conducted by researchers at the University of Wisconsin Comprehensive Cancer Center compared 5,878 women who were listed on breast cancer registries in Wisconsin, Massachusetts, Maine, and New Hampshire, with 8,216 women in a control group. Researchers found:

- A significant drop in breast cancer risk among women 20 years old or younger who had breastfed for six months. During their reproductive years these women had about half the risk of women who had never breastfed after pregnancy.
- For women who breastfed after age 30, the chances of getting breast cancer during their reproductive years were similar to those of women who never breastfed.
- No matter what their age when they nursed, after menopause every woman's risk was virtually the same.

Basically, the findings indicated that the longer you nurse when you are young, the more you reduce your risk of getting breast cancer, at least before menopause.

In 1995 Dr. Louise Brinton, an epidemiologist at the National Cancer Institute, published her analysis of data gathered on 2,477 women in three states, 1,211 of whom had been diagnosed with breast cancer between 1990 and 1993. Most of the women had developed premenopausal breast cancer. On evaluating the information about pregnancy and breastfeeding among the women, Dr. Brinton found only a small benefit from breastfeeding—about a 10 percent reduced risk of breast cancer. The women in the study had nursed an average of 30 weeks, supplementing the feedings with formula when the infants were about 14 weeks old. Dr. Brinton noted that a woman would probably be more likely to increase her protection against the disease with longer periods of breastfeeding.

In another study by Dr. Brinton and one by researchers at the State University of New York in Buffalo, women who themselves were breastfed were shown to have a 30 percent lower risk of developing breast cancer than women who had been bottle-fed. The researchers did not know why this added protection occurred, and obviously there is more to learn.

CONNECTIONS TO CONSIDER

In summation, pregnancy appears to reduce the risk of breast cancer after menopause. According to the Wisconsin study, breastfeeding reduces the risk of getting breast cancer *before* menopause. While it looks as if, together, pregnancy and breastfeeding will provide some protection against breast cancer throughout your life, nothing is certain. Even women who are at lowest risk still get the disease. What medical experts are starting to realize, however, is that a woman may be able to change some sort of cancer-causing mechanism in her body by making certain decisions early in life . . . decisions that include having a baby, breastfeeding, and, as you will see in later chapters, maintaining a certain diet and even exercising. That there are connections between reproductive choices and risk of breast cancer is clear, but only time and research will help us understand what mechanisms, hormonal or otherwise, are being touched by the choices a woman makes.

PART II

You Can Protect Your Breasts

A Breast Self-Examination: When You Have a Good Teacher, You *Can* Overcome Your Ambivalence

"Once in a blue moon I'll examine myself. I'm not very good at it."
—PATRICIA M., AGE 58

"I examine myself regularly and I'm very confident that nothing's there."
—LORNA C., AGE 45

"I'm bad at it, and lately I've heard that women who gain weight in their abdomen are at higher risk for breast cancer. That's just where I've put on the pounds."

—RACHEL D., AGE 50

"No, I don't examine my breasts, but hey, I'm only 31. I don't think it's a big deal at my age."

—MARCIE S., AGE 31

These women are all in my care. I have counseled them about monthly breast self-examination (BSE) and taught them how to do it, but as three of four revealed, most women do not routinely examine their breasts. It is estimated that only about one-third of women in the United States practice BSE every month, and roughly half do it only once in a while. Why don't more women perform BSE more frequently? Studies cite the fear of both missing and finding "something," the reluctance some women have about touching their bodies, and the fact that, as many women report, they do not really know what they are looking for because no one has shown them exactly how to do a breast self-examination.

In my books and my practice I have always advocated and will continue to advocate monthly breast self-examination for all women, even teenagers. However, that advocacy includes the caveat of proper personal instruction in BSE at a reputable health center, breast cancer center, or from a private practice physician or health care professional skilled in teaching BSE (yes, instruction for BSE is presented later on in this chapter, but it is no substitute for one-on-one training).

I regard breast self-examination as a commonsense approach a woman can take in the health care of her breasts, although recently BSE has moved into the realm of a "health issue." Dr. Susan Love, director of the UCLA Breast Center and author of *Dr. Susan Love's Breast Book*, has been quite vocal in her opinion that the importance of BSE as a tool in detecting cancer and saving lives has been exaggerated. She is joined by other breast cancer experts and activists who question the value of BSE in early detection and wonder whether the technique is psychologically damaging to women because it makes them think of their breasts as "the enemy."

My professional experience with a patient roster of almost 10,000 women has given me the opportunity to hear many women of different ages tell me how they found their breast cancers themselves during routine breast self-exams. Although there is no definitive scientific study that proves that BSE reduces a woman's chance of dying of breast cancer, over the years I have talked to a great number of women who feel that they have saved their lives with their own hands.

For good breast health, a woman should be examined by a physician at least once a year, and depending on her age, family history, and known risk of breast cancer, have annual breast screenings either with mammography, ultrasound, or both (see Chapters 4 and 5 for a comprehensive look at breast screening methods). Then, I think BSE can be viewed as something extra a woman does for herself rather than a directive she must fulfill.

THE VALUE OF BSE

The scientific proof that breast self-examination can help women detect breast cancer early and save their lives does not exist because large, randomized studies to determine the value of BSE have not been completed. One randomized clinical trial is currently under way in Russia. Sponsored by the World Health Organization, the Russian study randomly selected over 193,000 women aged 40 to 64 in Moscow and St. Petersburg to be in either study or control groups. They will be followed for 15 years. If 50 to 70 percent of the women in the study group practice BSE, the researchers are hoping to find a 30-percent drop in the rate of death from breast cancer. In 1994 a Finnish study of almost 29,000 women who turned in calendars recording their BSE schedules over two years showed their breast cancer death rates to be 25 percent lower than that of the overall Finnish population. However, the study depended on a select, record-keeping group of women who were not chosen at random.

In a much smaller 1991 study, Dr. Polly Newcomb compared 209 Seattle-area women who had advanced-stage breast cancer with 433 women who were cancer free. Dr. Newcomb determined that 80 percent of the women in each group had practiced BSE, and her conclusion was that women who examined their breasts were just as likely to develop late-stage breast cancer as those who did not. However, Dr. Newcomb went on to find that most of the women had poor BSE techniques. Among the small number that were proficient, the rates of advanced-stage breast cancer dropped by 35 percent.

So the research is scant, but experts at the National Cancer Institute continue to say that women who do regular, careful BSEs can feel lumps as small as one-quarter to one-half inch in their breasts. Eighty percent of breast lumps are harmless. They are benign fluid-filled cysts, fibroadenomas, or fibrocystic lumps. However, if a half-inch lump discovered during BSE were found to be cancerous, it would be likely that the disease would be at an early enough stage for a woman to be a candidate for breast-conserving lumpectomy (see Chapter 21). As Dr. Newcomb's study points out, if done in a thorough way, BSE should make a difference.

WHAT YOU FEEL WHEN YOU EXAMINE YOUR BREASTS

When you examine your breasts every month, you can tell right away when a lump is new, but at first you might not be familiar with how your body feels. BSE is a way to know how your body is evolving. At different times of your life, your breasts feel different. In your reproductive years, you can feel your breasts respond to your menstrual cycle. In the first week after your period, before ovulation and the rise of estrogen and progesterone, breasts feel smoother than they do in the last two weeks of the cycle. *The reduced lumpiness during the first week after your period is the reason for recommending regular BSE at that time.* As you move closer to menstruation, milk glands and ducts swell and enlarge, making lumpiness more apparent in the second half of your cycle. The fact is, though, that a normal breast can remind you of cottage cheese whenever you feel it. So you need to get to know the territory that is yours, whether you are in your reproductive years with breasts responsive to menstrual cycling; pregnant with fuller breasts; postmenopausal with breasts that are generally less glandular and lumpy; or have breasts with scar tissue from surgery or breast implants.

As described later, when you use the pads of the three dominant fingers on each hand, minus the pinky and thumb, to examine yourself monthly,

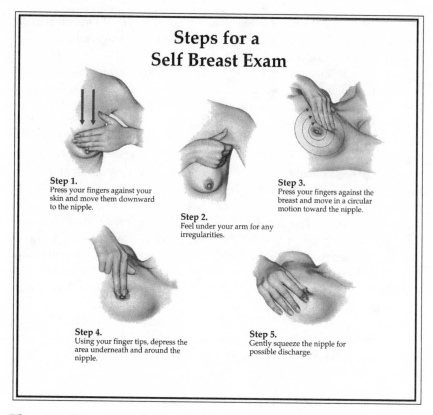

**Steps for a
Self Breast Exam**

Step 1.
Press your fingers against your
skin and move them downward
to the nipple.

Step 2.
Feel under your arm for any
irregularities.

Step 3.
Press your fingers against the
breast and move in a circular
motion toward the nipple.

Step 4.
Using your finger tips, depress the
area underneath and around the
nipple.

Step 5.
Gently squeeze the nipple for
possible discharge.

These steps for a breast self-exam can be included in a BSE using either a vertical strip, circular, or wedge pattern of examination. © 1994 Tim Peters and Company, Inc., Peapack, NJ 07977, 800-543-2230.

you will be able to tell whether something is different. Most detectable growths are about one-half inch in diameter, so you do not have to feel that you are on a mission to find something the size of a grain of sand. Remember, 80 percent of breast lumps are harmless, and you will know when you have found something new in your breast. A new growth will stand out.

It is interesting to note that 20 years ago, using research from the early 1960s on how fast breast cancer metastasizes, Dr. Bernard Fisher at the University of Pittsburgh calculated that one cancer cell could double into two cells in approximately 100 days. At that rate it would take 10 *years* for 100 billion cells to form, the amount necessary for a one-centimeter—one-half-inch—lump, which is the usual size of a lump you can feel. As some cells do grow faster or have inexplicable growth spurts, a one-centimeter cancer might be younger than 10 years, but on average, when you feel a lump that turns out to be cancerous, you have already been living with it for about a decade.

EXAMINING A BREAST MODEL

Every woman should examine a silicone breast model for the "feel" of different types of breast lumps. Once you know what the texture of hard and soft, small and large lumps feels like, you will never forget it. Your doctor may have a silicone breast model in his office and may offer you the opportunity to examine it during your next checkup. The most thorough way to examine a silicone breast model, however, is to find a MammaCare instructor in your area.

The BSE method called *MammaCare* is taught at a number of health clinics and breast cancer centers, and by women's health-care professionals. (To locate a MammaCare teacher near you, contact MammaCare at the 800 number on the next page, ask your doctor for a referral, or call the nearest branch of the American Cancer Society, or the health clinic of a major teaching hospital or cancer center in your area.) With this method a woman learns how to do a BSE by first feeling the consistency of a clear, silicone breast model. Wearing an examining gown, she lies down on a table, and the instructor places the silicone breast model on her chest. The breast model has varying smooth and wavy textures and three or four lumps placed at different depths and areas.

Using the "palpation" technique, a woman presses the flat pads of her three middle fingers on her right or her left hand into the silicone breast skin, moving her three fingers as one, in a tiny circle. (See box on page 50)

Next she learns how to palpate with different degrees of pressure: pressing lightly on the surface of the breast model, then applying more pressure to feel midway in the breast, and finally, pressing all the way down to the base of the breast. This helps a woman understand how various types of lumps can be discovered at different depths. The instructor helps her pupil identify a lump that feels like a piece of gravel midway in the breast; a larger, squishier lump toward the base; and another lump that's round like a pea.

As part of the MammaCare instruction, after a woman has examined the clear silicone breast, she then examines her own breast to feel the differences and similarities. Then, an opaque, flesh-colored silicone breast model in which the lumps cannot be seen is placed on the woman's chest. Using the vertical strip pattern for BSE, which is described later on in this chapter, a woman then locates the lumps in this second breast model.

When a woman discovers a growth, she should immediately consult her physician and go for a mammogram or ultrasound screening. If the screening suggests a malignancy, she still has a few weeks to decide what to do. Because the lump has been growing a long time, another two or three weeks to consult with more than one breast surgeon, gather information, and weigh a second opinion will not make a difference in her recovery. Decision making need not be rushed.

THREE TECHNIQUES FOR BSE

Three BSE techniques have been widely used. Women examine their breasts using vertical strip, circular, or wedge patterns. Although the circular style of breast self-examination is the most traditional, research comparing different BSE techniques has shown the vertical strip to be more effective. I would like to see every woman examine her breasts monthly, no matter which technique she chooses:

• **Vertical Strip or Grid** BSE is taught as part of the breast self-examination instruction of the MammaCare program that is being offered at more and more large teaching hospitals, cancer centers, and health clinics. (For information, contact MammaCare, P.O. Box 15748, Gainesville, FL 32604; 800-626-2273; or check the Web site: *http://www.mammacare.com.* An instructional package with videotape and silicone breast model may be purchased, although a 45-minute session with an instructor is more valuable.) With the vertical strip, a woman starts under her collarbone, near her shoulder, and works her way down the outside of her breast to the bottom of her bra line. After covering one vertical line, she moves her fingers about one-half inch inward and works her way back up to her collarbone. Row after row, alternating down and up, she follows the pattern like a mower going over a lawn, until she reaches her breastbone.

• **Circular or Clock** BSE starts at the 12 o'clock position just below the collarbone. A woman then moves her fingers to 1 o'clock and travels around the outermost part of her breast, stopping at each hourly position until returning to 12 o'clock again. She then moves her fingers one-half inch in toward her nipple and travels around her breast again. A woman usually makes about four trips around her breast before she reaches her nipple and completes the breast self-examination.

• **Wedge or Pie** BSE starts at the nipple. From the nipple a woman works her way outward toward her collarbone. For this technique, I suggest that a woman imagine her breast as a pie cut into quarters, or quadrants, with each quadrant containing four half-inch slices. She examines the length of each slice, each time starting from the nipple and moving outward to the collarbone, then to the outermost part of the breast, to the bottom of the bra line, to the breastbone, and finally, back to the collarbone and her starting point.

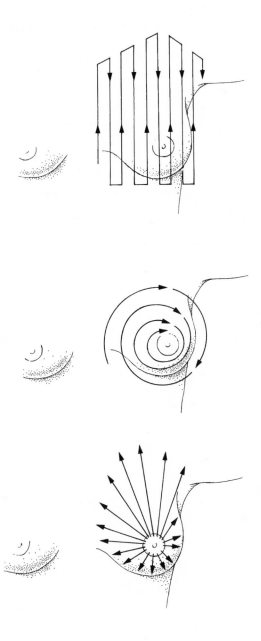

Three patterns for BSE, from top to bottom: Vertical strip or grid, circular, wedge or pie.

FOR ALL BREAST SELF-EXAMINATIONS: THE PALPATION TECHNIQUE

No matter what pattern of BSE a woman chooses, the way she touches her breasts, or her palpation technique, should be the same. Palpation requires using the sensitive pads—not the tips—of the three middle fingers (excluding the thumb and pinky) on each hand. The right hand examines the left breast and vice versa. The three fingers move as one. A woman presses her skin firmly on the surface of the breast, midway, and deeply, but not too deeply—if she presses too hard she'll touch ribs—and with each press, makes a small rotary motion as if moving around the rim of a dime. Palpation allows a woman to disturb the skin on her breast and easily move it over the internal tissue.

I have chosen the more effective **vertical strip** to illustrate the fine points of a BSE.

WHAT TO DO

1. The vertical strip technique should always be practiced while lying in bed. A small pillow or a folded towel should be positioned under the shoulder of the breast you are examining. This centers and flattens the breast tissue evenly. You will examine your right breast first.

2. Place your right arm behind your head.

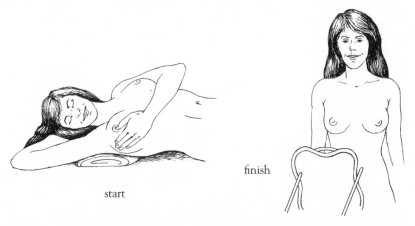

finish

start

At left, to start a BSE, it is best to lie in bed with a small pillow or folded towel underneath the shoulder of the breast examined; this flattens the breast tissue evenly. At right, to finish a BSE, breasts should always be examined in a mirror for anything unusual in their appearance.

3. Press the pads of the three middle fingers of the left hand, excluding the thumb and the pinky, against the skin just under your collarbone, near your shoulder.

4. Using the palpation technique (see box above), make small rotary motions, pressing your fingers down on your skin.

5. Press down along the outside of your breast. Follow your way down an imaginary bra line as you palpate down. When you feel the lower curve of your breast, at the bottom of your bra line, you may notice a ridge of firm tissue, which is normal.

6. When you reach the bottom of your bra line, move your fingers inward about one-half inch, and work your way back up to your collarbone. Imagine yourself mowing a lawn, going down, then up, and overlapping your rows a little.

7. Keep going up and down until you reach your breastbone in the center of your chest and are sure you have felt every part of your breast, including the nipple (where you can feel the breast tissue sink down a bit).

8. Repeat the vertical strip pattern on the left breast.

9. Squeeze the nipple of each breast gently between your thumb and index finger. Tell your doctor if you notice a discharge.

10. After you examine your breasts, look at them in a mirror. With your arms relaxed at your sides, see whether anything out of the ordinary catches your eye, such as a dimpling, redness, or swelling. Anything that makes you suspicious should be brought to your doctor's attention.

Where to Feel Most Carefully

A cancerous tumor may be a single, hard lump like a clump of gravel with a ragged edge, or a thickening. It is often but not always painless. According to information compiled during the 1980s by the U.S. Department of Health and Human Services:

- About 50 percent of troublesome lumps appear in the upper, outer quadrant of the breast, where breast tissue is most dense;
- 15 percent of breast cancers appear in the upper, inner quadrant of the breast;
- 18 percent in the nipple area;
- 11 percent in the lower outer quadrant;
- 6 percent in the lower inner quadrant.

A Tool for Examining Your Breasts

An Illinois company, Inventive Products Incorporated, gained Food and Drug Administration (FDA) approval for its product the Sensor Pad, which looks something like an inflated pancake but is actually a 10-inch polyurethane pouch filled with silicone lubricant. You perform your preferred breast self-examination technique on the pad while holding it over your breast. The Sensor Pad is designed to reduce friction and makes lumps easier to detect during BSE. The Sensor Pad is currently available by prescription and through health-care providers and clinics where women are taught how to use it, but the manufacturers are working for government approval to have the device sold over the counter.

BSE DURING PREGNANCY AND BREASTFEEDING

• **When a woman is pregnant,** even though her breasts are enlarged and somewhat lumpy, she should still continue monthly BSEs. Despite an expectancy-endowed figure, she will be able to feel a growth that stands out from the rest of her breast tissue, and as pointed out in Chapter 2, a breast cancer discovered during pregnancy can be quite aggressive. If a suspicious lump shows up, a woman should report it immediately to her obstetrician, who will probably suggest a breast screening with ultrasound rather than mammography to prevent exposure to radiation during the pregnancy.

An ultrasound screening that uses sound waves for an internal view of a breast (see Chapter 5) may be able to identify a benign cyst. If ultrasound does not indicate what the lump is, a woman may have no choice but to be evaluated through mammography and biopsy.

• **When a woman is breastfeeding,** a monthly BSE is easiest after the baby has finished nursing. Breasts are the softest when they have been emptied of milk.

BSE AFTER BREAST SURGERY

Whenever a woman in my care must have breast surgery, whether to remove a fibroadenoma or a lump, I suggest that before surgery she examine her breast carefully and mentally note its contours. Normally, as a breast heals, scar tissue forms near a surgical incision in the skin. If you know what your breast felt like without scar tissue, then you can recognize the scar tissue and identify changes other than those you can trace to your surgery.

BSE WHEN YOU HAVE BREAST IMPLANTS

Whether breast implants are filled with silicone or saline, a woman can still feel a mass or tenderness in the natural breast tissue surrounding the implant. As with any type of breast surgery, the operation to insert a breast implant will result in scar tissue forming around the incision and possibly around the implant itself. It is important for a woman to be able to identify the implant and the scar tissue during BSE and then recognize changes in the remaining breast tissue. For every woman with a breast implant, I think an occasional breast screening with magnetic resonance imaging (MRI), which does not involve any exposure to radiation, is advisable. MRI is gaining recognition not only as the best method for detecting leakage from a breast implant but also as a breast screening method that may be better than mammography for women who have implants. (See Chapter 5.)

BSE FOR A LIFETIME

A woman should begin breast self-examination as a menstruating teenager, and make it a habit for the rest of her life. A woman can discover a lump when she is 90 years old; in fact, the greatest number of breast cancers are discovered when women are between 60 and 80. But even reading this chapter is not enough for learning a self-examination technique. I urge you to find personal instruction in breast self-examination from your own doctor, at a health center, or through a MammaCare program. BSE is an easy, inexpensive way to enhance the health care of your breasts, and it is most effective when taught one-on-one.

CHAPTER FOUR

When to Have a Mammogram: A Recommended Timetable

A woman has a mammogram (an X ray of her breasts) to diagnose a symptom, such as a newly discovered lump in her breast, to screen her breasts because she has a family history of breast cancer, or because she is over age 40 and is having a routine checkup. Of course, the "age" part of that statement is debatable. The question of whether a woman, at age 40, should have her first mammogram and begin routine screenings is a controversy with no settlement in sight. Everyone agrees that when women 50 and older have annual mammograms, breast cancers are detected early and women's lives are saved, but many researchers argue that the screening of younger women does not save lives and can even expose women to unnecessary radiation and needless biopsies.

Meanwhile, the number of cases of breast cancer among women under 50 is rising. The American Cancer Society estimates that in 1996 more new cases of breast cancer will be diagnosed among women aged 40 to 49 (33,400 cases) than among women 50 to 59 years old (30,900 cases). All things considered, if you were my patient and you were in your forties, I would recommend a baseline mammogram for you today.

WHY AGE IS AN ISSUE

The reason women over age 50 have annual mammograms today can be traced back to the 1960s, when the Health Insurance Plan of New York (HIP) enrolled 26,000 women in a study that included four years of annual mammography and physical examination. At seven years a follow-up of the study showed a 30-percent reduction in breast cancer mortality in the group offered screening compared with the control group. At 14 years another follow-up showed mortality continued to be reduced by 24 percent. There was no clear-cut benefit for women who were younger than 50, however, and for more than 30 years researchers have been trying to determine whether mammographic screenings every one to two years for women in their forties would substantially reduce their rate of death from breast cancer.

The Breast Cancer Detection Demonstration Project (BCDDP), a joint project of the American Cancer Society and the National Cancer Institute (NCI) in the 1970s, reported that in 280,000 women 42 percent of cancers were detected by mammography alone, and one-third of these were in the early stages. In the Dutch city of Nijmegen, all female residents over 35 were invited to have mammograms every other year from 1975 to 1982. Because of early detection, there was an implied 52-percent reduction in deaths from breast cancer among the women screened. A two-county study in Sweden also showed that mammography could detect breast cancers approximately 1.5 to 2.5 years before they could be felt by women or their doctors. While these investigations did not answer the question of whether mammography would significantly lower the mortality rate for breast cancer among *younger* women, it did lead to a cry for mammography for early detection.

In response the American Cancer Society and the NCI advised women at that time to get their first or *baseline* mammograms at age 40 and to have mammograms every one to two years through their forties and annually beginning at 50. Still, there was no substantial evidence to indicate that when women in their forties had mammograms, they would live longer. Meanwhile, these younger women were exposed to radiation and in many cases, because their mammograms were difficult to interpret, underwent unnecessary biopsies.

To help resolve the issue of whether mammography adequately benefits younger women, the National Breast Screening Study (NBSS) of Canada was conducted between 1980 and 1988. It involved 50,430 women aged 40 to 49 at 15 urban medical centers in six Canadian provinces. The women were randomly assigned to receive either a yearly physical breast examination and mammogram or the usual care following an initial breast exam. The results indicated that with regard to mortality, mammography offered no benefit to women under 50. In fact, there were 38 breast cancer deaths in the group screened by mammography and only 28 breast cancer deaths in the usual care group. The higher number of deaths in the screened group may not have been considered statistically significant but nevertheless caught scientists by surprise.

Then highly respected researchers and major health organizations, such as the American Cancer Society and the American Medical Association, began to find fault with the NBSS. Reports began to appear questioning the skill of the radiologists, outdated mammographic techniques, and the

WHY A MAMMOGRAM IS HARDER TO READ
IF A WOMAN IS UNDER 50

Breasts are mostly made up of fat, and fat looks gray on a mammogram. Other tissues, including cancerous tissues, appear white. A white area may be an unidentifiable mass, a star-shaped lesion that suggests cancer, or specks of calcium, called *calcifications*, which are usually benign but can be precancerous. Premenopausal women generally have dense breasts with a lot of glandular tissue that also looks white on a mammogram. Sometimes a radiologist can have difficulty identifying a suspicious area, because it does not stand out in the overall lightness of a younger woman's mammogram. However, this does not happen all the time and many younger women have had cancers detected through mammography. Although an older woman may sometimes have dense breasts, usually with age, glandular tissue shrinks and fatty tissue increases, making it easier to spot troublesome white areas on the mostly gray mammogram.

inadvertent inclusion in the screening group of women with late-stage, poor-prognosis breast cancer. The consensus in the worldwide medical community is that there is still no study that answers the question, "Will women live longer if they begin their routine mammographic screenings in their forties?" (Dr. Daniel B. Kopans, director of breast imaging in the radiology department at Massachusetts General Hospital, has said that for a breast screening study to have real statistical power and prove a mortality reduction of 20 to 25 percent for women aged 40 to 49, it would have to include almost 500,000 women. As of this writing, less than 200,000 women have participated in all of the world's trials combined.)

Taking this information into consideration, the NCI decided to withdraw its earlier recommendations related to mammography for women in their forties but took the position that women 50 or older should have routine screenings every one to two years, along with a breast examination by a physician. Researchers at the NCI are waiting to see whether new evidence may emerge from other studies over the next few years. A study in the United Kingdom will have results in 1998 or 1999, and the Göteborg study from Sweden looks promising. Started in 1982 among women 40 to 59 years old, the study involves 21,000 women who are undergoing two-view mammograms every 18 months and 29,000 women in a control group. Early findings show the breast cancer mortality rate among 40- to 49-year-olds to be 40 percent lower in the screened group. "Right now," says Dr. Larry Kessler, chief of the Applied Research Branch of the NCI, "we cannot responsibly tell women to get screened when we know it's going to cause them pain, biopsies, anxiety, and money, and we cannot promise a benefit."

Basing their decision on the same information that the NCI had, other health organizations, such as the American Cancer Society, the American Medical Association, and at least a dozen other groups have decided to *continue to recommend* that women begin mammographic screenings at age 40 and have them every one to two years until age 50, when they should begin having annual screenings. "Even in the absence of definitive data," explains Dr. Robert Smith, senior director for detection programs for the American Cancer Society (ACS), "the data are very compelling that mammography is beneficial. The ACS evaluates data from the trials as well as from other sources, and finds the inferential evidence to be sufficiently strong that we can recommend mammography for women in their forties as the only method that will potentially allow them greater treatment options and a potential to not die of this disease that they're diagnosed with."

The official policy in Sweden now is to begin screening women by mammography when they are 40. Australia and Iceland are following the Swedish policy. Most other countries with advanced mammographic technology, such as the United Kingdom, the Netherlands, and eight nations of the European Group for Breast Cancer, have decided against recommending mammography for younger women. They recommend that routine screenings start when women reach their fiftieth birthday.

Even as this book goes to press, more studies are coming out both advocating and opposing the recommendation for routine mammographic screenings for women in their forties.

Research "for": Three years of mammographic screenings at Thomas Jefferson University Hospital in Philadelphia resulted in a diagnosis of 743 breast cancers in women over age 40 and 177 of these among women aged 40 to 49. These were cancers too small to be felt and were the types associated with longer survival terms. Researchers at Thomas Jefferson concluded that not only should women in their forties have routine mammograms, but they should have them every year. And a 1995 published analysis of eight studies designed to assess the value of mammography in younger women was undertaken by a research team headed by Dr. Charles R. Smart, formerly of the NCI. This study found a 14-percent reduction in breast cancer deaths among screened younger women (this included the Canadian NBSS results). Without the Canadian findings, a statistically significant 23-percent reduction in mortality was calculated.

Research "against": A meta-analysis of 13 breast cancer studies from 1966 to 1993 by epidemiologists at the University of California in San Francisco indicates that although mammography reduces breast cancer mortality by 26 percent for women aged 50 to 74, it does not significantly reduce the mortality of women aged 40 to 49.

Mammogram showing tiny ductal carcinoma in situ (DCIS) and a cluster of microcalcifications. Improved mammography has increased the early detection of small, localized cancers and precancers. Courtesy of HealthSouth Diagnostic, Washington, DC.

MY RECOMMENDED TIMETABLE FOR MAMMOGRAPHY

Having read the results of randomized controlled studies of mammographic screenings of thousands of women and having personally examined women in their forties who discovered early-stage cancers through mammography, I concur with the ACS and the official policy of Sweden. I recommend that healthy women of every age receive annual physical breast examinations by their gynecologists. Then, I send all of my patients who are not at high risk for breast cancer for baseline mammograms at age 40 and encourage them to get repeat screenings every year or two. I advise women aged 50 or more to undergo annual mammograms as part of their yearly checkups. When a woman is at high risk for breast cancer, I consider her risk factors individually and counsel her as to the best time of her life to begin her screenings, usually sooner than age 40.

HOW TO GET THE BEST MAMMOGRAM

The best mammogram, or X ray of your breast, uses the high resolution, low-dose film screen technique. In the 1980s, xeromammography, a screening method created by Xerox that combines X-ray and Xerox techniques for a high-contrast (blue on white paper) image, was more commonly used. Today this technique is being phased out. While mammography equipment does not expose you to more than 300 millirads per view for film screened, xeromammography requires a slightly higher exposure to radiation—400 millirads per view—for results. In the Mammography Accreditation Program of the American College of Radiology (ACR), more than 12,000 mammography units exist in about 9,000 facilities in the United States, but 100 xeromammography units are still around. *Before undergoing a mammogram, always ask the hospital, X-ray, or mammography center whether they are using dedicated mammographic equipment with radiation exposure limited to 300 millirads.* Dedicated mammographic equipment is designed and used solely for the purpose of mammography—nothing else.

To be sure you are getting a high-quality mammogram, select a mammography facility accredited by the ACR and the U.S. Food and Drug Administration, which began a joint program of accreditation in October 1994. Radiologists should be certified by the American Board of Radiology and radiological technologists by the American Registry of Radiologic Technologists or a state agency.

At a top-notch facility, you should have no trouble finding an ACR certificate of accreditation and an FDA placard on display (you can also find out whether a facility is accredited by checking with the National Cancer Institute, 800-4-CANCER, or the American Cancer Society, 800-ACS-2345).

AN IMPORTANT NOTE TO REMEMBER: MAMMOGRAPHY, THE "GOLD STANDARD," IS STILL IMPERFECT

Statistics tell us that when women 50 or older undergo mammographic screenings, they are 30 percent less likely to die of breast cancer. No other method of screening for breast cancer can claim so much success in decreasing mortality, which is why mammography is considered the "gold standard." About 40 percent of breast cancers are discovered through mammography alone; 35 percent are found with a combination of mammography and physical examination of the breasts; and 15 percent are found by physical examination alone.

The value of a mammogram greatly depends on the quality of the mammographic X-ray equipment used, the skill of the radiological technicians who carry out the screening procedures, and the radiologists who interpret the images. A mammogram can detect a mass that is 0.5 centimeter, about one-fifth of an inch, which you probably would be unable to feel. Yet even with the most up-to-date technology and the most skilled technicians and radiologists, *experts estimate that 10 to 15 percent of cancers are missed* (mammography reports always cite this margin of error), and that this percentage is even higher for women under 50—in one study, mammography missed cancerous lumps 44 percent of the time in younger women.

Also, although a mass can be identified on a mammogram, whether it is benign or malignant, a fluid-filled cyst or a solid mass, cannot be determined. Ultrasound, which produces an image by bouncing sound waves off tissue, is often used to clarify the consistency of a suspicious mass. This may then be followed by fine-needle aspiration, a core-needle biopsy, or a surgical biopsy of a solid lump. (See Chapter 17.)

Thus, the gold standard is imperfect. So, if you feel a lump and a mammogram does not reveal anything suspicious, ask your doctor to investigate further, suggest a second-opinion radiologist or a breast surgeon for another reading of your mammogram, or perhaps allow you to undergo an ultrasound imaging. Trust your instincts and listen to your body.

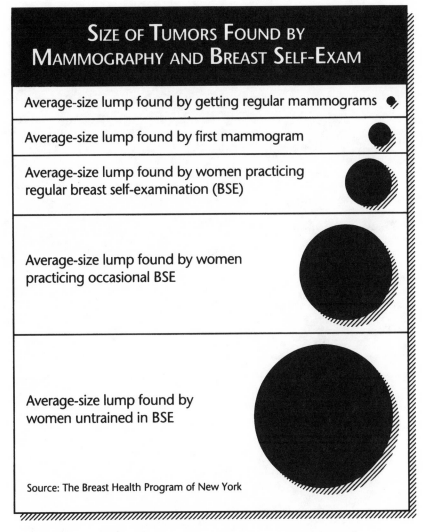

SIZE OF TUMORS FOUND BY MAMMOGRAPHY AND BREAST SELF-EXAM

Average-size lump found by getting regular mammograms

Average-size lump found by first mammogram

Average-size lump found by women practicing regular breast self-examination (BSE)

Average-size lump found by women practicing occasional BSE

Average-size lump found by women untrained in BSE

Source: The Breast Health Program of New York

Mammography is still the best method for earliest detection of a growth.

An accredited piece of equipment bears a round ACR seal. The accreditation program, which was voluntary when it was started by the ACR in 1987, became federally mandated in 1994. Today standards for quality control, quality assurance, image quality, and dosage of radiation to the breast must be met.

At an accredited center a radiologist who interprets mammograms must read a minimum of 480 mammograms per year. Such experts suggest looking

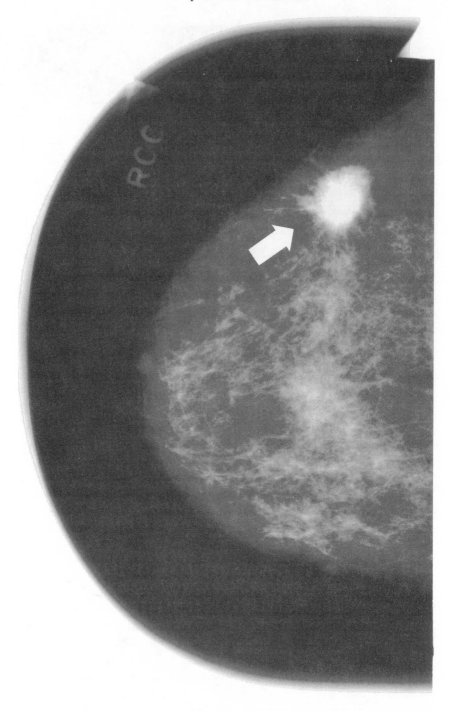

Mammogram showing a large invasive breast cancer, easily recognized by its irregular margins. Courtesy of HealthSouth Diagnostic, Washington, DC.

for a doctor who reads at least 10 to 20 mammograms a day. Women should ask about the number of mammograms read and done daily at the facilities they are selecting for their screenings (at least 20 to 30 is a good measure). In fact, do not be discouraged if you go to a mammography center that is busy and running behind schedule. Usually, the more mammographies undertaken at a center, the more skilled the staff is. You can also ask whether your mammogram will be read by *two* radiologists. If two experts interpret your mammogram, you can feel even more secure that the report you receive is accurate. If you are the least bit unsure of the interpretation of your mammogram, ask for a copy of the images and bring them to another radiologist or a breast surgeon for an additional reading.

A Note About Mammography Screening in Vans: If a mobile mammography screening is offered by a reputable mammography or medical center, the equipment in the mobile unit should be high quality and accredited by the ACR and FDA. Look for the ACR certificate of accreditation and FDA placard, just as you would when visiting a facility. I normally advise my patients to be screened at a main screening or medical center, however, because if a mammogram shows a suspicious area, the van may not have the equipment to screen that area more closely, and if your breast requires further scrutiny, you may be advised to report to the center anyway. Then you may be charged twice, once for the visit to the van and once for the follow-up visit to the center. It's a good idea to ask about fees for further screening before you choose mobile mammography.

MAMMOGRAPHY AND EXPOSURE TO RADIATION: PUTTING YOUR CONCERN INTO PERSPECTIVE

The permitted outer limit of radiation exposure during mammography is 300 millirads per film screen view—and an accurate mammography screening requires four views, two of each breast. Even though an outer limit of 600 millirads per breast seems high, radiation exposure from mammography is about 10 times less than it was in the mid-1970s. Why wasn't the dosage of radiation lowered many years ago? It has to do with the time it takes for technology to advance.

Today when you get a mammogram, the source of the radiation, the X-ray beam that traverses your breast, goes into a square black cassette that contains both film and an intensifying screen. This intensifying screen transforms the X-ray beam into light through a phosphorescent process and makes the X-ray beam glow onto the film. Over the years major film manufacturers, such as Kodak and Fuji, improved the quality and "glowability" of the screen, so that less radiation is needed from the X-ray beam to expose the film. At the same time, techniques for processing the film, manipulation of temperature and chemicals, and the chemicals themselves improved. Thanks to these advances, today there is far less exposure to radiation from mammography, and an eagle-eyed radiologist may be able to spot a growth that is only one-tenth of an inch in size. As Marie Zinninger, supervisor of the Mammography Accreditation Program of the ACR says, "We, the American College of Radiology, do not believe that there is a risk from the radiation of mammography, and the benefit of detecting cancer early is so much greater."

Still, we all know that our body's cells can be affected by radiation, so there is always some risk from exposure. Dr. Orhan Suleiman, chief of radiation programs for the FDA's Center for Devices and Radiologic Health, reports that although 300 millirads per view is the outer limit of radiation exposure to the breast during mammography, FDA research shows that the average dose to the average female breast is more likely to be 150 millirads (a woman with large, dense breasts may require a higher level of radiation for an accurate image). By way of comparison, a chest X ray exposes the lungs to an average dose of 7 millirads of radiation! Still, experts believe that the benefit of early cancer detection—*the odds of a woman having breast cancer detected between the ages of 40 and 50 is 1.6 percent, meaning 160 in 10,000 women will have their breast cancers discovered early*—outweighs the risk that a breast cancer will arise from radiation exposure during mammography.

Dr. R. Edward Hendrick, chief of the division of radiologic science at the University of Colorado Health Sciences Center, has collected the latest available figures on radiation dose and risk during mammography and reports that the data show that radiation risk is greater among younger women whose more rapidly dividing cells are more sensitive than among women over 40. The following table, from Dr. Hendrick's analysis published by the U.S. Department of Health and Human Services, gives a current best estimate of cumulative lifetime risk (figures are based on findings of the National Research Council's Committee on the Biological Effects of Ionizing Radiation or BEIR-V, 1990).

The table assumes annual mammographic screenings (two views to each breast), beginning at the specified age and continuing to age 75. The risk of radiation-induced breast cancer begins five to 10 years after exposure, with the probability of incidence peaking 15 years after exposure and the probability of mortality peaking 20 years after exposure. As you can see from the table, the younger you are, the more vulnerable your cells are to radiation exposure, but at age 40, when most women begin mammographic screenings, the risk drops considerably.

Again, bear in mind that most women do not begin having mammograms until they are 40, and then there is a considerable benefit: 160 per 10,000 women between 40 and 50 will have their breast cancers detected by mammography. Obviously, we all would like a screening method with no drawbacks, and techniques using less or no radiation are being investigated (see "Improving Breast Screenings for the Future" at the end of this chapter).

CUMULATIVE LIFETIME RISK OF BREAST CANCER MORTALITY* FROM ANNUAL MAMMOGRAPHY

Age at Start of Annual Screening	Cumulative Lifetime Risk of Breast Cancer Mortality (per 100,000 women)
20	54.1
25	41.9
30	30.9
35	21.4
40	13.8
45	8.9
50	3.9
55	1.5
60	0.4
65	0.04

Two views to each breast; 300 millirads exposure in each breast dose.
*L.W. Bassett, R.E. Hendrick, T.L. Bassford, et al., *Quality Determinants of Mammography, Clinical Practice Guideline No. 13*, AHCPR Publication No. 95-0632. Rockville, MD: Agency for Health Care Policy and Research, Public Health Service, U.S. Department of Health and Human Services, October 1994.

WHEN YOU DO HAVE A MAMMOGRAM

Even with its 10 to 15 percent margin of error, a mammogram is still the surest way to detect cancer at an early stage. So at some point, as part of caring for your whole body, you should have a mammogram.

First, choose an ACR/FDA–accredited facility for your mammogram, and ask whether you can know the results of the radiologist's reading before you leave. Why wait anxiously if you don't need to? If a facility will not have the results for you right away, make sure that its policy is to inform you within 10 days. Also, before you schedule your mammogram, ask about the fees. The cost of mammography can range from $50 to $250, and the more reasonably priced accredited centers are often just as good as those that are more expensive. Once you have settled on a center for your mammogram, then there are a number of ways to be sure you are getting the best possible image:

• Make sure that your breasts and underarm areas are free of talc and antiperspirant, which can cause a misreading of a mammography image. Flecks of talcum powder or aluminum, which can be an ingredient in anti-perspirant, can look like microcalcifications of the breast (usually benign, but sometimes precancerous bits of calcium) on a mammogram.

• Avoid getting tattoos on your breast. Sometimes the pigment in a tattoo can cast a shadow that resembles a calcification in a mammogram.

• Whether caffeine in the diet brings on breast cysts is uncertain. The latest research does not implicate caffeine, but I still tell the women in my care to avoid consuming coffee, tea, colas, and other caffeine-containing foods for at least a week before having a mammogram.

• Make sure that the radiologist knows whether you have had a breast implant or any other surgical procedure on your breast before the reading.

• If you are in your childbearing years and are sexually active without contraception, schedule your mammography during the first 10 days of your menstrual cycle, when you are least likely to be pregnant.

• The technique of mammography requires a total of four images, two images (a top-to-bottom, and a sideways view) of each breast. After you place your breast on an X-ray plate (which the technologist should wipe off with alcohol), a plastic plate compresses your breast horizontally. A top-to-bottom image is shot, and the X-ray plate is repositioned at the side of your breast. There is discomfort but usually no pain involved in having a mammogram. Some women, however, have very sensitive breasts and a mammogram momentarily hurts them. You can ask the technologist to ease the equipment and not squeeze down quite so hard if you hurt. (*Important to note:* Animal studies have shown that compression of cancerous tumors in rats has caused the number of malignant cells circulating in the blood to increase. In his 1992 preliminary study of breast compression, Dr. David Watmough of the University of Aberdeen in Scotland advises that special care be taken to use as little compression as possible when a woman with a known breast cancer is being screened by mammography.)

• Remember to hold your breath and remain perfectly still for the few seconds it takes to create the mammographic image. Any motion can blur the image and lead to a retake.

IMPROVING BREAST SCREENINGS FOR THE FUTURE

Researchers are striving to create screening techniques that will detect abnormalities in the breast in early stages, with greater accuracy, and with no or reduced exposure to radiation. Among the techniques being explored are:

Digital Mammography

A computer-assisted technique, digital mammography reduces radiation exposure but still requires an X-ray detector with an outer dosage of about 200 millirads for one image—and two are needed—of an average-size breast

UNDERSTANDING THE BASELINE
MAMMOGRAM

The "baseline" mammogram is the first one you have, at any age, and it is a reference point, a basis of comparison, for mammograms of your breasts in the near future. As time goes on and your number of screenings increases, radiologists refer to more recent images when making comparisons, so in effect, you are always creating a new baseline because your breasts change dramatically over the years. As you get older, the glandular tissue in your breast gives way to fatty tissue, and your breasts have less density. Thus a baseline mammogram when you had dense breasts at 40 is not the best point of reference when you are 55, and a radiologist will look at more recent mammograms when he does his reading.

(100 millirads per image less than traditional mammography), and 300 millirads for screening of a large, dense breast. Women should receive no more than 300 millirads per view during a traditional mammographic procedure, and to get an accurate image of a large, dense breast, radiation exposure may be maximized routinely. With digital mammography, there is no film screen or developed picture, because the image is computerized and enhanced on a video display terminal. This allows the radiologist to adjust the image electronically. A radiologist can zero in on a special area of the breast, heighten contrast, magnify, reduce the image, and detect the tiniest lesions. Since the image is in a computer, it can be transmitted in moments to doctors miles away for consultation. Digital mammography is currently being explored at university hospitals and other major research centers.

PET (Positron Emission Tomography)

In a PET scan tomogram, you are injected with a radioisotope that releases a nuclear substance called a *positron*. Concentrations of this isotope are taken up by cells of the breast and form "hot spots." A rapid sequence of film creates image "slices," or tomograms, which, when put together, produce a complete picture of a breast. By looking at the hot spots of a PET scan, a radiologist can find minute cancer growth and the spread of cancer in the lymph nodes, as well as a good view of very dense breasts. On the down side, sometimes false-positive results occur because the PET scan can make it difficult to distinguish between infections and cancer. The PET scan involves exposure to radiation, but its precision makes it worthy of continued investigation.

Ultrasound Computed Tomography (CT)

Currently being tested at the University of California/San Diego Center for Women's Health, ultrasound CT involves no radiation to get inside the breast for tomograms, those cross-sectional pictures or image "slices." The ultrasound equipment projects its images onto a computer screen for viewing. The entire screening, which requires seven or eight images to get a complete picture of your breast, takes about 20 minutes. You lie on your stomach on a table with a hole in it for your breast to drop through. In a warm water bath, your uncompressed breast is then surrounded by 1,024 tiny transducers, which generate echoes. From the low-frequency sound waves the computer can reconstruct the tomograms of your breast. The 10- to 12-millimeter slices become sharp images on the computer screen. California researchers are hoping that ultrasound CT will give better definition to the solid masses that are so difficult to identify in dense breasts.

Ultrasonography: The Crystal Scanner

Radiation free and operating with the use of sound waves, the Crystal Scanner may help detect breast cancer at a point when cells are just beginning to change their growth pattern. This would mean finding a potential cancer so early it would not even be classifiable as a tumor. Typically, ultrasonography has not been powerful enough to detect tiny tumors evident on a mammogram. However, ultrasonography techniques developed by the National Aeronautics and Space Administration (NASA) are so sensitive, they can find microscopic cracks in spacecraft materials. NASA's ultrasound equipment operates at frequencies many times greater than that of the sonogram instruments that medical professionals normally use.

The Crystal Scanner was created in October 1992, when the Supra Medical Corporation in Pennsylvania combined the sensitive ultrasonography techniques developed by NASA with its own high-resolution technology. The Crystal Scanner is capable of detecting a breast tissue irregularity as small as 50 microns, one-tenth the size of a grain of salt. Clinical studies on the effectiveness of this new technology began in fall 1994.

During a Crystal Scan a woman sits in front of the Scanner, which is shoulder high. She leans forward and rests her breasts on a special pad; there is no uncomfortable squeezing of her breasts like that during mammography. Ultrasound waves from both breasts are recorded simultaneously through an array of transducers built into the pad. The resulting ultrasound images appear on the scanner's video monitors. New image pattern recognition techniques help sonographers identify cancerous and noncancerous growths.

ALL IN ALL, MAMMOGRAPHY IS STILL THE BEST BREAST SCREENING TODAY

No matter how old you are, if you feel a suspicious lump, or even if you do not feel a lump but would like to allay an anxiety you have about breast cancer, you can schedule a mammogram. Every day, mammography saves lives! One 34-year-old woman had a mammogram simply because her mother had a dream that she had a problem with her breast. The daughter argued with her mother about it at first, because she thought that she was too young to be screened, but went for the X ray simply to placate her parent. Sure enough, a small malignancy was discovered. I tell you this story not to give dreams any special significance or to heighten your concern about breast cancer but to encourage you to use mammography whenever you think it may help you achieve better physical or emotional well-being. I especially encourage African American women to take advantage of this screening technique. The latest statistics show that African American women are more likely to die of breast cancer (31.2 per 100,000) than white women (26.0). One reason is the fact that many African American women are not being routinely screened, so that their cancers are more advanced by the time they are discovered. For all women, mammography is an important tool in the fight against breast cancer.

CHAPTER FIVE

Beyond Mammography: Other High-Tech Breast Tests You May Want

An unidentifiable mass shows up on your mammogram. Or, you are young, but your mother developed breast cancer when she was only 37. You know mammography is not recommended for young women who have dense breasts, but you want your breasts evaluated. What do *you* do?

There are times when mammography is not enough or when problems in your breasts require additional imaging or imaging more suited to your situation. That's where two other high-tech breast tests, ultrasound and magnetic resonance imaging (MRI), come in. (As mentioned in Chapter 4, the ultrasound of the future may someday vie with mammography as the ultimate breast screening method.) Also gaining attention for diagnostic capabilities are BBE (breast biophysical examination) and scintimammography. Although all of these tests are designed to find out what's going on inside a woman's breasts, each is special for different reasons.

ULTRASOUND

Ultrasound, also called *sonography*, is an imaging technique that uses high-frequency sound waves to produce an internal picture of a breast on a monitor. No radiation is involved in ultrasound, a test that doctors continue to regard as safe. A sonographer places gel on the skin of a woman's breast and with a transducer, a device much like a microphone, touches the skin. As the sonographer moves the transducer over a woman's breast, sound wave patterns, or echoes, are transmitted. These sound waves display the internal image of the breast on a screen. Today's ultrasound technology allows a woman to be evaluated by high-definition imaging (HDI), which has a sound beam that penetrates the breast more deeply. This increased depth gives a much more complete picture of a breast.

Most often ultrasound is used to determine whether a suspicious area on a mammogram is a solid tumor or a fluid-filled cyst. The ultrasound image helps a doctor guide a needle into the area for a biopsy or drain the cyst. (See Chapter 19 for more about biopsies.) With improved ultrasound, however, some doctors are now recommending its use for women with very dense breasts that are difficult to screen with mammography and for younger women (under 35) with a family history of breast cancer. Although standard ultrasound cannot detect the tiny precancerous specks called *microcalcifications* that mammography can, a recent study published in the August 1995 issue of the journal *Cancer* showed ultrasound to be effective in spotting breast cancers missed during mammography.

At the University of British Columbia, Dr. Paula Gordon performed ultrasound examinations on the breasts of 12,706 women who had come to her for screenings because they had a lump or some other problem. During ultrasound, Dr. Gordon unexpectedly detected 1,575 solid masses that could not be felt and were not visible on mammography. After further interpretations, biopsies, and surgery, 44 (2.8%) of these unexpected masses were confirmed cancers. For 16 women, this meant more than one cancer existed in their breasts. Because the majority of the masses discovered were benign, some women underwent further examination and needless biopsy (but this also happens with mammography). "The yield is as good as mammography," comments Dr. Gordon. Mammography finds about two to three breast cancers per 1,000 problem-free women, and in her study ultrasound found 3.5 cancers per 1,000 women who came to her with a preexisting problem. Nonetheless, she does not suggest that ultrasound replace the more specific mammography. What she would like to see is ultrasound examinations of women who have dense breasts and are at higher risk either because they have had cancer themselves or because they have a first-degree relative who has had breast cancer. Some of these women may be in their forties and may already be having routine mammographic screenings. Others would be younger, perhaps in their twenties, for whom mammography is not yet recommended. The problem with ultrasound readings, however, is that they are only as good as the interpretive skill of the sonographer using the equipment, and many sonographers are still absorbing the changes that have come with rapid advancements in the technology.

My Recommendation for When to Have an Ultrasound

I try to consider each case individually, but nevertheless, I do have a few general guidelines for suggesting an ultrasound breast examination. I feel that ultrasound is appropriate:

- When a woman has a "palpable" mass (one that can be felt during an examination), whether it has been seen on a mammogram or not. Ultrasound can determine whether the mass is solid and should be biopsied or a fluid-filled cyst that can be drained.
- When no lump can be felt, but a suspicious area shows up on a mammogram.
- When a woman is 30 or younger and has a sense that something does not "feel right" in her breasts. If a mass is found during an ultrasound screening, then she should have a mammogram.
- When a young woman with dense breasts and a family history of breast cancer in the premenopausal years is concerned about cancer and would like a breast test that goes beyond self-examination. However, I then recommend mammography for this high-risk woman when she is about age 35.
- When pregnant or breastfeeding women have cystic changes in their breasts that need evaluation.

MRI (MAGNETIC RESONANCE IMAGING)

Another way to get an inside view of breasts—without experiencing radiation—is with MRI (magnetic resonance imaging). Here's how an MRI works: Hydrogen is naturally present in the water within our bodies. An MRI machine contains a magnet that stirs up the hydrogen molecules. A technologist transmits a sequence of radio waves into the magnet, which is outfitted with a special receiver coil that relays information on agitated tissues to a computer. A calculation of the time it takes molecules to return to normal distinguishes cancerous from healthy tissue. Sometimes a dye is injected into a woman's body to enhance a reading of tumor tissue. Because both the dye and the fatty tissue in the breast are bright, however, it takes a skilled MRI expert to spot trouble.

At Baylor University Medical Center, Dr. Steven E. Harms, director of magnetic resonance imaging, thinks he is approaching a solution to this problem with a technique he devised called RODEO (rotating delivery of excitation off-resonance), which suppresses the fat signal on an MRI. In his studies, which now extend to 800 women with suspicious mammograms, Dr. Harms has identified breast cancers missed by standard mammography in 47 percent of the cases. His findings, however, also include false-positive readings (benign tumors labeled as cancerous) in 40 percent. Dr. Harms attributes half of the false-positive results to the precancerous conditions, however.

MRIs have been most helpful in screening women with silicone breast implants for signs of breast cancer or silicone leakage. The high density of the silicone obscures an estimated 22 to 83 percent of breast tissue from a mammogram but not on an MRI. Dr. Harms has also found that MRI can be useful in women who are contemplating breast-conserving surgery for breast cancer. Through MRI he has been able to identify the size and extent of tumors so that when surgery is performed, the margins are clear and no more tissue than necessary must be removed. An MRI is expensive (up to $1,000), but it still may cost less than the second surgery that would be needed to attain clear margins after lumpectomy. Still, you need to be aware that this is a fairly new idea. To suggest an MRI before breast-conserving surgery is not common practice; Dr. Harms is on the forefront of exploration into MRI usage.

My Recommendation for When to Have an MRI

When a woman has a breast implant, whether silicone gel or saline, an MRI is the best way to examine her breasts for cancer and detect any leakage from the implant. As mentioned above, silicone hides an estimated 22 to 83 percent of breast tissue from view during mammography.

BREAST BIOPHYSICAL EXAMINATION (BBE): STILL UNDER STUDY

A new test developed by Biofield Corp. in Roswell, Georgia, may help decrease the more than 700,000 breast biopsies performed every year for the 184,000 diagnosed breast cancers. During this noninvasive nonradiation test, 12 to 16 electrodes placed on a woman's breasts provide input into a computer. The breast biophysical examination (BBE) detects changes in the "electropotential" of your breasts. When a cancer develops, a cell's normally charged particles weaken and cause a shift in the breast's electrical impulses. From the electrode on the surface of a woman's breast, the BBE is able to detect the change and spot a cancer. A BBE takes only 15 to 20 minutes and thus far seems quite sensitive to cancer. In a preliminary study of 127 women, BBE was 97 percent sensitive, which means that it detected 97 of 100 existing breast cancers. It was 79 percent specific, which means it correctly identified 79 of 100 women who did not have cancer. These are very good results, and it will be a godsend for women who have suspicious mammograms if it can help eliminate the thousands of unnecessary biopsies that are being performed.

Biofield is working with the FDA, which will be involved in the analysis of multicenter clinical trials of BBE. As of this writing, 1,300 women are enrolled in double-blind testing of BBE at seven medical centers across the country. (Double-blind testing means that neither the examiners nor the women in the study know the results of the tests. The results will be revealed to a third party not connected with Biofield.) While BBE will be available in Europe in 1996, it will be a while before the FDA rules on its use in the United States.

SCINTIMAMMOGRAPHY: STILL UNDER STUDY

The goal of scintimammography, like BBE, is to reduce the thousands of unnecessary, expensive, and painful biopsies performed each year. Scintimammography uses a radioactive tracer to "light up" breast cancers that are viewed through a special scintimammography camera. The test takes about 35 minutes. First a woman is injected with the radioactive tracer, which under the brand name Cardiolite is commonly used to diagnose coronary artery disease. After a wait of approximately five minutes, she lies face-down on a special table shaped to allow her breasts to fall freely at the sides, where they can be viewed by the camera. A 10-minute side view and a 10-minute front view of each breast are photographed.

Results from early research by Dr. Iraj Khalkhali at Harbor/UCLA Medical Center in Torrance, California, show scintimammography detected breast cancer with over 90 percent accuracy among 147 women with 153 malignancies. There were 11 cases of false-positive results, women who had benign conditions that were diagnosed as cancer, and four cases of false-negative results in which women who were diagnosed as cancer-free ended up having cancer. Three cases of the false-negative results were among women who had cancer in the center part of their breasts, close to the breastbone. Several companies are now working to produce a special camera that will picture large breasts more completely. Scintimammography has been tested among 600 women in trials throughout the United States and Canada and among women in Europe. The FDA is analyzing data from the trials.

The use of scintimammography exposes women to 300 millirads of radiation, the same as mammography. Other noninvasive tests, such as the BBE, are getting good results without increasing a woman's exposure to radiation. Also, because the radioactive tracer is injected into a woman's bloodstream, it travels, and my concern is that it may affect her ovaries.

UPDATES ON ONCE-PROMISING BREAST TESTS

Thermography

The thermography technique for detecting breast cancer is based on the visualization of heat patterns in the breast, the idea being that cancerous tumors generate more heat than healthy tissue. Since it does not involve radiation, thermography appeared to be a safe and promising method for breast screening. Unfortunately, research over the years has not shown thermography to have a high rate of accuracy. At times cancers did not release sufficient heat, or they were buried in breast tissue where their temperatures could not be detected. Thermography is sometimes used in Europe as an aid in determining the aggressiveness of breast cancer, but as a breast-screening method, it is no longer in use in the United States.

Transillumination/Diaphanography

Transillumination, also called diaphanography, screens the breast by scanning it with light waves. Light transmitted through breast tissue illuminates various pathological conditions, in much the same way the beam of a flashlight seems to shine through one's hand in the dark. Transillumination is another imaging technique that does not involve radiation, and it once seemed promising as a safe breast screening method. In 1992, however, after studies from the National Institutes of Health (NIH) and Swedish researchers showed that transillumination was no more effective than manual breast examinations in detecting breast cancer, the FDA notified manufacturers that transillumination devices could not be marketed for breast screenings. It is best considered only an aid to other breast screening methods, with some doctors now using it only to get a better look at a cancer found during mammography or ultrasonography.

BE ALERT TO THE LATEST TESTS

As mentioned in Chapter 4, mammography remains the gold standard of breast screening methods for its ability to call attention to the tiniest precancers and cancers in the breast. Still, researchers are working to refine follow-up breast tests used in conjunction with suspicious mammograms. We are getting closer all the time to defining the diagnosis and reducing the number of biopsies performed on women every year. A woman should always ask her doctor whether any new, effective, safe test is available, whenever she needs a breast screening beyond mammography.

Yes, You Can Eat to Keep Your Breasts Healthy: The Latest on Foods That Fight Illness

"Don't eat too many almonds, they add weight to the breasts."
—COLETTE IN 1944, *GIGI*

Almonds? Targeting your breasts? The quotation above seems amusing until you realize that today's scientists are microscopically analyzing the components of what we eat and discovering undreamed-of connections between your food and your breasts. For at least the last five years, researchers at the National Cancer Institute (NCI) have been scrutinizing some of the small organic molecules that make up the *phytochemicals* in foods like garlic, citrus fruits, parsley, and carrots. In Greek, *phyton* means plant or "that which grows," so phytochemicals are, literally, plant chemicals. The NCI has been studying about 40 foods for the cancer-fighting potential of their phytochemicals, and many researchers outside the NCI have joined in the quest. The widespread work that is being done to define the cancer-fighting components of vegetables and fruits, however, is only one aspect of scientists' probe into the link between nutrition and breast health.

Researchers have produced a web of nutritional findings, which often seem conflicting. In this chapter we will take you through the main areas of nutrition under scrutiny and untangle the web of studies and opinions. The connection between diet and breast health will be clearly traced in:

- the fat in foods you eat
- fiber from grains, vegetables, and fruits
- the phytochemicals in vegetables and fruits
- antioxidants in vegetables and fruits

80

- garlic and olive oil
- the caffeine in coffee and other foods
- alcoholic beverages
- certain pesticides

Another reason that the diet/breast cancer connection is a hot topic among researchers today is because they are finding that certain food choices and types of cuisine affect the estrogen in your body, which in turn might affect your risk of breast cancer. Researchers are coming closer to concluding that a woman's chance of developing breast cancer is strongly linked to her exposure to her sex hormone, estrogen, during her lifetime. However, researchers are not exactly sure what components in which foods have the most effect, and they are also uncertain about the role that elevated levels of estrogen might play.

In another new wrinkle, not only what you eat but when you eat it has become important. Some researchers feel that by the time you reach your twenties, your diet may have already set the course of your health. This far-reaching but far from proven "window of vulnerability" theory is further explained in "The Fat in Your Foods" section. The latest issue aside, enough evidence exists to permit some practical approaches to eating for better breast health, and I have condensed my knowledge of the current scientific findings and the dietary advice set forth by the NCI into these following recommendations.

THE FAT IN YOUR FOODS

Because there is hope, but not proof, that a low-fat diet will make a difference in relation to breast cancer, two long-term, government-sponsored, clinical trials are going on as of this writing. These trials are testing the "window of vulnerability" theory, which holds that what you ate during your adolescence and early twenties—when the cells in your breasts, growing and dividing, were most vulnerable to dietary influences—determined your future breast health. With this theory growing more popular in the scientific community, speculation now abounds over whether adherence to a well-balanced, low-fat, high-fiber diet after age 50 carries any clout. Although we won't know the results for years, the ultimate findings of the following trials offer long-sought information about whether low-fat eating later in life can fight breast cancer:

- The Women's Health Initiative (WHI), a 10-year study, involves a $628 million commitment by the National Institutes of Health to get to the bottom of three major areas of concern to women: (1) whether a low-fat diet with only 20 percent of calories from fat prevents breast cancer, colon

MAKING THE HEALTHY EATING CONNECTION

The younger you are when you start eating with an awareness of the link between nutrition and the health of your breasts, the better your chances of keeping your breasts problem free. So, while the advice below is for women of all ages, I particularly encourage you to pass it on to someone younger—your daughter, sister, cousin, niece, granddaughter, or friend.

• Cut back on fat-laden foods, especially foods of animal origin, like meats and cheeses that are high in saturated fat. I advise eating red meat no more than once a week, choosing instead main courses with seafood, beans, rice, and pasta. Organizations such as the American Cancer Society and the NCI recommend limiting fat consumption to no more than 30 percent of daily calories and saturated fat to no more than 10 percent.

use sparingly
fats, oils, and
sweets

milk, yogurt
and cheese

meat, poultry,
fish, dry beans,
eggs, and nuts

vegetables

fruit

breads,
cereal,
rice,
and
pasta

Every day, by eating more of the fiber-rich foods at the bottom of the federal government's Food Guide Pyramid and less of the fatty foods at the top, a woman will have a more healthful diet. Illustration by Tony Kramer.

• Eat at least five, but, if possible, seven, kinds of vegetables and fruits every day. This is easier than it sounds. If you slice a banana into your breakfast cereal, and later at lunch have a salad with mushrooms, tomatoes, chickpeas, lettuce, and zucchini, you already have a total of six servings of vegetables and fruits—and you still have another meal to go.

• Include more high-fiber foods, such as whole grains, legumes, potatoes with their skins, and unpeeled fruits such as apples, peaches, and pears, in your menu. Americans eat only about 11 grams of fiber a day, and the NCI recommends doubling that intake to between 20 and 30 grams daily.

• Make olive oil your choice for cooking oil and salad dressings, and prepare foods with garlic as often as possible.

• Use moderation when drinking alcoholic beverages. Consult your doctor about your personal health history to know how a drink might affect you.

• Keep your calories at about 2,000 a day. The National Research Council's recommendation for women engaged in light to moderate physical activity is an average 2,200 calories per day for ages 19 to 50 and an average 1,900 calories per day for women over 50. I believe that 2,000 calories a day allows for an adequate amount of food, but a woman really has to gauge her individual situation. A heavier woman or a woman who feels that her activity is low for her energy intake, might want to eat less than 2,000 calories. On the other hand, a woman whose lifestyle includes a strenuous exercise regimen might easily increase her calories.

• Everyone benefits from a multivitamin every day. I recommend the following other daily vitamin supplements:

—for women who are thinking about starting a family, daily folic acid (80 micrograms [mcg]) to prevent neural tube birth defects and iron to counterbalance the iron lost in heavy menstrual bleeding (the iron supplement Slow FE has a high potency all-day release with few side effects; Slow FE-Folic Acid combines iron and folic acid in one tablet);

—for women under stress or on the birth control pill or occasionally suffering from premenstrual syndrome, vitamin B complex (100 milligrams [mg]) along with vitamin B6 (200 to 500 mg) for hormonal balance;

—for all women, vitamin E (400 international units [IU]), vitamin C (500 mg), selenium (100 mg), and beta-carotene (10,000 IU) for antioxidant protection (combating cancer-causing free radical cells in the body) and for any advantage the vitamins may offer in alleviating fibrocystic changes in breasts. A combination antioxidant supplement should also contain vitamins E, C, selenium, and beta-carotene.

Most important, make your daily eating a festival of foods, for variety is the key to good health.

cancer, and heart disease; (2) whether hormone replacement therapy prevents heart disease and osteoporosis; and (3) whether calcium and vitamin D supplements prevent osteoporosis and colon cancer. WHI is being carried out in 40 hospital and university centers across the country, and a diverse population of 63,000 women aged 50 to 79 have been recruited. It will probably be the year 2005 before we have a sense of the outcome of WHI.

• Results of the Women's Intervention Nutrition Study (WINS), an eight-year study sponsored by the NCI and conducted by the American Health Foundation, will be available about 2002. This trial, which involves 2,000 postmenopausal women with early-stage breast cancer, is designed to find out whether low-fat changes might be cancer-fighters *after* diagnosis. "We think there is good evidence that changes may work after breast cancer," says Dr. Ernst Wynder, president of the American Health Foundation. "Researchers test all kinds of chemotherapy and other modalities, so why not give diet a chance!" The low-fat diet will be superimposed on the standard surgical and medical treatments the women are receiving. Half of the women will get help to reduce their fat intake to 15 percent of their daily calories, and the other half, the control group, will be allowed diets containing up to 30 percent fat.

Exploring Fat as a Clue to Solving the Mystery of Breast Cancer

The interest in a possible cause-and-effect relationship between dietary fat and breast cancer started in the mid-1970s, when researchers doing population studies in different countries noticed a positive correlation between estimated per capita fat consumption and the number of women both developing and dying of breast cancer. As early as 1963 Dr. Wynder and his colleagues had reported that Japanese women diagnosed with breast cancer survived longer than American women in the same situation. His group had thought that the better survival among the women in Japan might be related to their lower-fat diets. After population studies were completed, Asian countries, particularly Japan, were shown to have the lowest numbers both for fat intake and breast cancer. Because breast cancer is believed to be a hormonally linked disease, scientists eventually began to compare the levels of total estrogen—which can be affected by food choice and cuisine—in the bloodstreams of different women.

Throughout the centuries, the diet in rural Japan had remained at 10 to 20 grams of fat a day, or one-fifth the fat of diets consumed by women in America. In 1990 researchers reported that measured estrogen was much lower among postmenopausal rural Japanese women, who also had lower rates of breast cancer, than for postmenopausal American women.

Epidemiologists then discovered that Japanese women who migrated to the United States and ate "Westernized" diets higher in animal fat developed breast cancer at the same rate as American women. So did their daughters, who also ate this higher-fat diet.

Fat intake continued to hold promise as a possible controllable risk factor for breast cancer until the results of the Nurses' Health Study were published in 1992. An original group of 121,700 nurses, aged 30 to 55, have been followed from 1976 and are still being followed. (Some have dropped out or died since the start of the study, but more than 100,000 nurses are still involved.) The study was initially created to examine the effects of oral contraceptives and cigarette smoking on the risk of major illnesses in women, but over time the study has broadened to include the health consequences of matters of lifestyle, such as diet, physical activity, and forms of estrogen replacement. Over 89,000 of the nurses were followed for eight years, and during that time they answered questionnaires about the food they ate. Among the nurses, 1,439 developed breast cancer. When the dietary habits of the women, as they reported them, were analyzed, fat intake ranged from 49 percent of daily calories down to 23 percent. Dr. Walter C. Willett, a respected epidemiologist at Harvard School of Public Health, and his colleagues concluded that *no association could be found between high- or low-fat intake and breast cancer.* Over the years Harvard researchers continued to report a lack of association between fat intake and breast cancer, and in 1996 the strongest evidence for "no connection" was presented. A team headed by Dr. David Hunter at the Harvard School of Public Health pooled data from seven studies that involved 335,000 women in four countries and concluded that there was *no relationship* between the amount of fat a women eats and her chance of developing breast cancer. Even women on very low-fat diets with less than 20 percent of their total calories from fat had no reduced risk of breast cancer.

Nevertheless, many scientists are not ready to scrap dietary fat as a contributor to breast cancer. Intercountry and migrant studies show correlations between diets high in animal fat and increased breast cancer, and in laboratory settings animals fed high-fat diets develop mammary tumors more readily than those consuming less fat. As for the Nurses' Health Study, Dr. Peter Greenwald, director of cancer prevention and control at the NCI, talks about "measurement error." Researchers have called into question the accuracy of the nurses' recall, because the study is based on responses to questionnaires. Then there is the issue of what constitutes a "low-fat diet." Only the seven-country pooled analysis includes women whose diets contained 20 percent or less of daily calories from fat. In the two major studies currently underway, low fat is the focus. The Women's Health Initiative keeps fat at 20 percent of daily calories and the Women's Intervention Nutrition Study lowers fat to 15 percent—much lower than the diets reported in the Nurses' Health Study.

What also may be coming to light is the effect of *calories*, rather than fat, on cancer risk. Some evidence suggests that calories may be more significant than their source. After World War II, researchers discovered that Dutch women who lived through a two-year famine that followed the German invasion when they were young adults were protected against breast cancer. More recently, laboratory studies with animals have shown that low-calorie eating inhibits the growth of tumors. In one study, more laboratory animals on low-fat unrestricted diets (they could eat whenever and how much they wanted) developed mammary tumors (43 percent) than did the animals on controlled higher-fat diets who ate 20 percent fewer calories (only 7 percent developed tumors).

While the roles of dietary fat and calories obviously need more exploratory research, I strongly recommend low-fat eating, which we know helps your heart and may help your breasts. I also believe that in the future, the subject of overall calories will overtake discussions on the pluses and minuses of individual foods. So in the meantime, keep those tempting second helpings and rich desserts at bay.

The Bad and the Good Fats in Meat, Cooking Oils, and Fish

MEAT AND SATURATED FAT

True, experts are at odds over what role dietary fat might play in the rising rate of breast cancer; true again, the issue is caught up in a net of questions about calories and may not be resolved for years, but all the same, researchers are drawn to investigations about whether the *kind* of fat a woman eats makes a difference. We consume three types of fatty acids: *saturated*, which are in animal products, some dairy products, and palm, palm kernel, and coconut oils; *polyunsaturated*, in vegetable and fish oils; and *monounsaturated*, also in vegetable oils.

In 1993 a study of over 62,000 postmenopausal women in the Netherlands found a small association between breast cancer and the saturated fat in the women's diets. However, lately more ties are turning up between breast cancer and meat itself than between breast cancer and saturated fat. In a survey from the University of Hawaii, 272 postmenopausal women who had been treated for breast tumors were asked to fill out food questionnaires, which then were compared with the questionnaires answered by 296 cancer-

free women. The risk of breast cancer was highest for obese women, especially those who ate a lot of sausage first of all, then meat, cold cuts, beef,
lamb, and whole-milk dairy products. A connection to meat was also found
in a 1994 study as part of the ongoing New York University Women's
Health Study, which is following over 14,000 women to learn the significance of the body's natural hormones and diet in relation to breast and other
cancers. Dr. Paolo Toniolo, professor of environmental medicine at NYU
School of Medicine, and his colleagues asked 180 women aged 35 to 65 who
had been diagnosed with invasive breast cancer, and 829 control subjects, all
from the NYU study, to respond to dietary questionnaires. When the results
were analyzed, the risk of breast cancer for frequent meat-eaters was almost
twice (1.87) what it was for those who ate meat rarely (1.0), while eating
poultry, fish, or dairy products did not seem to make a difference. No one
knows for sure whether increased saturated fat or something else in meat may
have led to the higher risk. Certain experts have speculated about hormones
given to cattle; others, about the effects of cooking. Whether grilling, frying,
or roasting meat, poultry, or fish, the browning or charring stage mutates
animal proteins into minute compounds called heterocyclic amines, which
are carcinogenic to laboratory animals. While researchers continue pursuing
these answers, it's worth remembering that meat lies in a circle of suspicion.

COOKING OILS WITH POLYUNSATURATED AND
MONOUNSATURATED FATS

In the late 1960s and early 1970s, concerns arose that polyunsaturated
fat may be more harmful to breasts than saturated fat. Researchers noticed
that the use of cooking oils such as corn and safflower oils and margarines
made from oils that contain mostly polyunsaturated fats had increased
steadily in the United States, side by side with the rise in breast cancer. At
the time, Dr. Kenneth Carroll, now director for human nutrition at the University of Western Ontario, conducted animal studies which found that
polyunsaturated fats induced more mammary tumors in rats than saturated
fats. Cooking with olive oil, a mostly monounsaturated oil that has not been
implicated in major tumor growth, is now beginning to catch on in America,
although it has been the Mediterranean way for centuries.

In the 1980s researchers started to hone in on a specific polyunsaturated
fat, linoleic acid, as the tumor-inducing culprit. (Recent figures show that
Americans get about 7 percent of their calories from linoleic acid, whereas
Italians, who have lower rates of breast cancer than Americans, get 2.4 percent of their calories from linoleic acid.) Feeding rats high levels of safflower
and corn oils (82 percent and 56 percent linoleic acid, respectively) significantly enhanced mammary tumors. The same high level of olive oil, which
has only 8 percent linoleic acid, brought on few tumors, however, and
resulted in minimal tumor growth. (For the latest on olive oil, see the section

"Garlic and Olive Oil" in this chapter.) Recent studies also have revealed that linoleic acid influences immune responses and thereby affects the body's ability to recognize and eliminate cancer cells. And linoleic acid is in the family of omega-6 fatty acids, which laboratory tests show enhances the metastasis of human cancer cells. In one study, Drs. David Rose and Jeanne M. Connolly of the American Health Foundation used linoleic acid to stimulate the growth of human breast cancer cells in a culture. More recently, in a scientific paper published in 1995, these researchers showed that mice injected with breast cancer cells and fed a diet that was 8 percent linoleic acid, had greater cell growth and metastasis than those mice that ate omega-3 fatty acids.

There's also the issue of what happens to linoleic acid during cooking. When linoleic acid and other polyunsaturated fats are heated, they oxidize (see more about oxidation in the section "Antioxidants in Vegetables and Fruits") into cells that are more likely to cause cancer. Olive oil, with mostly monounsaturated fat, has a different chemical structure than, for example, mostly polyunsaturated corn oil. Researchers have yet to explore the extent to which olive oil may oxidize, but this may be a key to why olive oil seems more healthful than other oils.

Based on all this evidence against polyunsaturated oils, I suggest olive oil as a first choice for cooking and salads.

FISH WITH POLYUNSATURATED OMEGA-3 FATTY ACID

The polyunsaturated omega-3 fatty acids in the oil of deep-sea, cold-water fish such as salmon, tuna, and sardines have consistently inhibited mammary tumors in animals under study. In the 1995 animal study referred to above, Dr. David Rose and his colleagues at the American Health Foundation found that diets of 8 percent omega-3 fatty acids experienced significant reductions in tumors and metastasis of their cancers, as compared with those mice fed diets of 8 percent omega-6 linoleic acid.

Throughout the 1980s and 1990s, research has continued to show that omega-3 fatty acids are protective. Fish oil won positive points in 1993 when Belgian researchers compared fats from animal, vegetable, and fish sources to breast cancer mortality by checking United Nations food balance sheets and breast cancer mortality rates of women from 30 countries from 1961 through 1986. When consumption of fish fat was up, mortality rates were down. (Mortality rates went up for animal and vegetable [cooking oil] fats.) In early 1995 Texas researchers found buoyed immune systems in 9 women who had surgery and/or chemotherapy and/or radiation therapy for breast cancer after 28 days of following low-fat, high-fiber diets that included cold-water fish. Disease-fighting helper T cells were boosted by the fish. Knowing the facts, it seems sensible to add cold-water fish to the types of foods you routinely eat.

CLA: A FAT THAT COMPLICATES THE FAT ISSUE

CLA, or conjugated linoleic acids, a fat found in dairy foods, turkey, and beef, seems to fight breast cancer, and as the research mounts in its favor, CLA is shaking the theories about how bad animal fat is for your health. It is complicating matters, because although it is closely related to the linoleic acid that enhances cancer, CLA does the opposite. In 1991 researchers at Roswell Park Cancer Institute in Buffalo, New York, discovered that as little as 0.5 percent CLA suppressed the growth of breast cancer in rats on a normal diet whose cancers had been chemically induced. More recently, researchers at Washington State University found that CLA inhibited *human* cell lines of breast cancer (and also colorectal cancer and melanoma). We are sure to be hearing more about this apparently "good" animal fat in the future.

FIBER FROM GRAINS, VEGETABLES, AND FRUITS

In the quest to find out how food might affect breast cancer, scientists focused on Finnish women, who have about 50 percent less breast cancer than American women, even though they consume high levels of dietary fat in butter, cheeses, and meats. Looking at Finnish diets, it became clear to researchers that one big difference was that the Finns eat a lot of fiber, mostly from whole grains. While Americans eat about 11 grams of fiber in their daily diets, the Finns take in about 30 grams. Researchers, mainly in Finland, the United States, and Australia, now have consistently shown fiber to have protective effects against breast cancer, although they were faced with a difference of opinion from the Nurses' Health Study. About 89,000 nurses in the study were followed for eight years while they answered questionnaires about their eating habits. Over the course of the study, 1,489 nursed developed breast cancer, and Harvard leaders reported that "no suggestion of a protective effect of dietary fiber was observed" when their findings were published in the *Journal of the American Medical Association* in 1992. Yet the evidence in favor of fiber has since mounted.

At the American Health Foundation, a year before the fiber findings from the Nurses' Health Study, Dr. David Rose divided a group of 62 women aged 20 to 50 into three subgroups and gave them supplements of wheat, oat, or corn bran. Although their fiber levels were brought up to 30 grams a day, their fat intake stayed the same. The women's hormone levels were measured at the beginning, middle, and end of the study, which lasted two months. The women in the wheat bran group had a significant reduction of estrogen in their bloodstream and higher amounts of estrogen excreted in their feces, because the wheat bran slowed down a bacterial enzyme that works to promote the body's reabsorption of estrogens from the intestine. Because it is believed that breast cancer risk increases with increasing levels of estrogen, a food that can lower estrogen levels is, indeed, protective.

More recently another researcher at the American Health Foundation, Dr. Leonard Cohen, reported that wheat bran fiber reduced the incidence of breast cancer tumors in animals. Dr. Cohen divided laboratory rats into four groups fed high-fat or low-fat diets, with or without wheat bran fiber, after they had been given a chemical carcinogen that induces breast cancer. Fifteen days later the rats in the low-fat, wheat bran group had the least cancer of all the groups. The rats on a low-fat diet alone and those on a high-fat diet with wheat bran had about the same mid-level range of disease; the animals on high-fat diet alone had a 90 percent cancer occurrence.

Additional support for the protective power of fiber in food came from Australia in 1994. In a case-control study, Dr. Peter Baghurst compared 451 women with breast cancer and 451 control subjects. Their responses to food questionnaires showed a drop in risk with a rise in dietary fiber. On average, these women consumed about 20 grams of fiber a day.

My belief is that by choosing whole-grain cereals and breads and brown rice over white, by eating more fibrous vegetables, such as beans, peas, cabbage, and carrots, by enjoying dried and fresh fruits you can eat unpeeled, such as apples, pears, and peaches, you are taking out health insurance for your breasts. Some experts acknowledge the possible cancer-fighting benefits of eating whole grains, vegetables, and fruits, but say they do not know whether fiber or other components in the food, such as the phytochemicals and antioxidants described below, are the top guardians of good health. No matter. Fiber still offers one more reason to eat a wide variety of plant foods.

THE "PHYTOCHEMICALS" IN VEGETABLES AND FRUITS

The National Cancer Institute entered the 1990s with its "Designer Foods" project, which over the years identified *phytochemicals*, natural chemical components of vegetables, fruits, and grains that could combat cancer. About 40 foods, among them garlic, flaxseed, citrus fruits, carrots, licorice root, and parsley, were brought into the lab for scientists to examine their chemical makeup. Other researchers, most notably those at the Strang-Cornell Cancer Research Laboratory in New York and Johns Hopkins in Maryland, also initiated investigations. Researchers have succeeded in discovering a number of new phytochemicals that can help protect your breasts from cancer by changing your estrogen levels:

• **Phytoestrogens** are plant chemicals that have a molecular structure similar to your body's own estrogen. Soybeans, alfalfa, apples, barley, carrots, cherries, coffee, fennel, garlic, hops, legumes, oats, parsley, potatoes, rye, sage, sesame seeds, sprouts, wheat, and yeast are some foods that contain varying amounts. The phytoestrogens are weak and do not have actual hormonal power, but they are great pretenders: your brain recognizes a phytoestrogen as the real hormone it is named after and instructs your ovaries to cut back on their estrogen output. This case of mistaken identity keeps true estrogen at a lower, more healthful level—although you can have too much of a good thing. Phytoestrogens came to light in the 1970s in Australia, when a high rate of infertility was discovered among ewes that had grazed in certain clover-covered pastures. The clover had a potent phytoestrogen! Whether it's phytoestrogens or something else at work, a few studies have shown that vegetarian diets can lower estrogen levels and affect fertility.

The phytoestrogens that have probably received the most attention are *genistein* and *daidzein*, primarily found in soybeans and soy products such as tofu. As early as 1980, researchers discovered that a soybean diet could protect laboratory rats that had been exposed to cancer-causing irradiation. Among the animals eating soybeans, 45 percent developed breast cancer, whereas 74 percent of the animals not eating soybeans were diagnosed with the disease. A recent case-control study of diet and breast cancer among women in Singapore showed that a decreased risk was associated with a high intake of soy products. (*Note:* The genistein in soy may battle breast cancer in two ways. In addition to its estrogen-lowering feature, German scientists discovered that genistein blocks a process called *angiogenesis*, which is the growth of new blood vessels. To expand, a breast tumor needs new vessels to spread from its core. By preventing the growth of the vessels, genistein keeps a tumor down.) Japanese women, who have low rates of breast cancer, eat about two ounces of soybean products a day. Researchers believe that Western women may be able to keep their breasts in better health by including soy and other plant foods with phytoestrogens in their diets.

• **Indole-3-carbinol** and **sulforaphane** are two phytochemicals found in the cruciferous—cabbage family—vegetables such as broccoli, brussel sprouts, cauliflower, and especially Savoy cabbage. Both of these phytochemicals change your body's estrogen balance, but they work differently:

The power of indole-3-carbinol has been backed up time after time in animal and human studies. Dr. H. Leon Bradlow, director of the laboratory of biochemical endocrinology at the Strang-Cornell Cancer Research Laboratory and a leader in the analyses of phytochemicals, explains that the indole-3 compound can actually squelch an active, potentially health-hazardous form of estrogen in women's bodies. In a woman's body, as estrogen metabolizes, it can become a "bad" 16α-hydroxylated (16α-OHE1) or a "good" 2-hydroxylated (2-OHE1) type. The 16α-OHE1 is more reactive and dangerous. Tissues from breast cancers have been found to contain more of the 16 oc-hydroxylated estrogen than surrounding noncancerous tissues. At the other end of the spectrum, the 2-OHE1 is favored for lowering the risk of breast cancer, and indole-3-carbinol induces estrogen to become this safer type. In his 1994 study of three groups of 20 women each, Dr. Bradlow and his associates gave one group 400-milligram capsules of indole-3-carbinol daily (the amount you would find in about half a head of cabbage), another group extra fiber in 20-milligram packets of cellulose mixed with fruit juice, and the third group placebo (fake) capsules. All the women otherwise ate normally. They were followed for three months. At the end of the first month, all but three women in the indole group had increased levels of 2-OHE1, while the women in the other two groups had no shift toward the safer estrogen. More studies are being done to find out whether lower levels of indole-3-carbinol will have similar effects.

Sulforaphane residing in the same cabbage-family vegetables as indole-3-carbinol was detected by Dr. Paul Talalay and his colleagues at the Johns Hopkins School of Medicine. In a recent animal study, when rats were given a cancer-causing chemical, 68 percent developed breast cancer, but of those that received low doses of sulforaphane, only 35 percent were diagnosed with breast cancer. Of the rats that received high doses of sulforaphane, only 26 percent got the disease. Sulforaphane changes the body's estrogen balance but in a way quite different from indole-3-carbinol. It stimulates the production of enzymes that increase the excretion of potentially harmful estrogens.

The search for more phytochemicals continues, even as we go to press.

ANTIOXIDANTS IN VEGETABLES AND FRUITS

We breathe in oxygen, which enters our bloodstream and travels to our cells, where enzymes begin the oxidation process. Oxidation provides us with energy, but this process has a price. Along with energy, it produces oxygen-free radicals, molecules that have lost one electron. These free radicals range throughout the body, causing trouble. They can inactivate enzymes, damage cell membranes, and attack DNA, the genetic material in the cell nucleus, which is how they can cause cancer. Your body has combatant antioxidants in the form of enzymes and other scavenger cells which can cancel out the free radicals, but they need help. This is especially true because our modern-day environment is shifting the balance. Free radicals are found in cigarette smoke and car exhaust fumes, and exposure to air pollutants, pesticides, certain industrial solvents, radiation, ultraviolet light, and certain medications and anesthetics tends to generate free radicals. In a chain reaction, as free radicals oxidize and destroy cells and tissue, they create more free radicals. They have to be stopped, and for years it has been believed that the antioxidant forces of compounds called carotenoids and vitamins A, C, and E in vegetables and fruits would do just that. With studies showing that the more beta-carotene people have in their blood, the lower their risk of cancer, major studies were undertaken to prove the power of the antioxidants, especially beta-carotene, but they did not work out the way it was thought they would. Beta-carotene was declared not only ineffective in fighting cancer and heart disease but possibly harmful.

Beta-Carotene Falls from Grace. Until 1994 studies on the protective effects of beta-carotene in relation to different types of cancer had been positive. The Nurses' Health Study and researchers from Australia and Canada had all shown that beta-carotene and even vitamins C and E were associated with lower risks of breast cancer. (*Note:* For the Nurses' Health Study, mentioned earlier in this chapter, researchers from Brigham and Women's Hospital in Boston and Harvard School of Public Health began surveying in 1976, among other things, the eating habits of over 89,000 women.) So it was a surprise when in 1994 a large, well-designed Finnish study showed that 14,500 male smokers taking 20 milligrams of beta-carotene a day for an average of six years developed 18 percent more lung cancer than smokers taking a placebo. Since that study, researchers have been cautious about pinning their hopes on a single component in food to fight disease. Then in the beginning of 1996, the NCI pronounced two large studies on beta-carotene ineffective.

The National Cancer Institute stopped the Beta-Carotene and Retinol Efficacy Trial (CARET) 21 months ahead of schedule, saying that *the beta-carotene supplements may have been more harmful than healthful.* The 18,314 people in the CARET study were all at high risk for lung cancer because they were smokers or asbestos workers. They took daily doses of either beta-carotene (30 milligrams), vitamin A (25,000 IU), or a placebo to see whether the supplements would give them greater protection against the disease. The reverse occurred. Lung cancer was 28 percent higher among the people who were taking the supplements, and the death rate was 17 percent higher.

On the same day as the CARET announcement, the 12-year Physicians Health Study ended without finding beta-carotene protective against cancer or heart disease. Over 22,000 doctors had taken beta-carotene (50 milligrams) or a placebo every other day, and there was no evidence of a health benefit.

The leaders of the Women's Health Study at Brigham and Women's Hospital in Boston then dropped beta-carotene from their investigation of the influence of beta-carotene, vitamin E, and aspirin on heart disease and cancer. They will continue studying vitamin E while acknowledging that the protective power of vegetables and fruits may not lie in a specific substance in the foods, but in the whole food.

Vegetables and Fruits Triumph. The blood levels of beta-carotene found in people who have lower risks of cancer can be directly linked to their consumption of foods containing carotenoid compounds. These are naturally present in the red, orange, and yellow pigments of vegetables and fruits. Pumpkins and the winter squashes, tomatoes, sweet potatoes, watermelon, carrots, cantaloupe, tropical fruits like papaya and mango, and dark green leafy vegetables such as spinach, kale, Swiss chard, and collard greens, are among the variety of foods that contain beta-carotene and other carotenoids, the antioxidant vitamin C, fiber, phytochemicals, and other nutrients. The disappointing findings about beta-carotene came from studies in which the antioxidant *was isolated in a supplement*. Beta-carotene may have to work in concert with other carotenoids and components in a food to be effective, and the same may be true of other antioxidants, such as vitamin C and E and the trace mineral selenium. Current wisdom suggests a variety of whole foods should be looked at as the best breast protection. A daily multivitamin that does not lean heavily on a particular vitamin, mineral, or micronutrient is a good health habit but no more important than consuming five to seven kinds of vegetables and fruits every day.

Awaiting Word About Selenium. Selenium, a trace mineral found in vegetables grown in selenium-rich soil, and in seafood and liver, first came to light in 1969 as a possible nutrient that may affect survival of cancer. Researchers discovered a lower cancer mortality rate among people who lived in areas of the United States where the soil was high in selenium. Since then animal studies have shown that high doses of selenium, which is believed to be an antioxidant, offer protection against cancer, but surveys of humans have had mixed results. The latest on selenium and breast health from the Nurses' Health Study was published in 1990 and shows that the trace mineral offers no protection against breast cancer. At the Arizona Cancer Center a double-blinded cancer prevention trial with selenium supplementation has been going on since 1983. Arizona is an area of the United States that is low in selenium, so the results of this investigation are awaited with great anticipation.

GARLIC AND OLIVE OIL

You can also make the most of the connection between your diet and the health of your breasts during food preparation. Cooking with garlic and olive oil shows strong protective effects:

Garlic's virtues as a health-giving herb have been cited since antiquity in medical folklore and literature. In countries where traditional dishes are made with garlic—in China, and of course, Mediterranean countries such as Spain, Italy, and Greece—breast cancer rates are much lower than in the United States. A number of interesting connections to breast cancer have been made recently:

A NOTE ABOUT ANTIOXIDANT SUPPLEMENTS

Although the ideal way to consume antioxidants is through food, many women are not eating a lot of the vegetables and fruits that offer healthful vitamins E, C, selenium, and the now tarnished beta-carotene, which is still viewed as healthful. A recent survey by researchers at the Centers for Disease Control and Prevention found that only 20 percent of 24,000 people were eating the recommended five servings of vegetables and fruits every day. So I encourage women of all ages to start taking antioxidant supplements: vitamin E (400 IU), vitamin C (500 mg), selenium (100 μg), and beta-carotene (10,000 IU) to strengthen the immune system and give breasts a greater chance at protection against cancer-causing free radical cells.

1. In test tube experiments, aged garlic extract comparable to five to 10 medium-size cloves has slowed the growth of human breast cancer cells.

2. At Roswell Park Cancer Institute in Buffalo, New York, Dr. Clement Ip has been feeding garlic cultivated with selenium fertilizer to rats with induced breast cancer, and tumor growth has been reduced sometimes as much as 75 percent.

Whenever garlic is bruised or cut, a biochemical reaction begins to produce the garlic-smelling sulfur compound allicin, which then decomposes into other compounds. The compounds formed in garlic change according to whether garlic is fresh or aged, raw or cooked, natural, abstracted or processed, in powder, pill, or capsule. At Penn State University, researchers doing laboratory tests found the garlic compound diallyl disulfide to be very effective in combating the spread of human cancer cells. Some garlic compounds are antioxidants that can stop the spread of potential cancer-causing free radical cells, while other garlic compounds block the formation of carcinogenic nitrosamines that are converted from the nitrites in cured meats and in plant foods grown in nitrite-rich soil. (Vitamin C also blocks nitrosamines.) Yet it's not only the scientific work that has been done on the relationship between garlic and cancer that moves me to recommend it as part of every woman's diet; it's also the anecdotal evidence of its power. In their best-selling memoir *Having Our Say*, the two 100-plus-year-old Delaney sisters shared one of their secrets of longevity: they chop up and swallow one clove of garlic every day. (They say that if you swallow without chewing, you won't get bad breath.)

Olive oil did not show a protective effect for breast cancer in a 1989 Italian study but a few years later stood out as protective in studies done in Spain and Greece, where olive oil is synonymous with eating. In the 1994 Spanish study, 762 women aged 18 to 75 with breast cancer and a control group of 988 cancer-free women were surveyed about their eating habits. The women who consumed the most olive oil were a third less likely to develop breast cancer than the women who consumed the least olive oil. In the Greek survey conducted by researchers from the Athens School of Public Health, the University of Athens Medical School, and the Harvard School of Public Health, 820 women with breast cancer and 1,548 women without it also responded to dietary questionnaires. Published in 1995, the survey found that among women of all ages, those who ate the most vegetables had a 48 percent lower cancer risk than those who ate the fewest, and those who ate the most fruits had a 32 percent lower cancer risk than those who ate the fewest. The risk of breast cancer was 25 percent lower among women who consumed olive oil more than once a day, and this protective effect was mainly found in postmenopausal women, who are at higher risk for breast cancer. In a newspaper interview, Dr. Dimitros Trichopoulos, a Harvard epidemiologist who coauthored the Greek study, is quoted as saying that "American women might actually experience as much as a 50-percent reduction in breast cancer risk if they consumed more olive oil." The idea is to replace the saturated and polyunsaturated fats in the American diet with the more healthful monounsaturated fats in olive oil. Greek women consume 42 percent of their calories from fat. While that's a high-fat diet, it's not high in animal fat; it's high in monounsaturated olive oil.

Many recommendations for healthy eating require people to take a new approach to food. Going the garlic and olive oil route, to me, seems an easy way to adjust one's diet. Adding garlic to meals and making olive oil a first choice in food preparation seem flavorful ways to possibly make a positive difference in your health.

The Caffeine in Coffee and Other Foods

For almost 20 years now, caffeine, a naturally occurring drug in coffee, tea, and cocoa, has been declared both guilty and innocent of contributing to benign breast lumps and, possibly, to breast cancer.

Caffeine and Breast Cysts. Ever since 1979, when Dr. John Minton, a surgeon at Ohio State University Hospital, reported that breast lumps, pain, and tenderness completely disappeared in 65 percent of his patients who eliminated all caffeine-containing coffee, tea, cola, and chocolate from their diets, caffeine has been highly suspect. Researchers questioned the accuracy of Dr. Minton's science then and two years later, when he did a follow-up study and reported that 83 percent of his patients were completely cured and 15 percent showed some improvement over the lumpiness and pain of what he called *fibrocystic breast disease*, a group of common, benign breast problems. (Doctors have recently started using the term *fibrocystic change* instead of fibrocystic breast disease when referring to various conditions in the breast.) Detractors said that Dr. Minton never did mammographic screenings or biopsies to identify and follow up on the types of lumps, whether they were in milk ducts, glands, or breast tissue. Also, because many breast conditions are related to hormonal shifts during the menstrual cycle, conditions may disappear on their own, making it harder for researchers to know whether they were influenced by dietary changes.

Through the years more careful studies have been done, and the results have only added to the confusion. Caffeine belongs to a group of compounds called *methylxanthines*. Other methylxanthines, such as theophylline and theobromine, are also in caffeine-containing food such as coffee, and a number of studies have looked not only at caffeine but at methylxanthines as a group. Still, whether caffeine is being studied alone or as one of several methylxanthines, some researchers have declared it bad for breasts, while others have pronounced it nothing to worry about. Most of these findings come from studies conducted in the 1970s and 1980s, because research interest in a possible caffeine/breast connection has waned in the 1990s. This leaves doctors looking at inconclusive findings and relying on their own judgment to advise women.

In the 1980s, for instance, the randomized trial of 56 women conducted by Drs. Allen and Froberg in Minnesota concluded that decreasing caffeine had no effect on breast pain or breast lumps. Dr. Allen divided the women into three groups: a control group made no dietary changes, a second group abstained from caffeine, and a third was on a cholesterol-free diet. There were no differences in reported breast pain or lumps discovered by examiners during the two-month study. However, a follow-up survey of these women then revealed that 42 percent of those who had eliminated caffeine reported a decrease in breast pain, tenderness, and lumpiness during the study. Thus, the study results were not supported by the follow-up.

Dr. Bruce Drukker at Michigan State University has searched without success for recent data on a caffeine connection. Despite the inconclusive findings, says Dr. Drukker, "When you talk to patients and when you talk to other physicians, women who rigorously decaffeinate themselves, I would say at least 60 to 65 percent notice some improvement in symptoms of premenstrual breast pain [and] other fibrocystic changes. They notice a change and feel that they are doing something effective."

In my practice, I also have noticed that many women can virtually eliminate cysts, pain, and tenderness in their breasts by eliminating caffeine. When a woman comes to me with signs of fibrocystic change, the first thing I suggest is that she cut down on her caffeine consumption. Although there are several hypotheses about a caffeine connection to breasts, the one heard most often relates to the enzymes adenosine and guanosine monophosphate phosphodiesterase. Methylxanthines interfere with the action of the enzymes, so that they accumulate in breast tissue and stimulate fibrocystic change. It seems quite possible, but no one can say with certainty, that this is how caffeine affects the breasts.

Caffeine and Breast Cancer. The concern about a possible link between caffeine and breast cancer arises from the fact that in certain species of mice, caffeine has made cancerous breast tumors grow. As for humans, in the 1980s an epidemiological study of Seventh-Day Adventist women who were coffee drinkers reported no increase in breast cancer risk. More recently the Iowa Women's Health Study, which assessed 34,388 Iowan women aged 55 to 69 over four years from 1986 to 1990, also found no apparent association between breast cancer and the amount of coffee or other caffeine-containing foods that the women consumed. Curiously, researchers evaluating the Nurses' Health Study (mentioned earlier) were surprised by the weak but significant caffeine connection they discovered. The more caffeine the nurses consumed, the *lower* their risk of breast cancer!

About Breast Cysts and Breast Cancer. Dr. Susan Love and associates made a strong case that cystic breasts *were not* a prelude to breast cancer in their work done in the early 1980s. Their conclusion supported Canadian studies that showed that the likelihood of finding breast cancer in women who had previous benign biopsies was 9 percent, compared with 15 percent for women who had not undergone earlier biopsies. Researchers have only shown that the presence of breast cysts may increase risk for breast cancer when a woman has a family history of breast cancer and has also been diagnosed with atypia (precancerous breast cells). In my own practice, I have seen women who have fibrocystic breast conditions develop breast cancer, while others did not. I believe that more studies should be done, and I advise women who are susceptible to fibrocystic change to eliminate caffeine from their diet. In general, I see a reduction in caffeine as a positive step toward better health care for women.

WILL ONE DRINK HURT? ALCOHOLIC BEVERAGES AND YOUR BREASTS

Yes, latest research does show that drinking increases a woman's risk for breast cancer, and as little as one drink a day will have an effect. An average lifetime consumption of one alcoholic beverage a day puts a woman at 39 *percent higher risk* than a nondrinker. That risk becomes 69 percent higher at two drinks a day and more than doubles at three drinks a day. This is the latest finding from a team of researchers headed by Dr. Matthew Longnecker, assistant professor of epidemiology at the UCLA School of Public Health, who has been investigating the association between alcohol and breast cancer for several years. Dr. Longnecker's previous research had found only a slight increase in risk connected with alcohol, but his latest study involved more than 15,000 women in four states and took into account lifetime as well as recent drinking habits. For those who do not think dinner is complete without a glass of fine wine, Dr. Longnecker did not find a link between wine and risk of breast cancer, although other studies have. His hypothesis is that alcohol increases estrogen levels in women.

In a 1993 controlled diet study of 34 women over six menstrual cycles, the women consumed about two drinks a day for the first half of the study and abstained from drinking during the second half. When a comparison was made, estrogen levels in their blood and urine rose in the first half of the study, when alcohol was consumed. The question then is whether higher estrogen levels cause the higher risk of breast cancer. They probably do, but that's as far as researchers will go right now. Also, there is another facet to consider:

An alcoholic beverage now and then is known to lower a woman's risk of coronary heart disease. A woman over 55 is at greater risk of having a heart attack than developing breast cancer, so she might benefit from drinking the one to three alcoholic beverages a week found to be beneficial in the Nurses' Health Study; on the other hand, a woman who is in the 45- to 55-year-old range is facing breast cancer as a more common cause of death than heart disease, so she might be better off if she abstains.

Because anything beyond moderate drinking is inherently unhealthy, there is no general recommendation to offer. My inclination is to suggest that a woman bear in mind the alcohol connection and ask her physician to guide her in making the decision that makes the most sense for her.

THE CHEMICAL CONNECTION: PESTICIDES AND OTHERS

A relation between pesticides and breast cancer was exposed in 1992, when a study headed by Dr. Frank Falck, Jr., then an assistant clinical professor of surgery at the University of Connecticut School of Medicine, found elevated levels of man-made chemicals called *organochlorines* in cancerous breast tumors. Organochlorines, man-made organic compounds derived from chlorine, are used in PVC (polyvinyl chloride) plastics and for bleaching, disinfecting, and dry cleaning. Pesticides, such as DDT (dichloro-diphenyl-trichlobethane) and Atrazine, are organochlorines, as are fluid insulators of electrical systems, such as PCBs (polychlorinated biphenyls). Although the use of DDT and PCBs was banned in the 1970s, they have seeped into the soil and water and remain in the food chain. In 1993 Dr. Mary Wolff, professor of community medicine at the Mount Sinai School of Medicine in New York, analyzed stored blood samples of 14,290 women enrolled in the New York University Women's Health Study from 1985 to 1991. Blood samples from 58 women who were diagnosed with breast cancer from one to six months after they entered the study were matched against those from 171 women who did not develop breast cancer. Levels of DDE, a derivative of DDT, and PCBs were measured. The result: the women with breast cancer had markedly higher levels of DDE. (No significant association with PCBs was found.) The women with high levels of DDE were four times as likely to develop breast cancer as the women with low levels. However, in 1994 Dr. Wolff was involved in a California-based study that *did not* report a strong association betweeen DDT, DDE, and breast cancer. So the pendulum is swinging in both directions right now.

Findings from Germany also have shown that chemical workers exposed to high levels of dioxin, another organochlorine, had high rates of breast cancer, and in Italy researchers were able to associate the commonly used pesticide and organochlorine Atrazine with ovarian cancer, another hormonally linked reproductive cancer.

What scientists have now learned is that organochlorines may mimic natural hormones. In particular, scientists have named DDT, its derivative DDE, and PCBs as *xenoestrogens*, chemical compounds in the environment that are similar to natural estrogen. Depending on the metabolic path estrogen takes in the body, it can change into a 2-hydroxylated form of "good" estrogen (2-OHE1) or a 16 oc-hydroxylated "bad" estrogen (16α-OHE1), which can stimulate cell division. Dr. H. Leon Bradlow of the Strang-Cornell Cancer Research Laboratory in New York and Dr. Devra Lee Davis, a senior advisor to the Department of Health and Human Services' assistant secretary of health, and their colleagues are researching whether the xenoestrogenic pesticides (besides DDT and PCBs, Atrazine, Kepone, Endosulfans, and y-Benzene hexachloride were also included in the study) affect estrogen metabolism for good or bad. (The intricacies of the study are explored in Chapter 8, pages 112–124.)

The bottom line is that Drs. Bradlow, Davis, et al. found that pesticides produced three to four times more of the "bad" 16α-OHE1 in cells, with DDT and its compounds being the most powerful creators of this "bad" estrogen. And surprisingly, it was found that even cells treated with a known animal carcinogen had more "good" estrogen and less "bad" than those cells exposed to pesticides.

Whether you call them organochlorines, xenoestrogens, or pesticides, chemicals such as DDT, Atrazine, Endosulfans, and PCBs add to the challenge of healthy eating. These chemicals linger in soil and water, especially in heavily sprayed farmlands. When you eat and drink them in food and water, they accumulate in your fatty tissue. Because the worst of these chemicals have been outlawed, their levels are dropping in the environment, but animals may still be eating food from soil once sprayed with DDT or drinking water that may have been tainted by PCBs and accumulating these chemicals in their fat. Therefore I believe you are more likely to get a greater dose of an organochlorine by eating foods that contain animal fat than if you consume its residue on a vegetable or fruit. While the organochlorines of today are not as potent as DDT and PCBs, we still cannot assume that they are "safe." The chemical/breast cancer connection is currently being explored as a component in six major studies funded by the NCI in collaboration with the National Institute of Environmental Health Sciences (NIEHS). Collectively, the six studies, known as the Northeast/Mid-Atlantic Study (NE/MA), are scheduled to run their course between 1993 and 1997. Until the results are in and we understand just what the connection may be, I am prompted to recommend a diet low in animal fats. (See Chapter 8 for more on environmental risks for breast cancer.)

SHAPING A PERSONAL APPROACH TO FOOD

It is revolutionary for the medical establishment to have embraced the idea of using the natural forces in food to fight illness. Diet and exercise, the subject of Chapter 7, are two areas of lifestyle in which researchers say your choices can make a difference. As wide-ranging and diverse as the studies are, general truths can be culled from the array of findings that exists. First, eating vegetables and fruits daily is good; it cuts your risk of getting certain cancers, perhaps by half. For you to know that is a start to shaping a personal approach to food. Second, corn oil and other polyunsaturated cooking oils and animal products, especially meat from four-legged animals, currently have a dicey reputation, and their inclusion in your diet should come with this awareness. On the other hand, the good word on fatty fish, garlic, and olive oil is growing. Meanwhile you are probably better off keeping caffeine and alcohol to a minimum.

Last, the number of calories you eat may, in the end, be just as important as what you eat, for calories contribute to body fat, which adds estrogen to your body. Because it is believed that breast cancer and other breast conditions are hormonally linked to estrogen levels, what happens to this hormone in your body, and how it responds to diet and exercise, may, in fact, be the key connection of all.

The Surprising Relationship Between Exercise and Your Breasts: Another Reason to Work Out

Every woman knows that exercise is good for her health, but *how good* it is sometimes gets lost. A growing body of research is showing that exercise is more important than anyone had realized. Exercise is on an equal footing with good nutrition when it comes to taking care of yourself. It is a major aspect of preventive health care, of being able to protect your body, and particularly your breasts, from disease. As astonishing as it may seem, the amount of exercise a woman does actually has a direct effect on her breasts. About four hours of workout a week can make breasts less vulnerable to breast cancer. With such a tremendous health benefit, exercise should fall into place as a *habit*, not an option.

A BREAKTHROUGH DISCOVERY: THE EXERCISE CONNECTION

In trying to find ways to fight breast cancer, researchers have struck gold with their discovery of a link between exercise and women's breasts. Exercise was named as a force in the fight against breast cancer by researchers at the University of Southern California (USC) School of Medicine in 1994. A team headed by Dr. Leslie Bernstein of the department of preventive medicine found that *women 40 and younger who worked out* (i.e., swimming, jogging, playing tennis, doing gymnastics, or dancing) *for four hours a week reduced their risk of developing premenopausal breast cancer by more than 50 percent.* And women who exercised one to three hours a week decreased their risk by about 30 percent when compared with inactive women. The greatest benefits were experienced by women who had borne children and those who had been physically active since their teens and twenties. *The healthiest women had formed lifelong exercise habits.*

In the course of their study the researchers interviewed over 1,000 young women: 545 who had been newly diagnosed with in situ or invasive breast cancer and 545 who formed a control group of women who were comparable but cancer-free. The same team of researchers is now analyzing their surveys of 3,000 *post*menopausal women (1,500 women diagnosed with breast cancer between the ages of 55 and 64 and 1,500 cancer-free women in a control group) to see whether the more physically active women developed breast cancer less frequently than the sedentary. Studies in the past have shown postmenopausal women who are heavier to be at greater risk of developing breast cancer than those who are lean. (The slimmer older women are often the ones who exercise more.)

When studied separately, exercise and body weight are each significant for having effects on hormonal levels, which in turn affect breast health. It is strongly suspected that a woman's lifetime exposure to the sex hormone estrogen has an impact on her risk of developing breast cancer, and exercise can have an influence on a woman's estrogen levels. The USC investigators are monitoring women in exercise physiology classes to learn exactly how physical activity may affect ovulation patterns and estrogen output. Studies in teenagers have shown that exercise changes hormonal levels and inhibits ovulation, but researchers have a hunch that exercise may affect estrogen even during ovulatory menstrual cycles. So far, scientific findings favor more exercise and less weight gain as you age. Frankly, I think that it is impossible to learn about the recently discovered connections between exercise, body weight, and breast cancer without feeling an urge to take up a sport or join a gym.

EXERCISE AND BREAST HEALTH

The Connection Grows

Evidence that exercise is beneficial to breasts has been showing up for some time. In the early 1980s, Dr. Rose Frisch, geneticist and currently associate professor emeritus at the Harvard School of Public Health, headed a team of researchers who surveyed 5,400 graduates of Radcliffe College from the classes of 1925 to 1981. The researchers compared the prevalence of breast and other reproductive cancers among college athletes (those who had been on a team or had run at least 10 miles a week in undergraduate school) and nonathletes. The athletes had a 35 percent lower lifetime risk of breast cancer and a 61 percent lower lifetime risk of cervical, uterine, and other reproductive cancers. The former athletes who had had pregnancies were at lowest risk for these diseases.

AN OPTIMAL WORKOUT

With the latest findings about the power of exercise to reduce the risk of breast cancer among premenopausal women and the mounting evidence that thinner, postmenopausal women have less risk of breast cancer, I advise the women in my care to **work out an hour a day at least four times a week.**

I recommend choosing a physical activity on the basis of how it suits your personality. Analyze your options and decide whether you would best fit into the group dynamic of a class, whether aerobics, dance, or the martial arts; the challenge of direct competition through a sport such as tennis or racquetball; or the solitude of running or cycling. You could be tempted to break the exercise habit if you are not well-matched to your activity.

In the early 1990s in Finland, a follow-up to a study of physical education and language teachers, which had shown a higher risk of breast cancer among the language teachers before menopause, showed a much closer ratio between the two groups after menopause, when the physical education teachers had become much less physically active.

The epidemiological study from USC researchers is the latest to report that breasts can benefit from physical activity and the first to be specific about the relationship between exercise and breast cancer. Researchers found that the average number of hours women spent exercising every week, from menarche to one year before diagnosis of breast cancer was a significant predictor of breast cancer risk. Women were surveyed for five years, from 1983 to 1989, and those who exercised about four hours a week had the lowest risk of breast cancer, *regardless of body size*. Whether small or tall, slender or heavy, they all benefited from exercise.

Support for the power of exercise is also coming from animal studies. A team headed by Dr. Henry J. Thompson of the AMC Cancer Research Center in Denver, Colorado, published its findings in the *Journal of the National Cancer Institute* in 1995. The team observed 125 laboratory rats exercising on a treadmill at four different levels of activity: zero, 35, 70, and 100 percent of maximal oxygen consumption. After the animals were injected with carcinogen-causing mammary tumors, they exercised 40 minutes a day, five days a week, for 26 weeks. The animals operating at a zero level had much higher rates of cancer and benign tumors than any of the more active animals—about eight times the cancer and more than four times the benign tumors of the 35-percent group. However, more intense exercise from the 70- and 100-percent groups did not bring about greater benefits.

This study may be sending the message that there is a plateau of activity, beyond which more substantial protection against breast cancer cannot be derived. Results of further animal and human studies comparing intensity of exercise to breast health will tell us more, but for now, the Colorado research confirms that an exercised body has healthier breasts.

About Exercise and the Estrogen Factor

There is growing evidence that a woman's lifetime exposure to her circulating sex hormones, particularly estrogen, increases her chances of developing breast cancer. As mentioned in Chapter 6 in relation to diet, the search is on to find ways of living that can regulate the estrogen factor and exercise is one that qualifies. Researchers believe that exercise starts a hormonal chain of events: it has an effect on the brain, which releases biochemicals that target the pituitary, the master gland that sends out messenger hormones to the ovaries, which in turn reduce their output of estrogen and progesterone. It appears that exercise can influence the menstrual cycle and inhibit ovulation, thereby reducing a woman's exposure to estrogen. The USC researchers thus logically assumed that the more than 50-percent reduction in breast cancer risk found among the premenopausal adult women who exercised three to four hours a week came about because their exercise regimens *reduced* their estrogen levels. Yet the women in the survey did not report menstrual irregularity, and many others had become pregnant, which meant that they were ovulating while they were exercising. So researchers are now looking into whether exercise affects the release of the sex hormones estrogen and progesterone *without* preventing ovulation.

In the past, studies among adolescent girls showed that vigorous exercise markedly affected menstruation. Well over a decade ago Dr. Rose Frisch reported the lack of menstrual periods among adolescent ballet dancers. Years later, in a report published in 1987, Dr. Leslie Bernstein and researchers at USC found that even teenage girls who exercised only moderately were less likely to ovulate, even when they continued to menstruate regularly. When exercise affects ovulation, less estrogen is produced throughout a menstrual month, and no progesterone is released in the second half of the cycle. Population studies also have found that the risk of breast cancer is lower for women who have fewer ovulatory cycles. Women who become pregnant or experience late menarche and early menopause have fewer ovulations in their lifetimes and are at less risk for breast cancer than never-pregnant women or those who have early menarche and late menopause. Women who have many uninterrupted years of fertility are more vulnerable to breast cancer because they have a much longer lifetime exposure to circulating estrogen. That is why exercise, with its seeming ability to lower estrogen, is so important.

Plus, the amount of body fat can increase estrogen—another reason exercise, which works to keep weight down, is so important. In fact, to reach menarche, a girl must weigh about 105 pounds, with about one-quarter of that weight in body fat. During the rest of her reproductive years she should weigh slightly more than she did at menarche if she wants to continue regular, monthly menstruation. We also know now that body fat creates an enzyme called aromatase, which can convert a steroid in your body called androstenedione into estrogen. Thus, the more fat you have, the more aromatase, and the higher your estrogen. In premenopausal women the amount of estrogen converted from the adrenal glands is minimal compared with what the ovaries produce, but the conversion becomes more significant for postmenopausal women, whose ovarian estrogen production has stopped. In the USC survey of women under 40, exercise created favorable results for breast health regardless of the woman's weight. Because these women were working out, they probably had little added fat to increase their estrogen levels. And it is probably a fair assumption that exercise kept their body fat down.

THE WEIGHT GAIN THAT EXERCISE CAN CONTROL

When and Where You Gain Weight Is Important to Your Breast Health

Gaining weight at certain places on your body and at certain times in your life affects the health of your breasts. In the past researchers analyzed the relation between body mass, a compilation of height and weight measurements, and breast cancer risk, but lately they are more interested in the placement and timing of weight gain.

WHETHER YOUR BODY IS APPLE- OR PEAR-SHAPED COULD AFFECT YOUR RISK OF BREAST CANCER

In 1991 researchers at the H. Lee Moffitt Research and Cancer Institute at the University of Southern Florida reported that women whose weight gain had shaped them like apples, with predominantly abdominal and upper body fat, had a different hormonal profile than women who gained mostly in their buttocks, hips, and thighs, giving them pear-shaped figures. The "apples" had lower levels of sex hormone binding globulin (SHBG), a hormone that binds the body's circulating "free" estrogen, than the "pears," who had more SHBG. Coinciding with their lower levels of unbound estrogen and higher amounts of free estrogen, more of the women diagnosed with breast cancer turned out to be apples.

"The more *bound* forms of estrogen you have, the less risk of the hormone acting on the breast; the more *free* forms you have, the higher the risk of the hormone acting without purpose on breast tissue. That's a theory that

THE IMPORTANCE OF BODY SIZE

Although the USC findings on the effects of exercise were not related to a woman's size, accumulating research shows that size does make a difference. Exercise benefited women of different body types, but some may have had more of an edge than others. Researchers have reported that:

• among postmenopausal women, higher levels of body fat were associated with an increased risk of breast cancer, but

• among younger, premenopausal women, body fat was not as easily correlated with breast cancer. Women who were heavier during their menstruating years did not show a higher risk for breast cancer. In fact, in some studies, thinner, younger women were more frequently diagnosed with breast cancer than their heavier contemporaries. For menstruating women it has been difficult to make a connection between body size and breast cancer.

The Theories: Why Body Size Affects Breast Cancer and How Exercise Is Involved

• After menopause your ovaries stop producing the sex hormones, but your body still manufactures estrogen. *Aromatase*, an enzyme produced by body fat, can convert androstenedione, a steroid released by the adrenal glands, into estrogen. So the more body fat you have, the more aromatase you have, and the more you convert androstenedione into estrogen. It is believed that after menopause, the higher a woman's estrogen levels, the more at risk she is for breast cancer. Exercise can keep body fat, and therefore estrogen, down.

• For menstruating women, the situation is more complicated. Women who are overweight during their reproductive years are already producing so much estrogen in their ovaries that the extra estrogen resulting from the enzymatic action of aromatase has a minimal effect. With this seemingly excessive production of estrogen no one really understands why some studies show heavier women to have less risk of breast cancer than thinner women with less body fat and therefore less estrogen. There is some speculation that high levels of progesterone in thin, premenopausal women may have an adverse effect, but this is a guess. My personal hunch is that some younger, thinner women may be dieting too severely, and their immune systems may be compromised by a lack of proper nutrition. They may be missing vegetables and fruits that are high in antioxidants. Since exercise was found to be beneficial no matter what a woman's body size, menstruating women should not be overly concerned about being thin. Exercise is a powerful protector against breast cancer, whether a woman is at her ideal weight or not. Also, where and when a woman gains weight complicates the relationship between body size and breast cancer.

has been established by our studies," explains Dr. Nagi Kumar, director of the department of nutrition at the Institute.

The good news is that the riskier weight around the middle is easier to lose than the pounds that seem to land lower, on the buttocks, hips, and thighs. Most women add lower body weight during times of hormonal changes such as puberty and pregnancy, but some women gain in the upper body too. In a follow-up study, Dr. Kumar and the Tampa team discovered that with weight loss, the first fat cells to fall away come from the upper body, helping women with apple figures. With weight loss and reduction of upper body fat, the researchers also saw a significant reduction in free estrogen and an increase in SHBG. This hormonal shift is much more favorable for maintaining healthy breasts. Exercise and diet are two ways to keep pounds down. Certain weight-bearing exercises can also target specific areas of the body for fitness.

BREASTS RESPOND TO WEIGHT GAINED AFTER AGE 30

If you have gained 10 pounds or more since you were 30, researchers suggest that you drop them. In 1995 Dr. Kumar and her colleagues published a paper, "Timing of Weight Gain and Breast Cancer Risk," in the medical journal *Cancer*. They looked at weight gain from puberty up to the time of diagnosis for breast cancer in 218 breast cancer patients and 436 cancer-free women in a control group. (The weight gained after age 25 is predominantly fat, because muscle and bone mass usually reach their peak when a woman is younger.) What they saw was that 63 percent of breast cancer patients had gained weight between age 30 and their current age, but only 49 percent of cancer-free women had put on pounds after age 30. The crucial years appeared to be between 30 and 39, when **for every 10-pound weight gain, researchers noted a 23-percent increase in risk of breast cancer.** Think about that if you gain 20 pounds! "It's typical for women to gain progressively throughout adulthood, every year a pound, every decade five or 10 pounds, so that by the time she is 60 a woman can be 40 or 50 pounds overweight, which is what we see in breast cancer patients," Dr. Kumar has told me. If that gain sits mostly in the upper body, a woman's breasts are being exposed to higher levels of free-floating estrogen.

The effects of weight gain show up in higher rates of breast cancer among heavier postmenopausal women. Before menopause, breast cancer does not strike heavier women at a higher rate, but girth adds to risk later on. Due to the increase of estrogen that results from an enzyme created in body fat, a heavier postmenopausal woman will have more estrogen than a thinner woman. Researchers at the University of Texas M.D. Anderson Cancer Center theorize that the increased estrogen created by the presence of body fat may be causing the increased recurrence of breast cancer that they found among heavier women.

For 10 years the researchers followed 735 pre- and postmenopausal women who had received chemotherapy for stage II and III breast cancer. A greater number of the postmenopausal women were overweight, but overall, women who were more than 20 percent over their ideal weight had 1.33 times the risk of recurrence (or 33% higher risk) than their more slender counterparts. "I think for every woman, the closer you are to your ideal body weight, the less likelihood of relapse from breast cancer, and also the less risk you have of heart attack," says Dr. Aman Buzdar, deputy chairman of breast, gynecological, and medical oncology at the University of Texas M.D. Anderson Cancer Center and one of the researchers involved in the study. At the University of Chicago Cancer Research Center, researchers are currently looking at the effect weight loss might have on the recovery of women at least 10 percent over their ideal weight who have been treated for stage I and II breast cancer. The influence of exercise and body weight on breasts undoubtedly will be in the news a lot more in the next few years, but even if we knew no more than we do today, all signs to good breast health point to low-fat eating with fresh fruits and vegetables, and regular exercise.

WORK YOUR BODY AND PROTECT YOUR BREASTS

Breasts on an exercised body have an edge on good health. The USC study found that the women who had lifelong exercise habits had lowered their risk of breast cancer. Exercise also keeps you trim, and after menopause, slimmer women have less risk of breast cancer. Although women who are trying to conceive must take care not to overexercise and affect their ovulation and fertility, moderate exercise has no "down" side. Yet even with all of its benefits to the body, 73 percent of women age 18 and older do not undertake even a minimal amount of moderate physical activity. At the start of 1995 a panel of experts from the U.S. Centers for Disease Control and Prevention and the American College of Sports Medicine recommended that every American adult accumulate 30 minutes or more of moderate-intensity physical activity on most, if not all, days of the week. They are referring to physical activity that will exercise your cardiovascular system. For people who are not on a regular exercise regimen, moderation is especially important so that joint and bone problems do not surface. For example, you could

METLIFE HEIGHT AND WEIGHT TABLE

Women

Height Feet Inches	Small Frame	Medium Frame	Large Frame
4 10	102–111	109–121	118–131
4 11	103–113	111–123	120–134
5 0	104–115	113–126	122–137
5 1	106–118	115–129	125–140
5 2	108–121	118–132	128–143
5 3	111–124	121–135	131–147
5 4	114–127	124–138	134–151
5 5	117–130	127–141	137–155
5 6	120–133	130–144	140–159
5 7	123–136	133–147	143–163
5 8	126–139	136–150	146–167
5 9	129–142	139–153	149–170
5 10	132–145	142–156	152–173
5 11	135–148	145–159	155–176
6 0	138–151	148–162	158–179

These are the weights of women aged 25 to 59, based on lowest mortality, which the MetLife insurance experts used as the best measure of good health. Weight is in pounds, with indoor clothing weighing 3 pounds and one-inch heels. Reprinted courtesy of Metropolitan Life Insurance Company, *Statistical Bulletin*.

initially choose to walk up stairs instead of taking an elevator, garden, and dance, and only later as your body strengthens, pursue more vigorous exercise such as running, swimming, or cycling. The message is "keep moving," but this call for motion is not being heard by enough women.

Because of sedentary lifestyles, one-third of American adults over age 20 (approximately 58 million Americans) are 20 percent over their ideal weight. An 8-percent increase in the number of overweight people has occurred between surveys taken from 1976 to 1980 compared with those from 1988 to 1991. For men and women aged 20 through 74, average body weight has jumped about 8 pounds. Adults are getting fatter and fatter, and so are children. The Center for Health Statistics reports that one in every five teenagers is overweight. In analyzing the 1990 Youth Risk Behavior Survey, researchers at the Centers for Disease Control and Prevention report that only 37 percent of teens engage in 20 minutes of vigorous exercise three times or more a week—down from 68 percent in 1984—while 35 percent of teens watch three or more hours of television each school day. Sedentary behavior and inexpensive fatty foods are leading to more obesity, which

IT HELPS TO HAVE COMPANY

After a long day of meeting obligations at home or in the office, most women feel too tired to exercise. Many people cannot afford personal trainers who can keep them on exercise schedules, but there is a way to motivate yourself to become physically active. I have noticed that women who make appointments to work out with their partners or friends are more likely to remain committed to exercise. Exercise can become a family affair, with wives and husbands, brothers and sisters, parents and children encouraging each other to stick to a fitness routine, at least one hour a day, at least four days a week. Once exercise is woven into your daily routine, you will be fit for life.

increases the odds of developing cardiovascular disease, diabetes, hypertension, stroke, and certain types of cancer, breast cancer among them.

It is ironic that while the population is exercising less, health and fitness experts are discovering and reporting more about the benefits of being active. The evidence points to a strengthened immune system and better breast health *if you begin an exercise regimen when you are young and continue throughout your life*. Also, exercise lifts the spirits. A brisk, 10-minute walk can immediately boost energy, release tension, and put you in a good mood. Exercise, along with diet and weight control, is an important mechanism of protection for your breasts. Other influences on breast health, such as environmental factors as described in Chapter 8, are not always within a woman's power to control. Exercise is. Exercise offers an opportunity to be in charge of your body.

Pollutants, Electromagnetic Fields, and Radiation: Exploring the Link Between Your Environment and Your Breasts

"What happens in a cell to change its orderly multiplication into the wild and uncontrolled proliferation of cancer? When answers are found they will almost certainly be multiple. Just as cancer itself is a disease that wears many guises, appearing in various forms that differ in their origin, in the course of their development, and in the factors that influence their growth or regression, so there must be a corresponding variety of causes."
—RACHEL CARSON, *SILENT SPRING*, 1962

As we near the twenty-first century, we have adopted an air of resignation about our intimate contact with potentially cancer-causing chemicals, radiation, and those highly suspicious electromagnetic fields that emanate from power lines as well as household appliances. Common sense would say that these combined ingredients of modern life must be contributing to the increased incidence of breast cancer, and researchers suspect, but have not specifically named, environmental health hazards for a woman's breasts. The search for proof continues. The long-held belief that there are many ways to affect a healthy cell and turn it into a cancer powers the drive to identify environmental connections. Thanks to the energy and tenacity of breast cancer activists, research money is being directed now more than ever before into studies exploring the possibility that some causes of breast cancer may be found in the environment.

Scientists are investigating three major areas, each of which is described in this chapter.

• **Chemicals** introduced into the environment through pesticides, herbicides, and plastics (including food wraps and containers); as by-products of industrial activity; and as bleaching, disinfecting, and dry cleaning agents. The organochlorines, organic compounds of chlorine bonded to carbon that have been linked to breast cancer, have chemical compounds that act like estrogens. Among the organochlorines are pesticides such as DDT (dichloro-diphenyl-trichloroethane) and Atrazine, PVC (polyvinyl chloride) plastics, and PCBs (polychlorinated biphenyls), which were once used as fluid insulators of electrical systems, and for cutting oils, lubricants, and plasticizers.

• **Electromagnetic fields (EMFs)** emanate from anything electrical and occur whenever an electric current is activated, such as when you turn on a household appliance or a computer. EMFs are also emitted by high-voltage power stations and power lines. The electrical current creates a magnetic field that can pass through most objects, including your body. The nearer you are to the source of electricity, the greater your exposure to its magnetic field. Scientists currently are at odds over whether EMFs cause cancer. On the one hand are physicists, who do not view EMFs as dangerous to health, but on the other are:

> —researchers who are observing the reaction of breast cancer cells to magnetic fields in the laboratory;
> —epidemiologists measuring magnetic fields in the homes of women who do or do not have breast cancer; and
> —investigators exploring the theory that exposure to EMFs increases breast cancer risk because it reduces the level of the cancer-fighting hormone melatonin that is released from the brain's pineal gland.

Something seems to be going on.

• **Radiation** is getting less attention from researchers than chemicals or EMFs, but it remains an environmental health hazard. Women over 45 especially have had more exposure to radiation than younger women, because of past medical practices. For example, the thymus gland of infants was once X-rayed, then there were regular chest X rays screening for tuberculosis, and on top of that, shoe stores used to make fluoroscopes of feet available for customers. New information about the effects of radiation is coming from scientific analyses of the lives of Japanese women who were exposed to radiation when the atomic bomb was dropped on Hiroshima and Nagasaki.

The possibility that breast cancer could be caused by environmental factors is being considered very seriously. Based on recent figures from the National Cancer Institute (NCI), the five areas in the United States with the highest breast cancer mortality rates per 100,000 in the population are (from highest to lowest): Washington, D.C., Delaware, New Jersey, Rhode Island, and New York. Hawaii has the lowest rate. Six major environmental studies funded by the NCI in collaboration with the National Institute of Environmental Health Sciences (NIEHS) are designed to find out what is happening in the environment of the industrialized northeastern United States. The six studies, collectively known as the Northeast/Mid-Atlantic Study (NE/MA), are scheduled to run from 1993 through 1997. In addition to the District of Columbia and the four states already mentioned, five other states with high rates of breast cancer are involved: Connecticut, Massachusetts, Maryland, New Hampshire, and Vermont. In addition, the NCI and NIEHS are coordinating investigations of two other areas hit with high rates of breast cancer: Long Island, New York, and Cape Cod, Massachusetts.

THE CHEMICAL CONNECTION

The first connection between cancer and the environment was made by a London physician, Sir Percivall Pott, in 1775. He believed that the scrotal cancer frequently suffered by chimney sweeps was caused by the soot that accumulated in their bodies. Dr. Pott's hunch has since been borne out, and unfortunately since then our environment has become more, rather than less, polluted.

Rachel Carson was the first scientist/author to bring the cancer-causing effects of the pesticide DDT to public awareness in her book *Silent Spring*, published in 1962. Two years later Rachel Carson died of breast cancer. More than 30 years later the studies on DDT and other chlorine-based chemicals used in agriculture and industry still have not reached resolution. The research, however, has taken a new turn in the last few years. Researchers formerly set their sights on finding out whether these and other potential carcinogens alter genetic structure; today, many investigators have shifted focus and are analyzing the ability of these chemicals to mimic estrogen. Here is what we know so far:

Population Studies Make a Link Between Chemicals and Breast Cancer

The connection between DDT and other organochlorine pesticides to breast cancer seemed strong in 1992, when a Connecticut study headed by Dr. Frank Falck, Jr., currently at the University of Michigan, found higher levels of the chemicals in the fatty breast tissue of women who had been diagnosed with breast cancer than in those who had benign breast disease. The use of DDT and PCBs, a group of more than 200 chemicals, was banned in the 1970s, but they linger in soil and water and still find their way into our foods. Also, because DDT was not banned in foreign countries, imported foods often have residues of the chemical.

Dr. Mary Wolff, professor of community medicine at the Mount Sinai School of Medicine in New York, was one of the researchers in the Falck study, and in 1993 she headed her own larger analysis. She analyzed stored blood samples of 14,290 women enrolled in the New York University

PROTECTING YOURSELF WHILE SCIENTISTS LOOK FOR ANSWERS

It will probably be the twenty-first century before we know for sure to what extent the environment may or may not be responsible for breast cancer. Yet even at our current level of knowledge, I feel that a woman can take some prudent measures:

• As mentioned in Chapter 6, eat red meat no more than once a week. The organochlorines of pesticides, herbicides, and cleaning products have seeped into the soil and water, and they are consumed by feeding animals. The chemicals then stay in the body fat of the animals. The result is that animal meat has a store of accumulated chemicals and more potential than plant foods to expose a woman to greater risk. I recommend the purchase of organically produced meats to minimize risk.

• Eat a total of at least five to seven fresh vegetables and fruits a day, preferably produce that has been certified organic and is not sprayed with pesticides and herbicides. Many vegetables and fruits contain phytochemicals (as explained in Chapter 6), which strengthen the immune system and help block the body's estrogen output.

• Consider installing a home water filter that can remove estrogen-promoting chlorine from tap water.

• Minimize your use of plastic food wrap and food containers, and do not use plastic dishes for microwave heating. Many plastics contain xenoestrogens that may leech into the food.

• Be cautious about exposing yourself to technological equipment. Turn off your computer unless you are actually using it, and reserve cellular phones for emergency calls.

• Be aware of the X rays you have undergone. Mammography is a necessary X-ray procedure, so take that into consideration when your dentist suggests routine X rays of your teeth.

• Try to reduce pollutants by phasing out carcinogenic chlorine products, such as bleach and other cleaners, that you use in your home.

• Try to help elect government officials who will initiate new environmental regulatory actions and preserve existing laws.

Women's Health Study from 1985 to 1991. Levels of DDE, a derivative of DDT, and industrial PCBs were measured in samples from 58 women who were diagnosed with breast cancer from one to six months after they entered the study and 171 women who did not develop breast cancer. The women with breast cancer had significantly higher levels of DDE, although no association with PCBs was found. The women with high levels of DDE were *four times as likely* to develop breast cancer as the women with low levels.

Dr. Wolff's study was supported by findings from Germany, where chemical workers exposed to high levels of dioxin, another organochlorine, also had high rates of breast cancer, and from Italy, where researchers were able to associate the commonly used pesticide Atrazine with ovarian cancer, another hormonally linked reproductive cancer. And then there is the news from Israel to consider. The breast cancer death rate has been falling since 1978, when Israel banned three major organochlorines: the pesticides DDT, BHC (alpha-benzene hexachloride), and lindane (gamma-benzene hexachloride). The pesticides had been used in cowsheds, and their levels in Israeli milk were 100 times higher than in the United States.

In 1994, however, Dr. Wolff was involved in a study headed by Dr. Nancy Krieger of the Kaiser Research Foundation. Entitled "Breast Cancer and Serum Organochlorines: A Prospective Study Among White, Black, and Asian Women," the study, published in the *Journal of the National Cancer Institute*, did *not* report the strong association between DDT, DDE, and breast cancer that other studies were reporting. (PCBs also did not generate an association, but this was similar to Dr. Wolff's earlier finding.)

Dr. Krieger and her colleagues analyzed stored blood samples taken from women in the San Francisco Bay area who had given their blood during health examinations in the 1960s. The researchers selected a random sample of 50 white women, 50 African American women, and 50 Asian women who developed breast cancer six or more months after the examinations and matched them by age and race with women who did not develop cancer. Follow-up analyses were conducted through 1990. Dr. Kreiger's group found that:

• Caucasian women experienced an increasing risk of breast cancer with increasing levels of DDE, a biological derivative of DDT, but the increases did not look statistically significant;

• In African American women there was a connection between risk of breast cancer and blood levels of DDE that was borderline statistically significant; and

• Asian women showed a decreased risk of breast cancer with increasing blood levels of DDE, but the relationship was not statistically significant.

• No association was found between PCBs and risk of breast cancer.

While Dr. Krieger and her fellow researchers concluded that "the data do not support the hypothesis that exposure to DDE and PCBs increases risk of breast cancer," some scientists who have analyzed the data feel that a link can be made, because there does seem to be some connection for white and African American women in the study.

We need to make sure, definitely, that there is no risk, because organochlorines are *everywhere*:

• In a 1994 study conducted by researchers at Ehime University in Japan, concentrations of organochlorines were found on islands in the South Pacific, an idyllic environment one would consider safe from industry pollutants. DDT, PCBs, CHLs (chlordane compounds), HCB (hexachlorobenzene), Aldrin, Dieldrin, Heptachlor, and Heptachlor Exposide were found in a wide variety of foods collected from Australia, the more remote Papua New Guinea, and the Solomon Islands in the South Pacific. Most of the people consumed the organochlorines through meat products.

• Virtually all of the breast milk taken from a 1995 sampling of nursing mothers in Victoria, Australia, was contaminated with DDT, DDE, HCB, and PCBs.

• In the United States the Environmental Protection Agency (EPA) is working on an exhaustive assessment of dioxins, a group of organochlorines that have become widespread in the environment due to smokestack emissions during the incineration of chlorine-based products, such as those used for the manufacture of paper. Dioxins travel with the wind, land on vegetation, and when consumed by animals, make their way into meat, fish, and dairy products. So far, the EPA's findings include increases in a variety of cancers among chemical industry workers and those exposed to high levels of dioxin; reproductive and fetal developmental problems in animals exposed to low levels of the chemical; and lower testosterone in men and endometriosis in women, as found during animal and human studies of dioxin. In other words, this ubiquitous group of organochlorines is wreaking hormonal havoc.

The Discovery of Xenoestrogens: Why Organochlorines and Other Chemicals May Increase Risk of Breast Cancer

Remember the word *xenoestrogens*, chemical compounds that act like estrogen when they get into your body. Xenoestrogens are found in organochlorine pesticides and herbicides; in plastics, including some food wraps and food containers; in paper and pulp production; in industrial detergents, chemicals, textiles, cosmetics, hair coloring, spermicides, and condom lubricants. Scientists searching for links between the environment and the rising incidence of breast cancer are now looking in this direction. The growing feeling among medical experts is that a woman's chance of developing breast cancer increases with her lifetime exposure to estrogen, and it now appears that xenoestrogens are another such source of exposure. Even

AN IMPORTANT FIRST . . . IF YOU LIVE NEAR A CHEMICAL PLANT

In 1994 the first report from a public health agency that officially recognizes a chemical connection to breast cancer was issued by the New York State Health Department:

The report declared that on New York's Long Island, women who lived near large chemical plants for years had a 60 percent greater chance of developing breast cancer after menopause than did women in the general population. State Health officials found that women who had lived for at least 10 years within about five-eighths of a mile from a chemical, rubber, or plastics plant developed breast cancer more frequently than did women who lived farther away from the plants. The officials compared 793 women diagnosed with breast cancer between 1984 and 1986 with a control group of 966 women who did not have breast cancer. The researchers looked at high traffic areas and distance from industry and discovered no greater incidence of breast cancer among women who lived near heavily traveled highways or nonchemical plants. But there was a higher incidence among postmenopausal women who lived within 1 kilometer or five-eighths of a mile from a chemical plant that was likely to have emitted pollutants and exposed the women for 10 or more years before their diagnoses. *Note:* The study did not find an increased risk among women who lived near chemical plants and developed breast cancer during their menstruating years.

though their chemical structures are different from a woman's own estrogen, xenoestrogens can unlock the estrogen receptors in her body and trigger potentially harmful estrogenic activity, even after menopause. These "bad" xenoestrogens should not be confused with the "good" *phytoestrogens* mentioned in Chapter 6. Here's the difference:

• Phytoestrogens are plant chemicals that have a molecular structure similar to estrogen. When you consume them through grains, legumes, and assorted vegetables and fruit, they actually lower your body's estrogen levels, protecting your breasts. Phytoestrogens do not have true hormonal power, but as the brain mistakenly recognizes them as estrogen, it instructs the ovaries to cut back on production of the real hormone.

• Xenoestrogens enter your body through contact with man-made products such as pesticides and plastics, which have chemical components. Xenoestrogens are more pervasive and more powerful than phytoestrogens and are able to stimulate an active, potentially cancer-causing form of estrogen in women's bodies. These latest findings about xenoestrogens are shedding new light on how a link between the environment and breast cancer might work.

At the U.S. Department of Health and Human Services, Dr. Devra Lee Davis, senior expert advisor to the assistant secretary for health, is involved in research on the link between breast cancer and xenoestrogens. In a recent study, Dr. Davis and her team found that organochlorine pesticides such as DDT, DDE, Kepone, and Atrazine significantly increased a form of estrogen linked to breast cancer. As mentioned in Chapter 6, in a woman's body, estradiol, the precursor to estrogen, can metabolize into a 16α-hydroxylated or a 2-hydroxylated type of estrogen, depending on its metabolic pathway. The 16α-type estrogen is more reactive and dangerous, and tissues from breast cancers have been found to contain more of the 16α form of estrogen than surrounding noncancerous tissues. In the laboratory study headed by Dr. Davis, human breast cells were exposed to the organochlorines, and an elevated ratio of 16α-hydroxylated estrogen occurred afterward.

OTHER XENOESTROGENS DISCOVERED IN PLASTIC WRAP, FOOD CANS, AND MORE SURPRISING PLACES

In 1988 at Tufts University School of Medicine, Drs. Carlos Sonnenschein and Ana Soto found that estrogenic activity was surfacing in the pristine environment of their laboratory. After pinning it down to a compound in the plastic of their new centrifuge tubes, they then wondered what might be going on in the environment. They found that xenoestrogens were in plastic coatings of canned food, including baby formula. Dr. Soto estimates that eight of 10 cans of food purchased in a supermarket today are shedding xenoestrogens that may leech into the contents. They also detected estrogen compounds in FDA-approved antioxidants used as preservatives in certain foods and candies, plastic food wraps and plastic containers, spermicidal jellies, lubricated condoms, detergents, synthetic leather, and hairspray. Although Dr. Soto does not claim to offer advice for everyone, she never allows a plastic dish or plastic food wrap to touch food being heated in a microwave oven.

To identify the presence of xenoestrogens, the Tufts researchers devised the E-Screen, a test that exposes human breast cancer cells that do not contain any estrogen to compounds with suspected xenoestrogens. The doctors want to see legislation passed that would require food companies and manufacturers to perform an E-Screen for estrogenic effects on any plastic components they use so that women no longer will unwittingly add estrogen to their lives. This is a cumulative problem. As Janet Raloff reported in *Science News* in 1993, "An unintended side effect of industrialization may be an environment that bathes its inhabitants in a sea of pollutants with estrogenic effects."

UNDERSTANDING THE ELECTROMAGNETIC FIELDS OF APPLIANCES AND POWER LINES

Another environmental assault on women's breasts may come from electromagnetic fields (EMFs), which exist virtually everywhere in our electrified world. Wherever you have electrical power, whether in a power station or a kitchen appliance, you have an electromagnetic field.

By definition, "electromagnetic" is one word that describes two different phenomena—electric fields and magnetic fields. An electric field results from the energy released by tiny charged particles called *ions*, while a magnetic field is created by the force and movement of these charged particles as they travel through an electric current. An important distinction between them is that electric fields stay contained in their circuitry, while magnetic fields fan out and penetrate whatever is in their range, even the human body. It is the magnetic field emanating from your hairdryer, blender, electric can opener, pencil sharpener, computer, vacuum cleaner, dishwasher, power tools, microwave oven, electric blanket, just to name a few sources—that is the potential problem of EMFs. Besides emanating from electrically powered machines or appliances, EMFs occur in the vicinity of high-voltage lines. EMFs lose their intensity with distance (in other words, the farther you are from electrical equipment, the weaker the fields).

Until 1979 no one thought that EMFs had an effect on living things, because their energy seemed too low to do any damage. Then, psychologist Dr. Nancy Wertheimer and physicist Dr. Edward Leeper looked at deaths from childhood cancers in the Denver area from 1950 to 1973 and reported that many of the young cancer victims lived close to electrical transformers and high-current distribution lines. Many epidemiological studies, mostly related to leukemia and brain cancers, have followed over the years with mixed results; a number of well-done studies support the Denver findings, although others do not.

Researchers took notice of EMFs in relation to breast cancer after three studies found higher than usual rates of breast cancer among male electrical workers. In 1994 an analysis of mortality among female electrical workers conducted by a team of three researchers headed by Dr. Dana Loomis, an epidemiologist at the University of North Carolina, found that women who held a variety of electrical jobs had a 38 percent higher rate of death from breast cancer than those in nonelectrical jobs. These findings came from a review of death certificates of women aged 20 and older who died of breast cancer between 1985 and 1989 and whose records indicated their occupations. The researchers then contrasted 68 women with breast cancer and 199 women who were cancer-free, all of whom had electrical jobs, with 27,814 women with breast cancer and 110,750 cancer-free women in other occupations. The strongest link to breast cancer was found among women who were telephone installers, repairers, and line workers. There were no higher rates of breast cancer among telephone operators, data entry staff, computer operators and programmers, and air-traffic controllers, occupations also related to the electrical field. Because the women with the highest rates of breast cancer were more intensely exposed to EMFs, the researchers concluded that their study offered evidence in support of EMFs as a possible cause of breast cancer.

Just how EMF exposure might lead to breast cancer is the next big question. A currently strong theory is that long-term exposure to extremely low-frequency EMFs suppresses the release of melatonin, a hormone that inhibits estrogen production. Estrogen, as we have mentioned, is considered key to the development of breast tumors, and researchers are realizing that without melatonin, estrogen levels can stay fairly high.

How EMFs May Promote Breast Cancer

Scientists have isolated noncancerous breast cells and exposed them to EMFs; they have also raised animals in electromagnetic fields in laboratories. In none of these experiments have they been able to grow cancers, so it appears more and more as if EMFs do not turn normal cells into cancerous ones but instead may promote a breast cancer that has already begun. In animal studies, female rats given breast cancer with an injection of carcinogen were then exposed to EMFs of 60 Hertz (Hz) power, the electric power used in the United States. Among these cancerous rats, those exposed to the EMFs produced 50 percent more tumors than those not exposed. What happened to the exposed rats, what caused them to become more cancerous, may have to do with the hormone *melatonin*.

The Melatonin Factor is the leading contender for being the missing link between EMFs and breast cancer. In 1987 Dr. Richard G. Stevens, a cancer epidemiologist at the Pacific Northwest Laboratory, a U.S. Department of Energy Lab in the state of Washington, offered a theory about melatonin. He based his thinking on the fact that in experiments, melatonin, the hormone released by the small pineal gland in the center of the brain, is affected by light and extremely low-frequency EMFs. The pineal gland releases melatonin during nighttime darkness, and animal studies had shown that the hormone then inhibits production of estrogen and prolactin, a hormone that stimulates the flow of breast milk. In other words, when melatonin is up, estrogen is down. Because other studies had shown that animals exposed to light during the night or EMFs had lower melatonin levels, Dr. Stevens proposed that women exposed to electric light long into the evening, and thereby EMFs, might also be experiencing lower melatonin levels. And with melatonin down, estrogen and the risk of breast cancer probably would rise. Over the years his theory has been borne out in animal studies, and since 1992 he has been involved in a case-control study of 800 women newly diagnosed with breast cancer and 800 cancer-free control subjects. Dr. Stevens and his team of researchers have left magnetic field meters in the women's homes to measure exposure to EMFs and have also been measuring levels of light in these homes. The results of his analyses are still pending.

However, there may be another link between EMFs and breast cancer. The prevailing belief has been that because EMFs have extremely low frequencies, they would not be powerful enough to cause genetic changes. However, at Columbia University, geneticist Dr. Reba Goodman has found that stress genes in breast cancer cells exposed to EMFs (at the typical 60 Hz level) overproduce certain proteins. These proteins then prevent chemotherapy from working on the cancer. She has also found that when breast cancer cells are exposed to EMFs, the proto-oncogene that they are housing—the gene that begins to multiply out of control—changes its genetic makeup to become more active. Dr. Goodman's research is still in progress, but her findings may change traditional thinking about the power of EMFs.

Other researchers are also continuing to investigate the possible EMF link. The studies investigating possible environmental causes of breast cancer on Long Island and Cape Cod are looking into EMFs, and in California Dr. Stephanie London at the University of Southern California has embarked on a study doing seven-day measurements of EMFs and investigating wire configuration coding in the homes of African American and Latina women, 600 of whom have breast cancer and 600 of whom are disease-free. The results of her study will be available in the year 2000.

AN AWARENESS OF RADIATION

The word "radiation" defines a wide spectrum of energy. At the low end of the spectrum is the nonionizing radiation released by television sets and computer monitors, and at the high end, the ionizing radiation of X rays and gamma rays from radioactive material. Radiation from radiowaves, microwaves, infrared light, visible light, and ultraviolet light exists in between.

It is the ionizing radiation at the high end of the spectrum that has the energy to break up the chemical structure of living organisms and create dangerous free radical cells in the body. These resulting free radicals are very active, and can easily alter their surroundings to make them cancerous.

Radiation in high doses causes breast cancer, but most women are not living in circumstances that expose them to high levels of radiation. Even

CONTROVERSY: THE AMERICAN PHYSICAL SOCIETY SAYS "NO" TO EMFS AND CANCER

In 1995 the American Physical Society, an organization representing the world's largest group of physicists, issued a one-page statement about EMFs and cancer. The statement was a summary of a report prepared for the Society by Dr. David Hafemeister, a physicist at California Polytechnic State University. Dr. Hafemeister reviewed more than 1,000 papers on aspects of research into EMFs and conducted interviews with specialists in the field. His report led the American Physical Society to conclude that the literature shows no consistent significant link between cancer and power line fields and to suggest that funding for research costs be virtually eliminated.

The EMR Alliance, a national umbrella organization representing citizen action groups involved in the EMF issue, was outraged and issued its own statement that the "EMF/cancer link is a very complex, highly debated issue," and "The American Physical Society has not been a participant in that debate." In the same statement, the EMR Alliance wrote that its own investigation found that the work of Dr. David O. Carpenter, a research biophysicist, dean of the School of Public Health at the University of Albany in New York—and as author of *The New York Power Line Project*, well known for his analyses of studies exploring the EMF/cancer link—was not included in the review. The EMR Alliance regarded this as a major oversight.

In the end, I feel that there is too much speculation and controversy over the role of EMFs in cancer to ignore the possibility that they may be a contributing factor to disease. Dr. David Savitz, a professor of epidemiology at the University of North Carolina School of Public Health, has conducted his own groundbreaking studies on the relation between EMFs and cancer, and I agree with him when he says, "The American Physical Society seems more confident than I would be that we will ultimately discover that these fields did not have adverse health effects. I think it is genuinely unknown right now what we will ultimately determine."

women working as radiological technologists have not been found to be in added jeopardy of developing breast cancer. I do recognize the concern about X rays, however, and older women who have undergone X-ray treatments on their thymus glands as infants or multiple chest X rays to check for tuberculosis in childhood should understandably be wary of further X rays. My recommendation is that women undergo X-ray procedures only when they are absolutely necessary and no other diagnostic tests will do. There has also been the recent discovery of the ATM gene (ataxia telangiectasia mutated). The cells of women with ATM are sensitive to radiation, thereby making them more susceptible to the early onset of radiation-induced cancer. Individual testing for ATM is not yet available, but we are sure to see it in the future as ongoing research reveals more about genetic influences on radiation sensitivity.

In terms of mammography, under normal circumstances the amount of radiation that a woman receives through regular mammography after age 40 would not put her at high risk of breast cancer. But if mammography is recommended for younger women, there is more cause for concern. In general, younger women are more vulnerable to radiation exposure, as shown through a recent analysis of breast cancer and radiation dose among Japanese women who survived the atomic bomb. Prepared by Dr. Charles E. Land, a health statistician at the Radiation Epidemiology Branch of the National Cancer Institute, the report showed that the number of radiation-related cases of breast cancer was greatest among women who were under 20 at the time of the bombings (55 of 205 cancers). Women who were 20 to 40 had fewer cases (38.5 of 259 cancers), and women over 40 the least (7.5 of 127 cancers). However, the young women who had been exposed to radiation before they were 16 lowered their risk of breast cancer if they gave birth early in life. The younger they were during their first full-term pregnancies, the healthier they remained. Childbirth after age 26 was not nearly as protective as before age 26. Dr. Land also told me that independent of age at first full-term pregnancy, breastfeeding also contributed to lowering the risk of breast cancer among young women exposed to radiation. However, a wide range of lactation time exists among Japanese women, with some women breastfeeding up to 72 months. So again, radiation in terms of mammography should not be a concern unless you are younger in years.

WHERE YOU LIVE AND WORK

Throughout this chapter I have attempted to raise your consciousness about your personal environment. Chemicals, EMFs, and radiation exist in our world. Since their effects are not completely known, precautions such as those recommended earlier in this chapter make sense. Good health also comes from trusting your instincts. For instance, if a room is newly painted and you think you should stay away until the fumes have dissipated, then do so. Environmental awareness, along with the diet and exercise regimens suggested in Chapters 6 and 7, offer health advantages not only for your breasts but for your entire body.

CHAPTER NINE

The Mind/Body Connection: Stress and Your Breasts

An awareness of the mind/body connection can improve the health of your breasts. What you feel in your mind sets off a crucial chain of events in your body: In a demanding or stressful situation, the signal for "good" or "bad" travels from your brain, via your central nervous system, to endocrine glands that then release hormones that affect your body's disease-fighting immune system. This mind/body interplay has spawned a field of medicine called *psychoneuroimmunology*, or PNI. Researchers have discovered that how stress is perceived is likely to affect both the release of stress hormones and the production of natural killer (NK) cells, which fight cancer. Interaction with other people during stress also activates the mind/body process. An important Stanford University study has shown that women with metastatic breast cancer who participated in support groups lived nearly *twice* as long as women who received treatment without group therapy.

In acknowledging their discoveries, many PNI researchers separate the power of the mind/body connection from the theory that personality traits influence health. They believe that everyone, regardless of personality, has the potential to benefit from their mind/body connection.

THE MIND/BODY CONNECTION CHALLENGES THE MYTH OF "THE CANCER-PRONE PERSONALITY"

Studies into a link between personality traits and illness have brewed high controversy. In the 1980s, research psychologist Dr. Lydia Temoshok proposed the existence of a type C cancer-prone personality. She described a type C as self-effacing, unassertive, and accepting—someone who doesn't complain because "why bother?" and who is likely to suffer cancer more severely than a person who is emotionally expressive. In a study of 58 people who had melanoma (skin cancer), Dr. Temoshok found that those who expressed their emotions about their illnesses had slower-growing tumors and stronger immune systems than those who thought it was useless to talk about their situations.

But Dr. Temoshok's type C personality was soon debunked by a major study conducted by Dr. Barrie Cassileth in 1985 at the University of Pittsburgh. After administering personality tests to a group of 204 people with advanced cancer and a group of 155 with stage I or II melanoma or stage II breast cancer, she found no relationship between the battery of personality traits measured and time of survival or recurrence of disease. Then in 1987 researchers at Vanderbilt University studied 49 women with advanced breast cancer for differences in personality traits such as self-esteem, sense of well-being, and feelings of being in control. They reported that there were no differences in personality that could predict how long each woman would survive with cancer.

More recently, in a 1993 issue of the medical journal *Lancet*, Stanford University's Dr. David Spiegel reported that personality traits were not predictors of survival among the 86 women with metastasized breast cancer whom he observed in his study on the effect of support groups. As he wrote in *Living Beyond Limits* (1993), "While the concept that certain personality attributes such as anger suppression may be more common in cancer patients is interesting, it lends itself far too easily to the problem of blaming the victim. If suppressing your anger makes tumors grow more quickly, then any growth of the tumor might be considered your fault. There is no proof that this is the case."

Now researchers are making a clear distinction between the mind/body connection and personality as an influence on health. The way a woman faces the suddenness of a stressful event, such as divorce, the death of a loved one, or the diagnosis of a disease, and how she copes with long-term stress, such as feeling trapped in a job she hates, is regarded as more important to health than overall personality. Scientists have shown that during stressful times, the stress hormones can be overproduced, thereby lowering immunity at intervals when the production of natural killer cells that fight cancer can drop too. But before going any further into the particulars, let me first offer the following recommendations for making the most of the mind/body connection, and combating the hard times:

HOW TO WORK THE MIND/BODY CONNECTION

• Review the stresses in your life. Can you zero in on an event or a situation that feels genuinely anxiety-provoking? If you can, slot some serious stress-relieving time in your schedule. Sometimes one simple, relaxing activity has the most profound effect. Every woman should have a stress reliever that makes her feel enriched. I know one woman who takes a half-hour morning walk in a park as a daily tonic, and another who goes to a two-hour drawing class once a week. For other women, the formality of a meditation or an imagery session works. The key is to find an activity that nurtures your spirit so you can tap into the potential for good health that comes from the link your mind makes with your body.

• When worry or illness besets you, being a member of a therapy or support group can give you a new outlook, as long as the group is one in which you can truly express your feelings.

• Let a realistic sense of hope come into your life. A false hope for a woman who has a family history of breast cancer is that she has nothing to worry about. This approach does not use the mind/body power. A woman is also ignoring the richness of the mind/body link when she surrenders to the feeling that nothing can be done to prevent the inevitable. Instead, I suggest having a realistic hope, one that springs from a belief that you are living each day fully, and that the steps you are taking to stay healthy, whatever they may be, are right for you.

THE PATH FROM THE PSYCHE TO STRESS HORMONES AND NATURAL KILLER CELLS

The Release of Stress Hormones

The idea that you could become physically sick during times of psychological stress has a long history. In ancient times, from A.D. 130 to 200, Galen reported seeing problems more often in "melancholic women." Teachings from this revered Greek physician, scientist, and scholar were regarded as gospel for centuries after his death. However, the mind/body connection was dismissed by physicians during the first half of the twentieth century. It was not until the 1950s that endocrinologists studying hormone levels in blood and urine discovered the link between the pituitary gland in the brain and the stress hormones released by glands in other parts of the body. Then the mind/body connection started being taken more seriously.

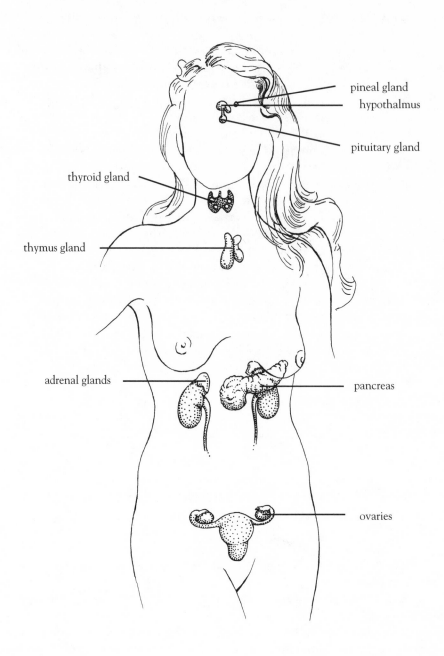

pineal gland
hypothalmus
pituitary gland
thyroid gland
thymus gland
adrenal glands
pancreas
ovaries

The location of the body's endocrine glands.

Today we know that two major biological systems strongly respond during times of stress: the nervous system and the endocrine (hormone-releasing) system. The two systems meet in the brain's hypothalamus. After recognizing stress, the hypothalamus (1) stimulates the sympathetic nervous system to quicken heart rate, breathing, and blood pressure, and (2) triggers the hormonal action of the endocrine glands by influencing the brain's master endocrine gland, the pituitary. The pituitary sends hormonal messengers to the adrenal glands, ordering them to release the stress hormones epinephrine (better known as adrenaline), norepinephrine, and cortisol. These hormones prepare the body for "flight or fight" by stimulating the heart to pump a greater supply of oxygen- and glucose-enriched blood to the muscles and increasing respiration, blood clotting activity, and sodium and water retention. Such hormonally produced changes were designed to be short term, but modern-day emotional stress can turn them into a long-term situation, and that's when the body suffers. Immune system organs, such as the thymus and spleen, can shrink, the lymph system can be affected, and there can be reduced activity and/or production of white blood cells and lymphocytes, which are responsible for bolstering the immune response. Medical experts now believe that stress-related diseases can arise from hormones that have lingered too long in the bloodstream.

Thus, more studies are being done to find out how the interaction of the mind and the body may affect risk of cancer and other diseases. As a follow-up to his study showing increased longevity among breast cancer patients in support groups, Dr. David Spiegel's team at Stanford is measuring changes in the stress hormone cortisol among group members. Physicians are becoming more aware of how sensitive breasts are to the body's hormonal balance, which is affected by the mind/body connection. We are on the verge of understanding what at one time seemed incomprehensible.

Natural Killer Cells and Your Breasts

Natural killer (NK) cells produced by our immune systems are able to recognize and kill cancer cells in the body. During the mid to late 1980s, Dr. Sandra Levy and her colleagues at the University of Pittsburgh focused their research on NK activity, especially in relation to breast cancer, and found a mind/body connection.

In 1985 they reported that women who had the greatest spread of breast cancer to neighboring lymph nodes also had the least number of NK cells. Along with their immunological status, the emotional, social, and biological conditions of the 75 women in the study were measured (after they were treated with either lumpectomy/radiation or mastectomy). The researchers believed that 51 percent of the changes in NK cells could be accounted for by three "distress indicators": (1) "adjustment," which the researchers described as a stoicism or passivity; (2) lack of social support; and

(3) fatigue/depression. The more women fell into these three situations, the less their NK activity, the greater their lymph node involvement, and the more advanced their cancers.

Dr. Levy and her group checked back with these women three months after they had been treated with radiation or chemotherapy and again checked their NK cells and distress indicators. As they reported in a 1987 issue of the *Journal of Clinical Oncology*, the researchers were surprised to find that NK cells were "seemingly unaffected by interim treatments." Again, they could predict women at higher risk by their distress indicators, correlated with their NK cell levels.

Dr. Levy's work on emotional distress and its potent effects on NK cell activity has piqued the curiosity of other researchers. It has been found that people who have a family history of cancer have lower levels of NK cell activity than people without such a history. At the Psychoneuroimmunology Lab of Memorial Sloan-Kettering Cancer Center in New York, Dr. Dana Bovbjerg has been looking into the NK cell activity among women with a family history of breast cancer, and he has found that they have higher levels of distress and report more intrusive thoughts about breast cancer than women at normal risk in the same community. His preliminary findings suggest that psychological factors, along with hereditary biological differences, may lower NK cells and immunity among women at high risk for breast cancer.

At the University of Pittsburgh, Dr. Andrew Baum has just begun looking into how stress may affect healthy women at high risk for breast cancer. He too is looking at changes in immunity (which can be evidenced by NK cells), along with behavioral and emotional changes that may affect whether a breast cancer actually develops in a woman who has a family history of the disease. Dr. Baum is in the process of recruiting about 100 women for a study that should have results in about 1998.

So it seems as if NK cells, which beat back cancer cells, can be subdued by distress, and according to Dr. Levy, that distress would reveal itself in a stoicism in coping with breast cancer, few social supports, and a tired, depressed feeling. This discovery is significant in our understanding of the mind/body connection.

THE HEALING POWER OF OTHER PEOPLE

"Lack of social support" was one of Dr. Levy's distress indicators that correlated with a drop in natural killer cells. What happens when there *is* social support is starting to surface, and the news is good. An important series of studies is going on at Stanford University School of Medicine under the guidance of psychiatrist Dr. David Spiegel. In the prestigious medical journal

Lancet in 1989, Dr. Spiegel and his colleagues reported *women with metasta-sized breast cancer who were in therapeutic support groups lived nearly twice as long as women who received treatment without group therapy*. Ten years before, 86 women with metastatic breast cancer had been randomly divided into two groups: one group, the control subjects, received only standard medical treatment; the other received standard medical treatment along with weekly one and one-half–hour group therapy sessions and lessons in self-hypnosis to help control pain.

The women in the therapy group met with therapists and other breast cancer survivors to talk about their experience, to discuss treatment, and to share their thoughts and feelings. This went on for one year. Ten years later, looking back on how the women had survived, it turned out that the women who had participated in group therapy had lived twice as long (an average of 36.6 months) as the women in the control group (an average of 18.9 months). Studies among the elderly have shown that social support can influence longevity, but Dr. Spiegel's study was the first scientifically controlled investigation into the effects of a group dynamic on survival. Perhaps other people acted as a buffer against stress; perhaps the group experience offered a sense of hope so that women followed their treatment regimens more closely; or perhaps a support group stabilized emotions and thereby influenced the immune system more positively. Note: In the support groups, the women did not have to worry about presenting themselves as "positive thinkers"; they expressed their feelings, positive or negative, about their breast cancers, and took an active role in helping and supporting others.

Today Dr. Spiegel is studying the effects of support groups on a different population of women with metastasized breast cancer and their spouses. He is looking not only at length of survival but at other mind/body changes. His research team is analyzing blood samples for different levels of stress hormones to get an idea of what happens to immune systems. He is also looking at the effects of group therapy on women with earlier-stage breast cancer that has not spread, to learn whether social support has positive influences on women who are healthier.

Dr. Spiegel's approach stems from his belief that you cannot control whether you have a disease, but you can control the quality of your life with an illness, and dealing with stress is part of that quality of life. Being free to talk about your hopes and feelings with family, friends, and members of a support group who understand what you are going through is a stress reliever that, as Dr. Spiegel's work already shows, clearly improves quality and length of life. Just how a social network can influence your overall health, and particularly the health of your breasts when you are not sick, has yet to be discovered, but connecting with others in what Dr. Spiegel calls "supportive expressive group therapy" may have a potential that has yet to be defined.

STRESS AND YOUR BREASTS

Stress can sometimes seem like a catch-all excuse for everything that goes wrong, but you cannot ignore the power of either a sudden stress, such as unexpectedly being fired from a job, or long-term stress, such as feeling trapped in a routine you hate. For good health, every woman needs a workable stress reliever, such as aerobic exercise, a relaxation technique such as meditation or imagery, or a creative outlet like cooking or carpentry. Your breasts are part of the body that is part of the mind/body connection. As the studies mentioned in this chapter show, women who have developed breast cancer or are at high risk seem to physically respond to the effects of stress. And psychoneuroimmunologists are only just beginning to understand how strong an effect those responses might have on one's health.

Wondering Which Course to Take? New Information About Medications and Operations

CHAPTER TEN

How Birth Control Pills and Fertility Drugs Affect Your Breasts

With so many scientific fingers pointing at the sex hormones, particularly estrogen, as being strong promoters of breast cancer, many are wondering whether women should expose themselves to drugs that contain these powerful substances. At the National Institute of Child Health and Human Development (NICHHD) and at the National Cancer Institute (NCI), large studies involving thousands of women are going on to investigate any possible links birth control pills and/or fertility drugs may have with breast cancer. Here is what is known so far, which may only be the tip of the iceberg.

BIRTH CONTROL PILLS: THE YOUNGER YOU ARE, THE MORE VULNERABLE YOU MAY BE

While many studies in the past have found no increased risk for breast cancer among women who were on the Pill, a growing body of medical evidence is showing that a risk exists. This evidence is also pointing to the fact that women who start on the Pill as teenagers and stay on it for more than 10 years may be the most vulnerable.

In a study published in 1995 a team of NCI investigators headed by Dr. Louise Brinton compared 1,648 women who were diagnosed with in situ (early, localized) or invasive breast cancer with 1,505 cancer-free women. These women who were from Georgia, Washington, and New Jersey, were under age 45 and had taken the low-dose, combination estrogen/progestin pills that have been available since 1975. They also had the opportunity to

135

be on the Pill for most of their menstruating years. The results: a 30 percent increase over normal risk for all women using oral contraceptives for six months or more, and for younger women, who had taken the Pill longer, an even greater risk for breast cancer. Women under 35 had a 70 percent higher than normal risk, which is almost twice the breast cancer risk of women who had used the Pill for less than six months or not at all. As for women who started taking birth control pills *before* age 18 and who used them *for more than* 10 years, they had *three times the risk*. Please note: researchers could not determine, however, whether this elevated risk lingers as women get older, stop the Pill, and enter the menopausal years.

When put into perspective, the risk for younger women is still low—the NCI describes the increase as accounting for only one additional in situ or invasive breast cancer per year for every 100,000 women aged 20 to 34 years—nonetheless, any link between birth control pills and breast cancer is unsettling. Other studies from Holland, New Zealand, England, Sweden, and the United States have reported similar increased risks of breast cancer among women under 45 who have used the Pill for four years or more and have also noted that the risk gets greater the younger you are and the longer you take the Pill. However, in these other studies, researchers have shied away from blaming the Pill itself and have considered other explanations. One is that the increase in breast cancer may be due to better screening, because women on oral contraceptives are examined more by doctors than women who use other methods of contraception. Another explanation is that the Pill causes a breast cancer that might have appeared later in life to appear earlier. Dr. Brinton believes otherwise.

She thinks the link between the Pill and an increased risk of breast cancer is "a real phenomenon. It has been observed consistently enough that we feel fairly confident that there is something going on in young women. We just don't know what it is. We don't know whether it's a unique characteristic of those women or if it had something to do with the type of pills they were exposed to or the way they were using the Pill. The thinking classically was that we would see a high risk of breast cancer associated with the use of high-estrogen-dose pills (those prescribed between 1960 and 1975), but we haven't really seen that. Now we are beginning to think that maybe it's not the dose of the estrogen or the dose of the progestin; maybe it has something to do with the balance of the hormones."

Today's combination estrogen/progestin (synthetic progesterone) oral contraceptives are available in different forms. They may be *monophasic* or *multiphasic*. Monophasic pills, which contain 1 milligram of progestin and 35 micrograms of estrogen, release a steady level of the hormones throughout the monthly cycle. The *multiphasic* pills, *biphasic* and *triphasic*, attempt to mimic the fluctuating hormonal patterns of the menstrual cycle. The *triphasics*, probably the most frequently prescribed oral contraceptives, "phase in" a varying low dosage of hormones in pills colored for the early, middle,

INVESTIGATING THE RISK FOR OLDER WOMEN: THE WOMEN'S CARE STUDY

At the National Institute of Child Health and Human Development (NICHHD), the Women's Care Study has just begun evaluating the relationship between oral contraceptives and breast cancer in the first generation of Pill takers, women who range in age from 35 to 64. Dr. Robert Spirtas, coordinator of the study, explains that between 1994 and 1998, researchers at medical centers with cancer registries in Los Angeles, Seattle, Detroit, and Philadelphia, expect to enroll 5,000 women with breast cancer, for comparison with 5,000 women without it. The Women's Care Study will offer an opportunity to look at the long-term effects of the earliest birth control pills which had high doses of estrogen and progesterone, on women who may also have used hormone replacement therapy once they entered menopause. Researchers also will look into whether women who are at higher risk for breast cancer because they have a family history or a genetic connection are at additional increased risk because they also were on the Pill.

and late phases of the cycle. (There is one *minipill* on the market which contains no estrogen, only progesterone, but because it has a higher pregnancy rate than other birth control pills, it is infrequently prescribed.) At the NCI an analysis is being undertaken to categorize the different types of birth control pills biochemically. Researchers hope that this analysis will offer clues to whether connections can be made between the increased risk of breast cancer and certain hormonal combinations of the pills.

Keeping Perspective on Birth Control Pills

It used to be advisable for women to stop taking oral contraceptives at 35, but today's pills, with their lower doses of hormones, do not produce the risks of stroke and blood clots that increase with age. In 1990 the FDA announced that healthy women over 35 could be offered the Pill if they were not at risk for potential complications. (Smoking offers the highest risk, although high blood pressure, diabetes, and a history of blood clots also limits the Pill as an option.)

While we have focused on research into the possible increased risk of breast cancer from the Pill, it is important to remember the Pill's benefits. Short of sterilization, the birth control pill is the most effective way to prevent unwanted pregnancy, with nearly 100 percent contraceptive protection. It also offers protection against endometrial (uterine lining) cancer and ovarian cancer. In fact, some doctors recommend the Pill to women who have a family history of ovarian cancer for its protective effect. The Pill also helps reduce the frequency of benign cysts and lumps in the breast. Even considering that oral contraceptives may raise the risk of breast cancer among pill-takers who are under 35, the risk is low to start with, and the Pill will only add the possibility of one more breast cancer per 100,000 women (according to the NCI interpretation of its latest study). Still, we see a link where we did not see one before. Until we have more solid information, I recommend that women stay on the Pill only 3 or 4 years at a time, then use a different form of contraception for a year or two, and return thereafter to the Pill for another few years.

FERTILITY DRUGS: NO KNOWN LINK TO BREAST CANCER

While research has linked fertility drugs to a higher risk of ovarian cancer, no one has discovered an increased risk of breast cancer. As of this writing, the most extensive look at fertility drugs has been conducted by researchers at the University of Washington and Fred Hutchinson Cancer Research Center in Seattle. A team of researchers headed by epidemiologist Dr. Mary Anne Rossino looked at the health records of 3,837 women who sought treatment in fertility clinics in Seattle from 1974 through 1986. They found ovarian cancer in 11 women. (Statistically, considering the low risk of ovarian cancer, the researchers expected to find no more than 4.4 cases. The 11 cases signaled a risk of ovarian cancer 2.5 times higher for women taking fertility drugs—more than twice the risk.)

Nine of the 11 women who developed ovarian cancer had taken clomiphene citrate (Clomid or Serophene), and five of the nine had used the drug for 12 or more menstrual cycles. For women who had been on the drug for a year or more, risk of ovarian cancer was 11.1 times higher than risk in women in the general population. On the positive side, no elevated risk was shown for women who used clomiphene citrate for less than a year or for women who used another fertility drug, human chorionic gonadotropin, for any period of time. The same team of researchers also looked at the risk of breast cancer from fertility drugs, especially clomiphene. The findings are reassuring, for they do not show greater risk.

What is important to remember, however, is that fertility drugs have been used with frequency only in recent years. With the advent of assisted reproductive techniques such as in vitro fertilization (IVF) and gamete intrafallopian transfer (GIFT), more and more women have taken drugs such as Clomid and Pergonal. These women are only just beginning to reach the menopausal, higher risk, years for breast cancer. Whether taking the drugs

A CONTRACEPTIVE TO PREVENT BREAST CANCER?

At the University of Southern California School of Medicine, researchers have been testing a contraceptive that uses a form of gonadotropin-releasing-hormone (GnRH), the brain hormone that has an influence on the levels of estrogen and progesterone produced by the ovaries. The researchers tested their theory that by injecting women with a GnRH agonist (a drug that competes with the body's own production of GnRH), they could block production of estrogen and progesterone, create birth control, and in addition, prevent the dividing of breast cells that normally takes place when these sex hormones rise. (Standard oral contraceptives keep sex hormone levels up.) For a year, women at high risk of breast cancer were injected with GnRH agonist every 28 days, which stopped their ovarian production of estrogen and progesterone. These hormones were then replaced orally, at levels similar to those used by postmenopausal women on hormone replacement therapy. From their experiment the researchers predict lifetime breast cancer risk would be reduced by about one-third if their contraceptive was used for five years; by more than 50 percent if used for 10 years; and by 70 percent after 15 years' use. We do not yet know where these findings will lead.

when they were younger will affect their health now that they are older is currently unknown, but finding out is one goal of a huge study undertaken by the NCI.

The four-year Follow-up Study of Women Evaluated and Treated for Infertility was started by the NCI in 1994. Researchers are looking at the long-term health effects on 10,000 women who were treated for infertility in the 1960s and 1970s. The researchers are particularly focused on exploring the effects of the fertility drugs clomiphene citrate and Pergonal. The reproductive cancer rates (including breast and ovarian cancers) of women who took fertility drugs will be compared with women in the general population.

A LAST WORD ON BIRTH CONTROL PILLS AND FERTILITY DRUGS

The Pill and fertility drugs, in their ability to affect a woman's hormonal balance and her breasts, are powerful. A woman should carefully consider their pros and cons before she chooses to use them. If she does, I recommend a breast examination by a physician twice a year, and regular breast self-examinations. I also encourage protecting the health of your breasts with a diet high in vegetables and fruits, exercise, and environmental awareness as described earlier in this book.

CHAPTER ELEVEN

How to Decide Whether Hormone Replacement Therapy Is for You . . . Even If You Have Survived Breast Cancer

When women who start experiencing symptoms of menopause think about replacing their waning estrogen and progesterone with prescribed hormones, many wonder what effect this might have on their breasts. "If I take them, will the hormones make me more vulnerable to breast cancer?" is a question often voiced. No straight answer is available, and to complicate an already confusing issue, some physicians are now contemplating hormone replacement therapy (HRT) to relieve the menopausal symptoms of women who have already battled breast cancer—women who, presumably, would be more susceptible to the effects of the sex hormones.

Trying to understand the connection between HRT and your breasts is like going to sea without a compass; the right course is not clear. A close inspection of the mixed reports leaves so much doubt about the issue that physicians carefully qualify their recommendations and ask that women have mammograms and physical examinations annually. From the evidence, physicians tell women to be cautious, because hormones might slightly increase their risk of breast cancer. However, many doctors like to focus on the positive: that HRT can stave off heart disease, bone-thinning osteoporosis, and if the latest reports hold up, colon cancer. The status of the HRT/breast cancer connection is often lost in the talk of what is good about hormones. This will not happen here.

This chapter includes two sections that try to make sense of the available research: one section focuses on the link between HRT and breast cancer in healthy women, and the other takes on the debate over whether women who have survived breast cancer should receive HRT. The current knowledge about HRT comes mainly from the analyses of the health

141

AN EMERGING PATTERN: HRT AND YOUR BREASTS

Hormone replacement therapy probably brings about a *slight* increase in the risk of breast cancer, which appears to start taking effect after a woman has been on HRT for five years or more.

Based on the current U.S. assessment that one in eight women may develop breast cancer during their lifetime, the experts say that a woman who never takes hormones has a 12-percent chance of developing the disease. Studies show that a woman who is on HRT for five years or more is facing a risk between 30 and 70 percent higher than the normal 12-percent risk. At the low end, 30 percent of 12 percent works out to be a *4 percent increase in risk*. With that 4 percent added on to the normal rate of risk, a woman on HRT for more than five years has a 16-percent chance of developing breast cancer during her lifetime.

patterns of women who have been followed over the years prospectively or whose health records have been scrutinized retrospectively by research teams. Both types of research are considered "inconclusive"—not as scientific as randomized, case-controlled studies—but all the same, they give us a lot to ponder.

FOR HEALTHY WOMEN: HRT AND THE BREAST CANCER CONNECTION

The sex hormones estrogen and progesterone are highly suspect in terms of a breast cancer connection, because it is known that they stimulate breast cells. In laboratory studies these hormones have made breast cancers grow in animals. Women whose ovaries were removed during their menstruating years have lower rates of breast cancer, and this is attributed to their lack of ovarian hormones. Women who experience early menarche and late menopause—giving them maximum exposure to estrogen throughout their lifetimes—are also at increased risk for breast cancer. Recently a study headed by Dr. Paolo Toniolo at the New York University School of Medicine and published in 1995 added to the evidence of a connection. Dr. Toniolo and his team looked at the association between blood levels of estrogens and the risk of breast cancer among more than 14,000 New York City women aged 35 to 65. The researchers found 130 breast cancers among 7,063 postmenopausal women during a period of five and one-half years.

Although estrogen levels of all women were in the normal range, those who developed breast cancer tended to have higher levels than those who remained cancer-free. All these observations have led scientists to theorize that adding sex hormones to a woman's biological makeup probably increases her chances of developing breast cancer, especially after menopause, when breast cancer rates are already higher.

A Swedish study in 1989 was the first to look at the effects of combining estrogen and progestin in hormone replacement therapy. (The study has been criticized for having too small a group on combined hormones to be significant, for lacking a control group, and for using a formulation of estrogens different from those commonly used in the United States and other countries.) For almost six years researchers at University Hospital in Uppsala followed 23,244 women who took hormones after menopause—two-thirds of the women took estrogen alone; one-third took a combination of estrogen/ progestin. Of the 253 who developed breast cancer, the rate among the women who took estrogen alone was almost *double* that of women who took no hormones; among those who took the combination hormones for four years or more, the rate of breast cancer was *four times as high* as the rate of women not on hormones. Thus, the inclusion of progestin in hormone replacement therapy after menopause (recommended to prevent an increase in risk of endometrial cancer brought on by taking estrogen alone) was shown to elevate the risk of breast cancer. So this study revealed another "damned if you do/damned if you don't" situation in terms of HRT.

Researchers in the United States and other countries have begun their own comparisons of female populations on hormones. Currently the Women's Health Initiative (WHI), the 10-year, $628 million research project under the auspices of the National Institutes of Health, is conducting a hormone replacement therapy study of 27,500 women. WHI researchers are mainly interested

---

THE BASICS OF HORMONE REPLACEMENT THERAPY

Today, for every woman who enters menopause with a healthy uterus, the recommended hormone replacement therapy (HRT) is a combination of estrogen and progesterone (usually in the form of synthetic progestin). Progesterone became paired with estrogen when it was discovered that "unopposed" estrogen increased the risk of developing endometrial (uterine lining) cancer. Progesterone brings about a healthy shedding of cells in the uterus and thereby prevents this increased risk. Estrogen alone, however, continues to be recommended to women who have undergone hysterectomies.

in whether hormone replacement therapy prevents heart disease and osteo-porosis, but important breast cancer information will surely surface, with results due in the year 2005. In the study women who have had hysterec-tomies are being randomly assigned to take either Premarin (conjugated estrogens) or placebo, while other healthy women are receiving Premarin plus Provera (a progestin/synthetic progesterone) or placebo.

Major meta-analyses are also going on. These studies take all the dif-ferent research results, reweigh the data, and recalculate the findings. According to Dr. Rena Bassilopou-Sellin, endocrinologist and associate pro-fessor of medicine at the University of Texas M.D. Anderson Cancer Center, "all of the studies are having a great deal of difficulty demonstrating a significant risk in anybody except in perhaps very specific subgroups, and even those groups are not the same from study to study; it depends on how the data are analyzed." Therefore, conflicting reports can make headlines at the same time, which is what happened when findings from two important studies, the Nurses' Health Study and the University of Washington Study, were published in 1995.

The Nurses' Health Study (mentioned in detail in Chapter 6) found an increased risk of breast cancer among women on HRT; the University of Washington Study found no link between the use of hormones and breast cancer. Although the research was done on different-size populations of women, the hormones were taken for different lengths of time, and the methodology of the studies was different, the opposing conclusions highlight the fact that we are still in the throes of a work in progress when it comes to reaching a conclusion about whether HRT increases a woman's chance of developing breast cancer:

In the Nurses' Health Study, the HRT findings involved about 70,000 women who were postmenopausal by 1990. Their questionnaires, which revealed what medications, including hormones, they had taken and whether they had been diagnosed with breast cancer were reviewed through 1992. Researchers reported that estrogen alone, estrogen plus progestin, and prog-estin alone, all appeared to *raise* the risk of breast cancer, but that age and the length of time the women took the hormones affected the significance of their risk. *The risk of breast cancer was* not *heightened when women were on HRT for five years or less, and the excess risk seemed to vanish two years after women stopped their HRT regimens.* However, women who were currently taking hor-mones and had been doing so longer than five years had an average increased risk about 40 percent greater than that of women not on hormones. Women aged 60 to 64, who were currently taking hormones longer than five years, showed the highest risk: about 70 percent greater than their contemporaries who were not on hormones.

The University of Washington Study compared a group of 537 women aged 50 to 64 from King County, Washington, who had been diagnosed with breast cancer between January 1, 1988 and June 30, 1990, with a group of

492 cancer-free women. About 60 percent of the women in both groups had taken hormones, and about 21 percent of the women in both groups had used combination estrogen/progestin HRT. Not only did the researchers fail to find an increased risk of breast cancer whether women did or did not use hormones, but in fact, women who used combination estrogen/progestin HRT for eight years or more had, if anything, a *reduced* risk of breast cancer.

In considering the results of both studies, it is hard to say whether the women taking the hormones had different risk factors and medical care. The Nurses' Health Study took in larger numbers of women and covered more years of follow-up than the Washington Study, but the Washington Study was a timely one and specifically designed to investigate present-day hormone replacement therapy. Back-and-forth findings like these on the issue of an HRT–breast cancer connection undoubtedly are going to go on for some time. *My belief is that women who choose to go on HRT slightly increase their risk of developing breast cancer, but that this rise must be weighed in terms of each woman's personal health history.* For example, HRT offers considerable health benefits for women who may be at high risk for heart disease and osteoporosis.

I also would like to see more attention paid to the results of the ongoing follow-up of the Breast Cancer Detection Demonstration Project (BCDDP), which began as a joint American Cancer Society/National Cancer Institute breast cancer screening program from 1973 to 1980. The BCDDP enlisted 283,222 women at 29 screening centers in 27 cities throughout the United States; a follow-up study of participating women was started by the NCI in 1979 and continues to this day. Between 1980 and 1989 information from about 50,000 of the women was analyzed to find out whether a relationship exists between taking estrogen alone (in a range of years, from under five to about 20) or as combination estrogen/progestin HRT (in a range of years, from under two to about four) and in situ (localized) or invasive breast cancer. Most of the women on hormones during those years were on estrogen alone; only a small percentage were on combination estrogen/ progestin. The follow-up found an overall slight increase in the risk of breast cancer among women who were on hormones when compared with nonusers, but what was new here was that *taking any type of hormones increased in situ more than invasive breast cancers.* (Bear in mind, however, that women who are on hormones, especially women in a breast screening program, are examined more frequently and thus are more likely to have an early in situ cancer detected than women who are not on HRT.)

Researchers also reported that women who took estrogen alone for 10 or more years had twice the risk of in situ cancers as women not on hormones, but the rate of invasive cancer did not rise with time. (It was hard to tell whether this applies to taking combination hormones, because the women in the study had taken combination HRT too short a time [less than five years] to evaluate an effect.)

WHY GO ON HORMONES AT ALL? THE PROS AND CONS OF HRT

Because the official word is that there is no conclusive proof that HRT affects the onset of breast cancer and that a woman who develops breast cancer may have done so with or without HRT, the best physicians today are trying to help women assess their own personal situation. It is a case-by-case process, and you and your doctor must decide what is best for you. HRT should not be prescribed lightly, but at the same time it should not be dismissed out of hand. It is definitely a source of mixed blessings.

Its benefits:

• HRT can eliminate severe menopausal symptoms that can include dizziness, nausea, heart palpitations, loss of concentration, frequent hot flashes, and vaginal dryness that leads to painful sexual intercourse. For many women, a continued, pleasurable sex life is the main reason to consider HRT.

• HRT greatly reduces the risk of heart disease and bone-thinning osteoporosis, two extremely severe health risks for women.

• HRT appears to offer protection against colon cancer.

• In several small studies estrogen has been found to improve memory for postmenopausal women, and there are early reports that HRT has improved the mental capacity of women with mild to moderate symptoms of Alzheimer's disease.

• HRT helps to maintain skin tone and elasticity as well as muscle mass.

Potential negative side effects of HRT:

• Possible weight gain, fatigue, depression, water retention, and irritability, to name a few. (Note: These symptoms can be alleviated by adjusting intake level and type of hormones.)

• After five years on HRT, risk of breast cancer may increase slightly. If HRT does not combine estrogen with progesterone and a woman has a uterus, there may also be an increase in the risk of endometrial (uterine lining) cancer.

• The estrogen in HRT can make existing fibroid tumors in the uterus grow until they cause pain and bleeding.

• HRT may contribute to existing conditions such as phlebitis, or liver, gallbladder, or thromboembolic (blood-clotting) disease.

You might want to consider HRT especially if you have: had a hysterectomy; risk factors for heart disease, such as smoking, high blood pressure, high-density lipoprotein cholesterol level below 35, diabetes, and a family history of heart disease or osteoporosis.

*You might **not** want to consider HRT if you have:* a family history of breast cancer (especially a mother or sister who developed breast cancer before menopause), fibroid tumors, phlebitis, or liver, gallbladder, or thromboembolic (blood-clotting) disease.

Your doctor should assess your health history with you, even though the final decision is ultimately yours. And if you choose HRT, you can help your body overcome potential risks by following a lifestyle that includes a low-fat diet high in vegetables and fruits, supplementation of antioxidant vitamins (beta-carotene, selenium, vitamins E and C), and at least four hours of exercise a week.

The finding of this study—the first of its kind showing a strong connection between hormones and in situ cancer—is one for all women to include in their mental assessment of whether to take HRT. And it reveals once again that the longer a woman stays on hormones, the greater may be her potential risk of breast cancer. Yet this, like all other studies on the HRT/breast cancer connection, needs further research before the finding should be considered proved.

FOR WOMEN WHO HAVE SURVIVED BREAST CANCER: IS HRT OFF-LIMITS FOREVER?

As more women survive breast cancer and live long into their menopausal years or enter menopause early due to the effects of chemotherapy, doctors have begun wondering whether HRT is viable for them. HRT can alleviate the menopausal symptoms of breast cancer survivors—the hot flashes, vaginal dryness, insomnia—and at the same time make its positive, heart-saving, bone-preserving health benefits accessible to them. The big question, of course, is, will a breast cancer survivor be more vulnerable to possible cancer-promoting effects of HRT than a woman who has never had breast cancer?

The *Physicians' Desk Reference*, better known as the *PDR* (guide to prescription drugs), states that hormones should not be given to anyone who has a history of having hormonally related cancers. So officially, HRT is off-limits to breast cancer survivors. But this has not stopped researchers from looking into the subject, because without randomized controlled studies, there is no conclusive proof that HRT actually promotes breast cancer among healthy women. (Again, my feeling is that HRT probably leads to a slight increase in risk.)

A number of analyses have been done using health records to compare the rate of breast cancer recurrence in survivors who have taken estrogen alone to the recurrence rate of survivors who have not used hormone therapy. Several of these analyses have concluded that estrogen, on its own, does not make the risk of breast cancer any higher among survivors than among the general population. Hormone replacement has even been seen as protective. A 1995 Australian study headed by Dr. John Eden of the Royal Hospital for Women offers evidence that estrogen may prove to be not only safe but even helpful for breast cancer survivors. In this study of 901 women who had received a range of surgical treatments and chemotherapy for a range of breast cancers, 90 had taken hormone therapy. Most of the women were using continuous, combined estrogen/progestin HRT. When compared with nonusers, the women on HRT fared much better: there were no deaths, and only 7 percent experienced a recurrence of breast cancer, compared with 10 percent of the group dying and 17 percent recurrence among nonusers. However, the use of hormones was gauged at a median 1.5 years—not a long time period. In studies looking for breast cancer risk among healthy women on HRT, effects of the hormones have not shown up until 5 years or more of hormone use. It is my feeling that this study is not of enough duration to support recommending HRT to breast cancer survivors.

In a small five-year pilot study still in progress at the University of Texas M.D. Anderson Cancer Center, Dr. Rena Bassilopou-Sellin is heading a team of researchers monitoring 160 women who have been treated for localized stage I or II breast cancer and have been disease-free for at least two years. The women are divided into one group that is on low- to moderate-dose estrogen—without progestin—and another that does not take any hormones. The women's cancers are mostly estrogen receptor negative (positive receptors are proteins that latch onto estrogen and, fueled by the hormone, grow; tumors with negative receptors are not stimulated by estrogen and do not grow). Midway through the study there has been no recurrence of breast cancer among any of the women in either group, and Dr. Sellin echoes the feelings of a growing body of physicians when she says, "I think that placing a taboo on HRT for breast cancer survivors does not make sense anymore. We have very, very limited safety information, and I would hate to be an early enthusiast and change a practice that has at least oncologically served us reasonably well. As this study matures and other studies begin to look at other subgroups or types of approaches, we will get some real data upon which we can base some recommendations."

Dr. Nicholas Robert, medical oncologist at Fairfax Hospital in Falls Church, Virginia, and cochairperson for the Eastern Cooperative Oncology Group's (ECOG) breast committee, is not only involved in researching HRT among breast cancer survivors (an NCI/ECOG study of HRT use among women on tamoxifen), but his committee has been involved in developing guidelines for physicians to use in this area. "Since we do not have a lot of good evidence for long-term hormone replacement for breast cancer survivors, what we are trying to do is to intelligently map out territory for some of the issues—what some of the tradeoffs might be—so that a woman can make intelligent decisions," Dr. Robert has explained.

The idea of prescribing HRT to breast cancer survivors at all is so new and the research data on the subject so scant that it seems too early to think about recommendations. However, because there is no conclusive proof that HRT increases the risk of recurrent breast cancer, a growing number of doctors want to improve the quality of life of breast cancer survivors and offer them the positive cardiovascular and bone-strengthening benefits of HRT. Some women who have been disease-free for a number of years and who have assessed their health with their doctors are already trying HRT. Women survivors who perhaps should not be considered for HRT are those who are genetically proved to be at risk for breast cancer or women who have had breast cancers with positive estrogen receptors.

My instinct is to exercise caution in this area. In laboratory experiments with genetically susceptible animals, hormones have promoted the growth of hormonally sensitive cancers. Before beginning any type of hormone replacement therapy, I think breast cancer survivors should wait for more research findings, especially from the more highly regarded randomized trials, where different groups are randomly assigned to receive either hormones or ineffective placebos. The symptoms of menopause, especially when brought on by chemotherapy, can be devastating, so it is understandable why women would want to consider HRT. And breast cancer survivors, who are at higher than normal risk of heart disease or bone-thinning osteoporosis, would certainly be drawn to hormone therapy. However, until more solid evidence can prove the safety of HRT for breast cancer survivors, I advise alternative treatments as the first line of defense.

Low-fat diets that include estrogen-blocking foods such as tofu (see Chapter 6) and exercise are known to minimize menopausal symptoms and prevent osteoporosis. Dietary supplements of vitamin B complex (100 mg), vitamin D (400 IU), calcium (1,500 to 2,000 mg), and iron help protect against cardiovascular disease, diabetes, and osteoporosis. Some physicians report that vitamin E (400 to 1600 IU daily) cures hot flashes, and some women in my care have reported successfully fighting hot flashes with the Chinese herb ginseng. I also recommend drinking eight glasses of water a day to flush the system and keep all the cells in balance.

A NEW DRUG TO FIGHT OSTEOPOROSIS

One of the major benefits of hormone replacement therapy has been the bone-strengthening power of estrogen. Recently the first of a new group of nonhormonal drugs designed to fight the bone-thinning disease osteoporosis has reached the market. Alendronate sodium (Fosamax) blocks the breakdown of bone during osteoporosis and allows the body's natural bone building to continue. So, if a woman taking calcium and vitamin supplements and exercising regularly still feels that she needs help in building bone mass, she now has an alternative to HRT. (The reported side effects of Fosamax are mild nausea, heartburn, gas, and abdominal pain.)

HRT: THE CHOICE IS YOURS

In all fairness, even with its drawbacks, HRT has quite a number of benefits and ought to be weighed by women entering menopause, but the alternatives should also be considered. Whatever you choose, for maximum health, combine your choices with a lifestyle that includes a low-fat diet (see Chapter 6) supplemented with antioxidants (beta-carotene, selenium, vitamins E and C), and a four-hour per-week exercise regimen (see Chapter 7).

CHAPTER TWELVE

When You Want to Reshape Your Breasts: The Latest Word on Cosmetic Surgery

"After nursing two kids, all I had left was nipples. Nipples. That was it. Six months before I had my implants, you couldn't pick up a paper without reading about silicone and all the problems. But I felt that with the saline implants, the risks were small. And I was willing to take those risks to get my breasts back again."

–A 38-YEAR-OLD WOMAN, TWO YEARS AFTER HER BREAST AUGMENTATION AND STILL PLEASED WITH HER DECISION TO UNDERGO COSMETIC SURGERY

On January 6, 1992, the FDA's moratorium on silicone gel implants set off shock waves that are still reverberating throughout the world of cosmetic breast surgery—because breast augmentation, or enlargement, was and still is the most common procedure requested by women who want to change the size and shape of their breasts. Implants may have changed since that fateful January day, but women's desire to seek cosmetic surgery for larger, smaller, higher, or more symmetrical breasts, has not.

I urge my readers to understand their motivation before they delve into the different aspects of the operations and the latest techniques described in this chapter. Cosmetic breast surgery can be quite beneficial if performed for sound reasons. I have seen women who have had cosmetic breast surgery that gave them pride in their body they had never had before. I am aware of breast reductions that have eliminated back problems and breast augmentations that have helped women regain their figures after breastfeeding. I believe that these best-case scenarios occurred because the women clearly understood why they were making an appointment with a plastic surgeon, and they did not have unrealistic expectations that their lives would be dramatically different after surgery.

GETTING THE BEST RESULTS: FIRST, SCHEDULE A CONSULTATION WITH YOURSELF

The operations that cosmetic surgeons perform last a lifetime; the scars are permanent. Therefore, it is vital that you understand your motivation for wanting breast surgery before you undergo any procedure. Every woman who is contemplating a change in her breasts should consider the following:

• **Why do I want this surgery?** The right reason for seeking cosmetic breast surgery pretty much boils down to: "I have always felt unhappy with the size (shape, appearance) of my breasts." You may have a medical reason, such as a breast reduction for large, painful breasts, but the motivation must be personal as well. Even feeling that you need the operation to further your career as an actress or model, for example, is valid, as long as *you* want the surgery. A woman should never consider having breast surgery for a boyfriend, spouse, or anyone else. This is *your* body! If you answer the question, "Why do you want this surgery?" with "My boyfriend wants me to . . . ," "My mother thinks my breasts are too big . . . ," "My husband likes women with large breasts . . . ," then you are *not* self-motivated. Having surgery to please someone else is flirting with danger to your mental health and, considering the potential of the mind/body connection, your physical well-being.

• **How does my mate feel about my desire to have surgery?** While a woman should never have surgery to please someone else—no operation, no matter how routine, is risk-free—she will need the support of the people close to her while she is healing. A partner whose attitude is either positive or "I am with you, whatever you want" is important to making this experience a good one. Sometimes a cosmetic surgeon who spots conflict in a couple will suggest postponing surgery until they are in agreement.

• **What are my expectations?** If you hope that reshaped breasts will change your life, then you are not a good candidate for surgery. A new figure may help you feel better about the way you look, which in turn may give you a more positive outlook, but to expect major life changes is a mistake.

• **What is my medical history?** A family history of breast cancer or other medical conditions such as diabetes and heart or pulmonary disease could be important in determining which procedures you should, or should not, have. While you are contemplating breast surgery, try to remember all the events in your breast health history that may affect your surgical options so that you can discuss them with a doctor.

CHOOSE THE RIGHT COSMETIC SURGEON
FOR YOUR NEEDS

Every woman wants to know that she has selected the doctor who will help her achieve her goals. Here is my best advice for finding the "right" cosmetic surgeon:

• **Get a meaningful recommendation.** A friend who has undergone cosmetic surgery herself, a family doctor, or an operating nurse is an excellent place to start. As always, your surgeon should be board-certified. (The American Society of Plastic and Reconstructive Surgeons operates a toll-free information line; call 800-635-0635 for a list of five ASPRS board-certified members near you.) Make a point of asking about the doctor's area of expertise. Only 40 percent of plastic surgeons work exclusively in cosmetic surgery, and while it is rare to find one focusing on just breasts (most also work with noses, eyelids, and liposuction), you will want to narrow your field of choice to a surgeon with experience in the technique you desire.

NOTE: A new patient came to me last year with horribly distorted breasts after a traditional reduction procedure. When I asked who had performed the operation, she gave me the name of a respected burn surgeon. "I told him what I was there for," she said, "and his response was, 'Oh, good. I haven't done one of those for a while.' " *Don't let this happen to you.*

• **Believe in first impressions.** Once you narrow your list to one or two candidates, use your time in the waiting room to form an impression. Often just by sitting in a doctor's office, observing your surroundings and the other patients, you can get a feel for whether you and a surgeon will be compatible aesthetically.

• **Take along pictures.** The more explicit you can be about your preferences, the clearer a surgeon can be about how closely he will be able to match the desired result. "If someone says, 'I want to be a C cup,' but then shows me a picture of a woman who's much larger, right away I have a better idea," a cosmetic surgeon told me recently.

Warning: Though many doctors now use two-dimensional computer visualization to give women some notion of how they might look postoperatively, this technique gives a necessarily idealized image. Often it is impossible to duplicate what the computer shows. For this reason, imaging is best viewed as an intriguing conversational tool.

• **Request a look at the doctor's own before-and-after photos.** If a doctor is unwilling to show you his own best and worst outcomes—understandable since the "bests" can set up false expectations, whereas the "worsts" may stem from factors beyond a surgeon's control (individual differences in scar formation, say)—ask for a random sampling of patients and/or textbook photos of operations gone wrong.

• **Ask for referrals to other patients who have had the surgery you are**

considering. A cosmetic surgeon usually has received permission from former patients to allow prospective patients to call them. He knows how important it is to a prospective patient to be able to talk to another woman who has undergone the surgery being considered. He should willingly give you names and numbers, although I should issue a caution here: One woman interviewed the former patient of a plastic surgeon at length before asking her informant's last name. It turned out that she had been chatting with the surgeon's wife! So much for an unbiased opinion!

• **Notice whether the surgeon is raising the issues that you considered privately in your consultation with yourself.** A good doctor will interview you while you are interviewing him and ask you why you want the surgery and what your expectations are. Cosmetic surgeons may decline to operate on women for physical reasons, such as women who are requesting surgeries that are inappropriate for their bodies, or for psychological reasons, such as those whose expectations cannot possibly be met through surgery. If a doctor declines to take you as a patient, ask for an explanation before you consult a different physician.

• **Ask for a thorough explanation of the risks involved.** Possible post-surgery effects of different breast operations are described in this chapter, but you want to know that your surgeon will tell you everything. Especially if you are considering more than one procedure, you want to be sure that your surgeon explains the pluses and minuses of each. This will also be an opportunity to assess how the two of you communicate.

• **Ask to schedule a second consultation.** During a first visit a woman is sizing up a doctor, but a second consultation can be a useful opportunity to get more specific. For instance, you can make sure that a board-certified anesthesiologist who specializes in aesthetic procedures will be present throughout your operation. That rule applies whether you will be under general or local sedation. Rare though it is, people have died during cosmetic surgery, almost invariably from the kinds of respiratory or cardiac problems that anesthesiologists are trained to monitor while the surgeon is busy doing other things.

KNOW THE FACTS ABOUT THE ACTUAL OPERATION

The Cost

As of this writing, a surgeon's fees usually range from $2,500 to $3,500 for breast augmentation; from $2,800 to $3,500 for a breast lift, and from $4,500 to $6,000 for breast reduction, with the highest prices in New York and California. While few insurance companies cover cosmetic surgeries, which they consider "elective procedures," breast reduction is often covered. Overly large breasts can play a role in medical problems from dermatitis to degenerative spinal disease. Many companies that agree to cover breast reduction, however, demand the removal of a certain amount of tissue, usually about a pound, from each breast, and this is not always feasible, especially if you are petite. Yet if less tissue is removed, the reduction may not be covered.

On the other hand, some insurance companies will not only refuse to pay for reduction, but they will not even cover reconstruction after *mastectomy!* And while compensation may be available for implant removal ($2,000 to $4,000), future implant-related problems generally are not.

The Pain Factor

The good news is that in general, cosmetic breast surgery involves relatively little discomfort. Dr. David Hidalgo, chief of plastic surgery at New York's Memorial Sloan-Kettering Cancer Center, says, "The breast has been described as a modified skin gland, and conceptually, that's right on target. Most of this surgery is superficial, involving only the skin and the tissue just underneath. No bones, organs, or even, in most cases, muscles, are affected, so there is not a lot of pain." The most discomfort comes with breast augmentation, because the implants are placed under the muscle, but even there, discomfort is confined to the few days after surgery.

The Breast Cancer Connection

No link has ever been found between cosmetic breast surgery and cancer of the breast. Ironically, one study has suggested a possible protective effect from silicone implants, but this finding may have occurred because doctors tended to shy away from using implants in women with family histories of breast cancer.

THREE STEPS TO TAKE BEFORE SURGERY

No matter which operation you have, there are three steps you can take beforehand to ensure the best of all possible outcomes:

- **Get a baseline mammogram.** This is especially important for women 35 or older or those with breast cancer in the family, but others may want to consider mammography, too. "I tell patients it's as if they decided to take up jogging after being sedentary," says Dr. Alan Matarasso, a plastic and reconstructive surgeon at Albert Einstein College of Medicine in New York. "Getting a baseline EKG before you change those numbers with exercise is always a smart idea." Dr. Matarasso also recommends a thorough breast examination by a doctor who specializes in treatment of breasts. Also, women who want breast augmentation should be checked for cysts to avoid needle aspiration once an implant is in place.
- **Avoid medications that promote bleeding.** These include aspirin, the

nonsteroidal anti-inflammatories, Alka-Seltzer, and vitamin E (your surgeon will give you a complete list), all of which are contraindicated for two weeks before the operation.

• **Learn all you can about the surgery you have chosen.** It would be hard to overstate the case for familiarizing yourself with the surgery you are about to undergo. Get to know your options—there may be quite a few—along with the special risks of each. Don't be afraid to ask questions—e.g., What kind of anesthesia will be used? (See box.) Will the surgeon put you in a seated position for part of the procedure (thought by many to be necessary for balanced, symmetrical results)? How can you help speed healing along?

RESHAPING YOUR BREASTS THROUGH SURGERY: THE PROCEDURES—BREAST AUGMENTATION, OR SURGERY FOR BIGGER BREASTS

An Update on the Silicone Breast Implant Controversy

*"Women considering breast implants deserve
to know whether these products are safe. . . .
I'm calling for a delay in the use of these
products until our advisory panel can meet
to consider new information. . . ."*
                    —FDA COMMISSIONER DAVID A. KESSLER, M.D.,
                                        ON JANUARY 6, 1992

At the time of Dr. Kessler's announcement, some 150,000 women were receiving silicone gel implants annually, 80 percent of them for cosmetic reasons alone. Reports had begun to surface linking the implants with connective tissue disorders in which the immune system attacks the body's own cells. The result is wide-ranging problems such as crippling joint pain and swelling (rheumatoid arthritis), hardened and thickened skin (scleroderma), skin rashes, and kidney damage (lupus), and some of these disorders are potentially fatal. A spate of lawsuits against Dow Corning, chief manufacturer of the implants, followed, resulting in Kessler's statement. Not long afterward an FDA advisory committee concluded that the moratorium should continue because safety of the silicone implants was still unproved.

The upshot: a snowballing of legal claims against Dow Corning—after a $4 billion class action settlement, the corporate giant filed for bankruptcy in May 1995—and a continuing controversy in which some feel that the FDA acted too little, too late, while others contend that Dow Corning was the victim of a panic attack. Meanwhile, for most women considering cosmetic breast augmentation, silicone implants are effectively off-limits until the FDA finishes its data-gathering mission—the target date is 1998.

UPDATE: A NEW DRUG FOR GENERAL ANESTHESIA

Most cosmetic breast surgery is done under general anesthesia (although augmentation is sometimes performed with only a local anesthetic), and this procedure has been made vastly simpler by a short-acting, revolutionary new drug called propofol (Diprivan), which is administered by injection.

In use since the late 1980s, propofol has one important advantage over its older counterparts: It does not lead to vomiting. Earlier drugs stayed in the bloodstream longer, were more toxic, and often caused postoperative retching, which raised blood pressure and increased the incidence of hematomas, or blood clots, underneath the skin. With propofol, these complications have been dramatically reduced. Also, propofol is nonaddictive. No matter how many injections are given during surgery (for longer procedures, several may be needed), there is no additive effect. An hour after an operation, people who have had propofol are fully alert.

UNDERSTANDING SILICONE'S PAST

Used for breast reconstruction and augmentation for 30 years before Dr. Kessler's announcement, silicone was originally developed as a sealant and coolant during World War II. But because silicone implants had entered the market before 1976, when the FDA was granted the authority to regulate medical devices, they were temporarily exempt from new safety requirements. However, the operative word is "temporarily"; Dow Corning and other manufacturers were required to gather evidence of their product's safety for the FDA.

What was not at issue was a drawback that had been well documented with both silicone and saline implants: a high (20 to 40 percent) incidence of capsular contracture, the formation of firm fibrous tissue around an implant. The body responds to any foreign object, a pacemaker or an artificial joint for instance, by forming a "capsule" around it. This can be a benefit with a breast implant, because capsule formation can hold it in place. The problem arises when capsules contract and force an implant into the smallest volume possible—a sphere. Then the implant can feel very firm and distorted. Lesser capsule formation is an aesthetic rather than a health issue, but severe capsular contracture can be painful. It was not capsular contracture, however, but the suspected silicone–autoimmune connection that prompted removal of the implants from the market pending further tests.

However, Silicone Does Not Seem as Bad as It Did in 1992. The courts have handed down multimillion-dollar awards on the presumption of autoimmune health risks related to silicone breast implants, but seven large epidemiological studies completed since the FDA action point to the opposite conclusion: **that there is no silicone–autoimmune system link.** (An eighth major study, which appeared in a 1996 *Journal of the American Medical Association*, showed a modest increase in risk. Dr. Charles Hennekens of Brigham and Women's Hospital in Boston considered surveys of over 400,000 women between 1962 and 1991, and found that one case of connective tissue disease a year might arise for every 3,000 women with implants.)

In a study published in 1994, scientists at the Mayo Clinic compared the medical records of all 749 women in Olmsted County, Minnesota, who had received silicone breast implants between 1964 and 1991, with twice that number of Olmsted County women who had not received implants. The Mayo scientists found five cases of connective tissue diseases in the implant recipients and 10 in the group of women who had never had implants— exactly what might have been expected if the implants had no effect.

In 1995, as part of the ongoing Nurses' Health Study, Dr. Matthew Laing and his colleagues, also working at Brigham and Women's Hospital, analyzed the health records of 87,000 nurses—1,183 of them with silicone breast implants—over a 15-year period, from 1975 to 1990, well before the silicone uproar began. Their finding: Women with implants were, if anything, *slightly less likely* than others to develop connective tissue diseases or even to complain of symptoms connected with "silicone syndrome" such as aches and pains, migraine headache, and fatigue. So convincing was this evidence that by February 1995, France, which had withdrawn silicone implants from the market, put them back, and 10 months later, in Great Britain, where sales had never stopped, the British Medical Devices Agency concluded once again that silicone implants were safe.

Nevertheless, the Controversy Continues. Critics contend that the studies have not adequately evaluated the risks of developing diseases as rare as those in question. They also point out that women with implants may have symptoms that don't conform to usual diagnostic criteria so that a causal connection may be missed. Another concern, as yet unsubstantiated, is that small amounts of silicone that leak from the implants could show up in breast milk. A 1994 study by two Long Island doctors at Schneider Children's Hospital/Albert Einstein College of Medicine, showed that six of eight breastfeeding infants of mothers with implants, all of whom were having digestive problems, had suffered esophageal damage, a possible early sign of scleroderma, an autoimmune disease. (Despite this provocative finding, Temple University pediatrician Jonathan Flick, in an editorial accompanying the study's publication in the *Journal of the American Medical Association*, advised breastfeeding mothers with implants to continue nursing. "The benefits of breast-feeding are well-established," he wrote, "while the potential adverse effects reported [by the researchers] are yet to be confirmed.")

It may be, as some have theorized, that some people are simply allergic to silicone and respond to its presence with autoimmune symptoms, while others suffer no ill effects. One research team claims to be close to isolating a gene that would make its carriers unusually susceptible to the presence of any foreign substance in the body, silicone included. Until the FDA concludes its evidence gathering, however, silicone remains a subject for debate and not a genuine cosmetic option.

Today's Available Option for Breast Augmentation: Saline Implants

Today, according to the American Society of Plastic and Reconstructive Surgeons (ASPRS), the number of breast augmentations is about 40,000 per year, an increase of some 8,000 since the low point in 1992. "It fluctuates with the media," explains Dr. David Hidalgo, chief of plastic surgery at Memorial Sloan-Kettering Cancer Center in New York. "When there are reports that implants are bad for you—meaning silicone implants—the numbers drop, but they always seem to come back. I'm seeing more women today for augmentation than I did five years ago, which can probably be accounted for both by the very real need for this kind of surgery and the perception of saline as a safer alternative." (And in most cases saline implants are the only kind available. With the FDA moratorium, today's silicone implants are only available to women enrolled in clinical trials involving silicone: women with mastectomies, serious breast injury or asymmetry, or those whose old implants have ruptured.) Because the FDA has deemed saline implants potentially less hazardous than their silicone counterparts, they have been kept on the market pending further study.

Indeed, the most common complaint about saline is that it feels and looks less natural than silicone gel. While viscous silicone more closely resembles the density of mammary tissue, saline feels like the salt water it is. Also, silicone gel retains a smoothness even when the implant is compressed; saline, a liquid, is less able to do this, and therefore ripples are sometimes seen.

Like a silicone gel implant, a saline implant is encased in a silicone shell (no substitutes for silicone, the most inert solid substance known, have yet been found) with a limited lifespan; most recipients will need to replace this at least once in their lifetime. No research data is available on just how implants eventually wear out. When a large volume of saline leaks, however, you'll know it; the breasts deflate within hours or days while the harmless saline is absorbed by the body.

(NOTE: When silicone gel leaks [or "bleeds"], the viscous gel stays, for the most part, in place, so that the breast's appearance may remain the same. Meanwhile, minute particles of silicone—which the body is unable to use or break down—may travel under the armpit and the pectoral muscle, potentially causing a host of complications if critics of silicone are correct.)

While a few experts have suggested a potential for bacterial and fungal infection after a saline leak, no complaints have been reported to date. Instead, the most serious medical reservations regarding these implants concern not the saline but the silicone shell. In 1994 doctors at the Mount Sinai Medical Center in New York examined more than 100 women whose saline implants had been removed for various reasons; about half had had implants in which the surface of the silicone shell was smooth, the others a newer form of textured silicone implants thought to further diminish the risks of capsular contracture. Their surprising finding? While there was no silicone in the breast tissue of the recipients of the smooth implant, virtually all the women with textured implants had silicone particles in surrounding tissue. Of these, three-fourths had tissue containing cells not occurring naturally in the breast—a sign of possible autoimmune reaction. Still, that isn't necessarily a cause for alarm, reports Dr. Michelle Copeland, a plastic and reconstructive surgeon at Mt. Sinai who coauthored the study. "The small doses of silicone we're talking about are not much when compared to a whole implant filled with gel. And there's no evidence that the fragments travel the way the gel does; they may be confined to breast tissue alone."

Certainly further studies are needed. It may be that this kind of "shedding" causes no problems—for that matter, it still has not been proved that silicone itself is dangerous. And, as Dr. Copeland puts it, "Everything's a trade-off—there may be advantages to the textured implant in terms of capsule formation and mammography. But a patient is entitled to all the information I have. So these are issues I discuss with anyone interested in augmentation so that together we can weigh the pros and cons."

Breast Implants of the Future

Since saline is not without its drawbacks, researchers are working on alternative fillers for implants, among them soybean oil and polyethylene glycol (PEG), a nontoxic compound used in toothpaste, hand lotion, and eye drops. Peanut oil implants are already available in Europe under a clinical trial. And the technique of liposuctioning the body's own fat to use in an implant shell is being done in Australia, Brazil, Japan, and other parts of the world. Yet while the fillers are different, the implant shells are still made of silicone.

Theoretically, all the new fillers could be safely absorbed or metabolized by the body in the event of an implant leak. They also have the advantage of being less opaque than existing implants—i.e., less likely to interfere with mammograms—while more like breast tissue to the touch. In view of the complex health and legal issues involved, getting them to the general public may be five or ten years away.

TEXTURED VS. SMOOTH: WHICH IMPLANT IS RIGHT FOR YOU?

Textured Implants

ADVANTAGES
- Less hard capsule formation. The rate of hard capsular contracture in women with textured implants is reportedly much lower, possibly because the texture prevents an organized capsule from forming.

DISADVANTAGES
- Possible "rippling." Some doctors have observed that the sandbar-like effect sometimes seen at the edges of saline implants is more common with the textured shell; other doctors disagree.
- Possible "shedding." Despite the need for further study, the Mt. Sinai finding that small particles of silicone from these implants make their way into surrounding tissue may be a factor for women concerned about possible autoimmune or breastfeeding implications.

Smooth Implants

ADVANTAGES
- Less observed rippling.
- No "shedding" according to the evidence to date.

DISADVANTAGES
- Higher risk of hard capsule formation.

As a result of this last factor, the textured implant is now the most popular in this country, used at an estimated rate of two to one. In general, surgeons believe they are aesthetically superior to smooth implants.

Decisions to Make with Your Doctor Before Breast Augmentation Surgery

ON SELECTING AN IMPLANT

Do you want a textured or smooth implant? See box above on advantages and disadvantages of each type.

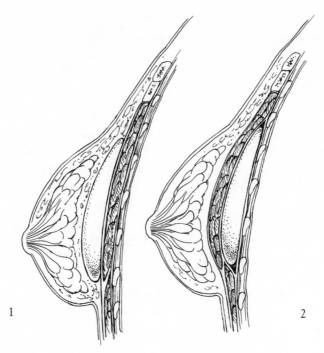

During breast augmentation, a saline breast implant can be either
1) subglandular, between the breast gland and the underlying muscle, or
2) submuscular, underneath muscle on the chest wall, generally the preferred
procedure.

Should your implant be round or shaped? (See box on "Sizing Up the Shape of Implanted Breasts.") Shaped implants are only available with textured surfaces.

ON THE PLACEMENT OF AN IMPLANT

An implant can be "subglandular," placed between the breast gland and the underlying muscle, or "submuscular," placed underneath muscles on the chest wall. Although some surgeons favor the appearance of subglandular implants, especially in women with highly developed pectoral muscles or a lot of loose breast skin, submuscular implants are generally preferred. (Although the musculature of the chest involves three muscles, the majority of surgeons perform subpectoral implants only.) When placed underneath the breast muscle, saline implants are less likely to ripple or have capsular contracture.

ON THE PLACEMENT OF THE INCISION

A small incision—from 1½ to 3 inches—can be made either under a woman's armpit, in the fold underneath her breast, or around her areola, the dark ring around her nipple. The implant is inserted through the incision

SIZING UP THE SHAPE OF IMPLANTED BREASTS

When Dr. Loren Eskenazi, a plastic and reconstructive surgeon in private practice in San Francisco, put ads in a local paper asking for volunteers to undergo a state-of-the-art scanning process to help her learn more about the real shape of women's breasts, she apparently hit a nerve. "A lot of the women who responded told me they had never been able to buy a bra that fit," Dr. Eskenazi told me, "and I knew from my practice that while implants came in all sizes, the shape choices were limited to round, round, and round."

In a study completed in October 1995, Dr. Eskenazi analyzed the size and shape of the breasts of 1,000 women, using the kind of sophisticated three-dimensional laser imaging that created special effects for *Jurassic Park* and *Terminator II*. "I looked at factors like the position of the breasts on the chest wall, their width, the fullness above and below," Dr. Eskenazi explained. "What I found is that real breasts tend to be fuller in the lower part than the top, a bit the reverse of the Wonderbra look."

As the years go by, breasts are more affected by gravity than other parts of the body, so Dr. Eskenazi is currently gathering data on what she calls "the fourth dimension," or time. Using her sophisticated imaging on women who come to her for augmentation, she performs four scans: (1) beforehand, to make sure women get the right implant, (2) postoperatively, and then twice more: (3) at six months, and (4) at one year. When viewed on a computer monitor, those scans answer important questions: Did the implants achieve the look the women asked for? Did the implants ripple? Did the augmented breasts keep their shapes? "Those are things we can only make educated guesses about now, so I'm creating an objective, quantified knowledge base that others will be able to draw on," Dr. Eskenazi has said.

At the moment Dr. Eskenazi is the only cosmetic surgeon using pre- and postoperative laser scanning, but manufacturers are taking note of women's desire for more realistic implants. In the fall of 1994, the first nonround saline implants were launched by Mentor and McGhan and are now widely available. Mentor also plans to produce a new line of implants based on Dr. Eskenazi's work.

and placed, as previously described, in a subglandular or submuscular fashion. Women with a poorly defined breastfold or a small areola diameter are good candidates for an armpit incision, which is least likely to disturb the breast gland and thus nipple sensation. (See box on "Endoscopic

'Bellybutton Surgery' " for a description of a more complicated breast augmentation procedure, which stirs controversy but remains an option.)

What to Expect During a Breast Augmentation Operation

Once you and your doctor have agreed on the type of implant, its placement, and the location of your incision, the operation can often be scheduled on an outpatient basis to keep costs down. (If you go this route, it is a good idea to make sure your doctor's office facility is accredited by the American Society of Plastic and Reconstructive Surgeons [ASPRS], which sets minimum standards on everything from ventilation to sterile technique.) A submuscular augmentation, the most prevalent kind, is performed with general anesthesia. (See box on "Update: A New Drug for General Anesthesia," page 157). The operation takes from one and one-half to three hours.

After surgery, women who have had breast augmentation with submuscular implants have reported feeling more discomfort than women who have undergone subglandular placements. Most of the discomfort from the submuscular surgery subsides within 48 hours, however. Skin sutures, if not of the "dissolving" type, are removed within five to seven days so that they do not leave marks, and most normal activities can be resumed. Strenuous exercise is allowed at four to six weeks.

After Breast Augmentation: Possible Postsurgery Effects

Infection and abnormal bleeding are a risk with any operation, but both are rare, from 1 to 2 percent, in augmentation surgery. Other complications include:

• **Hard capsular contracture.** According to the ASPRS, about 18 percent of women who receive saline implants experience severe internal scarring, the hard capsular contracture mentioned earlier. This can occur anywhere from two weeks to 15 years after surgery. As mentioned before, the likelihood of this happening is lessened with textured and/or submuscular implants. In the worst cases of hard capsular contracture, the breasts are hard, painful, and possibly deformed, and the implants must be removed. To prevent capsular contracture, women with smooth implants should massage the area twice a day. "By moving the implant," says Dr. Alan Matarasso, "you're putting an air pocket between it and the tissue, keeping the capsule from closing down."

• **Permanent loss or lessening of nipple sensation.** This happens in about 2 percent of cases, generally because sensory nerves have been stretched in the course of making the breast pocket. For the same reason there is also a slight chance of diminished feeling in the breast itself, especially in the case of a large implant that needs a large pocket.

ENDOSCOPIC "BELLYBUTTON SURGERY"

In a new and, what a number of doctors consider "questionable," alternative to standard breast augmentation techniques, an inch-long incision is made in the navel, and a tube with a tiny camera, or "endoscope" at the end, is inserted through the opening. The tube is then tunneled (through underlying skin tissue, not muscle) from the navel to an area just beneath the breast. Next, an implant shell is folded and inserted through the same tube. The camera helps the surgeon guide the implant shell into place under the breast tissue. Finally, the shell, which has a tiny nozzle similar to one you might find on a bicycle tire, is filled with saline by syringe and sealed before the tube is withdrawn.

- Advantages: Only one tiny scar at the navel, with none on the breasts or armpits.
- Disadvantages: Implants can only be placed under the gland (not under the muscle), increasing risks for capsular contracture and inaccurate mammography readings. While some surgeons report few problems with the procedure itself, others cite a high incidence of abnormal bleeding (from insertion of the viewing tube) and difficulty positioning the implant properly.

Even doctors wary of bellybutton surgery, however, may use the endoscope as a visualization tool during traditional breast augmentation, such as through the armpit. According to the American Society of Plastic and Reconstructive Surgeons, 17 percent of its members now use some form of endoscopic technique during breast augmentation surgery.

- **Breastfeeding problems.** See the box "Will Cosmetic Surgery Affect Your Ability to Breastfeed?" in this chapter.

BREAST REDUCTION (MAMMOPLASTY)

Most breast reduction involves fairly extensive scarring, but this is a drawback many large-breasted women are willing to accept. "These are my happiest patients," says Dr. David Hidalgo. "Any plastic surgeon will tell you that." Or as Dr. Alan Matarasso puts it, "I've never had a reduction patient say, 'The scars are worse than what I lived with before.' "

One of my own patients typifies the kind of woman who may seek a breast reduction. Married and 47 years old, she wore a double-D cup bra by the eighth grade and was horribly self-conscious about her shape. "Buying bras was a nightmare, going shopping for bathing suits a major trauma. While my friends were wearing bikinis, I was stuck with matronly one-pieces from the women's department, always with uncomfortable underwires." To camouflage her buxom figure, she took to wearing shapeless sweaters. But the physical problems could not be covered up. "Apart from the classic grooved shoulders and aching back, I had a dowager's hump I didn't know was from my breasts until I had surgery and it went away." Since her operation, she reports feeling more self-confident. She is buying bikinis and crop tops. And her sex life has undergone an exciting transformation. "It's not about my husband, who went along with the operation just because I wanted it, but about me. For the first time I'm seeing myself as a sexual, sexy person. And that affects you in bed. It's a bonus I never expected."

Your doctor will explain how much reduction is possible in your case: Most patients want to be a "B" cup, but that may not be feasible. "The base of the breast—the diameter—is a given, something no surgeon can change," reminds Dr. Alan Matarasso. "If you keep making breasts smaller and smaller, you'll eventually wind up with pancakes. You have to respect the natural contours of the chest."

Decisions to Make with Your Doctor Before Breast Reduction

A mammoplasty has three goals:

1. to diminish breast volume,
2. to make the areola/nipple complex higher and smaller, because overly large breasts tend to have overly large areolas, and
3. to eliminate any "ptosis" or sag.

Before a breast reduction can be performed, a woman and her doctor must agree about:

• **How much tissue will be removed?** The answer to this question will determine everything from the choice of procedure to the various refinements of the nipple/areolar complex. If a surgeon declines to do as large a reduction as you would like, by all means see someone else. Beware, though: there are always a few unscrupulous practitioners who will agree to do whatever you want whether or not it's sensible or safe.

• **What technique will be used?** Here again, the amount of tissue to be removed will be an issue, as will the skill and experience of your plastic surgeon. Other factors to consider: Are you sure you will never want to breastfeed? How important is it to you to minimize the risk of losing nipple sensation? There are literally dozens of variations on the basic procedures described in the section that follows and in the box "Some New Variations on Breast Reduction Methods." Together, you and your surgeon can choose a technique that fits your special needs.

What to Expect During a Breast Reduction Operation

After the amount of skin and tissue to be removed is determined, a pattern is drawn on the breast. In a traditional breast reduction technique, three incisions are made: one around the areola, another in a vertical line from the bottom of the areola to the crease under the breast, and a third along the length of the crease itself. Together these three incisions are called the "anchor" or "inverted T." (For departures from this traditional method, see the box "Some New Variations on Breast Reduction Methods.")

Contrary to popular myth, the nipple is not routinely removed and grafted back on, a procedure called "free nipple graft" that commonly results in lost sensation from severed nerves. More often, the nipple remains attached to the breast so that neurovascular function is maintained while tissue beneath and on either side of the nipple is removed. Nipple removal and subsequent grafting is usually necessary only in large reductions, perhaps 5 percent of cases. With today's improved techniques and in only a few exceptional cases, women have been able to breastfeed after a free nipple graft! (For more on breastfeeding after reduction, see the box "Will Cosmetic Surgery Affect Your Ability to Breastfeed?" in this chapter.)

Breast reduction surgery generally takes three and one-half hours or longer, depending on breast size. Sutures are removed five days after the operation, and all activities can be resumed within four to six weeks.

After Breast Reduction: Possible Postsurgery Effects

As with breast augmentation, there is a small risk of infection and abnormal bleeding from mammoplasty.

Other possible complications may include:

• *Diminished nipple sensation and breastfeeding ability*, as mentioned above. Again, see the box "Will Cosmetic Surgery Affect Your Ability to Breastfeed?" in this chapter.

• *Bad scarring.* What doctors call "exuberant healing," which may or may not include keloid, or raised, scars, is a problem in up to 20 percent of patients for reasons not completely understood. (New developments in scar treatment are discussed at the end of this chapter.)

• *Loss of tissue from the nipple-areolar complex.* This occurs to some degree in almost 4 percent of breast reduction operations, usually due to interruption of the blood supply. Again, the larger the reduction, the greater the risk. Correction is possible with surgical reconstruction (see Chapter 26).

A FINAL WORD

Gain weight after the operation, and your breasts will, too! Seldom is this a serious concern, but rare repeat reductions can be done through the old scars, often in the office under local anesthesia.

BREAST LIFT (MASTOPEXY)

The mammary equivalent of a facelift, mastopexy is most common among women aged 35 to 50, who account for 51 percent of these operations. Running a close second, at 34 percent, is a younger group, aged 19 to 34, whose breasts have "bottomed out" after pregnancies and nursing, or who have larger breasts on which gravity has taken an early toll. Surprisingly, 51- to 61-year-olds come in a distant third, representing only 12 percent of the women who choose to have breast lifts.

Decisions to Make with Your Doctor Before Undergoing a Breast Lift

CHOOSING THE TRADITIONAL OR "SMALL-SCAR" METHOD

Traditional Mastopexy. In a traditional breast lift, still the best procedure for severe ptosis, or sagging (see box on page 171), the scars are the same as for breast reduction. Incisions are made around the edge of the areola, vertically from the nipple to the breast crease, and in the fold itself, after which breast tissue and skin are removed through the inverted T incision. Indeed, a breast lift is virtually the same as a breast reduction, except that most of what is removed is skin rather than gland. The areola may or may not be made smaller. The traditional mastopexy leaves more scars than the small-scar method, but the latter technique has its drawbacks.

Small-Scar Mastopexy. Women with minimal sag and excess skin may be candidates for a small-scar or "circum-areolar" procedure, in which the incision is made around the areola only. Skin and tissue are removed through this incision. Since only a limited amount of skin can be removed by the small-scar method, tension from the remaining weight of the breast skin may cause the areola to spread and the breasts to be flatter than with traditional mastopexy. Depending on the particular technique used and the amount of glandular tissue involved in a breast lift, the small-scar mastopexy may be slightly more likely than a traditional breast lift to interfere with nipple sensation and breastfeeding function. (See the box "Will Cosmetic Surgery Affect Your Ability to Breastfeed?" in this chapter.)

IS MASTOPEXY ENOUGH?

Some women, on the advice of their plastic surgeon, choose to have a simultaneous breast reduction or augmentation to achieve the look they want. For example, very large-breasted women may choose a simultaneous reduction

SOME NEW VARIATIONS ON BREAST REDUCTION METHODS

Women whose too-large breasts are on the smaller side (with little "ptosis" or sagging), a group for whom the scarring drawbacks previously outweighed the benefits of reduction, may be candidates for one of the procedures described below. Remember that with any state-of-the-art technique, the skill of your surgeon is all-important; if one of these methods appeals to you, finding the right doctor may require some shopping around.

• **The vertical scar, or LeJour method.** Developed in Belgium a few years ago, this procedure eliminates the long incision in the breastfold and replaces it with removal of skin and tissue by the areola, using vertical incisions only. This is a procedure that is best for women with smaller, higher breasts, because breast tissue is moved to the top of the breast and allowed to drop over time. So please note that what you see after surgery is not what you get. It takes about six months for the tissues to remodel themselves, and most American women prefer the traditional longer scar to the long wait needed to see the final results.

• **The donut or Benelli reduction.** Popular in France, with its topless beaches and relatively small-breasted women, this procedure entails just two minimally visible scars, one around each nipple. Tissue is removed through these incisions alone. The hard part is removing as much skin as necessary with such small incisions. "This is a difficult operation, demanding a great deal of skill and judgment," says Dr. David Hidalgo. "If the surgeon is too ambitious, taking too much skin, he can really flatten the breast. You may also get a wider than normal scar around the nipple if there's too much tissue pulling on it, causing it to spread." *Prognosis:* Don't even consider this unless you're relatively small-breasted with minimal sagging and have a surgeon who feels comfortable with the technique.

• **Liposuction.** Here, two tiny incisions about the width of half a fingernail are made just under the areola and in the inframammary fold beneath the breast. Then a tiny vacuum tube is inserted and breast fat is literally sucked out. Liposuction is a relatively simple procedure; unfortunately, it is practical only for patients who have already had a reduction and want to be a bit smaller or for those with relatively small, high breasts largely composed of fat (rather than muscle or gland). To understand the limitations of liposuction, says Dr. Alan Matarasso, it helps to visualize the marbleized fat you might see in a steak. On a breast, "there's fat on the edges, around the gland, and marbleized fat throughout. Liposuction can't get at the marbleized fat," explains Dr. Matarasso, and only about 1 to 5 percent of women who want reductions can benefit from liposuction. As of this writing, researchers are working on developing ultrasonic instruments that may one day vaporize fat selectively, wherever it is, marbleized or not.

through the same incisions, for otherwise gravity may quickly undo the surgeon's work. Conversely, small-breasted patients are sometimes advised to have a simultaneous augmentation with saline implants to combat what many women call "the fried egg look." The breast, reduced in volume but possessed of the same chest wall dimensions, may appear unattractively flat.

For descriptions of both breast reduction and augmentation, see the appropriate sections earlier in this chapter.

What to Expect During a Breast Lift (Mastopexy)

The length of surgery depends on the type of mastopexy you have (see page 168) and whether you will be having a simultaneous breast reduction or augmentation. All mastopexies are done under general anesthesia. A traditional breast lift takes two to three hours in the operating room; the limited-scar method may require as many as four hours. (With simultaneous reduction or augmentation, another hour or so might be needed.) While some women stay in the hospital overnight, most go home the same day.

Sutures are removed five days later, when most activities can be resumed. Heavy lifting should be avoided for two weeks, and exercise that impacts the breasts, such as tennis, postponed for four weeks, and jogging for six.

After a Breast Lift: Possible Postsurgery Effects

As with any surgery, immediate complications may include infection and abnormal bleeding, but these are rare. Complications that are more likely to occur include:

• **Temporary loss of breast and nipple sensation.** This effect may last as long as six months. As described previously, the small-scar technique, which sometimes entails restructuring glandular tissue, has slightly higher risks of disturbing both nerve and breastfeeding function. However, permanent loss of breastfeeding ability is rare. (See the box "Will Cosmetic Surgery Affect Your Ability to Breastfeed?" in this chapter.)

WHAT CONSTITUTES "PTOSIS" OR SAGGING BREASTS?

You might think the question of whether or not a woman's breasts are sagging is a purely subjective observation. Not so. "Ptosis," or breast sag, as used by cosmetic surgeons, has specific criteria. When you stand in front of a mirror and look at yourself sideways, the nipple must be lower than the outer end (near your arm) of the inframammary crease, the fold just under the breast. Anything higher is not considered true sagging—from a medical point of view at least.

• **Scarring from tissue overgrowth.** This occurs at about the same rate as in breast reduction—roughly 20 percent of women experience this post-surgical effect. Among women who seek breast lifts, scarring may be viewed with less equanimity than among women who want breast reductions. Reductions are often undertaken for physical reasons, whereas breast lifts are more for beauty. The cosmetic benefits of breast lifts can be destroyed with bad scarring. In the worst cases, when scarring is unsightly, a surgical revision can be performed in a plastic surgeon's office, as explained in the section "Minimizing Scars" later on in this chapter.

SURGERY FOR BREAST ASYMMETRY

Most women are a bit "lopsided," with one breast larger or differently shaped than the other, or pointing in a different direction. About 40 percent of breasts are noticeably asymmetrical. In only 10 percent, however, is the problem severe enough to consider intervention.

Do you want to be bigger or smaller? All decisions about a woman's surgery for breast asymmetry will flow from this, and a woman must choose with her doctor the best and safest procedure for her. To correct asymmetry, doctors use one of three techniques:

• **Breast augmentation of the smaller breast.** The procedure is the same one described earlier in this chapter. With breast asymmetry, however, saline implants are not your only option. Silicone gel implants are allowed, provided you are enrolled in an FDA-approved clinical trial.

NOTE: A special disadvantage of augmentation for asymmetry is that an exact match is difficult. For this reason, your doctor may suggest a new inflatable saline or silicone gel implant, the Spectrum, which can be adjusted nonsurgically for up to six months. Even with the Spectrum, though, gravity will drag on the implanted and nonimplanted breasts at a different rate.

- **Reduction of the larger breast.** If all you need is some "tailoring"—i.e., one breast is just slightly larger than the other—you may be a candidate for liposuction, a suctioning of excess fat described in the box "Some New Variations on Breast Reduction Methods." The disadvantage of a traditional breast reduction with inverted-T incisions is that the reduced breast will have more scarring. On the plus side, exact matching of size and shape tends to be easier with reduction than with augmentation.

- **Reconstruction using the body's own tissue.** As described in Chapter 26, this is a difficult procedure that leaves scars both on the breasts and on the area the tissue is taken from, usually the abdomen or the back. Reconstruction with the body's own tissue is generally reserved for cases of severe congenital malformation, where the disparity between the breasts is great. A possible advantage if you are young: while most implants require eventual replacement, reconstruction is a once-in-a-lifetime event.

The possible postsurgery effects for breast asymmetry will depend on whether breast augmentation and/or breast reduction has been selected. The aftereffects of each type of surgery have been described earlier in this chapter.

AFTER THE OPERATION: MINIMIZING SCARS

The scars accompanying cosmetic surgery are permanent and can never be entirely erased. Some of the factors affecting them—such as how a woman heals—are beyond a doctor's control. Although many elements of scar production are still a mystery, surgeons are constantly finding new ways to minimize the visible effects. What follows is a guide to today's most helpful and innovative techniques:

- **Massage.** Often this is the first line of defense. Ask your doctor when after suture removal it is safe to massage so you do not break your suture line. Then rub the area in a circular motion two or three times a day for up to 20 minutes, using preparations from prescription steroid cream to aloe and vitamin E. "Though cortisone has a thinning effect, and aloe may have healing properties," one surgeon told me, "it's not so much the lubricant you're using but the act of massage that keeps the scarring down." Yes, this technique can be painful at first, but it can also be quite effective. This treatment may continue for several months.

- **Steroids.** Because of their ability to decrease redness, along with their thinning properties, steroids such as cortisone are frequently given by injection as well as topically, in a lotion or cream if scars have not settled down after a few months.

WILL COSMETIC SURGERY AFFECT YOUR ABILITY TO BREASTFEED?

The answer depends largely on the type of surgery you are considering. In general, the less a procedure interferes with breast gland and ducts, the less likely it is to affect a woman's ability to nurse. Here's what usually happens:

- **Breast augmentation.** Having an implant should not be a problem, although a few women (1%) lose lactation function with the circum-areolar incision. Textured implants, however, have been shown to shed small particles of silicone into surrounding tissue, and while we currently have no evidence that silicone—even from gel implants—shows up in breast milk, you may want to discuss the implications of this study with your doctor.
- **Breast reduction/mammoplasty.** Only 50 percent of these women are able to breastfeed postoperatively. For this reason, many women wait until after their childbearing years to have surgery. Risk increases with the donut and vertical scar methods and is highest for big-breasted women whose reductions require a free-nipple graft (entailing temporary nipple removal). It is very rare for a woman who has a free nipple graft to be able to nurse.
- **Breast lift/mastopexy.** This is a fairly superficial surgery, so unless large, pendulous breasts require a simultaneous breast reduction, mastopexy should not affect nursing at all.
- **Surgery for breast asymmetry.** The ability to breastfeed depends on whether the surgery involves a breast augmentation or reduction to remedy the imbalance. (See the considerations above.)

One Last Word

Before undergoing any type of cosmetic surgery on your breasts, be sure to let your surgeon know if breastfeeding is a concern for you. He will then be aware of your needs and able to recommend the best surgical approach.

- **Silicone sheeting.** This sheeting, a fabric-backed gel called Cica-Care, looks a little like thick Scotch tape and was originally developed by Dow Corning for treatment of burn victims. Today Cica-Care is manufactured by Smith-Nephew Roylan. No one is sure how it works to lessen scarring, but it usually does. One British study found a 100 percent success rate at improving the appearance of raised scars. Some doctors prescribe Cica-Care as a preventive measure immediately after sutures from the surgery have been removed. The sheeting is also effective for old scars. As for worries about a possible silicone-autoimmune disease link, most feel the difference in exposure level between topical and internal silicone precludes such concerns. (For more information about Cica-Care, call Smith-Nephew's technical assistance line, 800-558-8633.)

• **Surgical revision.** Raised or lumpy scars are cut away in this technique. "During the original operation," explains Dr. Alan Matarasso, "the skin is under tension, which is one of the elements that causes scars to form. When you revise tissue afterward, the skin is relaxed, so this kind of correction can really help." An outpatient procedure, revision can take up to one hour and is usually performed under local anesthetic.

Don't Forget to Ask "Why?" First

As I mentioned at the beginning of this chapter, whatever cosmetic surgery you choose, take the time beforehand to understand *why* you want the operation. You will be living with your choice for the rest of your life, so you want it to be a good one. A dancer with the New York City Ballet told me that she had undergone a breast reduction at age 22 because she felt that her large breasts were hurting her career. (Her breasts had grown after she had received hormone injections at age 19 to combat the amenorrhea [lack of menstruation] that is common among dancers.) Today at age 26 she says, "I have never doubted for a minute that I did the right thing." Ideally, if you choose to undergo cosmetic surgery, years later you too will still feel certain about your decision.

When You Are at High Risk for Breast Cancer: Should You Consider Preventive Mastectomy?

Perhaps 1 to 3 percent of mastectomies are performed on healthy breasts. A woman may be having surgery on a breast with a malignancy and feel that her chance of getting cancer in the other breast is high. Another may have a family history of two or more first-degree relatives with breast cancer, while another woman may have undergone a number of breast biopsies showing precancerous breast disease. All may be living with an anxiety that prompts them to request the surgery.

Although removing one or both breasts is a drastic step with no guarantee that the risk of breast cancer is eliminated, women may explore the option of preventive, or prophylactic, mastectomy, in an effort to stop breast cancer. And with the imminent availability of gene testing, the number of inquiries into prophylactic mastectomy is sure to rise. Right now a blood test for the mutated breast cancer gene BRCA1 exists, and researchers are working to create testing for two more recently discovered breast cancer gene mutations, BRCA2 and ATM. Although only an estimated 5 percent of women who will develop breast cancer have the mutated BRCA1 gene, a woman who does have it can face an 85 percent lifetime chance of being diagnosed, and she may want to take preventive action.

BEFORE YOU PROCEED

Seek Risk Assessment Counseling Before Any Surgery

The physical and psychological effects of a prophylactic mastectomy are profound, and any woman who considers this option should involve herself in risk assessment counseling before she proceeds. After having counseled women about the procedure for nine years at Johns Hopkins University, Dr. Michael Stefanek published a paper "Bilateral Prophylactic Mastectomy: Issues and Concerns," in the *Journal of the National Cancer Institute* in 1995. The first woman he saw in relation to prophylactic mastectomy was 28 years old and had a mother who had developed breast cancer in her early forties and two sisters who had been diagnosed with breast cancer in their early thirties. The surgeon who operated on one of her sisters told her, "I want to see you on the operating table next." In response to this scenario, Dr. Stefanek has told me, "One of the main goals [risk assessment counselors have] when a woman presents this type of family situation is to slow down the decision making, and explain to her that she is not in a medical emergency, that her risk over the next six months to a year is extremely low. Having a prophylactic mastectomy is such a difficult decision that we encourage women not to make it on the heels of a sister being diagnosed one or two months ago. Or if a family member has recently died, we suggest that a woman really absorb that a bit before making such a decision."

At the Strang Cancer Prevention Center in New York, genetic counselor Gladys Rosenthal explains the issues raised during counseling: "Our prophylactic mastectomy protocol is several sessions. We have sessions on genetic counseling, psychological counseling to discuss life situation, family support, the feelings of a partner, sexual issues and body image, and a session with a surgeon to understand what the surgery entails. The genetic counseling has to do with risk assessment: How high is the risk level, and what would be an acceptable risk for you? (No counselor can be definitive and say, 'We're giving you your risk; this is what you want to do,' because no one knows what an acceptable risk level for a particular woman is.) We also discuss the differences between developing breast cancer and dying of it. We want women to feel there is no rush to make this decision. We inform you that even with this preventive procedure, you cannot get your risk down to zero; it is almost impossible to remove all the breast tissue. Most important, we never recommend; the woman making the inquiry has to come to her own decision, and the only way to do that is to go into the issue very thoroughly and to search her feelings."

Before a woman even approaches a risk assessment counselor, however (the field of genetic/risk assessment counseling is specialized, so you will have to check with major cancer hospitals or breast cancer centers in your area to locate genetic/risk assessment programs near you), there are other aspects of prophylactic mastectomy to consider.

Consider the Reasons Behind Your Doctor's Opinion

Dr. Mary Daly, director of the family risk assessment program at Fox Chase

Cancer Center in Philadelphia, says that she has noticed that surgeons have always been very reluctant to remove healthy tissue and perform prophylactic mastectomy on women who have a family history of breast cancer but no disease. However, she has seen a change in attitude when it comes to women who have already been diagnosed with breast cancer. "Surgeons seem much more willing to consider prophylactic surgery on the opposite breast in that group of women," she says.

One NCI survey presented almost 1,500 Maryland surgeons (general, plastic, and gynecologic) with a scenario of a 35-year-old woman with a family history of breast cancer and an approximately 25 percent risk of developing breast cancer in the next 30 years. Most of the doctors surveyed were not inclined to recommend prophylactic mastectomy of both breasts. The overwhelming number voted for close surveillance of the woman with mammography, physician breast examinations, and breast self-examinations. Only 6 percent chose prophylactic mastectomy of both breasts as the treatment of choice, and of that group, most were plastic surgeons who would have been able to perform reconstruction.

The reluctance among most doctors for prophylactic mastectomy has to do with the obvious disinclination to remove healthy tissue, but other factors are also at work. First, there is the belief that cancer is a systemic disease, and a surgical approach to prevention is not appropriate. Many physicians are hoping for success in the field of chemoprevention, which is being explored right now with the drug tamoxifen (see Chapter 24). Also, gene testing is just around the corner. "We have been encouraging women to wait until they can be officially tested," explains Dr. Patrick Borgen, chief of the breast service, department of surgery at Memorial Sloan-Kettering Cancer Center in New York. "It would be a great tragedy to remove a woman's breast and then have her find out a year later that she did not have a genetic predisposition to breast cancer."

Then there is the fact that breast tissue extends from the collarbone down to the bottom edge of the ribs, and from the breastbone out to the muscle in the back of the armpit. No surgeon can remove all breast tissue, and no study has been able to prove that prophylactic mastectomy can prevent breast cancer from occurring in the remaining tissue.

So women should be wary if a doctor suggests prophylactic mastectomy. Some doctors are simply responding to what has come to be known as "cancerophobia," a woman's extreme worry that she is going to develop breast cancer. If you or someone you know is beset by this anxiety, I recommend finding a risk assessment counselor to talk with and putting any suggestion of surgery on the back burner. Although most doctors are not going to favor prophylactic mastectomy, there is more of an inclination to remove a healthy breast if one breast is already affected. Plus, some doctors feel that reconstruction of both breasts can then create symmetry.

A WARNING ABOUT TECHNIQUE

If you are considering preventive mastectomy, make sure you under-stand what technique a surgeon may plan to use. Do not agree to a *subcutaneous mastectomy*, whereby a surgeon makes a small incision, leaves the skin and nipple intact, removes most (80 to 90 percent) of the breast tissue and replaces it with an implant, either behind or in front of the pectoral muscle. *Women who have had this more cos-metically appealing procedure* (it leaves a certain amount of tissue and the nipple intact) *have developed breast cancer in the remaining tissue or the nipple.* Reputable cancer centers with up-to-date risk assess-ment programs will only discuss prophylactic mastectomy in terms of a *total mastectomy*, the same procedure that is performed on women who have already been diagnosed with breast cancer. With a total mastectomy, much more of the breast tissue is excised because the breast itself is fully removed. A new technique, a *skin-sparing mastectomy*, is being performed by a number of skilled sur-geons at major cancer centers. This surgery eliminates the elliptical saber slash incision that is left on a woman's chest after a traditional total mastectomy and replaces it with an around-the-nipple, small circular incision ($4^1/_2$ centimeters in diameter), that allows the sur-geon to remove breast tissue with the aid of fiberoptic retractors. (See Chapter 21 for a detailed explanation of mastectomy proce-dures.) With a skin-sparing mastectomy, reconstruction (discussed initially with a reconstructive surgeon during the counseling phase) is performed at the time of mastectomy, and the circular mastec-tomy scar is virtually nonexistent. (See Chapter 26 for reconstruc-tive techniques.)

Recognize That Little Is Known About the True Effectiveness of Prophylactic Mastectomy

We know very little about the true preventive value of prophylactic mastec-tomy of one or both breasts. Dr. Stefanek, who reviewed the literature on bilateral (both breasts) prophylactic mastectomy, reports that in a number of animal studies, prophylactic mastectomy was *not* effective in reducing breast cancer tumors. As far as how prophylactic mastectomy affects women, Dr. Stefanek refers to surveys of more than 2,000 subcutaneous mastectomies. (This is not a type of surgery that can be researched in a study.) Analyses of the surveys reported an incidence of breast cancer of 0.1 to 0.2 percent in remaining breast tissue. This is a low percentage, but the surveys had short follow-up times, and not all of the women surveyed were undergoing subcutaneous mastectomies because of breast cancer risk. Some of the women undergoing mastectomies had fibrocystic breast disease, and some with in situ (localized) breast cancer received total or radical mastectomies. Dr. Stefanek concluded that the low percentage may underestimate the risk of cancer, and that whether subcutaneous (which is no longer recommended at reputable breast cancer centers) or total, *mastectomy may reduce, but not likely eliminate*, the risk of breast cancer. Dr. Stefanek even cited an old study from 1965, where simple (now called "total") mastectomies were performed for benign breast conditions and 10 to 15 years after the surgeries, two cases of breast cancer occurred. *NOTE:* Researchers at Memorial Sloan-Kettering Cancer Center in New York are compiling a National Prophylactic Mastectomy Registry to gather information about this rarely performed procedure. Women who decide to undergo, or have undergone, prophylactic mastectomies can help by contacting: National Prophylactic Mastectomy Registry, Box 436, Memorial Sloan-Kettering Cancer Center, 1275 York Avenue, New York, NY 10021; 212-639-7870.

JUDGE YOUR RISK AS ACCURATELY AS POSSIBLE

In the 1995 survey of about 1,500 Maryland surgeons mentioned earlier, doctors responded that they would need to see a 40 to 55 percent lifetime risk of breast cancer in a woman before they would recommend prophylactic mastectomy as an option for fighting the disease. Yet risk is hard to judge. As Dr. Mary Daly explains, "Women tend oftentimes to overestimate their risk, and some women underestimate their risk. One of the key components of counseling is to take an objective look, see if you can quantify a woman's risk, and try to match the preventive options with the degree of risk so that we are not considering prophylactic mastectomy for someone who just had one first-degree (mother, sister, daughter) relative with what looked like a spread of cancer."

Risk factors, which include such variables as menstrual history, pregnancy history, family history, and results of any genetic tests for breast cancer genes (see Chapter 18), can be assessed by genetic counselors at breast cancer centers across the country. It is important to keep your perspective. A 1995 study of the results of counseling for 200 women whose relatives had been treated for breast cancer reported that almost two-thirds of the women continued to overestimate their risk three months later. They saw their lifetime risk to be more than 50 percent, when it was actually only estimated at 14 percent.

While blood tests for mutated breast cancer genes will help to pinpoint women at highest risk for breast cancer, women who have a family history but do not test positive for the genes will continue to find themselves in that gray area open to interpretation; it is my hope that they, along with carriers of the affected genes, will seek expert risk assessment counseling. While counselors cannot make the final decision for you, they are good at reminding even the highest-risk women of the option of close follow-up with annual mammography, frequent physical examinations by a physician, and monthly breast self-examinations, which can be chosen in lieu of prophylactic mastectomy. This course of early detection if a breast cancer develops may result in less extensive surgery than a prophylactic mastectomy.

IN THE FUTURE

As time goes on we will learn more of the results of the tamoxifen trial, which is assessing the effectiveness of the drug in the chemoprevention of breast cancer in premenopausal women (see Chapter 24). If researchers continue looking into chemoprevention, the future may well offer one or more systemic methods of fighting breast cancer that will outdate prophylactic mastectomy.

PART IV

Warning Signs That Your Breasts Need Attention

Nipples That Have Discharge, Soreness, or Other Conditions

The first question to ask yourself if you are neither pregnant nor breast-feeding, but fluid is leaking from your nipples, is, "What medications am I taking?" The connection between many widely used drugs and nipple discharge is stunning. Birth control pills, tranquilizers, and high blood pressure and ulcer medications are just a few sources of nipple discharge. In fact, a woman's nipples are susceptible to a range of situations that can cause them to leak or hurt: an imbalance of the hormone prolactin, clogged ducts, an abscess, warty growths. When it comes to the health care of breasts, breast cancer is inevitably on everyone's mind, but your breasts, and the nipples on your breasts, often need attention for many reasons that have nothing to do with serious disease. Fortunately the conditions that cause nipple discharge and pain, as described throughout this chapter, are mostly benign.

NIPPLE DISCHARGE

When Is It Normal?

A lactating mother grows accustomed to the letdown of her milk, but even a woman who is not nursing can notice a discharge from time to time. In fact, it is quite normal for most women in their reproductive years to notice nipple leakage, especially on occasions such as these:

• *During a breast self-examination*, a woman may squeeze her nipples and observe a clear or milky discharge. This is a common occurrence, and usually if one breast leaks, the other will too. Nipple squeezing, like the suckling of

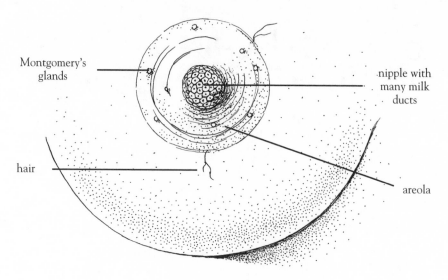

Montgomery's
glands

nipple with
many milk
ducts

hair

areola

Anatomy of a nipple. Note the openings of many milk ducts that have converged in the nipple. The nipple is encircled by the pigmented areola.

an infant, can send a message to the brain's pituitary gland to release the hormone prolactin, which in turn stimulates the production of breast milk. The practice of nipple squeezing during a breast self-examination is recommended because sometimes a bloody or suspicious discharge appears. An unexpected discharge from one or both breasts is alarming, but a single-breast discharge could signal a more serious problem. Either way, see a doctor immediately.

• *During sexual relations*, when a woman is erotically stimulated, the myoepithelial (small) muscles inside her breasts contract as her nipples become erect. Those tiny muscle contractions are the same ones that a new mother feels during breastfeeding. During lovemaking they can cause the breast and nipples to expel a light, clear discharge. If the discharge does not subside after sexual intimacy has ended and a woman's body returns to its normal, resting state, then a physician should be consulted.

• *While taking oral contraceptives or other medications such as some antihypertensive drugs, a variety of tranquilizers, antidepressants and antipsychotic drugs, Tagamet, and opiates such as morphine, methadone, and heroin*, a woman may notice a milky discharge. Sometimes the hormonal balance generated by these medications can affect the release of prolactin. Prolactin stimulates the breasts to produce milk, so an elevated level of this hormone may set off an unexpected milk production and a noticeable discharge.

• *When a woman stops taking the birth control pill*, her nipples might leak sometimes up to two or three years later. The hormonal balance created by an oral contraceptive can continue to affect the milk-producing hormone prolactin for a long time. When you squeeze your nipples, you see a pale whitish discharge from both breasts. You probably do not need to be concerned, but you should tell your doctor what is happening so that he can evaluate your condition. If the discharge is yellowish and seems to contain pus or blood, see a doctor immediately. The bottom line is, even though you may know that certain drugs you have taken may cause breast milk production, you should still consult a physician.

• *During pregnancy* a woman may notice many changes in her breasts, such as enlargement, soreness, a different skin tone, and a discharge of milk as her body prepares for breastfeeding. (See Chapter 2 for more about how your breasts respond to pregnancy.) It is a good idea to squeeze the nipples and check the color of a discharge before your next prenatal visit. If the discharge seems to be changing in color and is not milky but yellowish or bloody, inform your obstetrician. Any suspicious discharge is a cause for concern and a bloody discharge is suspect for breast cancer. It must be analyzed at a laboratory. According to the National Cancer Institute, breast cancer is the most common cancer in pregnant and postpartum women, occurring in about one in 3,000 pregnancies.

• *After an infant has been weaned,* a woman may find that she continues to leak milk for years thereafter due to the stimulation of her pituitary gland and its release of the hormone prolactin during breastfeeding. The milk-producing hormone prolactin may continue to stimulate the breasts. If a blood test shows that a woman's prolactin level is high, and her doctor has ruled out any malignancy or other possible causes of the discharge, such as a medication, then he is likely to prescribe bromocriptine mesylate (Parlodel). This medication can stop lactation, but it has also been related to heart attacks and strokes and is now recommended only in special cases.

For some women, nipple discharge is fairly common, natural, and inconsequential; other women rarely notice a leakage. The two seasons in a woman's life when she would be most likely to detect a discharge are during puberty and just before menopause; nipple discharge after menopause is unusual. Nipple discharge, especially if it occurs in both breasts, is normally nothing to worry about during the reproductive years, but it can be a sign of an underlying condition if the discharge is spontaneous—not connected to breastfeeding or an easily recognizable source of stimulation to the breasts such as those mentioned above—persistent, and comes from only one breast. A single nipple discharge is potentially more serious than leakage from both breasts.

If a woman does not fit into any of the situations described above but nevertheless experiences nipple discharge, she should ask herself, is this leakage:

appearing spontaneously?
persistently?
coming from one breast?

If the answer to these three questions is yes, then she must immediately see a doctor. She also should inspect the color and consistency of the discharge to help her doctor make the proper diagnosis.

What Does Your Nipple Discharge Look Like?

Nipple discharge may appear:

> milky
> multicolored
> yellow/green, containing pus
> clear, watery
> pink
> bloody

The first three types—milky, multicolored, and pus-filled—usually signal less serious conditions that can be treated medically. To determine treatment, a physician will test the discharge with a breast Pap test, which is similar to a Pap test of cervical secretions, and a laboratory culture. He will also order a blood test for prolactin levels.

The last three types—clear, pink, and bloody—may require a breast Pap test, a blood test for prolactin levels, and a mammogram, possibly in combination with a special screening called *galactography* (the technique of injecting water-soluble radiopaque dye into a leaking nipple duct and then performing a mammography). A doctor may also recommend a surgical biopsy to find out the cause of the discharge.

In one study, nipple discharge was a symptom in only 3.4 percent of 2,437 women with cancer, but even so, nipple discharge should not be ignored. Although by itself, nipple discharge is usually not a sign of breast cancer, only your doctor can officially tell you everything is all right.

What's Causing the Discharge?

MILKY, MULTICOLORED, OR YELLOW/GREEN
PUS-FILLED DISCHARGE

• **Milky:** *Galactorrhea* occurs when too much of the brain hormone prolactin is being produced by the pituitary gland. The result is a milky nipple discharge from *both* breasts that may vary from barely noticeable—occurring only when the breast is pressed or squeezed—to an obvious leak. Usually, if you have galactorrhea you have missed several periods during the time of your discharge. Your doctor can perform a blood test to determine whether you are living with an excess of prolactin. If a prolactin imbalance appears, your physician is then likely to suggest an X ray of your skull. Sometimes prolactin rises because you have an adenoma, a small tumor, on the pituitary gland in your brain. Usually the medication bromocriptine mesy-late (Parlodel), which is available for specially indicated cases, blocks the hormone, stops milk secretion, and reinstates menstruation and fertility. In rare cases, a prolactin imbalance is caused by a brain adenoma, a benign tumor, at the pituitary gland. If the adenoma is large and does not respond to Parlodel, surgery may be required.

• **Multicolored:** *Mammary duct ectasia* is a rare condition that occurs when the ducts become enlarged with glandular secretions. The resulting discharge is usually multicolored but can be a single color: green, yellow, white, brown, gray, or reddish brown. The swollen duct may create a tender, hard mass near the areola. You may also feel an itching or burning sensation as if your nipple is being pulled in. Duct ectasia usually appears when a woman is in her forties—anywhere from age 37 to 53, but the median age is 43. The condition normally clears up by itself, without treatment, but it is best to consult a physician, because duct ectasia should be monitored.

• **Yellow/green pus-Filled:** You probably have an *underlying infection* in your breast. It could be a mastitis, as explained in Chapters 2 and 16, which may cause a spot of tenderness in your breast or general breast pain. Your doctor can do a specialized breast Pap test of the discharge, and the sample can, in addition, be cultured in a laboratory to identify the problem. A broad spectrum antibiotic, in combination with hot compresses, will often cure the infection, and the discharge will disappear.

CLEAR, PINK, OR BLOODY DISCHARGE

When your nipple discharge is clear, pink, or bloody and comes from a single nipple, you must make an appointment to have it checked. It could be that you have *intraductal papillomas*, benign warty growths within the duct. You may have one or more of these noncancerous warts, which must be sur-gically removed. A doctor will perform a breast Pap test of the discharge for laboratory analysis, and he will no doubt recommend a mammogram, with or without a galactogram, as described earlier in this chapter. This technique helps a physician get a better fix on a growth, but it cannot tell him whether the growth is benign or malignant, so surgery is still needed.

You may ask, *why have surgery if the Pap smear of the discharge does not indicate abnormal cells?* Analysis of the discharge leads to a high rate of "false-negatives," meaning that the test may say "no abnormal or cancerous cells" when such cells are present. There is a reported 18 percent false-negative rate and 2.6 percent false-positive rate with the testing.

Usually when a nipple discharge is related to cancer, it is more likely to be bloody. The cells of a cancer located around the area of a milk duct bleed into the duct. Frequently you can feel a mass in your breast, but not always. In one study of breast cancers with a nipple discharge, there was no indica-tion of breast lumps in 13 percent of the cases. When a nipple discharge is clear, pink, or bloody, you just have to be more careful.

NIPPLE/AREOLA SORENESS AND PAIN

Your nipples can hurt during breastfeeding because a baby who sucks hard and long can crack them (see Chapter 2 for treatment of *cracked nipples*). Bacteria from the infant can then enter through the cracks and lead to infection and possible abscess (when an infection festers in one spot and pus builds). However, an abscess on the border of the areola can occur long after breastfeeding ends; it can also happen in women who have never breastfed, and even though the abscess—called a *subareola abscess*—is in one location, your entire nipple/areola area can hurt.

When You Have a Subareola Abscess

There is some discrepancy about the cause of an abscess, which can appear like a boil, on the edge of the areola. Conventionally, it has been thought to arise from a blocked, infected milk sinus (a collecting duct) in the nipple structure, but lately it has been suggested that small oily glands around that nipple can become infected, and ultimately form a subareola abscess. Whatever the source of the abscess, it is a red, painful, pus-filled swelling that starts out as an infection. So whenever you notice a tender, hot spot on your breast or in the area of the areola and nipple, consult a physician. This is an early sign of infection, and an antibiotic can kill the infection before it progresses into a subareola abscess.

Once an infection forms an abscess, antibiotics may still work, but at this later stage the abscess may very well require an incision for draining (see Chapter 2). The big problem with a subareola abscess is that even after treatment, it can recur every few months; antibiotics, incision, and drainage do not permanently resolve the condition. Then the abscessed gland and its attached ductal tract must be surgically removed. This means excising a small wedge of internal nipple/areola tissue after you have received a local anesthetic. A surgeon makes an incision that crosses the areola and goes into the nipple. A wedge of tissue is removed through the nipple/areola incision, which is then sewn closed, leaving only a thin, small scar. A subareola abscess is not a frequent occurrence, and by itself is never malignant. A doctor may want to perform a biopsy, however, to make sure no malignancy is in the area.

NIPPLE DERMATITIS

The skin on your nipples can become irritated, inflamed, and/or itchy, because during nursing, lovemaking, or in the course of wearing certain bras, the nipples are actively rubbed and touched. (A poorly fitting bra can cause friction and inflammation of the nipples.) Also, a woman can have an allergic reaction to the detergents used on her clothing or the perfumes and powders she uses on herself. Usually nipple dermatitis can be cured with ointments containing antibiotics or cortisone-like ingredients, or both, for about two weeks. You can usually find the source of the problem by eliminating detergents, perfumes, powders, bath oils, and ill-fitting bras. Then practice good breast hygiene, and use a soft cotton bra. If the problem does not disappear within two weeks of treatment, a biopsy may be recommended.

Sometimes nipple dermatitis is diagnosed when cancerous *Paget's disease* is the problem. One big difference is that nipple dermatitis usually involves both breasts, while Paget's disease appears on a single breast. Paget's disease produces a crusty flakiness of the nipple, without any involvement of surrounding skin. The eroded nipple can be biopsied in a procedure performed with a local anesthetic. Only one or two millimeters of tissue are needed for a pathologist to identify the cancer cells of Paget's disease. This could mean that ductal carcinoma in situ (DCIS) or invasive cancer exists somewhere in the breast, or that you have a cancer in the nipple. Your doctor will recommend a mammogram for diagnosis of a tumor.

Paget's disease begins slowly, and it may take some time before a palpable mass can be felt. If only the nipple is involved, the cancer may be treated by surgically removing the nipple alone, although in the past doctors have performed total mastectomies for this disease. Today reconstructive surgeons can create new nipples (see Chapter 26), but before permitting surgery, seek a second opinion.

INVERTED NIPPLES

As explained in Chapter 2, inverted nipples are nipples that are drawn inward by an adhesion of breast tissue that occurred during breast development. Massage and other treatments for inverted nipples are also discussed in Chapter 2. Inverted nipples are a cause for concern if you have not had inverted nipples all your life and notice that your nipples are suddenly retracting. This is the time to consult your physician, because nipples that are puckering inward may signal a possible malignancy.

PAY ATTENTION TO YOUR BREASTS

As part of the overall health of your breasts, your nipples need attention. Always try to notice any discharge, changes in shape and skin tone, and visit your doctor if you see anything that looks different or suspicious. The condition of your nipples is important to your overall well-being.

CHAPTER FIFTEEN

A Difference in Your Skin Tone

Breasts visibly respond to hormonal changes. During puberty and pregnancy, there is a deepening of the pigmentation of breasts. A girl going through menarche can see her breasts maturing, the areolae darkening and widening, and the nipples becoming more prominent. If breasts grow rapidly during adolescence or even due to a sudden weight gain, stretch marks may appear. Birth control pills, another source of hormonal change, also may darken skin tone and bring about breast enlargement and stretch marks. Similarly, a woman who becomes pregnant notices her breasts change almost immediately.

Sometimes a first sign of pregnancy is an added heaviness to a woman's breasts. The surface veins become more prominent, and the pigmentation of the areolae deepens in color. Fair women with pink nipples notice a change to light brown; women with darker skin tones and African American women see their brown nipples become very dark brown, brownish black, or black. Also, nipples become more erect and Montgomery's glands, the small, round, elevated oil glands around the periphery of the areolae, become more pronounced. As pregnancy progresses, the breasts may become so engorged that stretch marks become apparent. All this is normal, and routine massaging of the breasts, especially with lotions containing aloe vera or cocoa butter, can help soften the skin and prevent the onset of stretch marks.

With the breasts undergoing so many natural alterations, you may come to expect the unexpected, but two skin conditions do cause concern: one is a reddening of the breasts, and the other is a condition called *peau d'orange*, when the breast dimples, like the peel of an orange:

A REDNESS OF THE BREASTS

Usually when an area of your breasts looks red and inflamed, other symptoms are often appearing at the same time. The red spot may be painful, warm or hot to the touch, and/or swollen. The underlying cause is often *mastitis*, an infection that may or may not be linked to breastfeeding (see Chapters 2 and 16) and can be treated with antibiotics. A redness and swelling can also result from a more serious condition, an *inflammatory breast cancer* (see Chapter 22). So whenever you notice a redness, especially one accompanied by a lump or a swelling, consult your physician for a diagnosis. An inflamed or infected milk duct can be easily treated with antibiotics; a breast cancer is best fought through surgery and possibly adjuvant chemo and/or hormonal therapy, when it is found early.

PEAU D'ORANGE

Peau d'orange is not a change in pigment but a dimpling of the skin on a breast. The breast develops the dimpled texture of an orange peel because the ligaments that support breast tissue are being pulled inward by the presence of a large (almost 5-centimeter or 2-inch) tumor. Actually the tumor causes a swelling of the tissue, which in turn pulls on the ligaments and puckers the skin. This is usually the sign of an advanced breast cancer that has probably shed cells to other areas of the body. A woman must consult a physician immediately because the cancer causing peau d'orange can be aggressive.

APPEARANCES ARE IMPORTANT

I have tried to convey to the women in my care that they should not only be aware of the presence of breast lumps, but that they need to take the time to look at their breasts in a mirror and notice their overall appearance and any visible differences. Early signs of health problems often show up subtly, as in a change in the color or texture of the skin. A woman who is familiar with the healthy look of her breasts becomes alert to their most delicate changes, and when she sees something new, consults a physician to find out why, right away.

CHAPTER SIXTEEN

Your Breasts Hurt: Pain All Over or in One Spot

Our knowledge about breast pain, medically termed *mastodynia* or *mastalgia*, is just beginning to grow. Until lately, few researchers have investigated breast pain, because the existence of this very real condition was denied by physicians. It is hard to believe that as recently as the 1970s if there was no lump or easily definable cause for a woman's breast pain, her symptom was diagnosed as a state of mind. Currently we know that breast pain can be cyclic and related to the menstrual cycle; noncyclic and related to infection, injury, surgery, or other conditions; or linked to problems outside the breast, such as arthritis or back pain.

CYCLIC BREAST PAIN: CONNECTED TO THE MENSTRUAL CYCLE

Breast Pain in the Cycle of Life

There are certain seasons in a woman's life when the balance of the hormones estrogen, progesterone, prolactin, follicle-stimulating hormone (FSH), and luteinizing hormone (LH), shifts. Such changing hormonal levels can start, stop, or reconfigure a woman's menstrual patterns. Breast pain is merely one part of this biological transformation that occurs when you are:

• **Approaching Menarche.** In the teen years a girl's hormonal balance is unpredictable, and her breasts begin to activate a highly developed network of nerves and nerve endings which are connected to the hormonal impulses

---

BREAST PAIN: IS IT CANCER?

Three Points to Remember:

1. Breast pain alone is rarely a sign of breast cancer.
2. Breast pain that comes and goes during a menstrual month is *cyclic* and almost never linked to cancer.
3. Breast pain, when reported by women who were later diagnosed with breast cancer, has been persistent, *noncyclic* breast pain, which has almost always been accompanied by a lump.

---

coming from the brain and ovaries. This is when menstruation begins, and breasts begin to enlarge and develop, and a girl may feel breast pain for the first time. Sometimes the rapid breast growth that starts at about age 11, when breast buds appear, and ends around age 18, creates this tenderness in the breasts. The soreness may be intensified because hormonal changes can also cause breast cysts (fluid-filled sacs) to form during breast development.

• **Pregnancy.** As explained in Chapter 2, one of the earliest signs of pregnancy is breast enlargement and tenderness. Levels of the female hormones estrogen and progesterone, which normally drop with the onset of menstruation, continue to rise after conception and prevent menstruation from occurring. As pregnancy progresses, breasts can begin to tingle, and nipples can become extremely sensitive.

• **Breastfeeding.** Breasts can become engorged with milk and can swell, harden, and become quite tender. The pain caused by increased blood flow and milk production can be alleviated with the use of hot compresses, massage, and expression of milk, manually or with a breast pump (see Chapter 2 for details).

• **Approaching Menopause.** Breast tissue responds to many hormones, among them estrogen, progesterone, prolactin, oxytocin, and prostaglandins. At approximately age 43 (about 7 years before the last menstrual period), hormonal levels begin to fluctuate wildly, the length of menstrual cycles and the quantity of blood flow during menstrual periods can become unpredictable, and along with these changes a woman may notice that her breasts become fuller and more tender than usual before menstruation. This perimenopausal breast pain may be felt off and on until menstruation ceases and a woman enters her menopausal years. Breast pain should end with menopause, unless a woman chooses to take hormone replacement therapy (HRT), and then her breasts may respond to estrogen and progesterone supplementation. A woman on HRT should discuss adjustment of her hormonal dosage with her gynecologist if her breasts are tender and sore, and she should also be sure to have a yearly mammogram.

The fact that breast pain is intense in the early years, responds to hormonal disruptions such as pregnancy and breastfeeding, and ends after menopause basically tells us that hormonal changes, whether they are major watersheds in life or the monthly ups and downs of the menstrual cycle, are key to this condition.

Breast Pain During the Monthly Menstrual Cycle

Cyclic breast pain that comes and goes during the course of a menstrual month and is typically worse in the second half of the cycle just before menstruation, is the most common type of breast pain. Usually both breasts hurt, particularly in the upper outer quadrants. An overall lumpiness, which may be a sign of a fibrocystic condition (see Chapter 17), often goes hand in hand with the pain. While research has shown that a majority of women report breast pain during a menstrual month, the severity ranges from barely noticeable to so severe that a woman cannot sleep on her stomach or enjoy an affectionate hug. Because the pain pattern often changes, and some cycles produce more mastodynia than others, doctors find cyclic breast pain difficult to treat. Researchers have tried to find the hormonal connection that might be the precise source of breast pain, but thus far there is no scientific agreement on the subject.

Hormones affect cyclic breast pain, but exactly how they do this remains a mystery. Some women who have cyclic breast pain have normal levels of circulating hormones; others have decreased progesterone in relation to estrogen in the second half of the menstrual cycle; still others have pituitary glands that regulate the release of the hormone prolactin (which affects milk production and the breasts), based on their sensitivity to thyroid hormone. The trouble is, every time it looks like researchers are getting close to discovering the hormonal connection for breast pain, a new study comes along that disputes earlier findings. The latest theory is that hormonal receptors in the breast may have different sensitivities, based on the makeup of the cells, which depend on essential fatty acids in the body. Without a clear map to the source of cyclic breast pain, there is a wide variety of suggested treatments.

WHAT TO DO ABOUT CYCLIC BREAST PAIN

When you tell your gynecologist you are experiencing breast pain, the first thing he should do is perform a thorough breast examination to determine whether you have a lump or mass he can feel. If he detects a suspicious lump, he may ask you to undergo ultrasonography, mammography, or both (see Chapters 4 and 5). Also, he will want to evaluate your menopausal status and know whether you are taking medications, birth control pills, replacement hormones, or any other drugs that may affect hormonal balance. After analyzing a woman's health history, I often suggest that she keep a menstrual calendar for two months to record the severity of her breast pain (none, mild, moderate, extreme) every day. That way I can easily see whether her pain is cyclic and related to her menstrual cycle, or noncylic and occurring for other reasons. If her breast pain is cyclic, I can suggest a number of treatments, from changes in diet to medication:

• **Nonhormonal Treatments.** Whenever a woman reports any type of breast pain, I initially suggest that she change to a softer style brassiere just to see whether a new bra makes a difference. (See box "How to Get the Best-Fitting Bra, p. 199.") Some women have found that diuretics, sometimes called "water pills," which reduce water retention and bloating, offer relief. Others have made certain dietary changes to diminish breast pain. Many women have eliminated foods that contain caffeine, which belongs to a group of compounds called *methylxanthines*. As explained in Chapter 6, caffeine and methylxanthines have been linked to breast pain and breast lumps, but the pendulum swings back and forth on the issue of whether they are definite sources of these problems. Even so, I always recommend that women reduce or eliminate their caffeine consumption.

A low-fat diet (only 15 percent fat) reduced breast swelling, tenderness, and nodularity in 60 percent of the women in a group experiencing breast pain, and 20 percent in a control group. It seems that low-fat eating may not only play a role in preventing breast cancer (see Chapter 6) but may also be effective in fighting breast pain. A woman may also benefit from dietary supplementation with vitamins A, B complex, C, and E. Then there is evening primrose oil, a nutritional supplement that can be purchased over the counter in health food stores. Evening primrose oil contains vitamin K and essential fatty acids, including gamma-linolenic acid, which has been found to be deficient in some women who suffer premenstrual syndrome. If the theory holds up that women with breast pain may have hormone receptors that lack essential fatty acids, then evening primrose oil may help. A study at the Cardiff Clinic in England found evening primrose oil effective when two 500-milligram soft-gel capsules were taken three times a day for three to four months. Side effects included nausea and bloating. Some studies have shown that excessive amounts of evening primrose oil may lead to miscarriage, but I have not found this to be the case in my practice.

• **Hormonal Treatments.** Some women have breast pain severe enough to interfere with sleep, work, and relationships, and unless they are trying to conceive, a hormonally based medication may be recommended. Birth control pills change the balance of the sex hormones during a monthly cycle and can sometimes cause, sometimes alleviate, breast pain, depending on how a woman responds to them. If breast pain intensifies, of course, a woman should stop the pills immediately. In general, oral contraceptives are considered safe for young, healthy women, so if a woman in her twenties has serious breast pain and she has never been on the pill, this may be an avenue of treatment for her. If a woman's thyroid-stimulating hormone is elevated, it may possibly be causing an overproduction of prolactin, stimulating her breasts, and a doctor might prescribe the thyroid hormone, thyroxin, in such a situation.

The only FDA-approved drug for the treatment of breast pain is the antigonadotrophic medication danazol (Danocrine), which is a derivative of the hormone testosterone. Danocrine, which is often successfully prescribed for endometriosis, inhibits the release of the brain hormones FSH and LH; without these hormones, a woman will not ovulate. The lack of ovulation means that a woman will not experience menstrual flow, and her estrogen and progesterone will no longer fluctuate. Breast pain, which normally increases with the hormonal fluctuation of the menstrual cycle, is therefore prevented. The side effects of Danocrine, however, can include weight gain, bloating, breast reduction, breakthrough bleeding (occurring unexpectedly), and acne. Symptoms can often be overcome if a woman switches to a low-fat, low-salt diet and follows her doctor's recommendations for vitamin therapy.

If a blood test shows that a woman has an elevated level of the hormone prolactin, the drug bromocriptine mesylate (Parlodel) can be prescribed. Although in certain incidents Parlodel has been linked to heart attack and stroke, it is still an effective drug used in special cases to lower prolactin, stop production of breast milk, and alleviate breast tenderness. If you take Parlodel and experience nausea or vomiting, you should stop taking it immediately. Doctors have recommended for some women that a Parlodel tablet be inserted into the vagina, like a suppository. A multicenter European study found a significant drop in breast pain, tenderness, and heaviness with Parlodel but had a high dropout rate (36 percent) due to the side effects of nausea, vomiting, headache, dizziness, and fatigue. Tamoxifen (Nolvadex), which increases estrogen and progesterone levels in other parts of the body but blocks estrogen receptors in the breast, has also been studied as a treatment for mastodynia/mastalgia. While tamoxifen has been shown to be successful at alleviating breast pain, I think this is too powerful a medication to recommend because it carries with it the possibility of increasing a woman's risk of endometrial cancer. On the other hand, as explained in Chapter 24, tamoxifen is beneficial when used as adjuvant therapy to help prevent a recurrence of breast cancer.

NONCYCLIC BREAST PAIN: FROM INFECTION, INJURY, SURGERY, AND OTHER CONDITIONS

When breast pain cannot be connected to the hormonal ebb and flow of the menstrual cycle, it is considered "noncyclic." This type of breast pain is

---

MY RECOMMENDATIONS FOR NATURAL
TREATMENT OF BREAST PAIN

Over the years I have developed a list of drug-free recommendations for the women in my care who are experiencing either cyclic or noncyclic breast pain. Many of the women who have followed these recommendations have found relief:

- A low-fat, low-calorie diet. I have not advised a strict fat percentage or calorie count for a woman's daily diet, but instead I ask that a woman increase the number of fresh fruits and vegetables she eats every day and lower the amount of red meat and high-sugar, high-fat snack foods she consumes.
- Reduced caffeine consumption. If a woman does not want to eliminate caffeine from her diet, I suggest that she at least cut back. For coffee-drinkers who do not want to switch to decaf, I advise only 1 cup of caffeinated coffee a day.
- Exercise. Women who work out aerobically about 4 hours a week have found relief.
- Individual daily vitamin supplements. Daily intake of vitamin A (5,000 IU), B complex (100 milligrams [mg]), C (1,000 mg), E (400 IU).
- Evening primrose oil. A 500 mg capsule, twice a day.

---

much less common, affecting only about one of 10 women who have breast pain. Often described as a burning, sharp, ache that lasts for moments or days, noncyclic breast pain may surface in one spot or be a diffuse ache difficult to target.

Again, one of my first suggestions is to try a different style bra (see box "How to Get the Best-Fitting Bra"), because sometimes the solution to noncyclic breast pain can be as simple as a more comfortably fitting brassiere. Other possible causes of noncyclic breast pain are:

- **Mastitis.** As explained in Chapters 2 and 14, mastitis, a bacterial infection of the nipple and breast ducts, is more often seen in breastfeeding mothers who are more likely to be exposed to bacteria from their nursing infants. Nevertheless, a woman who is not breastfeeding may still become infected with bacteria such as Staphylococcus aureus or Streptococcus species, and her breast may become swollen, red, hot, and painful. Sometimes she may even come down with a fever. The best way to fight mastitis is with a broad-spectrum antibiotic and the application of hot compresses.

Sometimes, if mastitis is severe, a woman may need hospitalization and require intravenous antibiotic therapy.

• **Injury, Surgery, Radiation Therapy, Trauma.** Was there any time when you might have been involved in an accident and your breast was injured? A previous injury to the breast can cause pain in that spot for a long time. I have also met with women who years later have experienced pain at the site of a former biopsy or surgery on their breast. If radiation therapy damages skin tissue, pain may be an aftereffect. Basically, whenever the breast undergoes any sort of traumatic event, latent pain can be a consequence. Anytime you notice continuing pain, consult your physician. Sometimes a blow to a part of the body that has existing cancer cells can stimulate their growth, so it is important for a doctor to examine you carefully after an injury.

• **Weight Gain.** As explained in Chapter 7, the enzyme aromatase in body fat converts the steroid released by the adrenal glands into estrogen. Therefore, added weight increases the amount of estrogen in your body, and this hormonal change can make your breasts hurt. It is extremely important if you are overweight and have breast pain to exercise to lose weight and lower your estrogen levels.

• **Mondor's Disease.** In this rare condition, a phlebitis (inflammation) in the vein of the breast drains from the upper outer quadrant. Sometimes the skin pulls in because fibrosis, a type of scar tissue, arises along the linear path of the vein, down the outside of the breast. The breast can be very tender in the area, and the pain may last from one to six weeks. Symptomatic relief may come from analgesics and a warm heating pad applied to the area. In time the condition will subside on its own.

What to Do About Noncyclic Breast Pain

Noncyclic breast pain is harder to treat than pain that is clearly related to the hormonal shifts of the menstrual cycle. Hormonal therapy usually will not bring relief. Approaches to treatment for specific causes are mentioned above, but, of course, no treatment should be considered without first eliminating the possible presence of a lump. When you consult a physician for noncyclic breast pain, he should conduct a breast examination and recommend mammography and/or ultrasonography to rule out the possibility of breast cancer. Although breast pain alone is rarely a sign of breast cancer, pain that is noncyclic is more suspicious than pain related to hormonal changes, so it is always best to undergo a breast screening. Once I know that breast cancer is not an underlying cause of a woman's breast pain, I often recommend the nondrug treatments that also help alleviate cyclic breast pain (see box "My Recommendations for Natural Treatment of Breast Pain"). For drug therapy, danazol (Danocrine), a derivative of the hormone testosterone which blocks the fluctuation of estrogen and progesterone, sometimes works.

HOW TO GET THE BEST-FITTING BRA

(Note: Always measure while already wearing a brassiere.) To find the best-fitting, most comfortable bra, first be sure of your cup size:

• Measure your chest above your breasts, just under your armpits.

• Measure your chest around the prominent, nipple area of your bustline. (This will provide the "inches" for your bra size.)

• Compare the two measurements.

Comparison	Your Cup Size Is
The same:	AA
1 inch greater:	A
2 inches greater:	B
3 inches greater:	C
4 inches greater:	D

Once you have selected a bra, make sure it offers:

• Good breast position, so that your breasts lie halfway between your shoulder and elbow
• Ample support of your breast tissue
• No indentation at the shoulder straps
• A close fit at the breastbone
• Enough space to fit a finger under each cup
• A back strap in alignment with the base of the cups

WHEN BREAST PAIN COMES FROM OUTSIDE YOUR BREAST

Sometimes there is an inflammation of the costochondral junction, where the ribs meet the sternum (breastbone) in the middle of the chest. This causes *costochondritis*, a diffuse, midchest, arthritic pain that a woman may identify as breast pain. (Note: Both men and women can have costochondritis.) Anti-inflammatory medications such as Motrin and Anaprox can often bring relief.

When breast pain is hard to diagnose, a woman should remember that a consultation with a physiatrist (doctor of rehabilitative medicine) or an orthopedist may be in order for treatment. Sometimes a backache caused by the compression of nerves by vertebrae in the spine can send referred pain to the chest and breast. A fractured rib, angina, and heartburn can also cause chest pain that a woman may identify as breast pain.

MOST LIKELY IT'S HORMONES

My personal experience with caring for thousands of women has shown me that women are not concerned with breast pain itself as much as they are worried that breast pain may be a sign of breast cancer. Once again, I want to reassure women that cyclic breast pain is usually not associated with breast cancer, but noncyclic breast pain, particularly pain that exists in connection with a lump, could potentially signal a breast cancer. For the most part, breast tenderness and pain are hormonally connected to the menstrual cycle and not a major health concern, but no lingering pain in your body should be ignored. You should convey your symptoms to your physician so he can thoroughly evaluate your condition.

CHAPTER SEVENTEEN

You Find a Lump: It May Not Be Serious But It Should Not Be Ignored

It is always a pleasure to tell a woman that the lump that sent her to my office for an examination is a benign, fluid-filled cyst. Whenever you feel a lump in your breast, it is natural to fear the worst—the presence of a breast cancer. Hopefully that is not the case, but no assumptions can be made until a lump is examined by a doctor, and if necessary, biopsied. We are learning more and more about the makeup of breast lumps. For example, in health books I wrote years ago, I assured women that solid lumps called fibroadenomas were always benign, but today we know that certain types, those identified as *complex fibroadenomas,* may be related to an increase in a woman's risk of developing breast cancer. With advanced techniques in pathology analysis, lumps can be profiled more precisely than ever before.

Especially during a woman's reproductive years, a lump is more likely to be a cyst. In fact, two common, frequently felt lumps are soft cysts and firm fibroadenomas. These usually nonmalignant growths present a dilemma to physicians today. The techniques for determining whether a benign lump will someday produce cancerous cells do not exist. A cyst that does not collapse and disappear during an aspiration (needle draining) but remains in place becomes cause for concern. Other, rarer types of breast lumps may also be discovered; those caused by intraductal papillomas (warty growths), fat necrosis (damaged fatty tissue), duct ectasia (clogged ducts), or sclerosing adenosis (excessive growth of lobular tissue that creates calcium deposits). By becoming familiar with the texture of her breast tissue, a woman will know when a new growth appears.

Statistically, most breast lumps turn out to be benign, but the decision about whether to leave a benign lump in place is a challenge to doctors. Our

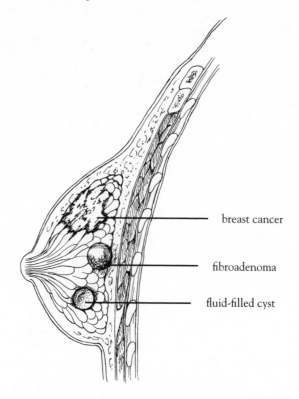

breast cancer

fibroadenoma

fluid-filled cyst

A breast lump may a hard, fixed cancer with irregular borders; a smooth, firm, solid fibroadenoma; or a soft, tender, fluid-filled cyst.

hope is that future noninvasive screening methods, particularly powerful ultrasound techniques, will be able to pinpoint whether cancerous cells are or are not germinating in a breast lump that otherwise shows signs of being nonmalignant. In any instance, women and their physicians must remain vigilant. A lump that is diagnosed as a cancer has the best chance of being treated successfully if it is detected at an early stage of development.

FIBROCYSTIC CHANGE: LUMPINESS VS. A LUMP

Fibrocystic breast disease used to be the catch-all diagnosis for any breast problem involving benign lumps, lumpiness, and breast pain. Today breast conditions are more precisely defined. The lumpiness or nodularity that you feel in your breasts in the second half of your menstrual cycle, after ovulation, is currently referred to as *fibrocystic change*, a natural occurrence that has nothing to do with disease. The overall lumpiness, and sometimes breast tenderness, that are part of fibrocystic change disappear as one monthly

WHAT A BREAST CANCER FEELS LIKE

In general, a cancerous lump is hard, fixed in the breast tissue, and painless, although on occasion it may be associated with pain. Breast cancers are more likely to be found when women are over age 40. As explained in Chapter 3, the best way to be able to know the feel of a cancerous breast lump is to examine a silicone breast model designed for the purpose of identifying different types of lumps (see page 51). A physician or qualified health professional who routinely instructs women in the technique of breast self-examination should have such a model.

When a premenopausal woman notices a lump, statistically it is more likely to be a soft cyst or firm fibroadenoma, not a cancer. Usually nonmalignant, cysts and fibroadenomas can sometimes develop into sites for breast cancer, so a woman still must consult her physician for an evaluation. Sometimes a postmenopausal woman who feels a lump learns that it is a cyst or a fibroadenoma that developed in her younger years and is only being detected postmenopausally, after her breasts have changed.

The bottom line is that every lump must be identified by a doctor.

menstrual cycle ends and a new one begins. Should a noticeable lump and, perhaps, breast pain remain persistent and unchanging through several menstrual cycles, you are experiencing something other than normal, fibrocystic change.

During a routine menstrual month, in the first week after your period, before ovulation and the rise of the hormones estrogen and progesterone, breasts feel smoother than they do in the last two weeks of the cycle. As you move closer to menstruation, milk glands and ducts swell and form cysts, fluid-filled sacs that make lumpiness more apparent and breasts more tender. This is the essence of fibrocystic change: a premenstrual, cystic swelling that may result in lumpiness either with or without pain, or sometimes, pain alone. (See Chapter 16 for more about breast pain.) It is important to remember that a healthy breast can always feel slightly lumpy, as if it contains cottage cheese, but there is a noticeable difference during the second half of the menstrual cycle, when that lumpiness becomes more pronounced. That's why it is always recommended that you perform a breast self-examination earlier, during the first two weeks of your menstrual month.

Women who are on hormone replacement therapy (HRT) to relieve menopausal symptoms should also notice how the texture of their breasts changes, especially if they are taking hormones in a sequential pattern that mimics the hormonal release of estrogen and progesterone during the menstrual cycle. When this is the case, postmenopausal women can experience the lumpiness and pain of fibrocystic change just the way younger, menstruating women do. Breast tenderness and swelling subside when women go off the replacement hormones estrogen and progesterone.

Whether a woman is menstruating, pregnant, perimenopausal, postmenopausal, on birth control pills or hormone replacement, whether she has scar tissue from injury, surgery, or breast implants, once she becomes familiar with the feel of her breasts, a new or different growth will get her attention. Most detectable growths are about one-half inch in diameter and not elusive. A woman who performs regular breast self-examinations will know a lump from her usual lumpiness. A new lump, whether hard or soft, will be large enough to stand out. She will know when she discovers "something," and hopefully, if she is in her reproductive years, that something will be a cyst or a fibroadenoma, which are described in greater detail later in this chapter.

The Effect of Diet on Fibrocystic Change

Whether a relationship between caffeine consumption and fibrocystic change is well founded has been debated for decades and is discussed at length in Chapter 6. I personally suggest that women in my care cut back on caffeine when they show signs of fibrocystic change. In my practice I have seen many women virtually eliminate cysts, pain, and tenderness in their breasts by eliminating caffeine. I also recommend a low-fat diet supplemented daily with vitamins A (5,000 IU), B complex (100 mg), C (1,000 mg), and E (400 IU.) A low-fat diet will also cut back on a woman's daily calories and keep her weight down. Staying slim has the advantage of lowering estrogen levels, and many experts believe that greater exposure to estrogen stimulates cell growth and adversely affects the breasts. The enzyme aromatase is produced by body fat, and through interaction with a steroid released by the adrenal glands, it causes estrogen levels to rise. The more body fat a woman has, the more estrogen. I recommend that women design their diets with low-fat menus that will keep their weight, and their estrogen levels, down.

BREAST CYSTS

Breast cysts are fluid-filled sacs that most often form in the upper outer portions of the breast and are surrounded by the milk glands, milk ducts, and fatty tissue that are the breast's normal components. A cyst can be microscopic, as small as a pea, or as large as a plum. Frequently a fast-forming cyst can pull on the nerves that encircle the breast tissue and cause pain. Cysts appear only after menarche. Most often they are small growths, tiny microcysts of 2 mm or less, in women between the ages of 16 and 50. They may appear with greater regularity when a woman enters her late thirties and forties, as the approach of menopause brings on hormonal disturbances. Unless a woman is on hormone replacement therapy, cysts often disappear with menopause. By the time you can feel a cyst, it is usually 3 mm or more in diameter and falls into the category of a large macrocyst, also called a "gross" cyst.

Evaluating a Cyst

Sometimes a woman can feel a lump that is obviously a soft and squishy cyst, but sometimes a lump that is a cyst is so deeply buried in breast tissue it feels hard. This hard lump is the kind that creates the most anxiety. But whether a growth has been discovered during a breast self-examination or through a breast screening such as a mammogram or a sonogram, if it does not disappear in the course of a menstrual month, it must be aspirated (drained) to verify its identity, no matter how sure you are it is a cyst.

The fine needle aspiration of a palpable cyst is an easy procedure, performed while a woman is on the examining table in the doctor's office. (A nonpalpable cyst is usually discovered on a mammogram and aspirated with the aid of ultrasound, as explained in Chapter 19.) Sometimes a physician first injects an anesthetic into the breast to numb the skin over the lump, but this is not always necessary. He holds the breast firmly in his hand, steadies the cyst, inserts a fine, thin needle into the cyst, and attempts to withdraw fluid. If clear, brown, green, or yellow fluid is extracted, the abnormality is most likely benign. Sometimes the fluid is milky because the cyst is a *galactocele*, a milk cyst caused by the thickening of breast milk in one of the acini. If the fluid is bloody, however, it is more suspicious and every doctor will send the specimen for cytological testing. All aspirated fluid should be sent for cytological analysis, although some breast specialists do not bother, trusting the appearance of the fluid to be a firm indication of a benign condition. I believe that all fluid should be analyzed.

Treating the Cyst

It is common for cysts to be tender or painful. As mentioned in Chapter 16, the only FDA-approved drug for the treatment of breast pain is the antigonadotrophic medication danazol (Danocrine), a derivative of the hormone testosterone. Certain cells of the breast are estrogen receptors; they are like keyholes waiting to be fitted with their estrogen "keys." Estrogen activates these cell receptors, stimulating them to grow and form cysts. Danocrine inhibits the release of the brain hormones FSH and LH; without these hormones, a woman will not ovulate, and her production of estrogen will be blocked. Thus, estrogen will no longer affect the breast, and without estrogen stimulation to the cell tissue, cysticness and tenderness disappear. Danocrine can be so effective for painless cysts. Although it is the designated drug for breast pain, it is also prescribed as a treatment for breast cysts that do not hurt. The side effects of Danocrine can include weight gain, bloating, irregular bleeding, and acne, among others.

Recurring Macrocysts

Macrocysts may be solitary or found in a cluster of cysts, and they often vanish on their own after a menstrual cycle has been completed. When a cyst remains in place through more than one menstrual cycle and is finally aspirated so that it collapses and disappears, it should be gone for good. When it returns in the same spot, a doctor may become wary of the lump. If after three aspirations it continues to recur, he may perform a surgical biopsy to learn more about the lump; every doctor should be concerned that the lump, even if benign, may become a future site for cancerous cell growth. Ultimately, the entire growth may have to be surgically removed to prevent the possibility of it becoming cancerous.

The Link Between Macrocysts and Cancer

Studies on whether the presence of cysts is connected to the development of breast cancer have had conflicting results. Some studies have shown that women with macrocysts have a two- to fourfold increase in breast cancer risk; others have shown very small or no increased risk. A recent Italian study followed over 1,000 women with macrocysts, aged 30 to 69, from 1983 to 1993. Fluid extracted from breast cysts was analyzed, and women who had a type 1 cystic fluid, with a high potassium/sodium ratio, were found to have a *fivefold increased risk* of developing breast cancer, compared with women who had a type 2 fluid, with a potassium/sodium ratio of less than 0.66. The analyses of cystic fluid for a possible cancer connection is a new approach to determining cancer probability. Until further research is completed, doctors remain uncertain about whether a woman who has experienced macrocysts is more susceptible to breast cancer.

When a Lump Is Not a Cyst

A lump that does not release fluid may be a solid fibroadenoma, the most common benign solid tumor in the breast, or one of the rarer types of breast lumps. A fibroadenoma is a smooth growth, whereas a cancerous tumor, which is also solid, often has a rigid configuration because it may contain calcium. A skillful physician who examines the breasts of all his patients can usually get a sense of what a mass may be when he touches a lump, but of

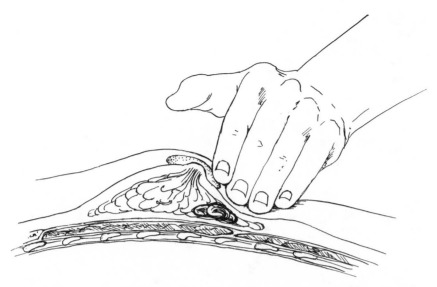

A doctor's examination of a woman's breast. The physician palpates a mass with the sensitive pads of his fingers. If he cannot determine the nature of the mass he will proceed with a fine needle aspiration and, depending on the results, recommend a sonogram or a mammogram, which may be followed by a biopsy.

course he must check out his suspicions using the latest diagnostic methods, such as needle aspiration and/or biopsy.

FIBROADENOMAS

A fibroadenoma can be a bit frightening to discover, because it is a firm, well-defined, painless lump and can immediately make you think you have cancer. Most fibroadenomas, which can be as small as peas or as large as oranges, are diagnosed as benign. The discovery of a slightly increased risk of breast cancer among women with complex fibroadenomas is a new finding that is described later in this chapter. Fibroadenomas are still the most common nonmalignant breast tumors diagnosed in women from menarche to age 25, although a fibroadenoma may appear any time after puberty, and are sometimes spotted on mammography in women in their sixties and seventies. They are twice as common among African American women than among women in other ethnic groups.

In a fibroadenoma, a mass or lump of fibrous tissue forms. Fibrous tissue is found throughout the body connecting muscle tissues. In fact, tendons are made of fibrous tissue. Fibrous tissue in the breast holds the breast in place.

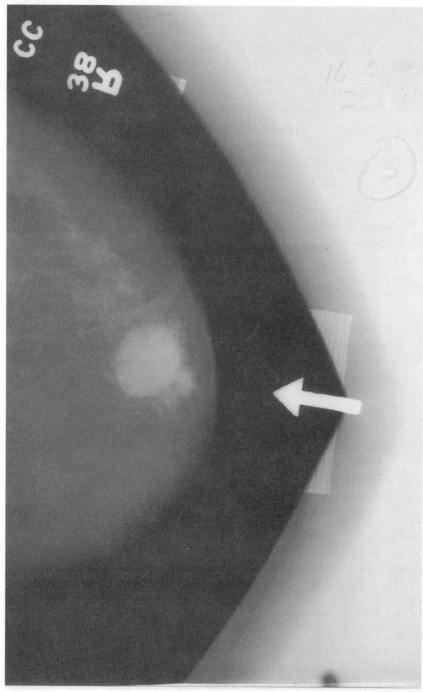

Mammogram of a large fibroadenoma, typically benign, with smooth borders. Some cancers may have smooth margins, so the mass should be biopsied. Courtesy of HealthSouth Diagnostic, Washington, DC.

The formation of a fibroadenoma may occur because of an unknown reason or possibly a hormone imbalance (recent studies have found the presence of estrogen receptors in fibroadenomas) or a blow to the breast. A fibroadenoma grows very slowly, and a doctor can often tell by the feel that a lump is a fibroadenoma. He can confirm his suspicions by withdrawing a biopsy sample of cells from a fine needle aspiration or a core biopsy method (see Chapter 19) performed with the aid of a mammogram or ultrasound screening. A new *high-definition imaging (HDI)* technique for ultrasound screenings is also proving effective in identifying breast lumps as benign and helping women avoid invasive biopsy procedures. You might ask your doctor about HDI if he suggests a core or surgical biopsy for a lump he suspects is a fibroadenoma.

Not Always, But Often, Surgery Is Needed

Once a fibroadenoma is positively diagnosed, whether it is removed or left in place depends on its size, location, and a woman's age. Younger women are less likely to be diagnosed with breast cancer, so a small fibroadenoma in a woman 25 or younger could safely remain in place. When fibroadenomas are large and discovered in women 40 or older, doctors are more inclined to remove them through excisional biopsy, just to be sure they are not cancerous. Sometimes a rare cancer called *cystosarcoma phylloides* can be discovered in a fibroadenoma, but this occurs only about 1 percent of the time in very large fibroadenomas. This is not a worrisome cancer because it tends to stay in place, but it continues to give basis to the belief that a big fibroadenoma is better off removed.

The Connection Between Fibroadenomas and Cancer

Recently researchers at Vanderbilt University conducted an analysis of the health histories of almost 2,000 women who had been diagnosed with fibroadenomas between 1950 and 1968. They found that over time women who had fibroadenomas had twice the risk of developing breast cancer than women who had never been diagnosed with the condition. Women who had what the researchers described as complex fibroadenomas, containing abnormal growths or cells such as microscopic cysts, sclerosing adenosis, epithelial calcifications, or papillary apocrine changes, had *three times* the risk (which increased to 3.72 times the risk when these women also had a family history of breast cancer). The risk was almost *four times* greater in women who had benign proliferative disease (the growth of abnormal cells) in the tissue neighboring fibroadenomas. The fibroadenomas do not in themselves become cancerous, but their presence is considered a marker for future trouble. The increased risk for breast cancer continued to remain elevated even as women aged.

The news about increased risk from complex fibroadenomas, heightened when a family history of breast cancer is involved, may change the approach to treating these growths. Physicians have been inclined to leave fibroadenomas alone, but after the results of this study, they may be more likely to surgically remove a fibroadenoma in the breast of a woman with a family history of breast cancer to analyze it for complex components. Also, women who have had fibroadenomas may be encouraged to begin mammographic screenings at age 35 or 40.

UNCOMMON KINDS OF BENIGN BREAST LUMPS

On rare occasions, the discovery of a lump results in the diagnosis of a benign condition that is not a breast cyst or a fibroadenoma but a warty growth, a fatty lump, a clogged duct, or a calcium deposit:

• **Intraductal papilloma.** As described in Chapter 14, this benign warty growth usually has the added symptom of nipple discharge with its palpable presence. Sometimes multiple intraductal papillomas occur, but if they do, they still tend to feel like one mass.

• **Fat necrosis.** This is actually a lump of damaged fatty tissue that can form at the site of a bruise or trauma to the breast from injury or surgery. It feels solid, irregular, and painless, and can easily be mistaken for a cancer. Sometimes the skin on a fatty lump can be red.

• **Duct ectasia.** A duct may become clogged by glandular secretions, and a condition called *mammary duct ectasia* can occur. This is described in detail in Chapter 14, because nipple discharge is an accompanying sign of duct ectasia.

• **Sclerosing adenosis.** Adenosis occurs when an excessive growth of tissue in the lobules of the breast produces lumps and causes pain. These lumps often show up as calcifications, small deposits of calcium, on a mammogram.

WHEN A LUMP IS DISCOVERED: TRUST YOUR INSTINCTS

Every unusual breast lump must be investigated. A woman's first, natural tendency is to want to ignore the discovery of a growth, but that feeling quickly passes, and I find that most women want a lump diagnosed as soon as possible. I counsel women to follow their instincts in regard to their bodies. I have heard too many stories of doctors advising women to "watch" a lump and return to their offices for periodic monitoring; meanwhile, the lump gets bigger. You must not hesitate to ask your doctor for a breast examination and

WHEN LUMPS ARE BIOPSIED: READING WHAT'S UNDER THE MICROSCOPE

Efforts are being made to reduce the number of surgical breast biopsies that are performed, through techniques such as fine-needle aspiration of cells and core biopsy, in which a large needle removes a tissue sample from a lump (these procedures are explained more fully in Chapter 19), but the main goal after you first feel a lump is to find out exactly what it is.

Whatever procedure your doctor performs, even if he identifies the lump as benign, you should ask for a copy of the biopsy pathology report and question him further. You want to know whether the lump shows any evidence of *atypia*, abnormal cell structure, or *hyperplasia*, excessive growth or proliferation. If either one of these conditions exist, you may have a greater chance of developing breast cancer, and your doctor should remove the growth and monitor you more closely. If a combination of the two, *atypical hyperplasia*, is found, then you are facing a breast cancer risk five times higher than average.

suggest a sonogram, mammogram, or even a biopsy procedure to learn the nature of your breast lump and rule out the possibility of breast cancer. A lump that turns out to be a breast cancer can be treated immediately, and the earlier a breast cancer is detected, the better a woman's chances of overcoming it. Women who are treated for early, localized breast cancer have a 96 percent survival rate and live healthy, productive lives.

PART V

When Breast Cancer Becomes a Personal Battle: Diagnosis, Treatment, Recovery

Genetic Codes and More: An Overview of the Growing List of High-Risk Factors for Breast Cancer

No one really knows what causes breast cancer, but the list of risk factors continues to grow and continues to surprise. In 1995, for example, Australian researchers who studied nearly 60 groups of immigrants who came to Australia and Canada from all parts of the world, discovered that when a woman moves to a different country, her risk of dying of breast cancer rises or falls to match the rate of her adopted land. The implication of the study is that no matter what a woman's early development might be, no matter what her menstrual and pregnancy patterns are, and regardless of the genes she has inherited, she is still strongly affected by outside influences such as diet, the toxins in her environment, and whether her lifestyle has included birth control pills or hormone replacement therapy. It casts into doubt the "window of vulnerability" theory, which holds that the future of your breasts is greatly determined by the food you ate when you were growing up—a time when breast cells were rapidly multiplying and dividing, and you were especially vulnerable to dietary influences. If adult women who move to new countries become susceptible to the same risk of breast cancer death as native-born women, then the impact of health choices made in the formative years may not be as powerful as some experts have suggested. However, this quandary is just one of many in the hunt for causes of breast cancer.

As we now know, breast cancer starts out as a change in the genetic material, the DNA (deoxyribonucleic acid), in the nucleus of certain cells. Dr. Mary Daly, director of the family risk assessment program at Fox Chase Cancer Center in Philadelphia, counsels women that most often these changes occur over a lifetime, from exposure to many things (some of which science has not even identified yet). Among the risk factors currently thought to have more impact than others are age; your family history plus your individual history of breast cancer; your hormonal history, including timing of your menarche, menopause, childbirth, and hormonal medications; and a history of benign breast disease. Among other possible but still unproven sources of DNA changes are dietary habits and environmental toxins—but you would need long-term exposure to these suspected influences to create DNA damage profound enough to cause cancer.

While the assault on DNA from external forces ensues, in certain families women are born with an inherited genetic mutation and have a greater chance of developing breast cancer. If you are in such a family, you will usually see breast cancer occurring in female relatives at young ages, and in both of their breasts. When only one female in a family develops breast cancer, the disease is not likely to stem from genetic inheritance. In families with inherited traits, genetic counselors can compile "pedigree charts" (much like family trees); these reveal the pattern of disease in relatives from one generation to another.

HOW IMPORTANT ARE RISK FACTORS?

We know more than we ever have about what may put an individual woman at high risk for breast cancer, but despite all the progress, and in the face of astounding scientific breakthroughs on the molecular structure of breast cancer genes, the majority of women who are diagnosed with breast cancer have none of the established risk factors. In fact, most breast cancer is considered *sporadic*, occurring spontaneously, with no definable cause. With the exception of having breasts and getting older—two factors that put women at highest risk for breast cancer—no one can say with certainty how meaningful any of the recognized risk factors may be.

In trying to trace the proportion of breast cancer cases that could be linked to risk factors, researchers at the National Cancer Institute analyzed data on 193 breast cancer cases diagnosed among 7,508 women between 1971 and 1987. They sought to calculate how four particular risk factors may affect the onset of the disease in the general population. In 1995 the researchers reported that about 41 percent of breast cancer cases in the United States could be attributed to having a family history of breast cancer (9 percent); having higher family income (19 percent); and never having experienced childbirth or only giving birth after age 19 (30 percent combined). Because many women in the study shared more than one of the four factors, the 41 percent total is less than the sum of the parts. More research is needed to find out how a woman's body responds to these factors and to explore other possible leads into the causes of breast cancer. Still, the analysis helps to shed some light on the kind of impact certain risk factors may have, and once again, the hormonal factor—childbirth—had the greatest significance.

RISK FACTORS FOR BREAST CANCER

What causes breast cancer? In most cases, experts don't know. Some estimate that known risk factors may account for only about half of all cases.

This table shows who falls into groups with higher risks . . . and how high those risks are relative to groups with the lowest risks. Comparing these "relative risks" can be tricky. For example, while a 90-percent increase in risk may sound high, it's less than two times the risk (that would be a 100-percent increase).

If you have:	Your risk is:	Than if you have:
Mother diagnosed with breast cancer		No first-degree relatives (mother, sister, or daughter) with breast cancer
before age 60	2 times higher	
after age 60	40% higher	
Two first-degree relatives with breast cancer	4–6 times higher	
Menarche at age 11–14	30% higher	Menarche at age 16
at age 15	10% higher	
First child born		First child born
at age 20–24	30% higher	before age 20
at age 25–29	60% higher	
at age 30 or older	90% higher	
No biological children	90% higher	
Menopause at age 55 or older	50% higher	Menopause at age 45–54
before age 45	30% lower	
Benign breast disease	50% higher	No biopsy or aspiration for benign breast disease
with proliferation	2 times higher	
with atypical hyperplasia	4 times higher	
Repeated fluoroscopy	50% higher to 2 times higher	No special exposure
Heaviest 10% of women age 50 or older	20% higher	Thinnest 10% of women

Tallest 10% of women		Shortest 10%
age 30–49	30% higher	of women
age 50 or older	40% higher	
Current use of birth		Never used birth
control pills	50% higher	control pills
Past use of birth		
control pills	No higher	
Current use of estrogen		Never used estrogen
replacement therapy		replacement therapy
age under 55	20% higher	
age 55–59	50% higher	
age 60 or older	2.1 times higher	
Past use of estrogen		
therapy	No higher	
1 alcoholic drink a day	40% higher	No alcoholic-
2 drinks a day	70% higher	beverage use
3 drinks a day	2 times higher	

Adapted from *New England Journal of Medicine* 327: 319, 1992.
Copyright 1996, CSPI, Reprinted/Adapted from *Nutrition Action Healthletter* (1875 Connecticut Ave. NW, Suite 300, Washington, DC 20009–5728; $24.00 for 10 issues).

Another attempt to gauge the severity of risk factors was made in the preceding table of "Risk Factors for Breast Cancer" that appeared in the *New England Journal of Medicine* a few years ago and more recently was adapted by the Center for Science in the Public Interest. This table, while helping to put matters in perspective, is far from the last word.

There is a bevy of research activity aimed at learning why more and more women are being diagnosed with breast cancer. The numbers keep climbing. In 1996 approximately 184,300 new cases of invasive breast cancer are expected to be diagnosed, and 44,300 women are expected to die of the disease. To find your place on the risk spectrum requires a comparison of your health history and habits with what is believed to be true about the significance of age, family and personal history of breast cancer, hormonal history, history of benign breast disease, as well as diet, exercise, and geographical location. What researchers do or do not understand about these factors and the latest on breast cancer genes can give you an understanding of your options. Basic biology cannot be altered, but as you will see, you can make a number of personal decisions to enhance the health of your breasts.

RECOGNIZED RISK FACTORS FOR DEVELOPING BREAST CANCER

If you are trying to gauge your chance of developing breast cancer or you have already been diagnosed with the disease and want to find out whether there is anything you can change to lessen your vulnerability in the future, an understanding of risk factors based on (1) biology and (2) lifestyle can certainly help. Genetic susceptibility, which affects 5 to 10 percent of women diagnosed with breast cancer, is a different, separate area of risk that is explained in the "Inherited Risk" section later in this chapter.

THE FORCES OF YOUR OWN BIOLOGY

Living a Long Life

About 77 percent of women who are diagnosed with breast cancer each year are over age 50. NCI figures show an overall one in eight chance of developing breast cancer in the course of a lifetime, but from birth to age 39 those odds are only 1 in 213. A dramatic jump occurs from age 40 to 59, when the odds go to 1 in 26, and from age 60 to 79, when the chance is 1 in 14. Another way of realizing how rapidly breast cancer climbs with age is to look at the fact that only one in 100,000 women between the ages 20 and 24 will develop breast cancer, while about 233 in 100,000 women aged 50 to 54 will. Breast cancer is the leading cause of death in women between the ages of 40 and 55.

Your Family History of Breast Cancer

Many women perceive their risk of developing breast cancer as higher than it actually is. In one study, two-thirds of 200 women whose relatives had been treated for breast cancer overestimated their risk at more than 50 percent when they were actually at an estimated 14 percent chance of developing breast cancer. In reality, women who are at greatest risk of developing breast cancer are those who are first-degree relatives (mother, sister, or daughter) of women who are diagnosed with breast cancer *before* menopause. From the results of population studies, researchers have reported that:

- Women whose mothers or sisters had cancer in *one* breast before menopause have twice the likelihood of developing the disease than women who do not have a family history.
- When cancer was found premenopausally in *both* breasts of a first-degree relative, a woman has four to five times greater risk.
- When breast cancer is diagnosed in a woman under age 40, especially when the cancer is in both breasts, the disease is most likely to be genetically linked.

- If women in three or more generations of a family have been diagnosed with breast cancer at young ages, the disease is without a doubt genetically linked.
- If breast cancer is diagnosed in a first-degree postmenopausal relative, a woman may have a slight increase in risk due to (1) a shared lifestyle that may include similar eating and exercise habits and place of residence, and (2) shared biological traits such as body type, and menstrual, pregnancy, and breastfeeding patterns, but this breast cancer is usually thought to be sporadic and **not** the result of a mutated gene.

Your Personal History of Breast or Other Reproductive Cancer

One of the strongest risk factors for the development of breast cancer in breast tissue is having had a breast cancer before. Microscopic breast cancer has been seen in the opposite, previously healthy breast of about 50 percent of women who have been diagnosed with breast cancer. And specifically:

- A diagnosis of *lobular carcinoma in situ* (a localized cancer) puts a woman at 10 to 30 percent higher than normal risk (which means 10 to 30 percent of the normal 12 percent risk) of developing invasive cancer.
- A diagnosis of *ductal carcinoma in situ* carries a greater 30 to 50 percent higher than normal risk of developing invasive cancer over the next 10 years.
- A history of uterine, ovarian, and even colon cancer has been associated with an increased risk of breast cancer.

Your Hormonal Health History

Most experts believe that a woman's exposure to her sex hormones, estrogen and progesterone, but particularly estrogen, affects her susceptibility to breast cancer. Estrogen affects cell growth in the breast, so it stands to reason that factors that influence a woman's lifetime exposure to sex hormones play a part in determining her risk. A woman who begins menstruating at age 10 and does not experience menopause until she is in her fifties will have a much longer exposure to fluctuating sex hormones than a woman who enters menarche at age 14 and becomes menopausal in her forties. In other words, **the earlier a woman starts menstruating and the later she reaches menopause, the higher her risk of developing breast cancer**.

Since it seems that the fewer menstruations a woman experiences in her life, the lower her risk of breast cancer, athletes, who are known to skip their menstrual periods, may also be at lower risk. Findings have shown that women who were athletes during their teens and twenties have a decreased risk of breast cancer.

Other events that affect menstruation are:

• **Pregnancy and breastfeeding.** Covered in depth in Chapter 2, pregnancy and breastfeeding also decrease the number of menstrual cycles a woman experiences and influence her hormonal exposure. As far as pregnancy is concerned, population studies have shown that the younger a woman is when she gives birth, the lower her risk of breast cancer *after* menopause. In general, women who give birth under age 30 have a lower breast cancer risk than women who either give birth over age 30 or who never give birth. But pregnancy also has a "down" side for mothers: being pregnant increases the risk of breast cancer for a number of years after childbirth, especially for women who conceive after age 30. Pregnancy's positive, protective influence is felt only after menopause, when having been pregnant and carried a newborn to term (preferably before age 30) lowers a woman's risk of breast cancer.

Meanwhile, the research on breastfeeding shows that any beneficial effect on risk would be felt in the reproductive years. Breastfeeding helps to protect a woman against breast cancer when she is young, but not after menopause; at that stage of life, whether a woman has breastfed or not does not seem to influence her chance of developing breast cancer. Also, the length of time a woman breastfeeds is important. Most beneficial effects have been experienced by women who were under age 30 when they breastfed if they nursed their infants for 6 months or longer. Breastfeeding was found to offer the greatest protection against breast cancer among postmenopausal Chinese women who had breastfed—because they had had several offspring—for almost a decade when they were younger! (Chinese women who breastfed only for up to a year had the same risk as those who had never breastfed.) Basically, results indicate that the younger you are and the longer you breastfeed, the greatest chance you have of bringing down your risk of developing breast cancer during the reproductive years. It has also recently been discovered that breastfed daughters have a reduced risk of breast cancer.

In summation, pregnancy fends off breast cancer when you are older, and breastfeeding fights the disease when you are young. **Women who give birth before age 30, and especially before age 20, lower their risk of developing breast cancer later in life, and women who breastfeed six months or more protect themselves against breast cancer before age 50.**

• **Spontaneous or induced abortion,** as it affects hormonal patterns and risk of breast cancer, is an area of some controversy. One population analysis of 845 women in 1994 concluded that women 45 or younger who had induced abortions, particularly after eight weeks' gestation, may have up to a 50 percent increased risk of developing breast cancer. The highest breast cancer risks showed up in women who underwent abortions when they were younger than 18, or at age 30 or older. Since this report, further surveys of more than 16,000 women in Wisconsin, Massachusetts, Maine, and New Hampshire found only a *slight* rise in breast cancer risk among women who have experienced either spontaneous or induced abortions. This latest survey makes the connection between abortion and breast cancer seem at this point, rather weak.

• **Birth control pills.** A growing body of medical evidence is showing that an increased risk of breast cancer exists among women who started on the Pill in their teens and stayed on it for more than 10 years (Chapter 10). For young women, the NCI describes the increased risk of being on the Pill as accounting for only one additional in situ or invasive breast cancer per year for every 100,000 women aged 20 to 34 years. Results from a major study investigating the Pill and breast cancer for women over 35 is due out in 1998. At the moment researchers do not know whether the increased risk they see among younger women on the Pill fades when they stop taking oral contraceptives and enter their menopausal years.

• **Hormone replacement therapy (HRT).** The issue of whether women in menopause who take either combination estrogen/progestin (synthetic progesterone) replacement hormones or estrogen alone increase their risk of breast cancer is explored in Chapter 11. Although some studies do not show an increased risk, the ones that do routinely find the risk to be from 30 percent to 70 percent higher than the normal 12-percent risk. The consensus of the research is that HRT probably brings about a modest increase in the risk of breast cancer, and that this risk appears to start taking effect after a woman has been on HRT for five years or more. Since HRT offers quality of life, freedom from menopausal symptoms, as well as protection against heart disease and bone-thinning osteoporosis, doctors are now considering the possibility of prescribing HRT for menopausal women who have survived breast cancer for a number of years. This new, radical way of thinking among doctors who feel that there is no, or only a slight, risk of breast cancer from replacement hormones, is reviewed in Chapter 11.

A History of Biopsy-Confirmed Benign Breast Disease

A woman who has consulted her doctor for breast lumps that turned out to be nonmalignant may nevertheless be at increased risk of developing breast cancer. As explained in Chapter 17, certain types of breast lumps—*soft cysts* and *firm fibroadenomas*—are suspect as risk factors. Some studies conclude that large macrocysts do not contribute to an increased risk, but others tag a two- to fourfold increase in breast cancer risk from the presence of macrocysts. One Italian study even found a fivefold increased risk, based on an analysis of the type of fluid aspirated from cysts. As for fibroadenomas, the presence of a *complex* fibroadenoma, which contains abnormal growths or cells, may triple a woman's breast cancer risk, and if the tissue surrounding the fibroadenoma has proliferative disease, she may face a quadruple risk. Much about the effect of benign breast disease depends on what shows up under the microscope after a biopsy. If a pathologist reports that any tissue samples contain *atypia*, abnormal cell structure, or *hyperplasia*, excessive growth or proliferation, a woman has a greater chance of developing breast cancer. If a combination of the two, *atypical hyperplasia*, exists, her risk may rise to five times higher than average.

FORCES FROM THE OUTSIDE WORLD

In analyzing population studies, researchers have been able to tell us what parts of the world, as well as what areas of the United States, have high rates of breast cancer. A look at these rates has led to further investigation of the environment in many of these high-risk locations, but geography is just a start for scientific detectives looking at how lifestyle forces relate to breast cancer. There are also personal habits to consider: What do women who may or may not develop breast cancer eat? How do they exercise? Do they smoke? Trying to find the combination of factors that will reveal themselves as promoters of breast cancer has kept a generation of scientists busy. Despite all the time and money expended, however, the answers remain elusive. Most researchers believe that repeated exposure to key elements in a woman's lifestyle have an impact on her cell DNA, but pinning down these elements has been difficult.

The recognized risk factors explained earlier (see box on pages 217–218), and a woman's genetic profile, as described later, are thought to be major influences on whether a breast cancer will develop. The risk factors listed below are considered to have some role in promoting the disease, but no one knows how big a part each may play.

Where You Live

The incidence of breast cancer is about five times higher in industrialized Western countries than it is in Asian countries. The highest rates of death from breast cancer are found, from highest to lowest, in the United Kingdom and Ireland, Malta, Belgium, The Netherlands, Denmark, and New Zealand. These are followed by Canada, Switzerland, the United States, Israel, Germany, Hungary, Austria, Italy, Australia, Argentina, and Czechoslovakia. Asian countries are way down at the bottom of the list.

The migration of Asian women to Western countries has alerted everyone to the importance of environmental and cultural elements. The daughters of Japanese women who moved to the United States developed rates of breast cancer comparable to U.S. women. And as the Australian study mentioned at the beginning of this chapter noted, most women moving to new countries as adults also take on the breast cancer rates of their adopted countries. To find out what is causing these changes, particularly whether they are the result of diet, is being investigated.

In the United States alone, death rates from breast cancer (calculated among white women from 1970 to 1992 government data) are highest in the Northeast, especially parts of New York, New Jersey, Massachusetts, Connecticut, and Rhode Island. High rates are also found in Vermont, New Hampshire, Pennsylvania, Delaware, Maryland, and scattered areas in the Midwest east of the Mississippi River. West of the Mississippi, only the San Francisco area has a high rate of breast cancer deaths. In an attempt to find out what causes these regional differences, NCI researchers recently took data from the 1987 National Health Interview Survey, adjusted for recognized risk factors among the population of white women, and reported that, statistically, the death rates for breast cancer are comparable across the nation. In other words, they thought that rather than being due to environmental issues, the divergent rates in different parts of the country could be traced to the fact that women with higher risk factors seemed to congregate in certain regions. All this still needs further study.

What You Eat

The possibility that breast cancer could be affected by a woman's food choices (see Chapter 6) has been scrutinized up, down, and sideways. The amount of fat in a woman's daily diet has always been a strong contender for gaining a spot on the list of recognized risk factors, but recent studies have disparaged its significance. While the results of two major research projects examining low-fat diets, the Women's Health Initiative and the Women's Intervention Nutrition Study, will not be in until after the turn of the century, mounting evidence makes fat intake seem less significant. Harvard researchers have been building a case *against* fat as an influence for some years now: the latest analyzed data on 335,000 women from seven studies in four countries shows that fat made no difference in breast cancer rates, even when women were on very low-fat diets containing less than 20 percent of daily calories as fat. It may be, though, that *calories* turn out to be more significant than fat in the diet, if studies of low-calorie eating among animals are supported in human studies. We already know that **obesity** heightens risk of breast cancer in postmenopausal women, because added body fat contains the hormone aromatase, which through an internal conversion process increases estrogen. In short, added body fat elevates estrogen.

A choice a woman can make when it comes to eating is to consume more fruits, vegetables, soy products, and foods high in phytochemicals, among them phytoestrogens, which help to block the production of biological estrogen and lower a woman's levels of the hormone.

Alcohol

The latest research into the lifelong drinking habits of several thousand women tells us that one alcoholic beverage a day increased breast cancer risk by about 40 percent; two drinks heightened risk by 70 percent, and three drinks doubled the risk. Dr. Matthew Longnecker, an epidemiologist at the National Institute of Environmental Health Sciences who headed the analysis, estimates that even though the numbers seem high, only about 4 percent of all breast cancers are linked to alcohol. While no one really knows whether it is the alcohol itself or other habits of drinkers that cause risk to rise, it has been shown that only two drinks a day can make estrogen blood levels climb.

What Is in Your Environment?

The chemicals in the environment—the organochlorines in pesticides such as DDT/DDE, Atrazine, Endosulfans, and PCBs—linger in soil and water. The worst of these, DDT and PCBs, have been outlawed, but they are still in the environment and therefore in our food and drink. Organochlorines appear to fall into a group of chemicals called xenoestrogens, which activate the production of estrogen in a woman's body. The xenoestrogens are also in the plastics of some food wraps, food containers, and the lining of food cans. No one knows how much environmental factors affect a woman's hormones and therefore her risk of breast cancer, but prevailing theories and findings are described at length in Chapter 8. Estrogen chemicals, the electromagnetic fields emanating from power lines as well as kitchen appliances, and exposure to radiation, primarily from medical X rays, are often referred to as factors that may possibly increase a woman's risk of breast cancer, but the issue of the environment is a hotbed of controversy.

Despite the controversy, I believe that since the persistent rise in breast cancer rates (1 percent a year since 1940, with a 4 percent per year jump between 1982 and 1987) coincides with the post–World War II introduction of pesticides, herbicides, and petroleum products into the environment; the increase in automobile emissions; and the popularity of electronic equipment, that the environment somehow plays a role in the onset of cancer. Although the unusual rise of breast cancer in the 1980s is often said to be due to better detection through mammography, I cannot help but wonder whether we felt any health effects from the radioactivity that entered the environment in that decade through nuclear accidents at Three Mile Island in Pennsylvania and at Chernobyl in the former Soviet Union. I encourage every woman to recognize personal choices she can make in her environment; for example, she can select organically grown foods, and when possible, ask for medical screenings that do not involve radiation. In general, she can and should be environmentally aware.

Your Exercise Regimen

When considering risk factors for breast cancer, not exercising may bring a woman closer to disease. Chapter 7 is devoted to the good news about the protective effects of a regular exercise regimen. Women in their childbearing years who work out for four hours a week reduce their risk of breast cancer by more than 50 percent. Exercising for one to three hours a week decreases risk by 30 percent, compared with inactive women. And because it is known that the body fat of overweight postmenopausal women has been linked to an increase in breast cancer, the lifelong benefit of staying slim through exercise seems clear.

Smoking

Smoking is bad for your health, and your breasts. Boston University researchers found that women who started smoking heavily (35 or more cigarettes a day) before they were 16 years old ran a greater risk of developing breast cancer than women who started smoking at age 16 or older. The findings, while sketchy, hint at the greater vulnerability of breasts when they are in a growth stage.

As for older women, American Cancer Society (ACS) researchers followed more than half a million women who were initially cancer-free for more than six years, and in 1994 reported that smokers were 25 percent more likely to die of breast cancer than nonsmokers or former smokers. Also, the longer a woman smoked and the more cigarettes she smoked a day, the more she increased her possibility of developing a fatal breast cancer, when compared with nonsmokers. At the time of the study, ACS did not point to smoking as a *cause* of breast cancer but thought smoking may lower immune responses, perhaps by reducing the number of natural killer cells that fight cancer, thereby causing smokers to succumb to the disease more frequently than nonsmokers. More recently, Swiss researchers at University Hospital in Geneva compared 244 women with breast cancer and over 1,000 cancer-free women, and suggested that both active and passive exposure to tobacco smoke *triples* the normal risk of developing breast cancer. (More precisely, they reported that when a woman smokes less than half a pack of cigarettes a day her risk doubles; 10 to 19 cigarettes brings 2.7 times greater risk; a pack or more a day, 4.6 times the risk.) What was very new in the study was the finding about *passive smoke*. Some researchers were astonished by the threefold increase in risk. Perhaps as investigations continue it will be discovered that passive smoke is more or less harmful, but whatever happens, the fact remains that smoking is bad for breasts.

INHERITED RISK: CRACKING THE CODES OF GENES THAT AFFECT BREAST CANCER

The majority of breast cancers are labeled *sporadic*, occurring for reasons that elude the experts. Only about 5 to 10 percent of all breast cancers are hereditary, but the discovery of genes responsible for these cancers, genes that have mutations—structural changes—that can tell a woman whether she may be at higher risk for breast cancer, has sparked interest in genetic testing.

There may be more genes than the two already isolated by geneticists, but right now the focus is on **BRCA1** on chromosome 17 and **BRCA2** on chromosome 13.

Everyone has these genes. In their normal, healthy states they prevent rapid cell division and the onset of breast cancer. When there is a mutation, however, the normal functioning of these genes is disrupted. In effect, the brakes are off, and the breast as well as ovarian cancer cells are free to grow and roam. The women in families with genetically linked breast cancers often develop the disease in their twenties and thirties. When it afflicts young women, breast cancer is often aggressive and deadly.

Work on the BRCA1 gene has come the farthest. Many different mutations that cause trouble have been found within the gene. It is thought to be responsible for 50 percent of hereditary breast cancers, or about 5 percent of all breast cancers. By comparing blood drawn from family members of different generations, geneticists can identify a BRCA1 mutation shared by relatives. A mutated gene can be carried by the father as well as the mother. The discovery that specific mutations on BRCA1 and BRCA2 genes are shared by the descendants of Ashkenazi Jews from Eastern and Central Europe (an estimated 1 percent of descendants share the BRCA1 mutation; prevalence of the BRCA2 mutation is under investigation) also shows that breast cancer gene patterns may be common to population groups as well as to families. (In the United States, Ashkenazi Jews make up about 1 percent of the Jewish population.) Gene testing for BRCA1 is now available at a number of institutions for women who meet a certain criteria.

NOTE: In 1995 researchers at the University of Texas/San Antonio reported that the *position* of a protein on the BRCA1 gene may play a part in identifying the risk and aggressiveness of nonhereditary breast cancer, which makes up about 90 percent of all cases of breast cancer. The scientists regularly found that a protein was either misplaced or absent from the nucleus of breast and ovarian cancer cells. Geneticists are conducting studies to learn whether the San Antonio findings can be supported.

Testing for BRCA2, which affects about 40 percent of hereditary breast cancers, or about 4 percent of all breast cancers, will soon be moving out of the research arena and will also become more widely available. Together, BRCA1 and BRCA2 may be responsible for 40 percent of breast cancers arising among women in their twenties. There is speculation about whether another gene, BRCA3, exists, but as we go to press, no one has found it.

The Dilemmas of Genetic Testing

There is a general wariness about whether widespread genetic testing is a good idea. If a woman is found to have an inherited BRCA1 gene mutation, for example, she has a 50 percent chance of developing breast cancer by age 50 and an 85 percent chance of developing the disease in her lifetime. Yet for a woman who is found to have this genetic susceptibility to breast cancer, it is unclear at this time what, if anything, she can do to avoid the disease.

The blood test for a mutation of BRCA1 is available at the writing of this book—but should you take it? Doctors require that a woman who is interested in being tested for an inherited, genetic susceptibility to breast cancer meet with qualified genetic risk assessment counselors about the ramifications of the test beforehand. A negative finding may alleviate the anxiety of higher risk and passing on a gene to another generation, but a woman still faces the same risk as every other woman in the country. A positive finding can stir up emotional problems, worry, and fear, and a woman still must rely on regular breast self-examinations and mammography, a screening known to miss breast cancers in the dense breasts of younger women more regularly than in older women. She then has to decide whether she should take the antiestrogen medication tamoxifen (currently under study as a preventive agent for high-risk premenopausal women), or whether to consider preventive mastectomy (addressed in Chapter 13). Moreover, if a health insurance company is informed about a woman's positive result, she might face the same denial of insurance or rate increase, that people who test positive for human immunodeficiency virus (HIV) have had to endure. And some employers might regard a woman who has a positive test as someone who might not be well enough to promote to a better job. That is why it is my strong belief that an employer should not be privy to a woman's personal health issues.

As complex as these issues about genetic testing may be, I believe that as genetic testing becomes more widely available, a greater number of women will decide to be tested. If "negative," women will know they are not at higher than average risk of developing breast cancer; if "positive," they will be alert to, and possibly help in the creation of, treatments that will undoubtedly be developed to fight the onset of genetically based breast cancer. Also, women who test positive will be even more attuned to the need to make the right lifestyle choices, such as exercising four hours a week, that help protect breast cell DNA.

ATM

For people who have a rare and progressive neuromotor disorder called ataxia telangiectasia (AT), death comes at an early age—in the teens, twenties, or thirties, usually of cancer. Israeli researchers discovered that about 1 percent of the world's population carry a flawed copy of the gene for AT from one parent and a normal copy from the other. This flawed gene is called ataxia telangiectasia mutated, or ATM. Scientists are trying to learn whether people with ATM are more susceptible to cancer and especially whether women who have ATM are more susceptible to breast cancer. The jury is still out on this. What is known is that people who have AT are extremely sensitive to radiation, and that ATM carriers, while not equally affected, also have heightened sensitivity. This link between ATM and radiation is the subject of studies designed to find out whether women who are carriers are at increased risk of breast cancer from radiotherapy or diagnostic x-rays, including mammography. The prevailing wisdom is that because early detection of breast cancer improves recovery and survival, mammography performed with dedicated, state-of-the-art equipment should help more than harm. As described in Chapter 4, research into highly sensitive ultrasonography, the Crystal Scanner, may be able to offer future breast screenings that are as effective as mammography but without radiation.

A LOOK AT THE NUMBERS: WHO IS MOST SUSCEPTIBLE TO BREAST CANCER?

In 1995 an estimated 182,000 new cases of invasive breast cancer were diagnosed, and in 1996, it is predicted that the numbers will climb to 184,300. While the incidence of breast cancer is rising, fortunately the number of women who are dying from the disease is falling. In 1995 more than 46,000 women died of breast cancer, in 1996 the estimate is a lower 44,300.

From 1940 to 1982 breast cancer rose at the rate of about 1 percent a year, but during each of the years between 1982 and 1987 the number of diagnosed cases climbed at the rate of 4 percent a year. This was alarming. Some experts attributed the increase to better detection through mammography, but others, while acknowledging improved breast screening technology, also believed the rise was real. Since 1987 the number of breast cancer cases seems to have stabilized at about 109 cases per 100,000 women. Although the overall figure for new cases is climbing, proportionately the rate appears to be leveling off. Of course, just why breast cancer has steadily risen since 1940 remains an unanswered question. Is it due to delayed childbirth? Having fewer babies? Environmental factors? The risk factors discussed in this chapter are only clues to causes, but I personally suspect that the increase in environmental toxins—pesticides, herbicides, and automobile emissions, to name a few—has strongly contributed, and that society's rapid growth has generated imperceptible stress in everyday life.

In an effort to understand how breast cancer strikes, statisticians have presented the disease in terms of age and race. The American Cancer Society says that about 77 percent of women who are diagnosed with breast cancer each year are over age 50. But recently there has been a change in breast cancer rates according to race. In 1992, African American women were diagnosed for breast cancer at an overall rate of 101 per 100,000; they were at lower risk than white women, who in the same year had an incidence of 113.1 per 100,000. However, African American women under age 50, who started out having lower rates of breast cancer than white women the same age, have now surpassed white women in this category. Among African American women under age 50, the number of cases has been rising over the last 20 years, from 25.8 per 100,000 in 1973, to 34 per 100,000 in 1992. Among white women under age 50 in matching years, numbers moved only slightly, from 29.3 to 31.7 per 100,000.

The data are harder to come by for other ethnic populations. In California between 1988 and 1992 Japanese women were diagnosed with breast cancer at a rate of 74 per 100,000; Chinese women, 52.1; Filipino, 73.8; Latina women, 69; Southeast Asian women, 31.8; and Korean women, 23.3.

And while there has been a recent decline in mortality rates for breast cancer, this has been only among white women. While rates dropped more than 5 percent among white women, African American women experienced a 2.6 percent **rise** in mortality. The drop in the number of white women who are dying of breast cancer has been attributed to improved screening, which detects the cancer at an early stage, a time when it can be more successfully treated. It is believed that African American women, whose rates of breast cancer had always been lower than white women's, may not have obtained mammograms on a regular basis. By the time cancers among African American women were discovered, they had already progressed to more advanced stages. It is also possible that lower-income African American women did not have easy access to medical care, and this is one of the reasons behind the politicizing of breast cancer. Annual mammographic breast screening should be available to every woman over 40 and particularly women over 50.

WHAT YOU CAN AND CANNOT CHANGE ABOUT YOUR RISK

Scientists do not completely understand how breast cancer begins. We live with the expectation that new links will be revealed, because as I have emphasized, most breast cancers fall into that *sporadic* category—they appear out of nowhere—and are diagnosed in women with few or no recognized risk factors.

That said, for the most part scientists believe that with the exception of established genetic connections, the extent of a woman's exposure to the sex hormones increases her likelihood of developing breast cancer. That exposure is determined by the onset of both menstruation and menopause. The earlier a woman's menarche and the later her menopause, the longer she will feel the effects of fluctuating estrogen and progesterone. A woman has no control over her basic biology, although she can make a decision about whether to take hormonal medications such as oral contraceptives and hormone replacement therapy. Decisions about whether and when to become pregnant and whether to breastfeed (and for how long) are also in her power, but these factors are complicated by modern lifestyles, and no woman should feel she must bear a child before she is 30 to protect herself against breast cancer. Many women who have become mothers under 30 have still been diagnosed with the disease. When it comes to risk factors for breast cancer, we are dealing with *probabilities*.

What strikes me as significant in the quest to find ways to reduce the risk of breast cancer are the reports relating external influences to a woman's DNA. As discussed in great detail, diet (Chapter 6); exercise (Chapter 7); and the environment (Chapter 8) offer areas in which women can have some control. A woman can include more pesticide-free fruits and vegetables in her diet, exercise about four hours a week, and try to lower her exposure to organochlorines and diminish the electromagnetic fields in her home and workplace. Whether a woman is attempting to prevent the onset of breast cancer, or even if she has been diagnosed with the disease, she *can* help protect the structure of her DNA by considering these external forces and creating a healthy, emotionally balanced lifestyle.

CHAPTER NINETEEN

A Suspicious Lump . . .
When a Biopsy Is Needed

What happens when a woman visits her doctor because she feels something during a routine breast self-examination, or her partner feels a lump during lovemaking? A breast screening is the first step in the scientific quest to learn the nature of a lump, and a mammogram or sonogram is necessary. The odds are in your favor that a breast lump will be benign, but diagnosis has become quite complicated.

First, there is the palpable (able to be felt) lump. Competent physicians can often tell what a lump is by its placement, by the way it feels, and by how it appears on a mammogram or sonogram, but they are concerned about possibly "missing" the presence of cancerous cells in a lump that appears benign.

Second, with improved breast screening methods, more and more tiny, nonpalpable (unable to be felt) abnormalities are showing up on mammography or high-resolution sonography. These must be identified, because they may be small *in situ* (localized, technically "in position") cancers, or they may harbor cells that contain *atypia*, abnormal cell structure, *hyperplasia*, excessive cell growth or proliferation, or *atypical hyperplasia*, a high-risk combination of the two. The tiny abnormalities cannot be evaluated by a doctor examining a woman's breasts because he cannot feel them during an examination. They are high-tech discoveries, and they require high-tech biopsies—medical procedures designed to remove cell or tissue specimens from the suspect area.

With more than a half-million breast biopsies performed each year—and perhaps as many as 80 percent proving to be benign—the push is on to find less surgically invasive ways to learn whether growths are cancerous. A generation ago, when it was possible to detect only large growths, a breast biopsy

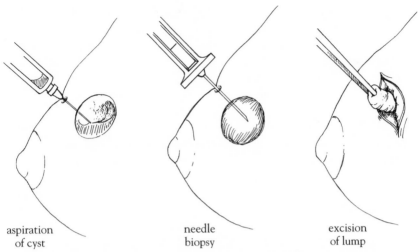

aspiration   needle   excision
of cyst   biopsy   of lump

From left to right: Fine needle aspiration of a cyst (FNA); a nonsurgical fine needle aspiration biopsy to obtain cells from a mass; and a surgical excisional biopsy to remove a lump.

meant general anesthesia and surgery to remove the lump. If a frozen sample of removed tissue was positive for cancer, a mastectomy was performed immediately, before a woman even came out of the anesthesia. Later on, when the two-step approach became common practice, women were allowed to recover from biopsy procedures; they then were told whether their frozen samples were benign or malignant and given time to adjust to the notion of further breast surgery.

Today new techniques are making it possible to identify cell structure from tissue samples so small they are extracted by needle during biopsy procedures that no longer require surgery. These miniature biopsies have become widespread because smaller and smaller breast abnormalities are being spotted on improved mammography and high-resolution sonography screenings. Still, there is no absolute rule about who gets what type of biopsy. The abnormality itself will, to a great degree, determine the kind of biopsy you have. Today's choices include:

• **Nonsurgical biopsies,** the *fine needle aspiration biopsy* and the larger *core needle biopsy*. The needles used to obtain tissue samples are selected based on the size of a woman's breast and the profile of the lump that is being investigated. Fine needles may be used by a doctor who has the expertise to aspirate a lump without imaging equipment, or fine and core needles may be guided by ultrasonography or computer-assisted mammography, a technique called stereotactic breast biopsy.

• **Surgical biopsies,** the *incisional* biopsy and the *excisional* biopsy. More invasive than the nonsurgical biopsy, *incisional* involves local or general anesthesia and the removal of part of a growth for microscopic examination of tissue; *excisional* requires local or general anesthesia and the removal of an entire growth. However, the widespread use of needle biopsies has practically ended the days of incisional biopsy. In particular, the core needle enables a doctor to remove a sample of tissue large enough for laboratory analysis. The excisional biopsy is still performed on large, questionable lumps. Doctors do not want to take the chance that somewhere down the road a technically benign lump may become cancerous, and they are also concerned about leaving behind surrounding tissue that may contain malignant cells.

THE FIRST STEP IS NOT NECESSARILY A BIOPSY

Your physician will assess an abnormality by examining your breasts and getting the results of your mammogram or sonogram. If a growth can be felt easily, he will either aspirate it to see whether it releases fluid and is a benign fluid-filled cyst or recommend a breast surgeon or radiologist/sonographer to perform the aspiration. If an aspiration reveals a solid lump, or a mammogram or sonogram shows other suspicious circumstances, such as the appearance of a starlike growth (usually a cancer), multiple abnormalities, or a cluster of microcalcifications in a woman's breast, a breast surgeon or radiologist/sonographer will suggest a biopsy. The type of abnormality you appear to have will guide the doctor's suggestion.

THE FINE NEEDLE ASPIRATION OF A LUMP

A Lump a Doctor *Can* Feel

No matter how it was discovered, when you and your doctor can feel a lump, the first step to take is usually not a biopsy but a needle aspiration to find out whether that lump is a benign, fluid-filled cyst. As explained in Chapter 17, with a palpable lump, especially a soft growth that a doctor suspects is a cyst, the goal is to learn whether or not the lump contains fluid. The presence of fluid usually confirms the cancer-free state of the growth.

If the lump is close to the surface, the procedure is fairly straightforward. An anesthetic can be injected into the breast to numb the skin (this is not always necessary). The physician holds the breast firmly in his hand, steadies the cyst, and inserts the fine, thin needle for what is called a fine needle aspiration (FNA). When he withdraws the needle, if fluid comes into the syringe, the lump is a cyst, and the problem is solved. If no fluid appears, the lump is solid and the woman must undergo a biopsy.

THE ACCURACY OF A BIOPSY

Radiologists perform a high percentage of today's nonsurgical biopsies, because the latest techniques involve high-resolution ultrasound and mammography. Good diagnostic centers are located in the breast cancer centers of major hospitals and in teaching hospitals across the country; your physician should be able to recommend one in your area.

For a surgical biopsy, your physician should recommend a board-certified breast surgeon.

The accuracy of both types of biopsy—nonsurgical and surgical—depends on:

- the skill of the doctor performing the biopsy,
- the quality of the tissue sample removed, and
- the precision of the pathologist's analysis of that sample.

Today core needle biopsy is considered so accurate that many doctors participating in the ongoing NCI-sponsored study comparing it to the "gold standard" surgical biopsy rejected the study protocol. Doctors trusted a benign diagnosis from a core biopsy and saw no need for surgical biopsy. This happened so often that the protocol for the study had to be changed, so that surgical biopsy was not mandatory in all cases.

A Lump a Doctor *Cannot* Feel

When a sonogram or mammogram detects a tiny abnormality that a doctor can see on the image, the first step is still fine needle aspiration to withdraw fluid. This is tricky, because the doctor cannot feel the growth and must use ultrasound imaging to help him guide the needle to its location. Fine needle aspiration with ultrasound is often performed by a doctor who is skilled in using sonography equipment (usually a radiologist/sonographer at a diagnostic center). High-resolution ultrasound uses high-frequency sound waves, or echoes, to picture the internal structure of the breast on the screen of a nearby monitor, which looks like a TV set. A transducer, which is something like a microphone, is placed on the breast after gel has been applied to the skin. The transducer sends and receives the sound waves that produce the internal breast image. The radiologist/sonographer locates the growth with the aid of the transducer and directs a fine needle into the abnormal area. The needle operates under vacuum pressure, so the doctor is immediately able to drain away any fluid. Again, if fluid appears, the growth is a cyst that will collapse, disappearing from the monitor. If fluid cannot be withdrawn, the growth is solid, and a biopsy is needed. The question then is, *what type of biopsy would offer a woman the greatest accuracy of diagnosis, and the least amount of surgery?* For an answer, doctors are turning to modern nonsurgical biopsies, performed with fine needles and fatter, core needles.

NONSURGICAL BIOPSIES

A Fine Needle Aspiration Biopsy (FNAB) of a Suspicious Lump or Area

Sometimes a fine needle—usually 23 to 27 gauge, or about the thickness of a straight pin—is used to determine whether a suspicious lump or area on a mammogram harbors cancerous cells. The needle, which is under the same vacuum pressure as the one used during an aspiration of a cyst, is inserted into the breast to withdraw tissue cells for cytological (cell) analysis. While a fine needle aspiration of cells is the least invasive method of performing a biopsy, many doctors do not want to rely on it because they are wary of having too small a cell sampling for an accurate diagnosis. A fine needle may pick up noncancerous cells and because its sampling is small, may miss cancerous cells that are nearby. Fine needle biopsies have reported sampling errors and false-negative rates (occasional findings of "no cancer" when malignant cells exist), but cytopathologists who work with radiologists and attend biopsy procedures report very low rates of error, even as little as 1 percent.

There are occasions when a fine needle aspiration biopsy works well. For example, when a mammogram pictures a starlike growth that is clearly a breast cancer, and the lump is palpable and near the surface, a fine needle aspiration biopsy (FNAB) of the lump can be performed by a breast surgeon. In this case, the surgeon may not need imaging technology to help him guide the needle. He can biopsy the lump with a fine needle in the same manner that he would aspirate a cyst. He holds the breast firmly in his hand, steadies the lump, and inserts the fine needle into the lump. By jiggling the needle he dislodges cells in the mass, and the vacuum pressure in the syringe allows him to withdraw cells. When a cancer seems fairly certain, all a doctor needs is a good sampling of cells for confirmation. If his experience tells him the lump is most probably a cancer, but the cells from a fine needle aspiration biopsy are "negative," then he will probably suggest a biopsy that will result in a larger specimen.

The suspicious lump or area that cannot be easily identified and/or cannot be easily felt requires more technology. When a doctor decides to perform a fine needle aspiration biopsy under these circumstances, the needle usually needs guidance from ultrasound or x-ray mammography, also called stereotactic imaging.

ULTRASOUND-GUIDED FINE NEEDLE ASPIRATION BIOPSY

A fine needle aspiration biopsy guided by ultrasound is similar to a fine needle aspiration of a cyst with ultrasound. A woman usually visits a diagnostic center where a radiologist/sonographer uses high-resolution ultrasound equipment to picture the internal structure of her breast on a monitor. The skin on the breast may be numbed by a local anesthetic, and a transducer, the microphone-like object used to touch her breast, receives and sends the sound waves that produce the image on the monitor. Once a radiologist/sonographer locates the suspicious area with the ultrasound equipment, he can guide the needle to it. After the needle is in place, a vacuum is created within the syringe, and cells are pulled into the needle. A doctor usually makes several insertions, called *passes*, of the needle into the area to ensure an adequate sampling of cells. Smears of these cells are made on glass slides, and the specimens are fixed and stained to preserve them and allow them to be read.

How Does a Doctor Know Whether the Cells He Withdraws Are the Suspicious Ones? Usually a doctor performing a biopsy puts cells on slides, fixes them with a special solution, and sends the slides to a laboratory, where a cytopathologist, a pathologist who specializes in cell analysis, evaluates them. This process takes 24 to 48 hours—a long time to wait for an answer about the status of a breast growth. Only then does a doctor learn whether he has captured or missed suspicious cells during the biopsy. Today another option exists.

A breakthrough in this procedure has come from the labors of Dr. Grace Yang, who adapted the cell-staining technique used with the Pap test for detecting cervical cancer, to create the new *Ultrafast Pap Stain* for diagnosing the slide smears from fine needle aspiration biopsies. Dr. Yang, the director of cytopathology at New York University Medical Center, occasionally teams up with Dr. Doreen Liebeskind at Park Avenue Radiologists, where the two women work together to achieve successful fine needle aspiration biopsies. Dr. Liebeskind gives Dr. Yang the cells she has biopsied immediately, and Dr. Yang determines whether the biopsy collected enough suspicious cells to indicate whether the abnormality is benign or malignant. If Dr. Yang does not have enough cells, Dr. Liebeskind immediately withdraws another specimen. This teamwork and the Ultrafast Pap Stain makes FNAB more accurate, and potentially much more popular. The Ultrafast Pap Stain is finding its way into diagnostic centers across the country.

Basically, Dr. Yang combined three existing discoveries in pathology for her new stain. She air-dries the cells removed from the biopsy needle, which flattens and enlarges them. Then she rehydrates the cells with salt water, making them transparent. Red blood cells that might compromise the analysis disintegrate at this point. Stain is applied, and different cells absorb different colors. The result is a slide with clearly visible cell structures that a skilled cytopathologist on the premises can easily read. Thus a woman can

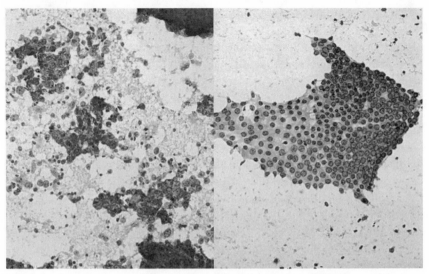

The Ultrafast Pap Stain used in conjunction with a fine needle aspiration biopsy method easily distinguishes between the malignant cells from a ductal carcinoma (left) and the benign cells from a fibroadenoma (right). Cell samples are shown at the same magnification. Courtesy of Grace Yang, M.D.

find out whether her cells are benign or malignant, and if malignant, what type of breast cancer she may have, all before she leaves the biopsy room.

"Ideally, this teamwork should happen for every fine needle biopsy that takes place, but most of the time it doesn't," Dr. Liebeskind says. "A physician will withdraw the sample, smear it on a slide, and have to hope that it is adequate. I work with a top cytopathologist, and if you have a top cytopathologist, a fine needle is as accurate as any other biopsy." Cytopathologists specialize in looking at individual cells, whereas pathologists interpret broader surgical specimens.

STEREOTACTIC FINE NEEDLE BIOPSY

Some suspicious lumps show up only on mammography, are deep in the breast, and cannot be felt by a doctor during an examination. These may be single areas of suspicion or tiny, scattered spots that often turn out to be microcalcifications, small calcified particles that may or may not harbor pre-cancerous or cancerous cells. The best way to target these areas for biopsy is with the use of stereotactic equipment, which involves the use of radiation to permit stereo x-ray images of the suspicious lesion or lesions. What you are actually getting is double-image mammography of the trouble spot, stereo views obtained by swinging the x-ray tube 15 degrees off-center in either direction. The two stereo images are viewed adjacent to each other on the same film, and from these images computer-generated coordinates are created. Once the doctor keys the coordinates into the stereotactic machine, the biopsy needle is automatically aligned with the lesion in question.

Some doctors have what is called "add-on" stereotactic equipment, which converts conventional mammography units for biopsy. Sometimes these are disparaged by radiologists who say that the add-on units, which require women to stand or sit as they normally would for a mammogram, with their breasts compressed between plates, is uncomfortable. In addition, the workspace for inserting the biopsy needle is cramped, and a woman would be too close a witness to this procedure, which would take place literally right under her nose. Women have fainted under such circumstances.

It is recommended that if you are going to undergo a stereotactic biopsy, which may be performed with a fine needle or a larger core needle (see below), that it be accomplished with *dedicated stereotactic equipment*. A dedicated stereotactic unit is only used for purposes of biopsy. A woman lies on her stomach on a special breast biopsy table, which has an opening through which she can lower her breast. The breast then is compressed between two plates for the stereotactic x-rays. The computer calculation of the abnormality allows the doctor to enter horizontal, vertical, and depth positions into the biopsy device. A woman's breast is numbed with a local anesthetic and the biopsy needle, which is in a device called a *biopsy gun*, is placed against a woman's skin and released. (Note: A fine needle may be inserted more than once into an abnormal area to ensure a sufficient sampling of cells.)

A Core Needle Biopsy of a Suspicious Lump or Area

ULTRASOUND-GUIDED CORE NEEDLE BIOPSY

Ultrasound is useful for women with multiple abnormalities in one or both breasts, lesions seen well on only one projection, and suspicious areas that only show up in an ultrasound image. Nursing mothers, who should avoid x-ray exposure, also should be biopsied only under ultrasound. Like an ultrasound-guided fine needle biopsy, a core needle biopsy with ultrasound is performed with the aid of a transducer. The transducer is placed on the breast, where it receives and sends the sound waves that produce the image of the internal breast on a monitor. A woman's breast is numbed with a local anesthetic before the core needle, which is 14 or 18 gauge and thicker than a fine needle (perhaps the width of a toothpick) is injected. The main difference between a fine needle biopsy and a core biopsy is the size of the needle. While a fine needle can be easily inserted into the breast, a doctor must make a nick in the skin to insert the wider core needle.

While looking at the ultrasound image, the radiologist directs the core needle to the abnormal area. The needle initially touches the edge of the lump or lesion, and the biopsy "gun" shoots the cutting edge in and withdraws a "core" specimen back into the needle. The needle makes a click when it moves and a cylinder of tissue is captured. The core needle can often be angled to get samples of tissue from as many as five different areas without having to be reinserted through the skin.

Whenever possible, I recommend ultrasonography for imaging during a biopsy to prevent a woman's being exposed to radiation. Unlike the fine needle biopsy, which withdraws small samples for cytological analysis of cells, there is enough tissue from a core biopsy to do a more in-depth, *histological* analysis, which can show more of the architecture of a growth. In about 48 hours a woman knows the nature of the abnormality. Current research is finding that the core biopsy is equivalent to surgical biopsy when it comes to diagnosing cancer, but doctors still are not ready to stop doing surgical biopsies. Needle biopsies do not reveal the margins of a cluster of calcifications, for example, and whether there is a microinvasion of cells (more about this in the section "Surgical Biopsies").

STEREOTACTIC CORE NEEDLE BIOPSY

For suspicious areas seen on mammography, a doctor may recommend a stereotactic core needle biopsy. The equipment is the same as that used for stereotactic fine needle biopsy, except for the use of the fatter, core needle. A core needle is used when doctors feel they need more tissue for analysis than a fine needle can provide and when there is a cluster of particles, called microcalcifications, to be identified. Radiologists have been pleased with the results of stereotactic core needle biopsy, performed while a woman lies prone on a special breast biopsy table, with an opening through which she can lower her breast. The core biopsy device, called a gun, is automated by a computer. The core needle is lined up according to the coordinates and inserted into the anesthetized breast through a nick the doctor makes in the skin. The 14- or 18-gauge needle is released, and once at its designated depth, can be angled to make three to five passes through a suspicious area to collect tissue samples. This can be done without making a new insertion in the skin. Because the core needle travels about $2^1/_2$ centimeters (about one inch) into the breast, this procedure would not be appropriate for a woman with small breasts.

After a stereotactic core needle biopsy, the needle's entry point on the breast is compressed manually for five to 10 minutes, and a compression bandage is placed on the wound. A woman should be examined by her doctor the next day for any bleeding, clotting problems, or other complications, although most women are usually fine. Women who undergo core needle biopsy rather than a surgical biopsy sometimes question, because of the amount of bleeding that can take place, whether it is an invasive procedure. Nevertheless, use of the stereotactic core needle biopsy is becoming more widespread, and a woman usually receives the results of the laboratory analysis of her biopsy specimen within 48 hours.

The University of Chicago acquired the first prone stereotactic table in the United States in 1986, and today Dr. Robert A. Schmidt, associate professor of radiology, reports that about half of all nonpalpable abnormalities considered for breast biopsy are being biopsied stereotactically. Also, stereotactic breast biopsies are being used to examine lumps that a doctor feels may have a 20 to 25 percent chance of being malignant as well as growths that seem highly suspicious—more than a 75 percent chance of being cancerous—to identify the cancer and help design its treatment. Dr. Schmidt estimates that over 1,000 dedicated stereotactic biopsy machines are now in use in the United States. These biopsies take less than an hour, do not require general anesthesia, cause less pain and scarring, and are less costly than the standard surgical biopsies.

ABOUT THE MAMMOTOME

Dr. Steve Parker of Radiology Imaging Associates in Colorado was one of the early pioneers of stereotactic breast biopsy. He has developed a new device, the Mammotome: a small probe that moves in a rotary fashion and can be used during stereotactic breast biopsy. The Mammotome can excise a large amount of tissue through a small needle hole in the skin, which is especially helpful in the case of clustered microcalcifications—very small, calcified deposits that are difficult to target. Still in its early stage of development, the Mammotome may become a possible option for examining certain types of breast problems.

SURGICAL BIOPSIES

An Incisional Biopsy of a Suspicious Lump

When a lump is large and can be easily felt by a doctor on examination, he may suggest removing a small slice of tissue for analysis. This is called an *incisional* biopsy, and it is performed in an outpatient facility or in the ambulatory surgery center of a hospital. A woman is given a local anesthetic or general anesthesia, and a small incision is made, usually over the suspicious lump. A portion of the growth is removed, sent to a laboratory for analysis, and a few hours later, the woman returns home.

Needle biopsies have nearly replaced incisional biopsies as methods of identifying breast lumps, so if your doctor wants to do an incisional biopsy, you should ask why. The procedure is costly and requires several hours, as opposed to the under-an-hour time it takes to perform a needle biopsy. An incision in the breast cuts through skin, fat, and tissue, leaving a scar. The incision may also be vulnerable to infection afterward. I recommend that a woman seek a second opinion when a surgeon suggests an incisional biopsy to diagnose a breast lump.

An Excisional Biopsy of a Suspicious Lump

A breast lump that is palpable (can be felt by a doctor on examination) is often surgically removed in an *excisional* biopsy, even if it is found to be benign during an initial needle biopsy. As mentioned in Chapter 17, a technically benign fibroadenoma may have surrounding tissue that gives it the quality of a complex fibroadenoma, a lump associated with a higher risk of breast cancer. A doctor will want to remove the fibroadenoma and its surrounding tissue for laboratory analysis to find out whether it falls into the "complex" category or not. In fact, a woman and her doctor often agree together to remove any type of large benign lump, just to be sure that it does not offer a site in which cancer may develop at a later date.

Therefore, an excisional biopsy is usually performed after a doctor has a reasonable sense of the palpable breast lump and suspects that it is probably benign; although it may contain atypical cells, it will not be a full-blown cancer. Reaching a conclusion like this requires a prior biopsy or a fairly certain identification through mammography or high-resolution sonography in combination with a clinical evaluation. If a doctor suggests an excisional biopsy, I recommend that, as with all surgery, a woman seek a second opinion. An excisional biopsy **is not** a lumpectomy. A lumpectomy is performed on a diagnosed breast cancer, and a margin of tissue surrounding the lump must be found to be cancer-free, or *clear*. In an excisional biopsy, it is not necessary to remove an extra margin of tissue, but a woman is still having a small portion of breast tissue removed, and she should ask her doctor first exactly where he plans to make an incision and what her breast will look like after surgery.

An excisional biopsy can be performed in an outpatient facility or in the ambulatory surgery center of a hospital. A woman may receive either a local anesthetic or general anesthesia. As with an incisional biopsy, a surgeon will usually make an incision over the lump, cutting through skin, fat, and tissue. The tissue surrounding the lump is spread apart, and the entire tumor is removed. To control bleeding from the operation, a doctor often uses electrocautery to seal off small blood vessels. Once the lump has been excised, the doctor uses dissolvable thread to stitch the tissue, fat, and skin, and close the incision.

All surgical biopsies require a woman to be in the operating facility for several hours. She should be able to return to her normal activities a day afterwards, but she may still be sore for a while. Her doctor will want to schedule follow-up visits to make sure that no complications, such as infection or hematoma (a blood blister that can form at the site of the incision), occur.

Wire Localization for a Lump a Doctor Cannot Feel

Improved mammograms detect the smallest abnormalities, such as tiny tumors and *microcalcifications*, specks of calcium that can be precancerous or signal the start of an early breast cancer. Microcalcifications are more suspicious if they are clustered in one area of the breast. To identify the nature of tiny tumors or microcalcifications, doctors often decide to perform wire-guided excisional biopsies.

This type of excisional biopsy is performed in much the same way it is for a lump a doctor can feel. A woman receives a local anesthetic so that a radiologist can localize, or mark, the spot for surgery with a thin wire. The radiologist performs a mammogram and uses the film image to guide a needle into the suspicious area of the breast. Then a wire (about the thickness of a hair) with a hooked end is passed through the needle. The hook fixes the needle in place, in the area of calcification or density; a second mammogram confirms its proper location. A woman, who until then is in the ambulatory surgery center of a hospital, is wheeled to the operating room. (Note: One of my patients was horrified that she would have to be wheeled through the halls with wire protruding from her breast; a friendly nurse offered to cover the exposed wire by placing a styrofoam cup over it, and then draping the patient's hospital gown over the cup.)

In the operating room, a woman may receive more local anesthetic, a sedative, or general anesthesia. After a surgeon makes the incision for the biopsy, he follows the wire and removes the tissue surrounding it. After the tissue is excised, it is sent to radiology and x-rayed to ensure that it is the suspicious area that appeared on the prior mammogram. Once a radiologist confirms that it is the correct tissue, the biopsy can be completed, and the X rays and tissue sent to a laboratory for analysis. As with excisional biopsy without wire localization, a woman should be back to normal in about a day. Any pain can usually be alleviated with a mild analgesic.

Because a surgeon does not know whether the suspicious area he removed contains all of the calcifications a woman might have, he will recommend that three to six months after surgery she have a mammogram to double-check a benign laboratory finding. If laboratory analysis reveals cancer, she will begin treatment, which starts with an understanding of the pathology report and consultations about further surgery (see Chapters 20 and 21).

HOW SUSPICIOUS BREAST LUMPS MAY BE DIAGNOSED IN THE FUTURE

BBE (Breast Biophysical Examination)

This new radiation-free technique measures the electrical potentials of breast tissue with an array of skin surface sensors. During BBE a woman lies on her back with her head elevated about 15 degrees for comfort. From 12 to 16 electrodes are placed over the center and margins of the suspicious lump, and also across a woman's breasts and fed into a computer. When a breast cancer

---

UNDERSTANDING THE PATHOLOGY REPORT

After a biopsy has been completed, you will have the pathology report on the nature of the lump. If a finding is malignant, it is time to consider the next step. The high-tech advancement of breast screening and biopsy procedures has led to the discovery of more cases of ductal carcinoma in situ (DCIS), a localized breast cancer, than ever before. A diagnosis of DCIS can result in a variety of treatment options, so the more a woman knows about the cells in her particular in situ cancer, the better she can decide what to do. Especially in the case of DCIS, a woman should seek a second opinion on her pathology report. What the laboratory report of a biopsy specimen can tell you and whether your case requires a second opinion are discussed in Chapter 20.

---

develops, a cell's normally charged particles weaken and cause a shift in the breast's electrical impulses. Developed by Biofield Corporation in Roswell, Georgia, BBE detects the shift, or *depolarization*, and in this way spots a cancer. BBE takes only 15 to 20 minutes and so far seems quite sensitive to cancer. As explained in Chapter 5, BBE will be available in Europe in 1996 but is still under study by the FDA in the United States. If it continues to be effective, it could certainly reduce the high number of breast biopsies.

High-Resolution Ultrasonography: The Crystal Scanner

Advanced, high-resolution ultrasound is being perfected so that a doctor can see the smallest abnormality, and in the case of the Crystal Scanner, that would be as small as 50 microns, one-tenth the size of a grain of salt. The Crystal Scanner was created in October 1992, when the Supra Medical Corporation in Pennsylvania combined the sensitive ultrasonography techniques developed by the National Aeronautics and Space Administration (NASA) with its own high-resolution technology. Clinical studies on the effectiveness of this new technology began in fall 1994.

With this advanced ultrasound equipment it might be possible to identify cancerous cells and eliminate the need for withdrawing specimens from the breast. Researchers from Supra Medical are also working on detection of cancer through an understanding of the length of time it takes for ultrasound waves to pass through tissue. Sound waves take longer to pass through a cancerous lesion than through benign tissue, and by calculating this effect, they aim to further refine the use of sonography.

Scintimammography

Scintimammography uses a radioactive tracer to "light up" breast cancers that are viewed through a special scintimammography camera. The goal of scintimammography is to reduce the high number of unnecessary biopsies performed yearly. The sensitive test exposes women to 300 millirads of radiation (the same dose limit as one screening image for mammography). A woman is injected with the radioactive tracer, which under the brand name Cardiolite is commonly used to diagnose coronary artery disease. After a wait of approximately 5 minutes, she lies face-down on a special table that allows her breasts to fall freely at the sides, where they can be viewed by the camera. A 10-minute side view and a 10-minute front view of each breast are photographed.

The technique is being pioneered by Dr. Iraj Khalkhali at Harbor/ UCLA Medical Center in Torrance, California. His research, described in Chapter 4, has prompted clinical trials in the United States, Canada, and Europe. The FDA is analyzing the data.

A TIME OF TRANSITION

We are in a transition period in medicine. Right now, high-tech screening methods are pointing out smaller and smaller suspicious growths and areas of abnormality in breasts, but when it comes to analyzing these masses, we still are playing "catch-up." Doctors need equally good high-tech methods for performing biopsies to define the nature of these growths so that women do not require invasive (surgical) procedures—especially as the majority of the findings have been benign.

I believe that the research that helps to develop noninvasive, radiation-free biopsies is the most progressive, and I am heartened by the work being done to create techniques such as BBE and the Crystal Scanner. Also, at Park Avenue Radiologists in New York, Dr. Doreen Liebeskind is involved in the development of a biopsy technique that could be used in conjunction with MRI (magnetic resonance imaging) and would be especially helpful for women under 50, who are still in their reproductive years and have dense breast tissue.

CHAPTER TWENTY

After the Biopsy:
What the Pathology Report
Will Tell You

"Benign" is the result in about 80 percent of breast biopsies, but thousands of women are among the approximately 20 percent whose biopsy reports show breast cancer. Suspicious lumps must always be identified. With the findings from a biopsy a woman and her doctor begin to develop a profile of a discovered malignancy. The pathology report of a biopsy is the first step in understanding how the disease has taken hold in your body, but like so many aspects of breast care, the report's finding can be controversial. Many women are now seeking second opinions on their initial biopsy reports even before surgery is discussed.

WHY A SECOND OPINION ON A BIOPSY REPORT MIGHT BE NEEDED

As mentioned, a second opinion on a biopsy report is becoming more commonplace, and I encourage women to seek the advice of a respected pathologist when the results are not clear-cut or when their common sense tells them that results do not correspond with the clinical signs of a suspicious lump. For example, a woman who receives a benign finding may still be haunted by a suspicious mammogram and the feel of a lump. On the other hand, every so often the newspaper headlines declare that a woman underwent a mastectomy for a cancer that was not there. Even if a woman has only her intuition to rely on, a second opinion from a respected pathologist who examines her slides and her report may prevent a mistake from becoming a tragedy.

The situation that usually generates the most interest in second-opinion pathology is the diagnosis of *carcinoma in situ* (a breast cancer that remains on site, technically "in position," where it originated in a duct or a lobule, and does not spread). One type, *ductal carcinoma in situ (DCIS)*, which remains on site in the duct, causes particular concern when it is diagnosed by a pathologist. One would think that by its nature, DCIS would cause little trouble because it is a stationary cancer. Not so!

The difficulties reside in these issues: DCIS is difficult for a pathologist to decipher; experts are struggling to understand how to evaluate conditions in the cells of DCIS that signal a risk of more aggressive, invasive breast cancer developing later on. Most of all, controversy rages over whether this type of cancer should be treated with some form of breast-conserving surgery, with or without radiation, or by mastectomy. When it comes to DCIS, nothing is clear-cut. We are hearing more and more about differences of opinion among pathologists who are, in effect, making medical judgment calls.

In a well-known study from Yale University, five of the country's top pathologists independently examined 17 slides that could be diagnosed anywhere along the spectrum of atypia (abnormal cells), hyperplasia (excessive cell growth), atypical hyperplasia (a proliferation of abnormal cells), and carcinoma in situ. There was not one case on which all five experts agreed. In a second, different study, six pathologists were given a uniform set of diagnostic guidelines to follow in reviewing slides. Under these specific directions, they still reached unanimous decisions in only 58 percent of the cases. In San Francisco Dr. Michael D. Lagios, medical director of the Breast Consultation Service at St. Mary's Medical Center, and the first to develop the concept of grading for diagnosis of DCIS, says that he and his team revise the initial diagnosis on 35 percent of the cases they review. "These represent cases that are presented as microinvasion (a tiny malignancy just beginning to spread), which in fact are not; cases of in situ or noninvasive cancer that become, on review, invasive, or turn out to be atypical duct hyperplasia, a much lower risk situation; and some cases that are actually presented as invasive cancer, which turn out to be absolutely benign disease."

HOW DIFFERENT TYPES OF BIOPSIES DETERMINE WHAT'S DETAILED IN THE PATHOLOGY REPORT

The amount of information a woman receives about her newly diagnosed breast cancer depends on whether she has undergone a fine needle aspiration biopsy (FNAB), a core biopsy, or a surgical biopsy. The surgical biopsy of part of a growth, an incisional biopsy, really is outdated. The excisional biopsy, surgical removal of all of a suspicious lump, is still performed. This provides the strongest profile of a discovered breast cancer, but often all a woman and her doctor must know is whether the area of concern is benign or cancerous, and evaluation of a fine needle aspiration biopsy by a

WHERE TO GO FOR A SECOND OPINION ON A BIOPSY REPORT

Pathological analysis is a combination of art and science, so a second opinion on a questionable diagnosis makes sense. In particular, when the diagnosis is DCIS, a woman is entering an area of medical controversy. Doctors do not have a firmly established approach to treating this type of breast cancer, and biopsy results are extremely important in influencing their later recommendations.

A second opinion on your biopsy slides and specimens can be requested from a pathologist at a breast cancer center or major teaching hospital other than the one at which your original report was prepared. Ask your doctor to refer your case to a pathologist at a different institution, or consult one of the experts listed in the breast pathology section of *The Best Doctors in America* (Woodward-White, 1992, available in libraries). You can also arrange to have your slides evaluated at the following second opinion services (fees cited are as of this writing):

• **Armed Forces Institute of Pathology, Civilian Consultation Program** in Washington, DC/For information, phone: 202-782-2110. The AFIP's Civilian Consultation Program provides a second opinion when a woman's biopsy slides and specimens are forwarded by a pathologist. The AFIP will make arrangements only through doctors. You can ask your doctor to have the pathologist contact the AFIP, which arranges to have the slides picked up and returned by Federal Express. After the AFIP completes its review, its second opinion report is sent to the physician. The turnaround time for diagnosis is three to four working days and the fee, which includes the delivery charge, is $120.

• **WomanKind Breast Cancer Consultation Service, St. Mary's Medical Center** in San Francisco, CA/For information, phone: 415-750-5848. Dr. Michael D. Lagios, the pioneer in DCIS diagnosis, is medical director of WomanKind's BCCS. This service accepts self-referrals from women seeking second opinions on biopsy reports of breast cancer, precancers, and atypia. When you contact Woman-Kind, an authorization will be faxed to you to sign and return. The signed authorization allows the service to request a Federal Express pick-up of your biopsy slides and mammograms. Within two days of receiving the slides and mammograms, Dr. Lagios himself reviews the material and writes the second-opinion diagnostic report, which is sent to you and your designated doctor. After the report is complete, you will be scheduled for a consultation with Dr. Lagios, either in person or by phone, about your case. The total cost is $525. If you want to discuss multiple aspects of your breast care with a team of physicians, WomanKind offers you the opportunity to meet with its Breast Cancer Consultation Panel, a team of St. Mary's doctors, which may include a pathologist, breast surgeon, reconstructive surgeon, radiation oncologist, and medical oncologist. The fee for an appointment with the panel is $50.

cytopathologist (a doctor who specializes in the analysis of cells) can tell them that.

When a FNAB is performed with a cytopathologist present, a woman can know before she leaves the doctor's office whether she has a breast cancer, what type it is, and how it is graded. If a cytopathologist is not on the premises, a woman will usually have to wait 24 hours (delays as long as 72 hours have been reported) for the results of her test. The results of a larger, core needle biopsy can be expected in about 48 hours, or two days. An FNAB results in cell, rather than tissue, samples, so a cytopathologist is not able to describe the architecture (the in situ vs. invasive nature) of a tumor and report its size. A core needle biopsy removes pencil-lead-sized "cores" of tissue, giving a doctor more to work with. A tissue sample from a surgical, incisional biopsy, which is fading with the popularity of core needle biopsies, provides a pathologist with a large specimen, a slice from the suspicious lump.

Samples from either type of needle or surgical biopsy can be evaluated in a laboratory with advanced, computerized equipment, and biochemical features of a growth can be included in a report. A doctor may request hormone receptor status, DNA analysis, and genetic biomarkers (discussed later on in this chapter). If an excisional biopsy is performed and a suspicious mass is removed with a margin of breast tissue, a pathology report can be quite complete. The results of an excisional biopsy may not be ready for 48 to 72 hours (two to three workdays). Even though a woman may want to know the results quickly, a pathologist may determine that he has to go deeper into the tissue, and this may add another day's wait.

WHAT A BIOPSY REPORT TELLS YOU

An initial biopsy report offers a diagnosis of your condition. From a fine needle aspiration biopsy, a cytopathologist (a doctor who evaluates cell samples, as opposed to a pathologist who examines tissue) can identify cell characteristics that signal either cancer or benign conditions such as fibrocystic change, nodularity, or fibroadenoma. Also, cytopathology can identify the abnormal cells of *atypia*, or the excessive cell growth of *hyperplasia*, or *atypical hyperplasia*, a combination of the two that puts a woman at higher risk of developing invasive breast cancer. Cytopathology cannot distinguish invasive from noninvasive disease, or certain atypias, in situ and invasive cancers that share a low nuclear grade (see below). These further distinctions require tissue samples from a core needle or surgical biopsy, which undergo a pathologist's scrutiny. When a doctor identifies breast cancer, he also reports on what type of cancer it is and describes how uniform or *well differentiated* the cancer cells appear (well-differentiated cells signal more controlled, less aggressive cancer; poorly differentiated cells indicate wild-looking, more aggressive cancer), and what their *nuclear grade* is (a low-grade cancer is less aggressive than a higher grade).

Type of Cancer

More than 75 percent of breast cancers are classified as *ductal carcinoma*, and about 7 percent as *lobular carcinoma*. (Sometimes a biopsy report will call a ductal or lobular breast cancer an *adenocarcinoma*.) It used to be believed that ductal carcinomas arose in ducts, while lobular carcinomas arose in lobules, the smallest group of end ductules; however, it is now recognized that the majority of both ductal and lobular carcinomas arise in lobules or terminal ductolobular units (TDLU). There are, however, about 20 percent of breast cancers confined to the ducts, classified as *in situ* or *intraductal carcinomas* (see below) or *Paget's disease*, diagnosed in the nipple. *Inflammatory breast cancer*, which is mostly characterized by swelling, redness, and warmth, may be diagnosed by a skin biopsy. In addition, three rare types of cancer can on occasion be discovered in the breast: *cytosarcoma phyllodes*, *angiosarcoma*, and *primary lymphoma*.

A fine needle aspiration biopsy may not be able to identify more than the presence of ductal or lobular carcinoma and its grade but with a core needle or surgical biopsy, a report may define the cancer as *invasive ductal (or lobular) carcinoma* or *ductal (or lobular) carcinoma in situ*.

Invasive ductal (or lobular) carcinoma may also be called *infiltrating ductal (or lobular) carcinoma*. Whatever the term, it means that the cancer has spread from its original site in a duct or a lobule and has started to grow into surrounding tissue. Invasive ductal breast cancer is the most common, accounting for about 75 percent of breast cancers, while invasive lobular breast cancer comprises only 5 to 10 percent of breast cancers. Lobular breast cancer is harder to spot on a mammogram because it does not always show up as a recognizable lump but instead creates an ill-defined thickening in the breast or infiltrates insidiously. Invasive lobular breast cancer also has a slightly higher chance (about 5 percent) of appearing in both breasts.

The three most common special types of invasive breast cancer are:

• *Tubular* cancers reproduce to a high degree the hollow, tubular shape of the breast ducts. These are slow-growing cancers and when small, rarely involve the lymph nodes.

• *Medullary* cancer is well circumscribed, resembles the gray matter of brain tissue (the medulla) in appearance, and has a favorable prognosis. True medullary cancer infrequently metastasizes but is often confused with high-grade invasive ductal carcinomas, which generally have a poorer prognosis.

• *Mucinous* (*or colloid*) breast cancers are recognizable by the mucin collected around the tumor cells. The more mucinous a tumor is, the more slow-growing it is.

Ductal (or lobular) carcinoma in situ may also be called *noninvasive ductal* (*or lobular*) *carcinoma* or *intraductal carcinoma*. Carcinoma in situ reveals itself as a proliferation of microscopic, malignant-appearing cells within ducts or lobules. In situ, or "in position," these cells do not invade the surrounding breast tissue, but ductal carcinoma in situ (DCIS) and lobular carcinoma in situ (LCIS) are worrisome for different reasons.

DCIS can be a *direct precursor* to invasive breast cancer, and is of greater concern than LCIS, a *marker lesion* indicating possible increased risk of developing invasive breast cancer in either breast. If a woman is diagnosed with LCIS in the left breast, for example, she has an equal chance of developing breast cancer in either the left or the right breast, but the risk is relatively small: about 0.9 percent per year cumulative for both breasts. The majority of women diagnosed with LCIS will never develop invasive breast cancer in their lifetimes.

Among women with high-grade DCIS, about 1 percent a year develop invasive breast cancer after lumpectomy. The risk is usually confined to the originally diagnosed breast, and generally to the actual site of the prior biopsy. In contrast to LCIS, which is characteristically multicentric (located in more than one quadrant of the breast), DCIS has been shown in recent studies to be largely unifocal (in one location) or multifocal (in more than one location but still within a single segment of the breast). In the past it has been estimated that about 25 percent of women with DCIS develop breast cancer, but Dr. Lagios has developed a classification system for DCIS based on nuclear grade and *necrosis*, the presence of dead cancer cells. He has created a new way of gauging the threat of invasive cancer.

He found that in over 10 years' follow-up, the local recurrence of cancer, particularly invasive cancer, was different for different subtypes. Breast cancer recurred in high-grade DCIS at a rate of 32 percent (16 percent were invasive breast cancers), but for intermediate- and low-grade DCIS, that rate dropped to 2.3 percent. This means that DCIS on a biopsy report, which is usually for an excisional biopsy done with wire localization, must be carefully evaluated by more than one pathologist. A woman risks overtreatment for DCIS and undergoing a mastectomy, when all she may need is breast-conserving surgery, removal of the area of in situ cancer along with a wide margin of tissue (radiation therapy may or may not be required; see Chapter 23).

At the Breast Center in Van Nuys, California, Dr. Melvin Silverstein, medical director and senior surgical oncologist, has created the Van Nuys Prognostic Index (VNPI) for classifying DCIS. VNPI ranks a growth according to a score of 1 (best) to 3 (worst) in each of three categories: (1) size of the growth, (2) margins that are widely clear of tumor, and (3) presence or absence of high nuclear grade and comedo-type necrosis. This formula led to scores ranging from 3 to 9 and was tested on 333 women (195 women were treated with breast-conserving surgery and 138 with breast-conserving surgery with radiation) to determine what treatment would have been most effective, based on the VNPI. The end result showed that on the low end of the spectrum, women with a score of 3 or 4 did extremely well with or without radiation. Women with scores of 5, 6, and 7 benefited from radiation, and women with an 8 or 9 had a high rate of recurrence despite radiation therapy. Mastectomy should be seriously considered for women who place on the high end of the scoring.

Most attempts to find out how aggressive a woman's diagnosed DCIS might be have focused on deciding whether the pattern of her in situ carcinoma was *papillary*, large flowerlike growths; *solid*, a grouping of cells with no spaces; *micropapillary*, a fingerlike grouping of cells within a duct; *cribriform*, a grouping of cells that contained holes, like those in a sponge, as they filled a duct; and *comedo*, an ugly collection of cells, many of them with necrosis, that filled a duct and created a white center, like a pimple about to ooze. Of these types, the comedo has been considered the most likely to signal the future presence of invasive cancer and the most worrisome, but a woman may have a mixture of types in a single diagnosis of DCIS. Both Doctors Lagios and Silverstein, in using new classification systems for the aggressiveness of DCIS, would like to see the names of pattern formation of cells phased out. As it turns out, much DCIS that is graded "high" or that has a lot of necrosis involves comedo (although not always), and as Dr. Silverstein points out, as far as treatment is concerned, other factors such as tumor size and margins play important roles. A woman must take the time to build a profile of her condition and assess her best course of action when she is diagnosed with DCIS. (While Dr. Silverstein is not involved in an organized second-opinion service [see page 248], a woman who has been diagnosed with DCIS may contact him at 818-787-9911, for information about making an appointment to discuss her case.)

With today's more sensitive mammography equipment, the American Cancer Society estimates that 25,000 new cases of DCIS will be diagnosed in 1996, representing about 13 percent of that year's breast cancers. Compare this figure to 1978, when a survey by the American College of Surgeons reported that less than 1 percent of all breast cancers were DCIS.

The following is a list of breast cancer classifications:

Ductal
   invasive
   in situ (also called intraductal or noninvasive)
   inflammatory
   medullary
   mucinous (colloid)
   papillary
   tubular
   other
Lobular
   invasive
   in situ (also called intraductal or noninvasive)
Nipple
   Paget's disease
   Paget's disease with in situ carcinoma
   Paget's disease with invasive ductal carcinoma
Undifferentiated carcinoma
Rare types of breast malignancies not considered carcinoma
   Cytosarcoma phyllodes
   Angiosarcoma
   Primary lymphoma

Size

Needle biopsy reports will not be able to give a precise measurement of a suspicious area or lump, but a doctor can make an educated estimate from the image seen on a mammogram or sonogram. As for surgical biopsies, when an entire lump or area is removed during an excisional biopsy, the pathologist can learn the exact size of a tumor. However, most women do not have excisional biopsies and must wait until they have had more definitive surgery, either a lumpectomy or other breast-conserving treatments, or a mastectomy, before they can know the size of their breast cancer. It is also after the more extensive surgery that a breast cancer is staged according to its TNM classification (T=tumor size; N=node involvement; M=metastasis). For now, if a woman has an excisional biopsy and gets a sizing of her tumor, a smaller tumor brings a more favorable prognosis. There is a direct relationship between the average maximum diameter of an invasive cancer and the risk of metastasis to the lymph nodes.

Nuclear Grading

The individual nuclei of cells can be assessed for their capacity to divide, and graded low, intermediate, or high, or on a scale of 1 to 3. The most rapidly

dividing cells are graded higher on the scale and are considered the more dangerous and aggressive. All needle and surgical biopsy results should include a
nuclear grading. A pathologist may also note whether cells appear to be well
differentiated, which is a sign that the disease is more stable and less aggressive, or poorly differentiated, in other words, wild-looking and faster-growing.

MOLECULAR TESTS INCLUDED IN A BIOPSY REPORT

The biopsy report is essentially an aid for helping a doctor predict the
behavior of a cancer. Dr. Mazhar Rishi, assistant chairman of the department
of gynecologic and breast pathology at the Armed Forces Institute of
Pathology in Washington, DC considers the two most important factors in
prediction are the size of a tumor (the smaller, the better) and the involvement of axillary lymph nodes (if lymph nodes removed during breast cancer
surgery are negative for cancer cells, the situation is much better than if they
are positive). "You want to know the size of a tumor, the involvement of
axillary lymph nodes, the grade, and the histology, which is how the cancer
looks under a microscope," explains Dr. Rishi, "and next you want to know
whether estrogen and progesterone receptors (ER and PR) are negative or
positive." These hormone receptor tests show a cancer's sensitivity to
estrogen and progesterone, and they help a doctor decide whether a woman
will respond to hormonal treatments.

Of course, an initial biopsy does not reveal lymph node status; this is
learned in the pathology report that follows breast cancer surgery (see
Chapter 22). Often on initial biopsy, a doctor requests only the main features of a cancer: its type, size, nuclear grade, and a description of its appearance. Needle and surgical biopsies offer these main features. Today, however,
the list of characteristics that can be discovered about a cancer is growing,
and the aggressiveness of a woman's disease can be exposed more clearly
than ever before. Science has provided pathologists with the technology to
perform advanced molecular testing on cells, which means they can now
identify estrogen and progesterone receptors, analyze DNA by computer, and
pinpoint specific biomarkers of cancer activity, such as finding extra copies,
or an "overexpression," of the HER-2/neu oncogene and its protein on the
surface of cancer cells. How much information does an initial biopsy report
contain? That depends.

Either a woman's doctor requests that certain diagnostic characteristics
be included in a biopsy report or the pathologist himself determines the
report's components. In addition to the main features of a discovered cancer,
he may ask for hormone receptor status after a needle or surgical biopsy. The
gathering of more extensive information is usually more likely if the initial
biopsy is surgical and results in a large tissue specimen. Often, additional
characteristics do not come until completion of breast surgery and removal of

lymph nodes. Briefly, molecular testing can reveal the following information about a breast cancer.

Estrogen and Progesterone Receptor Status

A receptor is like a lock, and a hormone, its custom-made key. When the hormone estrogen fits into a receptor in a cancer cell, that cancer is considered estrogen-receptor positive. A breast cancer cell may have receptors for both estrogen and progesterone; estrogen alone; or progesterone alone. When a breast cancer cell is estrogen-receptor positive, then the hormone estrogen attaches to the receptor in the cell and causes cellular changes. Postmenopausal women often have the less aggressive estrogen-receptor positive tumors, while women in their reproductive years are more likely to have estrogen-receptor negative breast cancers. When a woman has positive hormone receptors, a doctor can consider treating her with antihormonal drugs that will block the availability of the receptors.

Hormone receptor status can be difficult to cull from the small sample of cells withdrawn during a fine needle biopsy, but a top cytopathologist can often succeed. Information about estrogen and progesterone receptors and other biochemical features are routinely determined from core needle biopsies and surgical biopsies. As mentioned earlier, an analysis of these features may only be included in the pathology report of the mass in its entirety, following breast-conserving surgery or mastectomy.

DNA Analysis

The computer-calculated *flow cytometry* of a breast cancer's DNA—the amount of genetic material in the cells and its growth rate—is also an indication of the aggressiveness of a woman's disease. Flow cytometry appears on a pathology report as:

• PLOIDY

The DNA of normal human cells is defined as *diploid*, matching in genetic material. If extra material appears in the nuclei, the cells are called *aneuploid*. The abnormal aneuploid cells appear in about 70 percent of breast cancers. They are considered less favorable, and more aggressive than diploid cells.

• S-PHASE FRACTION

The S-phase fraction is an indirect estimate of the growth rate of a tumor. It refers to the fraction of tumor cells that are in the process of producing additional DNA in preparation for cell division. If a cancer has a high S-phase fraction, then it should be treated as more aggressive disease. Dr. Rishi has found that different labs measure S-phase fractions differently, "but generally 7 is considered to be the dividing line," he says. "If someone tells me the S-phase is 20, that's very high, but if I hear a 4 or 5, that's low. When you get the report, each lab tells you what their 'normal' or 'control' value is, and you have to compare your S-phase with that." S-phase fraction is second in importance to tumor size in estimating prognosis for node-negative breast cancers.

Biomarkers

High-tech molecular testing is enabling researchers to discover new genetic features of cancer cells. These new features, called *biomarkers*, have created a category of characteristics that a pathologist can explore during analysis of a biopsy specimen. Biomarkers offer more and more clues to cancer activity and more and more possibilities for the creation of drug treatments to counter cancer growth. One example is the discovery of extra copies of an oncogene (a gene that contributes to cancer) called *HER-2/neu* and its protein on the surface of cancer cells. This gene appears to be involved in more than 30 percent of breast cancers. The "overexpression" of HER-2/neu signals an aggressive cancer, one particularly resistant to chemotherapy. HER-2/neu immune serum is under investigation in the form of an antibody that would bind to the HER-2/neu receptor protein on the surface of the cancer cells and block the growth-promoting actions of the HER-2/neu oncogene.

Another biomarker is a mutation in the tumor suppressor gene p53, also known as TP53. The p53 appears to be involved in more than half of all breast cancers. The presence of the mutated gene in breast cancer cells has been associated with the progression of cancer.

Other biomarkers are found in a cancer cell's growth factors and telomerase (a ribonucleoprotein enzyme) activity. More biomarkers are being researched every day. By opening up a world of biomarkers through molecular biology, scientists are creating a new system for profiling a breast cancer and assessing the course of the disease. Right now, biomarkers enhance the basic TNM staging method, but if the genetic researchers prevail, someday a slew of biomarkers might be the elements doctors rely on to customize treatments for women who have been newly diagnosed with breast cancer.

GATHERING YOUR TEAM

A woman who learns she has a diagnosis of breast cancer starts to gather a team of doctors, which may include a pathologist, a breast surgeon, reconstructive surgeon, radiation oncologist, and medical oncologist. In the Resources section of this book you will find a list of ten top breast cancer centers in the United States where you can work with a team of physicians all under one roof. Even if you do not live near a major breast cancer center, you can contact the nearest one for a referral to doctors in your area, and you might also consider consulting the physicians at such a center for a second opinion. A diagnosis of breast cancer does not mean next-day surgery. You have some time—most breast surgeons estimate about 6 weeks—to decide what to do. A breast cancer usually takes years to grow to the point that it can be detected on mammography, so a woman has some weeks to consult with experts, gather second opinions, and develop a course of action that is suited to her needs, her personality, and her treatable disease.

When Your Doctor Says "Surgery," Which Is Best? Lumpectomy Versus Mastectomy

The most profound recent discovery about surgery for breast cancer is that lumpectomy plus radiation—removal of a malignant tumor and some surrounding tissue, followed by radiation therapy to kill any remaining cancerous cells—is as good as mastectomy for treatment of early breast cancer. There was a moment of uncertainty in 1994, when the National Cancer Institute (NCI) acknowledged that fraudulent data had been included in a historic U.S. government–sponsored study that had helped establish the effectiveness of the two treatments, frightening tens of thousands of women who had opted for the breast-conserving surgery. When the flawed data were eliminated, and the results reanalyzed, thank goodness everyone could rest easy: the conclusion remained the same. Women who undergo lumpectomy plus radiation do just as well as women who have mastectomies, in terms of both recurrence and breast cancer survival. Moreover, the study in question, the National Surgical Adjuvant Breast and Bowel Project (NSABP), was not the first—nor the last—to find that lumpectomy followed by radiation works as well as mastectomy.

A year later, researchers in England published an analysis of the results of 36 scientific studies involving more than 29,000 women worldwide that showed that survival and recurrence rates are identical whether women have had lumpectomies or mastectomies. Yet lumpectomy is not always right for everyone, nor is it the last word in breast cancer surgery. The *skin-sparing mastectomy*, a new variation on mastectomy that involves removing breast tissue but leaving the skin intact so that the breast can be immediately reconstructed, may soon take its place among the options more frequently offered to a woman facing surgery for breast cancer.

Unfortunately, none of these procedures are uniformly available. In some parts of the United States, doctors may not even give women a choice between a mastectomy or lumpectomy with radiation. Surveys indicate that the older the woman, the less likely she is to be offered lumpectomy. On the other hand, young women are not always informed that their chances for survival may be enhanced if their breast surgeries are scheduled from midway through the second half of their monthly menstrual cycles. If you are facing surgery for breast cancer, you will want to understand your options fully, so that your choice can truly be an informed one and your recovery worry-free.

THE LATEST SURGERIES FOR BREAST CANCER

Your surgical choices are, to some extent, limited by the size of the tumor in your breast, the size of your breasts, and whether the cancer is located in one spot or scattered in different areas of the breast. Whatever the case, below you will find explanations of the terms used for the types of breast cancer surgeries performed today. Because some of the terms are rather broad, be sure to ask your surgeon to be precise when he discusses your options with you:

- **Breast-conserving surgery (BCS):** Some form of lumpectomy designed to remove the tumor as well as some surrounding healthy tissue (the tumor "margins") in order to preserve the breast.
- **Lumpectomy:** The popular term for breast-conserving surgery that involves excising a tiny tumor and its margins.
- **Partial mastectomy:** Anything from what would be considered a lumpectomy to removing what might amount to half the breast.
- **Quadrantectomy:** Another term for lumpectomy, but one used to indicate that approximately one-quarter of the breast will be removed.
- **Wide excision:** Yet another way of saying lumpectomy, it means excising the tumor and some margins—but "wide" doesn't tell you how much surrounding tissue will be removed.
- **Segmental excision:** A third term used for lumpectomy. "Segment" does not really tell you anything about the extent of the surgery, just that in addition to the tumor itself, a section of healthy tissue will be removed.
- **Mastectomy:** A general term meaning removal of the breast.
- **Modified radical mastectomy:** The type of mastectomy most frequently performed in the United States today, it involves removing the breast and some underarm lymph nodes.
- **Total mastectomy:** Removal of the breast tissue alone; the lymph nodes are left in place. Sometimes called "simple" mastectomy, this procedure is usually reserved for women with *carcinoma in situ* (or "cancer in place") that has not infiltrated breast tissue.

- **Axillary dissection:** Removal of a section of fat in the armpit that contains lymph nodes to be examined in the laboratory for signs of cancer spread. Axillary dissection is done in the course of a modified radical mastectomy and through a separate underarm incision after lumpectomy.

- **Radical mastectomy:** Also called the *Halsted radical mastectomy* after the surgeon who introduced it in 1882. This type of surgery is seldom performed anymore, even though it was the standard treatment for breast cancer until the mid-1970s, when studies demonstrated that the modified radical approach was just as effective. In a radical mastectomy, the chest muscles and skin are removed in addition to the breast and underarm lymph nodes. The only time this operation is justified today are the rare cases in which the cancer has attached itself to the chest muscles.

- **Skin-sparing mastectomy:** This new procedure involves removing the breast tissue through a tiny incision around the nipple that leaves the skin intact so that the breast can be reconstructed immediately with insertion of an implant or through natural tissue reconstruction (see Chapter 26.) It is a variation on a "total" mastectomy but can also be done in place of a modified radical.

NOTE: Run as fast as you can from a doctor who mentions *subcutaneous mastectomy* to you. During this procedure, which is no longer performed by reputable breast surgeons, the breast skin and nipple remain intact, and most, but not all, of the breast tissue is removed through a small incision. In the past, many women who underwent this type of mastectomy, women who today would be given *total mastectomies*, were found to have developed breast cancer in the remaining tissue or nipple.

Weighing Your Options

After receiving a diagnosis of breast cancer, every woman has time to consider her next step. A delay of a few weeks, while you decide on a breast surgeon and understand the extent of your surgery, is not dangerous to your health. A breast cancer may grow for 10 years before it is a noticeable lump. A few weeks will not affect your recovery or your future.

You will definitely want to get a second opinion before scheduling surgery, whether or not you are comfortable with your doctor's recommendation. This is a time to seek confirmation and ask questions. If your doctor has advised a mastectomy, ask him whether you might be a candidate for lumpectomy, and if not, why not. If you do need or would prefer mastectomy, now is the time to consult a reconstructive surgeon about breast reconstruction. It is important to do this, even if you do not think you want reconstruction, or you do not want to think about it now. No woman deciding on surgery for breast cancer has to make up her mind on reconstruction immediately, but you may lose or limit your options forever if your surgery is not performed with the possibility of reconstruction in mind. (See Chapter 26, which explains the different techniques of breast reconstruction and why it is important for a woman who may undergo a mastectomy to meet with a reconstructive surgeon before her operation.)

Penny Pierce, an assistant professor of nursing at the University of Michigan who has studied the decision-making process, has found that many women are so overwhelmed by a breast cancer diagnosis that they simply do not hear what they are initially told about what treatment entails. She recommends bringing a friend or a sister along when you go to see the surgeon or consult another doctor for a second (or third) opinion. A friend may be more helpful than a spouse, who is also emotionally involved and may not grasp everything the doctor says. You also might want to bring a tape recorder so you can listen to what the doctor has told you when you get home.

Penny Pierce has learned that women facing surgery respond to the decision-making process in the following ways:

• Deferrers (41%) are primarily women in their mid-fifties or older who are inclined to follow their doctors' recommendations without fully investigating their options. After surgery they are more likely than other women to be angry and resentful about the outcome of their treatment.

• Delayers (44%) take time, usually several weeks, to make a decision until they arrive at a choice that feels right to them.

• Deliberators (15%) are the youngest group, the ones most likely to investigate their choices in depth by researching the medical literature and seeking second and even third opinions. These women tend to be comfortable with their choices but can be exhausted by the decision-making process.

Which type of decision-maker are you?

Timing Your Surgery

Some studies suggest that premenopausal women who have surgery between days 7 and 20 of their menstrual cycles are more likely to survive than those whose operations take place earlier or later in the month. No one knows why this should be so, but researchers have speculated that the body's natural killer cells that fight cancer may be more active at midcycle, when levels of the hormone progesterone are higher than at any other time of the month. Then, too, normal patterns of cell division and cell death in breast tissue during this phase of the cycle may be helpful.

Unfortunately, the timing issue is a lot more complicated than it sounds. In the first place, the women who do best with midcycle surgery have positive lymph nodes. And even those researchers who see a connection cannot be certain that the outcomes were not influenced by other factors, such as the extent of chemotherapy the women may have had, whether or not some had surgical biopsies before more extensive breast surgery, and at what point in the cycle those biopsies were performed. The trouble is that all of the studies done so far have merely looked back at surgical records and compared the timing of the operations with survival rates. The only way to prove conclusively that timing really makes a difference would be to recruit two identical groups of women who need similar treatment and see which group does best five to ten years after surgery.

In the meantime, most breast cancer surgeons are taking a "wait and see" attitude toward the question of timing, although some routinely schedule surgery for a woman in her midcycle on the theory that it cannot hurt and indeed, might provide a survival advantage.

Giving Your Consent

Whatever type of surgery you choose, you will be asked to sign an "informed consent" document before the operation. Look it over carefully, and make sure that it refers to the type of surgery you have agreed on with your doctor. If not, insist that it be changed before you sign it. By signing an informed consent form, you indicate that you understand the risks of surgery and anesthesia, that you may be given intravenous medications and blood transfusions if necessary, that any tissue removed during the surgery may be examined and disposed of. If there is anything on the form that you do not understand or that you object to, cross it out or refuse to sign until you can discuss it with your doctor. Sometimes, you may be able to obtain the informed consent form in advance so that you can look it over at leisure and contact your doctor about any concerns you may have before the day of your operation.

BREAST-CONSERVING SURGERY, OR LUMPECTOMY

Are You a Candidate?

The lumpectomy procedure was designed to "conserve" the breast so that after surgery your breasts still have a normal appearance, with only a small scar or slight asymmetry to indicate that a lump was removed.

Originally lumpectomy was developed for women with very small tumors (less than 2 centimeters, or about the size of a grape) located in the upper outer quadrant of the breast. Today, however, almost every woman with early invasive breast cancer can have breast-conserving surgery rather than mastectomy, providing the tumor is 4 centimeters or less (about 2 inches). Given that breast cancers today are found much earlier than in years past, the vast majority of cases, an estimated 80 percent, are diagnosed early and lend themselves to lumpectomy.

The Issue of DCIS. Ductal carcinoma in situ (DCIS), a cancer that remains on site in the duct, has in the past been considered "multicentric," in other words, able to appear in different areas of the breast; today it is seen more often as "multifocal," in different locations of one segment of the breast. So even though a DCIS may be only the size of a pencil point and does not in itself usually metastasize, surgeons have formerly recommended mastectomy. Today many doctors consider mastectomy overtreatment for DCIS, but the type of surgery that is recommended—whether it is a form of breast-conserving surgery with or without radiation, or a mastectomy— depends on the findings from a woman's biopsy. I suggest that a woman with diagnosed DCIS review Chapter 20 to get an idea of the complexity of biopsy analysis for this disease and to understand her need for a second opinion on her diagnosis. Whatever the surgery she finally undergoes, because DCIS usually does not spread, there will be no need for an additional incision in the area of her armpit and removal of lymph nodes.

As for larger tumors, not defined as either early or in situ, in 1994 researchers at Thomas Jefferson University Hospital in Philadelphia published a study suggesting that even women with relatively large tumors that have not yet spread to other parts of the body may be good candidates for lumpectomy with radiation. The researchers first treated the women with chemotherapy to reduce the size of their tumors and then performed the lumpectomies. At the study's end, 77 percent of the women treated in this manner were alive and cancer-free after five years, compared with only 56 percent of those who had mastectomies instead. The researchers estimated that about 40 percent of the 20,000 to 30,000 American women diagnosed with large tumors each year could be candidates for this type of breast-conserving treatment.

PERSONAL ISSUES TO CONSIDER

• The surgery involves removing the lump and a wedge of surrounding healthy tissue to make sure that the tumor margins are clear, or free of disease. The width of the margin is generally at least one centimeter in each direction. The smaller the lump, the less tissue surgeons have to remove, so the better your breast will look after the operation. If the lump is big and your breasts are small, you may not find the results cosmetically acceptable. Your breast may look so different from the other that you would be reminded of your surgery and the fact that you had cancer every time you looked in the mirror. Similarly, if you have more than one lump, or tiny microcalcifications scattered throughout the breast, lumpectomy may not be practical; you just won't have a normal-looking breast after the surgeon takes everything out.

• The size of your breasts can be a determining factor, too: if a woman's breasts are very small, removing even a tiny lump and its surrounding margins may add up to too much breast tissue to permit satisfactory results. At the other extreme, large pendulous breasts do not lend themselves well to lumpectomy because they would require unacceptably high doses of radiation as a follow-up.

• Women who have certain health conditions would not be good candidates for lumpectomy, primarily because the necessary radiation therapy would be harmful or lead to a poor cosmetic outcome. They include women with systemic lupus erythematosus or other collagen-vascular disease; the steroids used to treat their condition can impede healing. Also, pregnant women should not undergo lumpectomies because the follow-up radiation therapy could hurt their babies. (See box "Breast Cancer During Pregnancy," on page 272.)

A few other situations that may make lumpectomy unsuitable:

• There is more than one tumor (here, too, the issue is the appearance of the breast after the tumors and margins have been removed).

• There is a high risk of recurrence because the tumor is surrounded by extensive intraductal carcinoma in situ (EIC). Sometimes invasive breast cancer can have in situ components (not to be confused with DCIS, as discussed earlier) and so not all doctors agree that EIC indicates that mastectomy would be a better choice than lumpectomy. A 1987 study at Harvard suggested that women with EIC had a 35 percent local recurrence rate after lumpectomy, compared with only 3 percent of women without EIC, however, doctors at M.D. Anderson Cancer Center in Houston have found that women with cancer-free margins do well regardless of EIC.

Be Open to Options

There is no longer any doubt that for women who are offered the choice, lumpectomy with radiation is medically equivalent to mastectomy in terms of survival and recurrence, but some surgeons have been slow to accept it as a substitute. Studies have shown that doctors who are older, male, and practice in the Midwest, Southeast, and rural areas tend to be more biased toward mastectomy. Younger men as well as women physicians, especially those who specialize in cancer treatment and/or practice at urban medical centers, teaching hospitals, and the new multidisciplinary breast cancer centers, are more inclined to recommend lumpectomy plus radiation. The regional variations across the United States are quite striking. A recent survey demonstrated that women in the Northeast are most likely to be offered a choice between lumpectomy and mastectomy than women elsewhere, and that 20 percent of them elect lumpectomy. In the Midwest and South, lumpectomy rates are much lower and account for less than 10 percent of all breast cancer surgery, while in the West and Southwest, between 10 and 15 percent of all patients chose lumpectomy.

Why the geographical variations? No one knows for sure. Perhaps some areas lack the facilities and medical personnel needed to administer the radiation therapy that follows lumpectomy, but it is more likely that the differences boil down to medical preference. Doctors tend to practice medicine the way they were trained to do it, and training varies somewhat from one area of the country to another. As a result of these differences, many doctors change very slowly or only when prevailing trends force the issue. This is true not only of breast cancer surgery. Hysterectomy rates differ markedly from region to region (they're highest in the South, lowest in the Northeast), even though there are no known geographical differences in the rate of gynecological disorders. What all this comes down to is the fact that surgeons who have always done mastectomies for breast cancer may continue to recommend mastectomy despite all of the medical data showing that lumpectomy is just as effective. This same kind of resistance existed among surgeons back in the 1970s, when it was learned that modified radical mastectomy was as effective as the more extensive and disfiguring Halsted radical mastectomy.

And as mentioned, the kind of hospital you go to may influence whether you have a lumpectomy or mastectomy. A study of 5,892 non-Hispanic white women diagnosed and treated for breast cancer in 126 hospitals in California between 1984 and 1990 showed that lumpectomies were most commonly performed at teaching hospitals (where medical students are trained) and least commonly performed in nonteaching hospitals. At the teaching hospitals 50 percent of women with early breast cancers opted for lumpectomies, compared with only 30 percent of those treated at nonteaching hospitals. The statistics are even more striking at cancer centers. For example, at Memorial Sloan-Kettering Cancer Center in New York, between 65 and 70 percent of women with early breast cancer have lumpectomies—a much higher rate than that seen in many other large institutions.

Studies have also shown that doctors tend to offer lumpectomy to younger women more often than to their older patients, and that surgeons who perform lumpectomies on elderly women (those over 75) tend not to recommend radiation therapy as a follow-up. Interestingly, one recent study found that elderly women who had lumpectomies with no radiation had a higher rate of recurrence than younger patients who were treated with radiation, but both groups shared the same survival rate, proving yet again that a breast cancer recurrence is not a death warrant.

Recognizing these trends, a woman should not feel limited by where she lives, her age, race, health insurance, or the practices at her local hospital. Wherever you live, you should not have to travel far to find a breast surgeon who is experienced in performing lumpectomies on women who are good candidates for the procedure. The availability of a medical facility where you can have radiation therapy after your surgery may be more problematic, but

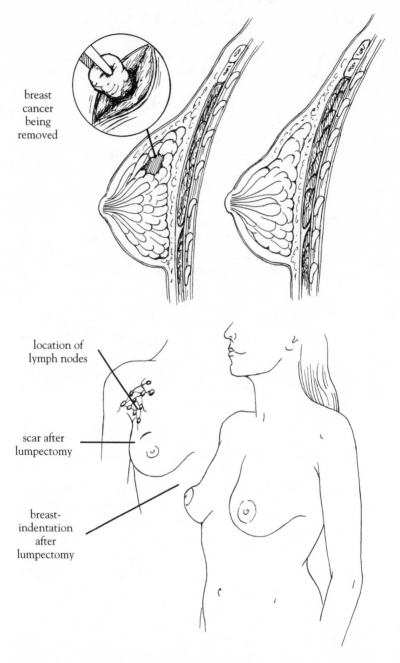

breast
cancer
being
removed

location of
lymph nodes

scar after
lumpectomy

breast-
indentation
after
lumpectomy

Breast conserving surgery: Lumpectomy. A surgeon makes an incision in one of Langer's lines of tension in the breast and removes a cancerous growth (inset). Depending on a woman's diagnosis, lymph nodes may or may not be excised for analysis through a separate incision in the armpit area. A diagnosis of ductal carcinoma in situ (DCIS) usually does not require axillary dissection.

this is a logistical issue to be considered only after you have been fully informed of your choices. Some states have tried to ensure that all the options are presented. Minnesota and Massachusetts have passed laws requiring doctors to inform all their patients of the full range of scientifically sound treatments for breast cancer. Fourteen other states publish standard-ized summaries of medically acceptable treatments that doctors must provide to all breast cancer patients. However, if you live in one of these states— California, Florida, Georgia, Hawaii, Illinois, Kansas, Kentucky, Maine, Maryland, Michigan, New Jersey, New Mexico, New York, and Texas—you should check to make sure that the information is up to date. Not all of these state summaries are kept current with the latest research.

What Happens During a Lumpectomy

Lumpectomy involves two incisions: one over the lump and, usually, another under the arm so the surgeon can remove some lymph nodes to see whether the cancer has spread beyond the breast. Occasionally both procedures can be done through the same incision if the tumor is located in the upper, outer area of the breast. For *carcinoma in situ* a woman does not need a second incision, because with this condition, there's no danger of lymph node involvement.

A lumpectomy generally takes from one to three hours. (Surgery will be longer if radioactive implants are inserted at the time of lumpectomy, a rarely used option discussed in Chapter 23.) These days breast surgery is increasingly being done as an outpatient procedure, meaning that you come into the hospital the morning of the operation and leave a few hours after it is over, when the effects of the anesthesia have worn off. If you are admitted to the hospital for the surgery, the amount of time you spend in the hospital varies widely, and to some extent may be dictated by what your health insur-ance will cover, but costs are not the only consideration.

Many women do not need any special care after lumpectomies and are more comfortable at home than in the hospital, but some doctors prefer to keep their patients overnight, and sometimes an overnight hospital stay is recommended to make sure that patients with asthma, heart conditions, or other medical problems recover uneventfully from anesthesia.

The Incision

One of the things you will want to discuss with your doctor before surgery is the placement of the incision. Yes, you may have a choice in the matter. A relatively small incision can be placed so that a scar will be as inconspicuous as possible and allow a woman to wear revealing bathing suits and low-cut necklines. Of course, the placement of the incision depends on the loca-tion of the tumor, but you do have some options within that parameter.

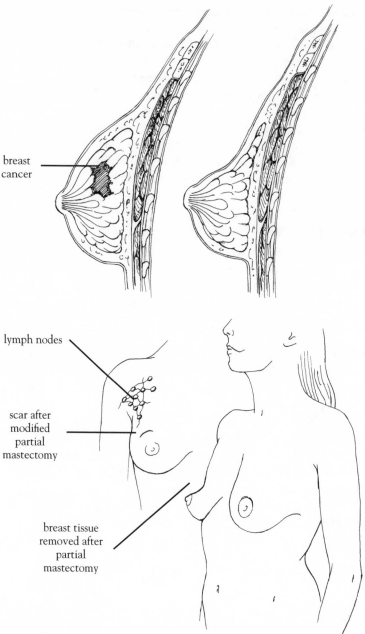

breast
cancer

lymph nodes

scar after
modified
partial
mastectomy

breast tissue
removed after
partial
mastectomy

Partial mastectomy. Sometimes the size, placement, and/or aggressiveness of a breast cancer requires more extensive surgery than a lumpectomy. A partial mastectomy varies in the amount of breast tissue removed, from a small segment to as much as half of the breast. A number of lymph nodes are usually excised for analysis through a separate incision in the armpit during the partial mastectomy procedure.

The main consideration is what your breast will look like after surgery. The smaller the lump and the larger the breast, the greater the likelihood that its general appearance will be unchanged, except for the scar. But sometimes, the incision will result in a repositioning of the nipple—it may end up a bit off center, pulled toward the incision, either higher or lower than it used to be, or to one side of the breast or the other. This can be avoided if the surgeon makes a *radial* incision, one that literally "radiates" from the center of the breast like the spoke of a wheel. The disadvantage of this choice is that part of the scar may show when a woman wears a more revealing garment.

If the tumor is in the upper part of the breast, the surgeon may be able to make an arc-shaped incision close to the areola so that the scar will not show in low-cut clothing. If the tumor is in the area of the breast nearest the armpit, the surgeon may be able to remove both the lump and the lymph nodes through the same incision, so that a woman is left with only one scar under the arm.

Recovery

Some women are fine, only a little uncomfortable, but some women suffer pain after a lumpectomy. In the main, feelings of illness and nausea are likely to be due to the effects of anesthesia (see box "What You Should Know About Anesthesia") and not the surgery itself. Before you go home, your doctor probably will prescribe painkillers (Percocet or codeine), but many women do not have to take the pills after the first day or two. However, you will have to favor the arm opposite the side of your surgery for a few days, because moving it too much can jiggle the breast and cause pain from the incision. Until the discomfort subsides, you will probably need a support bra to prevent your breast from moving too much, and at night you may feel more comfort sleeping with a pillow at your side. Your doctor may suggest some exercises to get your arm moving so that you can return to normal activity as soon as possible.

Many women go home with a drain in place to remove fluid that can collect around the incision in the armpit, although sometimes the drain is removed before the woman leaves the hospital. The drain is actually a soft plastic tube that travels from your armpit down along your side to a small bulb at your waist. It can be secured within your undergarments. You can detach the bulb and empty the fluid yourself until the doctor removes the apparatus—usually a few days to a week later, depending on whether the drainage seems complete. The incision on your breast will be covered by a dressing, which your doctor will remove a few days after surgery, during a post-op visit to his office. You may or may not have stitches that need removal; no stitches have to be removed if your surgeon used sutures that are absorbed by the body. You can shower as soon as the drain is removed, and, of course, if there's no drain, you can shower whenever the doctor removes the dressing.

WHAT YOU SHOULD KNOW ABOUT
ANESTHESIA

Most breast cancer surgery is performed while a woman is under a general anesthetic—basically asleep for the duration of the procedure. True, lumpectomies can be done with a local anesthetic that numbs the area of the breast where the incision will be made, but if a surgeon is going to do an axillary dissection to remove lymph glands from under a woman's arm, a local is not suitable—it cannot numb a large enough area. Local anesthesia is mostly used for biopsies, and it may sometimes be an option when surgery is performed for *carcinoma in situ.*

At the hospital on the day of your surgery, you will meet with the anesthesiologist, a medical specialist who administers anesthesia. Although you may have answered questions about your health history during a preoperation medical examination, the anesthesiologist will again ask about your medical history, whether or not you have any physical problems, including allergies, whether you are taking any drugs or have ever had any kind of adverse reaction to anesthesia or other drugs, and when was the last time you consumed any food. It is vital to answer these questions as thoroughly as possible. You also want to ask him:

What type of anesthetic do you plan to use?
Are there possible complications or risks?
How soon can I expect to wake up after surgery?
How soon will I be mobile?

A woman who is very anxious may be given a sedative, often Versed, a Valium-like drug, before surgery, explains Dr. Norman Levin, chief of anesthesiology at Century City Hospital in Los Angeles, but because this may slow recovery from the anesthetic, most women opt for the fewest drugs possible.

In the operating room you can expect to be hooked up to an intravenous (IV) drip, through which you will receive fluids, sedative, and painkilling drugs. You will drift off to sleep almost immediately from the effects of sodium pentothal, the first drug to hit your bloodstream. The actual anesthetic that will keep you asleep during surgery is administered a few minutes later, through a mask placed over your face after you are asleep. In some cases, a tube is placed in the windpipe to maintain respiration during sleep.

"The newer anesthetics are very good and cause a minimum of

nausea or vomiting, which oftens occurs with older agents," explains Dr. Levin. These anesthetics are also short acting, meaning that you wake up very soon after surgery has been completed, often on the way to the recovery room. Within one to two hours, the anesthetic wears off enough to enable you to get up. However, with general anesthesia, whether you have had a lumpectomy or a mastectomy, you are likely to feel fatigued for a few days after surgery.

MASTECTOMY

The most common operation for breast cancer today is the modified radical mastectomy, in which the breast tissue and underarm lymph nodes are removed; in a total mastectomy, breast tissue is removed but the underarm lymph nodes remain intact. Because all breast tissue is removed during total and modified radical mastectomies, there usually is no need for radiation therapy afterward. Today's "modified radical" is a far less extensive and less disfiguring surgery than the old Halsted radical mastectomy, in which the chest muscles beneath the breast are removed.

As mentioned earlier, if you are a candidate for a mastectomy, be sure to consult a reconstructive surgeon about breast reconstruction before surgery. (Chapter 26 describes the various methods of breast reconstruction.) You can have your breast rebuilt at the time of surgery or months or years later. Remember that even if you are not inclined to want reconstruction, your feelings at the time of surgery may change later on, so it is best to consult a reconstructive surgeon to be sure you keep your future options open.

Another issue to ask your surgeon about before mastectomy is whether or not to donate your own blood in advance. Blood transfusions are usually not necessary, but you may need some blood if you are having immediate reconstructive surgery. You can donate up to three units per week before surgery.

What Happens During a Modified Radical Mastectomy

During a modified radical mastectomy, the surgeon cuts away some of the breast skin and tissue above the biopsy scar. Unless he is performing a *skin-sparing mastectomy*, as described on page 274, he will make an elliptical incision that loops down below the nipple. (See illustration.) Reaching into the incision, the surgeon is able to remove breast tissue that extends up to the collarbone, down to the rib area, and over to the armpit. Once the breast tissue has been removed, the surgeon excises about 10 to 15 underarm lymph nodes. These and the breast tissue go to the pathologist for study.

BREAST CANCER DURING PREGNANCY

Fortunately, only 2 percent of all cases of breast cancer occur during pregnancy, affecting roughly one in every 3,000 to 10,000 pregnant women. When breast cancer strikes, there usually is no need to terminate the pregnancy or delay treatment. The type of surgery a woman has, however, depends on how advanced her pregnancy is.

Usually lumpectomy is not recommended. The follow-up radiation treatment could harm the baby if it occurs during the first or second trimester. If the cancer is found during the third trimester, surgery sometimes may be delayed until the baby is born, but because breast cancer during pregnancy is often highly aggressive, most doctors recommend immediate modified radical mastectomy.

If chemotherapy is needed during pregnancy, a woman must wait until after the first trimester. Studies have shown that when administered during the second and third trimesters, chemotherapy is not likely to harm the baby.

A modified radical mastectomy takes from two to four hours. A woman may enter the hospital the day of the surgery and stay there four or five days. Increasingly, however, mastectomy is being done as outpatient surgery. This is a cost-driven trend: a Johns Hopkins study published in 1994 showed that a woman who enters the hospital at 7 in the morning and leaves at 2:30 that afternoon can save $1,500 to $2,500 of the cost of a mastectomy, which ranges from $3,000 to $6,000. The Johns Hopkins team reported that one of the first women to have a mastectomy as an outpatient took a walk with her husband that afternoon and then went out to dinner!

Of course, outpatient surgery isn't for everyone, and cost isn't the only consideration. Having a breast removed can be more traumatic emotionally than it is physically, and many doctors and patients see the need for some hospital time to rest and begin to recover. A hospital stay should be discussed with your surgeon.

Recovery

Because the area around the incision tends to fill with fluid after surgery, you will probably wake up with some soft plastic tubing emerging from the incision to drain the wound. The drain generally remains in place for three or four days, until all the fluid has been siphoned. (Any fluid that accumulates later can be drawn off with a needle, but this potential complication of surgery is not worrisome, just a nuisance.) You will also

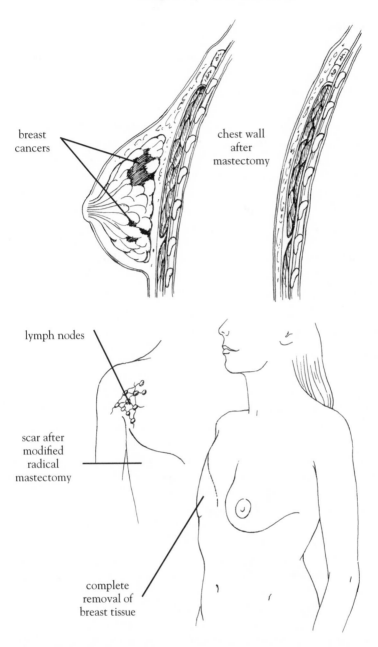

breast
cancers

chest wall
after
mastectomy

lymph nodes

scar after
modified
radical
mastectomy

complete
removal of
breast tissue

Modified radical mastectomy. A woman often has a choice between breast-conserving surgery or a more extensive modified radical mastectomy. Her breast cancer may be either large, aggressive, in more than one quadrant of the breast, or a combination of all three factors, and a modified radical is recommended. During a modified radical mastectomy, through one elliptical incision, a surgeon removes all of a woman's breast tissue and a selection of lymph nodes.

have a dressing over your chest that will be changed when the drain is removed.

Mastectomy scars have been getting smaller and smaller over the years. In general, however, the incision will leave a horizontal scar line across the chest. The nerves serving the breast are cut during surgery, permanently numbing the whole area. You may, in fact, find that touching the area brings about a tingly sensation known as *dysthesia*, similar to what you feel when your foot is asleep. Some women continue to feel as if their missing breasts hurt or missing nipples itch. This is a variation on the "phantom limb" syndrome that amputees report. It certainly does not happen to everyone, and when it does, it usually subsides as the brain recognizes that the nerve signals from the breast area have been interrupted.

Immediately after surgery you will not be able to move your arm well. Your doctor probably will recommend some exercises to get your arm moving so that you can resume normal activities as soon as possible. You will be up and around later in the day of the surgery or the next morning at the latest. You also will be urged to begin your arm exercises the day after surgery.

The Latest Innovation: The Skin-Sparing Mastectomy

This newest variation on mastectomy is not yet widely available, but Dr. Patrick Borgen, chief of the breast service department of surgery at Memorial Sloan-Kettering Cancer Center in New York, predicts that this innovation will be standard within about two years of the writing of this book. Essentially, *skin-sparing mastectomy* involves removing breast tissue through a small circular (about $4^1/_2$ centimeters in diameter) incision around the nipple. "Our operation is simply a modification of the total mastectomy. It is in fact, a total mastectomy, but it is done through a very small, minimally mutilating or disfiguring incision," Dr. Borgen explains.

Most women with early breast cancer are candidates for skin-sparing mastectomy. The surgery takes an experienced surgeon about an hour (more time will be needed for reconstruction). Immediately after the surgeon finishes removing the breast tissue, a reconstructive surgeon takes over to reconstruct the breast, using a saline implant or a fatty tissue flap transferred from a woman's abdomen, back, or buttocks (see Chapter 26 for a discussion of techniques for breast reconstruction). Women can usually expect to spend two nights in the hospital if their breast reconstruction involves an implant. The hospital stay will be longer, four to seven nights, if the breast is rebuilt using fat from elsewhere in the body. It takes the same amount of time to recover from skin-sparing mastectomy as it does to recover from any other mastectomy.

"Afterwards, it is very hard to tell that the patient has had a mastectomy," says Dr. Borgen. Another advantage: preserving the skin means that women have sensation in the rebuilt breast, which they generally do not have after other types of breast reconstruction. However, because the nipple and areola are removed during surgery, the rebuilt nipple/areola will not have any feeling.

The new procedure has been made possible by the latest in fiber optic retractors, surgical implements that enable doctors to remove all of the breast tissue through the small incision. Dr. Borgen explains that the big incision that was done in the past was more for the benefit of the surgeon than the patient. Skin-sparing mastectomy is technically challenging and exacting for the surgeon, but is, in fact, a total mastectomy. "The only thing we've eliminated is the big saber slash incision across the chest," says Borgen. If the lymph nodes are to be removed during surgery (they usually are not during a total mastectomy, but always are if the woman needs a modified radical), they are excised via an incision under the arm, the same as they would be if the surgery itself had been a lumpectomy.

Skin-sparing mastectomies are now being performed at a number of cancer centers and large medical centers, and the procedure is gaining popularity. If you are interested in exploring this option, ask your surgeon if he is familiar with the procedure or can refer you to someone who is.

REMOVING THE LYMPH NODES: AXILLARY DISSECTION

Whatever form of surgery you undergo, you probably will have some lymph nodes removed from your underarm. Although this procedure is routine in all breast cancer surgery, some experts are beginning to question the need, particularly among postmenopausal lumpectomy patients, the vast majority of whom have negative nodes. Those opposed to routine axillary dissection for these women contend that follow-up treatment (see Chapter 24) is the same, regardless of whether or not positive nodes are found. They also note that recovery from surgery is quicker without removing lymph nodes, and that radiation therapy can begin sooner. However, this view has not yet won many converts (if it ever will), and as things now stand, most women with breast cancer will have axillary dissection.

With mastectomy, the lymph nodes are removed after the surgeon has taken out all of the breast tissue, but without the need of a second incision. With lumpectomy, however, a second incision is necessary unless the tumor is in the upper, outer area of a woman's breast near her underarm, and the surgeon can reach the lymph nodes through the incision made to remove the tumor. The nodes are nestled in a wedge of fat in the armpit. To reach them, the surgeon makes a two-inch incision just beneath the underarm hairline. There's no way of determining in advance how many lymph nodes will be removed—they're usually pretty small. Most of the time the pathologist finds between 10 and 15 nodes, but there can be many more.

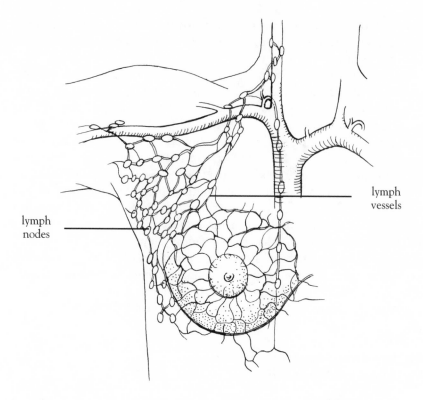

Lymphatic system of the breast. Lymph vessels drain into a network of lymph nodes located around the breast and armpit.

You may wake up with some tubes emerging from your underarm inci-sion to drain away any fluid that accumulates. Sometimes the drain will be removed before you leave the hospital, but often doctors send their patients home with the drain in place and remove it during a follow-up visit a few days to a week later.

The biggest problem with axillary dissection is the risk that the nerve that relays feeling from the back of your armpit to your brain may be severed during the surgery. The result will be an area of numbness that won't affect the use of your arm but will prove inconvenient when you shave under your arms—you won't be able to feel the entire area, so you'll have to be very careful with razors. Sensation may return if the nerve has been stretched, not severed.

Another potential complication is an inflammation in the basilic vein in the arm. If this develops, your arm will hurt or feel "tight." This is not as serious as it sounds. The inflammation usually subsides within a week. The only treatment is ice packs held against the affected arm, and aspirin. After the drain has been removed, sometimes a woman may still develop some swelling under the armpit from accumulated fluid. This is neither a common nor a serious occurrence and requires no treatment unless there is a lot of swelling. Then the fluid can be drained off through a needle.

Lymphedema

Lymphedema is a rare but serious complication of breast cancer surgery that stems directly from the removal of lymph nodes. It is swelling caused by an accumulation of lymphatic fluid that cannot drain normally when nodes have been removed. Usually, lymphedema develops as a result of an infection. Fortunately, this condition does not occur very often—in about 5 percent of mastectomies, and less often as a consequence of lumpectomy.

The symptoms of lymphedema can range from a very slight swelling, noticeable only because rings on your finger may seem a bit tighter, to an obvious enlargement of the arm. Lymphedema can develop soon after surgery or years later. Unfortunately, there is no reliable treatment so it is important to guard against it. You can do this by protecting your arm from injury that could lead to infection. Try to avoid cuts and any breaks in the skin, including injections and the drawing of blood. It also is a good idea to

---

SOFT TISSUE REHABILITATION: A NONTRADITIONAL APPROACH TO TREATING PAIN AFTER MASTECTOMY

Doctor-guided massage can help prevent the formation of adhesions and scar tissue after mastectomy, and painkillers can bring relief during the time of healing, but in some rare cases women do feel pain well after surgery. Soft tissue rehabilitation, a form of deep massage practiced primarily by chiropractors, physical therapists, and physiatrists (who are medical doctors) may offer relief. According to Dr. Wayne M. Winnick, a chiropractor in New York who performs soft tissue rehabilitation, this hands-on type of therapy involves an examination of the scar and the adjacent area for painful nodules, ropiness, abnormal tissue texture, and thickening, which are signs of adhesions and developing scar tissue. Once these changes are identified and located, the therapist uses friction massage, pressure, and sliding contact to break down the area and renew soft tissue. Soft tissue rehabilitation treatments are costly, however. According to Dr. Winnick, one treatment session can range from $75 to $100, and two treatments a week may be required for one to three months. This nontraditional approach to pain relief may not be covered by health insurance.

avoid wearing jewelry or clothing that fits tightly and to refrain from lifting heavy suitcases and bags of groceries with the affected arm.

If you do develop an infection or notice any swelling, be sure to get medical treatment promptly. Once lymphedema occurs, it can be hard to manage and impossible to cure. Keeping your arm elevated can help reduce swelling, and your doctor may recommend a special support sleeve or compression garment and physical therapy. In severe cases, swelling can be reduced with the aid of a special electric pump you can use to drain off liquid. There also are exercises to promote drainage and reduce swelling. For more information and a description of the exercises, contact the National Lymphedema Network, 2211 Post Street, Suite 404, San Francisco, CA 94115 or telephone 800-547-1133.

MOVING ON

After surgery for breast cancer, the next step is to await the results of the pathology report, which will profile your breast cancer and let you know whether your removed lymph nodes, and in the case of lumpectomy, the margins of tissue around the tumor, are positive or negative for the presence of cancer cells. There is nothing to do but rest and regain your strength until the findings are in. Whether you can breathe a sigh of relief because your results are negative, or whether you will need additional surgery because tissue margins are positive or adjuvant chemotherapy because lymph nodes are positive, is in the future. Right now your surgery is over, and your mind can focus on healing and good health.

CHAPTER TWENTY-TWO

Every Breast Cancer Has a Profile, and You Should Know Yours

The defining profile of a breast cancer emerges 48 to 72 hours after mastectomy, lumpectomy, or other forms of breast-conserving surgery, when the pathology report gives the cancer a name and describes its TNM staging (T=tumor size; N=node involvement; M=metastasis). This classification system is called the "gold standard" for gauging the severity of the disease. For women who have had lumpectomies or other forms of breast-conserving surgery, the report also shows whether the margins of tissue surrounding a tumor are free of cancer cells. If margins show the "positive" presence of cancer, a woman must return to the operating room for surgery that results in "clear" or "negative" margins.

A tiny tumor and no presence of cancer in the lymph nodes are the most favorable finding. While many pathologists do not use specific "TNM" initials in their reports, they do provide all the information that a TNM classification requires. In any event, the pathology report after surgery is a blueprint for the future, the basis for planning either no further treatment or more surgery; either chemotherapy, hormonal therapy, or chemoendocrine therapy, or a combination of the two. Upon learning the findings, a woman and her doctor can decide together which direction the course of her care will take. The time has not yet arrived when computerized molecular testing—for nuclear grade, DNA analysis, hormonal receptors, and the biomarkers a surgeon wants evaluated—outshines TNM staging in helping doctors make a prognosis.

TNM: CLASSIFYING A BREAST CANCER

The size of a tumor, the presence of cancer in a sampling of axillary lymph nodes, and any sign of a metastasis of cancer to areas outside the breast (termed "distant") have been classified by the National Cancer Institute (NCI) in the following TNM categories, from most to least favorable conditions:

T=Primary Tumor
TX: Primary tumor cannot be assessed
T0: No evidence of primary tumor
Tis: Carcinoma in situ (intraductal or lobular) or Paget's disease of the nipple with no associated tumor mass (Paget's disease with a tumor is classified according to the size of the tumor)
T1: Tumor 2.0 centimeters (cm) or less
    T1a: 0.5 cm but not more than 1.0 cm
    T1b: more than 0.5 cm but not more than 1.0 cm
    T1c: more than 1.0 cm but not more than 2.0 cm
T2: Tumor more than 2.0 but not more than 5.0 cm
T3: Tumor more than 5.0 cm
T4: Tumor of any size with direct extension to chest wall or skin
    T4a: extension to chest wall
    T4b: edema, including peau d'orange, ulceration of the skin of the breast, satellite skin nodules confined to the breast
    T4c: both T4a and T4b
    T4d: inflammatory carcinoma

N=Node involvement
NX: Regional lymph nodes cannot be assessed
N0: No regional lymph node metastasis
N1: Metastasis to movable axillary lymph node(s)
N2: Metastasis to lymph node(s) fixed to one another or other structures
N3: Metastasis to internal mammary node(s)

M=Distant metastasis
MX: Presence of distant metastasis cannot be assessed
M0: No distant metastasis
M1: Distant metastasis present

STAGES

The above TNM classifications, when grouped according to a breast cancer's features, place the cancer in a particular stage, which is usually cited on the pathology report. (Note: The lower the stage, the more favorable the prognosis.)

Stage O (in situ) breast cancer is: Tis, N0, M0
Stage I is: T1, N0, M0
Stage IIA is: T0, N1, M0—or—T1, N1, M0—or—T2, N0, M0
Stage IIB is: T2, N1, M0—or—T3, N0, M0
Stage IIIA is: T0, N2, M0
                T1, N2, M0
                T2, N2, M0
                T3, N1, M0
                T3, N2, M0
Stage IIIB is: T4, any N, M0—or—any T, N3, M0
Stage IV is: any T, any N, M1

STAGES AND SURVIVAL

Generally, a woman's chance of surviving for five years is not as good if her cancer is placed at a high stage rather than at a low stage. The latest NCI data show the following rates of survival at five years:

- 96 percent for cancer diagnosed at a stage when cancer is confined to the breast;
- 75 percent when cancer has spread to surrounding tissue;
- 20 percent when cancer has metastasized (note: only 6 percent of cancers are diagnosed at this stage).

Statistics for five-year survival also show that the rates for women with a low income are 9 percent lower than for upper-income women, and that low-income African American women are three times more likely than high-income white women to be diagnosed with advanced disease. Researchers are looking into whether this discrepancy arises because women with lower incomes do not have adequate health insurance or good access to medical care.

MOLECULAR TESTS

Current technology is providing pathologists with the capability to analyze breast cancer cells for nuclear grade based on their capacity to divide; the presence of hormonal receptors; DNA flow cytometry; and a variety of bio-markers, genetic features that offer clues to cancer activity. (Explanations of these enhanced characteristics of a breast cancer are provided in Chapter 20, which should be read in conjunction with this chapter.) Molecular testing may be undertaken by a pathologist who is working on a biopsied sample of a breast cancer, but most women will not have the results of molecular tests until after surgery.

IS A SECOND OPINION ON AN AFTER-SURGERY PATHOLOGY REPORT NEEDED?

Second-opinion services for confirming the pathology of a breast cancer (see Chapter 20), are often used in helping a woman determine how extensive her surgery should be, based on the type and aggressiveness of her cancer. Dr. Rishi finds that the majority of breast cancers diagnosed *after surgery* are straight-out invasive (also called infiltrating) ductal carcinoma that would not put women or their doctors into quandaries about further care. (See Chapter 20 for explanations of different types of breast cancers.) But because oncologists plan treatment with chemotherapy and/or hormonal therapy based on the findings of a woman's pathology report, the report's accuracy is essential. In the percentage of cases that are not straight-out invasive ductal carcinoma, or whenever a woman feels that her findings are not clear-cut and she wants further interpretation, she should ask her oncologist to suggest a second-opinion pathologist at an institution other than the one where her report was conducted or contact a second-opinion service.

Of all molecular tests, the diagnosis of estrogen and/or progesterone receptors in cells is the most important for influencing further treatment. Women who test positive for hormonal receptors are eligible for hormonal therapy with the drug tamoxifen, which is described in detail in Chapter 24. And Dr. Mazhar Rishi, assistant chairman of the department of gynecologic and breast pathology at the Armed Forces Institute of Pathology in Washington, DC says that biomarkers can become quite helpful in assessing further treatment of small cancers—those less than 1 cm that would not require further treatment using the standard TNM staging. Indeed the molecular features of these small tumors today may tell a doctor that chemotherapy *should* be considered.

NOW IS THE TIME TO STORE YOUR TISSUE SAMPLES

New biomarkers on cells are being discovered all the time, and no one knows which ones may lead to the creation of future treatments based on gene therapy. If an institution has the facilities, a woman should ask her doctor whether her tissue samples could be frozen and stored, so that pathologists can return to check for biomarkers that may be discovered later on. By saving her tissue samples, a woman can remain eligible for drug therapies that have not even been created yet.

But for now, once a woman has a profile of her breast cancer from an accurate pathology report, she and her doctor can begin to fit her treatment to her disease from the range of radiation and drug therapies currently available.

CHAPTER TWENTY-THREE

What to Expect During Radiotherapy

Today, radiation therapy, or radiotherapy, is almost always recommended as a follow-up to lumpectomy, to eliminate any cancer cells that might remain after that, or any other type of breast-conserving surgery. Researchers consistently find that radiotherapy is highly effective in preventing "local recurrences"—a return of the cancer in the breast where the first one occurred. In the short term (under five years), local recurrences may be 25 to 30 percent higher among women who do not get radiation therapy after lumpectomy. In a reanalysis of 12 years of follow-up of 4,000 women involved in the National Surgical Adjuvant Breast and Bowel Project (NSABP), local recurrences appeared in 35 percent of the women who only had lumpectomies but in just 10 percent of the women who had lumpectomies with radiotherapy. Even women with small tumors (under 1 cm) and negative lymph nodes—women who seem as if they might do very well having lumpectomies without radiation—still fare better with radiotherapy. A Harvard study showed that when women with this favorable pathology were followed up over five years, every year 3.6 percent of those who had lumpectomy *without* radiotherapy experienced local recurrence, whereas those who had lumpectomy *with* radiotherapy had no local recurrences.

No woman should doubt her decision of lumpectomy over mastectomy, because *lumpectomy **with** radiation is equivalent to mastectomy as a treatment for breast cancer*. The survival rates are the same *regardless* of which treatment is chosen. In fact, whether a woman has undergone a mastectomy, lumpectomy with radiation, or a lumpectomy alone, there are no statistically significant differences in long-term survival. A tumor's size and lymph node involvement are still the most important determinants of survival.

So why have radiation at all if it does not significantly enhance the odds of surviving breast cancer when compared with lumpectomy alone? First, prevention of local recurrence is important. Doctors know that without radiation therapy after lumpectomy 30 percent or more of all women eventually will develop a local recurrence, and they are in the process of understanding just how significant a local recurrence is. Some breast cancer specialists believe that local recurrences are "markers" of risk for a distant metastasis— that is, an indication that the cancer has already spread beyond the breast. How much of a risk? No one can say for sure. Most studies suggest that local recurrences that occur early (within three years of treatment) are more likely to mean that cancer has spread than those that occur later, and that the most worrisome recurrences usually are those that appear early on among women who did not have radiation therapy. Dr. Barbara Fowble, senior member of radiation oncology and cochair of the Breast Evaluation Center at Fox Chase Cancer Center in Philadelphia, reports that the chances of cancer spreading are considered remote if a local recurrence develops five years or more after treatment with lumpectomy plus radiation, and that even those recurrences that show up four to five years after treatment may not be meaningful in terms of cancer spread.

Another plus for radiation therapy is that it usually spares women from mastectomies. Without radiotherapy, there is a higher risk of local recurrence, which then might lead to mastectomy, which is more likely to be performed than a second lumpectomy. (Unfortunately, a woman who has a local recurrence after lumpectomy with radiation also usually requires a mastectomy, because the same breast cannot be irradiated twice. Excessive radiation could cause a breakdown of normal tissues, development of skin ulcers that won't heal, and, worse, radiation-induced sarcomas.) The bottom line is that even if 10 percent of women treated with radiation after lumpectomy develop local recurrences that lead to mastectomies, 90 percent of the women treated this way have still saved their breasts.

PUTTING OLD FEARS TO REST

In the past, doctors did not have good control over the direction of radiation, and even though a targeted cancer was successfully treated, sometimes years later other malignancies or heart disease surfaced as aftereffects of the treatment. Today, radiation oncologists, the medical specialists who formulate radiation treatments to fight breast cancer, do so knowing that high-energy X rays, gamma rays, or other sources of radiation can be aimed quite precisely at the area where malignant cells are most likely to be. The precise targeting of high-tech machines called *linear accelerators*, which accelerate radioactive particles and direct them as an external beam, enhances a doctor's ability to mount a carefully planned, local attack on breast cancer.

Radiotherapy works by disabling both normal and abnormal cells, but the normal cells recover quickly, while the abnormal cells die. So it is now unusual for women with breast cancer who have had radiotherapy to develop new tumors related to the radiation used in their care.

A study of 41,000 women diagnosed with breast cancer between 1935 and 1982 showed that fewer than 3 percent of all cases of breast cancer that later developed in the opposite breast could be attributed to the radiation therapy used to treat the first malignancy. The study also found that the increased risk occurred *only* among women treated when they were under the age of 45. This is a small danger, considering the effectiveness of radiation therapy and the fact that women who have had breast cancer once are three times as likely to develop a second breast cancer as women who have never had the disease.

More worrisome, perhaps, is a slightly increased risk of leukemia when radiation is paired with chemotherapy. However, NCI researchers who have documented the onset of this disease among more than 82,000 women treated in the 1970s and 1980s, noted that leukemia occurred most often in relation to chemotherapy involving melphalan, a drug rarely used today. Much safer was cyclophosphamide (Cytoxan), one of the most commonly used chemotherapy agents.

Overall, none of the risks of radiation therapy seems significant enough to offset the benefit of its use after lumpectomy and sometimes even after mastectomy.

RADIOTHERAPY AFTER MASTECTOMY

Radiation therapy is routinely recommended after lumpectomy. Occasionally, however, radiotherapy may be recommended after mastectomy. This might happen if the tumor was considered very large, and the surgeon is uncertain about whether all of the disease has been removed from tissue adjacent to the breast. Other instances when radiotherapy may be recommended after mastectomy are:

• If a woman is at high risk for a local recurrence in the chest wall area—in other words, if she has four or more positive lymph nodes or a tumor greater than or equal to 5 cm.

• After surgery for a large tumor that was reduced with chemotherapy before mastectomy. In these cases, radiation may be needed to sweep up cancer cells that may have escaped.

• After chest wall recurrence—that is, when a small malignant mass develops on the skin after mastectomy but has not spread to other parts of the body. Here radiation may be recommended after the lump is removed and followed, in most cases, by chemotherapy or hormone therapy.

WHO SHOULD NOT HAVE RADIATION THERAPY

Radiation therapy is not for everyone. It can be harmful in women with certain medical conditions and, under some circumstances, it can damage tissues in such a way that afterward the breast will not look normal. As discussed in Chapter 21, women with scleroderma or systemic lupus, which are collagen vascular diseases, are not good candidates for lumpectomy with radiation. Their tissues react abnormally to radiation, leading to more scar tissue than doctors like to see after treatment; skin ulcers may form that do not heal, and sometimes there is exposure of bone that does not heal. Although the risks are not as high with lupus, caution usually prevails, and lupus patients are discouraged from having lumpectomy with radiation. However, no such dangers exist with other conditions such as rheumatoid arthritis.

Large breasts may also make radiotherapy difficult because they require higher-energy radiation beams than smaller breasts. To deliver adequate radiation, the equipment used for treatment may have to be modified; if this cannot be done, large-breasted women may be referred elsewhere. That may mean traveling or living temporarily in another area to receive treatment at a facility with the necessary machinery. As a result, some large-breasted women may decide against lumpectomy and choose mastectomy initially.

CHOOSING A RADIATION ONCOLOGIST

If a woman is considering lumpectomy, her surgeon should discuss the involvement of radiation therapy with her and refer her to a radiation oncologist for a consultation. It is important to see a radiation oncologist before making the final decision about surgery, because a woman must be sure that she is a good candidate for radiotherapy. This is usually not a problem, but there are some circumstances under which radiotherapy should not be done (see box above). Because breast cancer recurrence is so high when lumpectomy is done without radiation, a woman may need to rethink her decision to undergo a lumpectomy if the radiation oncologist does not consider her a good candidate.

Certain radiation oncologists specialize in treating breast cancer patients. If a woman is being cared for at a comprehensive breast cancer center or a cancer or teaching hospital, a skilled and qualified radiation oncologist should be available to her. However, if she does not live near one of these centers or hospitals, she should carefully evaluate the treatment facilities and credentials of the radiation oncologists in her area and other medical personnel who will be involved in her care. Because radiation therapy requires that she present herself for treatment five days a week for five to seven weeks, she probably will be inclined to choose a center as close to her home or work as possible, but if the nearest center is not top-notch, she should not compromise her choice for the sake of convenience. Some women temporarily move to another city to undergo radiation therapy at facilities that offer the most skilled and experienced personnel and the highest quality of care. Here's what to look for when evaluating a radiation oncologist and radiation treatment facility:

• A radiation oncologist or radiation therapist who is certified by the American Board of Radiology or board eligible in radiation therapy and specializes in breast cancer treatment. Board certified means that a physician has completed a three- to four-year residency in radiation oncology and has passed a rigorous qualifying exam. Board eligible means that a physician has completed training and has worked in the field but has not yet taken the test.

• A facility with a qualified radiation physicist on staff. Qualified physicists have doctorates or master's degrees. They work with radiation oncologists in planning treatment and are responsible for taking the measurements of radiation beam characteristics. They are certified by the American Board of Radiology or the American Board of Medical Physics.

• Qualified radiation therapists and radiation nurses. The person you will see most often throughout your treatment is the therapist who will actually administer the radiation. Although his credentials are your main consideration, you also want someone with whom you can have a rapport and feel comfortable. Radiation therapists must complete a two- to four-year training program after high school graduation and should be certified by the American Registry of Radiologic Technologists. Radiation nurses are licensed registered nurses. They work with the doctors and will probably assist in your examinations. The nurses can also answer questions about the side effects of treatment and will be your link with the doctor if problems arise during or after your treatment.

• Dosimetrists should be board certified by the Medical Dosimetrist Certification Board. Dosimetrists calculate the dose of radiation to be administered and work with the radiation oncologist and radiation physicist to individualize treatment plans.

A woman can check the qualifications of the radiation oncologist in the Directory of Medical Specialists (available in most libraries), and ask if the facility is accredited by the American College of Radiology (800-ACR-LINE connects you with the ACR directly).

PREPARATION FOR RADIATION THERAPY

Depending on how quickly a woman heals, the first radiation therapy session may be scheduled as soon as two weeks after surgery. There is no medical reason to begin any sooner; in fact, if you are going to have chemotherapy, your radiation treatment may be delayed. If a woman does not need chemotherapy, the usual two- to four-week delay provides time to recover from surgery and to work some of the soreness out of the arm adjacent to the breast that had the surgery. This is important, because during treatment a woman lies on her back with that arm stretched above her head.

During a woman's first visit, the radiation oncologist and other team members decide exactly how and where to aim the radiation. While a woman is lying on an examining table, a machine called a "simulator" is positioned above her to take a variety of measurements. Among other things, the simulator determines where a woman's ribs, heart, and lung are in relationship to her breast and, more specifically, the area of the breast that will be treated. The information and measurements are fed into a computer that calculates the aim and angles of the radiation so that it goes to the right place and avoids other areas. To make sure that a woman's breast is in the same position every day, a mold in which she can rest her arm is usually used. A woman with very large breasts may be given a halter to hold the breast being treated in place.

A woman also receives some tiny tattoos to mark the area of the breast to be treated. These tattoo marks are very small dots of India ink that are usually barely noticeable, but they are important for two reasons: (1) they leave no doubt about where to aim the radiation and (2) should cancer develop in the opposite, normal breast a radiation oncologist will know not to irradiate the area outlined (due to the risks more radiation will pose to the skin). The alternative to tattoos is indelible ink, but ink can wash off over time, leaving future doctors in the dark as to the extent of the area treated. The tattooing may prick or sting a bit but is not really painful. The radiation therapist will do the tattooing, which takes about ten minutes. Most women need between nine and 15 tattoos, which wind up looking like freckles on the skin.

WHAT HAPPENS DURING RADIATION THERAPY

Radiation therapy is carried out once a day, five days a week for five to seven weeks. Each daily session takes only a few minutes. At the end of treatment, however, a woman may get a last "boost" of radiation for which she may have to check into the hospital for a day or two (see section that follows).

During the five to seven weeks only a small dose of radiation is given daily. Treatment is spread out over this long period of time to give damaged but

PRECAUTIONS TO TAKE DURING RADIATION THERAPY

Here are some simple precautions most doctors recommend to breast cancer patients undergoing radiation:

• To minimize skin irritation, do not wash breasts with perfumed or deodorant soaps that may react with the radiation and cause irritation. A mild soap, like Ivory or Neutrogena, paired with lukewarm water, is preferred.

• Do not use deodorant on the side that is being treated, because the aluminum in most deodorants can interact with radiation and cause a burn (like a sunburn). If you cannot imagine going without deodorant, check the labels of deodorants stocked in health or natural food stores and choose one that does not contain aluminum or ask your doctor to prescribe a deodorant that will not hurt you.

• Wear a soft, cotton bra with no underwiring because skin is especially sensitive, or go braless.

healthy cells a chance to repair themselves. Most women fall into the daily routine pretty quickly, although the first session can be unnerving. Essentially, a woman who has already been tattooed removes her shirt, bra, and any jewelry she may be wearing around her neck. Then she lies down on an examining table while the radiation machine is aimed toward the breast area. It takes five to 10 minutes for the radiation therapist to set up the equipment and make sure that the patient is positioned properly. Once everything is ready, the therapist leaves the room and turns on the machine. The actual treatment takes less than a minute, when the x-ray beam is repositioned so radiation can be delivered from another angle to another part of the breast. All told, a woman may lie on the table for 10 to 20 minutes. She must lie still without changing position, although she can breathe normally throughout the process. As with any X ray, she will not feel the radiation being delivered.

In addition to the daily treatment, a woman's blood probably will be tested from time to time to make sure that the radiation isn't affecting her red and white blood cells. This is just a precaution, because radiation rarely has any effect on the blood count of breast cancer patients.

The Boost

At the end of her treatment, a woman may receive a "boost" of another type of radiation delivered directly to the spot where the cancer was. Although a radiation therapist will use another type of radioactive particle (usually an electron beam delivered by a linear accelerator similar to the one used in earlier treatment), practically speaking, the boost will not seem different from earlier therapy. A woman reports to the radiation facility daily, five to 14 days. As her treatment progresses, she probably will notice some redness in the skin over the site.

Alternatively, a radiation oncologist may recommend an internal boost. If so, a woman will have to check into the hospital for two to three days to have some thin, hollow plastic tubes implanted in the area of the breast where the cancer was. The number of tubes and their placement depend on the size and location of the lump that was removed. A local or general anesthetic may be administered. Once the tubes are in place, the physician inserts some radioactive material, usually iridium-192, and the woman then returns to her hospital room. Her breast may feel somewhat sensitive, but most women do not complain of pain. During the hospital stay (about a day and a half on average), a woman must remain in her room because she now is radioactive. For this reason, nurses can spend only a limited amount of time in direct contact with her, and visitors must sit across the room. There is little danger to adults, but because even small amounts of radiation can be dangerous to pregnant women, relatives or friends who are expecting should wait until a woman returns home to visit.

In some cases, the internal boost actually may be given during the initial surgery. The thin plastic tubes and radioactive implants are inserted during surgery, after the breast surgeon excises the tumor but before the incision is closed. This difference in timing is based on the preference of a woman's radiation oncologist. When done in this fashion, the radioactive material can be placed in the exact spot where the lump was, explains Dr. Carl Mansfield, associate director of the radiation research program at the National Cancer Institute. This can be especially helpful for tumors located deep in the breast. After approximately two days, the implants are removed. Having the boost first shortens treatment time and cost, because afterward a woman needs only the five-week course of therapy (without the two additional weeks for an external boost). Also, she will not have to return to the hospital for an internal boost just a couple of days after her breast surgery.

Whether a woman has an internal boost first or last, the implants will be removed in her hospital room. She will not need anesthesia, because the procedure does not hurt; it just feels like having stitches removed. Once the implants are out, she should be able to go home. She will no longer be radioactive and will not have to limit her contact with others.

The choice of an external or internal boost depends on the amount of surgery a woman has had, the availability of electron beam therapy, and whether her radiation oncologist is skilled at performing the implant procedure. Today the external electron beam boost is much more common. (Most centers no longer use the implant.)

POSSIBLE SIDE EFFECTS

The frequent complaint among women undergoing radiation treatment for breast cancer is fatigue. A woman probably will not notice this immediately, but as treatment goes on, she may find that she is more tired at the end of the day than normal. Like surgery, radiotherapy stresses the body. However, there is no way to predict how tired a woman will be, when she will begin to notice fatigue, or whether she will be tired at all. Every case is different, but she should be able to continue to work and go about her usual daily activities. However, because fatigue *is* common, she may not want to schedule any major events during treatment or for the first month or so afterward.

Some women worry that they will be radioactive while they are being treated. This does not happen when radiation is delivered via an external beam. But as described earlier, when a woman has an internal "boost" she may have to take some precautions; until then, she can behave normally, with no fear of transmitting radioactivity.

Another common concern is that hair will fall out during treatment. This *never* happens to the hair on your head, but underarm hair can disappear with radiotherapy for breast cancer. Loss of head hair may occur as a result of chemotherapy (see Chapter 24), or from radiation for *brain* cancer, but otherwise, a woman's locks will stay in place.

After a few weeks of radiotherapy, a woman probably will notice a slight reddening of the skin over the area being treated. She may also have some swelling from water retention in the irradiated tissues. And after treatment is over, the irradiated skin may feel a little thicker than normal for a while, and a nipple may appear a bit crusty. All this is only temporary. One unlikely side effect is a type of arthritis called *costochondritis* that shows up as pain where your ribs and breastbone connect. Some women worry that the pain means the breast cancer has spread, but you can be pretty sure that it's only *costochondritis* if the area hurts when pressed. Aspirin and anti-inflammatory drugs used to treat arthritis can bring relief.

Radiation to the armpit will increase the small risk of lymphedema associated with breast cancer treatment, so you do need to be careful to protect yourself from infection (see Chapter 21). There is also a very small risk that radiation to the armpits can affect the nerves to the hand, causing some numbness in the fingertips.

The most serious after-effect of radiation treatment is *extremely* rare: a radiation-induced sarcoma, a cancer of the bone or connective tissues, estimated to occur in only two of every 1,000 women within 10 years of treatment.

Overall, however, most women tolerate radiation therapy quite well.

YOUR BREASTS AFTER RADIATION THERAPY

A woman's breasts may look different after radiation therapy. The redness that develops during treatment will fade, but she may notice that her skin is darker than it used to be and its pores larger. There may be other changes: skin may be thicker, and breasts firmer, than before treatment. Some women report that their breast is larger (because of fluid buildup), while others find that their breast is smaller (because of fibrous changes), but most see no difference in size.

THE FOLLOW-UP

Even after radiotherapy is over, a woman continues to see her radiation oncologist on a regular basis. During the first year visits often alternate between breast surgeon, radiation oncologist, and, if you have had chemotherapy, medical oncologist. Usually, a woman sees one doctor or the other every three months for the first three years. For five years after that, appointments are usually scheduled every six months, and she is more likely to see less of the breast surgeon and more of the radiation oncologist and/or medical oncologist. After the eight-year mark, a woman only sees the doctor who is overseeing her case once a year, and that is often the radiation oncologist, the physician who has the most experience in examining breasts that have been treated with radiation, or for women who have undergone chemotherapy, the medical oncologist.

When You Need Chemotherapy and Hormone Therapy: Seizing the Power of Cancer-Killing Drugs

In the last 20 years scientists have discovered that breast cancers are uniquely sensitive to a wide variety of new, powerful chemical and hormonal drugs. These systemic weapons in the war against breast cancer, used either separately or in combinations ranging from mild to highly aggressive, are extending the lives of tens of thousands of women annually. The greatest effects have been felt by women at high risk of suffering a recurrence of breast cancer after surgery, but women whose cancers have already reappeared in their breast or have metastasized beyond their breast to other parts of their body also have more optimistic prospects. In fact, in 1990 the Early Breast Cancer Trialists' (EBCT) Collaborative Group, which in 1985 published its first assessment of 133 clinical trials involving approximately 77,000 women, updated that promising analysis of women on systemic therapy after surgery for breast cancer. These studies are following women who underwent surgery for a primary breast cancer and were subsequently treated with either chemotherapy, the hormonal drug tamoxifen, or a surgical procedure called ovarian ablation, or were not treated at all.

In the five years since the first analysis showed that systemic drugs increased survival, the value of chemotherapy and hormonal therapy (based on tamoxifen) was even more evident. *In brief, chemotherapy directly attacks and destroys cancer cells; hormonal therapy deprives breast cancer cells of estrogen, an essential "growth food" for them.* The EBCT Collaborative Group reported that when the results of all trials of chemotherapy versus no chemotherapy were combined, the women on chemo clearly benefited: the overall odds of a recurrence of a breast cancer were 21 percent lower after chemotherapy, and the chances of dying of breast cancer were down 11 percent. The magnitude of these effects was even greater in women younger than 50. Tamoxifen lowered the overall rate of recurrence of breast cancer by 25 percent and reduced the odds of death by 17 percent. (Researchers found that ovarian ablation, a surgical procedure explained in the section "Understanding Hormonal Therapy," also lowered the rates of cancer recurrence and death, but this treatment was studied in only a small number of premenopausal women.) Word on the 1995 update, which had not yet been published when this book went to press, is that percentages show that chemo- and hormonal therapy continue to prevent recurrence and extend life.

Every day researchers continue to improve the effectiveness, safety, and side effects of existing treatments; to test new drugs that promise to extend medicine's ability to attack or control cancer; and to probe the mysteries of molecular biology for cellular features that can tell them more about breast cancer. If your doctor has recommended fighting your breast cancer *medically*—in other words, with chemotherapy and/or hormonal therapy—this chapter will help you understand why your particular treatment was suggested and what you may expect in the course of your care.

If your chemo- and/or hormonal therapy has been recommended by a doctor who is not a medical oncologist, be sure to consult such a specialist (see "Choosing the Right Oncologist for You"). A *medical oncologist* is a physician well-versed in the world of systemic therapy because he specializes in the medical, rather than surgical, treatment of cancerous tumors. (Note: Sometimes surgical oncologists make recommendations for systemic treatment, but a medical oncologist is the doctor of choice in this matter. In this chapter, the term *oncologist* refers specifically to a *medical oncologist*.)

A number of noted *medical breast oncologists*, physicians who subspecialize and focus on the treatment of women with breast cancer, have contributed to the comprehensiveness of this chapter. For the latest information on chemotherapy and hormonal therapy, we have relied on the knowledge and well-honed instincts of:

Dr. Maria Theodoulou, attending breast oncologist at The Breast/ Gynecological Oncology Service at Memorial Sloan-Kettering Cancer Center in New York;

Dr. C. Kent Osborne, chief of medical oncology at the University of Texas Health Science Center and director of the Breast Disease Clinic at the Cancer Therapy and Research Center, both in San Antonio; and

Dr. Silvana Martino, medical director of Westlake Comprehensive Breast Center in Westlake Village, California.

WHEN YOU NEED CHEMOTHERAPY AND/OR HORMONAL THERAPY

Whether undergoing chemotherapy or hormonal therapy, you will be taking anticancer drugs to fight your breast cancer *systemically*—throughout your body—as opposed to *locally*—through surgery or radiation at the site of your cancer. Drugs are given orally or intravenously and, once in the bloodstream, are carried throughout the body to attack migrant breast cancer cells—whether in microscopic or detectable amounts—elsewhere in the breast or lymph nodes, the bones or lungs, or wherever else they may have settled in. Chemotherapy and/or hormonal therapy are recommended in three different situations:

1. before breast surgery, to shrink a large or difficult-to-remove tumor down to operable dimensions, when it is called primary, or *neoadjuvant*, therapy,

2. after breast surgery has removed a tumor, when the drugs are considered *adjuvant* therapy, and

3. when a breast cancer has recurred or clearly metastasized, even when the malignant growth can be surgically removed.

CHOOSING THE RIGHT ONCOLOGIST FOR YOU

Some women like to have a medical oncologist involved in every phase of their decision making in regard to breast cancer, and they consult an oncologist at the first sign of trouble, at the point when a mammogram detects the presence of a possible cancer. More often—unless a tumor is so large chemotherapy is required to shrink it before surgery can be performed—women wait to consult an oncologist until a biopsy report or a pathology analysis after breast surgery tells them that a suspicious lump is cancerous. Even if a breast surgeon feels confident about recommending drugs for adjuvant therapy, it is always best for a woman to consult an oncologist who is focused on the medical treatment of cancer and more aware than a surgeon of new, effective drug combinations.

Even in situations that seem to hold less risk, an oncologist should still be consulted. It is the small—1 cm or less—early-stage breast cancer that can be the most difficult to analyze in terms of risk of recurrence. Recent research has shown subtle but critical differences in the pathology profiles of tumors that fall into this category. Researchers now know that some small tumors can be more aggressive than previously thought. Oncologists are experienced at assessing the pathological characteristics of a tumor and surrounding tissue and thus are valuable in interpreting a woman's medical treatment.

After surgery, it is not necessary to start chemotherapy immediately. A woman has time to choose an oncologist without influencing her prognosis. A recent study of women who were diagnosed with positive lymph node involvement after breast cancer surgery found no advantage in starting adjuvant therapy sooner than six weeks after surgery. Since every woman's breast cancer is unique, however, ask your doctor what he recommends as

BEFORE YOU START CHEMOTHERAPY OR HORMONAL THERAPY

The best systemic treatment for you may not be for anyone else. As oncologists emphatically point out, *there is no typical patient. The most sensible treatment for your breast cancer has to be worked out individually for you—and with you.* "Breast cancer," Dr. Theodoulou says, "has a hundred different varieties, and for each woman at the very same age, with the very same background, and sometimes even with the very same risk factors, it can be a very different disease." Dr. Ezra Greenspan, clinical professor of medicine at Mount Sinai School of Medicine in New York and founder of the Chemotherapy Foundation, finds breast cancer so strikingly varied from one woman to another that he claims "no two patients with breast cancer are alike."

As explained in this chapter, the treatment process begins with:

• choosing *an oncologist certified by the American Board of Internal Medicine*—someone who has the necessary training to treat breast cancer and who gives you the sense that together you can form an effective partnership for your health care. The process continues with:

• making sure that you have *an accurate pathology report.* If you have any misgivings about a pathologist's findings, get a second opinion. (The availability of second-opinion services is explained in Chapter 20.)

the time frame in which you should begin your adjuvant treatment. In general, Dr. Maria Theodoulou counsels that waiting more than six months to begin chemo- or hormonal therapy may mean canceling out any benefits the treatment might provide. Still, you have some time to consider the following recommendations and select the right oncologist for you:

• **Get a meaningful recommendation.** Ask your physician or breast surgeon to recommend a board-certified oncologist, a doctor certified by the American Board of Internal Medicine, whom he respects. Physicians always recommend doctors who share their professional standards. Because you will want to meet with more than one oncologist before you make your selection, breast cancer advocacy organizations are also a source for the names of board-certified *medical breast oncologists*, doctors who specialize in treating women with breast cancer. You may request the name of a breast oncologist from the National Alliance of Breast Cancer Organizations (NABCO), phone: 212-889-0606; SHARE, phone: 212-719-0394; Y-ME, phone: 800-221-2144. The National Cancer Institute's Cancer Information Service at 800-4-CANCER can provide you with listings for comprehensive cancer care centers in your area, as well as nearby medical societies. All of these are resources for the names of local oncologists. (If a biopsy has shown a less common type of cancer, such as inflammatory breast cancer, a woman can ask the NCI's Cancer Information Service for the names of oncologists who are conducting research in this area and are experts on the particular cancer they study. Also, sometimes the most advanced treatment is available through a clinical trial, a research study of drugs still considered experimental.) Of course, sometimes the most meaningful recommendation can come from a woman who has been treated by an oncologist and is pleased with the care she received. By joining a local breast cancer support group (check your telephone directory for the nearest chapter of the American Cancer Society to inquire about support groups; also NABCO and the Susan G. Komen Breast Cancer Foundation listed in the Resources section of this book maintain listings of support groups all over the country), you can meet other women who have survived breast cancer and ask them for their recommendations. I have found that even when you cast a wide net and inquire among many different sources, you usually find that one or two names consistently surface.

• **Select an oncologist who discusses your options with sensitivity and explains why he is recommending a specific treatment.** The drugs of chemotherapy and hormonal therapy, and their combinations, can have protocols—treatment programs—that continue for months and produce side effects, risks, and benefits. You want to choose a competent a doctor with whom you feel personally compatible, because you will have an ongoing partnership. You and your doctor are working together for the good health of your body. Ask yourself whether his explanations are simple and clear, if he has an approachable style, and if he exudes confidence about helping you triumph over your disease. If you feel he is as qualified personally as he is professionally, then you have chosen the right physician.

• **Ask a companion to accompany you when you visit an oncologist.** As mentioned in other chapters, when meeting with a doctor, whether it be a breast surgeon, reconstructive surgeon, or oncologist, you need another person to function as a "second pair of ears" on your behalf. The course of drug therapy for breast cancer can be complicated for a doctor to explain, much less for you to understand. A spouse, lover, family member, or close friend can offer emotional as well as practical support. The diagnosis of breast cancer can be so overwhelming it affects your ability to concentrate. That's why having another person with you who can be your advocate is so important.

• **Prepare in advance questions about side effects, risks, and benefits of the drugs you will be taking.** Because oncologists discuss the same drugs day after day, a doctor may go over the facts of your protocol too quickly for you to comprehend. Do not hesitate to ask the doctor to repeat himself or to explain more slowly and simply any possible side effects and treatments you may need for these side effects, possible complications that may be a result of your therapy, and benefits that may be in your future. You may want to bring a tape recorder to help you review the facts of the meeting later on. A woman can request a list of questions for her first meeting with an oncologist from the help hotline of the Susan G. Komen Breast Cancer Foundation at 800-I'M AWARE or 800-462-9273.

• **Consider an oncologist who is on the staff of a comprehensive breast cancer center.** These centers are being established by major hospitals all across the country. (See a list of 10 top breast cancer centers in the Resources section at the end of this book.) A breast cancer center gathers under one roof every professional a woman needs to see in the course of her care. The doctors on staff at such a center form her team: the radiologist who detects an abnormality in a mammogram, the breast surgeon who removes the breast cancer, the reconstructive surgeon, the pathologist who analyzes biopsied tissue samples and all the tissues removed during surgery, the radiation oncologist, the medical oncologist who recommends and supervises chemo- or hormonal therapy with anticancer drugs. At a comprehensive breast cancer center a woman also has access to an array of other professionals, such as psychiatrists and social workers who specialize in counseling women who are undergoing treatment for breast cancer.

THE IMPORTANCE OF AN ACCURATE PATHOLOGY REPORT

Your medical oncologist should insist on reviewing your mammogram, your pathology report, and the tissue specimens on which the report was based. *If you are referred to a medical oncologist who* **does not** *request all of this information, you should find someone else.* Whether you have a small tumor that has negative lymph nodes not showing signs of cancer or positive lymph nodes that clearly call for adjuvant therapy or a breast cancer that has returned or metastasized, an accurate pathology report is the first crucial step toward treatment. More and more women are realizing the need for an expert, second-opinion pathology review. You can ask your surgeon to recommend a pathologist at an institution other than the one where your current analysis took place, or you can contact one of the second-opinion services described in Chapter 20.

If your oncologist has confidence in the pathologist who did your evaluation and your case is fairly straightforward, a second opinion may be unnecessary. It is the tricky diagnosis that benefits from more than one analysis. For example, a breast cancer labeled "invasive" with "intraductal or in situ" components is more complicated to treat than a strictly invasive cancer. If a second-opinion pathologist disagrees with the initial report, it makes sense to go for a third opinion. Today many women are double- and triple-checking their pathology reports.

SCIENCE AND INTUITION: HOW ONCOLOGISTS DECIDE ON THE BEST TREATMENT FOR YOU

Certain women need systemic anticancer treatment at the outset: women diagnosed with inflammatory cancer and those who require tumor-shrinking therapy before surgery. The treatment protocol for these women is aggressive. After surgery for a woman's breast cancer has been performed, doctors must judge the postsurgical pathology report, decide whether breast surgery was complete, whether enough lymph nodes were removed during surgery to serve as a representative sample for the pathological evaluation, and whether a treatment regimen is needed. (On occasion, oncologists have suggested that a woman return to the operating room to have additional lymph nodes or breast tissue excised.)

Every woman's breast cancer is unique, and if chemo- and/or hormonal therapy is warranted, an oncologist will not only evaluate the individual nature of your cancer, but also your overall health, including medical problems other than breast cancer, and age. "I take into consideration each patient's *healthy age*," Dr. Theodoulou has told me. "I might have a woman who is 65 but looks and functions like a healthy 50-year-old, but if I have a 40-to-45-year-old patient with poorly controlled diabetes, underlying kidney insufficiency, and perhaps a heart attack already in her history, I want to treat her in a way that avoids worsening any of these conditions. Otherwise, if her cancer were to recur at some future point—which we have to think about, because nothing can be truly guaranteed in adjuvant therapy—these conditions, if worsened, might tie our hands." Your doctor will also assess your kidneys and liver—the two organs that clear drugs from your system— to make sure that there are no problems that might require a reduced dosage of drugs. Older women and younger women with suspicious symptoms are additionally given a full cardiac check-up. It is important to realize that sometimes a doctor's preference for one treatment regimen over another influences the treatment alternatives he offers, but you should feel that your treatment is being regarded as a cooperative undertaking between you and your doctor.

UNDERSTANDING YOUR NEED FOR TREATMENT

When Cancer-Killing Drugs Are Needed Before— or Instead of—Surgery

An oncologist may recommend chemotherapy for a woman who has:

• A *large—over 5 cm—tumor confined to her breast area*, which a breast surgeon has deemed inoperable. A 6-cm tumor in a small breast, for example, is so large that a surgeon cannot be confident of thoroughly clearing all the

IN HER OWN WORDS: DR. MARIA THEODOULOU, BREAST ONCOLOGIST, ON RECOMMENDING TREATMENT

"I won't make a treatment recommendation until I have done a *complete* head-to-toe physical. If a woman has positive lymph nodes, this includes a bone scan. If the pathology shows an aggressive cancer, or more than three positive nodes, I also order a CAT scan of the abdomen, chest, and pelvis.

"I review my patient's pathology with her, and I always draw a lot of pictures. We'll talk about what her tumor looks like and whether it came from the lobule or the duct. If it's invasive, we'll talk about what it means when the tumor breaks through the wall of that particular tissue. If she has positive lymph nodes, we'll talk about the number, the implication of lymph nodes being involved, and the different levels of lymph nodes where her dissection was. We talk about hormone receptors [see Chapter 20], what it means for a receptor to be on a cell, like a magnet drawing certain hormones that are circulating in her system, and what it means if her tumor is estrogen/progesterone-positive; estrogen-positive/progesterone-negative; estrogen-negative/progesterone-positive. We'll look at some of the newer tests that are done [DNA analysis and biomarkers as explained in Chapter 20]. I want my patient to understand exactly what her cancer looks like, because when we start talking about treatment, she needs to get into my head, to know what I'm concerned about.

"Based on all of this, I tell my patient how I see her prognosis. Is there a substantial chance that her breast cancer won't recur, and probably won't be one of the factors in her life she'll be worrying about? Or is her risk significant enough that I am worried it *is* going to be the most concerning factor in her immediate future—and we should be as aggressive as possible in treating her cancer. I always give my rationale for what makes me want to offer a particular regimen, and I always discuss alternatives, including different standard treatments, no treatment and it's implications, and investigational treatments. I explain what clinical trials are, what it means to a patient in a clinical trial. I talk about what the potential downside of different treatments may be, not just the short-term nausea, hair loss, and immune system suppression, but what may happen five or 10 years from now.

"If, after we consider everything, those long-term risks outweigh the potential benefits of treatment, I have to ask myself: What am I doing by giving potentially toxic therapy to someone who may not need it? Am I really improving her overall survival? But if the scale tips in favor of the benefits, then there is no question. I don't give statistics to my patients unless they ask for them, and then I reinforce the reality that they are only numbers,* and that breast cancer cells have never learned to read them. Above all, I stress that *I* am optimistic—that otherwise I wouldn't be suggesting adjuvant chemotherapy."

A note on "numbers": *Specific rates to describe risk categories and the effects that various treatments can have on these risks are computed differently from one medical study to another. So if you want to ask your doctor to statistically describe the risk associated with your cancer and the possible rate of improvement from a particular treatment, it is easiest to inquire in terms of "people." For example, in a group of 100 women with your type of breast cancer who do not undergo treatment, how many are expected to be disease-free in five years? In 10? How many will still be alive but no longer cancer-free? With treatment "A," how many **more** women will still be alive at these intervals? How many **more** women will also still be disease-free? If there are other treatment possibilities, what are the "people" numbers associated with them?*

malignant tissue during mastectomy. The first step, then, is three to four months, or cycles, of primary chemotherapy to shrink the tumor until it is small enough to allow adequate and complete surgery. After surgery, adjuvant chemotherapy is scheduled for several more months based on the pathology report of residual tumor, and finally radiation completes the sequence. (Hormonal therapy may be used if the tumor is hormonally sensitive.)

• *A 4-cm, or larger tumor, when the woman wants to preserve her breast.* Normally, doctors recommend a mastectomy for a tumor of this size, but Dr. Gianni Bonadonna, of the National Tumor Institute in Milan, Italy, worked out a program requiring only three cycles of chemotherapy that permitted 79 percent of the mastectomy candidates he studied to choose a safe and effective lumpectomy plus radiation instead. The degree of tumor response depended on the tumor's original size: the larger it was to begin with, the less it shrank. Response has no relation to patient age, menopausal status, DNA analysis of the tumor, or chemotherapy regimen (so the mildest drug therapy can be used). Although doctors in the United States are beginning to use this procedure to shrink tumors for breast-conserving surgery, it is still considered experimental; the medical establishment is awaiting statistics on local recurrence of cancer in the conserved breast.

• *An extensive tumor mass with cancerous skin involvement, often with retraction or ulceration of the skin (a stage IV tumor).* In the past these tumors were usually inoperable and incurable, but today aggressive and sustained chemotherapy is able to shrink them enough to permit surgery 80 to 85 percent of the time. On the other hand, sometimes the tumors disappear due to the chemotherapy, and surgery is no longer needed.

• *Metastatic breast cancer, which is usually spread too diffusely for surgery to be useful.* This type of widespread cancer is treated with chemo- and/or hormonal therapy. The one exception is the unusual metastasis that may be limited to a single, surgically accessible tumor somewhere other than in the breast; in this case, anticancer drugs might be used after surgery.

• *Inflammatory cancer, which used to kill 95 percent of women within a year of their diagnoses.* Aggressive, intensive chemotherapy regimens can gain rapid control of this inoperable form of breast cancer in the large majority (80 to 90 percent) of persons who have it. Although different studies report different survival rates, the specific numbers are not as important as the fact that a significant proportion of women who have been diagnosed with inflammatory cancer are surviving—many of them disease-free at five- and 10-year checkups. For women with inflammatory breast cancer, the latest research is being conducted at M.D. Anderson Cancer Center in Houston, John Hopkins Oncology Center in Baltimore, and the Mount Sinai Medical Center in New York.

When Cancer-Killing Drugs Are *Not* Needed After Surgery

Roughly 70 percent of the women diagnosed with breast cancer each year do not need chemotherapy or hormone therapy after surgery because their tumor is at *low risk* of recurrence. A low-risk breast cancer would be:

• *an in situ tumor diagnosed as having no cellular characteristics associated with a spreading cancer,*
• *a small, no bigger than 1 cm, tumor that a pathologist defines as a nonaggressive cancer.* In general, nonaggressive breast cancers have cells that are well differentiated, meaning that they still closely resemble the breast tissue from which they developed and have a low nuclear grade;
• *a tumor that has no associated malignant cells present in lymph nodes or surrounding tissue and no tiny malignant nodules near the tumor.*

The Gray Area: When Women Have Small Tumors and Negative Lymph Nodes

Oncologists evaluate tumor size and the presence of cancerous cells in lymph nodes, the profile of a breast cancer that emerges from the pathology report (which includes DNA analysis and molecular biomarkers), and then they consider the functional age of a woman's body based on her overall health. When the evaluation points to a tumor that falls into the gray area of decision making (described below), and may be more tenacious than it appears, these days doctors are more inclined to recommend systemic treatment. No one wants to let escape that one renegade cell that might start a cancerous growth somewhere.

Before Dr. Peter Rosen's landmark study—a 20-year follow-up of 767 node-negative women who had received mastectomy-only treatment, published at the end of 1993—most medical oncologists thought that women who had negative lymph nodes, with a tumor 2 cm or less, did not face enough of a risk of recurrence to warrant adjuvant treatment. Doctors were not aware that a breast cancer with an aggressive pathology profile could recur in a large enough number of women with 1- to 2-cm tumors to make systemic treatment worthwhile. When Dr. Rosen evaluated the women with stage I breast cancers who had undergone mastectomies almost three decades earlier (between 1964 and 1970), recurrence and survival statistics 20 years after surgery-only treatment showed that stage I women fell into low- and intermediate-risk groups. *Only the low-risk subset—one third of all the stage I women—actually showed the excellent prognosis that had for years been attributed to this entire group.*

The stage I women at **low risk** for long-term recurrence after surgery included those who had invasive duct or lobular tumors no more than 1 cm wide and women with special types of slow-growing invasive duct cancer: medullary, mucinous, papillary, tubular, and adenocystic, up to 3 cm wide. Twenty years later 87 percent of the women at low risk remained disease-free.

The women at **intermediate risk** had negative lymph nodes and tumors in the upper range of stage I (1 to 2 cm) and stage IIa (2 to 3 cm). At 20 years, 74 percent of the women with the larger, stage I tumors remained disease free, as did 72 percent of the women with stage IIa tumors.

This work lends support to the belief that the current TNM staging criteria for node-negative patients (see Chapter 22), with *T1* grouping together all tumors up to 2.0 cm and *T2* covering 2- to 5-cm tumors, should be revised to be more precise about risk.

Doctors are aware of the need to evaluate each woman's breast cancer individually, and often today's pathologists will describe the size of tumor, lymph node involvement, and metastasis without going into the technicalities of TNM staging in their reports. Even when a tumor meets all the classic staging criteria for an excellent prognosis—it is less than 1 cm, has negative nodes and clear margins—Dr. Theodoulou feels it is critical to hunt for evidence of cancer cells in lymphatic and blood vessels surrounding the tumor and to make sure that no poorly differentiated (wild-looking and more aggressive) tumor cells exist. "These all concern me," she says. "I would rather provide treatment for these women, especially for a young woman who, without that cancer, would have a very long lifespan. Women easily live to be 85 and 90, and I don't want to deprive a woman of that because I didn't take her cancer seriously enough."

Adjuvant Treatment Is the Rule: When Women Have Positive Lymph Nodes and/or Large Tumors

When a woman has a breast cancer that is 3.1 cm or more and/or lymph nodes that are positive for cancerous cells, she is considered at high risk for a recurrence or a metastasis of her cancer (a seeding of cells in other parts of her body), even after the mass has been surgically removed. The bigger the tumor and the higher the number of positive lymph nodes, the greater her risk. The risk jumps abruptly when more than three nodes are involved and rises again when more than 10 nodes are positive.

Postsurgery, adjuvant treatment with chemotherapy, hormonal therapy, or a combination of both is designed to attack undetectable but thriving microscopic clumps of cancer cells. (See the sections under "What Happens During Chemotherapy" and "Understanding Hormonal Therapy" for details on how these drugs are administered and how you may respond.)

• The drugs of *chemotherapy* work because they interfere with the ability of cells to divide and reproduce themselves. These drugs have a toxic quality needed to stop the spread of cancerous cells, but the very toxicity that kills a cancer can cause side effects that run the gamut from uncomfortable to debilitating. (See "Possible Toxic Effects" in this chapter.)

• The drugs of *hormonal therapy* home in on estrogen-responsive tumor cells and cut them off from estrogen, the hormone believed to have the strongest effect in stimulating growth. Usually estrogen and progesterone are both affected by the drugs of hormonal therapy. The hormonal receptor status of a woman's breast cancer and her menopausal status help determine whether she will benefit from hormonal therapy.

The goal of both therapies, of course, is to destroy the tiniest clumps of cells—potential *micrometastases*—that have spread outside the breast before they develop into new, more difficult-to-treat cancers.

When Aggressive or High-Dose Treatment Is Needed

The need for aggressive systemic therapy, which involves powerful drug combinations (the most potent falling under the category of high-dose chemotherapy), arises when a woman is facing advanced breast cancer: the return of the primary cancer in one breast or the other, or the spread of the primary tumor outside her breasts, in another area of her body, or the appearance of cancer in 10 or more lymph nodes. The treatment for metastatic breast cancer can be life-long. "I often tell a woman with metastatic disease that she needs to think of herself as if she has diabetes or high blood pressure. She would have to take medication to control either of those conditions for the rest of her life," says Dr. Silvana Martino. Oncologists consulted for this chapter all speak of women who have lived for 15 to 20 years with their metastatic breast cancer controlled by long-term chemotherapy.

WHAT HAPPENS DURING CHEMOTHERAPY

The cancer-killing drugs of chemotherapy interfere with the proliferation of cells by damaging DNA and stopping their ability to reproduce. The problem is that not all cells in the same tumor are vulnerable to interference in the same way; therefore, drugs are combined, to create regimens that can be more successful than single agents in their search-and-destroy missions. Even so, a woman must undergo a repeated number of treatments, or cycles, of her regimen to give these drugs the best chance of meeting all of the cancer-causing cells at their vulnerable time. Most of the body's healthy cells are not susceptible to chemotherapy because they do not reproduce as fast as cancer cells; their two-week period of reproductive inactivity protects them. Cells that normally reproduce faster than others—those in the ovaries, gastrointestinal tract, bone marrow, and hair follicles—however, are more vulnerable to the drugs of chemotherapy. That is why the most well-known side effects of chemotherapy have turned out to be the temporary suspension of menstruation or the onset of menopause (depending on a woman's age), nausea, diarrhea, and hair loss. Some women also experience an inexplicable weight gain of about 10 percent of their normal weight (see "An Overview of Chemotherapy Drugs and Their Range of Toxic Side Effects"). Also, bone marrow, which rapidly reproduces, can fall prey to the drugs; after a treatment cycle, production of red and white blood cells and platelets can plummet. This is called bone-marrow suppression and can result in fatigue and susceptibility to infection. The vulnerability of the bone marrow is the main reason for setting intervals between cycles of treatment. These intervals give the affected blood cells (red, white, and/or platelets) time to reproduce and return to a safe level.

As a general rule—but one with increasing exceptions—premenopausal women have most often been given chemotherapy, whereas postmenopausal women have most frequently received hormonal therapy. Lately a combination of the two, what's called *chemoendocrine* therapy, is looked at with increasing favor. Some women in their reproductive years are taking the hormonal drug tamoxifen after completing their chemotherapy, while postmenopausal women who are in good health aside from their breast cancers undergo chemotherapy regimens before taking tamoxifen.

Before going into how your chemotherapy may be scheduled and what you can expect during a chemotherapy session, however, here's a look at some of the drugs you may encounter:

About the Drugs of Chemotherapy and Their Combinations

The drugs most frequently used in breast cancer chemotherapy are:

Cyclophosphamide (Cytoxan)
Methotrexate
Fluorouracil (5-FU)
Doxorubicin (Adriamycin)
Vincristine (Oncovin)
Prednisone (which is thought to enhance the anticancer effect of other drugs)
(These are considered first-line drugs.)

Combinations for treatment can include up to six drugs. The oldest, mildest, and most commonly used combination is CMF (Cytoxan+methotrexate+fluorouracil). Next in line is CAF, with Adriamycin—the single most potent cancer-killing drug—replacing methotrexate. When it comes to metastatic breast cancer, taxol is the newest approved drug. You may also hear about thiotepa and cisplatin, among others.

Some of the more frequently administered chemotherapy combinations are:

CMF = Cytoxan, methotrexate, 5-FU
CAF = Cytoxan, Adriamycin, 5-FU
FAC = 5-FU, Adriamycin, Cytoxan (a higher Adriamycin dose than in CAF)
AC = Adriamycin, Cytoxan
A → CMF = the Milan regimen: four cycles of Adriamycin followed by eight cycles of CMF
CMFP = CMF + prednisone
CMFVP = CMF + vincristine, prednisone
CAFMV = CAF + methotrexate, vincristine
CMFVATN = CMF + vincristine, Adriamycin, thiotepa, tamoxifen (Nolvadex)

For women with aggressive, recurrent, or metastasized breast cancer, experimental high-dose chemotherapy, which often involves bone marrow transplants, can have two regimens: the first round of drug treatment may be a "conditioning" regimen to reduce the size of a tumor or to cleanse the bone marrow of cancer that has metastasized there. After this first round of drugs a woman undergoing high-dose chemotherapy may have her bone marrow or peripheral stem blood cells harvested. The second-round regimen lasts less than a week but involves intense, daily doses of powerful drug combinations. (See "High-Dose Chemotherapy with Bone Marrow Transplant.")

As explained throughout this chapter, your doctor will study your breast cancer profile and you, and individualize the chemotherapy regimen that he believes will most effectively fight your cancer and improve your health.

An Overview of Chemotherapy Drugs and Their Range of Toxic Side Effects

What follows is a rundown of different categories of cancer-killing drugs. Although they destroy cancer cells, these drugs carry certain toxic risks, which is another reason for a woman's oncologist to carefully monitor her treatment. The more intense the treatment, the more susceptible she becomes to side effects. Many new anticancer compounds are under study, but here are some of the more commonly used medications in chemotherapy:

ALKYLATING AGENTS

The most frequently administered alkylating agent is cyclophosphamide (*Cytoxan*). Alkylating compounds in more aggressive regimens include ifosphamide, melphalan (*L-Pam*), thiotepa, the platinum-derived drugs cisplatin (*Cisplatinum, Platinol*) and carboplatin (*Paraplatin*), and BCNU (*Carmustine*).

Possible Toxic Effects: Most alkylating drugs, especially thiotepa, BCNU, and carboplatin, have a suppressive effect on the bone marrow. Some have the greatest effect on white cells, others on platelets, and some on both. The effect of cisplatin on bone marrow is less worrisome, but cisplatin does carry a risk of kidney problems or nephrotoxicity, possible nerve damage that can lead to a loss of sensation in the hands and feet or imbalance, and hearing loss in the upper frequencies. A danger associated with BCNU is fibrosis of the lungs, which can be fatal. A possible side effect with Cytoxan, and also with ifosphamide, is bladder toxicity, but this can be controlled by drinking lots of water to keep the body adequately hydrated. A protective agent called *mesna* is also effective. Hair loss is especially common with Cytoxan. Thiotepa, which appears to be gaining again in popularity, can affect the brain in high doses. Symptoms include mildly inappropriate behavior, forgetfulness, confusion, and sleepiness.

One further word about alkylating agents, which are included in virtually all adjuvant chemotherapy regimens: over time there is a minuscule but established risk of developing acute nonlymphocytic leukemia. This occurs in one to 10 women for every 10,000 women treated over a 10-year period. Drs. Charles Shapiro and Craig Henderson, internationally respected breast cancer specialists, have concluded that "the magnitude of risk associ-

---

TREATMENT FOR WOMEN OF DIFFERENT AGES

Dr. Gianni Bonadonna, of Milan, Italy's National Tumor Institute, has done more research with CMF than anyone else. In 1995 he reported the 20-year follow-up of 386 women who comprised two groups of node-positive mastectomy patients (at all levels of risk) whom he had begun studying in 1973. One group of 179 women had no adjuvant treatment after surgery. The 207 women in the other group received twelve four-week cycles of CMF. After 20 years the chemotherapy with CMF proved to be most effective, especially for women in their reproductive years during their treatment (at the time, postmenopausal women were given less effective doses). Survivors included practically half of the CMF group (47%) but less than one-fourth (22%) of the untreated women. Although Dr. Bonadonna and others have spent years searching for still more effective regimens, he uses these CMF results to make several very important points:

- The impact after 20 years supports the long-term value of adjuvant therapy for breast cancer.
- Fear of the long-term side effect of other chemotherapy-caused cancers, especially leukemia, has not materialized.
- Unlike the premenopausal women in this study, many of the menopausal patients received significantly lowered chemotherapy doses. These lower doses—which were commonly given to older women—are responsible for what had seemed to be chemotherapy's lack of effect in older breast cancer patients. Dr. Bonadonna also cites a highly supportive recent study that analyzed different dose levels of drugs given to pre- and postmenopausal women. The results: menopausal status made no difference in treatment effect; all women responded well to higher doses.

---

ated with typical doses and durations of adjuvant CMF is probably too small to be of clinical significance."

ANTITUMOR ANTIBIOTICS

These include the powerful doxorubicin (*Adriamycin*) and mitomycin C.

Possible Toxic Effects: Bone marrow suppression, mouth sores, and injury to the skin if there is leakage at an injection site are the most common effects. Almost all women lose their hair. Mitomycin C poses the risk of kidney damage, and Adriamycin may disturb the heart rhythm for several days after the dosing. Although Adriamycin can damage the heart muscle, administering the drug very slowly reduces this risk, and simultaneously administration of a compound called *ICRF-187* (also called *ADR-529*) has been shown to protect the heart from damage—even when Adriamycin is given at twice the standard dose. Another new approach—now in clinical trials—encloses Adriamycin in a *liposome* capsule, which also appears to permit higher doses while protecting the heart.

The search for less toxic substitutes has produced:

• A synthetic relative called mitoxantrone (*Novantrone*). Although much larger doses of mitoxantrone can be given before heart damage occurs, it may not be quite as effective as Adriamycin.

• *Anthrapyrazoles*, scientist-designed drugs in which the problem-causing part of Adriamycin's chemical structure is altered. If their promise of highly effective anticancer activity that does not damage the heart is confirmed in clinical trials, then one or more of these drugs—biantrazole or losoxantrone are thought the most likely—may well replace Adriamycin and its relatives within the next few years.

ANTIMETABOLITES

These include methotrexate and fluorouracil (*5-FU*).

Possible Toxic Effects: Methotrexate can damage the kidneys, although this effect is prevented or greatly modified when leucovorin (*Wellcovorin*), a folic acid derivative, is administered 24 hours afterward. Since leucovorin can significantly increase 5-FU's suppressive effect on the bone marrow, it must be handled carefully when methotrexate and 5-FU are used together. A common side effect of methotrexate is mouth sores, and a less frequent but life-threatening one is fibrosis of the lungs. 5-FU can cause mouth sores and diarrhea, nerve damage, and skin discoloration around the injection site that fades very slowly.

Edatrexate is a new drug in phase II trials that promises to be significantly more potent against tumors than methotrexate, but toxicity—especially mouth sores—requires reduced dosing in most patients. Giving leucovorin after the dosing has shown excellent preliminary results in "rescuing" patients from mouth sores. Another new and promising antimetabolite is ICI D1694 (which will eventually be renamed).

VINCA ALKALOIDS

Derivatives of the periwinkle plant have produced vincristine (*Oncovin*) and vinblastine (*Velban*).

Possible Toxic Effects: Both drugs can severely damage the skin if they leak at the injection site. Nerve damage is possible but most likely in those with pre-existing neurologic diseases, pre-existing alcoholic- or dia-

betes-associated neuropathies, and increasing age. Vinblastine also suppresses the bone marrow.

Vinorelbine (*Navelbine*), a drug that is the result of efforts to find an
equally effective and significantly less toxic substitute, is in clinical testing.
Nerve damage is much less frequent, generally mild, and disappears after
treatment. An oral formulation may be very useful for prolonged outpatient
treatment.

EPIPODOPHYLOTOXINS

These include etoposide and teniposide, drugs under investigation.

Possible Toxic Effects: These drugs are associated with bone-marrow suppression and peripheral nerve damage. Although this damage is usually not
as frequent or severe as with the vinca alkaloids, if used after heavy treatment with a vinca alkaloid, the effects might be disabling.

TAXANES

Taxol (*Paclitaxel*) is derived from the bark and needles of the yew tree.
At the time of this writing it is approved as a single agent to treat metastatic
breast cancer and is being evaluated in adjuvant therapy. Taxol is also being
tested in combination with such other new drugs as edatrexate, vinorelbine,
and topotecan.

Possible Toxic Effects: Taxol is potent, and so are its side effects. An
intense allergic reaction—probably to the oil it is injected with rather than
the substance itself—is controlled by heavy antiallergy premedication and by
giving the drug very slowly over a prolonged period (periods from six to 96
hours are under study). Intense muscle and joint pains may occur for several
days after each injection, but starting Tylenol or Advil a few days beforehand can help prevent or minimize this. Nerve damage is also a risk,
although symptoms that do not disappear after treatment may respond to *tri-
cyclic antidepressants*. Coordination and intestinal problems are concerns.
Severe fluid retention limits repeated cycles.

Docetaxel (*Taxotere*), extracted from a plant related to the yew tree, is
currently the newest taxane. An extremely powerful anticancer drug with an
array of toxic effects, it has been approved by the FDA for use in the United
States.

RETINOIDS

These vitamin A derivatives are critical regulators of many normal human
biological functions, including cell growth, differentiation, and immunologic
function. Different retinoids seem to target different organs, and the retinoid
fenretinide in particular seeks out the breast. It has shown strong promise as a
treatment for breast cancer and is taken orally on a daily basis.

Possible Toxic Effects: Eye damage, the main concern, is avoidable by
taking a three-day "holiday" from the drug every month.

A large clinical trial is beginning in the United States comparing fenretinide alone to its use with tamoxifen, because this combination is more effective in animals than either agent alone. This synergistic relationship—when each combined drug makes the other significantly more potent—appears especially relevant to treating advanced breast cancer with breast-targeting retinoids.

PREDNISONE

This corticosteroid, which is well known for treating a variety of allergic problems, is thought to help fight breast cancer in two ways: it may have a mild effect on cell DNA, and it appears to enhance the cancer-killing effects of other chemotherapy drugs.

MISCELLANEOUS INVESTIGATIONAL DRUGS

Topoisomerase-I ("topo-I") interactive agents are chemically altered versions of camptothecin, an anticancer compound isolated from the stem, wood, and bark of the Chinese tree *Camptotheca acuminata*. Three compounds in this group are currently being studied for breast cancer treatment: topotecan, irinotecan, and 9-(AC) (short for 9-amino-camptothecin). (Topotecan is also being investigated in combination with taxol.) Some promising examples under clinical study that appear to be effective against breast tumors resistant to most other drugs are pyrazoloacridine and penclomidine (which can be given intravenously or orally). Other potential new drugs are fostriecin, clomesone, cyclopentylcytosine, bizelesin, and rhizoxin.

Shaping Chemotherapy Regimens

Every woman's chemotherapy regimen, also known as a protocol, is uniquely hers, but some generalizations can be found in the "Treatment Options" table.

Some important points about your chemotherapy regime also can be made about the following situations:

• *If you are in your reproductive years, and your breast cancer is small and your lymph nodes are "negative" for cancer, but your oncologist has advised adjuvant therapy,* you will probably receive the mildest chemotherapy regimen: Cytoxan+methotrexate+fluorouracil, referred to as CMF. Introduced in the late 1960s, when the concept of adjuvant therapy for breast cancer emerged, CMF was the first triple-drug combination used. It is still the most popular adjuvant regimen in breast cancer chemotherapy.

• *If you are in your reproductive years, and your breast cancer is large and you have lymph nodes positive for cancer,* you may still be treated with CMF. Women who have one to three positive lymph nodes but are not treated with CMF may receive either the more potent CAF or FAC, or a simplified

TREATMENT OPTIONS

Primary:	Adjuvant:	Can be considered:
Stage I Lumpectomy and axillary node dissection and radiation *or* Mastectomy	Chemotherapy if tumor does not have estrogen receptors *or* Tamoxifen if tumor has estrogen receptors	Eliminating adjuvant treatment for women whose tumors are smaller than 1 cm.
Stage II Lumpectomy and axillary node dissection and radiation *or* Mastectomy	Chemotherapy if tumor does not have estrogen receptors *or* Tamoxifen if tumor has hormone receptors	Both chemotherapy and tamoxifen for women whose tumors have estrogen receptors and whose lymph nodes have cancer cells
Stage IIIA Mastectomy *May be followed by* Radiation to the chest wall if tumors have invaded that region	Chemotherapy if tumor does not have hormone receptors *or* Chemotherapy and tamoxifen if tumor has hormone receptors	• High-dose chemotherapy with stem-cell transplant • Chemotherapy administered before surgery to shrink the tumor and thus reduce the size of surgery.
Stage IIIB Radiation to reduce tumor *May be followed by* Mastectomy	Chemotherapy if tumor does not have hormone receptors *or* Chemotherapy and tamoxifen if tumor has hormone receptors	• High-dose chemotherapy with stem-cell transplantation • Experimental drugs • Radiation or surgery to remove ovaries for premenopausal women
Stage IV Radiation to reduce tumor	Chemotherapy if tumor does not have hormone receptors	• High-dose chemotherapy with stem-cell transplantation

---

May be followed by

Mastectomy	*or*	• Experimental drugs
	Chemotherapy and	• Radiation or surgery
	tamoxifen if tumor	to remove ovaries for
	has hormone receptors	premenopausal women

Source: National Cancer Institute.
Reprinted from the October 1995 issue of the *Harvard Women's Health Watch*, © 1995, President and Fellows of Harvard College.

---

regimen called CA or AC (which omits the 5-FU). In these regimens the "A" stands for Adriamycin, so far the strongest single anticancer drug for advanced breast cancer. CAF and FAC both combine Cytoxan, Adriamycin, and 5-FU, but in FAC, the Cytoxan—which, unlike most chemotherapy drugs, can be given orally or intravenously—is given only intravenously; also, an additional dose of 5-FU is given on the eighth day of each cycle.

The three regimens CMF, CAF, and FAC are typically given for six months; CA is given for two and a half months.

• *If you are postmenopausal, your breast cancer is stage I, your lymph nodes are negative for cancer, and your cancer is estrogen-receptor positive,* the standard treatment is the hormonal drug tamoxifen.

• *If you are postmenopausal, your breast cancer is stage II (any number of "positive" lymph nodes, as long as the cancer has not spread beyond the nodes; a tumor greater than 2.0 cm but no more than 5 cm, even with "negative" nodes); or Stage III (a tumor greater than 5 cm with any number of "positive" lymph nodes; or a tumor that involves the chest wall or skin, but is "node negative"), and your cancer is estrogen-receptor positive,* chemotherapy may be part of a treatment plain that includes tamoxifen. Although it was long thought that estrogen-responsive breast cancers in menopausal women did not respond to chemotherapy, more recent research data—including Dr. Bonadonna's Milan study, which found A → CMF helpful for postmenopausal women—show that, for older women with higher-risk tumors, chemotherapy followed by tamoxifen—or **chemoendocrine therapy**—actually produces better results than either treatment alone.

• *If you are postmenopausal, your breast cancer is stage I to III regardless of node status, and your cancer is estrogen receptor-negative,* scientific observations together with clinical data now suggest that *tamoxifen,* which has been regarded as ineffective in controlling hormone-receptor-negative tumors, is beneficial in 10 percent of cases. (If a tumor is progesterone receptor-positive and estrogen receptor-negative, it is still considered estrogen receptor-positive. This is because a tumor need a positive estrogen receptor in order to create a positive progesterone receptor. So a woman should always have both receptors evaluated. With research also showing the effectiveness of chemotherapy, the most

THE CONTROVERSY OVER ADRIAMYCIN

The powerful Adriamycin is used without question to treat women who have recurrent or metastatic breast cancer. But can it be used in other situations? Large, well-designed studies have tested the effectiveness of the drug among women needing chemotherapy after surgery for earlier-stage disease, but the results run the gamut from increased survival to little difference to no difference.

A landmark study in Milan, Italy, found that in women with more than three positive lymph nodes, the timing and intensity of Adriamycin are critical to its cancer-killing potential. To begin with, one of the "no difference" studies—conducted by Dr. Gianni Bonadonna at Milan's Cancer Center—compared CMF alone with a two-step sequence of CMF+A. But then Bonadonna did a study in which he either alternated Adriamycin and CMF cycles or completed the Adriamycin portion up front, then administered CMF. Dr. Bonadonna found that bringing in Adriamycin's power at the very beginning and not diluting its intensity with an alternating regimen made the difference. His potent Adriamycin-containing combination called the *Milan regimen* is being used with increasing frequency (although CMF is still the traditional regimen). Called A → CMF, the regimen begins with four cycles of high-dose Adriamycin, then follows with eight cycles of CMF for a total of 33 weeks. Whether women had four to 10 positive lymph nodes, more than 10 positive lymph nodes, whether they were in their childbearing years or postmenopausal, Dr. Bonadonna found they all benefited from the A → CMF therapy.

When the number of positive lymph nodes rises above 10 or other high-risk factors—such as large tumor size, hormone-receptor-negative, poor differentiation—are present, the regimens often intensify *beyond* A → CMF. These extended regimens, which add to the CMF base, really do start to sound like alphabet soup and become much more potent. A few examples, explained in the section "About the Drugs of Chemotherapy and Their Combinations," are: CMFVP; CMFVATN; CAFMV. Needless to say, the more powerful the cancer-killing combination, the more intense the side effects.

helpful treatment for women in this category now appears to be combined chemoendocrine therapy. Two large NSABP chemoendocrine trials (each with a different "chemo" component) involving over 1,300 women support this combined therapy for node-positive postmenopausal women, regardless of receptor status. After three years, in one study 84 percent of the women on chemoendocrine therapy were disease-free, compared with 67 percent of the tamoxifen-only group; the other study had almost identical results: 83 percent of the women were disease-free on chemoendocrine therapy compared with 66 percent of the tamoxifen-only group.

• *If you have a stage IV breast cancer from a recurrence or a metastasis of your disease*, a wider variety of approved chemotherapy regimens exists than for adjuvant treatment of breast cancers in stages I through III. Also, there are many clinical trials in progress evaluating new drug combinations, intensities, and scheduling of drug dosages, high-dose chemotherapy with bone marrow transplant (see the section "High-Dose Chemotherapy with Bone Marrow Transplant"), and immunostimulating agents.

For a recurrent cancer, the treatment regimen may also be influenced by the length of time that has passed between the adjuvant therapy given after surgery and this recurrence. If it has been a fairly short time, such as a year or two, it is a fair bet—in hindsight—that the drugs making up your adjuvant regimen were not the most effective in fighting your particular cancer. Obviously, your doctor will want to select other anticancer drugs that attack these cancer cells in a different way. If, on the other hand, at least five years have passed before your cancer recurred or metastasized, your past treatment worked well. In this case some doctors advise repeating an adjuvant regimen that was effective against a particular cancer the first time around, but others think that a second treatment with the same drugs might give rise to cancer cells that will become drug resistant and thus more difficult to control. Whatever treatment you begin in stage IV will be continued for as long as your cancer remains under control and you are not experiencing any debilitating symptoms. If your situation changes, your doctor will probably revise your regimen.

How Chemotherapy Is Scheduled

For standard chemotherapy, the treatment periods and the intervals between them depend on a woman's protocol. Drugs are normally prescribed for a specific number of cycles over a scheduled number of months (except in the case of metastatic breast cancer, when the spread of the disease is its own gauge for treatment). A cycle covers the time it takes to complete an oral and/or intravenous round of drugs. A typical cycle lasts one month, but different regimens have different schedules. Intravenous drugs are administered in a doctor's office or a hospital, either weekly or twice a week, during the drug-taking cycles. A two- to four-week interval is scheduled between drug-taking cycles to allow the bone marrow to recover and start producing an adequate number of white blood cells again. (Bone marrow suppression, which creates a temporary reduction of infection-fighting white blood cells, is the most worrisome and universal side effect of chemotherapy.)

In all, the typical adjuvant chemotherapy regimen lasts about six months, with some regimens only four months and others as little as two and a half months. Past trials have shown that continuing treatment beyond six

HOW PROVEN IS YOUR CHEMOTHERAPY REGIME?

A *standard* chemotherapy regimen is one that is FDA approved for a particular stage of breast cancer. Treatment regimens under study are considered *investigational*, and while some investigational therapies have progressed only to small preliminary studies, others have advanced to large-scale *clinical trials*. As explained in the "Clinical Trials" section of this chapter, many women are participating in the ongoing research. In general, the higher the risk associated with a woman's diagnosed breast cancer, the greater the number of investigational treatments are open to her. Depending on the clinical trial a woman enters, she can become involved in the testing of new sequences or combinations of familiar drugs, the pairing of new drugs with known regimens, or the value of drugs that showed promise in preliminary studies. Researchers are constantly trying to improve existing drugs by creating new versions that are more effective and less toxic, and at the same time they are searching for cancer-killing formulas for treatments that may bring us closer to a cure.

months has no added benefit, but an alternative view of chemotherapy in patients at very high risk, championed by Dr. Ezra Greenspan at the Mount Sinai Medical Center in New York, holds that therapy should be extended significantly. Dr. Greenspan also does not end treatment abruptly but continues for at least a full year (and sometimes two), gradually lengthening the between-cycle intervals from monthly, to 6 weeks, to 2 months, to 3 months, and maintaining or somewhat intensifying the dosage.

Oncologists aim to match the aggressiveness of their recommended treatment to the aggressiveness of a woman's cancer, no matter what its stage. Treatment can therefore be varied in any or all of the following ways: higher dosage, longer treatment period, adding stronger drugs.

WHAT TO EXPECT DURING A CHEMOTHERAPY SESSION

With standard chemotherapy the drug Cytoxan is taken orally, but other drugs are administered intravenously, either in a doctor's office or a hospital. A chemotherapy session that involves intravenous drugs lasts about two hours and includes a blood test for evaluating white blood cells. Each session typically begins with some type of antianxiety medication (often Ativan) and antinausea drugs. While the IV is not painful, the drugs can feel cold as they flow into the bloodstream. Certain drugs, such as vincristine, require very careful supervision during the session because any leakage can burn surrounding skin.

Occasionally, the demands of a particular regimen or problems with a woman's veins require a small under-the-skin device (called a Mediport or Broviac) to feed the drugs into a major artery. Some of the more aggressive chemotherapy regimens and high-dose chemotherapy may require a complex device called a *Hickman* to be implanted in the upper chest during an ambulatory surgery procedure. This permits internal administration of powerful drugs.

Every woman should ask her oncologist about the devices that may be needed to administer her particular protocol of drugs. She should not be faced with any surprises on the day of her first intravenous chemotherapy session.

Coping with the Aftereffects of Cancer-Killing Drugs

As discussed, the side effects of chemotherapy can be nothing at all or quite severe; they vary from drug to drug and woman to woman. Hormonal therapy is generally milder. With chemotherapy, the side effects intensify with increasingly higher levels of drug dosages and the number of drugs in the mix. Some side effects are temporary, like fatigue, nausea, and hair loss. Some are long term or permanent, like menopause and nerve damage. Nausea and hair loss are the well-known side effects, but others are more debilitating and less familiar: possible depression with tamoxifen; the chance of nerve damage with vincristine and its analogues and taxol; premature menopause from Cytoxan; or the as-yet-unexplained weight gain that many women experience during treatment.

Fatigue, hair loss, nausea disappear once treatment is stopped. In fact, dramatic strides in coping with nausea have been made in the last several years with remedies called *antiemetic medications* ("emesis" is the medical term for vomiting). Ondansetron (*Zofran*) and granisetron (*Kytril*) prevent nausea and vomiting signals from traveling to the brain. Along with steroids and antianxiety medications such as Ativan, they ease the discomfort of chemotherapy.

However, there are more serious and lasting effects, such as heart muscle damage from Adriamycin or permanent nerve damage from vincristine. These health problems linger for a lifetime and must be weighed along with the benefits of treatments. What doctors worry about most, though, is the temporary—but very serious—situation each time chemotherapy lowers the number of white blood cells that normally protect the body against microbes in the environment. This periodic vulnerability to infection causes great concern. The drop in white blood cells is a situation that arises in the bone marrow, and management of blood-marrow problems depends both on the problem and the regimen:

• For very low white blood cell counts, injections of a growth factor, granulocyte-colony stimulating factor (G-CSF) stimulates production of stem cells. When used regularly in women receiving high-dose chemotherapy (described later on) G-CSF can be prescribed during standard treatment to help a woman regain a healthy white blood cell count. Side effects, which may include fever and bone pain, are temporary.

• If blood platelets are low enough to risk the possibility of internal bleeding, a platelet transfusion is ordered.

• For anemia, which reflects too few red blood cells, the genetically engineered hormone erythropoietin (*Epogen*, or *"EPO" for short*) is preferable to transfusions. (Erythropoietin is also a naturally occurring hormone that stimulates red blood cell production when levels begin to fall.) A simple injection is given every several days, and a daily iron pill is taken after breakfast to provide an adequate supply of iron for all the new red cells that will suddenly form.

The most important thing to understand about chemotherapy side effects is that each woman responds differently, and there is no way to predict what your experience will be like. "I can treat 10 women with CMF," Dr. Theodoulou says, "and I'll have some who don't even know [in terms of side effects] that they're being treated." Women who are not vulnerable to a side effect such as nausea know from the start, but if a first session provokes a bad reaction, "a caring physician is going to work at improving it for you, at finding what will hopefully change it from night to day for you," Dr. Theodoulou counsels. Many women have found that joining a breast cancer support group is a terrific way to cope with side effects. In such a group you can get first-hand information about what to expect, practical advice about dealing with chemo- and hormonal therapy, and strong emotional support from women who have been there.

MENOPAUSE, A SIDE EFFECT THAT CAN TAKE WOMEN BY SURPRISE

After standard chemotherapy, many women—starting with a small number under 30 but growing to a majority of women over 40—will experience permanent menopause. Cytoxan, a component of most regimens, is one of the cancer-killing drugs that can stop the ovaries from functioning. As Dr. Elissa Gretz, gynecologist with the Breast/Gynecology Oncology Service at Memorial Sloan-Kettering Cancer Center in New York, explains, "It is thought that the effect is age-based for the same reason that menopause itself is age-based. Women are born with their lifetime supply of eggs. They start out with hundreds of thousands and lose eggs regularly throughout their lives. A woman goes through menopause when her eggs have almost run out—when only about 400 are left. Chemotherapy that kills cancer cells can also kill eggs but this is not the whole explanation. Other etiologies must play a role."

Enlightened oncologists make efforts to inform and prepare the women in their care, but I have heard a number of my patients say that they were taken by surprise. The understanding of a gynecologist is very important at this time. A woman needs his help along with advice from other women who have had to cope with this situation. A sudden onset of the debilitating effects of menopause, including hot flashes, painful intercourse, a loss of concentration exacerbated by sleep deprivation, headaches, and dizziness, may occur. I recommend contacting breast cancer advocacy groups and local breast cancer support groups (see the Resources section at the back of this book) for recommendations on how to cope. The ENCOREplus YWCA health care program (800-95-EPLUS) and Y-ME programs offer valuable services for managing menopause. (A woman who is considering HRT after breast cancer should consult Chapter 11.)

For the woman whose period hasn't returned within 4 to 6 months after chemotherapy is finished, Dr. Marjorie Luckey, endocrinologist and director of the osteoporosis program at Mount Sinai Medical Center in New York, recommends a bone density evaluation to see whether medication is needed to protect her skeleton. *For women remaining on tamoxifen* (see section that follows), *the antiosteoporosis, bone-maintaining help they receive depends on their pretreatment menopausal status.* She explains that for premenopausal women who have suddenly been thrown into menopause, tamoxifen's effects on bone will be far weaker, and have less impact than the high levels of bone-maintaining estrogen these women had been producing. Postmenopausal women have already gone through that rapid phase of estrogen-depletion bone loss, and tamoxifen actually adds some estrogen to help prevent ongoing bone loss. However, the effectiveness of tamoxifen in preventing osteoporosis and bone fractures cannot be predicted in individual women. For this reason, monitoring with serial bone density measurements is recommended.

To measure bone density, *dual x-ray absorptiometry* (DEXA) is currently the technique of choice. Another option is a special CAT scan, which can assess the spine (the area most vulnerable to menopausal bone loss), but not the hip bones. At the least, a local radiologist or rheumatologist can get a *central plane x-ray* kit for measuring density of the hand bones.

UNDERSTANDING HORMONAL THERAPY

The drugs of hormonal therapy can block the estrogen supply that many breast cancers need for growth. As mentioned earlier, a pathology report profiles a woman's breast cancer and lets her know its hormone receptor status—whether a cancer has positive or negative receptors for estrogen and/or progesterone.

If a breast cancer is estrogen and/or progesterone receptor–positive, tamoxifen (*Nolvadex*), the most commonly prescribed drug for hormonal treatment of breast cancer, will probably be recommended. For women with positive receptors who experience a recurrence or metastasis of breast cancer and who were not given tamoxifen during earlier adjuvant therapy, the drug will be recommended now. If tamoxifen was previously used, or if this advanced cancer begins to progress again while a woman is on tamoxifen, an oncologist will turn to other hormonal agents, such as Megace or one of the aromatase inhibitors. (Arimidex, a new aromatase inhibitor, is a favorite of many top oncologists.)

About Tamoxifen

Tamoxifen is an estrogen-like compound that locks onto breast tissue estrogen receptors more easily than estrogen does—thus making the receptors unavailable to the hormone and its cancer-promoting effects. Because this blockade has to be maintained on a daily basis, tamoxifen is taken twice a day in 10-milligram (mg) tablets. Recent findings in Israel also show that tamoxifen fights breast cancer by reducing the enlarged blood supply that tumors need. And the result of years of research has led to the knowledge that tamoxifen should be taken for five years to be effective.

• **Beneficial Effects.** Although tamoxifen binds with estrogen receptors wherever they exist, in some parts of the body it acts like estrogen, while in others it doesn't. Tamoxifen does not mimic estrogen in the *breast* (which is what makes it so useful in treating breast cancer), but elsewhere it has estrogen's ability to stimulate bone production and prevent fatty plaques from accumulating in the blood vessels. These benefits are important virtues, because they help combat bone-thinning osteoporosis and heart disease, two serious health problems faced by older women. Tamoxifen therefore can confer the protection that otherwise might come from hormone replacement therapy.

• **Side Effects.** In the uterus, however, tamoxifen has an estrogenic effect that is not a virtue. It stimulates the endometrial tissue lining in the uterus, increasing the risk of an overgrowth of tissue, called *endometrial hyperplasia*, that can become malignant. The NCI places the risk of uterine cancer from five years of tamoxifen use at about one-tenth of 1 percent. Dr. Marc Lippman, director of the Lombardi Cancer Center in Washington, DC, interprets the risk in this perspective: tamoxifen causes one life to be lost to endometrial cancer for every 250 lives that it saves from breast cancer. (Colorectal cancer was raised as a possible risk of tamoxifen in a Swedish study, but Dr. Theodoulou points out that the women in this study took twice the dose used in the United States, that a family history of this cancer is a critical factor, and that women with this history can easily be monitored with a periodic colonoscopy. She sees no present risk of colorectal cancer associated with tamoxifen.) Tamoxifen can also bring on permanent menopause in women near the age of natural menopause. Even if menopause does not become permanent, a woman taking the drug may feel hot flashes and other symptoms created by a temporary, chemically induced menopause. The effects of long-term tamoxifen use are currently being studied in a huge ongoing preventive trial with healthy women deemed at high risk for breast cancer. (The NCI/NSABP Breast Cancer Prevention Trial involves observation and analysis of 16,000 pre- and postmenopausal women on five years of either daily tamoxifen or a placebo, with 5 years of follow-up. Results are not expected until 2002 or 2003.)

• **Use of Tamoxifen Among Postmenopausal Women.** Women who have entered menopause—whether naturally or prematurely—still produce estrogen, although at a minimal level that no longer comes from the ovaries but from the body's conversion of a steroid produced by the adrenal glands. But because this estrogen alone is enough to stimulate estrogen-responsive breast cancer, tamoxifen is especially helpful. Like a key in a lock, tamoxifen is able to fit into an estrogen receptor in the breast and prevent the real estrogen from taking hold and stimulating cancer cells.

• **Use of Tamoxifen Among Women in Their Childbearing Years: An Area of Controversy.** Women who have been diagnosed with breast cancer but have not reached menopause are normally treated with chemotherapy as adjuvant therapy after surgery. If a tumor is positive for estrogen receptors and a sustained interference with estrogen's influence is considered to be important as well, more and more often tamoxifen is prescribed once the chemotherapy is finished. (Experimental hormonal alternatives for women whose menstrual periods resume after chemotherapy are removal of the ovaries or use of a drug that temporarily shuts the ovaries down.) The near future may well see a much greater use of hormonal therapy among younger women, because recent research has found that premenopausal women who underwent *ovarian ablation*—destruction of the ovaries with a laser or by electrocauterization or complete removal of the ovaries—had a lowered risk of breast cancer recurrence and death, compared with that of women who had undergone chemotherapy. Hormonal therapy works like ovarian ablation.

Traditionally it was thought that tamoxifen had no effect on premenopausal women with estrogen-sensitive tumors, but more recent research raises the possibility that it may be very helpful for younger women *if* it is begun when chemotherapy is *over*, and *if* it is taken for a long enough period. Some of the earlier chemoendocrine studies simply combined tamoxifen with the chemotherapy regimen, ending both at the same time, but laboratory studies now show that tamoxifen and certain chemotherapy drugs actually work against each other in the test tube. Several human studies suggest this may also happen in people. In addition, tamoxifen treatment in many earlier chemoendocrine trials in younger women lasted for only one or two years, which is now seen as too short a time to make a difference. Current chemoendocrine trials are set up with six months or less for chemoendocrine therapy, followed by an extended period—typically five years, the recent limit set for benefit and safety—on tamoxifen.

Some specialists, though, are extremely cautious about using tamoxifen in women who are still menstruating until more is known about its effects in this group. There is a concern about creating *estrogen surges*. Theoretically, the ovaries could go into high-gear estrogen production in response to the body's estrogen receptors not being occupied with real estrogen. The pituitary-produced messenger hormones *luteinizing hormone-releasing hormone (LHRH)*, *luteinizing hormone (LH)*, and *follicle-stimulating hormone (FSH)*, which regulate the ovaries' estrogen production, respond to the absence of activity in normally estrogen-responsive breast tissue, so they signal the ovaries to churn out substantially more estrogen. The resulting estrogen surge makes many oncologists wary of giving tamoxifen to women whose ovaries are still functioning, because they believe there is not enough research available to know how the uterine lining will respond when a woman on tamoxifen is also in active estrogen production. (Note: After menopause, estrogen surges from the ovaries do not occur.) Again, doctors are awaiting the results of the Breast Cancer Prevention Trial described earlier.

• **Trying to Solve Problems of Tamoxifen.** Scientists are going in two different directions to overcome the disadvantages of tamoxifen:

1. One approach has been to tinker with the chemical structure of the drug, which has resulted in the creation of a compound called **tamoxifen methiodide**. This new compound has had highly encouraging results in mice, causing cancerous tumors to shrink substantially or go into remission. The drug has not yet been tested in humans.

2. The other approach has been to develop a compound that shuts off the effects of estrogen everywhere, a pure antiestrogen. **ICI 182,780** has been very successful in tamoxifen-resistant mice.

Other Drugs of Hormonal Therapy

Progestins such as *Provera* and *Megace* are alternative drugs for preventing the hormonal stimulation, or feeding, of breast tissue that could become cancerous; however, their common side effects include increased appetite, weight gain, and fluid retention.

Other drugs of hormonal therapy are used in *advanced* breast cancer—either when tamoxifen was already used in adjuvant therapy or once the disease has begun to progress despite tamoxifen. Some of these drugs—aromatase inhibitors, such as aminoglutethimide, and LHRH-inhibiting compounds—temporarily stop estrogen production by turning off the ovaries, in premenopausal women. In postmenopausal women, aromtase inhibitors block the normal hormonal conversion in the adrenal glands.

Aromatase inhibitors block the estrogen-producing enzyme aromatase; these drugs have shown promising results for lengthening survival. But because they disrupt all estrogen production (not just in the breast area), they remove estrogen's beneficial effects on bone strength and cardiovascular health. Also, in premenopausal women the disruption of estrogen production causes the ovaries to hyperactivate in their attempt to compensate. Dr. Paul E. Goss, director of both the Breast Group at the Toronto Hospital and the Medical Breast Group at Princess Margaret Hospital in Toronto, is planning a trial that will combine an aromatase inhibitor with an agent to suppress LH and FSH as well, thereby blocking ovarian stimulation. Aminoglutethimide (*Cytadren*), originally used to treat epilepsy, shuts down the activity of the adrenal cortex, which produces the sex hormones estrogen and testosterone. Cytadren stops postmenopausal estrogen production. A 1992 study found half the standard dose to be significantly helpful in treating metastatic disease. A 1994 study comparing it with tamoxifen found them equally effective, as well as a good sequential combination (switching from one to the other when the cancer began to progress). Among its side effects, however, are nausea, and it may require the use of thyroid medication.

The LHRH-inhibiting compounds, such as goserelin (*Zoladex*) and leuprolide (*Lupron*), suppress the production of certain pituitary hormones that stimulate the ovaries to produce estrogen. These drugs can cause hot flashes and nausea, however.

The male hormone testosterone (*Halotestin*), while suppressing the estrogen supplied to the breasts, can also cause masculinization, nausea, fluid retention and weight gain.

A SPECIAL LOOK AT THE APPROACHES TO TREATING METASTATIC BREAST CANCER

• *The most recent major addition to the arsenal of drugs for fighting breast cancer is Taxol,* derived from the bark of the yew tree. A variety of clinical trials are either combining taxol with other drugs for treating advanced breast cancer or using it alone in high-risk patients as adjuvant therapy. Taxol is as potent as Adriamycin but works very differently and has a different set of side effects (see page 311).

• *For metastases that do not involve a woman's vital organs and show a positive hormone receptor level*—indicating a less aggressive cancer—the NCI recommends a hormonal approach to disrupt the cancer's progress;

Tamoxifen or *oophorectomy* (surgical removal of the ovaries) is advised for women in their menstruating years;

Tamoxifen or perhaps *progestins*, hormonal drugs that work much like tamoxifen and are used if tamoxifen is no longer effective, for postmenopausal women.

Metastatic cancers in menopausal women, especially if they are over 65, are more often the kind that respond to hormonal therapy. If a breast cancer recurs while a woman is on adjuvant tamoxifen, the cancer has become resistant to the drug, and a doctor will recommend a different hormonal or chemotherapy option.

• *For metastatic tumors that involve the vital organs or are hormone receptor-negative*, the following chemotherapy combinations may be suggested:

CMF, CAF, CMFP, CMFVP, or possibly CA

A woman's doctor may want to place her on long-term chemotherapy or may think that hormonal therapy should be considered after a finite course of chemotherapy.

Dr. Hyman Muss, associate director for clinical research at Wake Forest University's Comprehensive Cancer Center in Winston-Salem, North Carolina, recommends that *all* postmenopausal women—regardless of the original tumor's receptor status—start treatment with hormone therapy *unless* their metastases are life-threatening. Two studies in older women have shown that starting with hormonal therapy does not diminish overall survival time, and compared with chemotherapy, the modest toxicity of hormonal therapy is highly desirable. Hormonal therapy has been beneficial in controlling cancer in all metastatic sites, including the brain—although women who have soft tissue or bone metastases are the ones most likely to respond.

For metastases that are already progressing rapidly or are life-threatening, there is no time to try hormonal therapy first. Dr. Muss considers combining hormonal therapy with chemotherapy from the outset or switching to it when chemotherapy ends. Women whose cancers respond to the chemotherapy regimen can go on a maintenance program of hormonal therapy alone after four to six cycles.

• *When metastatic breast cancer occurs in older women, coexisting health problems*—which have become common—may play an important role in treatment decisions and also influence a woman's ability to tolerate treatment and fight her cancer. When recommending a chemotherapy protocol, an oncologist carefully considers the existence and degree of other health problems.

It is particularly important to evaluate *kidney function* (creatinine clearance is the most common test), because three of the anticancer drugs that can be used against metastases—commonly methotrexate, and less commonly carboplatin and cisplatin—are excreted by the kidneys. A gradual decline of kidney function is a normal part of aging, so it takes very little additional loss in kidney function to impair this ability. If kidney function warrants it, the drug dose is lowered to accomplish two things: maintain a safe drug level in a woman's body and avoid stressing the kidneys.

Because drugs that can affect *the heart*—such as Adriamycin—do so more readily in older people, doses are often lowered and special attention is also given to other ways of reducing this effect. A technique called *infusion therapy* (very slow, prolonged IV delivery) lessens this potential. And an experimental agent—called **ICRF-187**—has shown exciting promise in protecting the heart from Adriamycin's impact.

There is also a brighter side to chemotherapy for a senior citizen. Fewer older women experience nausea and vomiting from it, and they seem psychologically more resilient in adapting to the impact that treatment makes on their lives.

Metastasis to the Bone

Breast cancer that metastasizes to the bone carries with it a unique set of serious problems because it alters the bones in two fundamental ways: (1) it impairs the marrow's ability to produce new blood cells, and (2) it causes certain bone cells to eat away critical amounts of bone.

In relation to bone marrow: If chemotherapy—which suppresses bone marrow function temporarily—is used, G-CSF (see pages 318–319) will be added to prevent white-cell production from dropping too severely. If this drug does not work, chemotherapy doses must be lowered. However, if consistent aggressive treatments continue, and a woman moves into the realm of high-dose chemotherapy, then her bone marrow or stem cells will have to be extracted to regenerate healthy bone marrow later on. (See "High-Dose Chemotherapy with Bone Marrow Transplant", page 327).

In relation to the bones themselves: Bone metastases also seriously weaken the skeleton—in some cases, catastrophically—and if widespread, flood the patient's system with what can be a life-threatening amount of calcium freed from the dissolving bones. Severe bone loss also causes pain. Bones normally maintain a healthy balance between two competing cell types that reside in the surface layer: *osteoblasts* make new bone at the same rate that *osteoclasts* destroy it. But breast cancer cells that travel to the bones secrete a chemical messenger that powerfully stimulates the osteoclasts, so bone is destroyed too fast for the osteoblasts to replace it. As cancer works on the bone, released calcium floods the system and causes *hypercalcemia of malignancy.* An increasingly fragile skeleton places some patients at risk for spinal fractures simply from normal walking.

Fortunately, a new group of drugs—the *bisphosphonates*—inhibits these osteoclasts and help treat bone loss, hypercalcemia, and pain. The few side effects are minimal and usually temporary, because these drugs home in exclusively on osteoclasts in bone surfaces. Whatever is not used is eliminated. *Aridia,* a bisphosphonate given by intravenous infusion, has been approved specifically for the hypercalcemia of malignancy. *Didronel* (etidronate), an oral bisphosphonate, has also been used against severe bone loss. *Fosamax* (alendronate), taken orally, was FDA approved in 1995 for treating osteoporosis. Endocrinologist Dr. Marjorie Luckey notes that Fosamax appears to be more potent than Didronel at muzzling the osteoclasts, thus allowing new bone to be laid down (and preliminary trials suggest it may be effective in treating hypercalcemia of malignancy). She recommends either Aridia or Fosamax for treating severe bone fragility.

CONTROLLING BONE PAIN

Bone pain is controlled in different ways at different stages. When metastases to the bone first develop, the initial focus is on stopping and reversing bone destruction, shrinking or eliminating the metastases with treatment, and using a bisphosphonate to stop further loss and rebuild bone. This diminishes or does away with the pain. Later, when neither chemotherapy nor hormonal therapy are working any longer, radiation therapy is very effective for relieving pain from metastases confined to a local area. You may have heard about the use of strontium to relieve bone pain, but this drug has not been shown to be very effective in relation to bone metastases of breast cancer.

For the woman who has diffuse pain in many places, several other possibilities—in addition to narcotic-like drugs—exist. Some patients are helped a great deal by a neurosurgical procedure called a *nerve block*, in which an injected agent temporarily deadens the nerve(s) carrying pain sensations. Also, the spinal cord itself can be treated to destroy those nerves permanently. The newest technique involves implanting a small catheter in the tiny space alongside the spinal cord, then infusing a local anesthetic to numb the nerves just in that area. Because this technique does not affect the brain in a noticeable way, it avoids all the unpleasant effects of systemic painkilling drugs.

Looking toward the future, research in animals has found that early use of these drugs actually prevents the progression of breast cancer metastasis to the bone. In studies now in progress outside the United States, these drugs are being provided to women after surgery to see if they effectively prevent bone metastasis.

HIGH-DOSE CHEMOTHERAPY WITH BONE MARROW TRANSPLANT

The effectiveness of adjuvant chemotherapy for breast cancer tends to improve as doses increase. This realization has led to the highly controversial practice of *high-dose chemotherapy*, most often a single brief cycle that involves dramatically increased dose levels and incorporates special techniques for coping with a variety of extremely toxic side effects, the most acute being the destruction of bone marrow. The need for renewing the bone marrow's life-sustaining ability to produce the blood cells that mature into infection-fighting white cells, oxygen-carrying red cells, and clot-making platelets gave birth to the *bone marrow transplant* (*BMT*).

Although high-dose chemotherapy no longer routinely involves a BMT, it still typically goes by this name. Today high-dose chemotherapy is increasingly paired with *peripheral blood stem cell transplant* (*PBSCT*), which does not require the surgery of BMT. But when high-dose chemotherapy does involve a bone marrow transplant, a woman's bone marrow is extracted *before* she receives the drugs and *after* her treatment is completed. This is the way the two-part bone marrow transplant procedure works: first, there is a "harvest," a 90-minute procedure requiring general anesthesia for the needle extraction of bone marrow from a woman's hip bones; second, there is the post–high-dose chemotherapy "transplant," when the extracted marrow, which was stored and treated, is intravenously returned. PBSCT, the new, nonsurgical advance in the BMT, is currently used with increasing frequency. Sometimes the two techniques are used together. It is important to remember that the high-dose chemotherapy regimens that these procedures support are still considered *experimental* when it comes to treating breast cancer.

The FDA has not yet approved high-dose chemotherapy with BMT because clinical studies proving its effectiveness have not been completed, and in fact, are progressing very slowly. Researchers are having a hard time enrolling patients for these trials, because most women who need high-dose chemotherapy are fighting for their survival and believe this procedure is their only hope. They will not enter a trial and risk being in a group that does not receive the high-dose treatment, and many oncologists are willing to provide the treatment outside clinical trials, especially for women with metastasized breast cancer.

Whatever high-dose combination of drugs is given, there are risks of permanent side effects, such as nerve damage, to weigh. According to Dr. George Raptis, director of the High-Dose Chemotherapy/Bone Marrow Transplant program at Memorial Sloan-Kettering Cancer Center in New York, although high-dose chemotherapy is safer than it was even five years ago (when up to 20 *percent* of the women who underwent this treatment died), the *risk of death* from severe treatment-related toxicities that defy treatment efforts is still very real. About 6 percent of women who undergo high-dose chemotherapy continue to die, but the mortality rate is usually lower at reputable teaching hospitals where the staffs are highly experienced. Controversy rages over whether the treatment—which may increase five-year survival from 18 to 25 percent—is worth the significant toxicities. Still, there remains a great demand for this procedure.

Oncologists' attitudes toward high-dose chemotherapy vary enormously. On one end of the spectrum are doctors who prefer to wait for the results of the BMT trials for high-risk primary breast cancer, sponsored by regional cancer research groups throughout North America and due by the year 2000. Meanwhile, many women not involved in any trials, women with metastatic or recurrent cancer, or women diagnosed with at least 10 positive lymph nodes, are being treated by willing oncologists.

As part of an early study, researchers at the Bone Marrow Transplant Program at the Duke Comprehensive Cancer Center at Duke University Medical Center in North Carolina, began offering adjuvant high-dose chemotherapy for high-risk breast cancer patients in 1987. An analysis of 85 women in the Duke program was published in 1993. With a four-cycle course of standard CAF chemotherapy followed by a high-dose program of Cytoxan+cisplatin+BCNU (also called *carmustine*), "we've been able to more than double the number of long-term disease-free survivors," says Dr. James Vredenburgh, director of Duke's Bone Marrow Transplant Program, with *long-term* meaning five years. However, Dr. Raptis cautions that the absence of a matched-comparison patient group (women judged equally likely to benefit from high-dose treatment but who received only the standard CAF therapy) makes it impossible to know whether these encouraging results are due to the high-dose treatment itself or simply that many of these carefully selected patients would be survivors no matter which treatment they received. The Duke group was compared with a broad collection of high-risk patients on standard treatment rather than a matching group. Although many other BMT centers have done similar small pilot studies with high-dose chemotherapy (mostly for women with 10 or more positive lymph nodes and some with less advanced disease) that "also shows a very good outcome for the most part," Dr. Raptis points out that "they also lack appropriate comparison groups, and their follow-up often hasn't been long enough." Follow-up should extend through the first five posttreatment years, the period in which a relapse in these high-risk women is most likely.

In the meantime, each woman considering high-dose chemotherapy must make her decision without conclusive proof. Every woman with advanced disease should discuss high-dose chemotherapy thoroughly with her oncologist and talk to other women who have undergone the treatment themselves. (See the Resources section for information about how to contact a local support group where you can meet women who have survived high-dose chemotherapy.) A woman must ask herself:

• Do my doctor and I believe that high-dose chemotherapy would be right for me?
• Am I willing to enroll in a randomized trial and risk being in the group that does not receive the treatment?

Because there are no proven cures for metastatic disease in actual practice, many women and their doctors feel justified in implementing this type of therapy, even if it is experimental.

Until the data are in, some larger BMT centers are analyzing their patient records in an effort to identify patient characteristics most often associated with successful treatment. Dr. Raptis emphasizes that the primary factor most often associated with success is having already achieved complete clinical remission with standard chemotherapy. Another frequent link to success is the lack of substantial metastasis to a vital organ and evidence of a good response to conventional chemotherapy.

Before High-Dose Chemotherapy: Harvesting the Bone Marrow and Peripheral Stem Cells

Bone marrow is harvested under general anesthesia. A hollow needle is repeatedly inserted into a woman's rear hip bones, which are rich marrow sources; each time it withdraws some marrow into a syringe. The marrow is frozen until it is needed for replacement, after a woman has received high-dose chemotherapy.

Peripheral stem cells—found mainly in the bone marrow, with a much smaller number circulating in the blood—are the primitive cells from which all healthy blood cells evolve. Stem cells are extracted from the circulating or *peripheral* blood through a process called *leukapheresis*, more commonly shortened to *pheresis*. First a woman receives several daily injections of a growth factor such as *granulocyte-colony stimulating factor (G-CSF)* to increase the number of stem cells in her circulating blood. Then she is connected to a leukapheresis machine by a slender tube temporarily inserted into a vein in her neck or chest wall. The machine continuously extracts stem cells from her blood as it repeatedly circulates through and returns to her body. The extraction process itself requires about two daily sessions (each one about four to five hours) to collect enough stem cells for one replacement.

In a new approach, moderately high-dose chemotherapy drugs, such as Cytoxan and taxol, are given to "mobilize" stem cells before G-CSF injections, as well as to begin treating the cancer. While G-CSF stimulates the marrow to produce more stem cells, the shot of chemo causes stem cells to flood out of the bone marrow and into the circulating blood. The combined drugs halve the number of pheresis sessions (only two or three days) and more than double the quantity of stem cells collected (enough for two transplant cycles with backup).

Leukapheresis involves withdrawal of the stem cells with the aid of a high-pressure machine, so the catheter used in the process must be able to withstand the pressure. After a woman has been given a local anesthetic, a doctor inserts a special, thick catheter in a large vein in her neck or chest wall. Leukapheresis itself begins 10 days after the chemo mobilization and ends in two or three days. Each day's session on the machine lasts two to four hours. Enough stem cells are collected and frozen to supply a woman with two transplants after high-dose chemotherapy.

Following chemotherapy, both bone marrow cells and / or peripheral stem cells can be injected back into a woman's bloodstream for travel to the spaces containing bone marrow.

The High-Dose Chemotherapy Experience

A high-dose chemotherapy treatment is a very intense session of approximately four days of intravenous infusions. The complete high-dose chemotherapy with bone marrow transplant and/or PBSCT procedure can take four to six weeks. Traditionally, this was all done in the hospital, but recently institutions are making outpatient facilities available. At Duke, for example, the once-typical 28-day hospital stay is now five or six days, after which a woman lives in a neighboring hotel and visits the outpatient clinic daily for careful monitoring and preventive medication. Of course the amount of time a woman spends in the hospital is dictated by the drugs in her protocol. Cytoxan, for example, requires an around-the-clock intravenous hydration and safety monitoring in the hospital.

Dr. James Vredenburgh, director of the Bone Marrow Transplant Program at the Duke Comprehensive Cancer Center at Duke University Medical Center in North Carolina, explains the high-dose chemotherapy experience there:

> All women get some initial chemotherapy to decrease the breast cancer cells, and in the past this was followed by a bone marrow harvest. Then five daily injections of G-CSF prepare them for leukapheresis, which is the only procedure we are doing today. Four days after leukapheresis, they enter the hospital for four days of high-dose chemotherapy. That night they get hydration and frequently a blood transfusion. A three-tube Hickman catheter has already been inserted in the upper chest area for giving the drugs and taking blood (to be removed when the patient's blood counts have returned to normal). Patients are heavily sedated throughout the drug-infusion period. They get continuous bladder irrigation and very aggressive hydration to limit adverse effects of the chemo, and the new antinausea drugs usually limit vomiting to an average of just once a day. As the chemotherapy ends, we stop the sedatives. The woman wakes up, and we make sure she is stabilized, and then we discharge her to a local hotel. She stays there for two to three weeks of daily clinic visits for monitoring and oral medication. She receives antibiotics to prevent infection, potassium and magnesium to stabilize her metabolic system, and antinausea medication. After the first couple of days out of the hospital, we inject her with her own marrow or stem cells. By the eighth day after chemotherapy, the number of infection-fighting white blood cells has generally

increased substantially, and by day 12 most women have reached an adequate platelet count.

Physicians were initially concerned about taking women out of a hospital's relatively germ-free environment, for fear problems with infection would arise. Ironically, the opposite has occurred. Not only are infections much less frequent, but women in this more comfortable environment experience significantly less physical toxicity and emotional stress. As Dr. Vredenburgh explains, "If you can maintain the psyche somewhat, then physically the patient does *a lot* better."

Post–Bone Marrow or –Peripheral Stem Cell Transplants

Many women who complete high-dose chemotherapy go into complete remission (with no evidence of metastatic disease on scans), but more commonly, women show a tiny little something—"ditsels," as Dr. Raptis calls them—that are impossible to identify as residual disease or scar tissue. The women then are monitored with full-body scans at intervals dictated by the programs they are in to check for possible progression. If these ditsels are scar tissue, they may take years to be reabsorbed, or they may be a permanent fixture. Cancer remnants may simply reflect fatally damaged cells that have not yet died.

Dr. Raptis feels that no stone should be left unturned to increase a woman's chances of remaining disease free. Women in both groups with a hormone-receptor–positive cancer should be placed on hormone therapy: tamoxifen for women who have not previously been treated with hormones, and Megace or Armidex for those who *have*.

Women who have any residual disease that can be surgically removed or irradiated also should have this done.

Checkups are most frequent during the first 18 months after high-dose chemotherapy with bone marrow support, as this is the period when progression is most likely to occur. Sometimes during these months women can become psychologically stronger by talking with other women who have been through high-dose chemo. Organizations offering information about high-dose chemotherapy and ways of finding support from other women are listed in the Resources section at the back of this book.

New Approaches: Tandem Transplants and Sequential High-Dose Chemotherapy

A single high-dose chemotherapy cycle puts a lot of women into remission, but the fact that metastases of the cancer can appear later has led to the testing of multicycles of high-dose chemotherapy. Two approaches under investigation are:

• **Tandem transplants,** which involve two cycles of high-dose chemotherapy and peripheral stem cell infusions, one after the other, with the same or different drug combination, leaving time in between for the blood cell count to recover. This tandem approach uses a drug combination, but each drug must be given at less than its maximum dosage, due to concerns about toxicity.

• **Sequential high-dose chemotherapy,** which is being developed at Memorial Sloan-Kettering Cancer Center in New York. It attempts to minimize dosage limitation. Since side effects are usually diminished when each drug is given alone but still at the maximally tolerated dosage, the experimental sequential program delivers two to three single-drug, high-dose cycles, each using a different individual drug at maximal dose. A peripheral stem cell infusion is included in each cycle.

WHAT HAPPENS AFTER SUCCESSFUL CHEMOTHERAPY AND/OR HORMONAL THERAPY?

When an anticancer drug treatment has achieved remission of disease, a woman continues to have follow-up visits with her oncologist to monitor her condition. The initial schedule of visits varies from doctor to doctor and depends on the diagnosed stage or aggressiveness of her breast cancer. Many women visit their doctor every three months for the first two years; every four months for the third year, every six months for the fourth year, and then annually starting at five years. Each visit involves a physical examination and blood tests to evaluate blood, liver, and bone function and biochemical markers that can indicate the presence of cancer. Any test showing a higher than normal value should be double-checked in four weeks. If the results of a repeated test continue to be abnormal, a scan for cancer in other organs is indicated. A woman should report any suspicious symptoms, no matter how minor they may seem, to her oncologist.

If a cancer recurs, your oncologist will discuss treatment options. If it has been five years since your last treatment, it is reasonable to use the same drugs again because they controlled your cancer effectively for that length of time. (Adriamycin is the exception, however, due to possible heart damage after a certain cumulative dose.) If the posttreatment interval has been shorter, your doctor will want to use different drugs, in the hope that they will be more lethal to your cancer.

PROMISING NEW TREATMENTS

Scientists are working on many aspects of cancer growth in their attempts to find more successful breast cancer-killing treatments. Today, advances are being made in the exploration and development of:

• better-targeted and more effective cytotoxic drugs to kill cancer cells outright,

- drugs to prevent or destroy the rich supply of blood vessels that support rapid growth and metastasis,
  - drugs to neutralize the growth factors that stimulate breast tissue,
  - techniques to stimulate and arm the immune system to destroy cancer cells.

The hope is that new, effective breast cancer treatments will be able to combine all of the above. Researchers are also looking into new ways to predict who will or will not benefit from adjuvant therapy and to give oncologists the ability to determine what drugs will be effective or ineffective before a woman begins treatment.

The following highlights some promising discoveries in research labs and clinics around the world.

Understanding pS2

Estrogen stimulates the production of a newly identified protein—called pS2—in breast cancer cells. This protein may be the key to distinguishing between which estrogen receptor–positive women will or will not respond to hormonal therapy. The presence of pS2 indicates a well-functioning estrogen pathway and a slower-growing cancer. In preliminary studies, women whose tumors produced little pS2 showed early recurrence and poor survival.

Urokinase Plasminogen Activator (uPA)

This enzyme, produced by all types of migrating cells, basically clears a path along which they can travel. Early research has found that aggressive cancers produce high levels of uPA, making this enzyme especially useful as a predictor of early relapse.

CDC25B

A member of a family of enzymes that supports cell division, CDC25B, when found in abnormal amounts, has been discovered in one-third of human breast cancers tested. When comparing women with high versus low/no CDC25B, researchers found that many more women in the high-level group experienced metastasis (42 percent versus 29 percent) and death by 10 years (37 percent versus 19 percent).

Gene Therapy: nm23 and MDR-1

Gene therapy for breast cancer is currently in development. Researchers hope to find ways to cure breast cancer by locating missing or defective genes that contribute to the disease and replacing them with copies of healthy genes; this is the essence of gene therapy. For example, the healthy **nm23** gene appears to suppress metastasis of breast cancer. When a cancer does not have the gene, the disease spreads more aggressively. Tumors with a defective nm23, one that produces just a small amount of the gene's protein, are associated with lymph node involvement, few estrogen receptors, poor histologic grade, increased recurrence rate, and reduced survival rate. Tumors with higher nm23 protein levels are well-differentiated, and women experience a longer disease-free period. On the one hand, nm23 is a predictive factor, but on the other it offers possibilities for gene therapy.

A variation on the gene therapy approach is the attempt to create bone marrow that is invulnerable to suppressive chemotherapy by infusing it with **MDR-1**, a gene that surfaces in tumor cells that have become resistant to certain drugs. Researchers who have isolated and cloned MDR-1 are attempting to place it in bone marrow. If they are successful, they might be able to prevent chemotherapy drugs from affecting bone marrow and suppressing production of blood cells.

Immune System Stimulants

Researchers fighting breast cancer through immune system stimulation are taking two approaches: (1) increasing the strength of the immune system by giving a woman one of the natural immune cell-stimulating compounds such as interferon, or one of the interleukins that the body produces when threatened by invading cells, or (2) altering some of a woman's existing immune cells in ways that will make them highly responsive to her breast cancer. A breast cancer vaccine (as described in the following section) is an example of this second approach.

Dr. H. Kim Lyerly, clinical director of the molecular therapeutic program at Duke University Medical Center, thinks that techniques that bring the immune system into play will prevent tumors from progressing rather than eradicate them. He sees their usefulness in breast cancers with a high risk of recurrence. Currently he is trying to harness the power of **IL-2 (interleukin 2)**, which triggers the body's immune system responses, particularly the production of T cells. Because injecting high amounts of IL-2 directly into the body is toxic, Dr. Lyerly has developed a technique for targeting added IL-2 specifically to the breast tissue surrounding the tumor. He extracts tumor cells, endows them with the gene for producing substantial amounts of IL-2, then re-injects them. The IL-2–stimulated cells then migrate to the breast. A phase I clinical trial is now in progress.

Cancer Vaccines

The concept of a vaccine's usefulness has begun expanding to include treatment as well as prevention and is being applied to a variety of cancers as well as other diseases. Research involving cancer vaccines is aimed at helping the immune system identify cancer cells. Scientists at Brigham and Women's Hospital in Boston—one of several groups of researchers working on breast cancer vaccines—have learned that a protein called **GP2**, which is involved in rapid cell division in the developing fetus but is normally fairly inactive in adults, appears to be active in breast and ovarian tumors. After encouraging results during test tube research, doctors are working on a vaccine for treating these cancers. Treatment begins with removing some of a woman's cytotoxic T cells (certain cell-killing white blood cells) from a sample of extracted blood, pairing these T cells with the GP2 protein in a test tube to stimulate their ability to recognize it, then injecting what have become "educated" T cells back into a woman's body. Once returned to a woman's bloodstream, large populations of educated T cells reproduce and stand ready to destroy anything that sports the GP2 protein.

New Drugs

Dr. Paul Goss, chief of both the Breast Group at the Toronto Hospital and the Medical Breast Group at Princess Margaret Hospital in Toronto, has identified a new aromatase inhibitor, a compound that blocks the estrogen-converting power of the enzyme aromatase. The new aromatase inhibitor, **liarozole**, disrupts estrogen production, and in hormonally fed cancer cells increases the cell differentiation that slows cancer growth. The therapeutic effect of liarozole in animals was profound, and Dr. Goss has just presented preliminary results of his first worldwide clinical trial.

Dr. Goss is also starting clinical trials with **flaxseed**, which contains both an aromatase-inhibiting substance and a compound that binds to estrogen receptors, just as tamoxifen does. Flaxseed prevents breast cancer in laboratory animals, and survey data suggest that it may be effective in humans.

A completely different type of drug being fashioned in the molecular biology laboratory is an **altered diphtheria virus toxin** that will destroy only those cells in breast tissue with a particular growth factor receptor (the EGFr) involved in aggressive cancers.

Angiogenesis Inhibitors

Angiogenesis describes the usually controlled growth of blood vessels needed for the maintenance of many normal body functions, like growth of the uterine lining, wound repair, muscle development, and the maturing of a fetus. Cancers stimulate an unchecked angiogenesis, or the growth of tumor-supporting blood vessels from the tissue surrounding a tumor. This over-grown network of blood vessels allows the tumor to progress beyond a microscopic size and eventually to metastasize.

Dr. Judah Folkman, director of the research laboratory at the Children's

Hospital in Boston and professor of surgery and cell biology at Harvard Medical School, is the dean of anti-angiogenesis research. Dr. Folkman and others have isolated various substances the body uses to control the formation of new blood vessels—working first in animals, then in people—to explore their ability to keep tumors from growing. Dr. Folkman is convinced that women whose breast cancers remain dormant for many years naturally produce an effective antiangiogenic substance during that time. In his research he attempts to block angiogenesis with **angiostatin**, a compound normally produced by the body, and **fumagillin**, an antibiotic secreted by an *Aspergillus* mold (and its synthetic analogues).

Dr. Folkman sees two types of advantages to antiangiogenic therapy, which other research supports. First, angiogenesis inhibitors greatly increase the effectiveness of chemotherapy drugs and radiation, so doses and toxicity can be lowered significantly while tumors are still effectively attacked. Second, once chemotherapy ends, continuing the angiogenesis inhibitor prevents growth and metastasis—without toxicity—indefinitely. Dr. Folkman calls this second effect "dormancy therapy" and equates it with the long-term treatment of diabetes and high blood pressure.

In fighting breast cancer, angiogenesis inhibitors may also make immune system therapies more effective.

Monoclonal Antibodies

A monoclonal antibody is like a nonworking key—painstakingly created in a molecular biology laboratory—made to fit a specific lock. By keeping the real key out, it makes sure that the door can't be opened. Creating a monoclonal antibody that latches onto a specific receptor or enzyme or protein, for example, neutralizes it, pulling it out of the system. For example, researchers are working with monoclonal antibodies to two different growth factor receptors—**EGFr** and **HER 2/neu**—found in high numbers in many tumors with poor prognosis. Some highly respected breast cancer researchers feel that monoclonal antibodies are extremely important in fighting the disease. At Memorial Sloan-Kettering Cancer Center in New York, research using a monoclonal antibody to the protein produced by the **HER 2/neu oncogene** is under way with women who have advanced-stage breast cancer resistant to chemotherapy. The monoclonal antibody for HER 2/neu deactivates the growth factor, and in doing so, it is hoped that it will halt the cancer's progress.

CLINICAL TRIALS: ONE MAY BE RIGHT FOR YOU

A clinical trial is a study that compares two different treatments by enrolling a large number of similar participants and randomly dividing them into treatment groups. One of the treatments in a clinical trial for breast cancer is always the best standard treatment available; the other is a newer treatment that has already shown itself to be at least as helpful. The trial is designed to answer the question: is the newer treatment equal or better? Women who participate in a clinical trial are carefully selected for very similar factors that could affect their cancer; this selection process helps researchers link recurrence and survival differences more directly to treatment. A large number of women are enrolled in these trials so that the final results can be applied to the population. The NCI is helping more and more community hospitals and doctors to become involved in this research; thus, a woman may be able to locate a clinical trial at an outreach center close to home.

Women who participate in randomized clinical trials receive the best available treatment now and help contribute to even better care for women who are diagnosed with breast cancer in the future. *The only progress in fighting this disease in the past 30 years has come through clinical trials, and further progress cannot materialize without them. Yet less than 5 percent of women with breast cancer enroll in clinical trials.* A scary misconception is that entering a clinical trial means that you are running the risk of getting ineffective treatment. This is *not* true. By the time a treatment reaches the stage of a randomized clinical trial, a great deal of research has already been done with animals, then with severely ill patients who thought they had nothing to lose by trying something new. *Being in a randomized clinical trial means that you will have excellent care in whichever group you are assigned to, whether it's the best current treatment for your particular cancer or an alternative treatment that is as good—and may be significantly better. Your care will be monitored and followed up by a highly trained and skilled research team* . . . and you will be helping to improve treatment for future generations of women—perhaps your daughters, nieces, and granddaughters.

A woman's greatest concern about entering a clinical trial may be the unsettling anxiety of not being able to choose which of the two treatments she prefers. In a clinical trial you do not know your treatment until therapy has been completed. Uncertainty, however, is always a built-in element of breast cancer treatment, and as one noted oncologist says about all chemo and hormonal therapy, "Breast cancer doesn't read the books or the numbers, and you can't know the outcome until you're there."

Clinical trials are ongoing for every stage and type of breast cancer. The investigative work described in the preceding section is only a sampling of the research involving clinical trials aimed at developing more effective methods of fighting breast cancer. To learn whether a clinical trial for your profiled breast cancer exists, you can call the NCI's Cancer Information Service at 800-4CANCER for information on clinical trials and to request their booklet *What Are Clinical Trials All About?* The National Cancer Institute also offers Physicians Data Query/PDQ for on-line computer users; PDQ includes the NCI database of information about clinical trials (see the Resources section for information on researching breast health care by computer).

On the Vanguard of Healing

As shown throughout this book, advances in surgical approaches, radiation equipment, and drugs to kill cancer and reduce debilitating side effects are improving the longevity and quality of the lives of women who survive breast cancer. What's called "standard treatment" is actually a dynamic approach to curing breast cancer, one in which doctors are constantly incorporating new discoveries.

In addition, physicians have become aware of how strengthening a woman's immune system can enhance the healing effects of the surgery, radiation, and chemotherapy they provide. A strong immune system produces more of the natural killer (NK) cells that destroy cancer. Many doctors who discuss diet and exercise as ways to boost a woman's immune system during and/or after standard treatment for breast cancer also recognize that reducing stress can heighten the body's resistance to disease. In a new twist, the medical establishment is now beginning to acknowledge the immune-strengthening potential of stress-reducing mind/body practices such as imagery, hypnosis, meditation, and prayer. For a woman who undergoes standard treatment, doctors are more frequently suggesting that these techniques be regarded as "complementary care," to be undertaken either during or after therapy.

An immune-strengthening mind/body practice that may enhance standard treatment should *not* be confused with unproved "alternative treatments," such as detoxification diets, herbal remedies, and cure-of-the-moment substances like shark cartilage, which some people turn to *instead of* standard care from qualified physicians. In this book, *standard treatments are considered the first line of defense against diagnosed breast cancer.* That said, the power of immune-strengthening mind/body practices are considered ways of continuing the battle that standard treatment starts.

A number of major medical institutions are expanding their cancer treatments to include complementary care. At Duke University Comprehensive Cancer Center, imagery, meditation, biofeedback, and prayer are offered to selected cancer patients in the course of conventional treatment. At certain medical centers in New York, complementary care may also include therapeutic touch, reflexology, hypnosis, yoga, acupressure, and instruction in the rituals of the Japanese tea ceremony.

These practices help a woman cope with the stress of her disease. Described in detail in Chapter 9, research in psychoneuroimmunology (PNI) has shown how during stressful times, the stress hormones can be overproduced, thereby lowering immunity at intervals when the production of natural killer cells that fight cancer can drop too. In other words, just how the mind perceives stress can alter the body's functioning. The research into complementary care is just beginning, and women who have breast cancer are benefiting from work done in many other areas. The most prominent discoveries, from diverse places, are described in this chapter.

THE POWER OF SOCIAL SUPPORT

An important series of studies is going on at Stanford University School of Medicine under the guidance of psychiatrist Dr. David Spiegel. In 1989 he and his colleagues reported in the prestigious medical journal *Lancet* that women with metastasized breast cancer who were in therapeutic support groups lived twice as long (an average of 36.6 months) as women in control groups (an average of 18.9 months) who had not received support. For one year, 86 women with metastatic breast cancer were randomly divided into two groups: a control group that received standard treatment and a group that received standard treatment along with weekly one-and-a-half-hour group therapy sessions and lessons in self-hypnosis to help control pain. Looking back 10 years later, researchers discovered that in a scientifically controlled investigation, social support could be shown to increase survival. Of course, it may not be only the social support but also self-hypnosis, or perhaps, women in the support groups followed their treatment regimens more closely. In any event, the results of this study have given rise to current investigations into the effect of support groups—not only on survival but on other mind/body relationships, such as production of NK cells—among women with earlier-stage breast cancer and other women with metastasized breast cancer and their spouses. The women in the studies do not have to be "positive thinkers," but they are encouraged to be themselves and to express themselves. Dr. Spiegel's focus is not on helping a woman gain personal control over a disease but rather on helping her affect the quality of her life with a disease.

For a woman to try to improve her quality of life after breast cancer makes enormous sense to me. Two aspects of complementary care that doctors and patients are acknowledging as helpful are: (1) meditative methods such as imagery, hypnosis, meditation, and relaxation; and (2) the spiritual approach. And as Dr. Spiegel's work shows, any effects may be more pronounced if complementary care is shared by women in support groups.

TAPPING INTO INNER CONSCIOUSNESS: IMAGERY, HYPNOSIS, MEDITATION, RELAXATION

Meditative methods such as imagery, hypnosis, meditation, and relaxation are well known. As long ago as 1978, when the best-selling book *Getting Well Again: A Step-by-Step Guide to Overcoming Cancer for Patients and Their Families*, by Dr. O. Carl Simonton, Stephanie Matthews Simonton, and James Creighton, was published, tapping into the mind/body connection through imagery gained national attention. The Simontons suggested a state of deep relaxation, followed by a mental picture of white blood cells aggressively battling cancer cells, and finally, the shrinking of a cancerous mass. Because the recommended imagery is combative, other experts have disputed the need for women to create these warring factions in their minds, saying that for some people, aggressive images increase stress, and stress reduction should be the goal. In his 1987 book *Healing Yourself: A Step-by-Step Program for Better Health Through Imagery*, Dr. Martin Rossman wrote that a gentle, healing image—whatever that may be—should be allowed to surface freely. He also suggested the creation of an "inner advisor," a symbolic representation of inner wisdom.

A number of researchers have recently been awarded government grants to explore the effectiveness of imagery, hypnosis, meditation, and relaxation on stress reduction and immune-system stimulation among women diagnosed with breast cancer. In the past, two respected studies conducted at the UCLA School of Medicine among malignant melanoma patients have revealed convincing connections that provide the basis for further investigation. One six-month study showed that men and women trained in relaxation techniques had increased the numbers and the activity of their NK cells, and in a six-year follow-up, the trained members of the study had longer rates of survival than the untrained control group. With regard to breast cancer, researchers in San Francisco have started to compare women diagnosed with breast cancer who are in support groups focused on meditation, visualization, and Eastern spiritual therapies such as yoga and tai chi, with women in more conventional cognitive and behavioral therapy support groups. These studies are being jointly undertaken by California Pacific Medical Center and the University of California at San Francisco.

The National Institutes of Health Office of Alternative Medicine is funding two significant investigations among women who have received standard treatment for breast cancer. One study at the University of Texas Health Science Center involves support groups and is evaluating the impact of imagery and relaxation techniques on the body's naturally produced immune system stimulants. The other study, at Good Samaritan Hospital and Medical Center in Portland, Oregon, is measuring NK cell activity among 25 women who will be trained in hypnotic imagery.

With the growth of scientific interest in the mind/body connection, a woman who wants to complement her standard therapy might contact the nearest comprehensive breast cancer center or major medical center for information about local breast cancer support groups who use these techniques.

THE SPIRITUAL APPROACH

In 1995 in the medical journal *Psychosomatic Medicine*, Dr. Thomas Oxman, a psychiatrist at Dartmouth Medical School, reported that in a study of 232 elderly people who had undergone open heart surgery, survival rates were three times higher among those who added strong religious belief to social support. So there is informal, but increasing, recognition that prayer may have a place in mind/body connection. One review in the *Journal of the American Medical Association* even showed that in more than 20 studies religious involvement had a positive effect on good health, including cases of cancer.

A frequently cited study on the power of prayer took place in the early 1980s when a group of born-again Christians prayed for people who came through the coronary care unit at San Francisco General Medical Center during a 10-month period. A group of 192 people received prayer, and a control group of 201 people did not; the result was that those who were prayed for, when rated on a scale of health factors, needed less medication and had better health.

There has been debate over whether prayer is beneficial alone, or because it often involves the social support of religious services. To understand what is going on, scientific studies on the link between spirituality and healing are being suggested by researchers such as Dr. Herbert Benson at Harvard Medical School, who has pioneered studies on the effects of transcendental meditation and health. The author of *The Relaxation Response*, he has found that people who meditate using a prayer or a phrase have reduced heart and respiration rates and blood pressure levels elevated by stress.

KEEPING COMPLEMENTARY CARE IN PERSPECTIVE

These are still the early days of research into stress-relieving methods and use of the mind/body connection in relation to breast health care. Social sup-

BEWARE OF "MIRACLE CURES"

The health-enhancing potential of the mind/body connection is a complement to the standard surgery, radiation, and chemotherapy treatments for women with breast cancer. These should not be confused with the so-called miracle cures that continue to surface in the media. For example:

Anecdotal reports of incredible recoveries have come from people who have been treated intravenously and orally with a medicine called *antineoplastons*, by Dr. Stanislaw Burzynski of the Burzynski Research Institute in Houston, Texas. The non–FDA-approved antineoplastons, which are reportedly nontoxic, are derived from peptides, small chains of amino acids or proteins, that Dr. Burzynski initially isolated from blood, then from urine; he now synthesizes them in a laboratory.

For decades Dr. Burzynski has functioned outside the medical establishment and treated patients without conducting the clinical trials that might allow his antineoplastons to be approved by the FDA. In an interview he said he had treated women with metastatic breast cancer with a 38 percent rate of response, but without scientific research to support his statement, it is difficult to know exactly how his drug may affect the disease. The FDA would like him to begin enrolling patients in phase II clinical trials. Currently his treatment is scientifically unproved, unapproved, and expensive—it has been reported that two years' treatment with antineoplastons may add up to $100,000.

Dr. Burzynski has been indicted in federal court on 75 counts that involve using an unapproved drug in interstate commerce and mail fraud. He denies all the charges. His case goes to trial in October 1996.

port, which has shown increased survival among women who have metastatic breast cancer, has given rise to widespread research into the power of people. And it seems that support groups, meditative methods, and spiritual undertakings have the potential to be regularly regarded as adjuncts to the powerful surgery, radiation, and drug treatments that scientific research has already sanctioned for breast cancer.

Breast Reconstruction: Is It for You?

"Going through the diagnosis of cancer, a mastectomy, and six months of chemotherapy was nothing but torture. It was exhausting, it took my spirit. Reconstruction gave me my spirit back."

—A 51-YEAR-OLD PUBLICIST,
18 MONTHS AFTER HER TRAM FLAP BREAST RECONSTRUCTION

More than half of the women who are diagnosed with breast cancer undergo mastectomies, and statistics show that most of them have their breasts reconstructed afterward. "Ten years ago probably fewer than 20 percent did, but there's been a dramatic turnaround," says Dr. Berish Strauch, chairman of the department of plastic and reconstructive surgery at Albert Einstein College of Medicine and Montefiore Medical Center in New York. "Eliminating the highest age group, I would say that over 80 percent of women who have mastectomies are choosing reconstruction today."

And there are reasons why growing numbers of women are making this choice:

First, the radical mastectomy, which required removal of the entire chest wall and made reconstruction next to impossible, has been virtually eliminated as a surgical treatment for breast cancer;

Second, new surgical refinements, such the total or "peg" back flap and others described in this chapter, have improved the techniques for breast reconstruction; and

Third, the recent and vastly encouraging finding that reconstruction has no effect on breast cancer survival and recurrence rates.

BEFORE A MASTECTOMY, TALK TO A RECONSTRUCTIVE SURGEON

Even if you are unsure about whether you will ultimately want to have "reconstruction," it is a good idea to consult a reconstructive surgeon from the outset of your treatment for breast cancer. Certain types of mastectomies are better suited to reconstruction, and certain reconstructions are better performed at the time of mastectomy, while you are still in the operating room. A consultation will give you the chance to know your options.

WHY IT IS *NEVER TOO SOON* TO CONSULT WITH A RECONSTRUCTIVE SURGEON

"When you're building a house you want to be around when the foundation is laid," says Dr. David A. Hidalgo, chief of plastic surgery at Memorial Sloan-Kettering Cancer Center in New York, "and likewise, the person performing your reconstruction needs to get in on the ground floor." Unless a reconstructive surgeon is called in at the start, a breast surgeon working alone may take a step that will later limit a woman's options for breast reconstruction.

Some of the variables that can make a difference are:

• **Radiation therapy**, prescribed as an adjunct to lumpectomy, can permanently thin and damage the skin of the chest wall; in the event of a subsequent mastectomy, this prior radiation can significantly limit the reconstruction techniques your surgeon will be able to use.

• **The type of incision and procedure chosen for a mastectomy.** The choice of a "skin-sparing" mastectomy (see Chapter 21), in which breast tissue is removed through a single tiny incision around the areola—a major improvement over the old-style, 12-inch mastectomy scar—may be inadvertently eliminated if a consultation with a reconstructive surgeon is not scheduled before a mastectomy is performed. This type of incision and mastectomy, explains Dr. Richard A. D'Amico, associate chief of plastic surgery at Englewood Hospital and Medical Center in New Jersey, "results in a breast with an almost 'scarless' appearance, a concept that has emerged from refinements in breast reconstruction with the body's natural tissue."

"Any discussion of the best we can do in reconstruction has to start with the skin-sparing mastectomy," says Dr. Hidalgo. "Not only is the minimal scar a plus, but you get a better shape by preserving all of the breast skin." But candidates for this new procedure must have a centrally located tumor,

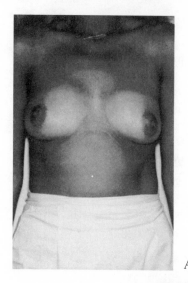

A

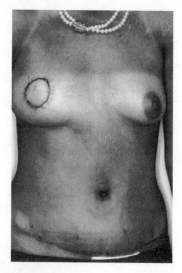

B

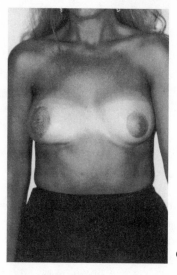

C

Breast reconstruction with natural tissue from a TRAM (abdominal) flap, performed immediately after a mastectomy of almost "scarless" appearance. (A) A 27-year-old woman before breast cancer surgery. (B) The same woman after a mastectomy in which both the nipple/areola area and internal breast tissue were removed through a circular incision around the areola. (A selection of lymph nodes also was removed through the same incision.) Breast skin was left intact and an immediate breast reconstruction followed using minimal skin and natural tissue from an abdominal (TRAM) flap. (C) The same woman after a later nipple reconstruction. The areola tattoo hides the circular incision, giving an almost "scarless" appearance to the reconstructed breast, a virtual match to the cancer-free breast. Courtesy of Richard A. D'Amico, M.D.

with a biopsy scar at the edge of the areola. "In large part it depends on the location of the tumor and the extent of the disease," Dr. Hidalgo says. Still, the numbers of mastectomy patients who qualify for skin-sparing surgery—currently just 20 to 30 percent—should grow significantly, he believes, as more surgeons learn the procedure and more women hear about it. "Sometimes a biopsy scar is arbitrarily placed, and all it would take to change that would be for the patient to speak up."

Skin-sparing mastectomies are followed by immediate reconstruction, either by the insertion of a tissue-expander implant underneath the pectoral muscle in the chest, or more often, by reconstruction with the body's own tissue, usually from the abdomen (both procedures are described later in this chapter). "For best results," says Dr. Hidalgo, "you need skin to replace the circle where the nipple was. And only a natural tissue reconstruction allows for that." (In most breast reconstructions, no matter what the method, the nipple/areola is rebuilt, if desired, as a separate outpatient procedure later.) Breast reconstruction after skin-sparing surgery is done at the time of the mastectomy; if you wait until the scar heals, the breast skin will contract and wrinkle, making it impossible for a surgeon to work with. *Even women who don't qualify for skin-sparing surgery, however, can often have scars minimized when the reconstructive surgeon is able to consult with the breast surgeon right from the start.*

If you know you must have a mastectomy, do not shy away from facing the issue of reconstruction before your surgery occurs, even if you think that reconstruction is the last thing on your mind. You now have options that may not be available to you later.

For insights into the latest techniques for breast reconstruction and help in guiding women who are considering this surgery, this chapter has benefited from the wisdom of the following physicians:

Dr. Richard A. D'Amico, associate chief of plastic surgery at Englewood Hospital and Medical Center in New Jersey;

Dr. Michelle Copeland, a plastic and reconstructive surgeon at Mount Sinai Medical Center in New York;

Dr. Loren Eskenazi, a plastic and reconstructive surgeon in private practice in San Francisco;

Dr. David A. Hidalgo, chief of plastic surgery at Memorial Sloan-Kettering Cancer Center in New York;

Dr. John McCraw, professor of plastic surgery at Eastern Virginia Medical School in Norfolk;

Dr. William Marx, chief of anesthesia service at Memorial Sloan-Kettering Cancer Center in New York;

Dr. Berish Strauch, chairman of the department of plastic and reconstructive surgery at Albert Einstein College of Medicine and Montefiore Medical Center in New York.

CHOOSING THE RIGHT RECONSTRUCTIVE SURGEON FOR YOU

Generally speaking, the same considerations addressed in Chapter 12 apply for selecting a reconstructive surgeon. Reconstruction is more complicated than cosmetic surgery, however, and for state-of-the-art technique, your best bet is a university or teaching hospital.

Note: Do not automatically choose the first person your breast surgeon recommends. "In the worst case scenario," says Dr. David Hidalgo, "you'll have an old-time doctor who doesn't want, say, a natural tissue reconstruction taking up his operating time. So the plastic surgeon, because he wants to keep the referral, winds up steering you in another direction, whether that's right for you or not."

Dr. Hidalgo advises seeing at least three reconstructive surgeons: You will want to ask each surgeon what kinds of operations he performs. How many of his reconstructions are with an implant, how many with natural tissue? Does he have microsurgical experience, and how often does he use these techniques? "Operating is like flying a plane," Dr. Hidalgo says. "You've got to do it often to keep your skills sharp." (Note: You will understand more about breast reconstruction procedures and how to interview doctors after you finish reading this chapter.)

If possible, bring a friend with you to function as a second, critical pair of ears. That kind of support can be crucial when breast cancer makes you feel powerless. Indeed, so strong are such emotions that one woman, herself a pediatrician, could barely stammer out the questions she would prepare before each visit with her plastic surgeon. "I'd decide one was just too silly and skip it altogether, only to get home and realize that was the very answer I needed."

According to Dr. Hidalgo, the most common misunderstanding about reconstructive breast surgery is the amount of time it takes. "No matter what you're having done, it's rarely as simple as 1–2–3." One woman, a TRAM flap (see pages 358–361) recipient, described her experience with the unexpected time-consuming nature of breast reconstruction: "First I was at the office every week or so for check-ups for infection. Then I went back for liposuction, because the breast turned out a little bigger than the other one. Then the nipple was constructed. And tattooed. And re-tattooed, to get the color right." Yet every time she looks at her reconstructed breast she is pleased and she says she would do it all over again.

ISSUES TO FACE WHEN YOU ARE CONSIDERING BREAST RECONSTRUCTION

Do You Want an Immediate Reconstruction?

In all women, the diagnosis of breast cancer sets off emotional shock waves that, for some, make it impossible to think beyond the mastectomy.

That was the case with a 53-year-old film editor. "I was totally freaked," she told me. "Adding one more element would have knocked me out of the box."

For other women, researching reconstruction during this harrowing period can be a way of regaining control. A 45-year-old lawyer confided, "I had a month between the biopsy and my surgery, and I used it to read everything I could get my hands on. The more I researched, the more I was struck by the uniformity of women's reactions to mastectomy—that terrible feeling of mutilation. I knew I wanted to avoid that. So there was no other choice for me but immediate reconstruction."

Even women who opt for immediate reconstruction, however, must eventually come to terms with the loss they have suffered. Two years after a mastectomy and immediate implant, one of my patients went through three months of paralyzing depression before a psychologist pointed out that she was grieving for the missing breast. Dissatisfied with her first implant, this woman has been happier since having it replaced with a new shaped implant (an option described in Chapter 12). "I've since realized that no reconstruction is as good as the original," she now says, "so maybe I should have waited. That way I'd have been comparing the new breast to a mastectomy scar instead of a normal breast." Still, she would do it all again, she says, "with a little more awareness of both the medical, and my own, limitations."

Another patient who delayed reconstruction because she didn't know she had an alternative says the best thing about her experience was that she can knowledgeably advise others not to repeat it. "The mastectomy scar was a constant reminder of my cancer. And it was hard to psych myself up for yet another operation. With an immediate reconstruction, I could have gotten on with my life."

By considering the following list of pros and cons, you may be better able to make your decision about reconstructive surgery:

ADVANTAGES OF IMMEDIATE RECONSTRUCTION
Fewer surgeries
Less money and recovery time invested
Aesthetic results as good or better
Less negative impact on body image
Less time to dwell on the cancer

DISADVANTAGES OF IMMEDIATE RECONSTRUCTION
Less time to make an informed decision
A longer initial surgery, with more potential for complications
Possible delayed mourning for the missing breast
Possible dissatisfaction when comparing the new breast to the old one

Is There Anyone Who Cannot Have Immediate Reconstruction?

Since chemotherapy, which interferes with healing, is normally postponed until two or three weeks after mastectomy, and a simultaneous reconstruction could theoretically add days or even weeks to the healing period (the latter extreme would be rare), women whose cancer affect the lymph nodes may be advised to postpone reconstruction until a later date. Failing this extreme sense of urgency, however, most doctors think that the brief delay reconstruction may cause to the start of chemotherapy makes no difference in treatment outcomes, and the latest research backs them up. Still, since only 38 percent of reconstructive surgeons are currently performing immediate reconstructions, in some areas it may be hard to find one. (For help, check the Resources section to contact the American Society of Plastic and Reconstructive Surgeons.)

Personal Issues Related to Reconstruction

To some extent, the procedure you and your surgeon decide on will be determined by your special needs. Is it important to look as normal as possible in the nude as well as clothed? How long a recovery period will you be able to manage, given family and work commitments? What are your feelings about altering the other breast? Regarding this last point, in the case of implants or larger breasts, a reduction or breast lift (see Chapter 12) may be necessary to match the reconstructed breast. And some doctors routinely favor reducing or lifting the opposite side. Nonetheless, many women cringe at the thought of unnecessary scars—as one woman put it, "I already look as if I've been through a war . . . which I have."

As for the effect of cosmetic surgery on cancer detection in the normal breast, the up side is that a reduction or mastopexy allows your surgeon to biopsy that breast (which previously may not have been possible). Where mammography is concerned, however, the news is mixed:

"Certainly a good mammographer can tell postoperative scar tissue from cancer, which is a different kind of calcification," says Dr. Loren Eskenazi, a plastic and reconstructive surgeon in San Francisco. "But you can get calcifications that are very confusing. And augmentation with implants definitely interferes with accurate mammogram readings. So I do surgery on the opposite side only if I have to, and in the case of implants, only after extensive counseling with the patient." (See Chapters 4 and 5 for more about the effectiveness of breast screenings after reconstructive surgery.)

HOW BREAST RECONSTRUCTION IS PERFORMED: IMPLANTS VERSUS NATURAL TISSUE

A breast may be reconstructed with either a saline implant (a procedure described in the augmentation section of Chapter 12) or the body's own tissue, called a "flap."

WHAT DOES INSURANCE COVER?

Read your policy carefully. Some companies pay for a prosthesis (an artificial breast) or reconstruction, but not both. (Obviously, if you're planning a delayed reconstruction, you'll be better off buying the prosthesis yourself.) Others cover reconstruction but draw the line at "aesthetic" procedures such as reduction and mastopexy; one even declined to ante up for nipple rebuilding on the reconstructed side! Find out, too, if all or only a portion of the cost will be covered and whether this will be based on an actual or preassigned cost. If you've had implants from previous surgery, check to see whether that will make a difference; some companies won't pay for reconstruction in women who have already had breast implants. And a few don't cover reconstruction at all!

If you object to something in your policy, by all means make your feelings known: Some women have found that by barraging their carrier with letters and having their doctors write on their behalf, they eventually get at least part of what they want. And if you have no insurance, consider that breast reconstruction is available at minimal charge through the plastic surgery departments of many teaching hospitals.

For the flap procedure, a portion of skin, muscle, and fat is harvested from another part of the body and moved to the chest area to create a new breast through the mastectomy incisions.

There are two types of flaps:

(1) **Pedicle** flaps are *attached* flaps, such as the one that can be taken from the back. The pedicle flap from the latissimus dorsi in the back is removed from that part of the back which is just below the armpit, not far from the breast area. This flap is left connected to a muscle stem (or "pedicle," meaning stalk), through which it gets its blood supply; the pedicle is then stretched and tunneled under intervening skin to the chest wall, where the flap is molded to the desired shape;

(2) **Free** flaps are *unattached*, meaning that the flap must be completely disconnected from a donor site, such as the buttocks, that is far away from the breast area. After a free flap is detached, the blood vessels are reconnected microsurgically—i.e., under a microscope—to vessels in the armpit or chest.

The most popular natural tissue flap, the TRAM (transverse rectus abdominis myocutaneous) or abdominal flap, can be moved as either a pedicle or free flap. The pedicle procedure, which involves less complicated surgery, is far more prevalent. (Free flaps, the TRAM included, account for only 3 percent of reconstructions in this country.) When it comes to rebuilding a breast, however, what is simplest may not always be best.

Although implants are the most straightforward method, surgically speaking, many women are reluctant to have a foreign object in their body, even one containing saline rather than silicone gel. (For a history of the silicone controversy that has raged throughout the 1990s, see Chapter 12.) Possessed of a limited lifespan, implants eventually must be replaced, often an important consideration for cancer patients who have had their fill of invasive medical procedures. And implants are firmer and sometimes rounder than a natural breast, making it difficult to match the opposite side.

With natural tissue reconstructions, women say their breasts look and feel more "normal," but this method means putting scars on other parts of the body. Furthermore, recovery time is longer. And the complication rate is higher: Even in pedicle operations performed under the best of conditions, part or all of the flap can die due to inadequate blood supply. What's more, after a temporary numb period in the reconstructed breast, recovered sensation may not be as good as that in an implant reconstruction covered by local breast skin, provided that the nerve endings of the skin are intact. (After mastectomy, the uniquely erotic sensation associated with the nipple is always lost.)

"If you look at it case by case," says Dr. David Hidalgo, "I would say that somewhere around 60 percent of reconstruction patients should have implants and 40 percent either a TRAM flap or another type of tissue reconstruction." His estimate is close to the national average: According to the American Society of Plastic and Reconstructive Surgeons, there were 63 implantations for every 34 instances of flap surgery in 1994. The following table is a summary of the basic differences between these two techniques.

A final point of comparison: Surgeon's fees for an implant run from $2,500 to $3,000; implant with tissue expander $3,000 to $3,500. Pedicle flaps can be as low as $5,000 (for a back flap) or as high as $8,000 (for a TRAM flap). And microsurgical free flaps tend to be the most costly of all reconstructive surgeries, from $6,500 to $8,500. (Remember that there will be hospital and anesthesia fees on top of these average figures.)

Now let's examine your options one at a time.

RECONSTRUCTION WITH AN IMPLANT OR EXPANDER

"To have scars anyplace I didn't absolutely have to didn't make sense to me," says a woman who chose implant surgery over natural tissue reconstruction. "And my stomach was too flat for a TRAM flap. I'd have had a pimple where my right breast used to be!"

IMPLANTATION VERSUS TISSUE RECONSTRUCTION*

	Expander/Implant	*Tissue Reconstruction*
Surgery	**Two** separate one-and-one-half to two-hour procedures	**One** six- to eight-hour procedure
General anesthesia	Required	Required
Hospitalization	Seven days with mastectomy; one day if done later	Seven to 10 days with or without mastectomy†
Scars	No new scars	Additional donor site scars
Shape and consistency	No natural sag, flat across front; firm	Very natural shape, very soft
Opposite breast (to match shape)	More changes usually required	Fewer changes usually required
Uncommon problems	Breast hardening with shape change	Abdominal weakness or bulge (TRAM flap)
Blood transfusion	None needed	Self-donation of two units preoperatively‡

* courtesy of Dr. David A. Hidalgo
† This varies, depending on the type of surgery performed and the doctor. In some cases, a hospital stay can be as short as two days.
‡ Often, this is drawn immediately before the operation, a new development explained later on in this chapter.

Basically there are two categories of implants: *fixed volume implants*, and those in which the volume can be adjusted after surgery (this last group is called *tissue expanders*). Both have a hard silicone shell that is generally filled with saline solution. Although silicone gel implants are still available for reconstruction, both liability concerns and the FDA requirement that recipients be enrolled in a clinical trial have made doctors reluctant to use them (fewer than 1 percent of implant reconstructions in 1994 involved silicone gel).

For a look at the general advantages and disadvantages of saline implants, see Chapter 12. A special drawback for reconstructive patients is these implants' tendency to ripple, an effect often markedly visible through the thin skin left at a mastectomy site. Moreover, directing postoperative radiation at an implant reconstruction will greatly increase capsular contracture risks (see Chapter 12). And of all the reconstructive options, this is the

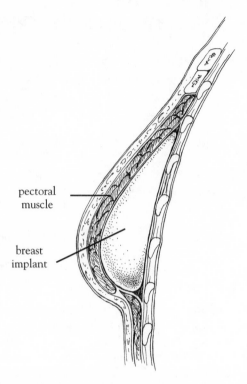

pectoral
muscle

breast
implant

Reconstruction with a breast implant. A woman who has enough healthy tissue remaining at her mastectomy site may be a candidate for breast reconstruction with a breast implant (inserted underneath the pectoral chest muscle). A breast implant may also be inserted underneath a latissimus dorsi flap of skin, tissue, and muscle transferred from a woman's back during a natural tissue breast reconstruction.

one most likely to necessitate surgical alteration of the other breast to achieve symmetry. Also, if you gain or lose weight later, the new breast, unlike a natural tissue reconstruction, will not get bigger or smaller along with the rest of you! Still, the vast majority of women who choose implants are ultimately pleased with their decision.

Candidates for a breast implant must have enough healthy tissue left at the mastectomy site to provide local cover. The best prospects are small-breasted women with little ptosis (sag) or those who've had a bilateral mastectomy and are happy with smaller breasts—large or sagging breasts are difficult to duplicate with reconstructive implants. Patients who have had prior radiation, which compromises the breast skin's healing and stretching abilities, are generally advised against this method, although some surgeons claim good results when the radiation dose has been low.

As for concerns that the implant could interfere with mammography, mammograms are performed on the remaining breast, not at the mastectomy site. If the remaining breast has an implant, a woman may be screened by displacement mammography, a technique described in Chapter 12, and magnetic resonance imaging (MRI) (see Chapter 5 for information about MRI breast screenings for women who have implants).

About Tissue Expanders

The basic procedure, along with its potential complications, is covered in the section on breast augmentation in Chapter 12. For reconstruction, though, things get a bit more complex: Because the mastectomy normally removes some breast skin along with the nipple, roughly 70 percent of reconstructive patients will not be able to have a permanent implant placed right away. Instead, they are given a tissue expander—an inflatable implant containing a metal port for fluid injection—to stretch the skin. The expander is inserted underneath the pectoral (chest) muscle in its deflated state, then, starting about two weeks after surgery, injected with a small amount of saline, a procedure repeated during weekly office visits over the next six to eight weeks. (Simultaneous chemotherapy can prolong the process by delaying the second stage of the procedure—the exchange of the expander for the implant—until about one month after chemotherapy is complete. This wait provides for the recovery of white blood cells, which must have high counts to prevent infection.) By the end of this period, the breast will have been inflated to up to one-third larger than the desired size, after which it is allowed to "settle" or "relax" for a month. Finally, the tissue expander is replaced with a permanent implant in a separate operation using the same incisions. During this second procedure—like the first one, it is usually performed on an outpatient basis—the surgeon may also want to adjust the implant's position, surgically remold the newly expanded tissue, and/or perform a reduction or lift on the other side. (For a new variation on the two-stage expander procedure, see the box that follows.)

In very rare cases, generally where existing breast skin has been irradiated and is too thin to stretch, the skin may tear, resulting in infection; when this happens, the expander is removed and replaced once the infection subsides. And as expansion proceeds, most patients experience a sensation of fullness that may be uncomfortable at times. "I wouldn't say the feeling was excruciating," one woman told me, "just very, very tight."

Again, though, implant recipients claim a high level of satisfaction. "I have patients who swear their implant reconstructions look better than any of the TRAM flaps they see in my lectures," says Dr. Richard D'Amico, (whose photos show the excellent results he achieved with both types of procedures). And for many women, this method, with its relatively short (10 to 14 days) recovery period, is the perfect solution. "I'll never forget the day I walked out of my surgeon's office with my new, partially inflated expander

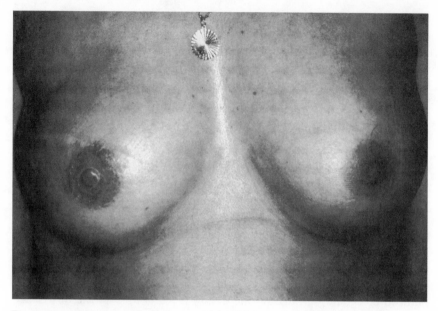

Breast reconstruction with a breast implant. This 40-year-old woman underwent a modified radical mastectomy with lymph node dissection. To reconstruct her breast, a temporary tissue expander was inserted under the pectoral muscle at the same time as the mastectomy. In three months the expander was replaced by a permanent saline breast implant positioned underneath the pectoral chest muscle. This breast implant reconstruction, combined with a later nipple reconstruction and areola tattoo, results in a very natural appearance. Courtesy of Richard A. D'Amico, M.D.

and realized I could play tennis without worrying I'd wind up with a pros-thesis in my armpit," one busy mother said. "I can't say cancer has brought me a lot of happy moments, but that was definitely a high point."

RECONSTRUCTION WITH NATURAL TISSUE

"I decided on a TRAM flap because the thought of a foreign body inside me gave me the creeps," says a 55-year-old realtor. "That was two years ago. Today I look in the mirror at the new breast and think, 'Wow, that's you. That's your flesh.' And using a part of my own body to fix myself is a mar-velous compensation for having a piece of me taken off."

True, breasts reconstructed by this method do feel like, well, breasts. "Comparing an average implant reconstruction to the average natural tissue reconstruction," says Dr. Richard D'Amico, "the natural tissue reconstruc-

HALFWAY BETWEEN IMPLANT AND EXPANDER: THE ADJUSTABLE SPECTRUM

In a recent development, some doctors are taking advantage of a new implant created by the Mentor Corporation to eliminate the usual second stage of implant reconstruction. Instead of inserting an expander at the time of the initial surgery, these surgeons are using an adjustable *permanent* implant called the Spectrum, in which the volume can be adjusted for up to six months. (The Spectrum is also used for cosmetic breast augmentation, as described in Chapter 12.) Once the desired volume is achieved, the injection port is withdrawn while the Spectrum remains in place.

"In an immediate reconstruction where a patient has had a skin-sparing mastectomy or one involving minimal skin loss," says Dr. Loren Eskenazi, "I can get as good or better results this way." Because she uses the Spectrum only in cases where breast skin has been left largely intact, there is seldom the need to later reshape the breast or correct placement of the implant, she says. In 1994 the new adjustable expander accounted for 6 percent of implant reconstructions in the United States.

tion is softer and more natural-looking, because the healthy tissue that's moved here—especially with the TRAM flap—is of essentially the same consistency as the tissue of the breast. It can also mimic ptosis, which makes for better symmetry."

The disadvantage is that you wind up with scars at the donor site. Also, because nerves here are severed, this area, like the reconstructed breast, goes through a temporary numb period. "For a year I felt as if I was wearing football padding—or living in somebody else's body," says a teacher who had TRAM surgery. Other patients experience a host of odd sensations while the nerves are regenerating. "I'd feel burning, I'd feel itching," a five-year flap veteran explains. "I'd scratch myself but feel as if I hadn't scratched. It took three years for my 'dead zones' to fully revive, with the breast area the first to come back. With the exception of the missing nipple, though, things feel pretty normal now." (Recovered sensation starts at the outer edges of reconstruction, gradually moving inward.)

Women who are not eligible for natural tissue reconstruction include those with inadequate body fat or extensive scarring at the site where the "flap" would be taken. In addition, medical conditions such as diabetes or heart disease may preclude such surgery, since flap reconstruction is a long operation, with a demanding recuperative period. (For a look at two new medical developments that have been a boon to patients both before and after surgery, see the box "Two Important Developments for Natural Tissue Reconstruction" in this chapter.)

In all flap procedures, there is, as I've mentioned, a possibility that a portion (more common) or all of the transferred tissue will die due to inadequate blood supply. Another potential complication: Delayed healing, estimated to occur in 30 percent of heavy smokers and previously irradiated patients. (For others, it is closer to 5 percent.) A less serious problem is the hardening of transplanted tissue, causing small, benign, subcutaneous lumps; in up to 10 percent of cases these are noticeable enough to necessitate corrective surgery through the original incisions. In addition, since some degree of seroma, or fluid build-up, is common postoperatively, patients must often live with plastic drains—foot-long tubes attached to grenade-shaped drainage bags—at the surgical sites for up to a week. "They're pliable and not all that uncomfortable," says one woman, "but I felt like a Christmas tree covered with ornaments for a while."

Now let's look at the different types of flap surgery, starting with the TRAM, the one Dr. D'Amico calls "the gold standard of natural tissue reconstruction."

From the Abdomen: The TRAM Flap (or "Tummy Tuck")

Used for two-thirds of natural tissue reconstructions, the transverse rectus abdominis myocutaneous, or TRAM flap, has two big advantages:

1. It feels like breast tissue, and
2. It allows for reconstruction of a larger breast.

Another plus, as suggested by this procedure's nickname ("tummy tuck"): The flap comes from an area many women are glad to see reduced!

Women who are good candidates for TRAM flaps have sufficient abdominal tissue, free of previous surgical scars. Because circulation here is more tenuous than in some flap donor sites, conditions such as obesity and heart disease are usually contraindications, as is heavy smoking. (Smokers who otherwise qualify may be given either a pedicle "supercharge" or free TRAM, as explained below.) Patients with back problems may also be advised against a pedicle TRAM, because the abdominal muscles help support the back.

ABOUT THE TRAM FLAP OPERATION

The overwhelming majority of TRAM flap surgeries are performed as single pedicle procedures—i.e., a bullet-shaped piece of skin and fat is cut away from one side of the abdomen but left attached to the nearest stalk of rectus abdominis muscle (there are two running side-by-side down the center

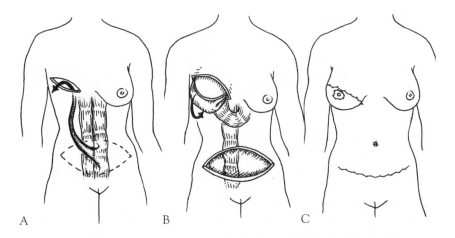

Breast reconstruction with natural tissue from a TRAM (Transverse Rectus Adominis Myocutaneous), or abdominal flap. (A) Two rectus abdominis muscles run side-by-side down the center of the abdomen; one of them is used for a natural tissue reconstruction of a breast after a modified radical mastectomy. (B) A bullet-shaped pedicle flap of skin, tissue, and muscle, still attached to the rectus abdominis, is tunneled under the skin to the chest wall, where it is shaped to form a breast mound through the mastectomy incision. (C) A nipple may be reconstructed at a later date; a woman will have a hip-to-hip scar across her abdomen, halfway between her navel and pubic area, and a scar around her navel. Not pictured: A breast reconstruction may be performed by shaping a breast mound with a TRAM flap that has been detached, cut away from the rectus abdominis; this requires microsurgery for reconnection of blood vessels at the chest. Illustration by Maya M. Puchkoff.

of the abdomen); next, the pedicle, with the flap still connected, is lifted from the abdomen and tunneled under intervening skin to the chest wall, where the flap is shaped to form a breast mound through the original mastectomy incision. The tip of the bullet is sutured to local tissue up toward the shoulder, the square part down at the inframammary fold. (For a better idea of how this works, see the illustration.)

The pedicle TRAM is far simpler surgery than the free TRAM, in which a portion of tissue is completely removed from the lower abdomen and microsurgically reconnected to blood vessels in the armpit. Still, despite lower risks of total flap death, pedicle TRAMs have a drawback:

With a pedicle TRAM, potential tissue yield is smaller, since the flap is dependent on the muscle for its blood supply. There are a number of "choke points" along the way that result in more tenuous circulation, especially farther from the main blood supply. As a result of this disadvantage, women with large opposite breasts may be advised to have a *bilateral* pedicle operation in which *both* muscle stalks are taken to supply one large, elliptical-shaped flap of tissue harvested from both sides of the abdomen. (When performed to reconstruct two breasts after a double mastectomy, the procedure is called a "double" TRAM.) There are aftereffects, however. A woman may experience abdominal weakness. A permanent layer of supporting Gore-Tex mesh is inserted where the muscles were to prevent the development of a hernia-like bulge, an uncommon complication most often seen in bilateral or double TRAMs. Another rare problem associated with such operations is total or partial loss of the navel, but when this happens, the navel may later be rebuilt.

As for the circulation drawbacks inherent in pedicle TRAM surgery, more and more surgeons are getting around them with an operation called a "turbo" or "supercharge," a procedure similar to the pedicle TRAM, in that the flap is taken from the upper abdomen and left attached to the muscle stem; here, though, microsurgical techniques are used to reconnect a few of the flap's blood vessels, as many as needed, to those in the underarm as well.

As I have mentioned before, the free TRAM in expert hands provides both better circulation and a larger flap. For these reasons, practitioners skilled in microsurgery often prefer the free flap for women at higher risk, such as those suffering from obesity or diabetes; women who are heavy smokers; thin or large-breasted women; or those with scars interrupting the abdominal muscle or the muscle's blood supply.

In both free and pedicle procedures, the incision runs from hip to hip halfway between navel and pubic hair—just slightly higher than it would be in a "bikini line" abdominoplasty. A few surgeons place the scar straight across the belly button, where better blood supply is an asset, but most consider this aesthetically undesirable.

The operation lasts four to eight hours or longer, with additional time for microsurgery and other procedures such as a reduction or mastopexy on the opposite breast. Although patients are generally up the next day—many are encouraged to get moving then, despite considerable initial discomfort—the hospital stay can be as long as 10 days. Most TRAM recipients are able to return to work four to eight weeks after surgery. But those who have had a pedicle flap may not be allowed to walk upright for one to three weeks. "That part was worse than I expected," says an accountant who overall "loves" her double-TRAM results. "Walking around bent over like a little old lady really kills the lower back."

Not surprisingly, those who have undergone double or bilateral surgery have the hardest recovery period. "My father attached a heavy rope to a post at the bottom of the bed so I could pull myself up," this woman tells me. "Otherwise, I would have been a beached whale for a month." Like others who have had both abdominal muscles removed, she will never be able to do a sit-up again—her only disability and "not a biggie since I've learned to get out of bed with my elbows," she says. Popular misconceptions to the contrary, sit-ups are generally not a problem when the TRAM is limited to a single muscle. (To stimulate circulation and help the remaining muscle more adequately do the work of two, many doctors prescribe regular abdominal exercises both before and after a pedicle TRAM operation.)

Indeed, to debunk another myth, TRAM flap recipients are even able to carry a pregnancy to term. Though this was previously thought impossible, the latest studies—admittedly small—seem to prove that notion wrong. "I tell patients they may need a Caesarian," says Dr. Hidalgo, "but otherwise, they should have no problem at all." Some surgeons even feel that last caution is unnecessary, having observed that C-sections are no more frequent among this group than any other.

Finally, there's one last fear that turns out to be groundless. While some women are afraid sex won't be as good after a pedicle TRAM, that may not be the case, according to a book editor who had her surgery three years ago. "At first I was worried because the abdominal stuff didn't seem to be working as well—my legs didn't move quite the way they used to. But a little physical therapy took care of that, and probably made for some improvement, since I got in the habit of working out. If anything, I'm more athletic in bed than I used to be."

From the Back: The Latissimus Dorsi ("LD") Flap

In this procedure, always performed as pedicle surgery, the latissimus dorsi muscle, behind the arm, is lifted from its origins in the back and tunneled forward to the chest. Surgeons remove an eye-shaped flap of tissue that remains connected to this muscle but is moved to the mastectomy site and shaped to replace the lost breast (see illustration). Because few patients have a lot of excess back tissue, this method often entails adding a submuscular implant as well. (For a discussion of implant pros and cons, see the implant section earlier in this chapter and in Chapter 12.) Expanders are not used, since the skin supplied by the flap is generally enough.

Due to the usual necessity for an implant—with all its potential complications—the latissimus is generally preferred for only three groups:

1. women with enough fat in the back area for a complete reconstruction;
2. those for whom the TRAM is contraindicated and who do not want an expander/implant reconstruction, and
3. women who have had prior radiation, in which case an expander is not recommended.

Of all the potential tissue donor sites, the latissimus dorsi offers the best circulation, an advantage after radiation, which compromises the blood vessels in the chest and permanently changes the skin so that it is not amenable to expansion.

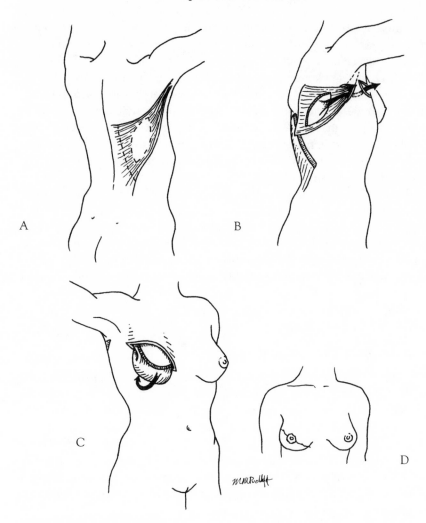

Breast reconstruction with natural tissue from the latissimus dorsi, or back flap. (A) An eye-shaped flap of skin, tissue, and muscle from the latissimus dorsi muscle behind the arm is lifted, but remains attached to the muscle. (B) The lifted LD or back flap is tunneled forward beneath the skin to the mastectomy site. (C) The back flap is shaped into a breast mound. (D) A nipple may be reconstructed at a later date. Not pictured: A latissimus dorsi flap may also be used to cover a breast implant, for a combination natural tissue/implant breast reconstruction. Illustration by Maya M. Puchkoff.

Still, a recent surgical refinement is making the back flap an option for increasing numbers of women. In this new procedure, called the *total or "peg" latissimus*, surgeons are able to harvest more tissue from the back by taking fat on the surface of the muscle as well as the eye-shaped flap. "In the standard latissimus," explains Dr. John McCraw, a professor of plastic surgery at Eastern Virginia Medical School in Norfolk, Virginia, and a pioneer of the new technique, "you take a small ellipse of tissue, plus the muscle without its fat covering. But that muscle often has a good pound of fat on it. And by taking that too, you can get enough to build an entire breast." A word of caution: The additional flesh harvested this way is rarely sufficient to match a large breast without adding an implant or reducing the opposite side.

Patients who have undergone breast reconstruction with a back flap tell me that there is always a slight feeling of tightness under the arm where the flap was moved forward. Also, apart from the volume limitations, the position of the scar may be a drawback. "A lot of people prefer the belly scar because it's hidden in a bathing suit or bikini," says Dr. Michelle Copeland, a plastic and reconstructive surgeon at Mt. Sinai Medical Center in New York. Not all women feel that way, though. "With the back flap," one says, "I don't have to look in the mirror and see the incisions every day. I've literally put all that behind me."

The horizontal scar, often placed within the bra line, can run as long as 12 inches, depending on the amount of skin needed to rebuild the breast. On the other hand, if only muscle and fat are needed, usually to provide additional cover for an implant, the flap can be harvested *endoscopically* (using a tube with a periscope-like viewing device called an endoscope at its end) through an incision of two inches or less.

Like most natural tissue reconstructions, the latissimus takes four to eight hours, during which air-filled bolsters are used to keep the patient in a three-quarter's sideways position that allows the surgeon to work on both back and chest. The hospital stay is two to seven days, the shorter maximum reflecting lower risks of delayed healing due to the back's sturdier blood supply. However, that does not mean that recovery doesn't take work.

"I was given a whole series of exercises," says a back flap recipient. "In one, I had to lie flat and use the affected arm to raise a wooden bar over my head. And it was five or six weeks before I could really do that."

Even after function is regained, some women feel they're never quite the same. "That makes sense," says Dr. Loren Eskenazi, "because you need the latissimus for pulling. Consensus is, there should be no problem unless you're an overhead tennis server or mountain climber, and in the extreme that's true. But in the mild, there is always going to be some little deficit."

Nonetheless, three years after her operation, a double latissimus patient who lost both muscles claims to have no disability whatsoever. "At first I couldn't reach for the cupboard to get a glass out," she says. "But now I play tennis, I take a step aerobics class, I jog. My doctor says I may have some trouble water skiing, but I doubt it. I'm planning to try it, just to prove him wrong."

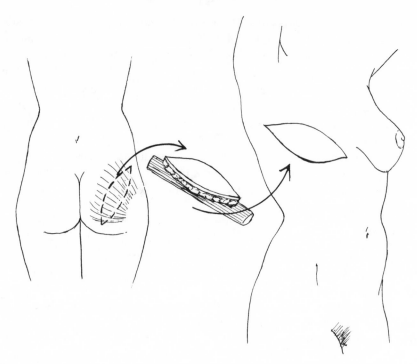

Breast reconstruction with natural tissue from the gluteus maximus, or buttocks flap. A flap of skin, tissue, and muscle is removed from the upper (as pictured) or lower gluteus maximus muscle, and transferred to the breast, where blood vessels are reattached through microsurgery. The buttock tissue is then shaped into a breast mound.

From the Buttocks: The Gluteus Maximus Flap

There are two possible donor sites here. One is the hip/flank area (called the *upper gluteus flap*), and another lower down, just above the buttock crease (the *lower gluteus flap*). Both are performed as free flaps due to their distance from the chest wall. Considering the length and complexity of surgery involved, these procedures are usually restricted to women under 45 who do not want an implant and lack a TRAM donor site. Not only does micro-surgery add to the operating time—the usual duration for a gluteal flap is eight to 10 hours or more—but there is another factor that makes surgery even more demanding when the upper flap is involved: Unlike free flaps from the abdomen or lower buttock, the upper gluteal flap, due to its circula-tory pattern, cannot be connected to the sturdy blood vessels of the armpit. Instead, it is attached to potentially smaller veins under the breast bone, necessitating the removal of an inch-long piece of rib.

Although doctors skilled in such techniques get good aesthetic results this way, with relatively low rates of flap death (1 to 3 percent), the number of surgeons trained to perform gluteal surgery are few. When available, however, this can be an excellent option, despite a rather grueling postoperative course.

"To avoid stretching the muscle, I had to lie flat for three days, which gives you one hell of a backache," says a 40-year-old architect who had a lower gluteal flap reconstruction three years ago. "They also put me in pressure boots that were pumped up and down day and night by a vacuum device. I hardly slept." (Note: The vacuum-pressured boots are also routinely used in TRAM reconstructions, to prevent venous thrombosis from developing during the postoperative stay in bed.)

Still, she says, that was a small price to pay, given the final result. "My breast looks terrific, an almost perfect match. Sensation is great now. And the scar, which runs horizontally all across my right buttock, is only visible in bathing suits with the leg cut high." Though some patients may be visibly flatter on the donor side, this woman says there is no appreciable difference between the size and shape of her buttocks, and physically, she has made a complete recovery. "Within six months, I was able to run and do Stairmaster. And even in the short term, it wasn't so bad. By the time I left the hospital, I was sitting down. To be honest, I felt worse after the C-section when my daughter was born."

DO YOU WANT YOUR NIPPLE/AREOLA RECONSTRUCTED?

At the moment, virtually all mastectomies include removal of the nipple/areola complex. The good news is that, thanks to today's improved techniques, more and more women are having their nipples rebuilt to their satisfaction. In 1994 such procedures accounted for 11 percent of reconstructive surgeries. "My TRAM reconstruction was great," says one patient, "but with the new nipple and areola, I'm even-steven, complete."

Generally, this finishing touch is added several months after the initial reconstructive surgery to give the swelling time to subside, allowing the surgeon to accurately place the new nipple. Usually performed as a same-day, outpatient procedure in the ambulatory surgery center of a hospital, nipple reconstruction takes one to two hours and is done under either local or general anesthesia, depending on the surgeon's and/or patient's preference. The areola may or may not be added at the same time.

Rebuilding the Nipple

In all these procedures, the flap used to form the projecting part of the nipple-areola complex, or nipple, is taken from the center of the breast. A portion of skin and underlying fat—in one popular technique this resembles a skate or ray fish, in another, a star—is cut away but not completely severed, then molded to form the new nipple and sewn in place.

TWO IMPORTANT DEVELOPMENTS FOR NATURAL TISSUE RECONSTRUCTION: HEMODILUTION AND PCA (PATIENT-CONTROLLED ANALGESIC)

Although patients seem to agree that any pain is well worth the gain, there is no denying that natural tissue reconstruction is a long, complex operation entailing blood loss that can cause significant weakness at first. The period just after surgery can be quite uncomfortable, but two new medical advances have proved helpful on both these fronts:

• **Preoperative self-donation of blood by hemodilution.** In this first improvement, currently used at many teaching hospitals, two to three units of the patient's blood are drawn immediately before surgery, after which the blood is replaced intravenously by the same amount of isotonic solution (a fluid routinely given during surgery to replace the normal fluid loss accompanying general anesthesia). "That way your blood gets diluted," explains Dr. Copeland, "so when you bleed during surgery, you're actually losing *less* blood." At the end of the operation, the units taken from the patient are given back to her, leaving her stronger than she would have been without this "extra" blood. At many hospitals, hemodilution has eliminated the need to plan for self-donation weeks ahead of time.

• **PCA, or Patient-Controlled Analgesic.** A Walkman-sized mobile unit that allows the patient to administer her own painkiller without overdosing, this device is called "a miracle" by Dr. William Marx, chief of the anesthesia service for Memorial Sloan-Kettering Cancer Center in New York. Usually administered intravenously, PCA delivers both a steady drip of narcotic such as morphine or demerol and a set amount of the drug whenever a patient hits a button. The device is programmed to prevent overdose and has been shown to reduce the amount of painkiller used overall. "If you didn't have the button to push," Dr. Marx explains, "you would call the nurse and by the time she got got there, you would be in more pain, requiring more of the drug. But since you're able to regulate the flow, you never hit the valleys—or the peaks. There's also a psychological plus in knowing you can help yourself. People handle pain better when they're in control."

In use for about a decade, PCA is currently available at most major hospitals. For breast reconstruction surgery, it is only given until a patient is able to eat solid food, after which oral painkillers are substituted. By then, though, Dr. Marx says, the worst of the discomfort is over. And for the two- to three-day period the patient is on PCA, "it's a wonderful example of modern technology making the postoperative period more tolerable."

In the past virtually all nipple reconstructions tended to flatten over time, a factor surgeons had to take into account when deciding on the new nipple's size. This is no longer the case, however. Dr. John McCraw's "fishtail" technique, which due to the amount of flesh required is possible only in natural tissue reconstructions, is a case in point. Not only is the fishtail shape of his flap designed for better projection, he says, it has another advantage, as well: An extra piece of skin on which the completed nipple will rest—"so it can't sink back into the hole it came from the way most other reconstructed nipples do." Though a few surgeons feel the nipple achieved this way has too much projection to look entirely natural, many have begun using Dr. McCraw's method or similar variations. "The whole area of nipple reconstruction has really progressed in the last few years," says Dr. Michelle Copeland. "Often it's hard to tell the real and the reconstructed nipple apart."

There is one distinguishing factor, though: A reconstructed nipple is permanently erect. "Never mind that I'm cold, hot, hugely aroused, or what-have-you, it's there," says a TRAM-flap recipient who was initially disconcerted by this aspect but has come to consider it "no big deal."

Rebuilding the Areola

Once the nipple has been reconstructed, the areola is added either immediately or in a separate outpatient procedure. Techniques vary but may depend on the type of nipple reconstruction used. In some, the areola is rebuilt from a skin graft, usually taken from the inner thigh crease (not, as often thought, the labia!). Skin tone here is often darker and a good match for the areola skin. As for notions that inner thigh grafts are always hairy, not so, Dr. David Hidalgo says. "When the graft is thinned out—which we do routinely—the hair follicles are usually cut off. In the rare case where a few hairs remain, electrolysis is an easy solution." All grafts for areola reconstruction can be done under local anesthesia and do not, for the most part, add much to recovery time. Since there is always a slight risk that the graft will die, however, many plastic surgeons favor other methods whenever adequate skin is available at the areola site.

In one new procedure requiring further study, Dr. Berish Strauch is re-creating the areolar ring with a scalpel by shaving off the outer layer of skin around the nipple; patients are then encouraged to sit under a sun lamp, since sunlight permanently darkens new scars. (A potential problem: It's not always possible beforehand to predict what kind of scar an individual will form.)

Currently, though, the most common method is an eminently simple one: tattooing. Aesthetically, this can work beautifully, but because tattoos tend to fade after a time, the shade chosen must initially be darker than that of the opposite areola.

Having the nipple/areola complex reconstructed has been very gratifying to women. "It was surprisingly traumatic having to stare at that empty white mound," says a TRAM flap patient who waited a year for nipple/areola reconstruction. "Getting the nipple was what made me feel whole again."

"SINGLE-STAGE" RECONSTRUCTION: THE BREAST AND NIPPLE IN ONE PROCEDURE

Although most doctors still do reconstructions in two basic steps—first the breast mound, then the nipple/areola—a few, generally at large teaching institutions, are performing single-stage reconstructions, where the nipple is rebuilt at the same time as the breast, often immediately after a mastectomy, preferably a skin-sparing mastectomy. Recovery time is the same as for a normal reconstruction, while surgery takes approximately an hour longer. And, according to Dr. Michelle Copeland, "For patients where the single stage is indicated, you can get excellent results this way." Be aware, though, that not every patient is a candidate for single-stage surgery.

Since implant reconstructions are harder to shape predictably (and the majority are done in stages, with a tissue expander), *only women electing natural tissue reconstruction are candidates.* Furthermore, some women will need a simultaneous reduction or lift on the opposite side to facilitate matching the new to the existing breast. To reduce operating time, two teams of reconstructive surgeons are preferred.

Later refinements of the single stage, such as fat suction or nipple repositioning, can be undertaken in the surgeon's office under local anesthesia. And as in any nipple reconstruction, tattooing is generally done afterward.

The advantage for you: lower costs and less time invested. Also, for many women, not having to live with "that empty white mound" or face another surgery are two more selling points.

ABOUT SCARS

Everyone forms scars differently, so your surgeon will not be able to predict how yours will ultimately look. Still, doctors are able to treat unsightly scarring more effectively than ever before. For a rundown of the latest methods, see Chapter 12.

THE AFTERMATH OF BREAST RECONSTRUCTION

Indeed, for many who choose it, breast reconstruction is the first step toward emotional healing and restored self-esteem. A patient who started exercising regularly to regain her strength after TRAM surgery says she's never been fitter—or looked better. Another, unhappy with her original bilateral latissimus reconstruction ("I had hoped to be bigger"), decided to have her doctor add implants so she could be the C-cup she'd always wanted to be. "This is not a process you'd choose to go through," she says, "but I've tried to make it a positive thing. And it's turned out to be. If you lined me up with 20 people who have not had mastectomies, you'd be hard-pressed to pick me out. Except that I'd be the one with the terrific body." Her one regret, she says, is that she didn't have reconstruction sooner.

The last word comes from a woman who opted for an immediate TRAM reconstruction. "Making the decisions I had to wasn't easy," she says. "And good as the new breast looks, it still isn't perfect. The nipple has shrunk a bit and maybe I'll have it fixed and maybe I won't. But the point is, I've got a breast. I can look in the mirror without seeing CANCER. When I notice the new breast at all, it's to give myself a mental pat on the back and think, 'Hey, you did OK for yourself.' "

CHAPTER TWENTY-SEVEN

The Wellness Attitude: Healthy Breasts Throughout a Lifetime

Breasts may be genetically influenced, but they are also sensitive to changes in a woman's body, her lifestyle, her environment, and the hormonally based drugs she takes. With the activism of today's women, who see the number of diagnosed cases of breast cancer climbing every year, breast health care has achieved a place of prominence in the minds of physicians and generated a bevy of activity in the world of research.

Yet even with all the attention placed on breast health, many issues are difficult to resolve. For example, researchers still debate the causes of benign breast problems, they can relate only about 50 percent of breast cancers to recognized risk factors, and they are at odds over how to treat the tiny in situ breast tumors detected by improved mammography. Any uncertainty that exists in breast health care, however, is companion to a growing body of information about breasts, how they function and respond. More than ever before, an understanding of how a woman can help protect the health of her breasts deepens every day.

THE ESTROGEN FACTOR

The mounting evidence that a woman's lifetime exposure to her circulating sex hormones, particularly estrogen, increases her chances of developing breast cancer, has led to consideration of an estrogen factor in breast health care. As discussed throughout the earlier chapters, aspects of a woman's lifestyle can mitigate estrogen levels. For instance, physical activity has been shown to affect levels of sex hormones, so a woman who works out regularly is, in effect, helping to maintain the health of her breasts. In fact, the latest research shows that the young woman who exercises four hours a week has a lower risk of breast cancer. And when a woman notices that she has gained abdominal and upper body fat, which gives her an "apple" shape, she can now be alert to the fact that this is linked to higher amounts of free estrogen in her body; for the sake of her breast health, she should take charge of her figure.

About half of this book is devoted to preventive health care for breasts and gives women the most up-to-date findings about the estrogen factor. It is my hope that mothers will share an awareness of estrogen levels with their daughters as they near menstruation. It is never too early to begin breast protection, and young women can learn that what they eat and drink, how they exercise, when they choose to become pregnant and breastfeed, and whether they use birth control pills or fertility drugs will affect their hormonal levels, and hence, the health of their breasts.

BREAST SELF-EXAMINATIONS AND BREAST SCREENINGS

In addition to being alert to the estrogen factor, a woman should include breast self-examinations (BSEs) in her preventive breast health care, and depending on her age, breast screening through mammography. Among women who adopt overall attitudes of what I like to call "wellness," BSEs and mammograms are second nature. Earlier chapters are devoted to effective BSEs, the controversy over when to have a mammogram—I recommend a baseline mammogram at age 40, a mammogram every 2 years until age 50, and then annually—and the effectiveness of sonography and other high-tech breast tests, a number without radiation.

New breast screenings will be available to women in the near future, and I advise all the women in my care to watch the headlines for new ways to screen breasts without radiation. Research into high-resolution ultrasound that can detect the cells of a breast cancer before they proliferate into a growth should come to fruition soon. The SupraScanner ultrasound system, for instance, is being tested for its ability to spot suspicious areas that are less than 1 mm and to distinguish malignant from benign tissue. Even women who are pregnant would be able to be screened without fear of affecting their unborn babies. Such early cell detection may also bring about methods of removal through needle aspiration, rather than surgery.

AWARENESS OF GENETIC BREAKTHROUGHS

Astounding discoveries are being made in relation to mutated genes associated with breast cancer. While there is no treatment yet as a result of locating mutations on BRCA1 and BRCA2 genes, an encouraging finding is that the BRCA1 gene appears to produce an ineffective protein on its surface rather than deep inside its cell. Drugs might be created to mimic a healthy protein of the BRCA1 gene. A healthy protein, which links with a receptor to prevent the spread of cancer, could then replace the ineffective protein that permits the spread.

While most researchers have refrained from genetic testing of women until issues of counseling, treatment, and the implications on health insurance and employment have been worked out, certain institutions have nevertheless made testing available to those who meet specific criteria. For example, the Genetics and I.V.F. Institute in Fairfax, Virginia, permitted testing of the mutated form of BRCA1 that shows up in 1 percent of Ashkenazi Jewish women (those of Central or Eastern European ancestry) much earlier than other institutions.

THE GOOD NEWS

For the first time in decades, the rate of death from breast cancer has *dropped*. According to the latest government statistics, breast cancer deaths declined by almost 5 percent between 1989 and 1992 (the latest year figures were available). This decrease is the largest since 1950. One of the reasons for this drop is that women are more aware of their breast health and the need for examinations and screening. This awareness must be encouraged to spread, because the overall decline fails to point out that among African American women, mortality rates increased 2.6 percent. It is believed that breast cancers among African American women are diagnosed at later stages, when the cancer is more aggressive. So I ask women to talk about the estrogen factor and communicate the ease of undergoing mammograms and sonograms either when breast problems arise, or later in life, when yearly mammography should be routine.

Women all over the world have made breast health care a global issue, working tirelessly for research into diet, exercise, and environmental influences on their breasts. They have fought for less invasive diagnostic breast tests and treatments. Women have also promoted and entered clinical trials and lobbied for faster approval of cancer-killing drugs. To its credit, the medical establishment has responded, but it is individual women who energize the drive for better breast health care, a drive that is foremost, a personal one. The Introduction of *The Complete Book of Breast Care* is entitled "Your Breasts: Your Pride and Your Worry." Ultimately, this book hopes to shine lights on the many opportunities a woman has to protect and maintain the good health of her breasts, so they are much less a worry, and much more a greater source of pride.

PART VI

Resources

Going On-Line for Information About Your Breasts: How to Use a Computer to Find Everything You Want to Know

When it comes to the health of your breasts, it is important to have confidence in your partnership with your personal doctor, but even so, a breast problem may arise that requires a breast specialist or a second-opinion physician. The computer is a wonderful way of getting yet another point of view. You can find the latest information quickly and easily from other, highly informed experts in the field of breast health care, with not just any computer, but one that uses an *on-line* service. Going on-line means gaining access to the world of computer information by hooking up your computer, through the telephone, to an on-line service.

As you progress through this chapter, we will lead you to selected on-line services, which have *sites* that are treasure chests of information, combinations of facts, institutional reports, and personal experiences that can help you initiate informed discussions with your doctor and reach clear decisions about your breast health care. By the time you finish reading this chapter, you will be able to review medical research—published studies, ongoing clinical trials, the latest breakthroughs—regarding your particular breast issue and also hear from other women who are, or were, in your situation.

FIRST, THE BASICS

What Going "On-Line" Means

Being on-line means that your computer is connected, through your telephone, to other computers throughout the world. To go on-line you need two things:

- A computer with a *modem*. A modem, a device built into the latest computers, converts signals so they can be transmitted over telephone lines. Your computer communicates with other computers through these signals. Modems range in speed from 300 bytes per second to over 28.8 kilobytes per second. A computer with a fast modem—at least 14.4 kilobytes per second— is the best one to use. (If the computer you use does not have a modem, you can buy one as an *add-on* feature; just remember to buy the fastest modem you can afford.)

- An account with an *on-line provider*. Private commercial companies have formed businesses to become on-line providers; in other words, they provide you with access to on-line services. These companies are somewhat like long-distance carriers, but instead of carrying your voice to another telephone, they carry your computer's signals into an electronic network of other computers, for a monthly service fee. The monthly subscription fee usually gives you about 20 hours of on-line time, with additional time billed hourly. In fact, to get your business, most services allow for a free "taste," anywhere from five to 10 hours of initial use without charge.

Finding an On-Line Provider

Finding an on-line service provider is as easy as buying a computer magazine at a newsstand. Advertisements with 1-800 numbers abound for (1) "fully featured" service providers such as CompuServe, America Online, Prodigy, and Delphi, which offer forums for discussion and information libraries; and (2) "single service" Internet providers such as EarthLink, Netcom, Pipeline, and IDT, which are strictly a means of getting to the Internet, with no special features or frills. After you choose a service and sign on with a credit card, you will receive by mail the necessary program installation disks or software. Installing the disks in a computer usually takes about 10 minutes—and you're *on-line*.

You're on Your Way

Once you have access to an on-line service, you're on your way. If you don't have a home computer, you might explore the on-line world at a computer-equipped café, or in an on-line computer at a library, a business, or a friend's house. Anyone, anywhere, who uses an on-line service can contact every other computer that is linked into the system. This web of connections allows you to *talk*, or write directly to others, post and read notices on *bulletin boards* or in *forums*, and enter various libraries and archives to view or retrieve historical as well as recent findings. You can directly contact institutions, private facilities, research and medical health care centers throughout the world, electronically, at your own pace.

There are three basic types of on-line services that allow you to *find*, *exchange*, and *download* (transfer found information into your computer's memory), images and messages: **(1) The Internet; (2) Commercial On-Line Services; (3) Bulletin Board Services.** Each type of service has a different format, style, and range of information on the health care of your breasts. What follows is an overview of what each of these services offers: *what* information is available, *where* it is located, and *how* to get there. For each service, we describe:

- Specific *site locations*, those treasure chests of information that can readily offer you answers to questions that wake you up in the middle of the night. With a click of your mouse, you can enter these sites electronically. Some sites offer general breast health care information, but most are dedicated to the prevention and treatment of breast cancer.
- Our Choice, our *best bet* in each of the services, for finding good information, presented in a thoughtful, easy-to-use manner, on breast health care and breast cancer.

Until now you might have been overwhelmed with the prospect of going on-line, but we will take you through the process one step at a time. We'll show you what's on the Internet, commercial on-line services, and bulletin board services, in that order.

THE INTERNET

The Internet is a decentralized electronic network where many private and nonprofit organizations, government agencies, universities, and other educational resources reside. You can access the Internet after you sign up with a provider. As mentioned earlier, companies such as Netcom, and IDT, as well as Microsoft and AT&T, are in business to provide you with a link to the Internet. Several avenues of communication, including E-mail (electronic mail), are on the Internet. You may already be aware of the names: *World Wide Web (WWW), UseNet,* and *Telnet.* To gain access to a particular Internet site, you must select the area you want to explore, such as WWW, and know a site's *electronic address.* We have included a number of electronic addresses for sites on the Internet, as well as on other on-line services, where you can find information about your breasts. Of all the areas on the Internet, you may find yourself using WWW the most. **The Web's format is so easy to use that instructions are hardly necessary, and there is so much information available and so much being planned for the future, that it is definitely the lane of preference on the information highway.**

ON THE INTERNET: THE WORLD WIDE WEB, USENET, TELNET—EXPLAINED
The World Wide Web is where individuals, organizations, businesses, and

a variety of institutions have *Web sites* with *Home Pages* (think of this as the first page of a brochure) that list their services and features. The WWW structure allows you to *jump* (move) to various other locations within the Web that have topics relating to a subject, such as breast health, that might appear on a Home Page. Using a format called *hypertext*, you can, by just *clicking* your mouse on a highlighted word or phrase, jump to a detailed explanation about the subject you are exploring. This unique and very powerful feature allows for an extraordinary wealth of information to be seamlessly linked and made easily accessible.

After going on-line to the Internet, just click the icon for WWW—this is also called the *Web Browser* button—that appears on your screen. Next, you will see a space for typing in the electronic address of the site you want. Type in the address and then double click or hit the "enter" key. Depending on the speed of your modem, you will soon be transported to that Web site. Then just scroll the Home Page of the site and click on the highlighted subject of your interest. Simple!

What do you do if you don't have a particular address to explore? Powerful tools called WWW *Search Engines* or *Web Spiders* take a command in the form of a key word or phrase, crawl through the Web, and find what you're looking for quickly and easily. (See more on Search Engines later on in this chapter.)

(An example of a Web site and address is: OncoLink: *http://cancer.med. upenn.edu/*)

The UseNet is a collection of topically named *newsgroups*; in other words, subject headings. Individuals can post specific messages, notices, and other forms of information under the different headings. The *UseNet* is in effect the largest bulletin board in existence. The information found here is loosely formatted and therefore sometimes hit-or-miss, but you can often find items of some interest. It is very important to remember, particularly when you are researching information on breast cancer, that the items found in this format are almost completely unedited. This means that they can be highly opinionated and may lack objective and scientific scrutiny. Even though the UseNet is not intended to carry commercially biased messages, there is no "filtering" system to ensure that this does not happen; UseNet is self-monitoring.

(An example of a *UseNet* cancer-related newsgroup is: *alt.support. cancer.*)

The Telnet allows you to operate computers at other locations as if you were actually *logged in* directly at the premises. When entering a *Telnet* site, you can open, but not change, files that are made available to you as a *guest login*, which, upon entering the system, you become. Once you connect with a site, just follow the instructions of the host computer terminal. Telnet makes available singular resource locations, usually at universities, government facilities, or other institutions. Unlike WWW sites, Telnet sites are *not* linked to each other. There are many locations on the Telnet that provide useful and helpful information on breast health and breast cancer, and many have, or will soon have, a WWW site as well.

(An example of a *Telnet* site is the National Cancer Institute's "Can-cerNet": *telnet://icicc.nci.nih.gov.*)

Useful Sites on the World Wide Web

Below are the *site names, electronic addresses,* and brief descriptions of what we consider to be, at the writing of this book, the best locations for breast health care information on-line on the World Wide Web. Site locations and their offerings are always changing, but the ones we have explored for you should continue to be available. Web sites are linked to other similar sites, so as new ones develop, older ones should have links to the new ones, so you can keep up with the changes. The most helpful sites we found, up to press time, are:

OncoLink (http://cancer.med.upenn.edu) is operated by the advisory board of the University of Pennsylvania Medical Center and Cancer Center. *OncoLink* has specific "pages" available for selection from its Home Page that are devoted to current newsworthy items and publications; media topics from CNN, The CancerNet, and both the *San Francisco Chronicle* and *Examiner*; upcoming meetings, speeches and seminars relating to cancer; lists of technical journals written and reviewed by career profes-sionals; and a clinical trials report, which tells you where the latest trials are and how you can participate. Through OncoLink, you can directly connect to other Web sites related to breast care and breast cancer. OncoLink also offers a comprehensive *List of Other Breast Cancer Sites* to review, with sites not included on the Web. OncoLink is very well organized and has a powerful search feature that allows you to type in key words to speed your hunt for information. This is an excellent place to begin your research because it provides a logical, friendly environment loaded with an extremely wide range of information.

NCI Clinical Trials Program (http://wwwicic.nci.nih.gov/proto/breast. html) is a site where you can find information about the National Cancer Institute's Intramural Clinical Program for breast cancer, in Bethesda, Mary-land. An on-line direct-link referral form is filled out on your computer screen and sent directly to their offices. Information can then be faxed or E-mailed directly to you. At this site you can call up information about ongoing breast cancer trials, with a list of criteria for women interested in being participants. Obviously, entering such a trial should only be consid-ered after consultation with your doctor and family.

NABCO/The National Alliance of Breast Cancer Organizations (http:// www.nabco.org/) is a central resource network of over 370 organizations that offers information about breast cancer and breast cancer–related events.

Through NABCO you can find links to other breast cancer sites. NABCO organizes its services into fact sheets: information on risk, detection, treatment, and follow-up care; *What's New*, a quarterly newsletter about the latest developments in medicine and science; National Support Groups, including a list of local breast cancer support groups; and a calendar of events.

The CancerNet (http://wwwici.nci.nih.gov/Cancernet.html) is one of the departments of the NCI, specifically designed to provide cancer information quickly and easily (in both English and Spanish) via the Internet. Information, including topics related directly to breast cancer, is updated monthly. From the CancerNet you can click on either of the words *CancerLit* or *PDQ* (in both *CancerLit* and *PDQ* you will only be able to research the last six months of articles and references.):

- **CancerLit (gopher.nih.gov:70/11/clin/cancernet/cancerlit/topics/breast)** is a bibliographic database of over one million resources from monthly publications, reports, and medical abstracts. When you go into CancerLit, you can choose from a list of monthly articles grouped under subject headings and dated, i.e., *Chemotherapy for Breast Cancer–December 1995*; *Surgery for Breast Cancer–November 1995*.

- **Physician Data Query (PDQ) (telnet://icicc.nci.nih.gov)** offers entry into the entire *NCI* database, where you can locate directories of physicians and organizations involved in cancer care; find information on diagnosis, prevention, and treatment of breast cancer; read reviews of approved drugs; and check references and abstracts of key medical papers and summaries of active trials and studies. PDQ is designed to provide information in two ways: one more technical, for health professionals, and the other an easier-to-read format for everyone else.

The *NCI* is the mother lode of information for many on-line sites that offer information on breast health care. It is enormously important, but due to its size and institutional structure, its site, the CancerNet and the services within it, can be intimidating if you are an on-line newcomer. You can access much of the findings relating to breast cancer from other more user-friendly sites and return to CancerNet later, when you've gained some on-line experience and confidence.

NOTE: If you think you may frequently use either CancerLit or PDQ, you may want to join the *NCI Information Associates* program, which offers full access to the *CancerNet*, *PDQ*, and *CancerFax*, and sends E-mail replies to requests made through CancerNet. Membership also includes 24 annual issues of *The Journal of the National Cancer Institute*. The annual fee is $100. For information about becoming a member of NCI Information Associates, call 800-624-7890.

HealthGate (http://www.healthgate.com) is a private company that provides unlimited access to both MedLine and CancerLit for a low monthly fee of $14.95. If you do not want to subscribe, HealthGate will charge you 25 cents per transaction for each reference you select. A brief description of each article is offered, and you only pay if you download. For more information about HealthGate call 800-434-4283.

AT-A-GLANCE: THE INTERNET'S WWW SITES

Site and Address	Description
OncoLink http://cancer.med.upenn.edu/	Breast care and breast cancer information from the University of Pennsylvania's Cancer News and Information Center.
NCI Clinical Trials Program http://wwwicic.nci.nih.gov/proto /breast.html	Clinical breast cancer trials and experimental treatment, from the National Institutes of Health Clinical Center in Bethesda, Maryland.
NABCO http://www.nabco.org/	A central resource network of breast cancer organizations.
HealthGate http://www.healthgate.com	A site for access to MedLine and CancerLit.
CancerNet http://wwwicic.nci.nih.gov/ Cancernet.html	A primary site of the NCI, which provides direct but limited access to CancerLit and PDQ.

Our Choice of Web sites: Although all of the sites above offer a different mix of information and services, *OncoLink* has developed the most advanced and complete site, offering access to the widest range of information. We recommend OncoLink as your first stop on the Internet.

COMMERCIAL ON-LINE SERVICES

Unlike the Internet, commercial on-line companies such as *CompuServe (CS)*, *America Online (AOL)*, *Prodigy*, and *Delphi* have created their own unique and separate structures, organized into *forums* and *interest groups*—sites where dialogues take place—libraries, and archives. These companies also offer a service not found in the Internet: system operators (*SysOps*), or interest group moderators, who monitor the forums and interest groups and offer technical advice; they can also edit, censor, or reject messages that are posted. On these services you can post and read messages, ask questions, and enter into ongoing computer conversations with health-care professionals and others who are looking for information about breast health care and/or breast cancer. Many informative *discussions* take place in these forums, and many long-term relationships begin here.

We suggest you take advantage of the free introductory time the services offer, and try a few to find the one that is most appropriate to you. Ask friends about their on-line favorites. All of the services also provide, at least to some extent, access to the Internet. So if you're going to subscribe to a commercial on-line service, it may not be necessary to have a separate service like Netcom for the Internet. Right now CompuServe and America Online are the most widely used services, and the ones we have chosen to explore.

GETTING TO SITES ON COMMERCIAL ON-LINE SERVICES

Useful Sites on Compuserve

CompuServe has a very rich environment for information about breast cancer in its *Forum* and *Library* sites. After going on-line with CompuServe, click on *Explore CompuServe* from the menu bar at the top of the opening page, then click *Professional*, then *Health & Medical* to go to a list of options: **The Cancer Forum, The Health Database+, Paper Chase,** and **Physician Data Query (PDQ.)**

In the **Cancer Forum,** you can go to the *Breast Cancer* section and read and/or post messages about subjects that interest you. This is the location to "leave" an opening question on any subject related to breast cancer, no matter how personal or naive it may seem. It is not unusual to get replies from almost any location in the world, from professionals offering advice, other women who have had similar concerns to yours, or even from husbands whose wives have had breast cancer. There is also a *Breast Cancer Library* section in the Forum, and a *Search Engine* available so you can find articles and references on a great variety of breast cancer issues in the library.

In **The Health Database+** you can retrieve information from consumer and professional publications on health care, disease prevention, and treatment. The publications range from newsstand titles such as *American Health, Parents Magazine,* and *Nutrition Today,* to professional journals such as *The New England Journal of Medicine* and *The Journal of the American Medical Association.* Articles on breast care and breast health can be found here. Additional charges range from $1 to $1.50 for each article read (viewed) or retrieved (downloaded).

PaperChase is a service of the Beth Israel Hospital in Boston, which is affiliated with Harvard Medical School. This site is designed to help you find information from the NCI's *CancerLit,* which offers articles and abstracts, and *MedLine*, which offers references to articles, at a cost of about $6 per search.

PDQ (described on page 380) is available from $2.00 to $7.50 for researching a group of up to five headings, depending on the category of the information you want to retrieve.

Any additional charges for these services are billed directly to your established on-line provider account. CompuServe also offers you a direct link with the Internet and all of its sites by clicking CompuServe's own **Web Browser** icon.

AT-A-GLANCE: COMPUSERVE'S SITES

Service/Forum Group	Description
CompuServe	A commercial on-line service: 800-848-8990
Professional	A category that appears when you click on the "Explore CompuServe" icon, at the top of the menu bar.
Health and Medical	A heading found in the *Professional* category; its subsites are listed below.
The Cancer Forum	A discussion forum found in the *Health and Medical* site.
Breast Cancer	A discussion forum found in the *Cancer Forum*.
Breast Cancer Lib.	A library devoted to breast cancer issues found in the *Cancer Forum*.
Health Database +	Information on general health issues from a variety of consumer and professional publications.
PaperChase	Information from the NCI via *CancerLit* (articles and abstracts) and *MedLine* (references).
PDQ	The *Physician Data Query* finds health/cancer information from a wide group of biomedical databases.

Useful Sites on America Online

America Online (AOL) offers two ways to obtain breast cancer information:

- In the **Main Menu,** click on **Reference Desk.** Then you click on the category *Health and Medical* and find three subsections dealing with breast care and breast cancer: **ACS (American Cancer Society), MedLine,** and **Women's Health.**
- You can also click on the *GoTo* caption in the menu bar at the top of the page, and then type in the key word *cancer*. This will bring you to the **Cancer Forum,** where a variety of categories are found that contain information on breast cancer.

As with CompuServe, with AOL you can also access the Internet and the Web sites we have described already, without having to join a separate service.

AT A GLANCE: AMERICA ONLINE'S SITES

Service/Forum Group	Description
America Online	A commercial on-line service: 800-827-6364
The Reference Desk	A category found on the *Main Menu*.
Health and Medical	A category found in the *Reference Desk*.
ACS	The American Cancer Society site for information on breast cancer is found in the *Health & Medical* site.
MedLine	Medical articles and abstracts.
Women's Health	A section on general issues concerning women's health and a link to *NYSERNet* (a Web site for breast cancer); it's found in the *Health & Medical* section.
The Cancer Forum	Found by typing keyword *Cancer* in the *GoTo* section. This forum has five main categories: *The American Cancer Society*; *Avon's Breast Cancer site*; *Pen Cancer Forum*; *The Cancer Journal from Scientific American*; *access to Cancer sites on the Internet.*

Our Choice of Commercial On-Line Services: CompuServe's Forums and Libraries. In CS we found a more useful structure and a richer content base for researching breast cancer. AOL offers a full network of services for breast care and cancer, but, to us it seems somewhat scattered. CS is more well organized.

THE BULLETIN BOARD SERVICES (BBS)

A Bulletin Board Service (BBS) is an individual connection to a particular site, usually set up by an institution or a commercial entity, that allows you direct access to its own database system without going into the Internet or through a commercial on-line service. You subscribe to a BBS just as you do to any other on-line service, and install its software, its user disks, in your computer.

Useful Bulletin Board Services

Grateful Med is an information retrieval program designed to simplify the process of searching the National Library of Medicine's Literature Analysis and Retrieval System, also known as *MedLars*. Upon subscribing, at a one-time cost of $29.95, you receive a user ID and password to gain access to the system. While on-line, you're billed at a rate of $18/hour for downloading the specified articles you choose after you review the search references (defined by using terms and words of your own choosing). Searches and retrievals occur rapidly; most average about $2 per search. Subscribers also have access to **MedLine** and **PDQ**. For information about subscribing to Grateful Med, call 800-638-8480.

AT-A-GLANCE: BULLETIN BOARD SERVICES

Service Name	Description
Grateful Med	The search program for the National Library of Medicine's (NLM's) bio-medical database *MEDLARS* (MEDical Literature Analysis and Retrieval System). For information: 800-638-8480

SEARCH ENGINES: HOW TO GET FAST ANSWERS

In most on-line sites, you can type the *key word* or *words* that best describe the subject of your research directly into an empty "field," then press the *Search* button. For instance, type in *breast cancer genes* if you want to find out the latest on genes and breast cancer, but don't just enter an abbreviated *dcis* if you want to find out about Ductal Carinoma In Situ, as you're probably going to get, as we did, Dartmouth College Information Service.

The tool to find your information fast is called a *Search Engine* when used within a particular site such as OncoLink and CancerNet. Not all health sites have them, but the ones that do usually have a *Search* button at the top or bottom of each page which, when clicked, provides access to the entry field and brief instructions on how to use the Search Engine.

A second method is to use search assistants or *Web Spiders* designed to search the Web itself, not just a particular site. These are very powerful tools, and we suggest three Web address sites to access these Web Spiders:

Yahoo - *http://www.yahoo.com/*
Alta Vista - *http://www.altavista.digital.com*
Lycos - *http://www.lycos.com*

Each one seems to search the Web using different selective criteria, so when we used the same key words and phrases, we got different results from each one.

Our Choice for Searching: The *Search Engines* within the breast cancer sites of *OncoLink* and *CancerNet.* Among the *Web Spiders,* we liked *Yahoo* for its range of "finds," and *Alta Vista* for its search format.

KEEP IN TOUCH BY BEING ON-LINE

There is so much information available on-line, it's hard to keep up with it all. Right now it probably seems a bit overwhelming. So much attention is being paid to breast health care that new information is announced almost every day, but that's what you want. Our best hope for prevention and proper treatment lies in intelligent use of what we already know and what is newly discovered. You need something to help organize all this information so you can find what you need, when you want it, in a manner that you can understand. This is when going on-line becomes so important; you keep in touch and up to date.

Almost daily new *Web Sites* are being created to address breast care issues. It is already phenomenal that within such a very short time, less than two years, there are so many Web sites relating to breast health care and breast cancer, either in operation, under construction, or ready for debut. We are poised at the beginning of the growth of the Web. Its ease of use and interactive potential will make turning to the Web almost commonplace when you want and need to find out the latest about breast care and breast cancer. On-line you will be able to locate information that can confirm a doctor's recommendation or lead you to research alternative care. With an on-line computer, you have immediate access and help.

LET US HEAR FROM YOU

We welcome any comments you have about this book, questions you have about your breasts, and suggestions for future editions. Send your E-mail messages to: stukane@ix.netcom.com

Where to Write, Phone, or Fax for Help

First, we would like to credit **SHARE**, 1501 Broadway, Suite 1720, New York, NY 10036; (212) 719-0364, fax (212) 869-3431. SHARE is a not-for-profit organization that provides information and emotional support services for women with breast and ovarian cancer and their families and friends. SHARE's services include support groups, a hotline in Spanish and English, a wellness program, education meetings, and advocacy opportunities in 14 sites throughout the New York area. SHARE's staff, volunteers, and the many women involved in SHARE's caring network offered invaluable assistance in the creation of this book.

BREAST HEALTH CARE

National Alliance of Breast Cancer Organizations (NABCO), 9 East 37th Street, 10th Floor, New York, NY 10016; (212) 719-0154, fax (212) 689-1213. NABCO's *Breast Cancer Resource List*, a 70-page booklet updated yearly, offers a comprehensive list of breast cancer support groups in the United States and Canada, breast cancer hotlines, and practical advice on how to find a breast surgeon, join a clinical trial, and log on to a breast cancer information database. The booklet also includes toll-free numbers for ordering videos, books, and brochures about breast cancer. To purchase the current *Breast Cancer Resource List*, send a self-addressed mailing label and a check for $3 to NABCO at the address above.

National Women's Health Network, 514 10th Street NW, Suite 400, Washington, DC 20004; (202) 347-1140, fax (202) 347-1168. Information packets and booklets on many aspects of women's health, including benign and malignant breast diseases, are available. A comprehensive listing of brochures may be requested.

Y-ME National Breast Cancer Organization, 212 West Van Buren Street, Chicago, IL 60607; (312) 986-8338, fax (312) 986-0020. National Hotline (800) 221-2141 (weekdays, 9 AM to 5 PM CST); 24-hour hotline (312) 986-8228. Y-ME is a nonprofit consumer-driven organization that provides information, referral, and emotional support to persons concerned about or diagnosed with breast cancer. Its toll-free national hotline is staffed by trained counselors and volunteers who have had breast cancer. Y-ME provides free written materials and publishes a bimonthly award-winning newsletter. A wig and prosthesis bank is available.

BREASTFEEDING

International Childbirth Educators Association (ICEA), P.O. Box 20048, Minneapolis, MN 55420; (800) 624-4934. The pamphlets *An Employed Mother Can Breastfeed When . . .* (50 cents); *Breastfeeding and the Working Mother* (30 cents), plus shipping and handling, are available. Quantity discounts may be arranged for each order.

La Leche League International, P.O. Box 1209, Franklin Park, IL 60131-8209; (708) 455-8317. A respected source of support and information about breastfeeding. Send a SASE to LLLI and request a copy of the LLLI directory, Number 504, which lists two key representatives in every area of the United States and 43 other countries. A woman may contact a particular representative for groups in her area. The league is very committed to the virtues of breastfeeding and offers over 200 information sheets, reprints, and booklets covering topics such as sore nipples, clogged ducts, breast infections, nursing twins, nursing an adopted child, and nursing while working. Send a SASE (business size) to request the catalog of publications, Number 501. For information in languages other than English, ask for the Translation List, Number 508.

ENVIRONMENTAL ASPECTS OF BREAST HEALTH CARE

The EMR Alliance, 410 West 53rd Street, Suite 402, New York, NY 10019; (212) 554-4073, fax (212) 977-5541, E-mail: emrall@aol.com The EMR Alliance is an international coalition of grassroots organizations and individuals concerned with the issue of electromagnetic fields (EMFs), which the alliance views as a significant threat to public health. Information packages on a number of EMF-related topics are available, including a compendium of EMF studies, powerline hazards, cellular phones, and electrical sensitivity. The quarterly journal *Network News* is included in a $50 annual membership ($60 outside the United States) or by subscription, $35 annually ($45 outside the United States). Contact Cathy Bergman-Venezia, president.

Massachusetts Breast Cancer Coalition (MBCC), 85 Merrimac Street, Boston, MA 02114; (800) 649-MBCC or (617) 624-0180, fax (617) 624-0176. The MBCC is committed to the prevention, cure, and ultimate eradication of breast cancer through activism, advocacy, and education. The organization presents and promotes various public awareness and educational programs, coordinates drives to increase funding for research, and focuses attention on the potential environmental links to breast cancer. Membership brochures are available on request. A suggested $25 annual membership fee includes a subscription to the quarterly newsletter *Stop the Epidemic!*

Women's Environment and Development Organization (WEDO), 845 Third Avenue, 15th Floor, New York, NY 10022; (212) 759-7982, fax (212) 759-8647. WEDO is an international activist, advocacy, and information network of 20,000 people worldwide. Its "Action for Cancer Prevention" campaign focuses on communicating information relevant to environmental connections to cancer. WEDO facilitates links between scientists, activists, and policymakers and responds to requests for information about public hearings. For information about obtaining briefing guides related to breast cancer and the environment; transcripts of public hearings on issues of breast cancer and the environment; or WEDO's Newsline publication, which updates cancer/environmental issues, contact Pamela Ransom. Costs will vary.

MAMMOGRAPHY AND OTHER BREAST SCREENINGS

National Cancer Institute (NCI), (800) 4-CANCER. Call for the nearest certified mammography provider or to check the status of your imaging center.

BREAST CANCER

A number of these listings have been adapted from the 1994–95 NABCO *Breast Cancer Resource List* and appear here with NABCO's permission. This list is revised annually and can be ordered for $3.00 by sending a check and a self-addressed mailing label to National Alliance of Breast Cancer Organizations at 9 East 37th St., 10th floor, NY, NY, 10016.

American Cancer Society; 800-ACS-2345. This national, toll-free hotline offers information on all forms of cancer and referrals for the ACS-sponsored "Reach to Recovery" program for breast cancer. Pamphlets such as *Breast*

Cancer Network Update, and *Breast Cancer Questions and Answers,* may be obtained by calling a local ACS chapter or state division, or the hotline.

The Cancer Information Service of the National Cancer Institute (NCI); (800) 4-CANCER. Offers information and direction on all aspects of cancer through its regional network. Provides free informational brochures and refers callers to medical centers and clinical trial programs. Spanish-speaking staff members are available.

NABCO, 9 East 37th Street, 10th Floor, New York, NY 10016; (212) 719-0154, is a nonprofit, national central resource for information about breast cancer. NABCO acts as an advocate for breast cancer patients' and survivors' legislative and regulatory concerns. Organizations and individuals who join NABCO's information network receive the quarterly NABCO *News,* customized information packets, the *Breast Cancer Resource List,* and special mailings. Annual membership is $40, tax deductible. For more information, write to NABCO at the address above.

Note: You may find different divisions or aspects of these major organizations in the listings below. They, along with other specialized organizations, were established to help you enter the company of smart, courageous women, at a time when you may feel alone.

WHERE TO FIND HELP

Risk Counseling

Strang Cancer Prevention Center, 428 East 72nd Street, New York, NY 10021; (800) 521-9356 or (212) 794-4900. Strang is a free national resource for breast cancer risk counseling and research into breast cancer risk. Strang operates a National High Risk Registry for purposes of research and educating participants. It also publishes a newsletter.

Memorial Sloan-Kettering Cancer Center, 205 East 64th Street, New York, NY 10021; (212) 639-5250. Memorial's service includes high-risk screening, genetic counseling, educational, and nutritional guidelines.

Women at Risk, Columbia-Presbyterian Medical Center, Breast Service, 161 Fort Washington Avenue, New York, NY 10032; (212) 305-9926. A research, diagnosis and treatment group for women at high risk of developing breast cancer.

IF YOU ARE DIAGNOSED

Planning Treatment

American College of Surgeons, 55 East Erie Street, Chicago, IL 60611; (312) 664-4050. Provides names of certified surgeons specializing in breast surgery, by geographical area.

American Medical Center (AMC) Cancer Information and Counseling Line; (800) 525-3777. Professional cancer counselors offer easy-to-understand answers to questions about cancer, provide advice and support, and will mail instructive free publications upon request. Equipped for deaf and hearing-impaired callers. Call weekdays, 8:30 AM to 5 PM, MST.

The Cancer Information Service of the National Cancer Institute (NCI); (800) 4-CANCER. As previously mentioned, information and direction on all aspects of cancer is provided through the NCI's national and regional networks. A Spanish-speaking staff member is available on request.

CANCERFAX; (301) 402-5874 or (800) 4-CANCER. This service allows access to the NCI's Physicians Data Query (PDQ) system by fax, 24 hours a day, 7 days a week, at no charge other than the charge for the fax call. Two versions of treatment information are available: one for health-care professionals and the other for patients, their families, or the general public. Information is also available in Spanish. Call for instructions and a list of necessary codes.

CANHELP, 3111 Paradise Bay Road, Port Ludlow, WA 98365-9771; (360) 437-2291 or (360) 437-9384. Will assist patients in making treatment choices by researching treatment options (including alternative therapies) based on your medical records. A personalized 10-15–page packet will be mailed within seven working days for $400. For emergency service (two working days) the cost is $550. Contact CANHELP to request information.

Clinical Trials Information Project (CTIP), P.O. Box 1551, Danville, CA 94526-1551; (510) 736-8155, fax (510) 736-2836, E-mail: info@ctip.org Answers requests for information about breast cancer clinical trials and research studies. CTIP explains what trials are, what questions to ask, and how to find out more. Directories of trials are available for selected regions.

Foundation for Informed Medical Decision Making, Inc., P.O. Box 5457, Hanover, NH 03755-5457; (603) 650-1180, fax (603) 650-1125, E-mail: 2ShareDecisions@dartmouth.edu This not-for-profit corporation has designed a set of computer and video programs, *Treating Your Breast Cancer: The Surgery Decision* and *Treating Your Breast Cancer: Adjuvant Therapy*, each to be used by a woman when planning her treatment. The 60-minute computer aspect of a program is an interactive disk that must be purchased by a physician who can enter in the specifics of a woman's condition. By using a customized computer program, a woman gains a precise understanding of the treatment options open to her. The 45- to 60- minute take-home video explores treatment options and contains interviews with women who have experienced the benefits and/or risks of different treatments. A woman may contact the Foundation for information on purchasing a video of a program ($49.95 each, plus shipping and handling) and suggest that her doctor contact the Foundation for information (cost, shipping, handling) on the computer aspect.

The Komen Alliance, The Susan G. Komen Breast Cancer Foundation, Occidental Tower, 5005 LBJ Freeway, Suite 370 LB74, Dallas, TX 75244; (214) 450-1777 or (800) I'M AWARE. This is a comprehensive program for the research, education, diagnosis, and treatment of breast disease. Call or write for information on screening, BSE, treatment, and support. The booklet *Caring for Your Breasts* is also available on audio cassette.

National Consortium of Breast Centers, P.O. Box 1334, Warsaw, IN 46581-1334; (219) 267-8058, fax (219) 267-8268. Requests for locations of breast centers must be made by geographical area. The consortium will provide a list of those breast centers in their registry in the requested area.

Alternative Medicine

Office of Alternative Medicine, Information Center, OAM/NIH, 6120 Executive Boulevard, Suite 450, Executive Plaza South, Rockville, MD 20892-9904; (301) 402-2466. At the National Institutes of Health the OAM investigates alternative medical treatments, helps integrate effective treatment into mainstream medical practice, and offers information packages.

Planetree Health Resource Center, 2040 Webster Street, San Francisco, CA 94115; (415) 923-3680, fax (415) 673-7650. A nonprofit, consumer-oriented center that houses a medical library open to the public. The center offers information on conventional medical and alternative health treatments, and prepares personalized packets of information for you. Write, phone, or fax to request a brochure, catalog, and price list.

Healthy Eating

American Institute for Cancer Research (AICR), 1759 R Street, NW, Washington, DC 20009; (800) 843-8114, fax (202) 328-7226. Established to provide information on cancer and nutrition, AICR publishes a newsletter, cookbooks, and a series of brochures. Especially valuable are the diet/nutrition brochures. Write to order written materials or a publications list. Callers who phone the hotline with nutrition-related cancer inquiries will be connected with a registered dietitian.

Garlic Information Center at New York Hospital–Cornell Medical Center; (800) 330-5922. Provides information about the role of garlic in preventing, treating, and managing disease, as well as information on garlic supplements.

Transportation

Airlifeline, 6133 Freeport Boulevard, Sacramento, CA 95822; (800) 446-1231, fax (916) 429-2166. This is a free nationwide service for flying qualified patients to treatment sites within a 500- to 700-mile radius.

Corporate Angel Network, Inc. (CAN), Westchester County Airport, Building 1, White Plains, NY 10604; (914) 328-1313. A nationwide program designed to give patients with cancer the use of available seats on corporate aircraft to get to and from recognized treatment centers. There is no cost or any financial need requirement.

Drugs

American Association of Retired People (AARP), Pharmacy Service, Catalog Dept., P.O. Box 19229, Alexandria, VA 22320. Members can use their nonprofit service to save on prescriptions delivered by mail. Good for tamoxifen (Novaldex). Write for a free catalog.

American Preferred Prescription, (800) 227-1195; **BioLogics—The RX Resource**, (800) 850-4036; and **Medi-Express RX**, (800) 873-9773, fax (516) 625-6099. These are services for ordering medications by mail. Bio-Logics specializes in hard to find and difficult to afford medication; Medi-Express RX specializes in oncology products. Each service has different policies regarding insurance, payment, and shipping. Call each company directly for more information.

Bristol-Myers Indigent Patient Assistance Program, Bristol-Myers Oncology Division, 2400 Lloyd Expressway, Evansville, IN 47721; (812) 429-5000. Provides chemotherapy (Cytoxan) free of charge to patients with financial need. Request must be made by patient's physician.

Zeneca Pharmaceutical Foundation, Patient Assistance Program. Contact Yvonne Graham at P.O. Box 15197, Wilmington, DE 19850-5197; (800) 424-3727. Provides tamoxifen to patients with financial need. Write or call for an application.

Your Appearance

American Hair Loss Council; (800) 274-8717. Call the hotline for information on hair loss.

Edith Imre Foundation for Loss of Hair, 30 West 57th Street, New York, NY 10019; (212) 757-8160, Wig Hotline (212) 765-8397, fax (212) 956-1769. Provides counseling and support as well as a selection of appropriate wigs. Patients can request financial assistance through their physicians.

External Reconstruction Technology, Inc., 4835 Benner Street, Philadelphia, PA 19135; (215) 333-8424, fax (215) 333-8808. External breast reconstruction is a nonsurgical procedure that sculpts a breast from a cast of your body and then colors it to match your skin tone. Write, phone, or fax for more information.

Look Good ... Feel Better; (800) 395-LOOK or (800) ACS-2345. This is a public service program sponsored by the Cosmetic, Toiletry and Fragrance Association Foundation in partnership with the ACS and the National Cosmetology Association to help women recovering from cancer handle changes in their appearance resulting from cancer treatment. The program's print and videotape materials are available both to patients and health care professionals. Instructional sessions run by ACS are offered in a number of locations. Written material and program also available in Spanish. Phone for information.

Y-ME Prosthesis and Wig Bank; (800) 221-2141. Y-ME maintains a prosthesis and wig bank for women in financial need. If the appropriate size is available, Y-ME will mail a wig and/or breast prosthesis anywhere in the country. A nominal handling fee is requested. Phone for information.

Lymphedema

The National Lymphedema Network, 2211 Post Street, Suite 404, San Francisco, CA 94115; (800) 541-3259, fax (415) 921-4284. This nonprofit organization provides patients and professionals with information about prevention and treatment of primary and secondary lymphedema, the latter resulting from complications of lymph node surgery.

Managing Pain

Cancer Care's Pain Resource Center, 1180 Avenue of the Americas, New York, NY 10036; (212) 221-3300. This is a program of Cancer Care, Inc. The center helps patients, their families, and health-care professionals learn the facts about cancer pain and its treatment by providing direct services, written materials, presentations, and referrals. Call or write for information.

Bone Marrow Transplants

The BMT Newsletter, 1985 Spruce Avenue, Highland Park, IL 60035;

(708) 831-1913, fax (847) 831-1943, is a bimonthly newsletter for bone marrow and peripheral stem cell transplant patients. A 157-page *Bone Marrow Transplants* book describing physical and emotional aspects of BMTs and PBSCTs is free to patients. The book *Mira's Month* ($5) helps prepare a young child for a parent's transplant. An attorney referral service to help resolve insurance problems and a "patient-to-survivor" telephone link are also available. Call 24 hours a day or leave a message on voice mail.

Chemocare; (800) 55-CHEMO, in New Jersey (908) 233-1103, fax (908) 233-0228. This national organization matches a patient or family with a volunteer who has survived a similar diagnosis.

National Bone Marrow Transplant Link, 29209 Northwestern Highway, #624, Southfield, MI 48034; (810) 932-8483 or (800) 825-2536. An information clearinghouse on bone marrow transplants with an additional service of linking women and family members with others who have been involved in the high-dose chemotherapy experience.

Plastic Surgery/Reconstruction

Einstein Direct, Albert Einstein Breast Cancer Program, 5401 Old York Road, Philadelphia, PA 19141; (215) 456-7383, fax (215) 456-3936. This support program, formerly called RENU, is staffed by trained volunteers who have had postmastectomy reconstruction. Hotline counseling and written materials are available.

American Society of Plastic and Reconstructive Surgeons, 444 East Algonquin Road, Arlington Heights, IL 60005; (708) 228-9900, (800) 635-0635 (referral message tape). Will provide written information and mail a list of certified reconstructive surgeons by geographical area after caller provides details on above (800) message tape.

Questions About Breast Implants

The Breast Implant Information Network, (800) 887-6828. Offers assistance and information to women who have, or are considering, breast implants. Material packets and newsletters available.

Claims Assistance Counsel, (513) 651-9770, fax (513) 621-6420. A group of court-appointed attorneys who provide assistance and information to women involved in legal issues relating to breast implants.

Emotional Support

Cancer Care, Inc. and the National Cancer Care Foundation, 1180 Avenue of the Americas, New York, NY 10036; (212) 221-3300, fax (212) 719-0263. A social service agency that helps patients and their families cope with the impact of cancer. Direct services are limited to the greater New York area, but callers will be referred to similar assistance available in their areas.

The Cancer Wellness Center/The Barbara Kassel Brotman House, 215 Revere Drive, Northbrook, IL 60062; (708) 509-9595, fax (708) 509-9596. Offers free emotional support to all cancer patients and families/significant others through its 24-hour hotline, support groups, relaxation/visualization groups, educational workshops, and library.

Chemocare; (800) 55-CHEMO, in New Jersey (908) 233-1103, fax (908) 233-0228. A national agency that provides one-to-one emotional support by matching a cancer patient or family with a volunteer who has had a similar diagnosis. Services are free and confidential.

The National Coalition for Cancer Survivorship, 1010 Wayne Avenue, 5th Floor, Silver Spring, MD 20910; (301) 650-8878, fax (301) 565-9670. A national network of independent groups and individuals concerned with survivorship and sources of support for cancer patients and their families. NCCS is a clearinghouse of information and an advocacy group for cancer survivors.

Reach to Recovery; (800) ACS-2345. A program of the American Cancer Society. Trained volunteers, who themselves have had breast cancer, visit newly diagnosed women to offer information and support. Call to request a visit.

The Wellness Community, 2716 Ocean Park Boulevard, Suite 1040, Santa Monica, CA 90405; (310) 314-2555, fax (310) 314-7586. Provides extensive support and educational programs that encourage emotional recovery and a feeling of wellness. All services are free. Contact The Wellness Community for information on several different locations around the country.

Y-ME National Breast Cancer Organization, 212 West Van Buren Street, Chicago, IL 60607, (312) 986-8338, fax (312) 986-0020. National Hotline (800) 221-2141 (weekdays 9 AM to 5 PM CST); 24-hour Hotline (312) 986-8228. Trained volunteers, most of whom have had breast cancer, are matched by background and experience to callers whenever possible. Y-ME offers information on establishing local support groups and has chapters in 12 states in addition to their Illinois home office. Y-ME also has started a hotline for partners.

REGIONAL SUPPORT GROUPS

NABCO maintains a comprehensive list of regional support groups for breast cancer survivors. The *Breast Cancer Resource List* can be obtained by sending a self-addressed mailing label and a check for $3 to NABCO, 9 East 37th Street, 10th Floor, New York, NY 10016. A woman may also be able to locate a local support group by contacting the American Cancer Society chapter in her area for a referral.

Emotional Support and Exercise

The YWCA of the USA, Encore Plus Program; (202) 628-3636 or (800) 95E-PLUS, fax (202) 783-7123. Provides supportive discussion and rehabilitative exercise for women who have been treated for breast cancer. Women receive information and referrals for breast screenings, peer group support, and land and water exercise.

Money Problems

Affording Care, 429 East 52nd Street, Suite 4G, New York, NY 10022-6431; (212) 371-4740. This not-for-profit organization provides financial information for coping with serious illness or injury. Seminars for patients and their advisors are offered. Free newsletter.

10 TOP COMPREHENSIVE BREAST CANCER CENTERS

Women may locate major Cancer Centers rigorously reviewed and supported by the National Cancer Institute by calling (800) 4-CANCER. In addition, in recent years a number of major medical hospitals and cancer centers have organized Comprehensive Breast Cancer Centers which provide all the services a woman needs under one roof. Breast screening, diagnosis, and treatment are performed by staff specialists. A woman who has been diagnosed with breast cancer works with a team of doctors she can call her own: a pathologist, breast surgeon, radiation oncologist, breast oncologist, genetic counselor, even psychological and nutritional counselors are available to her. Many women prefer this new approach to breast health care. Because space permits a limited listing, ten of the Top Comprehensive Breast Cancer Centers in the United States are shown below, alphabetically:

> **The Breast Center,** 14624 Sherman Way, Suite 600, Van Nuys, CA 91405; (818) 787-9911.
>
> **Comprehensive Breast Center at the Lombardi Cancer Center, Georgetown University Medical Center**, 3800 Reservoir Road NW, Washington, DC 20007; (202) 687-2122.

Dana Farber Cancer Institute Breast Evaluation Center (BEC), 44 Binney Street, Boston, MA 02115; (617) 632-3000.

Evelyn H. Lauder Breast Center/Iris B. Cantor Diagnostic Center of Memorial Sloan-Kettering Cancer Center, 205 East 64th Street, New York, NY 10021; (212) 639-5200.

The Mayo Clinic's Breast Clinic, 200 First Street SW, Rochester, MN 55905; (507) 284-9238.

Myer L. Prentis Comprehensive Cancer Center of Metropolitan Detroit, 110 East Warren Avenue, Detroit, MI 48201; (313) 833-0710.

Revlon/UCLA Breast Center at Jonsson Comprehensive Cancer Center, 200 UCLA Medical Plaza, Suite 510, Los Angeles, CA 90095; (800) 825-2144, (310) 825-2144.

Lynn Sage Comprehensive Breast Center at Northwestern Memorial Hospital, 333 East Superior, Chicago, IL 60611; (312) 908-5522.

Strang-Cornell Breast Center of the Strang Cancer Prevention Center, 428 East 72nd Street, New York, NY 10021; (212) 794-4900.

University of Texas M.D. Anderson Cancer Center Breast Clinic, 1515 Holcombe Boulevard, Houston, TX 77030; (800) 392-1611.

Activism

The National Breast Cancer Coalition (NBCC), 1707 L Street NW, Suite 1060, Washington, DC 20036; (202) 296-7477, fax (202) 265-6854. Although each individual can become active through contacting her elected officials, the most effective way a woman can help to change policy is to take part in a national movement. The National Breast Cancer Coalition was formed in 1991 as a public policy effort to involve women with breast cancer and those who care about them in changing public policy. The NBCC's goals include increasing breast cancer research funding and improving access to screening, increasing the influence that breast cancer survivors have over research, clinical trials, and national policy, and care for all women. The NBCC welcomes individuals as members of its National Action Network, and organizations that wish to join its more than 300 current member organizations and thousands of individuals. Many of the NBCC's members are local coalitions in more than a dozen states.

Bibliography

PART I—HEALTHY BREASTS ARE ALWAYS CHANGING

Chapter One—Understanding the Basics: Your Breasts Over Your Lifetime

Kitzinger, S. *Woman's Experience of Sex: The Facts and Feelings of Female Sexuality at Every Stage of Life.* New York: Penguin Books, 1985.

Lauersen, N.H., and E. Stukane. *Listen To Your Body.* New York: Simon and Schuster, 1982.

Love, S.M. *Dr. Susan Love's Breast Book,* 2nd ed. New York: Addison-Wesley Publishing, 1995.

Redmond, G. *The Good News About Women's Hormones.* New York: Warner Books, 1995.

Chapter Two—Transformed During Pregnancy and Breastfeeding: Your Breasts Are (Possibly) Better Off Afterward

Brinton, L.A. "Ways That Women May Possibly Reduce Their Risk of Breast Cancer." *Journal of the National Cancer Institute* 86 (1994): 1371–1372.

Gold, M. "Improving Skills to Support Breastfeeding." *The Female Patient* 19 (1994): 35–48.

Lambe, M., C. Hsieh, D. Trichopoulos, et al. "Transient Increase in the Risk of Breast Cancer After Giving Birth." *New England Journal of Medicine* 331 (1994): 5–9.

Levine, I.L., and N.T. Ilowite. "Sclerodermalike Esophageal Disease in Children Breastfed by Mothers with Silicone Breast Implants." *Journal of the American Medical Association* 271 (1994): 213–216.

London, S.J. "Breast-Feeding and Breast Cancer." *New England Journal of Medicine* 330 (1994): 1682.

London, S.J., G.A. Colditz, M.J. Stampfer, et al. "Lactation and Risk of Breast Cancer in a Cohort of U.S. Women." *American Journal of Epidemiology* 132 (1990): 17–25.

Mennella, J.A., and G.K. Beauchamp. "Maternal Diet Alters the Sensory Qualities of Human Milk and the Nursling's Behavior." *Pediatrics* 88 (1991): 737–744.

Newcomb, P.A., B.E. Storer, M.P. Longnecker, et al. "Lactation and a Reduced Risk of Premenopausal Breast Cancer." *New England Journal of Medicine* 330 (1994): 81–87.

Throen, H. "Pregnancy Affects Breast Cancer Survival." *Ob Gyn News*, September 1994, 17.

PART II—YOU CAN PROTECT YOUR BREASTS

Chapter Three—A Breast Self-Examination: When You Have a Good Teacher, You *Can* Overcome Your Ambivalence

Baines, C.J., and T. To. "Changes in Breast Self-Examination Behavior Achieved by 89,835 Participants in the Canadian National Breast Screening Study." *Cancer* 66 (1990): 570–576.

Gastrin, G., A.B. Miller, T. To, et al. "Incidence and Mortality from Breast Cancer in the Mama Program for Breast Screening in Finland, 1973–1986." *Cancer* 73 (1994): 2168–2174.

Morrison, A.S. "Is Self-Examination Effective in Screening for Breast Cancer?" *Journal of the National Cancer Institute* 83 (1991): 226–227.

Newcomb, P.A., N.A. Weiss, B.F. Storer, et al. "Breast Self-Examination in Relation to the Occurrence of Advanced Breast Cancer." *Journal of the National Cancer Institute* 83 (1991): 260–265.

Semiglazov, V.F., V.M. Moiseyenko, J.L. Bavil, et al. "The Role of Breast Self-Examination in Early Breast Cancer Detection (Results of the 5-Year USSR/WHO Randomized Study in Leningrad)." *European Journal of Epidemiology* 8 (1992): 498–502.

Semiglazov, V.F., V.N. Segaidak, V.M. Moiseyenko, et al. "Study of the Role of Breast Self-Examination in the Reduction of Mortality from Breast Cancer." *European Journal of Cancer* 29A (1993): 2039–2046.

Utian, W.H., T.B. Ades, A.U. Buzdar, et al. "Overcoming Your Patients' Fear of Breast Cancer." *Menopause Management*, November/December 1994, 18–28.

Chapter Four—When to Have a Mammogram: A Recommended Timetable

Baker, B. "Swedish Study Indicates Mammographies Benefit Women in Their 40's." *Ob Gyn News*, July 1994, 17.

Bassett, L.W., R.E. Hendrick, T.L Bassford., et al. *Quality Determinants of Mammography, Clinical Practice Guideline, No. 13.* AHCPR Publication No. 95-0632. Rockville, MD: Agency for Health Care Policy and Research, Public Health Service, U.S. Department of Health and Human Services, October 1994.

Beghe, C., L. Balducci, and H. Cohen. "Secondary Prevention of Breast Cancer in the Older Woman: Issues Related to Screening." *Cancer Control,* July/August 1994, 320–326.

BEIR 5. *Health Effects of Exposure to Low Levels of Ionizing Radiation.* Washington, D.C.: National Academy Press, 1990.

Black, W.C., R.F. Nease, Jr., and A.N.A. Tosteson. "Perceptions of Breast Cancer Risk and Screening Effectiveness in Women Younger Than 50 Years of Age." *Journal of the National Cancer Institute* 87 (1995): 720–726.

Boyd, N.F., J.W. Byng, R.A. Jong, et al. "Quantitative Classification of Mammographic Densities and Breast Cancer Risk: Results from the Canadian National Breast Screening Study." *Journal of the National Cancer Institute* 87 (1995): 670–675.

Byrne, C., C. Schairer, J. Wolfe, et al. "Mammographic Features and Breast Cancer Risk: Effects with Time, Age, and Menopause Status." *Journal of the National Cancer Institute* 87 (1995): 1622–1629.

Cady, B. "Approach to Mammographically Discovered Small Breast Cancer." *The Breast Journal* 2 (1996): 56–58.

Carroll, L. "New Data Back Mammograms in Women 40 to 49." *Medical Tribune* 1, December 1994 1.

de Koning, H.J., R. Boer, P.G. Warmerdam, et al. "Quantitative Interpretation of Age-Specific Mortality Reductions from the Swedish Breast Cancer Screening Trials." *Journal of the National Cancer Institute* 87 (1995): 1217–1223.

Elmore, J., C. Wells, C. Lee, et al. "Variability in Radiologists' Interpretations of Mammograms." *New England Journal of Medicine* 331 (1994): 1493–1499.

Faulkner, K., K.J. Robson, C.J. Kotre. "X-ray Mammography and Breast Compression." *Lancet* 340 (1992): 797–798.

Feig, S.A. "Determination of Mammographic Screening Intervals with Surrogate Measures for Women Aged 40–49 Years." *Radiology* 193 (1994): 311–314.

Fletcher, S.W., W. Black, R. Harris, et al. "Report of the International Workshop on Screening for Breast Cancer." *Journal of the National Cancer Institute* 85 (1993): 1644–1656.

Kaluzny, A.D., B. Rimer, and R. Harris. "The National Cancer Institute and Guideline Development: Lessons from the Breast Cancer Screening Controversy." *Journal of the National Cancer Institute* 86 (1994): 901–902.

Kopans, D.B. "The Accuracy of Mammographic Interpretations." *New England Journal of Medicine* 331 (1994): 1521–1522.

Miller, A.B. "The Role of Screening in the Fight Against Breast Cancer." *World Health Forum* 13 (1992): 277–285.

Scarbeck, K. "Quality of a Mammography Could Get Boost from Guidelines." *Ob Gyn News*, December 1994.

Swanson, G.M. "May We Agree to Disagree, or How Do We Develop Guidelines for Breast Cancer Screening in Women?" *Journal of the National Cancer Institute* 86 (1994): 903–905.

Thurfjell, E.L., and J.A.A. Lindgren. "Population-Based Mammography Screening in Swedish Clinical Practice: Prevalence and Incidence Screening in Uppsala County." *Radiology* 193 (1994): 351–357.

Vogel, V.G. "Mammographic Screening in Younger Women." *The Female Patient* 18 (1993): 21–27.

Watmough, D.J. "Breast Compression to Increase the Sensitivity of Lightscanning for the Detection of Carcinoma: Potential Hazard?" *Journal of Biomedical Engineering* 14 (1992): 173–174.

Watmough, D.J., K.M. Quan, and R.M. Aspden. "Breast Compression: A Preliminary Study." *Journal of Biomedical Engineering* 15 (1993): 121–126.

Chapter Five—Beyond Mammography: Other High-Tech Breast Tests You May Want

Gordon, P.B., and S.L. Goldenberg. "Malignant Breast Masses Detected Only by Ultrasound: A Retrospective Review." *Cancer* 76 (1995): 626–633.

Harms, S.E., and D.P. Flamig. "MR Imaging of the Breast: Technical Approach and Clinical Experience." *Radiographics* 13 (1993): 905–912.

Harms, S.E., and D.P. Flamig. "Present and Future Role of MR Imaging." *RSNA Categorical Course in Physics* (1994): 255–261.

Harms, S.E., and D.P. Flamig. "Staging of Breast Cancer with MR Imaging." *MRI Clinics of North America* 2 (1994): 573–584.

Harms, S.E., D.P. Flamig, W.P. Evans, et al. "MR Imaging of the Breast: Current Status and Future Potential." *American Journal of Roentgenology* 163 (1994): 1039–1047.

Harms, S.E., D.P. Flamig, K.I. Hesley, et al. "Fat-Suppressed Three-Dimensional MR Imaging of the Breast." *Radiographics* 13 (1993): 247–267.

Khalkhali, I., J. Cutrone, I. Mena, et al. "The Usefulness of Scintimammography (SMM) in Patients with Dense Breasts on Mammogram." *Journal of Nuclear Medicine* 36 (1995): 52.

Khalkhali, I., I. Mena, and I. Diggles. "Review of Imaging Techniques for the Diagnosis of Breast Cancer: A New Role of Prone Scintimammography Using Technetium-99m Sestamibi." *European Journal of Nuclear Medicine* 21 (1994): 357–362.

Khalkhali, I., I. Mena, F. Jouanne, et al. "Prone Scintimammography in Patients with Suspicion of Carcinoma of the Breast." *Journal of the American College of Surgeons* 178 (1994): 491–497.

Spieth, M., P. Vasinrapee, T. Evans, et al. "Spect Scintimammography for Lymphohadenopathy: Preliminary Clinical Findings." *Journal of Nuclear Medicine* 36 (1995): 52.

Taillefer, R., A. Robidoux, R. Lambert, et al. "99mTc-Sestamibi Prone Scinti-mammography in Detection of Primary Breast Cancer and Axillary Lymph Node Involvement." *Journal of Nuclear Medicine* 36 (1995): 52.

Weiss, B.A., G.A.P. Ganepola, H.P. Freeman, et al. "Surface Electrical Potentials as a New Modality in the Diagnosis of Breast Lesions: A Preliminary Report." *Breast Disease* 7 (1994): 91–98.

Chapter Six—Yes, You Can Eat to Keep Your Breasts Healthy: The Latest on Foods That Fight Illness

Abrams, A.A. "Use of Vitamin E in Chronic Cystic Mastitis." *New England Journal of Medicine* 272 (1965): 1080–1081.

Adlercreutz, H., T. Fotsis, C. Bannwart, et al. "Determination of Urinary Lignans and Phytoestrogen Metabolites, Potential Antiestrogens and Anticarcinogens in Urine of Women on Various Habitual Diets." *Journal of Steroid Biochemistry and Molecular Biology* 25 (1986): 791–797.

Adlercreutz, H., S.I. Gorbach, B.R. Goldin, et al. "Estrogen Metabolism and Excretion in Oriental and Caucasian Women." *Journal of the National Cancer Institute* 86 (1994): 1076–1082.

Adlercreutz, H., K. Hockerstedt, C. Bannwart, et al. "Effect of Dietary Components, Including Lignans and Phytoestrogens, on Enterohepatic Circulation and Liver Metabolism of Estrogens and on Sex Hormone Binding Globulin (SHBG)." *Journal of Steroid Biochemistry and Molecular Biology* 27 (1987): 1135–1144.

Allen, D.S., R.D. Bulbrook, M.A. Chaudary, et al. "Recurrence and Survival Rates in British and Japanese Women with Breast Cancer." *Breast Cancer Research and Treatment* 18 (1991): S131–S134.

Allen, S.S., and D.G. Froberg. "The Effect of Decreased Caffeine Consumption on Benign Proliferative Breast Disease: A Randomized Clinical Trial." *Surgery* 101 (1986): 720–730.

Armstrong, B.K., and R. Doll. "Environmental Factors and Cancer Incidence and Mortality in Different Countries, with Special Reference to Dietary Practices." *International Journal of Cancer* 15 (1975): 617–631.

Baghurst, K.I., and S.I. Record. "Fibre Consumption in the Australian Population: Results from a Recent Random Survey of the Victorian Population." *Proceedings of a Workshop on Chemistry and Nutritional Effects of Dietary Fibre.* Canberra, December 1991, 7–8.

Baghurst, P.A., and T.E. Rohan. "High-Fiber Diets and Reduced Risk of Breast Cancer." *International Journal of Cancer* 56 (1994): 173–176.

Barrett-Connor, E., and N.J. Friedlander. "Dietary Fat, Calories, and the Risk of Breast Cancer in Postmenopausal Women: A Prospective Population-Based Study." *Journal of the American College of Nutrition* 12 (1993): 390–399.

Bernstein, L., and R.K. Ross. "Endogenous Hormones and Breast Cancer Risk." *Epidemiologic Reviews* 15 (1993): 48–65.

Blot, W.J. "Alcohol and Cancer." *Cancer Research* 52 (1992): 2119S–2123S.

Blot, W.J., J.Y. Li, P.R. Taylor, et al. "Nutrition Intervention Trials in Linxian, China: Supplementation with Specific Vitamin/Mineral Combinations, Cancer Incidence, and Disease-Specific Mortality in the General Population." *Journal of the National Cancer Institute* 85 (1993): 1483–1492.

Boyd, N.F., L.J. Matin, M. Noffel, et al. "A Meta-Analysis of Studies of Dietary Fat and Breast Cancer Risk." *British Journal of Cancer* 68 (1993): 627–636.

Braden, L.M., and K.K. Carroll. "Dietary Polyunsaturated Fat in Relation to Mammary Carcinogenesis in Rats." *Lipids* 21 (1986): 285–288.

Bradlow, H.L., D.L. Davis, G. Lin, et al. "Effects of Pesticides on the Ratio of 16a/2-hydroxyestrone: A Biologic Marker of Breast Cancer Risk." Strang-Cornell Cancer Research Lab, New York, 1995.

Bradlow, H.L., J.J. Michnovicz, M. Halper, et al. "Long-Term Responses of Women to Indole-3-carbinol or a High Fiber Diet." *Cancer Epidemiology, Biomarkers and Prevention* 3 (1994): 591–595.

Brinton, L. "Ways That Women May Possibly Reduce Their Risk of Breast Cancer." *Journal of the National Cancer Institute* 86 (1994): 1371–1372.

Carroll, K.K. "Experimental Evidence of Dietary Factors and Hormone-Dependent Cancers." *Cancer Research* 35 (1975): 3375–3383.

Carroll, K.K. "Experimental Studies on Dietary Fat and Cancer in Relation to Epidemiological Data." In *Progress in Clinical and Biological Research, Dietary Fat and Cancer*, vol. 222, 395–408. New York: Alan R. Liss, 1986.

Carroll, K.K. "Fish Oils and Cancer. In *Health Effects of Fish and Fish Oils*, 395–408. St. John's, Newfoundland: ARTS Biomedical Publishers and Distributors, 1989.

Carroll, K.K. "Lipids and Cancer," in *Nutrition and Disease Update: Cancer*, 235–255. Champaign, Illinois: AOCS Press, 1994.

Carroll, K.K. "Nutrition and Cancer: Fat," in *Nutrition, Toxicity, and Cancer*, edited by I.R. Rowland, 439–453. Boca Raton: CRC Press, 1991.

Carroll, K.K., and H.T. Khor. "Dietary Fat in Relation to Tumorigenesis." *Progress in Biochemical Pharmacology* 10 (1975): 308–353.

Carroll, K.K., and H.T. Khor. "Effects of Level and Type of Dietary Fat on Incidence of Mammary Tumors Induced in Female Sprague-Dawley Rats by 7,12-dimethylbenz(a)anthracene." *Lipids* 6 (1971): 415–420.

Cassidy, A., S. Bingham, and K.D. Setchell. "Biological Effects of a Diet of Soy Protein Rich in Isoflavones on the Menstrual Cycle of Premenopausal Women." *American Journal of Clinical Nutrition* 60 (1994): 333–340.

Cauley, J.A., J.P. Gautal, L.H. Kuller, et al. "The Epidemiology of Serum Sex Hormones in Postmenopausal Women." *American Journal of Epidemiology* 129 (1989): 1120–1131.

Chlebowski, R.T., G.L. Blackburn, I.M. Buzzard, et al. "Adherence to a Dietary Fat Intake Reduction Program in Postmenopausal Women Receiving Therapy for Early Breast Cancer." *Journal of Clinical Oncology* 11 (1993): 2072–2080.

Clark, L.C., and D.S. Alberts. "Selenium and Cancer: Risk or Protection?" *Journal of the National Cancer Institute* 87 (1995): 473–475.

Cohen, L.A., M.E. Kendall, E. Zang, et al. "Modulation of N-nitrosomethylurea-Induced Mammary Tumor Promotion by Dietary Fiber and Fat." *Journal of the National Cancer Institute* 83 (1991): 496–501.

Cohen, L.A., D.P. Rose, E.L. Wynder, et al. "A Rationale for Dietary Intervention in Postmenopausal Breast Cancer Patients: An Update." *Nutrition and Cancer* 19 (1993): 1–10.

Cohen, L.A., and E.L. Wynder. "Do Dietary Monosaturated Fatty Acids Play a Protective Role in Carcinogenesis and Cardiovascular Disease?" *Medical Hypotheses* 31 (1990): 83–89.

Colditz, G.A. "Epidemiology of Breast Cancer: Findings from the Nurses' Health Study." *Cancer* 71 (1993): 1480–1489.

Colditz, G.A., M.J. Stampfer, W.C. Willett, et al. "Prospective Study of Estrogen Replacement Therapy and Risk of Breast Cancer in Postmenopausal Women." *Journal of the American Medical Association* 264 (1990): 2648–2653.

Comstock, G.W., T.L. Bush, and K. Helzlsouer. "Serum Retinol, Beta-Carotene, Vitamin E, and Selenium as Related to Subsequent Cancer of Specific Sites." *American Journal of Epidemiology* 135 (1992): 115–121.

Dorant, E., P.A. van den Brandt, R.A. Goldbohm, et al. "Garlic and Its Significance for the Prevention of Cancer in Humans: A Critical View." *British Journal of Cancer* 67 (1993): 424–429.

Dorgan, J., M.E. Reichman, J.T. Judd, et al. "The Relation of Reported Alcohol Ingestion to Plasma Levels of Estrogens and Androgens in Premenopausal Women." *Cancer Causes and Control* 5 (1994): 53–60.

Drukker, B.H. "Fibrocystic Change of the Breast." *Clinical Obstetrics and Gynecology* 37 (1994): 903–915.

Dupont, W.D., and D.L. Page. "Risk Factors for Breast Cancer in Women with Proliferative Breast Disease." *New England Journal of Medicine* 312 (1985): 146–151.

Dwyer, J.T., B.R. Goldin, N. Saul, et al. "Tofu and Soy Drinks Contain Phytoestrogens." *Journal of the American Dietetic Association* 94 (1994): 739–743.

Englyst, H.N., et al. "Dietary Fibre (Non-Starch Polysaccharides) in Cereal Products." *Journal of Nutrition and Dietetics* 2 (1989): 253–271.

Ernster, V.L., L. Mason, W.H. Goodson, et al. "Effects of Caffeine-Free Diet on Benign Breast Disease: A Randomized Trial." *Surgery* 91 (1982): 263–267.

Falck, F., Jr., A. Ricci, Jr., M.S. Wolff, et al. "Pesticides and Polychlorinated Biphenyl Residues in Human Breast Lipids and Their Relation to Breast Cancer." *Archives of Environmental Health* 47 (1992): 143–146.

Fosom, A.R., D.R. McKenzie, K.M. Bisgard, et al. "No Association Between Caffeine Intake and Postmenopausal Breast Cancer Incidence in the Iowa Women's Health Study." *American Journal of Epidemiology* 138 (1993): 380–383.

Freudenheim, J.L., J.R. Marshall, J.E. Vena, et al. "Premenopausal Breast Cancer

Risk and Intake of Vegetables, Fruits, and Related Nutrients." *Journal of the National Cancer Institute* 88 (1996): 340–348.

Friedenreich, C.M., G.R. Howe, A.B. Miller, et al. "A Cohort Study of Alcohol Consumption and Risk of Breast Cancer." *American Journal of Epidemiology* 137 (1993): 512–520.

Gapstur, S.M., J.D. Potter, T.A. Sellers, et al. "Increased Risk of Breast Cancer with Alcohol Consumption in Postmenopausal Women." *American Journal of Epidemiology* 136 (1992): 1221–1231.

Garland, M., S. Morris, M.J. Stampfer, et al. "Prospective Study of Toenail Selenium Levels and Cancer Among Women." *Journal of the National Cancer Institute* 87 (1995): 497–505.

Goldin, B.R., H. Adlercreutz, S.L. Gorbach, et al. "Estrogen Excretion Patterns and Plasma Levels in Vegetarian and Omnivorous Women." *New England Journal of Medicine* 307 (1982): 1542–1547.

Goodman, M.T., K. Mabuchi, M. Morita, et al. "Cancer Incidence in Hiroshima and Nagasaki, Japan, 1958–1987." *European Journal of Cancer* 30A (1994): 801–807.

Goodman, M.T., A.M. Nomura, L.R. Wilkens, et al. "The Association of Diet, Obesity, and Breast Cancer in Hawaii." *Cancer Epidemiological Biomarkers and Prevention* 1 (1992): 269–275.

Goodwin, P.J., and N.F. Boyd. "Critical Appraisal of the Evidence That Dietary Fat Intake Is Related to Breast Cancer Risk in Human Beings." *Journal of the National Cancer Institute* 79 (1987): 473–485.

Greenwald, P., G. Kelloff, C. Burch-Whitman, et al. "Chemoprevention." *CA: Cancer Journal for Clinicians* 45 (1995): 31–49.

Guo, W.D., W.H. Chow, W. Zheng, et al. "Diet, Serum Markers and Breast Cancer Mortality in China." *Japanese Journal of Cancer Research* 85 (1994): 572–577.

Hankinson, S.E., W.C. Willett, J.E. Manson, et al. "Alcohol, Height, and Adiposity in Relation to Estrogen and Prolactin Levels in Postmenopausal Women." *Journal of the National Cancer Institute* 87 (1995): 1297–1302.

Hems, G. "The Contributions of Diet and Child-Bearing to Breast Cancer Rates." *British Journal of Cancer* 37 (1978): 974–982.

Heyden S., and L.H. Muhlbaier. "Prospective Study of 'Fibrocystic Disease' and Caffeine Consumption." *Surgery* 96 (1984): 479–484.

Holmberg, L., E.M. Ohlander, T. Byers, et al. "Diet and Breast Cancer Risk: Results from a Population-Based, Case-Control Study in Sweden. *Archives of Internal Medicine* 154 (1994): 1805–1811.

Hopkins, G.J., and K.K. Carroll. "Relationship Between Amount and Type of Dietary Fat in Promotion of Mammary Carcinogenesis Induced by 7,12-dimethylbenz(a)anthracene." *Journal of the National Cancer Institute* 62 (1979): 1009–1012.

Howe, G.R., T. Hirohata, T.G. Hislop, et al. "Dietary Factors and Risk of Breast Cancer: Combined Analysis of 12 Case-Control Studies." *Journal of the National Cancer Institute* 82 (1990): 561–569.

Hunter, D.J., J.E. Manson, G.A. Colditz, et al. "A Prospective Study of the Intake of Vitamins C, E, and A and the Risk of Breast Cancer." *New England Journal of Medicine* 329 (1993): 234–240.

Hunter, D.J., J.E. Manson, M.J. Stampfer, et al. "A Prospective Study of Caffeine, Coffee, Tea, and Breast Cancer." *American Journal of Epidemiology* 136 (1992): 1000–1001.

Hunter D.J., J.S. Morris, M.J. Stampfer, et al. "A Prospective Study of Selenium Status and Breast Cancer Risk." *Journal of the American Medical Association* 264 (1990): 1128–1131.

Hunter, D.J., D. Spiegelman, H.O. Adami, et al. "Cohort Studies of Fat Intake and the Risk of Breast Cancer—A Pooled Analysis." *New England Journal of Medicine* 334 (1996): 356–361.

Hunter, D.J., and W.C. Willett. "Diet, Body Size, and Breast Cancer." *Epidemiologic Reviews* 15 (1993): 110–132.

Ingram, D. "Diet and Subsequent Survival in Women with Breast Cancer." *British Journal of Cancer* 69 (1994): 592–595.

Ip, C., and D.J. Lisk. "Bioavailability of Selenium from Selenium-Enriched Garlic." *Nutrition and Cancer* 20 (1993): 129–137.

Ip, C., and D.J. Lisk. "Enrichment of Selenium in Allium Vegetables for Cancer Prevention." *Carcinogenesis* 15 (1994): 1881–1885.

Jain, M., A. Miller, and T. To. "Premorbid Diet and the Prognosis of Women with Breast Cancer." *Journal of the National Cancer Institute* 86 (1994): 1390–1397.

Kardinaal, A.F.M., P. vant Veer, E.J. Kokl, et al. "Euramic Study: Antioxidants, Myocardial Infarction and Breast Cancer; Design and Main Hypothesis." *European Journal of Clinical Nutrition* 47, Suppl. 2 (1993): S64–S72.

Karmali, R.A., L. Adams, and J.R. Trout. "Plant and Marine n-3 Fatty Acids Inhibit Experimental Metastasis of Rat Mammary Adenocarcinoma Cell." *Prostaglandins Leukot Essential Fatty Acids* 48 (1993): 309–314.

Key, T., J.A. Chen, J. Wang, et al. "Sex Hormones in Women in Rural China and in Britain." *British Journal of Cancer* 62 (1990): 631–636.

Kreiger, N.K., M.S. Wolff, R.A. Hiat, et al. "Breast Cancer and Serum Organochlorines: A Prospective Study Among White, Black, and Asian Women." *Journal of the National Cancer Institute* 125 (1994) 556–561.

Li, J.Y., P.R. Taylor, B. Li, et al. "Nutrition Intervention Trials in Linxian, China: Multiple Vitamin/Mineral Supplementation, Cancer Incidence, and Disease-Specific Mortality Among Adults with Esophageal Dysplasia." *Journal of the National Cancer Institute* 85 (1993): 1492–1498.

Longnecker, M.P. "Alcoholic Beverage Consumption in Relation to Risk of Breast Cancer: Meta-Analysis and Review." *Cancer Causes and Control* 5 (1994): 73–82.

Longnecker, M.P., J.A. Berlin, M.J. Orza, et al. "A Meta-Analysis of Alcohol Consumption in Relation to Risk of Breast Cancer." *Journal of the American Medical Association* 260 (1988): 652–656.

Longnecker, M.P., P.A. Newcomb, R. Mittendorf, et al. "Risk of Breast Cancer in Relation to Lifetime Alcohol Consumption." *Journal of the National Cancer Institute* 87 (1995): 923–929.

Love, S.M., R.S. Gelman, and S. Silen. "Fibrocystic 'Disease' of the Breast—a Non-Disease. "*New England Journal of Medicine* 307 (1982): 1010–1014.

Martin-Moreno, J.M., W.C. Willett, L. Gorgojo, et al. "Dietary Fat, Olive Oil Intake and Breast Cancer Risk." *International Journal of Cancer* 58 (1994): 774–780.

Minton, J.P., H. Abou-Issa, N. Reiches, et al. "Clinical and Biochemical Studies on Methylxanthine-Related Fibrocystic Disease." *Surgery* 90 (1981): 299–304.

Minton, J.P., M.K. Foecking, D.I.T. Webster, et al. "Response of Fibrocystic Disease to Caffeine Withdrawal and Correlation of Cyclic Nucleotides with Breast Disease." *American Journal of Obstetrics and Gynecology* 135 (1979): 157–158.

Minton, J.P., T. Wisenbaugh, and R.H. Matthews. "Elevated Cyclic AMP Levels in Human Breast Tissue." *Journal of the National Cancer Institute* 5 (1974): 283–284.

Paganini-Hill, A., A. Chao, R.K. Ross, et al. "Vitamin A, B-Carotene and the Risk of Cancer: A Prospective Study." *Journal of the National Cancer Institute* 79 (1987): 443–448.

Parazzini, F., C. LaVecchia, R. Riundi, et al. "Methylxanthine, Alcohol-Free Diet and Fibrocystic Breast Disease: A Factorial Clinical Trial." *Surgery* 99 (1986): 576–581.

Pirke, K.M., U. Schweiger, R. Laessle, et al. "Dieting Influences the Menstrual Cycle: Vegetarian Versus Nonvegetarian Diet." *Fertility and Sterility* 46 (1986): 1083–1088.

Reichman, M.E., J.T. Judd, C. Longcope, et al. "Effects of Alcohol Consumption on Plasma and Urinary Hormone Concentrations in Premenopausal Women." *Journal of the National Cancer Institute* 85 (1993): 722–726.

Rose, D.P. "Diet, Hormones, and Cancer." *Annual Review of Public Health* 14 (1993): 1–17.

Rose, D.P. "Dietary Fat and Breast Cancer: Controversy and Biological Plausibility." In *Diet and Breast Cancer*, 1–17. New York: Plenum Press, 1994.

Rose, D.P. "Dietary Fiber, Phytoestrogens and Breast Cancer." *Nutrition* 8 (1992): 47–51.

Rose, D.P., A.P. Boyer, and E.L. Wynder. "International Comparison of Mortality Rates for Cancer of the Breast, Ovary, Prostate, and Colon, and per Capita Food Consumption." *Cancer* 58 (1986): 2363–2371.

Rose, D.P., M. Goldman, J.M. Connolly, et al. "High Fiber Diet Reduces Serum Estrogen Concentration in Premenopausal Women." *American Journal of Clinical Nutrition* 54 (1991): 520–525.

Savitz, D.A. "Re: Breast Cancer and Serum Organochlorines: A Prospective Study Among White, Black, and Asian Women." *Journal of the National Cancer Institute* 86 (1994): 1255–1256.

Schatzkin, A., D.Y. Jones, R.N. Hoover, et al. "Alcohol Consumption and

Breast Cancer in the Epidemiologic Follow-up Study of the First National Health and Nutrition Examination Survey." *New England Journal of Medicine* 316 (1987): 1169–1173.

Shamberger, R.L., and D.V. Frost. "Possible Protective Effect of Selenium Against Human Cancer." *Canadian Medical Association Journal* 100 (1969): 682.

Shimizu, H., R.K. Ross, L. Bernstein, et al. "Serum Oestrogen Levels in Postmenopausal Women: Comparison of American Whites and Japanese in Japan." *British Journal of Cancer* 62 (1990): 451–453.

Snowden, D.A., and R.L. Phillips. "Coffee Consumption and Risk of Fatal Cancers." *American Journal of Public Health* 74 (1984): 820–823.

Synderwine, E.G. "Some Perspectives on the Nutritional Aspects of Breast Cancer Research: Food-Derived Heterocyclic Amines as Etiologic Agents in Human Mammary Cancer." *Cancer* 74 (1994): 1070–1077.

Toniolo, P., E. Riboli, R.E. Shore, et al. "Consumption of Meat, Animal Products, Protein, and Fat and Risk of Breast Cancer: A Prospective Cohort Study in New York." *Epidemiology* 5 (1994): 391–397.

Trichopoulou, S.A., K. Katsouyanni, S. Stuver, et al. "Consumption of Olive Oil and Specific Food Groups in Relation to Breast Cancer Risk in Greece." *Journal of the National Cancer Institute* 87 (1995): 110–116.

Troll, W., R. Wiesner, C.J. Shellabarger, et al. "Soybean Diet Lowers Breast Tumor Incidence in Irradiated Rats." *Carcinogenesis* 1 (1980): 469–72.

Vatten, L.J., K.S. Bjerve, A. Andersen, et al. "Polyunsaturated Fatty Acids in Serum Phospholipids and Risk of Breast Cancer: A Case-Control Study from the Janus Serum Bank in Norway." *European Journal of Cancer* 29A (1993): 532–538.

Wang, D.Y., T.J.A. Key, M.C. Pike, et al. "Serum Hormone Levels in British and Rural Chinese Females." *Breast Cancer Research and Treatment* 18 (1991): S41–S45.

Welsch, C.W. "Caffeine and the Development of the Normal and Neoplastic Mammary Gland." *Proceedings of the Society for Experimental Biology and Medicine* 207 (1994): 1–12.

Welsch, C.W. "Interrelationship Between Dietary Lipids and Calories and Experimental Mammary Gland Tumorigenesis." *Cancer* 74 (1994): 1055–1062.

Willett, W.C. "Diet, Fat and Alcohol—Their Relationship to Breast Cancer—Epidemiological Aspects." From Palm Beach Breast Cancer Conference, February 1994, 17–19.

Willet, W.C. "The Search for the Causes of Breast and Colon Cancer." *Nature* 338 (1989): 389–394.

Willett, W.C., and D.J. Hunter. "Prospective Studies of Diet and Breast Cancer." *Cancer* 74 (1994): 1085–1089.

Willett, W.C., D.J. Hunter, M.J. Stampfer, et al. "Dietary Fat and Fiber in Relation to Risk of Breast Cancer: An 8-Year Follow-Up." *Journal of the American Medical Association* 268 (1992): 2037–2044.

Willett, W.C., M.J. Stampfer, G.A. Colditz, et al. "Moderate Alcohol Consumption and the Risk of Breast Cancer." *New England Journal of Medicine* 316 (1987): 1174–1180.

Wolff, M.S., P.G. Toniolo, E.W. Lee, et al. "Blood Levels of Organochlorine Residues and Risk of Breast Cancer." *Journal of the National Cancer Institute* 86 (1993): 232–234.

Wynder, E.L. "Nutrition and Metabolic Overload." *Resident and Staff Physician* 38 (1992): 63–70.

Wynder, E.L., and L.A. Cohen. "A Rationale for Dietary Intervention in the Treatment of Postmenopausal Breast Cancer Patients." *Nutrition and Cancer* 3 (1987): 195–199.

Wynder, E.L., L.A. Cohen, D.P. Rose, et al. "Dietary Fat and Breast Cancer: Where Do We Stand on the Evidence?" *Journal of Clinical Epidemiology* 47 (1994): 217–222.

Wynder, E.L., L.A. Cohen, D.P. Rose, et al. "Response to Dr. Walter Willett's Dissent." *Journal of Clinical Epidemiology* 47 (1994): 227–230.

Wynder, E.L., Y. Fujita, R. Harris, et al. "Comparative Epidemiology of Cancer Between the United States and Japan." *Cancer* 67 (1991): 746–763.

Wynder, E.L., T. Kajitani, J. Kuno, et al. "A Comparison of Survival Rates Between American and Japanese Patients with Breast Cancer." *Surgery in Gynecology and Obstetrics* 117 (1963): 196–200.

Chapter Seven—The Surprising Relationship Between Exercise and Your Breasts: Another Reason to Work Out

Ballard-Barbash, R. "Anthropometry and Breast Cancer: Body Size—A Moving Target." *Cancer* 74 (1994): 1090–1100.

Bastarrachea, J., G.N. Hortobagyi, T.L. Smith, et al. "Obesity as an Adverse Prognostic Factor for Patients Receiving Adjuvant Chemotherapy for Breast Cancer." *Annals of Internal Medicine* 120 (1993): 18–25.

Bernstein, L., B.E. Henderson, R. Hanisch, et al. "Physical Exercise and Reduced Risk of Breast Cancer in Young Women." *Journal of the National Cancer Institute* 86 (1994): 1403–1408.

Bernstein, L., R.K. Ross, R.A. Lobo, et al., "The Effects of Moderate Physical Activity on Menstrual Cycle Patterns in Adolescence: Implications for Breast Cancer Prevention." *British Journal of Cancer* 55 (1987): 681–685.

Bonen, A., A.N. Belcastro, W.Y. Ling, et al. "Profiles of Selected Hormones During Menstrual Cycles of Teenage Athletes." *Journal of Applied Physiology* 50 (1981): 545–551.

Bonen, A., W.Y. Long, K.P. MacIntyre, et al. "Effects of Exercise on the Serum Concentrations of FSH, LH, Progesterone and Estradiol." *European Journal of Applied Physiology* 42 (1979): 15–23.

Brinton, L.A. "Ways That Women May Possibly Reduce Their Risk of Breast Cancer." *Journal of the National Cancer Institute* 86 (1994): 1371–1372.

Brinton, L.A., and C.A. Swanson. "Height and Weight at Various Ages and Risk of Breast Cancer." *Annals of Epidemiology* 2 (1992): 597–609.

Ellison, P.T., and C. Lager. "Moderate Recreational Running Is Associated with Lowered Salivary Progesterone Profiles in Women." *American Journal of Obstetrics and Gynecology* 143 (1986): 1000–1003.

Frisch, R.E., A.V. Gotz-Welbergen, J.W. McArthur, et al. "Delayed Menarche and Amenorrhea of College Athletes in Relation to Age at Onset of Training." *Journal of the American Medical Association* 246 (1981): 1559–1563.

Frisch, R.E., G. Wyshak, N.L. Albright, et al. "Lower Lifetime Occurrence of Breast Cancer and Cancers of the Reproductive System Among Former College Athletes." *American Journal of Clinical Nutrition* 45 (1987): 328–335.

Frisch, R.E., G. Wyshak, N.L. Albright, et al. "Lower Prevalence of Breast Cancer and Cancers of the Reproductive System Among Former College Athletes Compared to Non-Athletes." *British Journal of Cancer* 52 (1985): 885–891.

Frisch, R.E., G. Wyshak, and L. Vincent. "Delayed Menarche and Amenorrhea in Ballet Dancers." *New England Journal of Medicine* 303 (1980): 17–19.

Heath, G.W., et al. "Physical Activity Patterns in American High School Students: Results from the 1990 Youth Risk Behavior Survey." AMA's *Archives of Pediatrics and Adolescent Medicine*, November 1994, 8.

Jurkowski, J.E., N.L. Jones, W.C. Walker, et al. "Ovarian Hormonal Responses to Exercise." *Medicine and Science in Sports and Exercise* 13 (1981): 109–114.

Kuczmarski, R.J., et al. "Increasing Prevalence of Overweight Among U.S. Adults: The National Health and Nutrition Examination Survey, 1960-1991." *Journal of American Medical Association* 272 (1994): 205–211.

Kumar, N.B., G.H. Lyman, K. Allen, et al. "Timing of Weight Gain and Breast Cancer Risk." *Cancer* 76 (1995): 243-249.

Schapira, D.V., N.B. Kumar, and G.H. Lyman. "Estimate of Breast Cancer Risk Reduction with Weight Loss." *Cancer* 67 (1991): 2622–2625.

Schapira, D.V., N.B. Kumar, and G.H. Lyman. "Obesity and Fat Distribution and Breast Cancer." *Cancer* 67 (1991): 523–528.

Schapira, D.V., N.B. Kumar, and G.H. Lyman. "Obesity, Body Fat Distribution and Sex Hormones in Breast Cancer Patients." *Cancer* 67 (1991): 2215–2218.

Sternfeld, B. "Cancer and the Protective Effect of Physical Activity: the Epidemiological Evidence." *Medicine and Science in Sports and Exercise* 24 (1992): 1195–1209.

Thompson, H.J., K.C. Westerlind, J.R. Snedden, et al. "Inhibition of Mammary Carcinogenesis by Treadmill Exercise." *Journal of the National Cancer Institute* 87 (1995): 45–47.

Vihko, V.J., D.L. Apter, E.I. Pukkala, et al. "Risk of Breast Cancer Among Female Teachers of Physical Education and Languages." *Acta Oncologica* 31 (1992): 201–204.

Chapter Eight—Pollutants, Electromagnetic Fields, and Radiation: Exploring the Link Between Your Environment and Your Breasts

Ahlbom, A., M. Feychting, M. Koskenvuo, et al. "Electromagnetic Fields and Childhood Cancer." *Lancet* 342 (1993): 1296.

Boice, J.D., J.S. Mandel, and M.M. Doody. "Breast Cancer Among Radiologic Technologists." *Journal of the American Medical Association* 274 (1995): 394–401.

Bradlow, H.L., D.L. Davis, G. Lin, et al. "Effects of Pesticides on the Ratio of 16a/2-hydroxyestrone: A Biologic Marker of Breast Cancer Risk." *Environmental Health Perspectives* 103 (1995): 147–150.

Carson, R. *Silent Spring*. Boston: Houghton Mifflin, 1962.

Council of the American Physical Society. *Powerline Fields and Public Health: Statement*. April 1995.

Davis, D.L., and H.L. Bradlow. "Can Environmental Estrogens Cause Breast Cancer?" *Scientific American*, October 1995, 166–172.

Davis, D.L., H.L. Bradlow, M.S. Wolff, et al. "Medical Hypothesis: Xenoestrogens as Preventable Causes of Breast Cancer." *Environmental Health Perspectives* 101 (1993): 372–377.

Demers, P.A., D.B. Thomas, K.A. Rosenblatt, et al. "Occupational Exposure to Electromagnetic Fields and Breast Cancer in Men." *American Journal of Epidemiology* 134 (1991): 340–347.

Dewailly, E., P. Ayotte, J. Brisson, et al. "Breast Cancer and Organochlorines." *Lancet* 344 (1994): 1707–1708.

Dewailly, E., P. Ayotte, and J. Brisson. "Protective Effect of Breast Feeding on Breast Cancer and Body Burden of Carcinogenic Organochlorines." *Journal of the National Institute* 86 (1994): 803.

Dewailly, E., S. Dodin, R. Verreault, et al. "High Organochlorine Body Burden in Breast Cancer Women with Estrogen Receptor-Positive Breast Cancer." *Journal of the National Cancer Institute* 86 (1994): 232–234.

EMR Alliance. "American Physical Society Ignores Decades of Research in Recent Statement." Press release, 1995.

Falck, F., A. Ricci, M.S. Wolff, et al. "Pesticides and Polychlorinated Biphenyl Residues in Human Breast Lipids and Their Relation to Breast Cancer." *Archives of Environmental Health* 47 (1992): 143–146.

Greene, G., and V. Ratner. "The Chemicals Around Us: A Toxic Link to Breast Cancer?" *The Nation*, April 1994, 866–869.

Heath, C.W., Jr. "Electromagnetic Field Exposure and Cancer: A Review of Epidemiologic Evidence." *CA: A Cancer Journal for Clinicians* 46 (1996): 29–44.

Kannan, K., S. Tanabe, R.J. Williams, et al. "Persistent Organochlorine Residues in Foodstuffs from Australia, Papua New Guinea and the Solomon Islands: Contamination Levels and Human Dietary Exposure." *Science of the Total Environment* 153 (1994): 29–49.

Krieger, N., M.S. Wolff, R.A. Hiatt, et al. "Breast Cancer and Serum

Organochlorines: A Prospective Study Among White, Black, and Asian Women." *Journal of the National Cancer Institute* 86 (1994): 589–599.

Land, C. "Studies of Cancer and Radiation Dose Among Atomic Bomb Survivors: The Example of Breast Cancer." *Journal of the American Medical Association* 274 (1995): 402–407.

Loomis, D.P. "Cancer of Breast Among Men in Electrical Occupations." *Lancet* 339 (1992): 1482–1483.

Loomis, D.P., D.A. Savitz, and C.V. Ananth. "Breast Cancer Mortality Among Female Electrical Workers in the United States." *Journal of the National Cancer Institute* 86 (1994): 921–925.

Loscher, W., M. Mevissen, W. Lehmacher, et al. "Tumor Promotion in a Breast Cancer Model by Exposure to a Weak Alternating Magnetic Field." Elsevier Scientific Publishers, 1993.

Marshall, D. "Breast Cancer: The Toxin Trail." *Lear's,* April 1994, 36–37.

Matanoski, B.M., P.N. Breysse, and E.A. Elliot. "Electromagnetic Field Exposure and Male Breast Cancer." *Lancet* 337 (1991): 737.

Mussalo-Rauhamaa, H. "Selenium and DDE in Breast Fat of Breast Cancer Patients: Their Relationship to Hormone Receptors in Breast Tissue." *Journal of the National Cancer Institute* 65 (1993): 1964–1965.

Perlmutter, D. "Organochlorines, Breast Cancer, and GATT." *Journal of the American Medical Association* 271 (1994): 1160–1161.

Quinsey, P.M., D.C. Donohue, and J.T. Ahokas. "Persistence of Organochlorines in Breast Milk of Women in Victoria, Australia." *Food and Chemical Toxicology* 33 (1995): 49–56.

Raloff, J. "EcoCancers: Do Environmental Factors Underlie a Breast Cancer Epidemic?" *Science News* 144 (1993): 10–13.

Reeves, K.T. "Organochlorines in the Environment and Breast Cancer." *British Medical Journal* 308 (1994): 1520–1521.

Rosenbaum, P.F., J.E. Vena, M.A. Zielezny, et al. "Occupational Exposures Associated with Male Breast Cancer." *American Journal of Epidemiology* 139 (1994): 30–36.

Saffer, J.D., and S.J. Thurston. "Cancer Risk and Electromagnetic Fields." *Nature* 375 (1995): 22–23.

Savitz, D. "Re: Breast Cancer and Serum Organochlorines: A Prospective Study Among White, Black, and Asian Women." *Journal of the National Cancer Institute* 86 (1994): 1255–1256.

Stevens, R.G. "Electric Power Use and Breast Cancer: A Hypothesis." *American Journal of Epidemiology* 125 (1987): 556–561.

Stevens, R.G., S. Davis, D.B. Thomas, et al. "Electric Power, Pineal Function, and the Risk of Breast Cancer." *FASEB Journal* 6 (1992): 853–860.

Taubes, G. "Fields of Fear." *The Atlantic Monthly* 11 (1994): 94–108.

Theriault, G., M. Goldberg, A.B. Miller, et al. "Cancer Risks Associated with Occupational Exposure to Magnetic Fields Among Electric Utility Workers in Ontario and Quebec, Canada and France, 1970–1989." *American Journal of Epidemiology* 139 (1994): 550–572.

Trichopoulos, D. "Are Electric or Magnetic Fields Affecting Mortality from Breast Cancer in Women?" *Journal of the National Cancer Institute* 86 (1994): 885–886.

Tynes, T., and A. Andersen. "Electromagnetic Fields and Male Breast Cancer." *Lancet* 336 (1990): 1596.

Vena, J.E., J.L. Freudenheim, J.R. Marshall, et al. "Risk of Premenopausal Breast Cancer and Use of Electric Blankets." *American Journal of Epidemiology* 140 (1994): 974–979.

Vena, J.E., S. Graham, R. Hellmann, et al. "Use of Electric Blankets and Risk of Postmenopausal Breast Cancer." *American Journal of Epidemiology* 125 (1987): 556–561.

Westin, J.B., and E. Richter. "The Israeli Breast Cancer Anomaly." *Annals of the New York Academy of Science* 609 (1990): 269–79.

Wolff, M.S., P.G. Toniolo, E.W. Lee, et al. "Blood Levels of Organochlorine Residues and Risk of Breast Cancer." *Journal of the National Cancer Institute* 85 (1993): 648–652.

Chapter Nine—The Mind/Body Connection: Stress and Your Breasts

Cassileth, B., E.J. Lusk, D.S. Miller, et al. "Psychosocial Correlates of Survival in Advanced Malignant Disease?" *New England Journal of Medicine* 312 (1985): 1551–1555.

Chorot, P., and B. Sandin. "Life Events and Stress Reactivity as Predictors of Cancer, Coronary Heart Disease and Anxiety Disorders." *International Journal of Psychosomatics* 41 (1994): 34–40.

Greer, S., and T. Morris. "Psychological Attributes of Women Who Develop Breast Cancer: A Controlled Study." *Journal of Psychosomatic Research* 19 (1975): 147–153.

Greer, S., T. Morris, and K.W. Pettingale. "Psychological Response to Breast Cancer: Effect on Outcome." *Lancet* 2 (1979): 785–787.

Hilakivi-Clarke, L., J. Rowland, R. Clarke, et al. "Psychosocial Factors in the Development and Progression of Breast Cancer." *Breast Cancer Research and Treatment* 29 (1994): 141–160.

Jamison, R.N., T.G. Burish, K.A. Waltson, et al. "Psychogenic Factors in Predicting Survival of Breast Cancer Patients." *Journal of Clinical Oncology* 5 (1987): 768–772.

Lerman, C., K. Kash, and M. Stefanek. "Younger Women at Increased Risk for Breast Cancer: Perceived Risk, Psychological Well-Being, and Surveillance Behavior." *Monograph of the National Cancer Institute* 16 (1994): 171–176.

Lerner, M. *Choices in Healing: Integrating the Best of Conventional and Complementary Approaches to Cancer.* Cambridge: The MIT Press, 1994.

Levy, S. "Host Differences in Neoplastic Risk: Behavioral and Social Contributors to Disease." *Health Psychology* 2 (1983): 21–44.

Levy, S., M. Herberman, M. Lippman, et al. "Correlation of Stress Factors with Sustained Depression of Natural Killer Cell Activity and Predicted

Prognosis in Patients with Breast Cancer." *Journal of Clinical Oncology* 5 (1987): 348–353.

Levy, S., and B. Wise. "Psychosocial Risk Factors and Cancer Progression." In *Stress and Breast Cancer*, edited by C.L. Cooper, 77–93. New York: John Wiley and Sons, 1988.

Morris, T.A. "Type C for Cancer: Low Trait Anxiety and the Pathogenesis of Breast Cancer." *Cancer Detection and Prevention* 3 (1980): 102.

O'Leary, A. and S. Miller. "Stress, Immune Function, and Health: Early Settlement of a New Frontier." *Clinical Immunology Newsletter* 11 (1991): 177–180.

Ramirez, A.J., T.K. Craig, J.P. Watson, et al. "Stress and Relapse of Breast Cancer." *British Medical Journal* 298 (1989): 291–293.

Roberts, C.S., V.J. Shannon, and N.L. Wells. "A Closer Look at Social Support as a Moderator of Stress in Breast Cancer." *Health and Social Work* 19 (1994): 157–164.

Spiegel, D. *Living Beyond Limits: New Hope and Help for Facing Life-Threatening Illness*. New York: Random House, 1993.

Spiegel, D., H. Kramer, J. Bloom, et al. "Effect of Psychosocial Treatment on Survival of Patients with Metastatic Breast Cancer." *Lancet* 10 (1989): 888–891.

Temoshok, L. "Personality, Coping Style, Emotion and Cancer: Towards an Integrative Model." *Cancer Surveys* 6 (1987): 545–567.

Temoshok, L., and H. Dreher. *The Type C Connection: The Behavioral Links to Cancer and Your Health*. New York: Random House, 1992.

Temoshok, L., B.W. Heller, R.W. Sagebiel, et al. "The Relationship of Psychosocial Factors to Prognostic Indicators in Cutaneous Malignant Melanoma." *Journal of Psychosomatic Research* 29 (1985): 139–153.

PART III—WONDERING WHICH COURSE TO TAKE? NEW INFORMATION ABOUT MEDICATIONS AND OPERATIONS

Chapter Ten—How Birth Control Pills and Fertility Drugs Affect Your Breasts

Brinton, L.A., J.R. Daling, J.M. Liff, et al. "Oral Contraceptives and Breast Cancer Risk Among Young Women." *Journal of the National Cancer Institute* 87 (1995): 827–835.

Chilvers, C., K. McPherson, M.C. Pike, et al. "Oral Contraceptive Use and Breast Cancer Risk in Young Women." *Lancet* 1 (1989): 973–982.

La Vecchia, C., E. Negri, S. Franceschi, et al. "Oral Contraceptives and Breast Cancer: A Cooperative Italian Study." *International Journal of Cancer* 60 (1995): 163–167.

Meirik, O., E. Lund, H.O. Adami, et al. "Oral Contraceptive Use and Breast Cancer in Young Women." *Lancet* 2 (1986): 650–654.

Miller, D.R., I. Rosenberg, D.W. Kaufman, et al. "Breast Cancer Before Age 45 and Oral Contraceptive Use: New Findings." *American Journal of Epidemiology* 129 (1989): 269–280.

Olsson, H., T.R. Moller, and J. Ranstam. "Early Oral Contraceptive Use and Breast Cancer Among Premenopausal Women: Final Report from a Study in Southern Sweden." *Journal of the National Cancer Institute* 81 (1989): 1000–1004.

Paul, C., D.C.G. Skegg, and G.F.S. Spears. "Oral Contraceptives and Risk of Breast Cancer." *International Journal of Cancer* 46 (1990): 366–373.

Romiu, I., J.A. Berlin, and G. Colditz. "Oral Contraceptives and Breast Cancer: Review and Meta-Analysis." *Cancer* 66 (1990): 2253–2263.

Rookus, M.A., and F.E. Van Leeuwen. "The Netherlands Oral Contraceptives and Breast Cancer Study Group: Oral Contraceptives and Risk of Breast Cancer in Women Aged 25–54 Years." *Lancet* 344 (1994): 844–851.

Rossing, M.A., J.R. Daling, N.S. Weiss, et al. "Ovarian Tumors in a Cohort of Infertile Women." *New England Journal of Medicine* 331 (1994): 771–776.

Spicer, D.V., and M.C. Pike. "Sex Steroids and Breast Cancer Prevention." *Monograph of the National Cancer Institute* 16 (1994): 139–147.

Spirtas, R., S.C. Kaufman, and N.J. Alexander. "Fertility Drugs and Ovarian Cancer: Red Alert or Red Herring?" *Fertility and Sterility* 59 (1993): 291–293.

Thomas, D.B. "Oral Contraceptives and Breast Cancer: Review of the Epidemiologic Literature." *Contraception* 43 (1991): 597–642.

Toniolo, P.G., M. Levitz, A. Zeleniuch-Jacquotte, et al. "A Prospective Study of Endogenous Estrogens and Breast Cancer in Postmenopausal Women." *Journal of the National Cancer Institute* 87 (1995): 190–197.

Velentgas, P. and J.R. Daling. "Risk Factors for Breast Cancer in Younger Women." *Monograph of the Cancer Institute* 16 (1994): 15–22.

White, E., K.E. Malone, N.S. Weiss, et al. "Breast Cancer Among Young U.S. Women in Relation to Oral Contraception Use." *Journal of the National Cancer Institute* 86 (1994): 505–514.

Whittemore, A.S., R. Harris, J. Intyre, et al. "Characteristics Relating to Ovarian Cancer Risk: Collaborative Analysis of 12 U.S. Case-Control Studies." *American Journal of Epidemiology* 136 (1992): 1184–1203.

Wingo, P.A., N.C. Lee, H.W. Ory, et al. "Age-Specific Differences in the Relationship Between Oral Contraceptive Use and Breast Cancer." *Cancer Supplement* 71 (1993): 1506–1517.

Chapter Eleven—How to Decide Whether Hormone Replacement Therapy Is for You . . . Even If You Have Survived Breast Cancer

Barber, H.R.K. "ERT and Breast Cancer." *The Female Patient* 20 (1995): 12–15.

Bergkvist, L., H.O. Adami, I. Persson, et al. "The Risk of Breast Cancer After Estrogen and Estrogen-Progestin Replacement." *New England of Journal of Medicine* 321 (1989): 293–297.

Birkhauser, M. "Hormone Replacement Therapy and Estrogen-Dependent Cancers." *International Journal of Fertility and Menopausal Studies* 39 (1994): 99–114.

Butler, W. "Hormone Replacement Therapy in Patients with Estrogen-Sensitive Malignancies." *The Female Patient* 20 (1995): 43–49.

Colditz, G.A., K.M. Egan, M.J. Stampfer. "Hormone Replacement Therapy and Risk of Breast Cancer: Results from Epidemiologic Studies." *American Journal of Obstetrics and Gynecology* 168 (1993): 1473–1480.

Colditz, G.A., S.E. Hankinson, D.J. Hunter, et al. "The Use of Estrogens and Progestins and the Risk of Breast Cancer in Postmenopausal Women." *New England Journal of Medicine* 332 (1995): 1589–1593.

Colditz, G.A., M.J. Stampfer, W.C. Willett, et al. "Type of Postmenopausal Hormone Use and Risk of Breast Cancer: 12-Year Follow-up from the Nurses' Health Study." *Cancer Causes and Control* 3 (1992): 433–439.

Davidson, N.E. "Hormone-Replacement Therapy—Breast Versus Heart Versus Bone." *New England Journal of Medicine* 332 (1995): 1638–1639.

Dupont, W.D., and D.L. Page. "Menopausal Estrogen Replacement Therapy and Breast Cancer." *Archives of Internal Medicine* 151 (1991): 67–72.

Dupont, W.D., D.L. Page, and L.W. Rogers. "Influence of Exogenous Estrogens, Proliferative Breast Disease, and Other Variables on Breast Cancer Risk." *Cancer* 63 (1989): 948–957.

Eden, J.A., T. Bush, S. Nand, and B. Wren. "A Case-Control Study of Combined Continuous Estrogen-Progestin Replacement Therapy Among Women with a Personal History of Breast Cancer." *Menopause* 2 (1995): 67–72.

Felson, D.T., Y. Zhang, M.T. Hannan, et al. "The Effect of Postmenopausal Estrogen Therapy on Bone Density in Elderly Women." *New England Journal of Medicine* 329 (1993): 1141–1146.

Gambrell, R.D., Jr., R.C. Maier, and B.I. Sanders. "Decreased Incidence of Breast Cancer in Postmenopausal Estrogen-Progestogen Users." *Obstetrics and Gynecology* 62 (1983): 435–443.

Kaufman, D.W., J.R. Palmer, J. de Mouzon, et al. "Estrogen Replacement Therapy and the Risk of Breast Cancer: Results from the Case-Control Surveillance Study." *American Journal of Epidemiology* 134 (1991): 1375–1385.

Marchant, D.J. "Supplemental Estrogen Replacement." *Cancer* 74 (1994): 512–517.

Newcomb, P.A., and B.E. Storer. "Postmenopausal Hormone Use and Risk of Large-Bowel Cancer." *Journal of the National Cancer Institute* 87 (1995): 1067–1071.

Persson, I., J. Yuen, L. Bergkvist, et al. "Combined Oestrogen-Progestin Replacement and Breast Cancer Risk." *Lancet* 340 (1992): 1044.

Potter, J.D. "Hormones and Colon Cancer." *Journal of the National Cancer Institute* 87 (1995): 1030–1040.

Schairer, C., C. Byrne, P.M. Keyl, et al. "Menopausal Estrogen and Estrogen-Progestin Replacement Therapy and Risk of Breast Cancer." *Cancer Causes and Control* 5 (1994): 491–500.

Seachrist, L. "What Risk Hormones? Conflicting Studies Reveal Problems in Pinning Down Breast Cancer Risks." *Science News* 148 (1995): 94–95.

Stanford, J.L., N.S. Weiss, L.F. Voigt, et al. "Combined Estrogen and Progestin Hormone Replacement Therapy in Relation to Risk of Breast Cancer in Middle-Aged Women." *Journal of the American Medical Association* 274 (1995): 137–142.

Toniolo, P.G., M. Levitz, A. Zeleniuch-Jacquotte, et al. "A Prospective Study of Endogenous Estrogens and Breast Cancer in Postmenopausal Women." *Journal of the National Cancer Institute* 87 (1995): 190–197.

Wingo, P.A., P.M. Layde, N.C. Lee, et al. "The Risk of Breast Cancer in Postmenopausal Women Who Have Used Estrogen Replacement Therapy." *Journal of the American Medical Association* 257 (1987): 209–215.

Chapter Twelve—When You Want to Reshape Your Breasts: The Latest Word on Cosmetic Surgery

Angell, M. "Do Breast Implants Cause Systemic Disease?" *New England Journal of Medicine* 330 (1994): 1748–1749.

Bryant, H., and P. Brasher. "Breast Implants and Breast Cancer—Reanalysis of a Linkage Study." *New England Journal of Medicine* 332 (1995): 1535–1539.

Deapen, D., and G. Brody. "Re: Induction of Plasmacytomas with Silicone Gel in Genetically Susceptible Strains of Mice." *New England Journal of Medicine* 87 (1995): 315–316.

Gabriel, S.E., W.M. O'Fallon, and L.T. Kurland. "Risk of Connective-Tissue Disease and Other Disorders After Breast Implantation." *New England Journal of Medicine* 330 (1994): 1697–1702.

Hennekens, C.H., I.M. Lee, and N.R. Cook. "Self-Reported Breast Implants and Connective-Tissue Diseases in Female Health Professionals." *Journal of the American Medical Association* 275 (1996): 616–621.

Levine, J.J., and N.T. Ilowite. "Sclerodermalike Esophageal Disease in Children Breastfed by Mothers with Silicone Breast Implants." *Journal of the American Medical Association* 271 (1994): 213–241.

McLaughlin, J.K., J.H. Olsen, S. Friis, et al. "Re: Breast Implants, Cancer, and Systemic Sclerosis." *Journal of the National Cancer Institute* 87 (1995): 1415–1416.

Vasey, F.B., and N. Aziz. "Breast Implants and Connective-Tissue Disease." *New England Journal of Medicine* 333 (1995): 1423.

Chapter Thirteen—When You Are at High Risk for Breast Cancer: Should You Consider Preventive Mastectomy?

American Cancer Society, Surveillance Research. "Age-Specific Probabilities of Developing Breast Cancer." *Breast Cancer Facts and Figures* 1995, 5.

Daly, M.B., C. Lerman, C.B. Sands, et al. "Breast Cancer Risk Factors Are

Underestimated Among High Risk Women." *Breast Cancer Research and Treatment* 27 (1992): 177.

Gail, M.H., L.A. Brinton, D.P. Byar, et al. "Projecting Individualized Probabilities of Developing Breast Cancer for White Females Who Are Being Screened Annually." *Journal of the National Cancer Institute* 81 (1989): 1879–1886.

Hoskins, K.F., J.E. Stopfer, K.A. Calzone, et al. "Assessment and Counseling for Women with a Family History of Breast Cancer." *Journal of the American Medical Association* 273 (1995): 577–585.

Houn, F., K.J. Helzlsouer, N.B. Friedman, and M.E. Stefanek. "The Practice of Prophylactic Mastectomy: A Survey of Maryland Surgeons." *American Journal of Public Health* 85 (1995): 801–805.

Lerman, C., and R. Croyle. "Psychological Issues in Genetic Testing for Breast Cancer Susceptibility." *Archives of Internal Medicine* 154 (1994): 609–616.

Lerman, C., K. Kash, and M. Stefanek. "Young Women at Increased Risk for Breast Cancer: Perceived Risk, Psychological Well-Being, and Surveillance Behavior." *Monograph of the National Cancer Institute* 16 (1994): 171–176.

Lerman, C., E. Lustbader, B. Rimer, et al. "Effects of Individualized Breast Cancer Risk Counseling: A Randomized Trial." *Journal of the National Cancer Institute* 87 (1995): 286–292.

Schatzkin, A., A. Goldstein, and L. Freedman. "What Does It Mean to Be a Cancer Gene Carrier? Problems in Establishing Causality from the Molecular Genetics of Cancer." *Journal of the National Cancer Institute* 87 (1995): 1126–1130.

Stefanek, M.E. "Bilateral Prophylactic Mastectomy: Issues and Concerns." *Monograph of the National Cancer Institute* 17 (1995): 37–42.

Stefanek, M.E. "Counseling Women at High Risk for Breast Cancer." *Oncology* 4 (1990): 27–38.

Stefanek, M.E., K.J. Helzlsouer, P. Wilcox, et al. "Predictors of and Satisfaction with Bilateral Prophylactic Mastectomy." *Preventive Medicine* 24 (1995): 412–419.

PART IV—WARNING SIGNS THAT YOUR BREASTS NEED ATTENTION

Chapter Fourteen—Nipples That Have Discharge, Soreness, or Other Conditions

Adashi, E.Y. "Diagnostic Evaluation of Hyperprolactinemia." *Resident and Staff Physician* 31 (1985): 16PC.

Baker, B. "Cytology of Nipple Discharge Worthwhile Only in Isolated Instances." *Ob Gyn News*, February 1995, 8.

Fiorica, J.V. "Breast Disease." *Current Opinion in Obstetrics and Gynecology* 4 (1992): 897–903.

Fiorica, J.V. "Nipple Discharge." *Obstetrics and Gynecology* 21 (1994): 453–460.

Fiorica. J.V. "Special Problems: Mondor's Disease, Macrocysts, Trauma, Squamous Metaplasia, Miscellaneous Disorders of the Nipple." *Obstetrics and Gynecology* 21 (1994): 479–485.

Gliedman, M.L., P.J. Deckers, R.G. Margolese, et al. "Problems in the Management of Carcinoma of the Breast." *Contemporary Surgery* 44 (1994): 351–362.

Chapter Sixteen—Your Breasts Hurt: Pain All Over or in One Spot

Baker, B. "Reassure Patients with Breast Pain That Cancer Is Unlikely." *Ob Gyn News*, March 1995, 6.

Boyd, N.F., V. McGuire, and P. Shannon. "Effect of a Low-Fat High Carbohydrate Diet on Symptoms of Cyclical Mastopathy." *Lancet* 2 (1988): 128–132.

Gately, C.A., R.R. Maddox, G.A. Pritchard, et al. "Plasma Fatty Acid Profiles in Benign Breast Disorders." *British Journal of Surgery* 79 (1992): 407–409.

Gately, C.A., and R.E. Mansel. "Management of Cyclical Breast Pain." *British Journal of Hospital Medicine* 43 (1990): 330–332.

Horrobin, D. "The Effects of Gamma-Linolenic Acid on Breast Pain and Diabetic Neuropathy: Possible Non-Eicosanoid Mechanisms." *Prostaglandins, Leukotrienes, and Essential Fatty Acids* 48 (1993): 101–104.

Kumar, S., R.E. Mansel, M.I. Scanlon, et al. "Altered Responses of Prolactin, Luteinizing Hormone and Follicle Stimulating Hormone Secretion to Thyrotrophin Releasing Hormone/Gonadotrophin Releasing Hormone Stimulation in Cyclical Mastalgia." *British Journal of Surgery* 71 (1984): 870–873.

Kumar, S., R.E. Mansel, D.W. Wilson, et al. "Daily Salivary Progesterone Levels in Cyclic Mastalgia Patients and Their Controls." *British Journal of Surgery* 73 (1986): 260–263.

Maddox, P., and R. Mansel. "Management of Breast Pain and Nodularity." *World Journal of Surgery* 13 (1989): 699–705.

Onnis, A., G. Nardilli, B. Mozzanega, et al. "Progestinic Treatment of Mastodynia: New Suggestion for the Follow-up." *European Journal of Gynecology and Oncology* 1 (1984): 11–15.

Redmond, G. *The Good News About Women's Hormones.* New York: Warner Books, 1995.

Sitruk-Ware, R., N. Sterkers, and P. Mauvais-Jarvis. "Benign Breast Disease: Hormonal Investigation." *Obstetrics Gynecology* 53 (1979): 457–460.

Chapter Seventeen—You Find a Lump: It May Not Be Serious But It Should Not Be Ignored

Baker, B. "Gross Cystic Disease Raises Cancer Risk." *Ob Gyn News* 30 (1995): 13:1.

Drukker, B.H. "Nonsurgical Treatment of Breast Disease." *Obstetrics and Gynecology Forum* 4 (1990): 3–5.

Dupont, W.D., D.L. Page, F.F. Parl, et al. "Long-Term Risk of Breast Cancer in

Women with Fibroadenoma." *New England Journal of Medicine* 331 (1994): 10–15.

Fiorica, J.V. "Fibrocystic Changes." *Obstetrics and Gynecology* 21 (1994): 445–452.

Fiorica, J.V. "Special Problems: Mondor's Disease, Macrocysts, Trauma, Squamous Metaplasia, Miscellaneous Disorders of the Nipple." *Obstetrics and Gynecology* 21 (1994): 479–485.

Hindle, W.H. "Fibrocystic Breast Disease—Not a Diagnosis." *The Female Patient* 18 (1993): 41–48.

Isaacs, J.H. "Benign Tumors of the Breast." *Obstetrics and Gynecology* 21 (1994): 487–497.

Nellist, C.C. "Some Fibroadenomas Are Breast Cancer Risks." *Ob Gyn News*, September 1994, 13.

PART V—WHEN BREAST CANCER BECOMES A PERSONAL BATTLE: DIAGNOSIS, TREATMENT, RECOVERY

Chapter Eighteen—Genetic Codes and More : An Overview of the Growing List of High-Risk Factors for Breast Cancer

Bell, M.C., and E.E. Partridge. "Early Breast Carcinoma: Risk Factors, Screening, and Treatment." *Contemporary Ob/Gyn* 40 (1995): 31–51.

Bhatia, S., L.L. Robison, O. Oberlin, et al. "Breast Cancer and Other Second Neoplasms After Childhood Hodgkin's Disease." *New England Journal of Medicine* 334 (1996): 745–751.

Blot, W.J., and J.K. McLaughlin. "Geographic Patterns of Breast Cancer Among American Women." *Journal of the National Cancer Institute* 87 (1995): 1819–1820.

Calle, E.E., C.A. Merris, P.A. Wingo, et al. "Spontaneous Abortion and Risk of Fatal Breast Cancer in a Prospective Cohort of United States Women." *Cancer Causes and Control* 6 (1995): 460–468.

Colditz, G.A., B.A. Rosner, and F.E. Speizer. "Risk Factors for Breast Cancer According to Family History of Breast Cancer." *Journal of the National Cancer Institute* 88 (1996): 365–371.

Colditz, G.A., W.C. Willett, D.J. Hunter, et al. "Family History, Age, and Risk of Breast Cancer." *Journal of the American Medical Association* 270 (1993): 338–343.

Daling, J.R., K.E. Malone, L.F. Voight, et al. "Risk of Breast Cancer Among Young Women: Relationship to Induced Abortion." *Journal of the National Cancer Institute* 88 (1994): 1584–1592.

Gail, M.H., and J. Benichou. "Assessing the Risk of Breast Cancer in Individuals." *Cancer Prevention*, June 1992, 1–15.

Gammon, M.D., J.E. Bertin, and M.B. Terry. "Abortion and the Risk of Breast Cancer: Is There a Believable Association?" *Journal of the American Medical Association* 275 (1996): 321–322.

Goldgar, D.E., S.L. Neuhausen, L. Steele, et al. "A 45-Year Follow-up of Kindred 107 and the Search for BRCA2." *Monograph of the National Cancer Institute* 17 (1995): 15–19.

Hunter, D.J., D. Spiegelman, H.O. Adami, et al. "Cohort Studies of Fat Intake and the Risk of Breast Cancer—a Pooled Analysis." *New England Journal of Medicine* 334 (1996): 356–361.

Kash, K.M., J.C. Holland, M.P. Osborne, et al. "Psychological Counseling Strategies for Women at Risk of Breast Cancer." *Monograph of the National Cancer Institute* 17 (1995): 73–79.

Kliewer, E.V., and K.R. Smith. "Breast Cancer Mortality Among Immigrants in Australia and Canada." *Journal of the National Cancer Institute* 87 (1995): 1154–1161.

Longnecker, M.P., P.A. Newcomb, R. Mittendorf, et al. "Risk of Breast Cancer in Relation to Lifetime Alcohol Consumption." *Journal of the National Cancer Institute* 87 (1995): 923–929.

Madigan, M.P., R.G. Ziegler, J. Benichou, et al. "Proportion of Breast Cancer Cases in the United States Explained by Well-Established Risk Factors." *Journal of the National Cancer Institute* 87 (1987): 1681–1685.

Newcomb, P.A., B.E. Storer, M.P. Longnecker, et al. "Pregnancy Termination in Relation to Risk of Breast Cancer." *Journal of the American Medical Association* 275 (1996): 283–287.

Rosner, B., and G.A. Colditz. "Nurses' Health Study: Long-Incidence Mathematical Model of Breast Cancer Incidence." *Journal of the National Cancer Institute* 88 (1996): 359–364.

Shattuck-Eidens, D., M. McClure, J. Simard, et al. "A Collaborative Survey of 80 Mutations in the BRCA1 Breast and Ovarian Cancer Susceptibility Gene." *Journal of the American Medical Association* 273 (1995): 535–541.

Sorensen, T. "Is There an Inherited General Susceptibility to Cancer?" *New England Journal of Medicine* 333 (1995): 1633–1635.

Sturgeon, S.R., C. Schairer, M. Gail, et al. "Geographic Variation in Mortality from Breast Cancer Among White Women in the United States." *Journal of the National Cancer Institute* 87 (1995): 1846–1853.

Thompson, J.A., G.L. Wiesner, T.A. Sellers, et al. "Genetic Services for Familial Cancer Patients: A Survey of National Cancer Institute Cancer Centers." *Journal of the National Cancer Institute* 87 (1995): 1446–1455.

Weber, B.L. "Clinical Implications of Basic Research: Susceptibility Genes for Breast Cancer." *New England Journal of Medicine* 331 (1994): 1523–1524.

Ziegler, J. "Geographic Variation in U.S. Breast Cancer Death Rates." *Journal of the National Cancer Institute* 87 (1995): 1831–1832.

Chapter Nineteen—A Suspicious Lump: When a Biopsy Is Needed

Anderson, A.H. "Breast Cancer: Will FNA Change Your Role?" *OBG Management*, September 1991, 17–27.

Dershaw, D.D., B.A. Caravella, and L. Liberman. "Limitations and Complications in the Utilization of Stereotaxic Core Breast Biopsy." *The Breast Journal* 2 (1996): 13–17.

Drukker, B.H. "Breast Cysts and Solid Lesions: The Role of Fine-Needle Aspiration." *Current Opinion in Obstetrics and Gynecology* 6 (1994): 492–494.

Fechner, R.E. "Frozen Section Examination of Breast Biopsies: Practice Parameter." *American Journal of Clinical Pathology* 103 (1995): 6–7.

Janes, R.H. and M.S. Bouton. "Initial 300 Consecutive Stereotactic Core-Needle Breast Biopsies by a Surgical Group." *American Journal of Surgery* 168 (1994): 533–536.

Kerin, M.J., N.N. Williams, K.J. Cronin, et al. "Stereotactic Cytology in a Regional Breast-Screening Program." *British Journal of Surgery* 81 (1994): 221–222.

Masood, S. "Recent Updates in Breast Fine-Needle Aspiration Biopsy." *The Breast Journal* 2 (1996): 3–12.

Parker, S.H. "Percutaneous Large-Core Breast Biopsy." *Cancer* 74 (1994): 256–262.

Parker, S.H., J.D. Lovin, W.E. Jobe, et al. "Stereotactic Breast Biopsy with a Biopsy Gun." *Radiology* 176 (1990): 741–747.

Pressler, V., T. Namiki, J. Cieply, et al. "Stereotactic Fine Needle Aspiration of Mammographic Lesions." *Journal of American College of Surgeons* 178 (1994): 54–58.

Sarfati, M.R., K.A. Fox, J.A. Warneke, et al. "Stereotactic Fine-Needle Aspiration Cytology of Nonpalpable Breast Lesions: An Analysis of 258 Consecutive Aspirates." *American Journal of Surgery* 168 (1994): 529–531.

Schmidt, R.A., "Stereotactic Breast Biopsy." *CA: A Cancer Journal for Clinicians* 44 (1994): 172–191.

Skolnick, A.A. "New Data Suggest Needle Biopsies Could Replace Surgical Biopsy for Diagnosing Breast Cancer." *Journal of the American Medical Association* 271 (1994): 1724–1728.

Chapter Twenty—After the Biopsy: What The Pathology Report Will Tell You

Bell, M.C., and E.E. Partridge. "Early Breast Carcinoma: Risk Factors, Screening, and Treatment." *Contemporary Ob/Gyn* 40 (1995): 31–51.

Hutter, R.V.P. "The Role of the Pathologist in the Management of Breast Cancer." *CA: A Cancer Journal for Clinicians* 41 (1991): 283–296.

Lagios, M.D. "Duct Carcinoma in Situ: Implications for Current Breast Cancer Management." *New Perspectives on Breast Cancer* 1 (1996): 1–4.

Lagios, M.D. "Ductal Carcinoma in Situ: Controversies in Diagnosis, Biology, and Treatment." *The Breast Journal* 1 (1995): 68–78.

Lagios, M.D. "Heterogeneity of Duct Carcinoma in Situ (DCIS): Relationship of Grade and Subtype Analysis to Local Recurrence and Risk of Invasive Transformation." *Cancer Letters* 90 (1995): 97–102.

Lagios, M.D. "Morphologic and Biochemical Prognostic Variables for Early TINO Breast Carcinoma." *New Perspectives on Breast Cancer* 1 (1995): 1–4.

Page, D.L., and M.D. Lagios. "Pathologic Analysis of the National Surgical Adjuvant Breast Project (NSABP) B-17 Trial: Unanswered Questions Remaining Unanswered. Considering Current Concepts of Ductal Carcinoma in Situ." *Cancer* 75 (1995): 1219–1222.

Rosai, J. "Borderline Epithelial Lesions of the Breast." *American Journal of Surgical Pathology* 15 (1991): 209–221.

Schnitt, S.J., J.L. Connolly, F.A. Tavassoli, et al. "Interobserver Reproducibility in the Diagnosis of Ductal Proliferative Breast Lesions Using Standardized Criteria." *American Journal of Surgical Pathology* 16 (1992): 1133–1143.

Silverstein, M.J. "Intraductal Breast Carcinoma: Two Decades of Progress?" *American Journal of Clinical Oncology* 14 (1991): 534–537.

Silverstein, M.J., M.D. Lagios, P.H. Craig, et al. "The Van Nuys Prognostic Index for Ductal Carcinoma in Situ." *The Breast Journal* 2 (1996): 38–40.

Silverstein, M.J., D.N. Poller, J.R. Waisman, et al. "Prognostic Classification of Breast Ductal Carcinoma in Situ." *Lancet* 345 (1995): 1154–1157.

Chapter Twenty-One—When Your Doctor Says "Surgery," Which Is Best? Lumpectomy vs. Mastectomy

Abrams, J.S., P.H. Phillips, and M.A. Friedman. "Meeting Highlights: A Reappraisal of Research Results for the Local Treatment of Early Stage Breast Cancer." *Journal of the National Cancer Institute* 87 (1995): 1837–1845.

Angell, M., and J.P. Kassirer. "Setting the Record Straight in the Breast-Cancer Trials." *New England Journal of Medicine* 330 (1994): 1448–1449.

Bailler, J.C. "Surgery for Early Breast Cancer: Can Less Be More?" *New England Journal of Medicine* 333 (1995): 1496–1498.

Baker, B. "Opinions Diverge Over Best Setting for Care of Breast." *Ob Gyn News*, July 1994, 18–19.

Bonnema, J., A. Wersch, A.N. Geel, et al. "Early Discharge from the Hospital of Patients Being Operated On for Breast Cancer." *Cancer Researcher Weekly*, October 1994, 19.

Early Breast Cancer Trialists' Collaborative Group. "Effects of Radiotherapy and Surgery in Early Breast Cancer: An Overview of the Randomized Trials." *New England Journal of Medicine* 333 (1995): 1444–1455.

Ernster, V.L., J. Barclay, K. Kerlikowske, et al. "Incidence and Treatment for Ductal Carcinoma in Situ of the Breast." *Journal of the American Medical Association* 275 (1996): 913–918.

Fisher, B., J. Costantino, C. Redmond, et al. "Lumpectomy Compared with Lumpectomy and Radiation Therapy for the Treatment of Intraductal Breast Cancer." *New England Journal of Medicine* 328 (1993): 1581–1586.

Fisher, B., S. Anderson, C. Redmond, et al. "Reanalysis and Results After 12 Years of Follow-up in a Randomized Clinical Trial Comparing Total Mastectomy with Lumpectomy with or Without Irradiation in the Treatment of Breast Cancer." *New England Journal of Medicine* 333 (1995): 1456–1461.

Goodman, A.A., and A.L. Mendez. "Definitive Surgery for Breast Cancer Performed on an Outpatient Basis." *Archives of Surgery* 128 (1993): 1149–1152.

Hofer, D., and L. Wise. "Therapy Update: Controversies, Choices and Conclusions." *Consultant*, March 1994, 385–394.

Jacobson, J.A., D.N. Danforth, K.H. Cowan, et al. "Ten-Year Results of a Comparison of Conservation with Mastectomy in the Treatment of Stage 1 and 2 Breast Cancer." *New England Journal of Medicine* 332 (1995): 907–911.

Johantgen, M.E., R.M. Coffey, R. Harris, et al. "Treating Early-Stage Breast Cancer: Hospital Characteristics Associated with Breast-Conserving Surgery." *American Journal of Public Health* 85 (1995): 1432–1434.

Laino, C. "Data Endorse Greater Lumpectomy Use." *Medical Tribune* May 1994: 16.

Orange, L.M. "Timing of Surgery Critical for Premenopausal Breast Cancer Patients." *Ob Gyn News*, September 1994, 17.

Pommer, R.F., and S.A. Fields. "Breast Cancer in Pregnancy, a Diagnostic and Therapeutic Challenge." *Western Journal of Medicine* 163 (1995): 70.

Senie, R.T., and D.W. Kinne. "Menstrual Timing of Treatment for Breast Cancer." *Monograph of the National Cancer Institute* 16 (1994): 85–90.

Tartter, P.I., G. Beck, and K. Fuchs. "Length of Hospital Stay Following Mastectomy." *American Journal of Surgery* 168 (1994): 320–324.

Thomas, R., and M. Pack. "What Is the Role of Axillary Lymph Node Dissection in Early Breast Cancer?" *Cancer Researcher Weekly* May 1994, 21.

Chapter Twenty-Two—Every Breast Cancer Has a Profile, and You Should Know Yours

American Joint Committee on Cancer: "Breast." *Manual for Staging of Cancer*, 149–154. Philadelphia: J.B. Lippincott, 1992.

Bell, M.C., and E.E. Partridge. "Early Breast Carcinoma: Risk Factors, Screening, and Treatment." *Contemporary Ob/Gyn* 40 (1995): 31–51.

Hutter, R.V.P. "The Role of the Pathologist in the Management of Breast Cancer." *CA-A Cancer Journal for Clinicians* 41 (1991): 283–299.

Menard, S., N. Cascinelli, F. Rilke, et al. "Re: Prediction of Axillary Lymph Node Status in Breast Cancer Patients by Use of Prognostic Indicators." *Journal of the National Cancer Institute* 87 (1995): 607.

Sainsbury, J.R.C., T.J. Anderson, D.A.L. Morgan, et al. "Breast Cancer (ABCs of Breast Diseases)." *British Medical Journal* 309 (1994): 1150–1154.

Chapter Twenty-Three—What to Expect During Radiotherapy

Abrams, J.S., P.H. Phillips, and M.A. Friedman. "Meeting Highlights: A Reappraisal of Research Results for the Local Treatment of Early Stage Breast Cancer. Is Breast Irradiation an Essential Component of BCT?" *Journal of the National Cancer Institute* 87 (1995): 1837–1845.

Clark, R.M., M.N. McCulloch, M. Levine, et al. "Randomized Clinical Trial to Assess the Effectiveness of Breast Irradiation Following Lumpectomy and

Axillary Dissection for Node-Negative Breast Cancer." *Journal of the National Cancer Institute* 84 (1992): 683–689.

Craighead, P.S. "Postoperative Radiotherapy After Conservative Surgery in Patients with Early Breast Cancer." *Journal of the National Cancer Institute* 87 (1995): 317–318.

Early Breast Cancer Trialists' Collaborative Group. "Effects of Radiotherapy and Surgery in Early Breast Cancer: An Overview of the Randomized Trials." *New England Journal of Medicine* 333 (1995): 1444–1455.

Fisher, B., S. Anderson, C.K. Redmond, et al. "Reanalysis and Results after 12 Years of Follow-up in a Randomized Clinical Trial Comparing Total Mastectomy with Lumpectomy with or Without Irradiation in the Treatment of Breast Cancer." *New England Journal of Medicine* 333 (1995): 1456–1461.

Fowble, B. "Conservative Surgery and Radiation for Stage 1 and 2 Breast Cancer: Identification of a Subset of Patients with Early Stage Breast Cancer for Whom Breast-Conserving Therapy May Be Contraindicated." *The Breast Journal* 2 (1996): 65–70.

Fowble, B. "The Role of Radiotherapy in the Treatment of Ductal Carcinoma in Situ—The Challenge of the 1990's." *The Breast Journal* 2 (1996): 45–51.

Hellman, S., and R.R. Weichselbaum. "Radiation Oncology and the New Biology." *The Cancer Journal*, September/October 1995, 1.

Mansfield, M.M., L.T. Komarnicky, G.F. Schwartz, et al. "Ten-Year Results in 1070 Patients with Stages 1 and 2 Breast Cancer Treated by Conservative Surgery and Radiation Therapy." *Cancer* 75 (1995): 2328–2336.

Chapter Twenty-Four—When You Need Chemotherapy and Hormone Therapy: Seizing the Power of Cancer-Killing Drugs

Abrams, J.S., T.D. Moore, and M. Friedman. "New Chemotherapeutic Agents for Breast Cancer." *Cancer* (supplement) 74 (1994): 1164–1176.

Allred, D.C., G.M. Clark, A.K. Tandon, et al. "HER-2/neu in Node-Negative Breast Cancer: Prognostic Significance of Overexpression Influenced by the Presence of in Situ Carcinoma." *Journal of Clinical Oncology* 10 (1992): 599–605.

Anand, A., A. Anand. "Paclitaxel in Doxorubicin-Resistant Metastic Breast Cancer Patients." *Journal of the National Cancer Institute* 87 (1995): 1642.

Anzano, M.A., C.W. Peer, J.M. Smith, et al. "Chemoprevention of Mammary Carcinogenesis in the Rat: Combined Use of Raloxifene and 9-cis-Retinoic Acid." *Journal of the National Cancer Institute* 88 (1996): 123–125.

Bonadonna, G. "Evolving Concepts in the Systemic Adjuvant Treatment of Breast Cancer." *Cancer Research* 52 (1992): 2127–2137.

Bonadonna, G., and P. Valagussa. "Dose-Intense Adjuvant Treatment of High-Risk Breast Cancer." *Journal of the National Cancer Institute* 82 (1990): 542–543.

Bonadonna, G., P. Valagussa, A. Moliterni, et al. "Adjuvant Cyclophosphamide,

Methotrexate, and Fluorouracil in Node-Positive Breast Cancer." *New England Journal of Medicine* 332 (1995): 901–906.

Bonadonna, G., U. Veronesi, C. Brambilla, et al. "Primary Chemotherapy to Avoid Mastectomy in Tumors with Diameters of Three Centimeters or More." *Journal of the National Cancer Institute* 82 (1990): 1539–1545.

Bornstein, J., R. Auslender, B. Pascal, et al. "Diagnostic Pitfalls of Ultrasonographic Uterine Screening in Women Treated with Tamoxifen." *Journal of Reproductive Medicine* 39 (1994): 674–678.

Carlson, R.W. "High-Dose Chemotherapy with Bone Marrow–Stem Cell Rescue in the Treatment of Advanced Stage Breast Cancer." *The Breast Journal* 2 (1996): 97–98.

Champlin, R. "Dose-Intensive Therapy with Autologous Bone Marrow Transplantation for Treatment of Breast Cancer." *The Cancer Bulletin* 45 (1993): 532–537.

Cobleigh, M.A. "Breast Cancer and Fenretinide, an Analogue of Vitamin A." *Leukemia* 8 (1994): S59–63.

Coccini, G., G. Bisagni, G. Ceci, et al. "Low-Dose Aminoglutethimide with and Without Hydrocortisone Replacement as a First-Line Endocrine Treatment in Advanced Breast Cancer: A Prospective Randomized Trial of the Italian Oncology Group for Clinical Research." *Journal of Clinical Oncology* 10 (1992): 984–989.

Cook, L.S., N.S. Weiss, S.M. Schwartz, et al. "Population-Based Study of Tamoxifen Therapy and Subsequent Ovarian, Endometrial, and Breast Cancers." *Journal of the National Cancer Institute* 87 (1995): 1359–1364.

Folkman, J. "Tumor Angiogenesis in Women with Node-Positive Breast Cancer." *The Cancer Journal* 1 (1995): 106–106.

Gale, K.E., J.W. Andersen, D.C. Tormey, et al. "Hormonal Treatment for Metastatic Breast Cancer: An Eastern Cooperative Oncology Group Phase 3 Trial Comparing Aminoglutethimide to Tamoxifen." *Cancer* 73 (1994): 354–361.

Ganz, P.A., R. Day, J.E. Ware, et al. "Baseline Quality-of-Life Assessment in the National Surgical Adjuvant Breast and Bowel Project Breast Cancer Prevention Trial." *Journal of the National Cancer Institute* 87 (1995): 1372–1382.

Gianni, L., E. Munzone, G. Capri, et al. "Paclitaxel in Metastatic Breast Cancer: A Trial of Two Doses by a 3-Hour Infusion in Patients with Disease Recurrence After Prior Therapy with Anthracyclines." *Journal of the National Cancer Institute* 87 (1995): 1169–1175.

Goldhirsch, A., and R.D. Gelber. "Understanding Adjuvant Chemotherapy for Breast Cancer." *New England Journal of Medicine* 330 (1994): 1308–1309.

Goldhirsch, A., W.C. Wood, H.J. Senn, et al. "Meeting Highlights: International Consensus Panel on the Treatment of Primary Breast Cancer." *Journal of the National Cancer Institute* 87 (1995): 1441–1445.

Greenspan, E.M. *The Breast Cancer Epidemic in the US: An Informed Woman's Guide to Breast Cancer. How 15,000 More Lives Can Be Saved Each Year. A*

Medical Oncologist's Perspective. New York: The Chemotherapy Foundation, 1986.

Greenspan, E.M. "Has the Cure of Breast Cancer with Chemotherapy Become a Reality?" *Cancer Investigation* 12 (1994): 98–99.

Hortobagyi, G.N., and A.U. Buzdar. "Current Status of Adjuvant Systemic Therapy for Primary Breast Cancer: Progress and Controversary." *CA: A Cancer Journal for Clinicians* 45 (1995): 199–226.

Hortobagyi, G.N., D. Frye, A.U. Buzdar, et al. "Decreased Cardiac Toxicity of Doxorubicin Administered by Continuous Intravenous Infusion in Combination Chemotherapy for Metastatic Breast Carcinoma." *Cancer* 63 (1989): 37–45.

Kennedy, B.J. "Age-Related Clinical Trials of CALGB." *Cancer Control* March/April 1995, 14–16.

Koh, E.H., A.U. Buzdar, F.C. Ames, et al. "Inflammatory Carcinoma of the Breast: Results of a Combined-Modality Approach—M.D. Anderson Cancer Center Experience." *Cancer Chemotherapy Pharmacology* 27 (1990): 94–100.

Kornblith, A.B., D.R. Hollis, E. Zuckerman, et al. "Effect of Megestrol Acetate on Quality of Life in a Dose-Response Trial in Women with Advanced Breast Cancer." *Journal of Clinical Oncology* 11 (1993): 2081–2089.

McNeil, C. "In the Clinic: Where Paclitaxel and Docetaxel Stand." *Journal of the National Cancer Institute* 87 (1995): 1107–1108.

Mort, E.A., L. Esserman, D. Tripathy, et al. "Diagnosis and Management of Early-Stage Breast Cancer." *Journal of Clinical Outcomes Management: Obstetrics and Gynecology ed.* 1 (1995): 1–16.

Muss, H.B. "Breast Cancer in the Elderly: Treatment of Metastatic Disease." *Cancer Control* March/April 1995, 39–42.

Roberge, A.E., and J.K. Erban. "Today's Adjuvant Therapy in Breast Cancer: Who Should Receive What?" *Cancer Control* May/June 1995, 209–217.

Schwartsmann, G., A.W. Dekker, and J. Verhoef. "Complication of Cytotoxic Therapy." In *Oxford Textbook of Oncology*. Oxford: Oxford University Press, 1995.

Seidman, A. "The Emerging Role of Paclitaxel in Breast Cancer Therapy." *Clinical Cancer Research* 1 (1995): 247–256.

Seidman, A.D., T. Portenoy, J. Yao, et al. "Quality of Life in Phase 2 Trials: A Study of Methodology and Predictive Value in Patients with Advanced Breast Cancer Treated with Paclitaxel plus Granulocyte Colony-Stimulating Factor." *Journal of the National Cancer Institute* 87 (1995): 1316–1322.

Sledge, G.W., Jr., and W.J. McCaskill-Stevens. "Chemotherapy for Breast Cancer: How Are We Doing? Can We Do Better?" *The Breast Journal* 2 (1996): 59–63.

Speyer, J.L., M.D. Green, A. Zeleniuch-Jacquotte, et al. "ICRF-187 Permits Longer Treatment with Doxorubicin in Women with Breast Cancer." *Journal of Clinical Oncology* 10 (1992): 117–127.

Stewart, S.K. "Bone Marrow Transplants." Highland Park, *BMT Newsletter*, 1992.

Tormey, D.C., R. Gray, M.D. Abeloff, et al. "Adjuvant Therapy with a Doxorubicin Regimen and Long-Term Tamoxifen in Premenopausal Breast Cancer

Patients: An Eastern Cooperative Oncology Group Trial." *Journal of Clinical Oncology* 10 (1992): 1848–1856.

Wood, W.C., D.R. Budman, A.H. Korzun, et al. "Dose and Dose Intensity of Adjuvant Chemotherapy for Stage 2, Node-Positive Breast Carcinoma." *New England Journal of Medicine* 330 (1994): 1253–1259.

Chapter Twenty-Five—On the Vanguard of Healing

Barrett, S. "Questionable Cancer Treatment: Nutritional, Herbal, and Biological Approaches." *Nutrition Forum* 12 (1995): 53–57.

Brigden, M.L. "Unproven (Questionable) Cancer Therapies." *The Western Journal of Medicine* 163 (1995): 463–467.

Fallowfield, L. "Has Psychosocial Oncology Helped in the Management of Women with Breast Cancer?" *The Breast Journal* 2 (1996): 107–113.

Glentzer, M. "Desperate Measures." *Good Housekeeping* 222 (1996): 84–85.

Holland, J., ed. *Textbook of Psycho-Oncology*. Oxford, England: Oxford University Press, 1997 (to be published).

Lerner, Michael. *Choices in Healing: Integrating the Best of Conventional and Complementary Approaches to Cancer*. Cambridge: The MIT Press, 1994.

Locke, S., and D. Colligan. *The Healer Within: The New Medicine of Mind and Body*. New York: E.P. Dutton, 1986.

Parker, S. "Spirituality Is an Often Untapped Resource." *Ob Gyn News*, February 1996: 41.

Podolsky, D.A. "New Age of Healing Hands: Cancer Centers Embrace Alternative Therapies as 'Complementary Care.' " *US News & World Report* 120 (1996): 71–72.

Spiegel, D., G.R. Morrow, C. Classen, et al. "Effects of Group Therapy on Women with Primary Breast Cancer." *The Breast Journal* 2 (1996): 104–106.

Stehlin, I.B. "An FDA Guide to Choosing Medical Treatments." *FDA Consumer* 29 (1995): 10–15.

Wittman, J. In Search of Life. "*Ladies Home Journal*," March 1994, 72–76.

Chapter Twenty-Six—Breast Reconstruction: Is It for You?

Baker, B. "Elective Contralateral Mastectomies Increase with Better Reconstruction." *Ob Gyn News*, June, 1994: 16.

Berger, K., and J. Bostwick. *A Woman's Decision: Breast Care, Treatment, & Reconstruction*. 2nd. ed.St. Louis, Missouri: Quality Medical Publishing, 1994.

Hartrampf, C.R., M. Scheflan, and P.W. Black. "Breast Reconstruction Following Mastecomy with a Transverse Abdominal Island Flap: Anatomical and Clinical Observations." *Plastic Reconstruction Surgery* 69 (1982): 216.

Stephenson, J. "Concern Over Implants Puts Focus on Alternatives for Breast Reconstruction." *Ob Gyn News*, February 1994, 3.

Web, M.S. "Reconstruction's Place in Breast Cancer Management." *Contemporary Ob/Gyn*, August 1994, 83–90.

INDEX

Abscesses, 39–40, 188
Abortion, 221–222
Acini, 15, 34, 40
Adenocarcinoma (*see* Carcinoma in situ)
Adolescence, 18–20
Adrenal glands, 20, 24, 27, 128
Adrenal steroids, 16
Adrenocorticotropic hormone (ACTH), 17
Adriamycin (*see* Doxorubicin)
Affording Care, 398
African American women, 13, 19, 73, 116, 117, 190, 229–230
Age, as breast cancer risk factor, 219, 229
Aggressive systemic therapy, 305–306
Airlifeline, 394
Alcoholic beverages, 83, 98–99, 218, 224–225
Alendronate sodium, 150
Alkylating agents, 308–309
16 alpha-hydroxyestrone, 10
Altered diphtheria virus toxin, 336
Alveoli, 15
American Association of Retired People (AARP), 394
American Board of Internal Medicine, 297

American Board of Medical Physics, 288
American Board of Radiology, 288
American Cancer Society (ACS), 4, 58, 59, 61, 63, 82, 145, 226, 229, 252, 384, 390
American College of Radiology (ACR), 63, 65, 68, 288
American College of Sports Medicine, 109
American College of Surgeons, 392
American Hair Loss Council, 394
American Health Foundation, 84, 88–90
American Institute for Cancer Research (AICR), 393
American Medical Association (AMA), 59, 61
American Medical Center, 392
American Physical Society, 123
American Preferred Prescription, 394
American Registry of Radiologic Technologies, 288
American Society of Plastic and Reconstructive Surgeons (ASPRS), 153, 159, 396
America Online, 376, 381–382, 384, 385
Aminoglutethimide (Cytadren), 323, 324

Ampullae, 15, 34
Analgesic, patient-controlled, 366–367
Anatomy, 13–15
Androstenedione, 24, 106
Anemia, 319
Anesthesia, 157, 164, 270–271
Aneuploid cells, 255
Angiogenesis inhibitors, 336–337
Angiostatin, 337
Anthrapyrazoles, 310
Antianxiety medications, 317
Antibiotics, 39, 40, 188, 197, 309–310
Antiemetic medications, 318
Antimetabolites, 310
Antineoplastons, 343
Antioxidants, 92–94, 95, 108, 150
Antitumor antibiotics, 309–310
Areolae:
    breast lift and, 168
    breast reduction and, 166, 167
    color of, 13
    defined, 13
    hairs of, 13
    reconstruction of, 365, 367–368
    release of milk and, 36
    sexual response of, 25
    subareolar abscess and, 188
    tattoos, 346
Arida, 326
Arimidex, 321
Arizona Cancer Center, 94
Armed Forces Institute of Pathology,
    Civilian Consultation Program,
    248, 282
Aromatase, 106, 107
Aromatase inhibitors, 321, 323–324, 336
Asian women, 13, 116
Aspiration of cysts, 205, 234–236
AT (ataxia telangiectasia), 228
Athens School of Public Health, 96
Athletes, 31, 103
Ativan, 317–318
ATM gene, 124, 228–229
Atrazine, 113, 116
Atypia, 223, 232, 247
Atypical hyperplasia, 217, 223, 232,
    247, 250
Axilla, 13
Axillary dissection, 260, 275–278

Baghurst, Peter, 90
Baseline mammograms, 58, 59, 71, 155

Bassilopou-Sellin, Rena, 144, 148
Baum, Andrew, 130
BBE (see Breast biophysical
    examination)
BCNU, 308
Benelli reduction method, 169
Benson, Herbert, 342
Berstein, Leslie, 9–10, 102–103, 105
Best Doctors in America, 248
Beta-carotene, 83–84, 93–94
Beta-Carotene and Retinol Efficacy
    Trial (CARET), 93
Biofield Corporation, 77, 244
BioLogics-The RX Resource, 394
Biomarkers, 256
Biopsies, 3, 211, 232–243
    accuracy of, 235
    core needle, 233, 235, 239–241, 247
    fine needle aspiration, 233, 236–239,
        247, 249
    pathology report (see Biopsy
        pathology report)
    stereotactic guided, 233, 238–241
    surgical, 234, 241–243, 247, 249
    ultrasound guided, 235–240
Biopsy gun, 239
Biopsy pathology report, 244, 246–257
    information in, 249–254
    molecular tests included in, 254–256
    second opinion on, 246–249
    type of biopsy performed and, 247,
        249
Biphosphonates, 326
Birth control pills, 135–140, 184–185,
    195–196, 218, 222, 230
Blood donation, 271, 366
Blood supply, 14
Bloody nipple discharge, 187
BMT Newsletter, 395–396
Board certification, 288
Body fat, 26–27, 105–107
Body shape, 106–108
Body weight, 25–27, 103, 106–110, 198,
    217, 224
Bonadonna, Gianni, 302, 309, 315
Bone:
    breast cancer metastasis to, 326–327
    density evaluation, 320
    pain control, 327
Bone marrow, 306, 326
    transplants, 327–333, 395–396
Boost treatments, 290–291

Borgen, Patrick, 177, 274
Bottle-feeding, 33
Bovbjerg, Dana, 130
Bradlow, Leon, 91–92, 100
Bras, 22, 33, 38, 188, 195, 197, 199, 269, 290
BRCA1 and BRCA2 genes, 175, 372
Breast abscess, 39–40
Breast asymmetry, surgery for, 171–173
Breast augmentation (implants), 151, 156–165
  anesthesia, 157, 164
  for asymmetry, 171–172
  breastfeeding and, 41, 158–159, 173
  breast self-examination and, 56–57
  cost of, 154
  endoscopic "bellybutton" surgery, 165
  future, 160
  incisions, 162–164
  magnetic resonance imaging and, 76
  outpatient, 164
  placement of, 162
  post-surgery effects, 164–165
  saline, 159–160, 162
  selection of, 161–162
  shape of, 163
  silicone, 41, 56–57, 76, 151, 156–159
  textured vs. smooth, 161
Breast biophysical examination (BBE), 77, 243–244
Breast cancer:
  biopsies and (see Biopsies)
  birth control pills and, 135–140
  breast cysts and, 98, 201, 206, 222
  breastfeeding and, 29, 42–43, 221
  caffeine and, 98
  carcinoma in situ (see Carcinoma in situ)
  chemicals and, 99–101, 112–120
  chemotherapy and (see Chemotherapy)
  classification of, 253, 279–281
  cosmetic surgery and, 155
  diet and (see Diet)
  electromagnetic fields and, 113, 120–123
  estrogen and, 9–10, 105–107, 141–150, 220, 370–371
  exercise and, 9–10, 31, 102–111
  feel of lump, 203
  fertility drugs and, 138–140
  fibroadenomas and, 209–210

history of, as risk factor, 220
hormonal connection to, 9–10
hormone replacement therapy and, 24, 141–150
increased incidence of, 9, 218, 225, 229
inflammatory, 191, 303
information resources, 390–391
intermediate-risk, 304
lifetime odds for, 9
low-risk, 303, 304
metastatic, 303, 305–306, 324–327
mortality, 3, 59, 61, 68–69, 88, 120–121, 230, 372
natural killer cells and, 129–130
personality and, 126
during pregnancy, 272
pregnancy and risk of, 30–32, 221
preventive mastectomy and, 175–180
profile, 279–283
progesterone and, 9–10, 141–150, 220
radiation exposure and, 67–69, 113, 122–124
radiotherapy (see Radiotherapy)
risk factors (see Risk factors for breast cancer)
sporadic, 226
stress and, 129–131
survival rates, 281
tests (see Breast tests)
treatment of (see Breast cancer treatment)
types of, 250–253
warning signs (see Breast cancer warning signs)
"Breast Cancer and Serum Organochlorines: A Prospective Study Among White, Black, and Asian Women," 116
Breast cancer centers, 256, 299, 398–399
Breast Cancer Detection Demonstration Project (BCDDP), 59, 145
Breast cancer genes, 175, 179–180, 227
Breast cancer treatment:
  clinical trials and, 337–338
  complementary care, 339–343
  information resources, 392–393
  new, 333–337
  (See also Chemotherapy; Radiation therapy; Surgery)

Breast cancer warning signs:
  breast lumps (*see* Breast lumps)
  breast pain, 193, 198, 200
  nipple dermatitis, 189
  nipple discharge, 186–187
  skin tone, 190–191
Breast Center, The, 398
Breast-conserving surgery (BCS):
  defined, 259
  (*See also* Lumpectomy)
Breast cysts, 21, 201, 202
  aspiration of, 205, 234–236
  breast cancer and, 98, 201, 206, 222
  caffeine and, 96–98
  evaluation of, 205
  examination for, 206–207
  recurring macrocysts, 206
  size of, 204–205
  treatment of, 205–206
Breast examinations:
  by physician, 3, 206–207
  self (*see* Breast self-examinations)
Breastfeeding, 15, 21, 32–43
  appearance of breast after, 41
  beginning, 36–37
  breast asymmetry surgery and, 173
  breast augmentation and, 41,
    158–159, 173
  breast cancer and, 29, 42–43, 221
  breast lift and, 41, 170, 173
  breast milk content, 37–38
  breast pain in, 193
  breast reduction and, 41, 173
  breast self-examinations during, 56
  complications, 38–41
  duration of, 37
  health tips, 38
  information resources, 389
  milk production stimulation, 33–36
  positions for, 35, 36
  sexual quality of experience, 26
  weaning, 41
Breast Implant Information Network,
  396
Breast implants (*see* Breast
  augmentation)
Breast lift (mastopexy):
  breastfeeding and, 41, 170, 173
  in combination with breast reduction
    or augmentation, 168, 170
  cost of, 154
  post-surgery effects, 170–171

  pre-surgery decisions, 168
  procedure, 170
  sagging breasts, defined, 171
Breast lumps, 4, 201–211
  benign, risk factors for breast cancer
    and, 217, 222–223
  biopsies (*see* Biopsies)
  cystic (*see* Breast cysts)
  fibroadenomas, 201, 202, 207–210,
    222, 242
  fibrocystic change, 96–98, 194,
    202–204
  instincts and, 210–211
  uncommon kinds of, 210
  (*See also* Breast self-examinations)
Breast milk, 37–39
Breast models, 51
Breast pain, 192–200
  from breast cysts, 205–206
  from costochondritis, 199
  cyclic, 192–196
  hard to diagnose, 199
  information resources, 395
  nipple, 188
  noncyclic, 193, 196–198
  post-lumpectomy, 269
  post-mastectomy, 277
  from reconstruction surgery, 366–367
Breast pump, 38, 39
Breast reconstruction, 344–369
  aftermath of, 369
  for breast asymmetry, 172
  choosing the surgeon, 348
  consultation for, 260–261, 345
  immediate, 348–350
  implants, 347, 350, 352–356
  increasing use of, 344
  information resources, 396
  with natural tissue (*see* Natural tissue
    reconstruction)
  nipple/areola, 346, 365, 367, 368
  personal issues related to, 350
  skin-sparing mastectomies and, 345,
    347
Breast reduction (mammoplasty),
  165–170
  for asymmetry, 172
  breastfeeding and, 41, 173
  cost of, 154
  goals of, 166
  insurance coverage, 154–155
  new variations on, 169–170

post-surgery effects, 167
pre-surgery decisions, 166–167
repeat, 168
scarring, 165, 167
techniques, 167
Breasts
    anatomy of, 13–15
    appearance following breastfeeding,
        41
    beauty of, 10
    cancer of (*see* Breast cancer)
    development of, 16, 18–21, 23–25
    elevation of, 13
    engorgement of, 38–39
    functioning of, 15
    heredity and, 20, 26
    hormones and (*see* Hormones)
    infections of, 39–40
    information and care of, 3–9
    instincts and care of, 4–9
    lifestyle and health of, 26–28
    lumps in (*see* Breast lumps)
    massaging (*see* Massage)
    menopause and, 23–24, 31
    menstrual cycle and (*see* Menstrual
        cycle)
    milk-filled, when bottle-feeding, 33
    mind/body connection and, 16
    pain in (*see* Breast pain)
    perimenopause and, 23
    postmenopause and, 24
    in pregnancy (*see* Pregnancy)
    sex and, 25–26
    skin tone, 190–191
    stress and, 125–132
    surgery and (*see* Cosmetic surgery;
        Surgery)
    tests of (*see* Breast tests)
Breast self-examinations (BSE), 4,
    47–57, 371
    during breastfeeding, 56
    with breast implants, 56–57
    breast models and, 51
    distinguishing new lumps, 204
    menstrual cycle and, 49
    nipple discharge and, 183–184
    over lifetime, 57
    palpation technique, 54
    patterns, 52–56
    during pregnancy, 32, 56
    size of detectable growths, 50
    size of tumors found by, 65

steps in, 50
after surgery, 56
value of, 48–49
Breast surgery (*see* Surgery)
Breast tests, 371
    biopsies (*see* Biopsies)
    breast biophysical examination
        (BBE), 77, 243–244
    information resources, 390
    magnetic resonance imaging (MRI),
        57, 76–77
    mammograms (*see* Mammograms)
    once-promising, 78–79
    positron emission tomography (PET),
        71
    scintimammography, 78, 245
    self-examinations (*see* Breast self-
        examinations)
    ultrasound, 72, 74–76, 244
Brigham and Women's Hospital, 336
Brinton, Louise, 42–43, 135–136
Bristol-Myers Indigent Patient
        Assistance Program, 394
British Medical Devices Agency, 158
Bromocriptine mesylate, 33, 41, 185, 196
Broviac, 318
BSE (*see* Breast self-examinations)
Bulletin Board Services (BBS), 385
Burzynski, Stanislaw, 343

Caffeine, 96–98, 197
Calcifications, 60
Calories, 83, 86, 101, 224
Cancer (*see* Breast cancer)
Cancer Care, Inc., 397
Cancer Care's Pain Resource Center,
    395
CANCERFAX, 392
Cancer Forum, 382–384
CancerLit, 380
CancerNet, 380, 381
"Cancer-prone personality," myth of,
    125–126
Cancer vaccines, 335–336
Cancer Wellness Center, The/The
        Barbara Kassel Brotman House,
        397
CANHELP, 392
Carboplatin (Paraplatin), 308
Carcinoma in situ (CIS):
    ductal, 220, 244, 247, 251–253
    lobular, 220, 251–253

Caretinoids, 93
Carpenter, David O., 123
Carroll, Kenneth, 87
Carson, Rachel, 114
Cassileth, Barrie, 126
CAT scan, 320
CDC25B, 334
Center for Health Statistics, 110
Central plane x-ray kit, 320
Cerebral cortex, 16
Chemical plants, 118
Chemicals, environmental, 99–101,
    112–120, 225, 229
Chemocare, 396, 397
Chemoendocrine therapy, 306
Chemotherapy, 294–333
  choosing the medical oncologist,
      296–299
  combined with hormone therapy, 306
  drugs, 307–312
  follow-up, 333
  function of, 306
  high-dose, with bone marrow
      transplant, 327–333
  importance of accurate pathology
      report, 299
  indications for, 296
  metastatic breast cancer and, 303,
      305–306, 324–327
  promising new treatments, 333–334
  recurrence rates and, 294–295
  regimens, 312–317
  risks of radiation therapy with, 286
  scheduling, 316–317
  sessions, 317–318
  side effects, 306, 308–312, 318–320
  treatment protocol, 300
  treatment recommendations,
      300–306
Chest wall recurrence, 286
Chicago, University of, 241
  Cancer Research Center, 109
Childbearing, as breast cancer risk
      factor, 216, 217, 221, 230–231
Cica-Care, 173–174
Circular BSE technique, 52, 53
Cisplatin (Cisplatinum, Platinol), 308
CLA (see Conjugated linoleic acid)
Claims Assistance Counsel, 396
Clinical trials, 317, 337–338
Clinical Trials Information Project,
    392

Clock BSE technique, 52, 53
Clomid, 138
Clomiphene citrate, 138, 139
CMF (Cytoxan+methotrexate+
    fluorouracil), 307, 309, 312, 315,
    325
Cohen, Leonard, 90
Colloid cancers, 251
Colostrum, 34, 36, 37
Comedo, 252
Commercial on-line services, 381–385
Complementary care, 339–343
Complex fibroadenomas, 201, 242
Comprehensive Breast Center at the
    Lombardi Cancer Center,
    Georgetown University Medical
    Center, 398
CompuServe, 376, 381–383
Computers, 375–387
Conjugated linoleic acid (CLA), 89
Connolly, Jeanne M., 88
Consciousness, inner, 341–342
Consent, 262
Cooking oils, 87–88
Copeland, Michelle, 160, 347, 363, 366,
    368
Core needle biopsy, 233, 235, 239–241,
    247
Corn oil, 87, 88
Corporate Angel Network, Inc., 394
Corpus luteum, 21
Cosmetic surgery, 151–180
  for breast asymmetry, 171–173
  breast augmentation (see Breast
      augmentation)
  breast cancer and, 155
  breastfeeding and, 41, 173
  breast lift (see Breast lift)
  breast reduction (see Breast
      reduction)
  cost of, 154–155
  pain factor, 155
  pre–procedure steps, 155–156
  scar minimization, 172–174
  self-consultation, 152, 174
  surgeons, 153–154
Costochondritis, 199, 292
Cracked nipples, 36, 40
Creighton, James, 341
Cribiform pattern, 252
Crystal Scanner, 72, 244
Cyclic breast pain, 192–196

Cyclophosphamide (Cytoxan), 286, 307, 308, 317
Cystosarcoma phylloides, 209
Cysts (*see* Breast cysts)
Cytopathologists, 238
Cytoxan (*see* Cyclophosphamide)

Daidzein, 91
Daly, Mary, 176–177, 179, 215
D'Amico, Richard A., 345, 347, 355–357, 358
Danazol (Danocrine), 196, 198, 205–206
Dancers, 31
Danocrine (*see* Danazol)
Davis, Devra Lee, 100, 119
DDE, 115–117
DDT, 99–100, 113, 114, 116, 226
Decision-making process, 261
Deferrers, 261
Delayers, 261
Deliberators, 261
Delphi, 376, 381–382
Dermatitis, nipple, 188–189
Diaphanography, 79
Didronel, 326
Diet, 80–101, 224
    alcoholic beverages, 83, 98–99, 218, 224–225
    antioxidants in vegetables and fruits, 92–94
    caffeine, 96–98
    calories, 83, 86, 101
    fats, 27–28, 81, 84–89
    fiber, 83, 89–90
    fibrocystic change and, 204
    Food Guide Pyramid, 82–84
    garlic, 94–95
    information resources, 393–394
    low–fat, 27, 81, 84, 85–86, 149, 197, 204
    olive oil, 27, 87–88, 95–96
    personal approach to, 101
    pesticides in, 99–101
    phytochemicals in vegetables and fruits, 90–92
Digital mammography, 70–71
Dioxins, 117
Directory of Medical Specialists, 288
Discharge, nipple, 183–187
DNA, 215, 216, 231
    analysis, 255–256

Docetaxel (Taxotere), 311
Doctors, team of, 256–257
Donut reduction method, 169
Dosimetrists, 288
Dow Corning, 156, 173
Doxorubicin (Adriamycin), 307, 309–310, 314, 315, 325, 333
Drains, 269, 272
Drukker, Bruce, 97
Dual x-ray absorptiometry (DEXA), 320
Ductal carcinoma:
    invasive, 250–251
    in situ (DCIS), 220, 244, 247, 251–253, 263
Duct ectasia, 210
Duke Comprehensive Cancer Center, 340
    Bone Marrow Transplant Program, 329
Dysthesia, 274

Early Breast Cancer Trialists' (EBCT) Collaborative Group, 294
EarthLink, 376
Eastern Cooperative Oncology Group (ECOG), 149
Edatrexate, 310
Eden, John, 148
Ehime University, Japan, 117
Einstein Direct, Albert Einstein Breast Cancer Program, 396
Electromagnetic fields (EMFs), 113, 120–123, 225
Electronic address, 377
EMR Alliance, The, 123, 389–390
Endocrine glands, 16, 17
Endometrium, 21, 23
Endoscopic "bellybutton" surgery, 165
Engorgement, 38–39
Environmental Protection Agency (EPA), 117
Environmental risk factors, 112–124
    chemicals, 99–101, 112–120, 225, 229
    electromagnetic fields, 113, 120–123, 225
    geographic location, 223–224
    information resources, 389–390
    radiation exposure risk, 67–69, 122–124, 225
Epipodophylotoxins, 311
Erythropoietin (Epogen), 319

E–Screen, 119–120
Eskenazi, Loren, 163, 347, 350, 357, 363
Estrogen, 16
  body fat and, 27
  breast cancer and, 9–10, 105–107,
    141–150, 220, 370–371
  breast development and, 16, 19, 20
  dietary fiber and, 90
  exercise and, 31, 105–106
  hormone replacement therapy and,
    24, 141–150
  hormone therapy and (see Hormonal
    therapy)
  menstrual cycle and, 20–21
  perimenopause and, 23
  phytochemicals and, 90–92
  postmenopause and, 24
  pregnancy and, 29
Estrogen/progestin pills, 135–136
Estrogen receptor status, 255
Estrogen surges, 323
Etoposide, 311
Evening primrose oil, 195, 197
Excisional biopsy, 234, 242, 247, 249
Exercise, 9–10, 31, 102–111, 197,
    225–226, 398
Exercises, 22, 25, 40
Extensive intraductal carcinoma in situ
    (EIC), 264
External Reconstruction Technology,
    Inc., 395

Falck, Frank, Jr., 99, 114
Family history of breast cancer, 216,
    217, 219–220
Farber, Dana, Cancer Institute Breast
    Evaluation Center (BEC), 399
Fasciae, 14
Fat:
  body, 26–27, 105–107
  dietary, 27–28, 81, 84–89, 149
Fatigue, post-radiation therapy, 292
Fat necrosis, 210
Fertility drugs, 138–140
Fetal breast development, 16, 18
Fiber, dietary, 83, 89–90
Fibroadenomas, 201, 202, 207–210, 222,
    242
Fibrocystic change, 96–98, 194, 202–204
Fine needle aspiration, 234–236
Fine needle aspiration biopsy, 233,
    236–239, 247, 249

Finnish diets, 89
Fisher, Bernard, 50
Fish oil, 88
Fixed volume implants, 353
Flap reconstruction (see Natural tissue
    reconstruction)
Flaxseed, 336
Flick, Jonathan, 158–159
Flow cytometry, 255–256
Fluoroscopy, 217
Fluorouracil (5-FU), 307, 310
Folic acid, 83
Folkman, Judah, 336–337
Follicles, 20–21
Follicle-stimulating hormone (FSH), 17,
    20, 323, 324
Follow-Up Study of Women Evaluated
    and Treated for Infertility, 139
Ford, Betty, 4
Fosamax, 326
Foundation for Informed Medical
    Decision Making, Inc.,
    392–393
Fowble, Barbara, 285
Free flaps, 351
Free radicals, 92–93, 122
Frisch, Rose, 103
Fruits, 82, 83, 90–94, 115
Fumagillin, 337

Gail, Mitchell H., 30
Galactoceles, 40, 205
Galactography, 186
Galactorrhea, 186
Galen, 127
Garlic, 94–95
Garlic Information Center, 394
Gene therapy, 334–335
Genetic research, 26, 226–229, 371–372
Genetic testing, 227–228
Genistein, 91
Geographic location, as risk factor for
    breast cancer, 223–224
Getting Well Again: A Step-by-Step Guide
    to Overcoming Cancer for Patients
    and Their Families (Simonton, et
    al.), 341
Gluteus maximus flap, 364–365
Gonadotropin-releasing hormone
    (GnRH), 37, 139
Gonadotropins, 17
Goodman, Reba, 122

Good Samaritan Hospital and Medical Center, Portland, Oregon, 342
Gordon, Paula, 75
Goserelin (Zoladex), 324
Goss, Paul E., 324, 336
GP2 protein, 336
Graafian follicle, 21
Granisetron (Kytril), 318
Granulocyte-colony stimulating factor (G-CSF), 330
Grateful Med, 385
Greenspan, Ezra, 297, 317
Greenwald, Peter, 85
Gretz, Elissa, 319
Grid BSE technique, 52–56
Group therapy, 130–131
Growth hormone, 16, 17, 38

Hafemeister, David, 123
Hair loss information sources, 394–395
Halsted radical mastectomy, 260
Hard capsular contracture, 164
Harms, Steven E., 76–77
Harvard School of Public Health, 96
Healing Yourself: A Step-by-Step Program for Better Health Through Imagery (Rossman), 341
Health Database+, 382, 383
HealthGate, 380–381
Health Insurance Plan of New York (HIP), 58–59
Hemodilution, 366
Henderson, Craig, 308–309
Hendrick, Edward, 68–69
Hennekens, Charles, 158
Heredity, 20, 26
HER–2/neu oncogene, 256
Hickman, 318
Hidalgo, David, 155, 159, 165, 169, 345, 347, 348, 352, 367
High-definition imaging (HDI), 75, 209
High-dose chemotherapy, 327–333
High-resolution ultrasonography, 244
Hoffman's exercise, 40
Hope, realistic sense of, 127
Hormonal therapy, 294, 295, 320–324
  choosing the medical oncologist, 296–299
  combined with chemotherapy, 306
  follow-up, 333
  importance of accurate pathology report, 299

indications for, 296
  for metastatic breast cancer, 324–325
  new drugs, 336
  regimens, 313–316
  side effects, 318, 321–322
  tamoxifen, 196, 294–295, 306, 313–314, 320–323
  treatment protocol, 300
  treatment recommendations, 300–306
Hormonal treatment of breast pain, 195–196
Hormone receptor status, 255, 320
Hormone replacement therapy (HRT), 24, 141–150, 193, 203–204, 218, 222
Hormones:
  birth control pills (*see* Birth control pills)
  breast cancer and, 9–10
  breast growth and health over lifetime and, 16–21, 23–25
  in breast milk, 37–38
  exercise and, 103
  milk production stimulating, 34–35
  mind/body connection and, 16, 126–130
  pituitary, 16, 17, 20, 21, 25, 34–35, 105
  (*See also* Estrogen; Progesterone)
Hunter, David, 85
Hypercalcemia of malignancy, 326
Hyperplasia, 217, 223, 232, 247, 250
Hypnosis, 341–342
Hypothalamus, 17, 29, 128, 129, 162

IDT, 376
Ifosphamide, 308
Imagery, 341–342
Immune-strengthening practices, 339–343
Immune system stimulants, 335
Implants:
  for breast augmentation (*see* Breast augmentation)
  for breast reconstruction, 347, 350, 352–356
  information resources, 396
Imre, Edith, Foundation for Loss of Hair, 395
Incision:
  breast implant, 162–163
  lumpectomy, 266, 267, 269
  modified radical mastectomy, 271, 273

Incisional biopsy, 234, 241, 247, 249
Income level, as breast cancer risk
    factor, 216
Indole-3-carbinol, 91–92
Induced abortion, 221–222
Infections, 39–40
    mastitis, 39, 191, 197–198
    nipple discharge and, 187
Inflammatory breast cancer, 191, 303
Information, 3–9
Information resources, 375–399
Informed consent, 262
Infusion therapy, 325
Injury, breast pain and, 198
Inner consciousness, 341–342
Instincts, 4–9
Insulin, 16
Insurance coverage, 154–155, 351
Interleukin-2 (IL-2), 335
International Childbirth Educators
    Association (ICEA), 389
Internet, 377–381
Intraductal papillomas, 187, 210
Invasive ductal or lobular carcinoma,
    250–251
Inventive Products Incorporated, 55–56
Inverted nipples, 40, 189
Iowa Women's Health Study, 98
Irinotecan, 312
Iron supplements, 83

Japanese women, 84–85, 223, 230
Journal of Clinical Oncology, 130
Journal of the American Medical
    Association, 89, 158, 342
Journal of the National Cancer Institute,
    104, 116

Kessler, David A., 156
Kessler, Larry, 60–61
Khalkhali, Iraj, 78, 245
Kidney function, 325
Komen, Susan G., Breast Cancer
    Foundation, 298, 299, 393
Komen Alliance, 393
Kopans, Daniel B., 60
Krieger, Nancy, 116
Kumar, Nagi, 108
Kushner, Rose, 4

Lactation suppression, 33, 41
Lagios, Michael D., 247–248, 251, 252

Laing, Matthew, 158
La Leche League International, 37, 389
Lancet, 126, 131, 340
Land, Charles E., 124
Latissimus dorsi flap, 361–364
Leeper, Edward, 120
LeJour method, 169
Leucovorin, 310
Leukapheresis, 330
Leukemia, 286, 308
Leuprolide (Lupron), 324
Levin, Norman, 270–271
Levy, Sandra, 129–130
Liarozole, 336
Liebeskind, Doreen, 237, 238, 245
Ligaments, 14
Linear accelerators, 285
Linoleic acid, 87–88
    conjugated, 89
Lippman, Marc, 321
Liposuction, 169–170
Living Beyond Limits (Spiegel), 126
Lobes, 14, 15
Lobular carcinoma:
    invasive, 250–251
    in situ (LCIS), 220, 251–253
Lobules, 14, 15
London, Stephanie, 122
Longnecker, Matthew, 98–99, 225
Look Good . . . Feel Better, 395
Loomis, Dana, 120
Love, Susan, 48, 98
Lower gluteus flap, 364
Low-fat diet, 27, 81, 84, 85–86, 149,
    197, 204
Luckey, Marjorie, 320, 326
Lumpectomy, 242, 253
    candidacy for, 262–264
    defined, 259
    incision placement, 266, 267, 269
    vs. mastectomy, 258–260, 262–265, 267
    personal issues to consider, 263–264
    procedure, 266, 267
    quadrantectomy, 259
    radiation therapy and (see Radiation
        therapy)
    recovery, 269
    types of, 259
Luteinizing hormone (LH), 16, 17, 20,
    21, 323, 324
Luteinizing hormone-releasing hormone
    (LHRH), 323

Lyerly, H. Kim, 335
Lymphedema, 277–278, 292, 395
Lymph node removal, 260, 275–278
Lymph node status, 254, 305
Lymph system, 14

Macrocysts, recurring, 206
Magnetic resonance imaging (MRI), 57, 76–77, 355
MammaCare, 51, 52
Mammary artery, 14
Mammary duct ectasia, 187
Mammograms, 4, 58–73
    accuracy of, 64
    age issue, 58–61
    baseline, 58, 59, 71, 155
    choosing the facility, 69
    before cosmetic surgery, 155
    cost of, 69
    digital, 70–71
    information resources, 390
    preparation for, 69–70
    procedure, 70
    quality of, 63–67
    radiation exposure risk and, 67–69, 124
    recommended timetable, 63
    size of tumors found by, 65
    stereotactic biopsies, 233, 238–241
Mammography Accreditation Program, American College of Radiology (ACR), 63
Mammoplasty (see Breast reduction)
Mammotome, 241
Mammotrope differentiating peptide, 38
Mansfield, Carl, 291
Marker lesions, 251
Martino, Silvana, 295
Marx, William, 347, 366, 367
Massachusetts Breast Cancer Coalition, 390
Massage
    following breastfeeding, 41
    scar minimization with, 172
    soft tissue rehabilitation, 277
    to stimulate milk let-down, 36–37
Mastalgia, 192–200
Mastectomy, 252, 253
    breast reconstruction and, 345, 347
    defined, 259
    vs. lumpectomy, 258–259, 262–265, 267

modified radical, 259, 271–274
partial, 259, 268
preventive, 175–180
radical, 260, 271
skin-sparing, 178, 258, 260, 274–275, 345, 347
subcutaneous, 178, 260
total, 259
types of, 259–260
Mastitis, 39, 191, 197–198
Mastodynia, 192–200
Mastopexy (see Breast lift)
Matarasso, Alan, 155, 164–166, 174
Mayo Clinic, 158
    Breast Clinic, 399
McCraw, John, 347, 363, 367
MDR-1 gene, 335
Meat, 86–87, 115
Medical history, 152
Medical oncologists, 295–299
Medi-Express RX, 394
Mediport, 318
Meditation, 127, 341–342
MedLine, 384
Medullary cancer, 251
Megace, 321, 323–324
Melatonin, 38
Melatonin factor, 121
Melphalan (L-Pam), 286, 308
Memorial Sloan–Kettering Cancer Center, 179, 265, 337, 391
    Evelyn H. Lauder Breast Center/Iris B. Cantor Diagnostic Center, 399
Menarche, 9, 105, 106, 142, 192–193, 217, 220, 230
Menopause, 23–24, 31, 105, 142, 143, 146, 149, 193, 205, 217, 230, 319–321
Menstrual cycle, 19–21, 23, 26, 31
    breast pain during, 194, 195, 200
    breast self-examinations and, 49
    exercise and, 105
    fibrocystic change and, 202–203
    risk factors for breast cancer and, 220–222
    timing of surgery and, 261–262
Mentor Corporation, 357
Mesna, 308
Metastatic breast cancer, 303, 305–306, 324–327
Methotrexate, 307, 310
Methylxanthines, 97–98

MetLife height and weight table, 110
Microcalcifications, 75, 242–243
Micrometastases, 305
Micropapillary pattern, 252
Milk ducts, 14, 15, 34
Milk glands, 14–16, 19, 24, 34
Milk let-down, 36
Milk production stimulation, 33–36
Milk reflex, 35
Milk ridge, 16, 18
Mind/body connection, 16, 125–132, 341–342
Minipill, 137
Minton, John, 96–97
"Miracle cures," 343
Mitomycin C, 309–310
Mitoxantrone (Novantrone), 310
mm23 gene, 335
Modems, 376
Modified radical mastectomy, 259, 271–274
Moffitt, H. Lee, Research and Cancer Institute, 106
Molecular tests, 254–256, 281–282
Mondor's disease, 198
Monoclonal antibodies, 337
Monophasic pills, 136
Monounsaturated fats, 86–88
Mons veneris, 19
Montgomery's glands, 13, 184, 190
Mortality rates, 3, 59, 61, 68–69, 88, 120–121, 230, 372
MRI (see Magnetic resonance imaging)
Mucinous cancers, 251
Multiphasic pills, 136–137
Muss, Hyman, 325

National Alliance of Breast Cancer Organizations (NABCO), 297, 379–381, 388, 390, 391, 398
National Bone Marrow Transplant Link, 396
National Breast Cancer Coalition (NBCC), 399
National Breast Screening Study (NBSS), 59–60
National Cancer Care Foundation, 397
National Cancer Institute (NCI), 4, 49, 59, 60–61, 63, 80, 82, 84, 90, 93, 101, 113–114, 135, 136, 139, 145, 177, 216, 222, 258, 281, 286, 338, 390

Cancer Information Service, 298, 338, 391, 392
CancerNet, 380
Clinical Trials Program, 379, 381
Information Associates Program, 380
National Coalition for Cancer Survivorship, The, 397
National Consortium of Breast Centers, 393
National Institute of Child Health and Human Development (NICHHD), 135, 137
National Institute of Environmental Health Sciences (NIEHS), 101, 113–114
National Institutes of Health (NIH), 79, 81
Office of Alternative Medicine, 341–342
National Lymphedema Network, 278, 395
National Prophylactic Mastectomy Registry, 179
National Research Council, 83
National Surgical Adjuvant Breast and Bowel Project (NSABP), 258, 284, 315–316
National Women's Health Network, 388–389
Natural killer (NK) cells, 129–130, 339, 340
Natural tissue reconstruction, 172, 346, 347, 350–353, 356–365
  flap types, 351
  gluteus maximus flap, 364–365
  hemodilution, 366
  latissimus dorsi flap, 361–364
  patient-controlled analgesic, 366–367
  single-stage, 368
  TRAM flap, 346, 351–352, 356–361, 369
  vs. implantation, 353
Nausea, 318
Necrosis, 210, 251
Nervous system, 129
Netcom, 376
Newcomb, Polly, 49
New England Journal of Medicine, 30, 218
New York University Women's Health Study, 87, 99–100
9-(AC), 312

Nipples:
  anatomy of, 184
  during breastfeeding, 15
  breast lift and, 168
  breast reduction and, 166, 167
  care during breastfeeding, 36–37
  changes in pregnancy, 190
  color of, 13
  cracked, 36, 40
  dermatitis, 188–189
  discharge from, 183–187
  on fetal milk ridge, 18
  internal view of, 14
  inverted, 40, 189
  lumpectomy surgery and, 269
  milk ducts in, 34
  nursing infant stimulation of, 34–35
  painful, 188
  position of, 13
  post-surgical loss or lessening of
    sensation in, 164, 167, 168, 170
  reconstruction of, 346, 365, 367, 368
  sensitivity in pregnancy, 30
  sexual response of, 25
  sore, 188
Nipple shield, 40
Noncyclic breast pain, 193, 196–198
Noninvasive ductal or lobular
  carcinoma, 251–252
Northeast/Mid-Atlantic Study
  (NE/MA), 113–114
Nuclear grading, 250, 251, 253–254
Nurses' Health Study, 85–86, 89, 93, 94,
  144, 145, 158
Nursing (see Breastfeeding)

Obesity, 224
Office of Alternative Medicine,
  Information Center, 393
Oils, dietary, 82, 87–88
Olive oil, 27, 83, 87–88, 95–96
Omega-3 fatty acid, 88
Oncogenes, 256
OncoLink, 379, 381
Oncologists:
  medical, 295–299
  radiation, 287–288
Ondansetron (Zofran), 318
One-step procedure, 4
On-line providers, 376
On-line services, 376–386
Oophorectomy, 324

Oral contraceptive pills (see Birth
  control pills)
Organochlorines, 99–101, 113, 116,
  117, 119, 225
Orgasm, 25
Osborne, Kent, 295
Osteoblasts, 326
Osteoclasts, 326
Osteoporosis, 150
Ovarian ablation, 295, 322
Ovaries, 20–21, 142, 324
Ovulation, 105
Oxman, Thomas, 342
Oxytocin, 16, 17, 25, 34–35, 38

Paget's disease, 189, 250, 253
Pain:
  bone, 327
  breast (see Breast pain)
Palpation technique, 54
Pancreas, 128
PaperChase, 382–383
Papillary pattern, 252
Pap test, 187
Parker, Steve, 241
Parlodel, 33, 41, 185, 196
Partial mastectomy, 259, 268
Pathology reports:
  biopsy (see Biopsy pathology reports)
  post-breast surgery, 279–283, 297,
    299
Patient-controlled analgesic, 366–367
PCBs, 99–100, 113, 115–117, 225
Peanut oil breast implants, 160
Peau d'orange, 191
Pectoral squeeze exercise, 22, 23
Pedicle flaps, 351, 352
Peg latissimus flap, 362–363
Penn State University, 95
Pergonal, 138, 139
Perimenopause, 23
Peripheral blood stem cell transplant
  (PBSCT), 328, 330–332
Personal environment (see
  Environmental risk factors)
Personal history of breast cancer, 220
Pesticides, 99–101, 112–119, 225
PET (see Positron emission tomography)
Physician Data Query (PDQ), 338, 380,
  383
Physician's Desk Reference (PDR), 147
Phytochemicals, 90–92, 115

Phytoestrogens, 91, 118
Pie BSE technique, 52, 53
Pierce, Penny, 261
Pineal gland, 128
Pipeline, 376
Pituitary gland, 16, 17, 20, 21, 25,
    34–35, 105, 128, 129
Placental hormone, 16
Planetree Health Resource Center, 393
Plastic food wrap, 115, 117, 119
Plastic surgery (see Cosmetic surgery)
Polyunsaturated fats, 86–88
Positron emission tomography (PET),
    71
Postmenopause, 24, 109
Prayer, 342
Prednisone, 307, 312
Preeclampsia, 9
Pregnancy, 21, 29–32
    breast cancer during, 272
    breast cancer risk and, 30–32, 221
    breast pain in, 193
    breast self-examinations during, 32,
        56
    nipple discharge during, 185
    response of breasts during, 29–30
    sexual response of breasts during,
        25–26
    skin tone changes in, 190
Premarin, 144
Prentis, Myer L., Comprehensive
        Cancer Center of Metropolitan
        Detroit, 399
Preventive mastectomy, 175–180
Prodigy, 376, 381–382
Progesterone, 16
    breast cancer and, 9–10, 141–150,
        220
    breast development and, 16, 19
    hormone replacement therapy and,
        24, 141–150
    menstrual cycle and, 21
    pregnancy and, 29
Progesterone receptor status, 255
Progestin, 135–136, 143, 144, 148
Prolactin, 16, 17, 34, 35, 184–187
Propofol, 157
Prostaglandins, 21
Provera, 323–324
pS2, 334
Psychoneuroimmunology (PNI), 125,
    340

Ptosis, 171
Puberty, 18–19
PVC plastics, 113

Quadrantectomy, 259

Race, as risk factor for breast cancer,
    229–230
Radial incision, 269
Radiation exposure risk, 67–69, 113,
    122–124, 225, 286
Radiation nurses, 288
Radiation oncologists, 287–288
Radiation physicists, 288
Radiation therapy, 284–293
    breast pain from, 198
    breast reconstruction and, 345
    choosing a radiation oncologist,
        287–288
    contraindications for, 287
    differences in breasts after, 293
    follow-up, 293
    after mastectomy, 286
    possible side effects, 292
    precautions during, 290
    precise targeting in, 285
    preparation for, 289
    procedure, 289–291
    recurrence rates and, 284, 285
Radical mastectomy, 260, 271
    modified, 259, 271–274
Radiotherapy (see Radiation therapy)
Raloef, Janet, 120
Raptis, George, 328, 330, 332
Reach to Recovery, 397
Reconstruction (see Breast
        reconstruction)
Recovery:
    lumpectomy, 269
    modified radical mastectomy, 272,
        274
Reddening of breasts, 191
Referrals, 153–154
Relaxation techniques, 341–342
Releasing factor, 20
Religious involvement, 342
Retinoids, 311–312
Revision, surgical, 174
Revlon/UCLA Breast Center at Jonsson
        Comprehensive Cancer Center,
        399
Rishi, Mazhar, 254, 282

Risk assessment counseling, 175–176
Risk counseling information resources, 391
Risk factors for breast cancer, 215–231
    age and susceptibility, 229
    control over, 230–231
    estrogen exposure and, 9–10, 105–107, 141–150, 220, 370–371
    forces from the outside world (see Environmental risk factors)
    forces of your own biology, 219–223
    genetic research, 226–229
    importance of, 216, 218–219
    race and susceptibility, 229–230
    table of, 217–218
    (See also Diet)
Robert, Nicholas, 149
Rockefeller, Happy, 4
Rose, David, 88–90
Rosen, Peter, 304
Rosenthal, Gladys, 176
Rossino, Mary Anne, 138
Rossman, Martin, 341
Roswell Park Cancer Institute, 89

Safflower oil, 87
Sage, Lynn, Comprehensive Breast Center at Northwestern Memorial Hospital, 399
Saline breast implants, 159–160, 162, 350
San Francisco General Medical Center, 342
Sarcoma, radiation–induced, 292
Saturated fats, 86–87
Savitz, David, 123
Scarring:
    breast lift surgery, 171
    breast reduction surgery, 165, 167
    lumpectomy, 268, 269
    mastectomy, 273, 274
    post-surgery minimization of, 172–174
Schmidt, Robert A., 241
Scintimammography, 78, 245
Scleroderma, 41, 287
Sclerosing adenosis, 210
Search engines, 378, 385–386
Second opinion:
    for breast surgery, 260
    on pathology reports, 246–249, 282

Segmental excision, 259
Selenium, 83–84, 94
Self-examinations (see Breast self–examinations)
Sensor Pad, 55–56
Sequential high–dose chemotherapy, 333
Sex hormone binding globulin (SHBG), 106, 108
Sexual response, 25–26
Shapiro, Charles, 308–309
SHARE, 297–298, 388
Silent Spring (Carson), 114
Silicone:
    breast implants, 41, 56–57, 76, 151, 156–159
    breast models, 51
    sheeting, 173–174
Silverstein, Melvin, 252
Simonton, O. Carl, 341
Simonton, Stephanie Matthews, 341
Simulator, 289
Single-stage reconstruction, 368
Skin-sparing mastectomy, 178, 258, 260, 274–275, 345, 347
Skin tone, 190–191
Small-scar mastopexy, 168
Smart, Charles R., 61
Smith, Robert, 61
Smoking, 226
Social support:
    healing power of, 130–131, 340–343
    information resources, 397–398
Soft tissue rehabilitation, 277
Solid pattern, 252
Sonnenschein, Carlos, 119–120
Soto, Ana, 119–120
Southern California, University of, School of Medicine, 102–106, 109, 139
Soybean oil and polyethylene glycol breast implants, 160
Spectrum, 357
S-phase fraction, 255–256
Spiegel, David, 126, 129–131, 340, 341
Spiritual approach, 342
Spontaneous abortion, 221–222
Stanford University School of Medicine, 130–131
State University of New York, Buffalo, 42–43
Stefanek, Michael, 176, 178–179

Stereotactic breast biopsy, 233
    core needle, 240–241
    fine needle, 238–239
Steroids, 172, 318
Stevens, Richard G., 121–122
Stitches, 269
Strang Cancer Prevention Center, 391
    Strang-Cornell Breast Center of, 399
Strauch, Berish, 337, 344, 367–368
Stress, 125–132, 341–342
Subareola abscess, 188
Subcutaneous mastectomy, 178, 260
Sulforaphane, 92
Support groups, 129–130
Supra Medical Corporation, 72, 244
SupraScanner ultrasound system, 371
Surgeons, cosmetic, 153–154
Surgery, 258–278
    anesthesia, 157, 164, 270–271
    axillary dissection, 260, 275–278
    biopsy, 234, 241–243, 247, 249
    breast pain and, 198
    breast reconstruction (see Breast
        reconstruction)
    breast self–examinations after, 56
    cosmetic (see Cosmetic surgery)
    for fibroadenomas, 209
    informed consent, 262
    lumpectomy, 242, 253
    mastectomy (see Mastectomy)
    timing of, 261–262
    weighing options, 260–261
Surgical revision, 174
Survival rates, 281, 284
Swedish milk cups, 40
Sympathetic nervous system, 129
Systemic lupus, 287

Talalay, Paul, 92
Tamoxifen (Nolvadex), 196, 294–295,
        306, 313–314, 320–324
Tamoxifen methiodide, 323
Tandem transplants, 332–333
Tattooing, 289, 346, 368
Taxanes, 311
Taxol (Paclitaxel), 311, 324
T cells, 336
Telnet, 378–379
Temoshok, Lydia, 125–126
Teniposide, 311
Terminal ductolobular units (TDLU),
        250

Testosterone (Halotestin), 324
Tests (see Breast tests)
Texas, University of:
    Health Science Center, 342
    M. D. Anderson Cancer Center, 109,
        264, 303
    at San Antonio, 227
Theodoulou, Maria, 295, 297, 300,
        301–302, 304, 319, 321
Thermography, 78
Thiotepa, 308
Thomas Jefferson University Hospital,
        61, 263
Thompson, Henry J., 104–105
Thymus gland, 128
Thyroid gland, 128
Thyroid-stimulating hormone (TSH),
        16, 17
Tissue-expander implants, 347, 353,
        355–356
Tissue samples, storage of, 282–283
TNM classification, 253, 279–281
Toniolo, Paolo, 87, 142–143
Topoisomerase-I interactive agents, 312
Topotecan, 312
Total latissimus flap, 362–363
Total mastectomy, 259
TRAM flap, 346, 351–352, 356–361, 369
Transillumination, 79
Transportation information resources,
        394
Triphasic pills, 136–137
Tubular cancers, 251
Tumor size, 253, 254, 262, 280, 296,
        300, 302, 305
Tumor suppressor gene p53, 256
Type C personality, 125–126

UCLA School of Medicine, 341
Ultrafast Pap Stain, 237, 238
Ultrasound, 72, 74–76, 244
    core needle biopsy guided by,
        239–240
    fine needle aspiration biopsy guided
        by, 237–238
    fine needle aspiration guided by,
        235–236
Upper gluteus flap, 364
Urokinase plasminogen activator
        (uPA), 334
U.S. Centers for Disease Control and
        Prevention, 109, 110

U.S. Department of Health and Human Services, 119
U.S. Food and Drug Administration (FDA), 55, 63, 77, 137, 151, 156, 157, 159, 317, 328, 343, 353
UseNet, 378
Uterine contractions, 25, 26

Vaccines, cancer, 335–336
Van Nuys Prognostic Index (VNPI), 252
Vans, mammography screening in, 67
Vasopressin, 17
Vegetables, 82, 83, 90–94, 115, 339–343
Vertical scar method, 169
Vertical strip BSE technique, 52–56
Vinblastine (Velban), 310–311
Vinca alkaloids, 310–311
Vincristine (Oncovin), 307, 310–311, 318
Vinorelbine (Navelbine), 311
Vitamin A, 93, 195, 197, 204
Vitamin B6, 83
Vitamin B complex, 83, 149, 195, 197, 204
Vitamin C, 83–84, 93, 195, 197, 204
Vitamin D, 149
Vitamin E, 83–84, 93, 149, 172, 195, 197, 204
Vredenburgh, James, 329, 331–332

Washington, University of, 144–145
Watmough, David, 70
Weaning, 41
Web Spiders, 378, 386
Wedge BSE technique, 52, 53
Wellness attitude, 370–372
Wellness Community, The, 397
Wertheimer, Nancy, 120
What Are Clinical Trials All About? (NCI), 338

White blood cell counts, 318–319
Wide excision, 259
Willett, Walter C., 85
"Window of vulnerability" theory, 81
Winnick, Wayne M., 277
Wire-guided excisional biopsies, 242–243
Wisconsin, University of, Comprehensive Cancer Center, 42
Witch's milk, 18
Wolff, Mary, 99–100, 114–116
WomanKind Breast Cancer Consultation Service, St. Mary's Medical Center, 248–249
Women at Risk, 391
Women's Care Study, 137
Women's Environment and Development Organization (WEDO), 390
Women's Health Initiative (WHI), 27, 81, 84, 86, 143–144, 224
Women's Intervention Nutrition Study (WINS), 84, 86, 224
Workout, optimal, 104
World Wide Web, 377–378
Wynder, Ernst, 84

Xenoestrogens, 100, 117–120, 225
Xeromammography, 63
X-rays, 113, 115, 122–124, 225

Yang, Grace, 237
Y-ME, 298, 320, 389, 397
    Prosthesis and Wig Bank, 395
YWCA of the USA, Encore Plus Program, 320, 398

Zeneca Pharmaceutical Foundation, 394
Zinninger, Marie, 68

NIELS H. LAUERSEN, M.D., Ph.D., is a noted, board-certified, New York obstetrician/gynecologist. A gifted surgeon, practitioner, and researcher, he is an attending physician at Lenox Hill Hospital, as well as a clinical professor of obstetrics and gynecology at New York Medical College. Long an aggressive advocate for women to become active participants in their health care, Dr. Lauersen has written many books on women's health care issues. He is the author of *It's Your Pregnancy* and *Childbirth with Love*, and the coauthor of *It's Your Body: A Woman's Guide to Gynecology*, *The Endometriosis Answer Book*, *A Woman's Body*, and *Getting Pregnant*. Along with Eileen Stukane he is the author of *Listen to Your Body*, *You're in Charge: A Teenage Girl's Guide to Sex and Her Body*, and *PMS: Premenstrual Syndrome and You*. He has written over 100 scientific papers and is a regular guest on local as well as national radio and television shows. *The Complete Book of Breast Care* continues Dr. Lauersen's tradition of empowering women by addressing their issues of concern.

EILEEN STUKANE is a noted women's health and nutrition writer. She is the coauthor of the women's health books *Listen to Your Body*, *PMS: Premenstrual Syndrome and You*, and *You're in Charge: A Teenage Girl's Guide to Sex and Her Body*. She is also the author of *You're Pregnant and Your Dreams Are Driving You Crazy*. Her monthly "Healthy Eating" nutrition column appeared in "Food and Wine" magazine for eight years, and her articles have appeared in numerous national publications. She lives in New York City.